One Foot in the Palace

One Foot in the Palace

The Habsburg Court of Brussels and the Politics of Access in the Reign of Albert and Isabella, 1598-1621

Dries Raeymaekers

Leuven University Press

Published with support of

Universitaire Stichting van België

and

Universiteit Antwerpen
Universiteit Antwerpen – Prinsstraat 13 – B-2000 Antwerpen

ISBN 978 90 5867 939 0
D / 2013/ 1869 / 42
NUR: 697

Translation: John R.J. Eyck
Cover illustration: Frans Francken de Jonge with Paul Vredeman de Vries, *Ballroom scene at the court in Brussels*, c.1610, oil on panel, 68,6 x 113,3 cm, inv.nr. 244 © Royal Picture Gallery Mauritshuis, The Hague
Lay-out and typesetting: Friedemann BVBA

GPRC
Guaranteed
Peer Reviewed
Content
www.gprc.be

Table of Contents

Preface

In the springtime of 1725, the Habsburg emperor Charles VI had a quite uncommon command remitted to the Council of State in the Austrian Netherlands. The emperor charged the councilors with providing him as many data as possible about the household of the archdukes Albert and Isabella and about that of their successor as governor in Brussels, the cardinal-infante Ferdinand of Austria (1634-1641). In its clarity, the imperial decree left nothing to be desired:

> 'You shall attempt to verify with distinction the number, the degree and the wages of their entourages, of the two sexes, and of everything else as regards to the formation of the household and the ceremonial, (...) and you shall draft, if possible, distinct reports with the names of the knights and ladies who have served the said Royal Persons, which you shall send to me without delay (...).'[1]

It was a remarkable assignment. Why at that moment did the emperor suddenly show so much interest in an episode from history, which had already slipped past long ago?

Much more than on historical interest, the imperial decree was based on a purely political consideration. Earlier that year Charles had named his sister Maria Elisabeth as governess of the Austrian Netherlands. A few months later the archduchess would depart from Vienna for Brussels. The emperor realized all too well, however, that the appointment of Maria Elisabeth would be received with distrust by many. Despite a long tradition, a century had already passed since the old palace on the Coudenberg hill in Brussels had housed a female governor. On top of that, the Austrian regime in the Southern Netherlands – at that moment barely ten years young – could not count on very much enthusiasm in terms of the local populace. Charles' weak position on the international chessboard prevented him from conducting vigorous policy moves. His attempts to put through institutional and economic reforms came up empty time and again. Should the emperor still want to gain the support of his subjects in the Netherlands, he would have to go looking for ways to give force to the legitimacy of Austrian rule. In that sense, his request for information about the household of the archdukes and the cardinal-infante was not in the least illogical. It was Charles' intention to create a glistening gubernatorial court in Brussels, a magnificent site

[1] '*Vous tacherez de vérifier avec distinction le nombre, les degrez et gages de leurs familles des deux sexes, et de tout le surplus qui regardera la formation de la maison et du cérémonial, (...) et ferez former du tout, s'il est possible, des relations distinctes avec les noms des chevaliers et dames qui ont servy les dittes Royales Personnes, lesquelles vous me remettrez sans delay (...).*' ARA, *RvS* 157, s.f.: *Établissement de la maison de l'archiduchesse Marie-Elisabeth, 1725* (article 15).

that would call forth the memory of the illustrious courts the city had known in the early seventeenth century. The best way to realize that, in his judgment, consisted of copying the composition and the organization of the princely households at that time as faithfully as possible:

> 'While the journey is being prepared of the Most Serene Archduchess Maria Elisabeth, my most cherished and most beloved sister, it is a precise duty to form and establish her household and entourage with the splendor that corresponds to her Royal Blood, and seeing as in times past the same offices have been held by the Most Serene Archduke Albert and after his death the Most Serene Infanta Isabella his wife, legitimate daughter of mylord King Philip II, and mylord Cardinal Infante, brother of mylord King Philip IV (...).'[2]

This anecdote is significant in several respects. In the first place, it suggests that conducting a grandiose household made up part of a political strategy with conscious intentions. It is striking that in his decree Charles explicitly referred to the fact that all persons involved were of royal blood. Obviously the emperor wanted to emphasize that Maria Elisabeth – just like her illustrious predecessors – was a full member of the Habsburg dynasty, which not only could strengthen the legitimacy of her authority as governess *de jure*, but also evoked the presumption of continuity with the past. The creation of a princely household according to an ages-old model allowed that association to be accentuated. In the second place, the anecdote makes it apparent that even the composition of a princely entourage depended to a great degree on political motives. Charles appears to have wanted to make use of the opportunity to engage a number of noble families from the Southern Netherlands in royal service and in that way affirm their bonds with the House of Habsburg. Finally, the anecdote implies that the households of Albert and Isabella and the cardinal-infante were perceived long after their disappearance as examples to be emulated. Not coincidentally, these three considerations constituted the central points of departure for the research project *Changing Formats: Court and Household in the Habsburg Netherlands (1598-1647)*, a two-part study that began in 2005 at the universities of Ghent and Antwerp. As a whole, the project embraced in-depth research into the political significance of

2 '*Entre temps que l'on diffère le voyage de la Serénissime Archiduchesse Marie Elisabeth ma très chère et très amée soeur, c'est un devoir précis de former et establir sa maison et famille avec le lustre qui correspond à son Royal Sang, et comme desià des temps passez ont possedé les mesmes charges à Bruxelles le Sérénissime Archiduc Albert et depuis sa mort la Sérénissime Infante Isabelle sa femme, fille légitime du Seigneur Roy Philippe Second, et le Seigneur Cardinal Infant, frère du Seigneur Roy Philippe Quatre (...).*' ARA, *RvS* 157, s.f. (article 16).

the court in Brussels during the first half of the seventeenth century, giving special attention to the role of the princely household. In that sense, it sought to connect with the historical discipline of *court studies*, which has especially taken off since the 1980s within the historical sciences.

The book at hand encompasses the results of the project *Changing Formats* for the period 1598-1621 – one of the rare time frames in which the early modern court in Brussels enjoyed a sovereign status.[3] In spite of relatively great attention given to the archducal reign during past eras in historiography, the court of Albert and Isabella could not count on much interest until now. The most detailed studies date from the beginning of the twentieth century and are highly antiquated as a consequence. After these, historians seemed to have foremost in mind the role of the court as the focal point for art and culture. Its political function came up for discussion only tangentially in a few brief contributions, which seldom were placed within a broader context. More recently the various essays in the collection *Albert & Isabella, 1598-1621*, edited by Werner Thomas and Luc Duerloo (Turnhout, 1998), together form a commendable and important addition to the extant knowledge of the matter, but here too the research remains of necessity limited to one or a few specific aspects. The same applies to other recent studies, which are generally intended to be introductory and in many cases only ruminate over what was already known earlier. A detailed analysis, in which the political significance and the workings of the archducal court are thoroughly studied, has never been undertaken before.

As will become obvious from the following chapters, the historiography concerning the archducal reign was dominated in the late nineteenth and twentieth centuries by the debate over the political autonomy of Albert and Isabella. The emphasis lay on the often difficult relations between Brussels and Madrid, on the presence of Spanish diplomats and functionaries in the Southern Netherlands, and on the presupposed influence of the latter on decision-making. Strangely enough, this debate seldom was concerned with the court and the household of the archdukes. Nevertheless, research into early modern courts in Europe has sufficiently demonstrated by now that the princely court not only played a key political role as the seat of central power, but also fulfilled an important symbolic function with regard to the *representatio maiestatis* – the display of princely majesty and authority by means of ceremonies, rituals and a profound religiosity. That same research has pointed out as well – in contrast to what was often assumed in the past – the notion that the members of the royal

[3] The second panel of this research project diptych was carried out by Birgit Houben. See Houben, B. *Wisselende gedaanten. Het hof en de hofhouding van de landvoogden Isabella Clara Eugenia (1621-1633) en de kardinaal-infant don Fernando van Oostenrijk (1634-1641) te Brussel.* Unpublished doctoral dissertation, Universiteit Gent, 2009.

household not only occupied themselves with domestic duties, but also could exercise significant influence on policy as confidants and counselors of the prince. That a solid understanding of these elements is indispensable for unraveling the mechanisms of early modern decision-making, is a scholarly conviction which international literature in the matter applies as self-evident at present; still, in the historiography concerning the archducal reign this truth has yet to see the light of day.

This book means to investigate to what degree and in what way the court of Albert and Isabella answers to current theories concerning the political significance of the early modern court. In doing so, it will employ a broad perspective, in which attention is given not only to the structure, the organization and the composition of the archducal household – aspects about which very little is known – but also to topics which at the moment are advancing scholarly debate, such as the interaction between the so-called politics of access and the acquisition of princely favor. Various historians have demonstrated that the right of access to the prince was a precious commodity in the administrative constellation of the Ancien Régime. The opportunity to abide in the immediate proximity of the prince translated more often than not into the acquisition of political power and influence. From this optic, it is perhaps not surprising that Gaston Spínola, one of Albert's courtiers, advised his friend and brother-in-arms Charles of Arenberg to 'always keep one foot in the palace' (*tener siempre un pie en palacio*) in order to look out for his interests.[4] This book applies Spínola's advice as the common thread that ties all the chapters of this story together.

In connecting with present trends in research, this study aims to remedy (in part, in any case) the lacuna with regard to knowledge concerning the archducal court. In addition, it attempts to introduce a few innovative insights that can place into a new light extant knowledge as concerns the archducal reign and – in a broader context – as concerns the nature and the workings of early modern politics. Doing so, attention is given, among other things, to the problem of the supposed link between 'nation' and 'loyalty' during the Ancien Régime, to the common corporate culture that characterized the various Habsburg courts of Europe, and to the role that a princely favorite could play in an average-sized yet complex principality like the Archducal Netherlands.

In the period preceding the completion of this book, I had the good fortune to be able to count on the scholarly, practical and moral support of a great number of sympathetic advocates. A sincere word of thanks is thus in order here.

[4] ACA, 38/4, file 133, f. 5: Gaston Spínola, count of Bruay, to Charles of Arenberg, princely count of Arenberg and duke of Aarschot, March 16, 1613.

When I first met Luc Duerloo in November 2004, I could not yet estimate how our relationship would evolve during the years that followed. At present many colleagues seem to see us as two peas in a pod, and perhaps that is the most fitting description of the solid bond that has grown between us. Luc proved to be not only a very erudite but also a very warm and caring supervisor. He succeeded like no other in making me think about the subject matter treated in this book, without wanting to impose his own ideas or to determine mine. I am especially thankful to him for his infinite advice, his incisive comments, and his rock-solid belief in my capabilities.

At the time of my dissertation, Birgit Houben was my steadfast *compagnonne de route*. Together we spent many hours in various archives at home and abroad. I am very thankful to her for her pleasant company, for her helpfulness and for the many talks when we encouraged each other. To Birgit's supervisor and my co-supervisor René Vermeir, I am very appreciative for all the archival and additional tips he provided me in the past years, for his indefatigable industry in reading over the manuscript and for the confidence he always put in me.

The Department of History at the University of Antwerp offered me the stimulating environment necessary to bring this book to a happy conclusion. I have always felt at home there and I would very much like to thank all my colleagues explicitly for the enjoyable atmosphere over the past years. May those who follow count as representative among them: Michael Auwers, Stefanie Beghein, Veerle De Laet, Brecht Deseure, Wannes Dupont, Dries Lyna, Nicolas Mazeure, Jeroen Puttevils, Steven Thiry, Bart Tritsmans, Laura Van Aert, Ilja Van Damme, Veerle Vanden Daelen, Maarten Van Dijck, Gerrit Verhoeven and Reinoud Vermoesen. I reserve a special and very warm word of thanks for Carolien Van Loon, whose sparkling presence was always a source of joy and friendship.

Elsewhere, too, in the academic world, I was able to meet many pleasant colleagues, both inside and outside Belgium. I gladly express my sincere thankfulness for their help and advice while this book was coming to its fruition. In that context, special mention goes to Sebastiaan Derks for his incessant interest as well as his willingness to read and listen. I found inspiration, interest and enthusiasm as well from Hans Cools, Harald Deceulaer, Jeroen Duindam, Liesbeth Geevers, José Eloy Hortal Muñoz, Richard Kagan, Mirella Marini, Jonathan Spangler, Fabian Persson, Magdalena Sánchez, Violet Soen, Patricia Stoop, Erik Swart, Klaas Van Gelder, Cordula Van Wyhe, Griet Vermeesch and Coen Wilders. To the members of the Board of Directors of The Society for Court Studies, I would also like to give my heartfelt thanks for their smooth collaboration over the past years, in particular Philip Mansel and Malcolm Smuts.

Publishing a book is an adventure. My good friend and editor at Leuven University Press, Veerle De Laet, deserves lavish praise for her tireless efforts in guiding me through it. She made the entire process seem like a picnic, and I am tremendously grateful to her. Thanks are also due to the University Foundation in Belgium, the Research Foundation Flanders, the University of Antwerp and Radboud University Nijmegen, who graciously funded the project.

Any historical research stands or falls on the availability and accessibility of its sources. I would like very much to express my appreciation to H.Ill.H. the Duke of Arenberg, who was so kind as to grant me access to his rich family archive in Enghien. Furthermore, I received at just the right times the very appreciated help of specialists for whom the language of Cervantes has no secrets, namely, Maria Raeymaekers, Javier Calvo and Myrjam Vleugels. Mary Hollingsworth and Gert Vleugels helped me with the translation of a few Italian letters. Any possible remaining carelessness is naturally my own.

I reserve an especially loving word of thanks for my parents and brothers. Their unconditional support was and is always indispensable in everything I undertake in my life. I am terribly thankful for all the opportunities they have offered me through the years, and for the warm home where I was able to grow up.

And, finally, Anneleen Arnout brought color into my life at a moment when everything looked dull and dreary. To be able to make history with her is my highest happiness.

– DR

Illustrations & Plates

Tables & Charts

Abbreviations

ACA	Arenberg Archives and Cultural Centre, Enghien
AGPR	Archivo General del Palacio Real, Madrid
AGS	Archivo General de Simancas, Valladolid
AHN	Archivo Histórico Nacional, Madrid
ARA	Algemeen Rijksarchief, Brussels [National Archives of Belgium]
ASV	Archivio Segreto Vaticano, Vatican City
Aud	*Audiëntie*
BaL	*Barberini Latini*
BAV	Biblioteca Apostolica Vaticana, Vatican City
BFZ	Biblioteca Francisco de Zabálburu, Madrid
BL	British Library, London
BNF	Bibliothèque Nationale de France, Paris
CCE	LONCHAY, H., CUVELIER, J. & LEFÈVRE, J., eds. *Correspondance de la Cour d'Espagne sur les affaires des Pays-Bas au XVIIe siècle.* 6 vols. Brussels, 1923-1937.
CODOIN	*Colección de Documentos Inéditos para la Historia de España.* 112 vols. Madrid, 1842-1895.
DuiS	*Duitse Staatssecretarie* [German Secretariat of State]
HHStA	Haus-, Hof- und Staatsarchiv, Vienna
IVDJ	Instituto Valencia de Don Juan, Madrid
MsF	*Manuscrits Français*
NA	National Archives, Kew
NF	*Nunziatura di Fiandra*
OOMM	*Órdenes Militares*
RA	Rijksarchief in Brussels (site Anderlecht), Anderlecht [National Archives of Belgium – Anderlecht site]
RAH	Real Academia de la Historia, Madrid
RK	*Rekenkamer* [Chamber of Accounts]
RvS	*Raad van State* [Council of State]
SAA	Stadsarchief, Antwerp [City Archives of Antwerp]
SOO	*Secretarie van Staat en Oorlog* [Secretariat of State and War]
SP	*State Papers*
SyC	*Salazar y Castro*

Currency values

In the accounting ledgers or *libros de razón* of the archducal household (cf. ARA, *RK* 1837 and 1838), an entire gamut of currencies and accounting units is used interchangeably. Generally amounts are expressed in *maravedis* (a very small and, consequently, unwieldy unit), but often also in (Spanish) ducats and sometimes in *escudos* or *reales*. Mostly – but not always – these amounts are converted into guilders (florins, fl.), worth 20 stuivers each. To the degree it is possible, this conversion is also continued in this book. On the basis of the data recovered in the accounting ledgers, the following rates apply:

1 ducat	= 375 *maravedis*	= fl. 2.757	
1 *escudo*	= 350 *maravedis*	= fl. 2.57	
1 *real*	= 34 *maravedis*	= fl. 0.25	
1 guilder	= 136 *maravedis*	= 4 *reales*	= 0.4 *escudos*
1 stuiver	= 6.8 *maravedis*		

Prelude

On the morning of September 27, 1595, a feverish busyness dominated the harbor of Barcelona. Along the quays of the Catalonian capital no less than 27 galleys were moored, the holds of which were stowed full of baggage and provisions. Eight ships were under the command of the Spanish nobleman Don Diego de Mendoza. The nineteen remaining galleys had been sent from Genoa, sailing under orders of Carlo Doria, duke of Tursi, who as captain of the fleet followed in the footsteps of his famous great-uncle, the Genoese admiral and statesman Andrea Doria. Mendoza and Doria had been summoned to Barcelona with a weighty task in mind. Shortly after midday, their entire fleet would lift anchor and set a course for Savona, Italy, with numerous Spanish nobles, soldiers, servants and lackeys on board.[1] This illustrious company constituted the entourage of a passenger of royal blood, whose embarkation inaugurated the beginning of a new chapter in the political history of Europe. That passenger was Cardinal-Archduke Albert VII of Austria (1559-1621), son of the Habsburg emperor Maximilian II and nephew of King Philip II of Spain.[2]

Approximately one month earlier, on August 28, Albert had left Madrid to make that transfer in Barcelona for Italy. From there he would journey further overland to Brussels, where in the name of his uncle he would take up the function of governor of the Spanish Netherlands. The appointment fell to Albert rather unexpectedly. For many years it was known that Philip had in fact conceived of a different future for his nephew. Already in 1577, at the request of the king, Pope Gregory XIII had named the then 17-year-old archduke as cardinal.[3] It was a strategic move, the sole objective of which was to prepare the way for Albert's ultimate destiny: the archbishopric of Toledo. On account of the exceptionally long life of his predecessor, Archbishop Gaspar de Quiroga, Albert could not be proclaimed Primate of Spain until 1594, however, and he would not carry the title for long. Scarcely a year later, the sudden death of his older brother Ernst of Austria made a political reorientation necessary. In 1593, Archduke Ernst had been appointed by Philip II as governor of the Netherlands. The king had hoped that when the new administrator assumed his post, he would

---

1 The anecdote is based on a contemporaneous account from the hand of the Spanish cleric Juan Roco de Campofrío. This report was published in 1973 as Roco de Campofrío, J. *España en Flandes. Trece años de Gobierno del Archiduque Alberto (1595-1608).* Madrid, 1973.

2 Albert was the tenth child and the fifth surviving son of Maximilian II and his spouse Maria, a sister of Philip II. For a complete biography, see Duerloo, L. *Dynasty and Piety. Archduke Albert (1598–1621) and Habsburg Political Culture in an Age of Religious Wars.* Farnham, 2012.

3 The appointment was announced during the Consistory of March 3, 1577. Not until three years later, on February 12, 1580, did Albert receive the cardinal's hat. Cf. Duerloo, *Dynasty and Piety*, 22-23.

bring about a positive turning point in the Low Countries, tormented as they were by war and rebellion; yet he saw his plans thwarted when Ernst, consumed by a persistent illness, lost his life on February 20, 1595. His death created a vacuum of power that had to be filled as quickly as possible. The perilous situation in the Netherlands would not bear any long drawn-out appointment proceedings: it had to be treated with haste. Philip found himself obliged to put away his well-considered plans. On April 26, he designated his confidant Albert as successor to Ernst. Although the decision was not in keeping with his original intention, the king would not be sorry about it. As the former viceroy of Portugal (1583-1593), the cardinal-archduke had been tried and tested in politics, and his upbringing at the strict religious Spanish court had seen to it that Albert was devoted to the Catholic faith with heart and soul.[4] Philip, who also harbored a great personal inclination toward his nephew, would not have hesitated long in entrusting to him his tumultuous territories on the North Sea.

The organization of Albert's departure for the Netherlands started pretty well immediately after his appointment. An undertaking of that scope assumed minute preparations.[5] The required funds needed to be collected, the necessary personnel acquired, the correct number of coaches and beasts of burden bought or hired. Diego de Arze, Albert's clerk, was assigned to look into which nobles and servants would take part in the journey. His colleague Pedro de Mendoza calculated the number of mules necessary for transporting the baggage. Don Juan de Toledo, one of Albert's *gentilhombres*, was sent to Barcelona to make arrangements for the crossing to Italy.[6] The organization turned out to be a sinecure least of all: ultimately the departure would have to wait four months. Not that they struggled with a lack of experience in moving households at the Spanish court. The numerous moves of the royal household between the Real Alcázar in Madrid and the surrounding residences of Aranjuez, San Lorenzo del Escorial and El Pardo demanded great financial and logistical efforts annually. In April 1583, for example, approximately 50 coaches and not less than 100 beasts of burden were procured to transport only a portion of the royal household to the Pardo situated nearby, good for a sum of 95,393 *maravedis* (approx. 700 fl.) – at that time a small fortune.[7] The relatively short excursions in the vicinity of Madrid,

[4] Concerning these episodes in Albert's life, see Jordan Gschwend, A. 'In the Shadow of Philip II, *El Rey Lusitano*: Archduke Albert of Austria as Viceroy of Portugal (1583-1593),' in: Thomas, W. & Duerloo, L., eds. *Albert & Isabella, 1598-1621: Essays*. Turnhout, 1998, pp. 39-46; Caeiro, F. *O Arquiduque Alberto de Austria. Vice-rei e inquisidor-mor de Portugal, cardeal legado do papa, governador e depois soberano dos Países Bajos*. Lisbon, 1961 and Martínez Millán, J. 'El archiduque Alberto en la corte de Felipe II (1570-1580),' in: Thomas & Duerloo, *Essays*, pp. 27-37.

[5] Concerning the preparations with regard to Albert's journey to the Netherlands, see RAH, *SyC* A-61, f. 20: *Las cosas que en el Bureo sean acordado en xx de julio 1595.*

[6] *Ibidem.*

[7] AGPR, *Sección Administrativa: Viajes y Jornadas* 778. Loc. cit. the minutes for the year 1583.

however, were nothing compared to the journey that awaited the cardinal-archduke. Albert and his retinue would need to withstand rain, wind and cold lasting more than five months, at times stopping in large cities or at friendly courts, other times in small villages or abbeys. In view of the fact that the kingdom of France was seen as enemy territory at that moment, the travel route carefully outlined in advance led them of necessity to Italy, from where the *camino español* would bring them over the Alps at wintry temperatures and subsequently via Franche-Comté and Luxembourg to the final destination.[8] Not for nothing in contemporaneous sources the voyage was designated with a capital letter as *la Jornada*.[9] For most participants it was the journey of their lives, an unmistakably perilous undertaking, with which they put their futures in the balance.[10]

In view of this not very encouraging prospect, it comes as no surprise that not everyone felt called to accompany the cardinal-archduke to his new residence. A number of members of his retinue claimed to be too old, too poor or too sick to be able to take part in the journey, or chose not to trade the Madrid they knew well for an unknown Brussels.[11] Among them was the clerk Diego de Arze himself, who put forward that his 'advanced age, poverty and many daughters' did not allow him to leave Spain.[12] Others, however, grabbed their chance and sold all their worldly possessions to set up a new existence in faraway *Flandes*. Some of those with wanderlust but lesser fortunes put themselves deep into debt to be able to finance their participation. Most left their wives and children behind in the hope of having them come over later. Those who could afford it took their families with them. A few found their final resting place during the voyage: they did not survive *la Jornada*.[13] For the travelers who did reach their destination, the first confrontation with the Netherlands must have been a strange experience. Awaiting them was a grey, cold country, devoid of sun, tormented by the persistent violence of war and inhabited by a people who since forever and a day had the reputation of taking a wary rather than willing position over against anything that was called Spanish. There was, however, not much time to pause and reflect on that. Once arrived in Brussels, work immediately needed to be done on the development of a fully functioning household, which on the highest as well as the lower levels could run as smooth as a well-oiled machine. Both palace and city had to be explored, contacts secured with local purveyors, housing sought, extra personnel

[8] Concerning the famous *camino español*, see Parker, G. *The Army of Flanders and the Spanish Road, 1567-1659*. Cambridge U.P., 1972.

[9] See e.g. IVDJ, ms. 26-I-10, ff. 188-198: *Relación de la Jornada que el Serenissimo Archiduque Cardenal Alberto hiçó de España a Flandes en los annos de 1595 y 1596 (por Bernardo Gómez de la Vega)*.

[10] For a detailed report of the journey, see Roco de Campofrío, *España en Flandes*, 8-81.

[11] RAH, *SyC* A-61, ff. 43-66: *Consulta de las pretensiones de los criados de Su Alteza.*

[12] RAH, *SyC* A-61, f. 59.

[13] RAH, *SyC*, passim.

acquired. And if there were already talk of being homesick, then there was no other choice but to swallow these feelings and make the best of it. Spain was far away, and only a few would ever see the place of their birth again.

Though continually augmented and expanded through the years, the extensive royal retinue that embarked that morning in Barcelona would form the nucleus of the archducal household in Brussels lasting more than three decades. In that capacity, the traveling companions would be privileged witnesses to one of the most amazing periods in the history of the Habsburg Netherlands. From nearby they experienced how on July 13, 1598, the archduke laid down his cardinal's hat on the altar of the Black Madonna in Halle, and how, as a secular prince a few months later, he entered into marriage with the eldest daughter of Philip II, the infanta Isabella Clara Eugenia (1566-1633). Approximately one year later, they saw how Albert and his bride were festively received in Brussels and how the sovereign reign of the princely pair took its start. During the subsequent years the archducal court would develop into one of the political and diplomatic nerve centers of Europe. In the process many courtiers and servants of Albert and Isabella would be not only spectators and extras, but also play active supporting and leading roles. In this book, their story will be reconstructed.

Introduction

On May 6, 1598, a gravely ill Philip II signed the Act of Cession. With that he sealed the transfer of sovereignty over the Habsburg Netherlands and Franche-Comté to his daughter Isabella Clara Eugenia and her prospective spouse Albert of Austria (cf. Plates 1 and 2 in the color section of this book).[1] By way of dowry, the archdukes, as they would come to be known, received theoretical dominion over all regions in the Low Countries except for the prince-bishopric of Liège. In reality, the reach of their power was limited to the areas that had remained loyal to Habsburg rule after the outbreak of the Dutch Revolt, with the duchy of Brabant and the county of Flanders as driving forces. Via the transfer of power to his daughter the king hoped to force a breakthrough in the conquest of the rebellious provinces in the north, which had defended themselves by every means possible against his authority. It would be Philip's final attempt to settle the conflict. Four months later, on September 13, 1598, he breathed his last.

Historiography traditionally bookmarks the beginning of a notable political, economic, religious, and cultural revival in the Habsburg Netherlands when Albert and Isabella assumed their posts as sovereign princes.[2] Initially, however, the archducal reign certainly did not start without a hitch. The Treaty of Vervins, which sealed the peace between Spain and France in 1598, might well have brought quiet to the country's southern borders; in the north the animosities went on undiminished. The United Provinces, knowing themselves to be supported by England, proved to be not only especially stubborn but also quite successful opponents of Habsburg authority in the Low Countries. In the Habsburgs' own ranks an acute lack of money, mutinies, and quarrels within the army leadership saw to it that military successes as yet remained outstanding. In 1600, the Battle of Nieuwpoort, in which the archducal troops came out on bottom, would go down in history as one of the most bloody of the Eighty Years' War. In 1604, the turn-around followed, when Archduke Albert and his field commander Ambrogio Spínola succeeded in taking the harbor city Ostend from the rebels after a lengthy siege.[3]

---

1 The text of the Act of Cession can be found in Brants, V., ed. *Recueil des Ordonnances des Pays-Bas. Règne d'Albert et d'Isabelle.* 2 vols. Brussels, 1909.

2 For an overview, see Thomas, W. 'La Corte de los Archiduques Alberto de Austria y la Infanta Isabel Clara Eugenia en Bruselas (1598-1633). Una revisión historiográfica,' in: Crespo Solana, A. & Herrero Sánchez, M., eds. *España y las 17 provincias de los Países Bajos. Una revisión historiográfica (XVI-XVIII).* Córdoba, 2002, pp. 358-386.

3 Concerning the siege, see Thomas, W., ed. *De val van het Nieuwe Troje. Het beleg van Oostende, 1601-1604.* Exhibition catalogue. Leuven, 2004.

Although the news was received with jubilation in all of Habsburg Europe, there could in fact scarcely be any talk of resounding victory. The undertaking had dragged on more than three years in total and demanded thousands of lives. Yet the occupation of this strategic bulwark proved to be a psychological turning point. After the fall of Ostend the archducal troops again felt strengthened. In 1605, they conquered Blokkersdijk, Oldenzaal and Lingen. The year after that, Groenlo and Rheinberg fell. All the same, Albert and Spínola wanted for the necessary means to continue with this élan. Deserters and mutineers quickly raised their ugly heads again. The news of the arrival of a silver treasure fleet in Spain provided a short sigh of relief, but Albert realized quickly that total conquest of the United Provinces was simply not realistic. The costs were too great, as were the losses. After 1606, the desire for an accord made itself felt more and more strongly in both the Northern as well as the Southern Netherlands. Physically and mentally, both parties were at the end of their wits, and in financial respects, too, the many war campaigns had struck deep wounds. The stalemate was complete: exhausted, they gathered around the negotiating table. The provisional ceasefire announced in March 1607, however, could not be put through as a formal peace treaty. Despite all attempts political and religious division stood in the way of absolute reconciliation. In 1609, mutual consideration turned of necessity into reluctant consensus. For a period of twelve years, it was agreed, the animosities would be suspended.

After decades of political chaos the Twelve Years' Truce (1609-1621) brought a vitally necessary period of quiet to the Habsburg Netherlands. In the domestic arena the policies of Albert and Isabella could now be fully unfurled. One of the most prominent elements of these was the codification of the unwritten common law, which not only put an end to statutory insecurity and judicial caprice, but created as well the legal framework that was necessary to break through the societal impasse squeezing the country since the Dutch Revolt broke out.[4] A targeted recovery program was drawn up to put the affairs of the disrupted society in order. High up on the agenda came the slackening economy, which they tried to breathe new life into via all manner of intervention. The establishment, for example, of the so-called 'Mountains of Mercy' [*Bergen van Barmhartigheid*], a network of charitable credit institutions, was to reduce the immense poverty in the cities.[5] In the countryside initiatives were taken to make the largely depopulated villages and smaller rural communities attractive

[4] In that context, see Martyn, G. *Het Eeuwig Edict van 12 juli 1611: zijn genese en zijn rol in de verschriftelijking van het privaatrecht.* Brussels, 2000; and Martyn, G. 'Het recht ten tijde van de aartshertogen: codificatie en enkele fundamentele wetten,' in: Thomas, W. & Duerloo, L., eds. *Albert & Isabella, 1598-1621: Essays.* Turnhout, 1998, pp. 249-254.

[5] See Soetaert, P. *De Bergen van Barmhartigheid in de Spaanse, de Oostenrijkse en de Franse Nederlanden (1618-1795).* Brussels, 1986.

while expanding the land area for agriculture. These and other measures did not miss their intended effect. The population numbers exhibited a gradual trend upward, and buying power also notably increased, which was reflected in the development of local industry specialized in costly luxury products.

Even so, where economic recovery remained modest on account of the blockade of the Scheldt River by northern troops, there could still be talk of a genuine revival in the religious arena. In the fight against Protestantism the Counter-Reformation pulled out all the stops, financially backed in the process by the strict Catholic archdukes, who flew the princely virtue of *pietas* – one of the ideological pillars of the Habsburg dynasty – high among the banners of their principles.[6] Under their impetus began the rebuilding of churches and monasteries that had been laid to waste during the Iconoclasm of 1566 and subsequent unrest. Recently established religious orders, such as the Discalced Carmelites, were prodded to settle in the Netherlands and to make the populace attracted to the Catholic faith again. The Jesuits, too, received the necessary financial support to dedicate themselves with renewed fervor to the education of the youth. Everywhere in the country initiatives in the spirit of the ideals of the Council of Trent came into being.[7] The organization of religious processions and parades, in which the participation of the populace was actively sought, guaranteed a very visual and tangible form of religious propaganda. In that context, the expansion of the shrine of pilgrimage at Scherpenheuvel [Montaigu], where Marian devotion took to the heights, was the crowning achievement.[8] The success of this politics was not long in coming. Without any doubt the triumph of militant Catholicism in the Habsburg Netherlands can be counted among the greatest accomplishments of the archducal regime.

The revival with which the reign of Albert and Isabella would be historiographically associated thus was carried out in pretty much all areas of public life. It need not come as a surprise then, either, that the archdukes would go down in history as bearers of peace and prosperity. Already at the very beginning of their rule the princes were presented in contemporaneous literature and dramaturgy as heroic liberators of a destitute people.[9] The iconographic program that was exhibited on the occasion

6 Duerloo, L. ' 'Pietas Albertina.' Dynastieke vroomheid en herbouw van het vorstelijk gezag.' *Bijdragen en Mededelingen betreffende de Geschiedenis der Nederlanden*, 112 (1997) pp. 1-18; Duerloo, L. 'Archducal Piety and Habsburg Power,' in: Thomas & Duerloo, *Essays*, pp. 267-283.

7 The classic works about this are Pasture, A. *La restauration religieuse aux Pays-Bas catholiques sous les archiducs Albert et Isabelle (1596-1633)*. Leuven, 1925; and Elias, H.J. *Kerk en Staat in de Zuidelijke Nederlanden onder de regeering der aartshertogen Albrecht en Isabella, 1598-1621*. Antwerp, 1931. See also Put, E. 'Les archiducs et la réforme catholique: champs d'actions et limites politiques,' in: Thomas & Duerloo, *Essays*, pp. 255-265.

8 See Duerloo, L. & Wingens, M. *Scherpenheuvel. Het Jeruzalem van de Lage Landen*. Leuven, 2002.

9 Porteman, K. 'Albrecht en Isabella in de letterkunde van hun tijd,' in: Thomas & Duerloo, *Essays*, pp. 309-318.

of their Joyous Entries into a number of cities in the Southern Netherlands even ascribed mythical characteristics to the archducal couple in that context.[10] While they still lived, the benevolence and rectitude of Albert and Isabella would be repeatedly praised in panegyric verse; yet the trumpets blared loudest shortly after they died, when diverse eulogies and biographies fitted to them an image of holiness.[11] It was a strongly hagiographic approach, which would exercise much influence on later historians with regard to the archducal period.[12] In nineteenth- and early twentieth-century Catholic religious historiography, too, the rule of Albert and Isabella was traditionally depicted as a triumphant transformation in national history.[13] With their beneficent administration inspired by fear of God and virtuousness, they succeeded in uniting the different regions of the country and in preserving the Catholic religion, so that judgment read. As true *Patres Patriae* the archdukes thus stood at the cradle of the sovereign and independent Belgian nation-state, which in 1830 would be recognized as such.[14]

The sovereignty debate

With the abundant attention paid to the supposed influence of the archducal reign on the creation of the subsequent Belgian state, an old controversy stepped into the spotlight, one that would dominate scholarly debate far into the twentieth century. Already during their rule questions were raised about the sovereign status of Albert and Isabella. Three centuries later those same doubts – also under the influence of the up and coming liberal and anti-clerical movement in historiography – proved yet to offer fodder for discussion.[15] Although the archdukes officially enjoyed political autonomy, many have argued that in practice the princes were least of all in the position to sail an independent course.[16] In the background the Spanish government, continually

[10] Thomas, W. 'Andromeda Unbound: The Reign of Albert & Isabella in the Southern Netherlands, 1598-1621,' in: Thomas & Duerloo, *Essays*, pp. 1-14.

[11] A small sampling of the supply: Courvoisier, J.J. *Le sacré Mausolée ou les parfums exhalant le tombeau de la sérénissime princesse Isabelle...* Brussels, 1634; de Montgaillard, B. *Le Soleil Eclipsé, ou Discours sur la vie et mort du Sérénissime Archiduc Albert Prince Souverain des Pais bas et de Bourgogne*. Brussels, 1622; Miraeus, A. *De vita Alberti Pii, sapientis, prudentis Belgarum Principis commentarius*. Antwerp, 1622; Puteanus, E. & Francquart, J. *Pompa funebris (...) Alberti Pii, archiducis Austriae...* Brussels, 1622.

[12] For a good analysis, see Papy, J. & Van Houdt, T. 'The Image of Archduke Albert in Seventeenth-Century Funeral Literature,' in: Thomas & Duerloo, *Essays*, pp. 319-334.

[13] This vision carries great weight, for example, in Hennequin de Villermont, M. *L'Infante Isabelle, gouvernante des Pays-Bas*. 2 vols. Paris, 1912.

[14] Thomas, W. 'La Corte de los Archiduques,' 359.

[15] See e.g. Discailles, E. *La légende des bons souverains: les archiducs Albert et Isabelle*. Brussels, 1910.

[16] See e.g. Blaes, J.-B. 'La Belgique au XVIIe siècle. Le gouvernement de l'archiduc Albert,' in: Blaes, J.-B. *Études historiques sur le XVIe siècle*. Brussels, 1863, pp. 133-193.

looking over the couple's shoulders, held the strings firmly in its hands. Political and military initiatives were only approved after having the pros and cons weighed in advance by Isabella's half-brother Philip III and his councilors. According to critics the Archducal Netherlands were therefore little more than a Spanish protectorate.[17] The sovereign status of Albert and Isabella was merely papering over the cracks: in reality, policy was dictated from Madrid. So as to give force to that argument, reference was made among other things to the Act of Cession, which in 1598 regulated the gift of Habsburg possessions in the Low Countries to the infanta and her spouse, the secret clauses of which stood in the way of a fully autonomous administration. The remaining presence of Spanish troops in the Netherlands was only one such clause, but it was seen by most authors as decisive. Real independence was after all difficult to harmonize with a military apparatus that was led and financed by a major 'foreign' power. On top of that it was an open secret that archducal authority stood or fell with the monetary support of Spain. The sovereignty of Albert and Isabella, so the verdict read, was an empty shell.

During the first decades of the twentieth century the sovereignty debate predominated historiography concerning the archducal period. One after the other, all manner of extreme and less extreme standpoints came under consideration in the process.[18] An important contribution was provided by the Belgian historian and archivist Joseph Lefèvre, who in 1924 would introduce a concept that for dozens of years would continue to guide the direction of the scholarly interpretation of the reign of Albert and Isabella. In his article about the power relationships characterizing the archducal regime, Lefèvre posited that the political administration and the military leadership in the Habsburg Netherlands were almost fully in the hands of a limited group of Spaniards, whom he arranged for sake of ease under the moniker '*le ministère espagnol*.'[19] According to Lefèvre, this ministry consisted in the main of a series of successive Spanish ambassadors and secretaries of State and War in Brussels; of a few leading functionaries such as the *veedor general* (controller-general), the *pagador general* (paymaster-general) and the superintendent of the military court of justice; and of the citadel commandants in the garrison cities of Antwerp, Ghent, and Cambrai.

[17] For an historiographical overview in this matter, see Noens, V. *Het standpunt van het Madrileense hof inzake de onafhankelijkheid van de aartshertogen met betrekking tot binnenlandse aangelegenheden.* Unpublished master's thesis, Universiteit Gent, 2006.

[18] See e.g. Brants, V. *L'autonomie internationale de la Belgique sous les archiducs Albert et Isabelle (1598-1621).* Macon, 1901; Gossart, E. *La domination espagnole dans les Pays-Bas à la fin du règne de Philippe II.* Brussels, 1906; Lonchay, H. 'Philippe II et le mariage des archiducs Albert et Isabelle.' *Académie Royale de Belgique, Bulletin de la Classe des Lettres et des Sciences Morales et Politiques et de la Classe des Beaux-Arts,* 6 (1910) 364-388; Lefèvre, J. 'La souveraineté d'Albert et d'Isabelle.' *Revue Générale Belge,* 89 (1953) 967-983.

[19] Lefèvre, J. 'Le ministère espagnol de l'Archiduc Albert, 1598-1621,' *Bulletin de l'Académie Royale d'Archéologie de Bruxelles,* 1 (1924) 202-224.

That their observatory and regulatory presence constituted a significant hindrance to the independence of the archdukes was a fait accompli for Lefèvre. Political freedom of movement for the princes, after all, was noticeably constrained by the Spanish-oriented policy vision held by the members of this 'ministry': 'To maintain and extend the rights of the king of Spain, that is their collective aim. It seems evident that their presence has been a severe limitation to the liberty of the prince.'[20]

As concerns biographical information, Lefèvre's study still forms a valuable addition to the knowledge of the political scene in the Habsburg Netherlands at the beginning of the seventeenth century. In spite of this, Lefèvre's argumentation sets up a few pertinent questions that in a way qualify the validity of his analysis. Thus the author started out for instance from the implicit position of a solid correlation between 'nation' – a concept that must always be employed with the requisite circumspection in an early modern context – and political loyalty, which did not necessarily have to be the case. That problem will be treated in detail later on in this book (cf. Chapter III). For now it suffices to indicate that Lefèvre's concept of the *ministère espagnol* strengthened the conviction supposing that the exercise of power in the Archducal Netherlands had been the object of conflict between two groupings, distinguished on 'national' grounds. In so doing, the 'Spanish' party, propagating a strong policy vision oriented to the king, stood diametrically opposed with respect to a rather recalcitrant 'indigenous' – Lefèvre used the term *belge* [Belgian] – party, swearing loyalty to the archdukes. Thus, according to Lefèvre, the fault lines cutting through politics ran parallel to the gulf that separated the two contending nations from each other. In that way he reduced decision-making in the archducal period to a process subject to disputes of an unmistakably nationalistic nature. Even if this vision had been based on a contemporaneous perception of the problem, the question remains as to how much it actually approaches reality.

A second aspect that causes Lefèvre's argumentation to lose its force is the fact that the author's attention concentrated on what nowadays would be described as the formal structures of power. Apart from a few exceptions the article exclusively discussed prominent figures from the diplomatic world and from the political and military administration. Not coincidentally, it is a matter here of the creation and evolution of domains that were seen by historians at that time as crucial conditions for the formation of the modern state. Lefèvre displayed little to no interest for structures and processes that seemingly functioned in the background and where power manifested itself as less pronounced and visible, yet certainly as no less real. Wholly

[20] '*Maintenir et étendre les droits du roi d'Espagne, en cela consiste leur programme à tous. (...) Que leur présence ait été une limitation accentuée de la liberté du prince, cela paraît évident.*' Lefèvre, 'Le ministère espagnol,' p. 224.

in accordance with the historiographical norms of his times, the author employed a paradigm in which politics was seen as the resultant force of policy actions and points of view that – if not exclusively, then at least primarily – came to fruition inside the established institutions of the state apparatus.

Lefèvre's approach was sharply contested in 1964 by Charles H. Carter, who publicly denounced its pronounced nationalistic bias.[21] In a commendable attempt to find consensus in the different standpoints regarding the autonomy of Albert and Isabella, Carter placed the emphasis on the gravity of that question, gave an overview of the extant standpoints, summed up their pros and cons, and in the end came to the conclusion that the independence of the archdukes was to a strong degree contingent upon the concrete situations and the nature of the individual cases it was tested against. An unequivocal solution to the problem surrounding the sovereign status of Albert and Isabella consequently did not pertain to the possibilities. It was an extremely nuanced position, supported even today by most historians. Nevertheless it needs to be pointed out that Carter's analysis put the emphasis just as strongly on the traditional structures of power. In spite of his rejection of Lefèvre's vision, even for Carter the political and military administration was central, and the less tangible ways of power remained beyond examination. The same applies to the authoritative study published in 1976 by Hugo De Schepper and Geoffrey Parker, who posited that 'a good deal of the history of the South Netherlands in the early seventeenth century will fail to make sense' without a clear answer to the question about the political autonomy of the archdukes.[22] For that reason the authors investigated how the Collateral Councils tried to direct and influence the policy of Albert and Isabella, as well as what role the Spanish ministry played. In an attempt to justify their line of questioning, they put forward that 'we do not fully understand how any government of an early modern state made decisions, because we do not fully understand how the governmental processes worked.'[23]

---

[21] Carter, C.H. 'Belgian 'Autonomy' under the Archdukes, 1598-1621.' *The Journal of Modern History*, 36 (1964) 245-259.

[22] De Schepper, H. & Parker, G. 'The Formation of Government Policy in the Catholic Netherlands under 'the Archdukes', 1596-1621.' *The English Historical Review*, 91 (1976) 241-254. Op. cit. p. 242.

[23] *Ibidem*, p. 241. The authors based their argumentation on a citation from Geoffrey Elton: 'No one can hope to write about any aspect of Tudor history without the solid grasp of realities and probabilities, without the deep understanding of the records before him which administrative history (...) alone can supply.' See Elton, G.R. *Studies in Tudor and Stuart Politics and Government, papers and reviews 1946-1972*. 2 vols. Cambridge, 1974. Op. cit. vol. I, p. 259.

The emergence of court studies

Without wanting to detract from the individual accomplishments of the studies mentioned, each of which in its way signified enrichment for scholarly knowledge with regard to the Archducal Netherlands, it can be postulated that they shared a common weak point. In their treatment of the political regime they employed one after the other a quite rigid focus, which in the main was directed at the institutional history of these regions. They thus cultivated the conviction supposing that the 'governmental processes' would have been played out within the fold of a number of well circumscribed political organs, which constituted a foreshadowing of what in the twentieth century would come to belong to the standard trappings of the modern state (the government councils, the secretariats, the representative bodies of the estates, etc.). One of the endeavors of this book is to demonstrate that such a one-sided vision is in no way possibly capable of sufficiently deciphering the early modern decision-making process in all its complexity, let alone for drawing conclusions about the nature and the workings of policy. That, moreover, is definitely not a revolutionary standpoint. In 1987 already, the British historian David Starkey deemed that 'the emphasis on institutional history appears fully justified. But institutions, the institutional historian too easily forgets, are not self-sufficient entities.'[24]

Determining that the administrative institutions in England at the time of the Ancien Régime functioned within the wheelworks of the personal monarchy – a political context that for the large part was subjected to unpredictable variables like patronage, nepotism, favoritism, the granting of favors, and princely caprice – led Starkey to argue that early modern politics cannot be grasped without paying attention to the personal identity of the prince, to the specific form of exercising and delegating power which issued forth from that, and to the princely court as the central *locus* of decision-making.[25] Characteristic of this point of view is the importance attached to the personal role of the monarch as 'source of secular authority and the most prominent distributor of offices and honors,' as well as the weight given to the degree to which the monarch is both physically and mentally 'accessible' for his subjects.[26] In that way the prince could choose to rely to a greater or lesser degree on the advice of an entourage, whether limited or not, or even delegate a portion of his power to privileged individuals who outlined the policy in his stead. If he opted, on

---

24 Starkey, D. 'Introduction: Court History in Perspective,' in: Starkey, D. et al. *The English Court from the Wars of the Roses to the Civil War*. London-New York, 1987, pp. 1-24. Op. cit. p. 6.

25 *Ibidem*.

26 The citation derives from Adamson, J. 'The Making of the Ancien-Régime Court, 1500-1700,' in: Adamson, J., ed. *The Princely Courts of Europe. Ritual, Politics and Culture under the Ancien Régime 1500-1750*. London, 1999, pp. 7-41. Op. cit. p. 7.

the contrary, for an elevated position, receiving as little external influence to integrate as possible, then he needed to distance himself literally and figuratively from an all too meddlesome environment. The way in which the dominion of successive English princes manifested itself – whether it be more 'participatory' or 'detached,' according to Starkey – went beyond not just the mere institutional framework but was defining for the workings of the political order as a whole.[27] Choosing one of either extremes led to varied policy-making with regard to the distribution of power and demanded, therefore, varied strategy in terms of those who wanted to acquire that power. Both ways of acting, Starkey says, can essentially be traced back to contrasting methods of dealing with the relationship between prince and subject and, consequently, to the vision of 'kingship' as an abstract matter.[28] Inherent in it was the duality between the prince as a *person* (i.e. the natural body of the prince as individual) and the princely *persona* (i.e. the princely authority and *maiestas* symbolized by his body), an idea that was elaborated in 1957 by the medievalist Ernst H. Kantorowicz.[29] Nowhere was that foggy twilight zone as blatantly present as at the early modern court, where the dividing line between the private and the public life of the ruler was inevitably quite visible, yet at the same time paper-thin.

With this conclusion Starkey wanted to fix the attention of political historians on what according to him was 'a natural goal for any man of ambition' from the late fifteenth until the early nineteenth century.[30] In his optic the English court during the Ancien Régime was the forum *par excellence* where power was traded, not simply for the sake of the administrative institutions circling around it, but above all by means of the interaction that came about between the prince and the noble elites. Thus Starkey started out from the position, for example, that the most important political organ was not the Privy Council, as populated by councilors and jurists, but instead the Privy Chamber, the most secluded space of the palace, where noble chamberlains made up the staff.[31] In view of the fact that the Privy Chamber enclosed the private quarters of the monarch, access to it was strictly regulated. The few who had permission to enter this *sanctum sanctorum* of the palace and to approach the prince were in the main members of his household. They not only fulfilled domestic and ceremonial duties, but combined their office with positions in administrative, financial, diplomatic, and military domains as well. In that way they functioned as intermediaries between the prince and other strata of society, making them – Starkey

---

27 Starkey, 'Introduction,' 8.

28 *Ibidem.*

29 Kantorowicz, E.H. *The King's Two Bodies: A Study in Mediaeval Political Theology*. Princeton U.P., 1957.

30 Starkey, 'Introduction,' 2.

31 See in that context also Starkey's doctoral dissertation: Starkey, D. *The Development of the Privy Chamber, 1485-1547*. Unpublished doctoral dissertation, Cambridge University, 1973.

says – crucial pawns on the political chessboard. In the heavily monitored Privy Chamber these courtiers succeeded, on top of that, in grabbing the ear of the prince, in gaining his favor, and in rousing his confidence and affection. Here, in the personal quarters of the ruler, where the private and public spheres flowed over into each other, decision-making did not run according to standard administrative procedures but according to the unwritten natural laws of the 'politics of intimacy.'[32]

Starkey's vision, influencing a generation of historians, broke in a daring way with the scholarly theories that for years had dominated historiography about Tudor and Stuart England.[33] Ironically enough, the most important representative of this traditional movement was none other than Geoffrey Elton, Starkey's former teacher, which perhaps may be the explanation for the not very subtle ferocity with which both historians entered into debate with each other.[34] Without beating around the bush, Starkey argued that the distinction Elton defended between 'court' and 'government' simply did not exist in early modern England. The princely court *was* the government, and the palace of the prince was the seat of the government. This bold proposition rested on the conviction – however varied and diffuse it might be – that political power in essence emanated from the figure of the prince: 'In a personal monarchy, unless the monarch wished, it could be no other.'[35] With that Starkey provided sharp criticism of Elton who saw the court as one of the 'points of contact' of that politics, to be sure, but at the same time started from the position that the government itself was a matter of central institutions like the Privy Council and the parliament.[36] In this way, according to Starkey, Elton created an unjustifiable differentiation between 'politics' on the one hand and 'government' on the other, in which the first term can be associated with individual rivalry, factional infighting, conflict of interest and backroom politics, and the second with professionally educated bureaucrats who endeavored to steer the day-to-day administration in the right direction in spite of everything.[37] On top of that, Elton started from the position of a similar distinction between the 'courtier' and the 'councilor,' where both figures not only employed the same strategies and objectives, according to Starkey, but often were also one and the same person.[38]

---

[32] *Ibidem.*

[33] Mears, N. 'Courts, Courtiers, and Culture in Tudor England.' *The Historical Journal*, 46 (2003) 703-722.

[34] See e.g. the polemic in *The Historical Journal*: Elton, G.R. 'Tudor Government.' *The Historical Journal*, 31 (1988 no. 2) 425-434 and Starkey, D. 'A Reply: Tudor Government: The Facts?' *The Historical Journal*, 31 (1988 no. 4) 921-931.

[35] Starkey, 'Introduction,' 19.

[36] Elton, G.R. 'Tudor Government. The Points of Contact, III: The Court.' *Transactions of the Royal Historical Society, 5th series*, 26 (1976) 211-228.

[37] Starkey, 'Introduction,' 11.

[38] *Ibidem*, p. 13.

Though the debate between David Starkey and Geoffrey Elton degenerated into a severe and at times quite biting polemic in the course of time, both historians started out in fact from the same position: they were in agreement that the early modern court deserved more scholarly attention than it had received until then. In that context Elton wrote, 'We all know that there was a Court, and we all use the term with frequent ease, but we seem to have taken it so much for granted that we have done almost nothing to investigate it seriously.'[39] The question, rather, was in what way that was supposed to occur. Even Starkey, in defiance of his criticism of the institutionalistic historiography of his teacher, said that he wanted to approach the court as an administrative institution, yet in that case from a broad perspective that connected politics with aspects like ceremonial, material culture, interpersonal relationships, and conspicuous consumption.[40] In doing so, he was one of the inspirations of the so-called *New Tudor political history*, which since the 1990s prevailed in the research on the matter and which endeavored to couple the early modern decision-making process to a more social and cultural interpretation of politics. Essentially, this historical movement starts out from the position 'that politics was less about institutions (...) than the interaction between those institutions, people, and ideas.'[41] For that reason it concentrates not just on the purely institutional side of the matter, but it endeavors to employ an interdisciplinary approach that is oriented to a mix of archival research and the study of political culture and ideology, dynastic strategies, social networks and clienteles, factional formation, patronage, the (mental) life-world of the nobility, contemporaneous literature, dramaturgy, iconography, and even architecture. In the process the princely court stands more than ever front and center as 'the main forum for policy-making' during the Ancien Régime.[42]

The turn from a merely institutional toward an alternative, more socio-culturally oriented angle not only brought forth new and elucidating syntheses about the Tudor era, but also stimulated methodological discussions about political historiography and its processes, and even about the functioning of early modern politics itself.[43] In that way it inspired as well historical research into princely courts and households on the European continent, where since the 1970s a similar turning point had arisen (albeit not everywhere, and not always at the same tempo). Especially influential in that context was the German sociologist Norbert Elias, whose study *Die höfische Gesellschaft* (completed in 1933, but not published until 1969) saw to a radical break

[39] Elton, 'Tudor Government. The Points of Contact,' 211.
[40] Starkey, 'Introduction,' 2.
[41] Mears, 'Courts, Courtiers, and Culture in Tudor England,' 704.
[42] *Ibidem*, p. 722.
[43] For a long list of examples in this matter see the overview in Mears, 'Courts, Courtiers and Culture in Tudor England,' passim.

with regard to the visions of the early modern court at that time.[44] Where the latter was seen by nineteenth-century historians as an archaic institution that was scarcely worth studying, and depicted again as autocratic, corrupt and pompous in later Marxist historiography, Elias acknowledged a key role for the court as the engine of a triumphant absolutism. In Elias' vision the court functioned as a battleground in which the different elites of the principality contested each other for the attention and affection of the prince. Thanks as well to the introduction of refined court ceremonial and a frugal distribution of favors, the prince succeeded in making the courtiers more and more dependent on his person. In that way, according to Elias, the theretofore weighty political role of the nobility was fettered for the advantage of a state apparatus becoming increasingly more powerful. The familiar image of the court as a 'golden cage' for the tamed aristocracy can be seen as illustrative for this approach.

In the past decades Elias' theories were spared criticism least of all. Above all, the interaction, seen as self-evident, between the development of the absolutist court, the disappearance of nobles' power, and the emergence of the modern state was repeatedly called into question.[45] Nevertheless, *Die höfische Gesellschaft* proved to be crucial for the heights to which research into early modern courts has been taken in the non-Anglo-Saxon world. Since the publication and the translation of Elias' work, an abundance of scholarly studies has appeared concerning the countless princely courts in Europe, from large surveys employing the general thrust to well-wrought analyses exposing the daily life at a specific court down to the smallest detail.[46] In France, Spain, Germany, Austria, and Italy, important research centers have been established in the meantime, occupying themselves exclusively with 'court studies.'[47] In addition to mutual contacts, more and more collaborative connections are also coming into being between these continental schools and their Anglo-Saxon counterpart, which

---

[44] Elias, N. *Die Höfische Gesellschaft. Untersuchungen zur Soziologie des Königtums und die höfische Aristokratie*. Neuwied, 1969.

[45] See e.g. Duindam, J. *Myths of Power. Norbert Elias and the Early Modern European Court*. Amsterdam U.P., 1995.

[46] An entire library can be filled with the number of studies concerning courts and their households; examples in this matter are to be found in abundance in the footnotes in this book. An extremely selective list ought to mention the three most important surveys in any case: Dickens, A.G., ed. *The Courts of Europe. Politics, Patronage and Royalty, 1400-1800*. London, 1977; Asch, R.G. & Birke, A.M., eds. *Princes, Patronage and the Nobility: The Court at the Beginning of the Modern Age, c. 1450-1650*. Oxford U.P., 1991; and Adamson, J., ed. *The Princely Courts of Europe: Ritual, Politics and Culture under the Ancien Régime, 1500-1750*. London, 1999. For a historiographical overview, see Vázquez Gestal, P. *El espacio del poder. La corte en la historiografía modernista española y europea*. Valladolid, 2005.

[47] France: *Centre de Recherche du Château de Versailles*; see also the Internet project *La Cour de France du Moyen Âge au XIXe siècle* (http://cour-de-France.fr/). Italy: *Centro Studi Europa delle Corti*. Spain: *Instituto Universitario 'La Corte en Europa'* (Universidad Autónoma de Madrid). Germany: *Residenzen-Kommission* (Akademie der Wissenschaften zu Göttingen), see also the *Rudolstädter Arbeitskreis zur Residenzkultur*. In Austria, the Institut für Geschichte of the Universität Wien administers the research project *Patronage- und Klientelsysteme am Wiener Hof*. A list of websites can be found in the bibliography.

again comes to the benefit of the comparative approach.[48] All in all, it can be postulated that as an area of study court studies – despite a difficult start – has grown into a fully-fledged as well as full-grown branch of historiography, with its own forums for debate and even its own scholarly journal.[49] That does not take away from the fact, however, that, in addition to embarrassing lacunae and ambiguities, great differences of opinion still exist concerning the role and the function of the early modern court as well as the effectiveness of diverse research methods.

In the past years, various historians have argued convincingly that extant historiography with regard to the courts and their households has been plagued by all manner of shortcomings.[50] In spite of necessary commendable attempts, knowledge concerning the way in which the princely court interacted with other echelons of the political universe is still limited. After years of debate, the scholarly theories with regard to networking, patronage, clientelism, and factional formation are at a very high level, yet they are underpinned with too few concrete examples concerning the way in which these aspects influenced political decision-making.[51] There seems as well to exist an overestimation of culturally inspired topics like ceremonial, ritual, and representation, where the socio-economic character of the court still could reckon with little interest until now.[52] At present, the heretofore overestimated institutional dimension is again done away with as unfashionable, whereby the scales have perhaps tipped too far in the other direction. Furthermore, the comparative approach – inasmuch as it is being applied – concentrates in the main on early modern European princely courts, whereas it would perhaps gain more with a larger geographical *and* chronological distribution. The comparison with courts in non-Western cultures,

---

48 Active since 1995 in the Anglo-Saxon world is *The Society for Court Studies*.

49 See Smith, H. 'Court Studies and the Courts of Early Modern Europe.' *The Historical Journal*, 49 (2006) 1229-1238. The journal of *The Society for Court Studies* is *The Court Historian*.

50 See e.g. Duindam, J. 'Van cohabitatie naar coëxistentie? Hofhouding en staatsbestuur in vroeg-modern Europa.' *Tijdschrift voor Geschiedenis*, 115 (2002) 254-273; Duindam, J. 'De herontdekking van het vorstelijk hof.' *Tijdschrift voor Geschiedenis*, 108 (1995) 361-376; and, as already cited, Mears, 'Courts, Courtiers, and Culture in Tudor England.' Further see Dean, T. 'The Courts. A Historiographical Problem.' *The Journal of Modern History*, 67 (1995) 136-151; Chaline, O. ' 'Combien de royaumes nous ignorent': la cour dans l'historiographie française.' *Annali di Storia moderna e contemporanea*, 2 (1996) 384-392; and Fantoni, M. 'The Future of Court Studies: The Evolution, Present Successes and Prospects of a Discipline.' *The Court Historian*, 16/1 (2011) 1-6.

51 Quite a number of studies concerning patronage and clienteles in the early modern period have already appeared. Leading the way in that context is the research of Sharon Kettering. See e.g. Kettering, S. *Patrons, Brokers and Clients in Seventeenth-Century France*. New York, 1986; Kettering, S. 'The Historical Development of Political Clientelism.' *The Journal of Interdisciplinary History*, 18 (1988) 419-447; Kettering, S. 'Brokerage at the Court of Louis XIV.' *The Historical Journal*, 36 (1993) 69-87; and Kettering, S. *Patronage in Sixteenth and Seventeenth Century France*. Ashgate, 2002. See also the different contributions in Mączak, A. & Müller-Luckner, E., eds. *Klientelsysteme im Europa der frühen Neuzeit*. Munich, 1988.

52 Research into the economic history of the early modern court received an important impetus with the publication of Aymard, M. & Romani, M.A., eds. *La cour comme institution économique. Actes du douzième congrès international d'histoire économique, Séville-Madrid, 24-28 août 1998*. Paris, 1998.

for example, seldom comes up for discussion.[53] The interdisciplinary approach also remains all too often inadequate. Court studies, to be sure, extends its hand more and more often to art history and architectural history, yet it would also be aided with a more structural approach to sociology, political science and gender studies.[54] There exist, therefore, still many pitfalls for the court historian, and the direction in which the historiography concerning courts and their households needs to evolve must be well considered.

That there is room for improvement, however, is not to say that historians are not on the right track. Since the 1980s, as an area of study, court studies has fundamentally redrawn the landscape of political historiography concerning the early modern period. The focus on administrative institutions has made room for a more holistic approach, in which the process of state formation still plays a role, though it does not stand front and center any longer. In that regard, John Adamson concludes that

> 'perhaps the defining characteristic of the new court history is methodological: an attempt to emancipate the study of court politics and institutions from the anachronistic structures of 'absolutism', and court culture from crudely functionalist modes of analysis and the equally distorting concept of 'propaganda'. In the process, the new court history inevitably calls into question a closely related historical trend: the analysis of European ancien régimes in terms of statebuilding, in which the importance of early modern institutions is gauged according to the extent that they 'anticipate' modern structures of bureaucratic power.'[55]

Court studies and the court of the archdukes

From the preceding it would appear that the early modern court has grown into an important topic in the historical sciences for a few decades now. As regards the courts in the Low Countries, the reaction was somewhat longer in coming, but since the

---

53 An important exception is Duindam, J., Artan, T. & Kunt, M., eds. *Royal Courts in Dynastic States and Empires*. Leiden, 2011.

54 The history of familiar and less familiar princesses can reckon with more and more interest in recent years. See e.g. Sánchez, M.S. *The Empress, the Queen and the Nun: Women and Power at the Court of Philip III of Spain*. Johns Hopkins U.P., 1998; Campbell-Orr, C., ed. *Queenship in Britain, 1660-1837: Royal Patronage, Court Culture, and Dynastic Politics*. Manchester U.P., 2002; Campbell-Orr, C., ed. *Queenship in Europe, 1660-1815: The Role of the Consort*. Cambridge U.P., 2004; and Cruz, A.J. & Suzuki, M., eds. *The Rule of Women in Early Modern Europe*. University of Illinois Press, 2009. See also Hirschbiegel, J. & Paravicini, W., eds. *Das Frauenzimmer. Die Frau bei Hofe in Spätmittelalter und Früher Neuzeit* (Residenzenforschung 11). Stuttgart, 2000; and Keller, K. *Hofdamen. Amtsträgerinnen im Wiener Hofstaat des 17. Jahrhunderts*. Vienna, 2005.

55 Adamson, 'The Making of the Ancien-Régime Court,' 40.

1990s progress has been made here, too. Above all research into the courts and their households is meeting with much success most recently – albeit with great differences in quality.[56] In so doing, it has rightly concentrated not only on the court of the princes of Orange but also on the smaller and less familiar courts.[57] For the Southern Netherlands research has limped somewhat more behind, but here, too, improvement is noticeable. In this way the court of the governess Margaret of Austria in Mechelen, for instance, could in the meantime reckon with some interest shown – albeit to a limited degree as yet.[58] As regards the court of Brussels, the attention has gone primarily to the Burgundian period instead, and to the first half of the sixteenth century.[59] Apart from a few brief and not always evenly elucidating contributions, the role and the significance of the court in Brussels in the late sixteenth and seventeenth century remained underexposed for the large part.[60] On account of the historiographical

---

[56] See e.g. Mörke, O. 'Sovereignty and the Authority. The Role of the Court in the Netherlands in the First Half of the Seventeenth Century,' in: Asch & Birke, *Princes, Patronage, and the Nobility*, pp. 455-477; Mörke, O. 'De hofhouding van het huis Oranje-Nassau in de zeventiende eeuw,' in: Frijhoff, W., Burke, P. & Te Boekhorst, P., eds. *Cultuur en maatschappij in Nederland 1500-1850. Een historisch-antropologisch perspectief.* Heerlen, 1992, pp. 39-77; Zijlmans, J. 'Aan het Haagse hof,' in: Keblusek, M. & Zijlmans, J., eds. *Vorstelijk vertoon. Aan het hof van Frederik Hendrik en Amalia.* Zwolle-The Hague, 1997, pp. 30-45; Israel, J. 'The Courts of the House of Orange, c. 1580-1795,' in: Adamson, *The Princely Courts*, pp. 119-139; Zandvliet, K. 'Het hof van een dienaar met vorstelijke allure,' in: Zandvliet, K., ed. *Maurits. Prins van Oranje.* Zwolle-Amsterdam, 2000, pp. 36-63; and Delen, M.-A. *Het hof van Willem van Oranje.* Amsterdam, 2002.

[57] See e.g. Nijsten, G. *Het hof van Gelre. Cultuur ten tijde van de hertogen uit het Gulikse en Egmondse huis (1371-1473).* Kampen, 1992.

[58] Concerning the Mechelen court, see Eichberger, D. 'A Cultural Centre in the Southern Netherlands: The Court of Archduchess Margaret of Austria (1480-1530) in Mechelen,' in: Gosman, M., MacDonald, A. & Vanderjagt, A., eds. *Princes and Princely Culture 1450-1650.* 2 vols. Leiden, 2003, volume I, pp. 239-258. See also the different contributions in Eichberger, D., ed. *Dames met klasse. Margareta van York/ Margareta van Oostenrijk.* Exhibition catalogue. Leuven, 2005. See also Steurs, F. *Het Keizershof en het hof van Margareta van Oostenrijk te Mechelen.* Mechelen, 1879.

[59] See e.g. Paravicini, W. 'Die Residenzen der Herzöge von Burgund, 1363-1477,' in: Patze, H. & Paravicini, W., eds. *Fürstliche Residenzen im spätmittelalterlichen Europa.* Sigmaringen, 1991, pp. 207-263; and Paravicini, W. 'Expansion et intégration. La noblesse des Pays-Bas à la cour de Philippe le Bon.' *Bijdragen en Mededelingen betreffende de Geschiedenis der Nederlanden*, 95 (1980) 298-314. See also the different contributions in Gunn, S.J. & Janse, A., eds. *The Court as a Stage. England and the Low Countries in the Later Middle Ages.* Woodbridge, 2006. For later periods, see Martínez Millán, J., ed. *La Corte de Carlos V.* 5 vols. Madrid, 2000; and Kerkhoff, J. *Maria van Hongarije en haar hof (1505-1558). Tot plichtsbetrachting uitverkoren.* Hilversum, 2008.

[60] See e.g. Coremans, V. 'L'archiduc Ernest, sa cour, ses dépenses: détails sur son voyage de Prague à Bruxelles (1593-1595).' *Compte rendu des séances de la Commission Royale d'Histoire ou recueil de ses bulletins*, 13 (1847) 85-147; and Lefèvre, J. 'La Cour de l'Archiduc Léopold-Guillaume, 1647-1652.' *Archives, Bibliothèques et Musées de Belgique*, 5 (1928) 65-77. More recently the courts of the archduke Leopold-Wilhelm and the governor Don Juan José of Austria were put under the magnifying lens, see Echevarría Bacigalupe, M.A. 'Los gastos de un gobernador general en Flandes: el archiduque Leopoldo Guillermo (1647-1652).' *Letras de Deusto*, 33 (1983) 175-186; Mertens, J. & Aumann, F., eds. *Krijg en Kunst. Leopold-Willem (1614-1662). Habsburger, landvoogd en kunstverzamelaar.* Exhibition catalogue. Bilzen, 2003; Hortal Muñoz, J.E. 'La casa del Archiduque Ernesto durante su gobierno en los Países Bajos (1593-1595),' in: Álvarez-Ossorio Alvariño, A. & García García, B.J., eds. *La Monarquía de las Naciones. Patria, nación y naturaleza en la Monarquía de España.* Madrid, 2004, pp. 193-205; and Roegis, E. *Het hof van don Juan José de Austria, landvoogd in de Habsburgse Nederlanden (1656-1658).* Unpublished master's thesis, Universiteit Gent, 2006.

debate concerning the import of the archducal period in Belgian history, the court of Albert and Isabella could still count on the most interest exhibited, even though the harvest is relatively meager here too.[61] On top of that, research into the question was defined for a long time by an historiographical agenda that had been fixed in the late nineteenth and early twentieth century. In that, the focus was not only on the traditional administrative institutions but also on the rivalry between the Spanish and the 'indigenous' presence in the Netherlands. Even until today historians have found it difficult to shake off the influence of this institutional and polarizing approach.

In light of the sovereignty debate the archducal court was and is generally described as a bulwark of Spanish authority in the Netherlands.[62] From a certain angle that need not be surprising: as the following chapters will demonstrate, the court was in many areas seemingly a faithful copy of its pendant portrait in Madrid. That applied both to the organization of its household as well as to the court ceremonial in vogue there. Even the language of communication and the fashion at court were Spanish. Yet appearance does not necessarily say anything about content. On top of that, the idea of the 'Spanish bastion' relies not so much on the composition of the household of Albert and Isabella as it does on the presence of various Spanish diplomats, functionaries, and army officers in and around the Brussels palace.[63] As was previously cited, the role of the actual archducal household in this matter was seldom taken into account. For reasons to be discussed later on, an analysis of the composition, the activities, *and* the political significance of that household could cast new light on the autonomy of the archdukes. In that context, for example, the fact was already indicated that Albert and Isabella – to the degree their reign advanced – took more and more courtiers into their service whose origins were in the Southern Netherlands and Burgundy, and that the Spanish presence in their household became

[61] The most important studies are: Gossart, E. *L'auberge des princes en exil. Anecdotes de la cour de Bruxelles au XVIIe siècle*. Brussels, 1905; Klingenstein, L. *The Great Infanta: Isabel, Sovereign of the Netherlands*. London, 1910; Hennequin de Villermont, M. *Le duc et la duchesse de Bournonville et la cour de Bruxelles*. Brussels, 1904; Hennequin de Villermont, M. *L'Infante Isabelle, gouvernante des Pays-Bas*. 2 vols. Paris-Tamines, 1912; Saintenoy, P. *Les arts et les artistes à la cour de Bruxelles*. 3 vols. Brussel, 1932-1935; and De Maeyer, M. *Albrecht en Isabella en de schilderkunst. Bijdrage tot de geschiedenis van de XVIIe-eeuwse schilderkunst in de Zuidelijke Nederlanden*. Brussels, 1955.

[62] See e.g. García García, B.J. 'La Corte de los Archiduques en Bruselas.' *Torre de los Lujanes*, 44 (2001) 59-75.

[63] For this, the various contributions of Joseph Lefèvre may be seen as representative: Lefèvre, J. 'Don Juan de Mancicidor, secrétaire d'État et de Guerre de l'archiduc Albert (1596-1618).' *Revue belge de Philologie et d'Histoire*, 4 (1925) 697-714; Lefèvre, J. 'L'aumonerie militaire à l'époque de l'archiduc Albert, 1598-1621.' *Revue belge de Philologie et d'Histoire*, 7 (1928) 113-129; Lefèvre, J. 'Les ambassadeurs d'Espagne à Bruxelles sous le règne de l'archiduc Albert (1598-1621).' *Revue belge de Philologie et d'Histoire*, 2 (1923) 61-80; Lefèvre, J. 'Les chatelains militaires espagnols des Pays-Bas à l'époque de l'archiduc Albert (1598-1621).' *Revue belge de Philologie et d'Histoire*, 9 (1930) 831-852; Lefèvre, J. 'L'intervention du duc de Lerme dans les affaires des Pays-Bas (1598-1618).' *Revue belge de Philologie et d'Histoire*, 18 (1939) 463-485; and Lefèvre, J. *La Secrétairie d'État et de Guerre sous le Régime espagnol (1594-1711)*. Brussels, 1934.

increasingly smaller.[64] Consequently, it can be posited that the balance between the different nations at court gradually tilted to the advantage of the local elites.

Some caveats are necessary, however. Naturally, numerical superiority does not necessarily translate into political supremacy. On top of that, there is still the question as to what degree the courtiers' origins tell something about their political affinity. That kind of argumentation relies perhaps all too strongly on the traditional interpretation of the archducal reign, in which the rivalry between the Spanish 'overlords' and the native populace stood front and center.[65] One of the positions of this book is that the stereotypical image of the court has been in large part based on an historiographical paradigm that was in full force in the first half of the twentieth century, and in which the idea of Spanish tyranny in the Southern Netherlands was dominant.[66] The sharp edges have been filed down in the meantime, yet under the surface this vision still exercises the obligatory influence even today, in the sense that the focus on this 'national' conflict still prevails in the literature. In that way, Jonathan Israel wrote in 1997, for instance, that 'regarding high matters of state at the court of Albert and Isabella, nothing could be clearer than that only the views of Spanish commanders, officials and diplomats (...) really counted while the voice of the Archdukes' Netherlandish courtiers, whether nobles, churchmen or bureaucrats, was an entirely minimal one.'[67] A little later on he posits that '(...) the diplomacy and the decision-making process at the archducal court were almost exclusively run by Spaniards, whereas court ceremony, publicity, etiquette, formal announcements and presenting of gifts to fellow rulers, as well as judicial and administrative supervision were the domain of the autochthonous nobility.'[68] The author repeated the same standpoint again in the survey *België in de Zeventiende Eeuw* ['Belgium in the Seventeenth Century'], which was published in 2006.[69]

Although Israel is one of the few historians to emphasize the importance of the court of Albert and Isabella as a political and diplomatic nerve center, he nevertheless appears to hold a rather traditional opinion as regards the *modus operandi* of that court. Where the 'high affairs of state' – a somewhat misleading concept in a political

[64] Lanoye, D. 'Structure and Composition of the Household of the Archdukes,' in: Thomas & Duerloo, *Essays*, pp. 107-119.

[65] See Gossart, *La domination espagnole dans les Pays-Bas*; Lonchay, 'Philippe II et le mariage des archiducs Albert et Isabelle' and Lefèvre, J. 'La souveraineté d'Albert et d'Isabelle.'

[66] See in that context Stengers, J. 'Le mythe des dominations étrangères dans l'historiographie belge.' *Revue belge de Philologie et d'Histoire*, 59 (1981) 382-401.

[67] Israel, J. 'Chapter 1: The Court of Albert and Isabella, 1598-1621,' in: Israel, J. *Conflicts of Empires. Spain, the Low Countries and the Struggle for World Supremacy 1585-1713*. London, 1997, pp. 1-21. Op. cit. p. 6.

[68] *Ibidem*, p. 7.

[69] Israel, J. 'Het tijdperk van de Aartshertogen, 1598-1621,' in: Janssens, P., ed. *België in de Zeventiende Eeuw. De Spaanse Nederlanden en het prinsbisdom Luik*. 2 vols. Ghent, 2006, volume I, pp. 28-32.

context in which dynastic interests namely took priority – were fully in the hands of Spaniards according to Israel, the role of the courtiers from the Southern Netherlands was apparently 'limited' to the domains of public relations and administration. Disregarding the observation as yet that this approach builds really quite strongly upon the classic conceptions concerning the '*ministère espagnol*' from Joseph Lefèvre, the question still remains as to whether the distinction proposed here between two apparently contrasting political spheres was indeed as rigid as the author makes it appear. Israel's vision seems to start from the position that the domain of diplomatic relations, for instance, had nothing to do with the world of ceremony, publicity, formal announcements and gift-giving – a conclusion that stands contrary to the conceptions many specialists of early modern diplomacy hold at present. In the same way Israel's line of argumentation suggests an opposition between 'officials and diplomats' on the one hand and 'courtiers' on the other. It is questionable whether this kind of vision is in keeping with the perception contemporaries held.

Building on the debate already launched in the nineteenth century, the attention of historians of the archducal reign generally has gone and goes to the formal political structures and processes that were traditionally associated with the concept of 'decision-making' and that – not coincidentally – left behind copious written remains in the archives. In emulating recent tendencies in research into early modern courts and their households, this study wants to adjust today's image of the archducal court, taken from the standpoint that political power could also make itself manifest in very informal and often less tangible ways. The focus on the institutional framework passes over a great number of things that could influence the decision-making process, not least of which is the role of the archdukes' personal entourage. The excessive attention paid to the rivalry between the Spanish and the indigenous peoples does no justice, on top of that, to the cosmopolitan character of the court, which must be seen not so much as a Spanish bastion, as in fact one of the great power bases of the Habsburg dynasty. The reciprocal rivalry between those from Spain and those from the Southern Netherlands did indeed really exist, yet may not be seen as the only explanatory, let alone as the ever-decisive factor in the greater story. That kind of approach mistakes the characteristic identity of the archducal court as the forum *par excellence* where individual and familial favors were strived for, and where political conflicts of a diverse nature were fought out. These are the elements that have been tremendously ignored in the sovereignty debate.

The question arises, then, in what way the court needs to be studied to create a more nuanced image. The answer to this presupposes in the first place an accurate demarcation of the subject to be studied. The literature concerning the archducal reign, often refers to 'the court,' yet in fact historians seldom make clear what the concept comprises precisely. In the most cases the term is employed as a vague synonym for 'the government,' or by refraction for 'government circles.' In other cases it seems, then again, to denote the administrative organization, or a certain subdivision of it. Sometimes the term is used as a catch-all phrase for everyone in and around the Brussels palace; sometimes it refers only to the immediate entourage of the princes. In other words, there is much written about 'the court,' but unanimity concerning the concrete interpretation of that concept is far to be found. Even the introductory article by Paul Janssens in the collection *De centrale overheidsinstellingen van de Habsburgse Nederlanden* ['Institutions of Central Government in the Habsburg Netherlands'] offers little consolation in that area.[70] As indicated above, to study the court from a merely institutional angle does not suffice in any way. That kind of approach underestimates the multi-faceted and multiform nature of the early modern court, which as a 'protean institution' – to borrow an adequate term from R.J.W. Evans – constituted a nexus of political and social/cultural structures, networks, and processes that go beyond the merely institutional aspect.[71]

Already in 1991, Ronald Asch wrote that 'if the whole state apparatus is identified with the court, the word 'court' becomes virtually meaningless. Any discussion of the role of the historical court has, therefore, to start with the problem how to define the court.'[72] With that, Asch put his finger on the sore spot, for a conclusive definition has until now not been found. In the context of the kingdom of France, Norbert Elias described the early modern court as 'the vastly extended house and household of the French kings and their dependents, with all the people belonging to them.'[73] That kind of interpretation leaves room for play yet at the same time raises the question as to the precise boundaries of the court. The opinions about this are divided. Where David Starkey seemed to want to reduce the court to the private apartments of the prince, the American historian Perez Zagorin employed, for example, a much broader angle, in which the term 'court' was coupled to the whole administrative organization – even out into the provinces.[74] Between both these extremes can be found a whole gamut of usable and less usable definitions. This book pretends least of all to offer a ready-made solution for the problem set up by Asch. The reality is that the early modern

---

[70] Janssens, P. 'Het vorstelijk hof,' in: Aerts, E., Baelde, M., Coppens, H. et al., eds. *De centrale overheidsinstellingen van de Habsburgse Nederlanden (1482-1795)*. 2 vols. Brussels, 1994, volume I, pp. 163-171.

[71] Evans, R.J.W. 'The Court. A Protean Institution and an Elusive Subject,' in: Asch & Birke, *Princes, Patronage, and the Nobility*, pp. 481-491.

[72] Asch, R.G. 'Introduction: Court and Household from the Fifteenth to the Seventeenth Centuries,' in: Asch & Birke, *Princes, Patronage, and the Nobility*, pp. 1-38. Op. cit. p. 7.

[73] English translation taken from Elias, N. *The Court Society*. Translated by E. Jephcott. Oxford, 1983. Op. cit. p. 41.

[74] Starkey, 'Introduction,' 5; and Zagorin, P. 'The Court and the Country: A Note on Political Terminology in the Earlier Seventeenth Century.' *The English Historical Review*, 77 (1962) 306-311.

court can be defined in different ways, because it simply did have several functions, which are difficult to capture within one description. On top of that, two of these functions were seemingly also opposed to each other. On the one hand, the court was the private residence of the prince and, consequently, the environment *par excellence* where the latter could screen himself off from the outside world with the help of a strict court ceremonial. On the other hand, the court constituted the connection between the prince and the broad political universe around him, not in the least through the different networks of power that branched off from his household to the other echelons of society.

Although both functions may seem to be opposed to each other, still it is indeed striking that in both cases a crucial role was set aside for the immediate entourage of the ruler. The courtiers had not only direct access to the prince – which meant that they could exchange thoughts with him at all times and could talk him round to their way of thinking – but were at the same time intermediaries between the prince and his subjects – and as such mediators between the center of power and the periphery. For that reason historians start out from the position that the princely household occupied a strategic position in the early modern political order. In what follows this standpoint will be gone into more in depth.

The role of the household

In his book *Vienna and Versailles: The Courts of Europe's Dynastic Rivals, 1550-1780*, Jeroen Duindam points out that just about all contemporaneous definitions of the early modern court make mention of a union between 'household' and 'government.'[75] They agree that both personally serving the ruler as well as the administration of the realm fell under the responsibility of the princely court. As opposed to what nowadays is the case, these functions were therefore not perceived as separate domains during the Ancien Régime. The symbiosis between them both stood as self-evident. According to Duindam, however, that does not take away from the fact that a gradual tendency arose toward more rationalization and bureaucratization from the late middle ages through to the eighteenth century. That tendency would make the characteristic identity of (and the discrepancy between) both spheres increasingly more visible over time, without coming to an absolute split, all the same.[76] In nineteenth-century historiography this evolution would be explained as a natural process that necessarily had to precede the formation of the modern state, where

[75] Duindam, J. *Vienna and Versailles. The Courts of Europe's Dynastic Rivals, 1550-1780.* Cambridge U.P., 2003. Op. cit. p. 3.

[76] *Ibidem.*

(ideally, in any case) a strict separation between the personal entourage of the head of state and the administrative organization dominates. Duindam rightly argues that this teleological and anachronistic vision antedates the 'isolation and marginalisation of the household': 'An obsession with the antecedents of the modern state prevented [historians in the nineteenth century] from granting the household its proper place, and from understanding the crucial unrecorded and informal component of collegial decision-making.'[77]

Although more or less pronounced according to the specific circumstances, government and household continued to overlap each other till far into the eighteenth century. Whereas the English language is tied to the nomenclature '*household*' and '*government*,' in the Dutch language the interwoven nature between both spheres is perhaps better expressed via the single term '*hofhouding*,' which in principle allows both the domestic as well as the administrative component to be taken into consideration too. Nevertheless the word was and is generally associated simply with domestic activities, and in the meantime it has also acquired that meaning in Van Dale's *Groot woordenboek van de Nederlandse taal* ['Great Dictionary of the Dutch Language'], in which the word '*hofhouding*' is described as 'the entire household of a (specifically, princely) court, including those servants belonging to it.'[78] On top of that, in nineteenth-century historiography the term acquired a pejorative undertone, as if the existence of the princely household had for a long time stood in the way of the formation of a modern, professional bureaucracy. As a result, historians mistook the rightful place of the early modern princely household as a relevant and full-fledged political entity. In no way did that household form the backdrop, doomed to disappear, against which decision-making was played out, but was actually its very stage.

In this book, emulating the argumentation of Duindam, the supposed distinction between the princely domestic household and the princely government is cast off as an anachronistic historiographical construction. As Mia Rodríguez-Salgado also noted in that context, 'such a division is not only difficult, it is false.'[79] During the period studied here *domus* and *res publica* were inseparable and connected with each other in continual interaction. It is, however, seemingly not simple to bring this premise into accord with the multifaceted character of the household. Rather than a monolithic institute, it seems in its entirety to have constituted a nexus of different domains, functions, and objectives. Thus, in the context of the fifteenth-century English court, for example, the *Liber Niger Domus Regis Angliae* spoke already of a symbiosis between

[77] *Ibidem*, p. 7.

[78] Den Boon, T. & Geeraerts, D., eds. *Van Dale Groot woordenboek van de Nederlandse taal.* Utrecht, 2005.

[79] Rodríguez-Salgado, M.J. 'Honour and Profit in the Court of Philip II of Spain,' in: Aymard & Romani, *La cour comme institution économique*, pp. 67-86. Op. cit. p. 76.

the *domus providencie*, which was occupied with the logistical support of the prince and his entourage (the kitchens, the bakery, the chandlery, etc.), and the *domus magnificencie*, which meant not just the more respectable departments (the chapel, the wardrobe, etc.), but also the staff that took on certain advisory and administrative roles for themselves (the Knights and Esquires of the Body, the Gentlemen and Yeomen Ushers, etc.).[80] This contemporaneous partitioning illustrates, on top of that, that the princely household was in essence a complex social configuration, in which hundreds of individuals of different rank and standing lived and worked next to one another. It raises the question how that kind of pluriformity is in keeping with the political interpretation postulated in this book. The idea that the princely household united domestic and political responsibilities in itself seems at first only applicable to the 'higher' dignitaries alone, who in addition to a domestic function held actually administrative or diplomatic responsibilities too.

All the same, care needs to be taken against an all too modern approach to early modern politics. Where the 'lower' echelons of the princely household naturally did not occupy themselves with day-to-day administration, their role may not altogether be pushed aside. Rather, it is a matter of employing a vision that the household in its totality can be seen as an institution for which the core responsibility is defined as 'the making and maintaining of kingship.'[81] As was cited previously, the tense relationship, inherent to that kingship, between the natural and the symbolic body of the prince presupposed a distinction between his private and his public lives. This book means to start out from the standpoint that the princely court – as opposed to what is often assumed – was not just responsible for the first, but also for the second domain. The day-to-day care of the *person* of the prince was only one aspect of the service that the household guaranteed. In addition to that, the court also was responsible for the support and the display of the princely *persona*, which went beyond the individual. Its activities were not limited to the merely domestic, therefore, but extended just as well to the administrative and organizational domains, to the construction of the regime as well as the formation of the image that was connected to it. As such, the internal structure, the organization, the composition, the distribution of duties, the ceremonial, and the scale of the early modern princely household did not constitute isolated elements at all. They were factors attuned to one another, which in mutual coherence contributed to the creation and representation of princely power. The role of the household was, consequently, significant in several respects. It not only

[80] Morgan, D.A.L. 'The House of Policy: The Political Role of the late Plantagenet Household, 1422-1485,' in: Starkey, D. et al. *The English Court from the Wars of the Roses to the Civil War*. London-New York, 1987, pp. 25-70.

[81] For an extended discussion, see the introduction in Costa Gomes, R. *The Making of a Court Society. Kings and Nobles in Late Medieval Portugal*. Cambridge U.P., 2003.

contributed in a very concrete, practical way to the support of the prince, but also participated fully in the ritual with which he accentuated his elevated and sacred position as the chosen ruler. In that sense the presence of the household, just as the pomp and pageantry and the extravagant opulence of the court, was a manifestation of the princely *maiestas*. That which in antiquated, Marxist-inspired historiography was often done away with as an aberrant outgrowth of autocracy and social inequality constituted in reality an essential component of the visual politics with which kingship – as an abstract matter – was evoked and conveyed.

The mixed nature of the court was, consequently, counterbalanced by the common characteristic connecting all members of the princely entourage with each other: each of them provided one or more services to the prince and contributed in this way to the *representatio maiestatis*. In exchange the prince saw them in his turn as *familiares*, making up a part of his extended *familia*. In the last will and testament of Archduke Albert that relationship was symbolically compared with the affective bond between parents and children: '*(...) a todos mis criados, a los quales he tenido y tengo como por hijos (...)*.'[82] It is tempting to connect this phrase with the childlessness of the archdukes. The disputed historiographical discipline of psychohistory would in any case really have to bite into it. Rather than proof of the suggestion supposing that Albert and Isabella would have projected their parental love onto their servants for dearth of progeny, the phrase has to be interpreted as a metaphor for a relationship that was based on mutual loyalty. As thanks for their service during the life of the archduke, the members of his *familia* received a number of favors and financial advantages after his death. At the same time the hope was expressed that they would continue to commit themselves to the House of Habsburg in the future. In that sense the relationship between both parties was structured by the expectation of reciprocity. That is not to say, however, that a certain form of fondness between the princes and their servants did not pertain to the possibilities. It is an illusion to think that their relationship always rested on merely pragmatic grounds and remained shielded from human emotions like friendship and sympathy under any circumstances. Many members of their household lived and worked over decades in the immediate proximity of the princes, and there is no doubt that a few among them were able to build up an affective bond with their masters in the course of those years. Even so, though, it is also an illusion to think that that kind of bond brought no political consequences along with it.[83] In an administrative constellation dependent on one single ruler to a large degree, forms of affection between prince and subject were by definition politically relevant.

---

[82] ARA, *Papiers du Comté de Mercy-Argenteau* 125: Last will and testament of Archduke Albert.

[83] See in that context Miller, P.N. 'Friendship and Conversation in Seventeenth-Century Venice.' *The Journal of Modern History*, 73 (2001) 1-31.

Building further on the theories sketched here, the book at hand means to study the household of Albert and Isabella as a multiform whole in which various roles and functions converged. It means to go in search of not only the concrete workings of their household, but also the way in which that household participated in political and diplomatic life. Doing so, it starts out from the conviction that decision-making in the archducal period came into being not only in the organizational and administrative institutions that are generally associated with policy, but also in the private apartments of the princes where the so-called 'politics of intimacy' set the tone. These themes will be illuminated from the interaction between access, acquisition of favor, and political influence at court.

Consequently, this study means to demonstrate that the archducal household was in the first place a political entity. Still, an important nuance needs to be taken into account, one that in current historiography with regard to courts and their households does indeed get overlooked. The princely household was a political organ that operated not so much *around* as much as *alongside* traditional institutions. The difference between both these modifiers seems negligible, yet that is not so. The term 'around' wrongly suggests that there would be a question of a fundamental opposition between both these spheres, as if the 'legitimate' and formal channels of power had been 'circumvented' in a sinister way by informal decisions, scarcely under control, made in the corridors and back rooms of the palace. In that way anachronistic discourse threatens to raise its ugly head again. It can be speculated whether during the Ancien Régime there was indeed a question of a radical distinction between a 'formal' and an 'informal' political sphere. These kinds of terms bear witness to an all too modern vision of early modern decision-making. Just as the boundaries between 'public' and 'private' were much less clearly delineated in the seventeenth century than is the case at present, so too the difference between 'formal' and 'informal' was not perceived as such in this period. Rather, there was talk of one overarching system in which power came into being and was distributed in various ways. The word 'alongside' is, consequently, better suited for describing the workings of the princely household: after all, it was a matter not so much of a contrasting, as it was of a complementary sphere within the early modern political order.

Sources and methodology

Research into the archducal court and household is subject to various advantages and disadvantages. In view of the success of court studies during the past decades, that research can build further on a great number of models, theories, and approaches, which have already proven their value in the historiography concerning early modern courts. At the same time literature about this Brussels case is especially scarce. The research is thus obliged to start from a position of very limited concrete knowledge. Hence, this book is a pioneering study and as such cannot possibly offer an answer to all the questions that could be posed concerning the court and its household. Consequently, it is a matter of making a few thematic and methodological choices that have an impact on the scope of the whole body of research yet, nevertheless, hand on a solution for the most urgent problems. In that way, this book hopes to prepare the way for further research.

In view of the fact that a good grasp of the workings of the archducal court is indispensable for being able to go into rather abstract topics like access and acquisition of favor, this study opts in the first place for offering an answer to questions concerning the organization and the composition of its household -- 'structuralistically' inspired, to be sure, yet nevertheless crucial. In the second place it means to enter into debate with the dominant visions of the archducal court, which leave very much to be desired. In that way it hopes to give a new turn to the classic approach to the reign of Albert and Isabella. Doing so it makes use of a selection of theories that are central to the literature concerning courts and their households, and that seem especially useful as well with the context of the archducal court. In that way, for instance, in the following chapters the importance of access and favoritism is gone into more in depth as mechanisms exercising much influence on the decision-making process.

In order to be able to offer even an answer to the simplest questions concerning the archducal court, this research must make use of a great number of unpublished sources. The archival situation, though, is far from ideal. Usually studies concerning the early modern court start out with the documents at hand such as court indices and ordinances. Even so, only a handful of court indices remain preserved for the archducal period, and court ordinances have yet to come to light. That means that research into the structure and organization of the archducal household needs to build further on 'secondary' data from accounting ledgers, chronicles, travelogues, and political and diplomatic correspondence. On top of that the subject of this study is not of such a nature that the relevant information allows itself to be easily unmasked. The politics of intimacy are by definition not very tangible. Whoever goes in search of matters brewing under the surface must be able to read above all between the lines. In that context family correspondence seems to offer already more consolation than the exchange of political letters.[84] All the same, one thing or the other results in research that is of necessity based on the multitude of circumstantial evidence. That

[84] In that context, the archive of the Arenberg family in Enghien proved to be of inestimable value.

is, however, less problematic than it seems: just by making use of less than self-evident sources and apparently irrelevant anecdotes looked over in classic historiography, this book is able to cast new light onto decision-making in the Archducal Netherlands.

The problem of sources is only one of various difficulties to which this research is subject. So, for example, an important conceptual problem arises in connection with the archducal household, for what precisely is being studied? Depending on the angle employed, the concept 'household' lends itself to different interpretations and, consequently, also to different methodological approaches. Whoever looks at the household from a merely institutional standpoint, and on that account concentrates on the formal description of courtiers' and servants' duties, risks underestimating their political and symbolic role, which was not recorded in official court ordinances. That kind of approach produces useful data but threatens to reduce the importance of the princely household to the purely domestic domain. Inversely, it is just as invalid to research the members of that household apart from a certain institutional framework, even though it be because they did indeed really enjoy a peculiar status in legal and financial regard. Yet it cannot be forgotten that their household was also a social configuration, a community of independent individuals who nevertheless shared certain attitudes and a certain cultural ethos. In that sense, a biographical and/or prosopographical method can again lead to interesting results. Rather than making a choice between different approaches, it is a matter of employing a golden mean and of studying the courtiers and servants to the extent it is possible from a multifocal perspective.

With that thought in the back of the mind, an important question intrudes: who precisely is meant when discussing the members of the archducal household? 'I am no courtier (although I live at court),' wrote Juan de Mancisidor, Albert's secretary of State and War, in 1612.[85] His statement demonstrates at once that the answer to the question about the composition of the household was not obvious.[86] Does it concern just courtiers and servants who held an official, remunerated function in the princely household, or is it on the contrary about all the individuals who, one way or another, made up part of the court (and if so, where then did 'the court' end, and how was it related to its 'household')? Or, in even broader terms, is it perhaps about the persons who belonged to the princely 'entourage' in the very full sense of the word (and if so, where does one then draw the borderline)? As ingeniously as this theoretical problem may be tackled in practice, its ultimate solution always remains –

85 AGS, *Estado* 2294, s.f.: Juan de Mancisidor to Juan de Ciriza, November 14, 1612. Concerning Mancisidor, see Cuvelier, J. 'Don Juan de Mancicidor, secrétaire d'Etat et de Guerre de l'archiduc Albert, 1596-1618.' *Revue belge de Philologie et d'Histoire*, 4 (1925) 698-714.

86 See the discussion concerning this in Duindam, *Vienna and Versailles*, pp. 47-51.

and is, consequently, in this book too – arbitrary. Most historians leave the answer to the problem therefore as an open question or hide behind the unavoidable or handy excuse that the time, financial means, and/or nature of the historical sources allowed them simply justifies a necessarily artificial demarcation of the object of study. In no way does that have to be held against them: the problem they are wrestling with has always provided for confusion, not in the least at the early modern courts themselves. In 1613, the archdukes enacted an ordinance that rendered an explanation concerning the jurisdiction to which the courtiers and servants of their court were subjected. In it Albert and Isabella declared that 'as there may exist doubt as to whom we consider to be our servants and courtiers, we declare as such all those who find themselves registered or enrolled in the ledgers of our Court and household, of whatever quality, nation or condition they be (...).'[87]

According to this contemporaneous definition the members of the household are those who are named as such in the accounting ledgers and personnel rosters of the court. This definition is problematic even without considering the fact that historians today are dependent on the question whether and in what state of completeness these kinds of archivalia have been preserved. Where, for example, does one rank the many 'courtiers' who indeed held an official function in theory and received remuneration for it, but who seldom or never stayed at court in practice? Or, inversely, what about persons who spent time in the proximity of the prince often or even every day, but who did not exercise any well-defined position? Just as little as other studies, so too this book does not pretend to give preference to an all-encompassing vision toward that which helps put the problem out of the way. It is moreover doubtful whether that kind of *deus ex machina* is indeed to be devised at all. For want of a wieldy definition, this definition from 1613 will therefore be used in this book as an elastic guideline, albeit with the necessary circumspection. Although normative in nature, it reflects in any case who was seen in a legal sense as belonging to the archducal household. In that sense, it has the effect of showing the way without being absolute on that account.

Arrangement of the book

During a colloquium in 2006 concerning the princely households of Habsburg Europe in the period 1555-1665, Luc Duerloo argued that the early modern court can in essence be seen as a battleground of conflicts, or more specifically, as an arena in

[87] '*(...) comme il y pourront tomber doubte quels nous tenons pour nos domestiques et courtisans, nous declarons pour tels tans ceux qui se trouveront enrollez ou assentés es livres de nostre Cour et maison, de quelle qualité, nation, ou condition ils soyent (...).*' ARA, *RvS* 158: *Règlement de l'Archiduc Albert du 9 juillet 1613 du ressort des judicatures (touchans ceux estans domestiques de la Cour).*

which various pressure groups with conflicting interests fought each other for power and princely favor.[88] The analysis of these conflicts – and of the different ways in which rulers endeavored to deal with them – can furnish an important contribution to the knowledge of the mechanisms of decision-making in this period. According to Duerloo, the Habsburg empire exhibited a striking internal coherence in doing so, in the sense that all members of the dynasty employed a similar strategy for reconciling, controlling, or compelling the conflicting interests at their courts. In the process it was not simply about the great Habsburg courts in Prague, Vienna, and Madrid, but also about the courts of the younger members of the dynasty in Innsbruck (1564–1665) and Graz (1564–1619) and about a multitude of smaller courts in places like Hall in Tyrol, Mergentheim in the lands of the Teutonic Order, and Saverne in the prince-bishopric of Strasbourg. To create harmony in the chaos of their courts, the Habsburgs had at their disposal a number of common 'instruments of conciliation,' according to Duerloo, the study of which is indispensable for a good grasp of the complex characteristic identity of the Habsburg dynasty.[89] The most important instruments, says Duerloo, were *access*, *patronage*, *ethos*, and *hierarchy*. Jointly and in mutual interaction with each other, these four elements constituted the pillars of corporate culture that connected all Habsburg courts with each other. Not coincidentally they played a crucial role at the court of Albert and Isabella too, and they figure prominently in all chapters of this book as a consequence.

This study consists of two parts. In Part I the 'anatomy' of the archducal household is put under the magnifying lens. In view of the fact that no one book can begin without clearly situating its subject, the first chapter can be seen as a necessary overture. It sketches the background against which the story is played out and introduces the most important characters. In so doing a few core questions stand front and center, which are necessary for grasping the further course of the book. They concentrate in the first place on the organization, the structure, and the workings of the archducal household. What did that household actually look like? Where does one have to situate it? Who made up part of it? How did it function, and with what goal? Which ceremonial was in vogue there? What were the core responsibilities of the personnel? The questions seem simple, yet for a good grasp of the argumentation that comes up for discussion in the following chapters, knowledge of the answers to them is indispensable. In this chapter, on top of that, it will become clear that the archducal court was in the first place a Habsburg court, and in that sense shared a

[88] Duerloo, L. *Patronage and Ethos at the Habsburg Courts of Europe*. Paper presented at the colloquium *A Constellation of Courts: The Households of Habsburg Europe, 1555-1665*, organized by the universities of Antwerp and Ghent (Brussels, Paleis der Academiën, November 3-4, 2006).

[89] Raeymaekers, D. 'The Households of Habsburg Europe: Conference Report.' *The Court Historian*, 12/1 (2007) 91-94.

common cultural and religious ethos with the other Habsburg courts of Europe. At the same time, however, it meant to be profiled as an independent, self-aware and, above all, sovereign court.

The second chapter builds further on the first and studies the scale of the court and the extent of the archducal entourage. How large was the court of Albert and Isabella, and how did it relate to other courts in Europe? On the basis of data from personnel rosters, remuneration indices, and other historical sources, a – necessarily tentative – estimate is made of the number of courtiers and servants connected to the archducal household, and of the evolution of that number across time. From this it will become obvious that the extent of the household cannot be seen separately from political motives. The financial aspect comes up for discussion in this chapter as well. Via an extended analysis of the remuneration of court personnel and of the budgets of different court departments, the chapter endeavors to offer an answer to the question about the financial impact of the household on the archducal treasury. In all of that, to the extent it is possible, comparison is made with other early modern courts and their households in Europe, whereby the reciprocal hierarchy among the different princely courts is to be exposed.

The third chapter poses the question about the composition of the archducal household. It researches the mechanisms that lay at the foundation of the formation of the entourage of Albert and Isabella and discusses the different criteria employed in doing so. Who was taken into service, and why? Who had no chance for a position in the household, and why not? In all of that, the question of the correlation between 'nation' and political loyalty stands front and center, and it is demonstrated that the origins of the courtiers were important, to be sure, yet were certainly not the only aspect that was taken into consideration as well in the selection of courtiers. After all, the latter also had to answer to the ethos current at court, which reflected the values and norms of Habsburg policy. In that sense the 'recruiting process' was a much more complex matter than is generally presupposed.

Part II goes more in depth into the political role of the courtiers. One of the most important instruments for being able to pacify the different groupings at court was providing the right of access to the person of the prince. This topic comes up for discussion in the fourth chapter, which goes in search of the 'politics of access' at the archducal court. The acquisition of access was for most courtiers an important motivator to aspire to a position in the archducal household. In order to prevent this instrument of conciliation from growing into an instrument of confrontation, this privilege had to be 'distributed' with much care and frugality. In this way, then, it will become clear that the right of access was a desired privilege that could be both monopolized as well as constrained and that, in that way, brought with it great political consequences. At the same time the organization of access is coupled in this chapter to the acquisition of princely patronage and, resulting from this, to the acquisition of political power and influence.

The fifth chapter builds further on the fourth and means to investigate how the courtiers concretely participated in the business of politics. In doing so, not only the political discord that arose at the Brussels court is looked at, but also the way in which the courtiers made the connection between the court and other echelons of society. On the basis of a few case studies, it will be demonstrated that the members of the archducal household were locked up in a golden cage least of all but, on the contrary, played an active role as politicians and diplomats. From this, among other things, it will become obvious that the historiography concerning the archducal reign has until now given disproportionately much attention to relations between Brussels and Madrid, whereby other important topics – like its relationship with the Holy Roman Empire – have not or have only marginally been studied. On top of that, it will be demonstrated as well that the *raison d'état* in this period was even much more coupled to dynastic interests than is generally assumed, and that an all too modern vision of the early modern process of state formation cannot suffice for fully getting to the bottom of political decision-making in this period.

In the sixth and last chapter, finally, an aspect is studied that in the historiography concerning the archducal reign has never before come up for discussion. It is fully dedicated to the Spanish nobleman Don Rodrigo Niño y Lasso, count of Añover, who as Albert and Isabella's high steward, grand chamberlain, *and* master of the horse accumulated the three most prominent positions in their household and – as this chapter means to demonstrate – in the long run evolved into the *gran privado* or great 'favorite' of the archdukes. With that, this book seeks to connect with theories today about favorites in early modern politics, a topic that in recent years has caused some commotion in the historical sciences. An extended analysis of Añover's *curriculum vitae* and career at the archducal court will not only create more clarity concerning the way in which the immediate entourage of Albert and Isabella directly exercised influence on policy, but also concerning the question whether and how a difficult matter to grasp like favoritism could flourish in the Archducal Netherlands.

Chapter I
Setting the Stage

'La Corte degli Arciduchi, in questa parte del servitio delle persone lor proprie, & in generale ancora di tutto il resto, può contendere veramente con ogn'altra delle più fiorite, e più splendide, che siano in Christianità.'[1]

Guido Bentivoglio
Relationi

On the night of February 3, 1731, the old palace on the Coudenberg hill in Brussels went up in flames.[2] The exact cause of the disaster is difficult to track down. More than likely a scatterbrained lady-in-waiting neglected to snuff her candle in going to sleep and thus involuntarily sealed the fate of the princely residence.[3] In no time the fire spread to the adjacent quarters. The governess at that time, Archduchess Maria Elisabeth, could only narrowly escape and be brought to safety; other residents were less fortunate.[4] Powerless, the people of Brussels looked on as the destructive fire reduced a great deal of the palace to ashes. Only the Court Chapel was more or less spared, yet it offered a desolate aspect in the middle of the scorched-black ruins. During the following four decades the remains of 'the burnt court' [*la Cour brûlée*], as it was called in the vernacular, would continue to dominate the panorama of Brussels. Plans for rebuilding were proposed, evaluated and, just as quickly, disposed of again. The complete reorganization of the site was not embarked upon until 1775. What little remained for recalling past glories had to make room for setting up the strained, classicist-inspired Place Royale. On that same spot only a few decades later the building

1 Bentivoglio, G. *Relationi del Cardinal Bentivoglio*. Brussels, 1632, p. 160. [Original edition: Bentivoglio, G. *Relationi fatte dall' illustrissimo, e reverendissimo signor cardinal Bentivoglio in tempo delle sue nuntiature di Fiandra, e di Francia. Date in luce da Erycio Puteano*. Antwerp, 1629.]

2 A report on the occurrences in Gachard, L.-P. 'L'incendie du palais royal de Bruxelles (3 février 1731),' in: Gachard, L.-P., ed. *Études et notices historiques concernant l'histoire des Pays-Bas*, vol. III. Brussels, 1890, pp. 194-232.

3 Basing itself on the official report that was drawn up as occasioned by the disaster, Louis-Prosper Gachard situated the source of the fire in the kitchens of the palace. See Gachard, 'L'incendie,' 198. An unofficial (and presumably more faithful) version, however, posits that the fire arose in the quarters of a lady-in-waiting to governess Maria Elisabeth, named Capellini. See Smolar-Meynart, A., Vanrie, A., Soenen, M. et al. *Het paleis van Brussel. Acht eeuwen kunst en geschiedenis*. Exhibition catalogue. Brussels, 1991, p. 148.

4 Gachard, 'L'incendie,' 198-199.

of the present royal palace was begun.[5] There was no lying about its symbolism. Once the Napoleonic regime ceased to exist and the monarchy was triumphantly restored, the earlier center of government rose again like a phoenix from its ashes. Literally resting on the foundations of a centuries-old structure, the new palace symbolized a massive and tangible incarnation of continuity.[6]

Whoever visits the Place Royale today has to have a lively imagination at his disposal in order to visualize for himself how the district was formerly dominated by the contours of the famous *Aula Magna*. In that ceremonial hall Charles V, tired of fighting, ceded the throne, and Alexander Farnese held his splendid wedding party. Only underground, where archaeologists have exposed the vaulted cellars of the old palace, do a number of storage places and the so-called Isabella Street recall an effervescent and sparkling life at court, which has belonged to the past for a long time now. At present an almost hallowed silence rules, but at the beginning of the seventeenth century a world of busyness unfolded in these cellars. Servants and hallboys ran hastily back and forth, in search of casks of wine or beer, smoked hams, fragrant spices, game pies, preserved fruits, or olives. Whipped on by the booming commands of their superiors, they hurried with their tasty cargo to the palace kitchens, where a team of cooks and kitchen help transformed the ingredients into the most exquisite dishes. Four hundred years later the clamor there has been silenced, and the harried hustle and bustle have made room for staid reservedness. Nothing suggests that for centuries this hushed space constituted the logistic hub of an enormous complex in which the political history of the Netherlands would take shape. As opposed to the palaces of Versailles, Schönbrunn, or Hampton Court – princely residences that have withstood the test of time and are deeply imbedded in an historical frame of reference – the former palace on the Coudenberg hill no longer occupies a place of significance in the collective memory. The catastrophe of 1731 appears to have effected the demise not only of the building *per se*, but also of interest in the early modern court at Brussels in its entirety. Taking into note that for centuries the Brussels court was one of the great centers of power in Europe, that decline can at least be called remarkable.

Even when Cardinal-Archduke Albert took up his residence there in February 1596, the Coudenberg palace already had a turbulent history behind it. Supposedly erected around the end of the eleventh century, the medieval fortress was inhabited by the dukes of Brabant from the twelfth to the fourteenth century. During their reign

---

[5] Smolar-Meynart, *Het paleis van Brussel*, 269-302.

[6] Concerning the urban planning operations in Brussels in the nineteenth and early twentieth century, see Verschaffel, T. 'The Embellishment of Brussels under Leopold I and Leopold II.' *The Court Historian*, 12/2 (2007) 193-214.

Brussels acquired the unofficial status of the seat of government, a reputation that would be confirmed in the fifteenth century by the regular presence of the dukes of Burgundy. By means of requisite expansion and ornamentation, they built the castle of their predecessors into a renaissance idyll furnished with opulent apartments and an extensive game park. It was Philip the Good who embarked upon building the *Aula Magna* in 1451, though he did not shrink back from having the city administration foot the bill for the costs.[7]

While the court grew into a fully-fledged governmental and administrative center over the years, Brussels transformed slowly but surely into a genuine capital. Noble families settled on or in proximity to the Coudenberg hill and had their palatial townhouses built there, the one more luxurious than the other.[8] The artistic sensibility of Burgundian court life as well as its pomp and pageantry acquired great fame across all of Europe. Artisans, merchants, artists, actors, mountebanks, beggars and other fortune seekers came down to Brussels, attracted by the concentration of wealth to be found there. Under the first Habsburg rulers the trend continued steadily along. Charles V took up residence in the palace and expanded it with a new chapel consecrated in 1553.[9] Although the emperor had an ambulatory court and often found himself abroad, the building on the Coudenberg hill was and remained his most important residence in the Netherlands.[10] During Charles' absence his sister Mary of Hungary took over the administration. The governess settled into the palace as well and had, among other things, an imposing arcade added to it. Gradually the building acquired the façade and the structure that is known only thanks to iconographic sources handed down to today. These preserved engravings and paintings show an impressive edifice, one that seems to have grown organically over successive renovations rather than being consciously conceptualized. In that context the seventeenth-century French geographer Pierre Bergeron spoke of 'a large and spacious building' with 'a large number of halls, chambers, antechambers,

[7] The palace's architectural history has been studied by Krista De Jonge. See De Jonge, K. et al. 'Building Policy and Urbanisation during the Reign of the Archdukes: The Court and its Architects,' in: Thomas, W. & Duerloo, L., eds. *Albert & Isabella, 1598-1621: Essays*. Turnhout, 1998, pp. 191-215; De Jonge, K. 'Der herzogliche und kaiserliche Palast zu Brüssel und die Entwicklung des höfischen Zeremoniells im 16. und 17. Jahrhundert,' in: *Jahrbuch des Zentralinstituts für Kunstgeschichte*, V/VI (1989-1990) pp. 253-282; De Jonge, K. 'Le palais de Charles-Quint à Bruxelles. Ses dispositions intérieures aux XVe et XVIe siècles et le cérémonial de Bourgogne,' in: Guillaume, J., ed. *Architecture et vie sociale. L'organisation intérieure des grandes demeures à la fin du Moyen Age et à la Renaissance. Actes du colloque tenu à Tours du 6 au 10 juin 1988*. Paris, 1994, pp. 107-125 and De Jonge, K. ' ' 't Hof van Brabant' als symbool van de Spaanse hofhouding in de Lage Landen.' *Bulletin van de Koninklijke Nederlandse Oudheidkundige Bond*, 98 (1999) 183-197. For an antiquated yet still useful study, see Saintenoy, P. *Les arts et les artistes à la cour de Bruxelles*. 3 vols. Brussels, 1932-1935.

[8] Though very antiquated, Henne, A. & Wauters, A. *Histoire de la ville de Bruxelles*. 3 vols. Brussels, 1845 remains one of the standard works concerning the history of Brussels.

[9] De Jonge, 'Building Policy and Urbanisation,' 191.

[10] De Jonge, 'Der herzogliche und kaiserliche palast,' 253.

cabinet rooms and diverse apartments, the whole built comfortably rather than nicely or well, because it possesses an ancient structure.'[11] His English contemporary John Evelyn kept it in his diary at an 'antient confus'd building, large & irregular.'[12] Erected around a central rectangular inner courtyard, the building was flanked on its southern exposure by the public Place des Bailles, and on its northern exposure by the palace gardens (cf. Plate 3).

In emulating their predecessors, Albert and Isabella also showed themselves to be ardent patrons of architecture.[13] Under the direction of the renowned court architect Wenceslas Cobergher, they had a great many architectural operations carried out, which were supposed to increase the grandeur and the comfort of the palace. Already shortly after he assumed his post Archduke Albert had the residential wing of the palace renovated. A few year later the entry gate to the palace was renewed and expanded with a monumental belltower, crowned by a wooden cupola. In 1608, a second gallery on top of the existing one was erected by Mary of Hungary, and a year later Cobergher added an extra storey and a new roof to the central wing of the palace. In 1620, the private oratory of the infanta was rebuilt and evidently refurnished with much care, for the French ambassador Jean Péricard reported that the private chapel was 'very magnificent,' and 'filled with one of the greatest collections of carefully enshrined relics one can look at in the Christian world.'[14] Even more than the palace complex itself, the gardens were taken firmly in hand. The garden architect and engineer Salomon de Caus, who enjoyed as excellent a reputation as Cobergher, had *grottos* and hydraulic machines built there, stylized flower beds laid out, and water organs and fountains erected.[15] With that he transformed the park into a paradisiacal place, in which it was pleasant to pass the time according to contemporaries. The English nobleman Charles Somerset, who visited the court at Brussels in 1612, formulated it as follows: '[The Archduke] hath a house of greate pleasure both for fine groves and walkes and waterworkes, and also he hath adjoyning unto them a fine little parke of fallow deare, a verie fine sweete place, as anie Prince can have.'[16]

---

[11] *'(...) un grand et spacieux bastiment (...) grand nombre de (...) salles, chambres, antichambres, cabinets et appartements divers, le tout plus commode que beau ny bien basty, pour estre de structure (...) à l'antique.'* Michelant, H., ed. *Voyage de Pierre Bergeron ès Ardennes, Liège et Pays-Bas en 1619*. Liège, 1875. Cited in Smolar-Meynart, *Het paleis van Brussel*, 103.

[12] de Beer, E.S., ed. *The Diary of John Evelyn*. 6 vols. Oxford, 1955. Op. cit. vol. II, p. 70.

[13] For and overview of the different reconstructions in the archducal period, see De Jonge, 'Building Policy and Urbanisation,' passim.

[14] *'(...) le plus magnifique (...) et remply de grande quantité de reliques pretiecement enchassées qui se puisse veoyr en chrestieneté.'* BNF, *MsF* 16133, f. 164: Jean Péricard to Secretary of State Pierre Brulart, marquis of Puisieux, January 15, 1621.

[15] Lombaerde, P. 'Pietro Sardi, Georg Müller, Salomon de Caus und die Wasserkünste des Coudenberg-Gartens in Brüssel.' *Die Gartenkunst*, 3 (1991) 159-173.

[16] Brennan, M.G., ed. *The Travel Diary (1611-1612) of an English Catholic Sir Charles Somerset, edited from the manuscript in the Brotherton Collection University of Leeds*. Leeds, 1993, pp. 286-287.

While the old Brussels palace was the most important residence of the archdukes, it was not the only one. During the summer months Albert and Isabella usually stayed in the castle of Mariemont – built in former times by commission of Mary of Hungary – and they preferred to hunt most of all in the woods around the moated fortress at Tervuren.[17] Both castles were in proximity to Brussels but far enough away from the suffocating commotion of the city as to provide the necessary peace and quiet. Furthermore the princes regularly visited the many cities in the Southern Netherlands, where they lodged in local mansions, fortresses, or abbeys. Consequently the Coudenberg palace constituted certainly not the only but indeed the central setting against which the story of the archdukes was played out. Here the lifeworld of Albert and Isabella unfolded; here their reign took shape; here was their authority most tangible. Populated by a colorful company of noble lords and ladies, diplomats, clergy, councilors, military, clerks, pages, and servants, the Brussels palace functioned as the physical space *par excellence* which contemporaries made one and the same with 'the court.' If only for that reason alone, it is worth the effort to take a look behind the scenes of this stately building.

This first chapter means to penetrate into the many chambers and halls that the residence of Albert and Isabella was rich in, and research how daily life there was organized in practice. In so doing it concentrates in the first place on the structure and the workings of the archducal household (which is defined here in the minimalist sense as all of the court departments and divisions which were responsible for the smooth functioning of the actual household of the princes); on the court ceremonial that was in vogue there (understood here as all of the customs and activities that structured daily life at court); and on the courtiers and servants who officially made up part of that household according to the remuneration lists as well as the court indices from that time.[18] Doing so the necessary attention is devoted to the introduction of a number of leading characters who will play an important role further on in this book. The chapter ends with an interpretative exposition concerning the significance of the court ceremonial in the political context of that time.

---

[17] Concerning the castle of Mariemont, see Demeester, J. 'Le domaine de Mariemont sous Albert et Isabelle (1598-1621).' *Annales du Cercle Archéologique de Mons*, 71 (1978-1981) 190 and Wellens, R. 'Deux documents relatifs à l'agrandissement du domaine de Mariemont sous les Archiducs Albert et Isabelle.' *Annales du Cercle archéologique du Canton de Soignies*, 23 (1964) 1-14. Concerning the hunting palace of Tervuren, see Wauters, A. *Histoire des environs de Bruxelles*. 3 vols. Brussels, 1855, vol. III, pp. 388-390.

[18] In that sense, this chapter builds further on the brief but nevertheless especially useful article by Lanoye, D. 'Structure and Composition of the Household of the Archdukes,' in: Thomas & Duerloo, *Essays*, pp. 107-119. It is very much indebted as well to the as yet unpublished study of Hortal Muñoz, J.E. 'The Household of Archduke Albert of Austria from his Election as Governor of Flanders until his Investiture as Sovereign Prince of the Low Countries: 1595-1598,' *Revue belge de Philologie et d'Histoire*, in press. I thank Dr. Hortal for his willingness to put this text at my disposal.

Reconstructing the archducal household

A fundamental problem, which hampers research into the archducal household to a serious extent, concerns the want of court ordinances that tell something more about the specific workings of that household. Whereas these sorts of regulations usually form the point of departure in the historiography concerning early modern courts and their households, for this Brussels case – except for a few dossiers concerning the status and the privileges of the courtiers – no similar documents have come to light.[19] That is lamentable, for although these ordinances are of a normative nature and thus only describe the court in theory, they nevertheless offer valuable information concerning the ideal that the archducal household was supposed to answer to.[20] In this case it means that historians have to make do with other types of sources that reflect the required information often less accurately or only partially. Thus, it comes down to compensating for the lack of court ordinances with indirect data from chronicles, travelogues, accounts, personnel rosters, correspondence, and so forth. In that way the structure and the workings of the archducal household can be reconstructed to a certain degree. As concerns the archducal period, historians have various sources at their disposal, which can be helpful in this process.

In his *Relationi* Guido Bentivoglio, who held the position of the apostolic nuncio in Brussels between 1607 and 1615, gave a short description of the household of Albert and Isabella.[21] His account offers a brief yet solid sketch of the various court departments, supplemented with details concerning the most important courtiers. Bentivoglio's findings can subsequently be compared with data from the so-called *libros de razón* or accounting ledgers of the archducal household, which in addition to an overview of personnel, remunerations and financial transactions contain a veritable treasure of information concerning daily life at court.[22] Unfortunately only the indices from the period of 1612-1618 remained preserved, such that historians are less well informed about the first decade of the archducal reign. That lacuna can only be filled in part by making use of a number of court indices in which the names of the

[19] See ARA, *Geheime Raad – Papieren Roose en De Paepe* 1591, ff. 299-300: *Arrêté de l'archiduc Albert du 6 juillet 1611 prescrivant des règles à observer dans sa maison*; ARA, *Aud* 1259: *Documents relatifs au logement des troupes: 1. Logement des gens de cour et ordements de la ville de Bruxelles de 1600 à 1619*; ARA, *RvS* 158, ff. 8-16: *Reglement de l'Archiduc Albert du 9 juillet 1613 du ressort des judicatures (touchans ceux estans domestiques de la Cour)*; and ARA, *Aud* 33/1-2, no. 21: *Translat de l'espagnol des privileges des Domestiques des Archiducs en françois et autres papiers touchant la jurisdiction de l'alcalde*.

[20] Paravicini, W. 'Europäische Hofordnungen als Gattung und Quelle,' in: Kruse, H. & Paravicini, W. *Höfe und Hofordnungen 1200-1600* (5. Symposium der Residenzen-Kommission der Akademie der Wissenschaften in Gottingen. Residenzenforschung 10). Stuttgart, 1999, pp. 13-20.

[21] Bentivoglio, *Relationi*, pp. 157-161.

[22] ARA, *RK* 1837 (period 1612-1615) and 1838 (period 1616-1618). For more information about these interesting ledgers, see Lefèvre, J. 'Les livres de raison de l'archiduc Albert (1612-1618).' *Archives et bibliothèques de Belgique*, 42 (1971) 156-163. For similar data beginning with 1610, see ARA, *SSO* 666.

courtiers and servants were written down and arranged by department.[23] Depending on the completeness of these lists and on reasons that gave occasion for their redaction, these enumerations can furnish a contribution not only to the reconstruction of the organizational structure of the household but also to a better grasp of its extent and composition over time. Provided the requisite adjustments and additions can be distilled from other historical documents, the combination of these types of sources introduced here produces several interesting assessments.[24]

Although the historical sources put us in the position to reconstruct the organigram of the archducal household for the large part, the want of court ordinances sees to it that the concrete workings of the various departments, just like the exact descriptions of servants' duties, is not simple to track down. As already mentioned, historians have to make do with data that have fallen rather coincidentally into the sources. Yet there is one possibility for finding out more about the 'work conditions' at the Brussels court. The National Archives [Algemeen Rijksarchief/Archives Générales du Royaume] in Brussels has preserved a few manuscripts from the hand of Francisco Lozano and his son Juan, in which they offer an overview of the organization of the court at the time of Cardinal-Infante Ferdinand of Austria and the successive governors in the Southern Netherlands until around 1700.[25] Both Lozano the father and his son were connected to the princely household in Brussels (in the time periods of 1634-1685 and 1656-1701, respectively) and based their findings on their own experiences as well as on the older writings of chroniclers Olivier de la Marche and Jules Chifflet, among others.[26] Although the manuscripts cover in principle a later period, the authors frequently refer to the circumstances at the time of the archdukes, and they clearly demonstrate

23 The following court indices were consulted (in chronological order): ARA, *Aud* 23/10 [= idem as ARA, *Aud* 33/4, ff. 61-65] (c. 1595); ASV, *Borghese* I 913, ff. 339-344 (c. 1597); ARA, *Aud* 33/4, ff. 66-72 (1603); SAA, *Privilegekamer* 1627 (1605); ARA, *Aud* 33/3 (1605); ARA, *Aud* 20, ff. 16-26 (1611); ARA, *RvS* 157 (1620); ARA, *RvS* 157 (1624).

24 I made use of [Anonymous]. *Relation de Flandres. État de la cour et maison des archiducs en 1610. Document inédit du temps enrichi de notes généalogiques et historiques.* In: *Souvenirs de la Flandre-Wallonne. Recherches historiques et choix de documents relatifs à Douai et au Nord de la France*, vol. VI). Paris-Douai, 1866, pp. 1-25; Van der Straeten, E., ed. *Den Lyste van den Musiciens van den Capelle van haer Hoocheden.* In: Van der Straeten, E. *La musique aux Pays-Bas avant le XIXe siècle. Documents inédits et annotés.* 8 vols. Brussels, 1867-1888, vol. II, pp. 10-11; Chifflet, J. *Aula Sacra Principum Belgii; sive commentarius historicus de Capellae Regiae in Belgio, Principiis, Ministris, Ritibus atque universo apparatu.* Antwerp, 1650; de Seur, J., ed. *Rolle des noms, gages et pensions des conseilliers, ministres et autres officiers de leurs altesses sérénissimes...fait en l'an 1609.* In: de Seur, J. *La Flandre illustrée par l'Institution de la Chambre du Roi à Lille.* Rijsel, 1713; de Reiffenberg, F.A.F., ed. *Itinéraire de l'archiduc Albert, de la reine d'Espagne Marguérite d'Autriche et de l'infante Isabelle, en 1599 et 1600, tiré d'une relation contemporaine et manuscrite.* In: *Nouveaux Mémoires de l'Académie Royale des Sciences et Belles-Lettres de Bruxelles*, 14 (1841) 3-33; and Francquart, J. & Puteanus, E. *Pompa funebris (...) Alberti Pii, archiducis Austriae...* Brussels, 1622.

25 ARA, *Handschriftenverzameling* 821, ff. 1-93: *Plan ou Estat de la maison royale dans ces estats de Flandres* and ARA, *Handschriftenverzameling* 822: *Notice de touts les Emplois de la Cour et de la Chapelle Royale de Bruxelles.*

26 See the introduction to ARA, *Handschriftenverzameling* 821, ff. 1-4.

that the court ceremonial – at least in a normative sense – exhibited much continuity throughout the seventeenth century. Provided one takes note of the requisite caveats, the works of both Lozanos may be seen, then, as trustworthy sources.

On top of that, in the following sections it will become clear that the organization of the archducal court was to a great extent comparable to those of other Habsburg courts in Europe and, specifically, to the organization of the Spanish court in Madrid. The indirect information that can be drawn out of the 'secondary' sources generally proves to accord well with what would be expected on the basis of court ordinances in Madrid. Inasmuch as it can be verified, the rules and regulations that applied in the archducal household were based on those that were applicable in the *Corte y Casa* of Philip II and Philip III. This determination at once provides accountability for filling in the gap mentioned with regard to the functioning of the Brussels household with data concerning its pendant in Madrid, where necessary – and inasmuch as a comparison seems acceptable. At the same time it justifies the choice to keep the overview of the archducal household limited to a short and to-the-point sketch, in which only the most important points are touched upon. A detailed description of the range of responsibilities of the archducal household is necessarily unattainable in the context of this book. On top of that the interested reader can seek consolation in Spanish historiography, in which the successive *Casas* of Charles V, Philip II and Philip III have already been studied in detail.[27]

The development of the Spanish-Burgundian court model

In September 1599, Archduke Albert announced that no less than six nobles from the Netherlands would be dubbed knights in the Order of the Golden Fleece. The announcement involved Prince Philip William of Orange – the oldest son of William the Silent – and furthermore the duke of Aarschot, the marquis of Havré and the counts of Ligne, Egmont and Solre.[28] The originally Burgundian Order of the Golden

[27] See the recently published overviews of the Instituto Universitario 'La Corte en Europa': Martínez Millán, J., ed. *La Corte de Carlos V*. 5 vols. Madrid, 2000; Martínez Millán, J. & Fernández Conti, S., eds. *La Monarquía de Felipe II: la Casa del Rey*. 2 vols. Madrid, 2005. Martínez Millán, J. & Visceglia, M.-A. *La Monarquía de Felipe III: La Casa del Rey*. 2 vols. Madrid, 2008. See further also Hofmann, C. *Das Spanische Hofzeremoniell von 1500-1700*. Frankfurt, 1985; Mayoral López, R. *La Casa Real de Felipe III (1598-1621). Ordenanzas y Etiquetas*. Unpublished doctoral dissertation, Universidad Autónoma de Madrid, 2007; Rodríguez Villa, A., ed. *Etiquetas de la Casa de Austria*. Madrid, 1913; Varey, J.E. 'Professional Ceremonial of the Spanish Court in the Seventeenth Century,' in: *Studia Iberica. Festschrift für Hans Flashe*. Bern-Munich, 1973, pp. 643-652 and Varey, J.E. 'Further Notes on Processional Ceremonial of the Spanish Court in the Seventeenth Century.' *Iberomania*, 1 (1974) 71-79.

[28] The ceremony would take place on December 24, 1599. ASV, *NF* 11, f. 740: Nuncio Ottavio Mirto Frangipani to Cardinal-Secretary of State Aldobrandini, December 24, 1599.

Fleece, instituted in 1430 by Philip the Good, was one of the most prestigious orders of chivalry in Europe. Since the duchy of Burgundy had been taken into the Habsburg Empire, the Order was presided over by the Spanish king, who as its grandmaster had the right to designate new members. This kind of appointment was quite desired, and there is no possible doubt, then, that the selection of six leading noblemen from the Netherlands made up part of a well-considered tactic to tighten the weakened bonds between the Habsburg dynasty and the local aristocracy anew. This round of appointments proved, however, to have yet another favorable side-effect. Ottavio Mirto Frangipani, the papal nuncio in Brussels at that time, was able to report that Albert's announcement had a calming effect on the heated feelings at court, which had flared high on the occasion of the introduction of a new court ceremonial, cobbled from the Spanish model.[29] One of the new elements included the high nobility's being no longer permitted to kneel on cushions specially provided for the celebration of the mass – a prerogative that not only spared their knees but was also seen as an important symbol of distinction. Another measure concerned stricter control of access to the princely apartments, whereby the nobles were no longer authorized to approach the princes whenever they wished. According to the nuncio, the new rules could count on quite a lot of criticism. The nobility from the Southern Netherlands accused the archduke of putting aside local traditions and of wanting to organize his court just like that of the king of Spain. In view of the fact that Albert himself was no king, the courtiers saw the reforms as excessive and inappropriate.[30]

In her article about the symbolic value of the court at Brussels, Krista De Jonge notes that there is something remarkable going on with this criticism.[31] The courtiers from the Southern Netherlands were of the opinion that the reforms of 1599 went against the ages-old traditions in the Netherlands. They saw the new court ceremonial as something 'Spanish,' not in keeping with the rules they were used to in Brussels. That is notable in view of the fact that Spanish etiquette at that time was in essence based on regulations that had formerly been in force at the court of the Burgundian dukes and that had thus come to be developed among other things in Brussels. This Burgundian model made its entry at the Spanish court under Charles V, where

[29] '*Por simil dechiaratione cessa in gran parte il murmure ch'haveva cominciato a'lor dare la riforma della Cappella, et del palazzo nell' universale malamente intesa cosi per essere quella dicha Cappella qui stretta di prima, essendose tolti li coscini che se preparavano al nuntio, alli Grandi, et Signori del Tosone per ingenocchiarse, come per vederse l'altra pallazzo fuor dell' aspettation commune, persuadendose ogn'uno di poter vivere con l'Arciduca secondo il solito con li Duchi di Brabanza.*' ASV, *NF* 11, ff. 705-706: Nuncio Ottavio Mirto Frangipani to Cardinal-Secretary of State Aldobrandini, September 18, 1599.

[30] *Ibidem*: '*Questi riformi sono qui stimati per eccesso, poiche S.A. non essendo Re, voglia governata la sua Corte et servita a simiglianza di quella del Re di Spagna, con distintion di camere, porte serrate, et portinario in ciaschuna, lo che disegna mal principio, non altromene ch'il disordinato appetito di suditi, col qual vorrebbino in un subito tirar il lor Principe dalla vita Spagnola alla fiammenga,*'

[31] De Jonge, ' ' 't Hof van Brabant' als symbool van de Spaanse hofhouding,' 187.

Philip II adopted it afterward. Consequently, the Spanish ceremonial was a direct derivative of the tradition that had been maintained in the Netherlands for ages. Yet the reforms of 1599 were experienced by the local courtiers not only as 'new,' but also as 'foreign.' This indicates that, since its introduction at court in Madrid, the Burgundian ceremonial had fundamentally deviated from the rules that were in vogue at the Brussels court. One thing or another demands a word of explanation here.

'The court of the archdukes,' as Guido Bentivoglio noted in his *Relationi*, 'is composed like that of the other Habsburg princes, who in general have modeled their courts according to the example of the dukes of Burgundy.'[32] Even so, the conclusion of the nuncio needs to be placed in the right context. At the beginning of the seventeenth century the organization of the court Bentivoglio was talking about still recalled this Burgundian tradition only to a limited extent. That tradition had come to be developed two centuries before that at the court of the same name and would acquire great luster namely through the memoirs of Olivier de la Marche.[33] Based on the late-medieval example of the French court, yet possibly also hearkening back to influences from Flanders and Brabant, the household of the Burgundian dukes was characterized, among other things, by a very hierarchically built structure and great participation from the nobility.[34] In addition to the personal quarters of the prince (the *Chambre*), that structure consisted of six domestic departments: the *Paneterie*, the *Échansonnerie*, the *Cuisine*, the *Fruiterie*, the *Écuyerie* and the *Fourrière*.[35] While the court steward directed their household from day to day, noble *écuyers* in turn made up the servants in the different divisions. The range of their responsibilities consisted among other things of serving the duke at table, a very ritualized process in which the *écuyer tranchant* carved the meat and the *échansonnier* poured the wine. The strict etiquette followed in doing so not only provided for an impressive visual spectacle but also solidified the elevated position of the prince. To an increasing extent his role as *primus inter pares* had to make room for an emphatically distinct status as rightful and chosen ruler. The serving presence of nobles in the princely entourage was thus in several respects significant. In the first instance their participation in the care of

[32] Bentivoglio, *Relationi*, 157.

[33] de la Marche, O. 'Sensuyt l'estat de la maison du duc Charles de Bourgogne, dit le Hardy,' in Beaune, H. & d'Arbaumont, J., eds. *Mémoires d'Olivier de la Marche, maitre d'hotel et capitaine des gardes de Charles le Téméraire IV.* Paris, 1888, pp. 1-94.

[34] Paravicini, W. 'The Court of the Dukes of Burgundy. A Model for Europe?' in: Asch, R.G. & Birke, A.M., eds. *Princes, Patronage and the Nobility: The Court at the Beginning of the Modern Age, c. 1450-1650.* Oxford U.P., 1991, pp. 69-102.

[35] For an explanation concerning the Burgundian court ceremonial, see Hofmann, *Das Spanische Hofzeremoniell*, 50-64. See further also the successive publications of Werner Paravicini in the journal *Francia*: Paravicini, W. 'Die Hofordnungen Philipps des Guten von Burgund.' *Francia*, 10 (1982) 131-166; 11 (1983) 257-301; 13 (1986) 191-211; and 15 (1987) 183-231. See also Cartellieri, O. *La Cour des ducs de Bourgogne*. Paris, 1946.

the duke affirmed the bonds of loyalty between the regime and the social elites. At the same time the introduction of a refined court ceremonial and the concomitant distribution of domestic positions of honor created new possibilities for the nobility to profile itself as the leading social class. Whereas the norms and values of the second estate had rested for ages on its role in warfare, now room was also made for a frame of reference in which life at court occupied a central position.

While the years advanced and various Burgundian dukes succeeded each other, the structure of their households remained to a great extent unmodified. Rather than a method of creating order in the household, the organization at court made up part of a conscious political strategy that served to confirm its continuity with previous regimes. That tradition was continued even after the complex of Burgundian lands had been taken into the Habsburg imperium. The court ordinances drawn up in 1497 for Philip the Fair and in 1515 for his son Charles V were clearly inspired by the ideal that Olivier de la Marche had described in his memoirs.[36] Yet after the passage of time very many organizational modifications would be applied. When, in 1545, Charles' court controller Jean Sigoney embarked upon a revision of the ceremonial, he concluded, dissatisfied in a way, that only the service at table was still in keeping with the old Burgundian customs that the emperor's predecessors had kept.[37] Above all, adjustments had been put through with regard to the protection of the personal life of the prince.[38] If in the foreground the table ceremonial exhibited more and more similarity with a strictly orchestrated, public glorification of the princely *persona*, then in the background the privacy and isolation of his physical *person* were taken into account to an increasing extent. That was expressed, among other things, in the ordinances of 1497 and 1515, which contained clear guidelines concerning the access to the princely apartments.[39] At the same time architectural operations like the expansion of the number of antechambers saw to it that the private life of the ruler was withdrawn from view more and more. With time the creation of detachment would in that way come to make up part of the consecration of the prince, which was elementary in the Burgundian court ceremonial, and which will be expanded upon in a later chapter.

---

36 Delen, M.-A. *Het hof van Willem van Oranje*. Amsterdam, 2002. Op. cit. p. 31.

37 Hofmann, *Das Spanische Hofzeremoniell*, 58-59. Concerning the ceremonial at the court of Charles V, see De Ridder, A., ed. *Les règlements de la Cour de Charles Quint*. In: *Messager des sciences historiques* (1893) pp. 392-418 and (1894) pp. 36-52, pp. 180-201 and pp. 280-291 and De Ridder, A. 'La Cour de Charles-Quint.' *Mémoires de la Société littéraire de l'Université catholique de Louvain*, 14 (1889) 41-213.

38 Concerning these adjustments, see Martínez Millán & Fernández Conti, *La Monarquía de Felipe II*, vol. I, pp. 132-133.

39 De Jonge, K. 'De voornaamste residenties in Mechelen. Het hof van Kamerijk en het Hof van Savoyen,' in: Eichberger, D., ed. *Dames met klasse. Margareta van York/Margareta van Oostenrijk*. Exhibition catalogue. Leuven, 2005, pp. 57-66.

All the same, during the reign of Charles V another important development arose, which would prove to be defining for the further evolution of the Burgundian court model. After the death of his grandfather Ferdinand of Aragon in 1516, the young Charles journeyed to the Iberian peninsula to claim the crown of the Spanish hereditary lands. He did not take them into hand without much effort, though. Only two years later, in 1518, would the *cortes* of Castile and Aragon swear loyalty to their new prince. It produced a noticeable territorial expansion for Charles, which, to be sure, also brought the requisite problems along with it. In cultural, political and institutional respects his territorial patrimonium was characterized by enormous diversity. The wariness of the Spanish populace toward his councilors, who had come primarily from the Low Countries, led rather quickly to complaints about the greed of those *flamencos*, with Charles' confidant Guillaume de Croÿ as the main target.[40] Should the king want his as yet unstable regime to acquire the necessary legitimacy, then he needed to meet the characteristic regional identities as well as their attained rights up to a certain degree. His decision to honor the existing royal household in Castile – albeit with the necessary reforms – played along with that. More than any other institution the *Casa y Corte de Castilla* constituted the incarnation *par excellence* of the Kingdom of Castile. Seen politically, its complete replacement with a court organization cobbled from the Burgundian model was therefore unthinkable. Of necessity the *Casa de Castilla* would continue to function during the following decades of Charles' reign independently of the *Casa de Borgoña*, though at the same time Castile would exercise much influence upon Burgundy.[41]

In 1531 Charles, having meanwhile been elected emperor of the Holy Roman Empire, entrusted the administration of the Netherlands to his sister Mary, the widow of the fallen King Louis II of Hungary. As opposed to her predecessor Margaret of Austria, whose court was in nearby Mechelen, the new governess settled into the Brussels palace. In view of the fact that the emperor was mostly abroad, the residence on the Coudenberg hill had for a few decades only been sporadically inhabited. Charles permitted his sister to introduce a new household there, and left her the choice between a ceremonial '*à la mode d'Austria*' – by which he meant the hereditary Habsburg lands of Austria and Hungary – or one '*à la mode de Bourgoigne*'.[42] In emulation of the old tradition Mary chose the Burgundian model. On account of the difference in status (gubernatorial versus sovereign), but also because it concerned in essence the entourage of a woman, Mary's household would deviate on different points from that of her brother, though. The court ordinance that was drawn up

[40] Elliott, J.H. *Imperial Spain*, 1469-1716. London, 2002 [Original edition: 1963]. Op. cit. pp. 144-159.

[41] Martínez Millán & Fernández Conti, *La Monarquía de Felipe II*, vol. I, pp. 53-61 and pp. 134-135.

[42] Cited in: Delen, *Het hof van Willem van Oranje*, 34.

for her in 1555, gave for example much less attention to the rules of access for the *Chambre*, which undoubtedly had to do with the fact that Mary could make no claim on the ideal of splendid isolation reserved for sovereign princes.[43]

After the death of Charles V in 1558, his son and successor Philip II settled permanently in Spain. Already in 1535, the then eight-year-old Philip had received his own household in the Castilian style, which, to be sure, was strongly influenced by traditions from Aragon and Portugal.[44] In 1548, at the command of his father Philip's household was completely reorganized according to the Burgundian model, in conformity with the new ordinance of Jean Sigoney.[45] Although the reorganization was received under much protest, political motivations lay at the basis of the decision.[46] With the introduction of the Burgundian court ceremonial, typified by great participation from the nobility, the emperor wanted to promote the integration of the social elites – coming from diverse compass points of the Habsburg realm – into the entourage of his son.[47] Seen politically, however, it was still unthinkable to do away with the *Casa de Castilla* altogether. Although very reduced in scope, this *Casa* continued to exist alongside the *Casa de Borgoña*, with mutual influence and even a partial overlap as a consequence. Even so, as far as the personal care of the prince and his family was concerned, the Burgundian household was preferred over its Castilian pendant, which in the words of Mia Rodríguez-Salgado was characterized instead by 'an odd assortment of offices' of which, above all, the Court Chapel and the division of the hunt mattered.[48] Nevertheless the coexistence of both traditions was characteristic for the reign of Philip II, and the evolution of the Burgundian ceremonial in the second half of the sixteenth century can only be grasped in light of the influence of the *Casa de Castilla*.

---

[43] *Ibidem*, p. 35 and Kerkhoff, J. *Maria van Hongarije en haar hof (1505-1558). Tot plichtsbetrachting uitverkoren*. Hilversum, 2008. Op. cit. p. 137.

[44] Martínez Millán & Fernández Conti, *La Monarquía de Felipe II*, vol. I, p. 61. Surrounding this, see also Rodríguez-Salgado, M.J. 'Honour and Profit in the Court of Philip II of Spain,' in: Aymard, M. & Romani, M.A., eds. *La cour comme institution économique. Actes du douzième congrès international d'histoire économique, Séville-Madrid, 24-28 août 1998*. Paris, 1998, pp. 67-86. Op. cit. p. 67.

[45] Martínez Millán & Fernández Conti, *La Monarquía de Felipe II*, vol. I, p. 61 and pp. 136-137. See also Rodriguez-Salgado, M.J. 'The Court of Philip II of Spain,' in: Asch & Birke, *Princes, Patronage and the Nobility*, pp. 205-244.

[46] It is contested among historians of the matter whether the introduction of the Burgundian court ceremonial into the household of the prince aroused much criticism. Cf. the discussion in Redworth, G. & Checa, F. 'The Courts of the Spanish Habsburgs 1500-1700,' in: Adamson, J., ed. *The Princely Courts of Europe. Ritual, Politics and Culture under the Ancien Régime 1500-1750*. London, 1999, pp. 43-65 (namely, pp. 47-51) and Nader, H. 'Habsburg Ceremony in Spain: The Reality of the Myth.' *Historical Reflections*, 15 (1988) 293-309 (namely, p. 296). See also Mayoral López, *La Casa Real de Felipe III*, p. 37.

[47] Martínez Millán & Fernández Conti, *La Monarquía de Felipe II*, vol. I, p. 136.

[48] Rodríguez-Salgado, 'Honour and Profit,' 69.

While the court at Madrid gradually developed into one of the most impressive of Europe, the Brussels court had to surrender quite a lot of its former luster. Political circumstances hindered the expansion of the court at Brussels as a stable administrative and cultural center, and the relatively rapid succession of governors after Mary of Hungary saw to it that even their respective entourages were not allotted any long life. Under Margaret of Parma the Burgundian ceremonial continued more or less to be maintained, but after that its evolution becomes unclear.[49] Court ordinances are wanting for this period, and it is still questionable whether governors-general who were not of royal blood, such as the duke of Alba and Luis de Requeséns, did indeed keep a household in the classic sense of the word. More than likely they had a limited entourage at their disposal, yet their peculiar status prevented them from conducting a court roster on a princely scale. Then again, the household that Archduke Ernst brought along with him to Brussels in 1594 was based on the Austrian court model that was current in Central Europe.[50] Though also originally inspired by the Burgundian court ceremonial, this model, too, had evolved very much over the years, such that in the meantime it differed fundamentally from the tradition familiar in Brussels.[51]

The observation by the nuncio Bentivoglio supposing that the household of Albert and Isabella would rest on the ages-old organization of the *maison de Bourgogne*, has to be interpreted in the right context as a consequence. At the time when the nuncio wrote down his report, the notion of a Burgundian ceremonial had not referred for a long time to the model that had come into being in former times under the dukes of Burgundy. Rather, it referred to a mishmash of influences that deviated in many ways from the idealized image that Olivier de la Marche had postulated in his memoirs. Although the Burgundian model still made up its core in theoretical respects, the court ceremonial under Charles V and Philip II had devolved into a medley of different traditions, among them perhaps those of Flanders and Brabant, yet in any case those of Castile, Aragon, and possibly even Portugal. On top of that, the accent came to fall more and more emphatically on an attitude of reservedness and *gravitas*, one inspired by the Counter-Reformation and later made one and the same with typical Habsburg tradition.[52] The *Casa de Borgoña*, which had defined the

[49] Delen, *Het hof van Willem van Oranje*, 37.

[50] Hortal Muñoz, J.E. 'La casa del Archiduque Ernesto durante su gobierno en los Países Bajos (1593-1595),' in: Álvarez-Ossorio Alvariño, A. & García García, B.J., eds. *La Monarquía de las Naciones. Patria, nación y naturaleza en la Monarquía de España*. Madrid, 2004, pp. 193-205.

[51] Duindam, J. 'The Burgundian-Spanish Legacy in European Court Life: A Brief Reassessment and the Example of the Austrian Habsburgs,' in: Cauchies, J.-M. & Noflatscher, H., eds. *Pays bourguignons et autrichiens (XIVe-XVIe siècles): une confrontation institutionelle et culturelle*. Publication du Centre Européen d'Études Bourguignonnes (XIVe-XVIe s.) 46: Rencontres d'Innsbruck (29 septembre au 2 octobre 2005). Neuchâtel, 2006, pp. 203-220.

[52] Redworth & Checa, 'The Courts of the Spanish Habsburgs,' 59-61.

face of the court in Madrid at the end of the sixteenth century, was consequently still Burgundian only in name. In practice the royal household had fashioned for itself a character entirely of its own, which, to be sure, exhibited traits of an older precedent, yet differed substantially from it as far as the rest was concerned. This medley of styles, which rapidly acquired the connotation of 'Spanish,' was the model that Bentivoglio denoted and that would be introduced at the court of the archdukes. The nuncio left no doubt remaining in any way that the court at Brussels was a faithful copy of the court in Madrid both in terms of organization and structure as well as in terms of ceremonial. 'In general it can be posited that both courts were cobbled from the same model,' he noted.[53] That 'model' was in essence neither Burgundian nor Spanish, but rather typically 'Habsburg' in character. To clarify this conclusion the following section goes deeper into the question of how the imitation of the court model from Madrid was concretely translated at the court in Brussels.

Structure and organization of the archducal household

Just like the *Casa de Borgoña* in Madrid, the household of Albert and Isabella numbered four overarching divisions.[54] The *Capilla* or Court Chapel provided for the religious services and the musical ministrations, while the *Casa* (House), the *Cámara* (Chamber) and the *Caballeriza* (Mews) jointly attended to actually serving the princes. The palace guard or *Guarda* held a peculiar position in the sense that it did not directly make up part of the actual household, but was responsible for the physical security of the archdukes and – in a broader context – for the monitoring of their residence and entourage.[55] Each division was in its turn subdivided into several departments, which were responsible for well-described duties and authorizations. This set-up was characterized by a strict hierarchy among the divisions, as shown in historical sources in which the diverse articulations are constantly arranged in accordance with the same pattern. The remarkable stability of this structure is striking too. Except for the gradual growth in the number of staff members, the organization of the different departments seems to have scarcely undergone modification throughout

[53] Bentivoglio, *Relationi*, 161.

[54] See also Lanoye, 'Structure and Composition,' 107.

[55] In the literature, the *Caza* or division of the hunt is also sometimes arranged with the household. This rather important aspect of life at court, however, falls outside the purpose of this book, and consequently does not come up for discussion. Whoever desires more information concerning this can go to Liesenborghs, P. *Het edele vermaak. De jacht in de Spaanse Nederlanden onder de Aartshertogen.* Unpublished master's thesis, Katholieke Universiteit Leuven, 2005, and the article derived from this: Liesenborghs, P. 'Het edele vermaak. De jacht in de hofcultuur van de Spaanse Nederlanden onder de Aartshertogen.' *Ons Heem*, 60 (2007) 6-14.

the archducal time period. This assessment does not point so much to the efficiency of the system, however, as to the importance of continuity with tradition already cited earlier.

A characteristic feature that distinguished the court of Brussels from its counterpart in Madrid is the fact that Albert and Isabella kept a joint household. Except for the *Cámara*, which was responsible for the individual care of the princes and consequently was split up into a male and a female section, they did not have separate households at their disposal. That was exceptional in comparison with other European princely courts, and the reason for it is not clear right away. The most obvious explanation perhaps should be sought in a purely pragmatic consideration. After all, in one of her letters to the duke of Lerma, the infanta declared straightforwardly that a joint household offered not only more comfort to the servants but also was simply more advantageous on financial grounds.[56] There was, however, possibly another reason for the basis of deciding not to split the archducal household.

Where the classic partitioning between the household of the prince and that of his consort usually went hand in hand with a mutual difference in status in countries like Spain, France or England, that kind of distinction was not obvious in Brussels. Although the Archduke in practice had most affairs of state at heart, he shared sovereignty over the Netherlands with the infanta by law.[57] This remarkable status of co-sovereignty was still unheard of at the beginning of the seventeenth century. In the fifteenth century, to be sure, the Catholic Monarchs Ferdinand and Isabella both possessed sovereign status, and in the sixteenth century the short-lived marriage of Philip II with Mary Tudor also would have produced a similar situation. In these cases, however, it was not a matter of co-sovereignty in the strict sense of the word. Seen technically, Ferdinand was sovereign in Aragon but not in Castile, where his spouse was the rightful princess. In the same way Philip II was sovereign in Spain but not in England – for Mary the inverse applied. Consequently, with the marriage of the archdukes for the first time the special situation arose in which both princes were co-sovereign in one and the same principality. As opposed to other princely couples Albert and Isabella possessed equal hierarchical status, which was altogether translated into the architectural arrangement of the palace.[58] Whereas the personal quarters of Albert were found on the first storey of the residential wing, those of Isabella were

56 Rodríguez Villa, A., ed. *Correspondencia de la Infanta Doña Isabel Clara Eugenia de Austria con el Duque de Lerma y otros personajes*. Madrid, 1906. Op. cit. p. 44 f.: The infanta Isabella to the duke of Lerma, Feast of the Ascension, 1606.

57 Thomas, W. 'Andromeda Unbound. The Reign of Albert and Isabella in the Netherlands, 1598-1621,' in: Thomas & Duerloo, *Essays*, pp. 1-14.

58 De Jonge, 'Building Policy and Urbanisation,' 193 and De Jonge, ' ' 't Hof van Brabant' als symbool van de Spaanse hofhouding,' 191.

placed in the second storey. Both floors numbered exactly as many rooms, and with the addition of a second processional arcade on top of the existing one, the apartment of the infanta was completely put on equal footing with that of her consort.[59]

In the political context sketched here the decision not to split the archducal household was far from illogical. Any possible split-up could arouse the impression that the household of the infanta enjoyed less prestige than that of her spouse, which would put the balanced power relations between the two princes under pressure. In times of political instability conflicts over rank and precedence among the entourage of Albert and that of Isabella were anything but desirable. On the other hand it should be noted that the presupposed hierarchical balance between the princes was nuanced. After all, in a legal sense the sovereignty over the Netherlands did belong to the infanta, who as the daughter of Philip II was his rightful hereditary successor.[60] During the public oath-taking of the archdukes in 1600 it was Isabella consequently – and not her spouse – who symbolically got the sword of sovereignty belted on (a fact that she found really amusing by the way).[61] Only by the grace of her marriage was this sovereign power transferred in part to Albert. In practice it is striking, then, that the Archduke pretty much always gave precedence to his spouse in ceremonial questions. So, for example, foreign ambassadors and diplomats as a rule first went to an audience with Isabella and only after that with Albert.[62] It would, however, be wrong to deduce from this that the role of the archduke was limited to that of prince-consort. He did indeed stand at the head of the government and was – at least during the first years of his reign – the supreme commander of the army. Seen from that standpoint, the choice of a joint household was rather an affirmation of Albert's status as co-sovereign beside Isabella, and not the inverse.

In theory the day-to-day direction of the archducal household was in the hands of four dignitaries, who each took over the administration of one of the large divisions. The *capellán mayor* or grand chaplain stood at the head of the *Capilla*, while the members of the *Casa*, the *Cámara* and the *Caballeriza* answered, respectively, to the *mayordomo mayor* (high steward of the household), the *sumiller de corps* (grand chamberlain) and the *caballerizo mayor* (master of the horse). Within each division their authority was almost but not quite fully absolute. They doled out the commands, monitored the execution of them, and – even more important – had the financial budget assigned to them more or less autonomously at their disposal. On top of that these four superiors were authorized to take an oath of obedience from those servants put to work in their

59 *Ibidem*.
60 Thomas, 'Andromeda Unbound,' 13.
61 Rodríguez Villa, *Correspondencia*, p. 10: Isabella to Lerma, January 29, 1600.
62 See e.g. ASV, *Borghese* III 113, f. 184: Nuncio Lucio Morra to Cardinal-Secretary of State Borghese, August 19, 1617.

division.[63] Seen hierarchically, though, the *mayordomo mayor* was first in rank, in the sense that he not only took the oath of the subordinates of the *Casa*, but also of the *sumiller de corps* and the *caballerizo mayor*.[64] As such his jurisdiction extended over the complete archducal household, with the exception of the *Capilla*.

The *Capilla*

In the court indices reflecting the structure of the archducal household, and by refraction those of most Habsburg courts in Western and Central Europe, the Court Chapel is pretty much always mentioned as the first division. Taking into note the symbiotic relationship between the Habsburg regime and the Catholic religion, that need not come as any surprise. In their study concerning the *Capilla Real* of Philip II, José Martínez Millán and Henar Pizarro Llorente conclude that the Court Chapel was an essential component of the royal household in Madrid.[65] As the environment *par excellence* in which the ideological bases of the policies of the Spanish prince were conceived and made known, the Chapel constituted not only the spiritual conscience of his politics but was also of inestimable importance for the legitimization of the regime. Rubén Mayoral López even goes a step further and posits that for that reason the *Capilla Real* may be counted as one of the most fundamental institutions of the Spanish monarchy.[66] Though in essence charged with the spiritual well-being of the palace inhabitants and the musical embellishment of religious services, the Court Chapel profiled itself as the watchdog of religious orthodoxy in the country, as occasioned by Philip II's politics of confessionalization. In other words, it not only provided for the spiritual needs of the prince and his courtiers but also emerged as a theological advisory board that drew up the moral and spiritual outlines of the regime in minute detail.[67] Under its impetus the ideological doctrine came into being upon which Philip's rule was grounded and which would lie at the base of the ultimate *Monarquía Católica* that he had in his sights. The impact of the *Capilla Real* on the organization of state was consequently gigantic, certainly when taking into account the influence the chaplains, preachers and father confessors could exercise on the actions and the intentions of the strict Catholic prince.[68] Furthermore, the power of the

[63] Only the male servants were expected to make this oath. See Mayoral Lopez, *La Casa Real de Felipe III*, 211.

[64] Mayoral López, *La Casa Real de Felipe III*, 233.

[65] Martínez Millán, J. & Pizarro Llorente, H. 'La capilla real: integración social y definición de la ortodoxia religiosa,' in: Martínez Millán & Fernández Conti, *La Monarquía de Felipe II*, 517-544.

[66] Mayoral López, *La Casa Real de Felipe III*, 47 f.

[67] Concerning the Spanish *Capilla Real*, see Carreras, J.J. & García García, B.J., eds. *La Capilla Real de los Austrias. Música y ritual de corte en la Europa Moderna*. Madrid, 2001. See also Nelson, B. 'Ritual and Ceremony in the Spanish Royal Chapel, c. 1559 - c. 1561.' *Early Music History*, 19 (2000) 105-200.

[68] Martínez Millán, J. & Pizarro Llorente, H. 'La capilla real,' 517-518.

Court Chapel was expressed also in a very tangible way: to it fell spiritual jurisdiction over all courtiers and servants of the court. Consequently, it was the responsibility of the Court Chapel to monitor compliance with religious regulations as well as to judge the behavior and devotion of its 'parishioners.' Should the royal household want to be an example for all the populace to emulate, then the actions and the thoughts of the courtiers needed to accord with the religious-ideological standpoints propagated by the Court Chapel, so the motto went. The exuberant lifestyle that went hand in hand with court life was, then, a favorite subject of the preachers, who never shrank from bringing up concrete excesses in their sermons.[69]

Just like in Madrid, the Court Chapel in Brussels was one of the most important forums where the symbiosis between the regime and the Catholic religion was celebrated and evoked. It was sufficiently demonstrated already in the 1920s and 1930s that the regime of Albert and Isabella was a driving force behind the promotion of Tridentine Catholicism.[70] In 1997, all the same, Luc Duerloo would convincingly demonstrate that this militant devotion was oriented not only to the Catholic revival in the Netherlands but also to the restoration and the affirmation of princely authority.[71] 'The pious support that Albert and Isabella provide to the Counter-Reformation,' Duerloo posits, 'is sincerely meant, to be sure, but for that reason still not unimportant. The archducal religious zeal is also and as much a crucial element in the Habsburg strategy oriented to the dynastic mandate of governing the Southern Netherlands as natural princes, of being endorsed anew by the inhabitants of those regions.'[72] The religious practices at the court in Brussels fulfill the function of catalyst in that process. Inspired by the ideal of the *Pietas Austriaca* – the profound experience of piety that characterized the Habsburg dynasty – the court profiled itself as a beacon of light for spirituality and Christian devotion.[73] Life ticked to the rhythm of the liturgical calendar, with special attention for the ecclesiastical high holy days like Christmas, Easter, and above all the Feast of Corpus Christi. The special archducal veneration before the Eucharist was expressed among other things in the organization of a series of religious ceremonies and processions in honor of the Most Holy Miraculous Sacrament, a fourteenth-century relic preserved in the Brussels

---

69 Mayoral López, *La Casa Real de Felipe III*, 47 f.

70 See, namely, Pasture, A. *La restauration religieuse aux Pays-Bas catholiques sous les archiducs Albert et Isabelle (1596-1633)*. Leuven, 1925 and Elias, H.J. *Kerk en Staat in de Zuidelijke Nederlanden onder de regeering der aartshertogen Albrecht en Isabella, 1598-1621*. Antwerp, 1931.

71 Duerloo, L. 'Pietas Albertina. Dynastieke vroomheid en herbouw van het vorstelijke gezag.' *Bijdragen en Mededelingen betreffende de Geschiedenis der Nederlanden*, 112 (1997) 1-18. See also Duerloo, L. 'Archducal Piety and Habsburg Power,' in: Thomas & Duerloo, *Essays*, pp. 267-283.

72 Duerloo, 'Pietas Albertina,' 18.

73 The standard work concerning this is still Coreth, A. *Pietas Austriaca. Ursprung und Entwicklung Barocker Frömmigkeit in Österreich*. Vienna, 1959.

cathedral of Saint Gudula. In addition the traditional Habsburg Marian cult was also strongly observed by the archdukes. The celebration of the seven Marian holidays – the Immaculate Conception (December 8), the Feast of the Purification of the Virgin (February 2), the Annunciation (March 25), the Visitation of the Blessed Virgin Mary (July 2), the Assumption (August 15), the Nativity of Mary (September 8) and the Presentation of the Blessed Virgin Mary (November 21) – as well as the traditional court pilgrimages to Our Lady of Laeken and to the Black Madonna of Halle may be seen as exemplary in that respect.[74] The expansion of the shrine of pilgrimage at Scherpenheuvel [Montaigu], where Marian devotion was propelled to unknown heights, was without a doubt the crown on that work.[75]

In that kind of climate diffused with the fear of god, it need not come as a surprise that Aubertus Miraeus, the Antwerp dean of the cathedral chapter and court chaplain, wrote in his biography of Archduke Albert the following: 'Holy, I say, was his Court, for the reason that it seemed more like a Monastery of very God-fearing People and of clergy leading a devout religious Life, than a Palace of Secular People.'[76] Without a doubt it was Miraeus' intention to accentuate the exceptional devotion of the archduke shortly after his death, and yet it can be safely assumed that his statement was in no way exaggerated. More than any other princely court in Europe at that time, the court of Albert and Isabella was immersed in an atmosphere of strict religious orthodoxy and penance, in which all members of the archducal household were expected to take part. A clear outward expression of that was the establishment of the Brotherhood of Saint Ildefons, which made the union – characteristic of the Brussels court – between the Eucharist, Marian devotion, and the veneration of the saints. Archduke Albert founded this confraternity in 1588 in Lisbon, but moved its seat in 1603 to the priory of the Church of Saint Jacques-sur-Coudenberg in Brussels.[77] Membership was exclusively reserved for courtiers, with the understanding that joining was not as much desired as in fact obligatory – whoever did not present himself of his own volition could expect a stiff penalty.[78] Membership presumed among other things that members were devoted to the doctrine of the Immaculate Conception. The members were presumed as well to take turns accompanying the Viaticum whenever someone

[74] Duerloo, 'Pietas Albertina,' 5.

[75] Concerning Scherpenheuvel [Montaigu], see Duerloo, L. & Wingens, M. *Scherpenheuvel. Het Jeruzalem van de Lage Landen*. Leuven, 2002.

[76] Original citation: '*Sanctum voco, nec blandior aut adulor, utpote quae Monasterii potius religiosissimi atque ab omni contagione liberi speciem referret.*' Miraeus, A. *De vita Alberti Pii, sapientis, prudentis Belgarum Principis commentarius*. Antwerp, 1622, p. 105.

[77] Castan, A. 'Les origines et la date du Saint-Ildefonse de Rubens.' *Mémoires de la Société d'émulation du Doubs, 5e série*, 9 (1884) 15-107.

[78] The index of the confraternity is preserved in the Rijksarchief in Anderlecht, *Kerkelijk Archief van Brabant* 6915 (= microfilm 1647): *Register van de Broederschap van de Heilige Ildefons, ca. 1690.*

from their ranks was in the throes of death. On top of that, every year on January 23, a special celebration of the mass was held in honor of Saint Ildefons, in the presence of the entire court.[79] In that way, willing or not, the courtiers were involved in the strict religious practices at court, whereby the intertwining between the Habsburg dynasty, the aristocracy and religion was emphasized once more.

According to the Burgundian intellectual Jules Chifflet, who gave a description of it in his *Aula Sacra Principum Belgii*, the Court Chapel was partitioned into the so-called Capella Minor, the *capellanes de Oratorio* of which led the daily religious services in the private chapels of the archdukes, and the Capella Maior, which took care of the high mass sung on Sunday in the great palace chapel and was composed of the *capellanes de Altar*, the musicians, and the choristers.[80] In addition, a number of preachers, servants, and father confessors also made up part of the Court Chapel.

THE *CAPILLA*

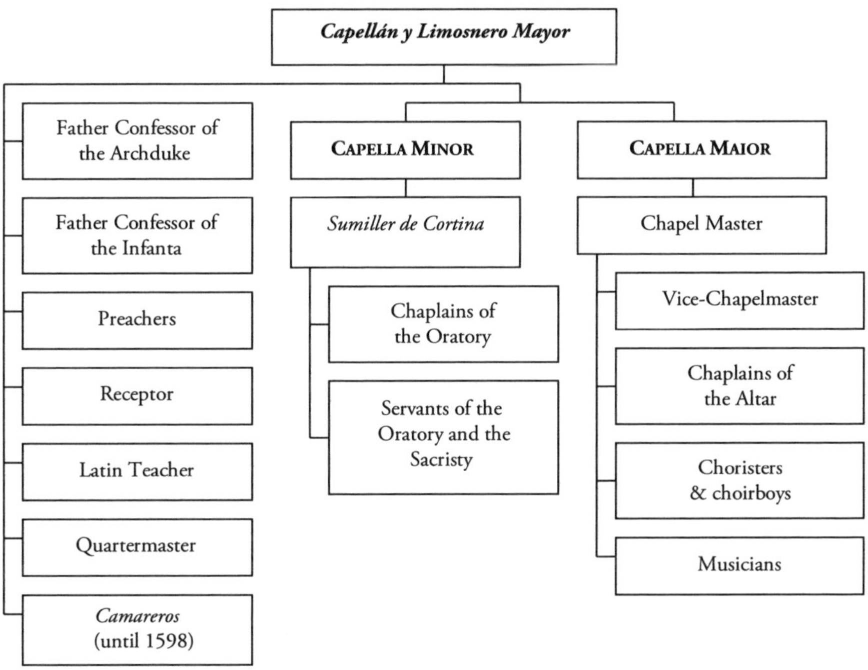

[79] Duerloo, 'Pietas Albertina,' 7.

[80] Chifflet, J. *Aula Sacra Principum Belgii; sive commentarius historicus de Capellae Regiae in Belgio, Principiis, Ministris, Ritibus atque universo apparatu*. Antwerp, 1650.

As said previously, the *Capilla* came under the direction of the *capellán mayor*, who usually combined this function with that of *limosnero mayor* (grand almoner) and consequently had the say-so over the distribution of alms which were handed out monthly and on holidays to 'old and poor people, prisoners, sick women, poor orphan children, girls who were going to marry, people with burn injuries, and merchants who had gone to ruin through misfortune.'[81] The commission of the grand chaplain consisted of steering the spiritual services provided at court in the right direction, which implied a diverse range of responsibilities.[82] The practical organization of daily religious services was one of his most important responsibilities. He consulted with the princes when and where the daily celebration of the mass would take place, saw to it that all the servers were informed of this, designated the chaplains and preachers who had to preside over the service, commissioned the cleaning of the palace chapel, and defined with what ornamentation it had to be adorned. In addition he also functioned as the personnel manager: he took the oaths of the servants of the Court Chapel, appointed the chaplains who were assigned to the pages and the body guards of the archdukes, and took care of the punctual payment of remunerations and honoraria of his subordinates. Finally, the leading position of the *capellán mayor* was also literally reflected in the rules of precedence of the court ceremonial. During ceremonial processions he followed immediately behind the princes and next to the *mayordomo mayor*. He could enter the quarters of the archduke at all times without permission, even if the latter was sick, and they went to communion together in the private oratory.[83]

The privileged position of the grand chaplain is perhaps best depicted on the basis of Illustration 1 (below), in which can be seen very clearly how the placement of the pews in the palace chapel reflects the rules of precedence among the courtiers.[84] During celebrations of the mass the *capellán mayor* sat in a place of honor next to the *cortina*, the ceremonial curtain behind which the princes usually took their places and which – just like the tabernacle – was only opened during the consecration. The association between divine and secular power was clearly accentuated as a result: each time when the tabernacle opened and the Holy Sacrament was revealed to the faithful

---

[81] '*(...) des gens anciens et pauvres, prisoniers, femmes malades, orphelins pauvres, filles à marier, et gens brulez du feu, marchans distruict par la fortune.*' ARA, *Handschriftenverzameling* 821, f. 7.

[82] For a complete overview of the responsibilities of the grand chaplain, see Mayoral López, *La Casa Real de Felipe III*, 65-66.

[83] *Ibidem.*

[84] This order is confirmed in a report by the Venetian ambassador Giorgio Justiniani from 1605. See Hagemans, G., ed. *Voyage par la France, la Flandre et l'Allemagne rapporté par l'Excellentissime Giorgio Justiniani, à son retour à Venise de son ambassade ordinaire en Angleterre, 1605*. In: Hagemans, G., ed. *Relations inédites d'ambassadeurs Vénitiens dans les Pays-Bas sous Philippe II et Albert et Isabelle* (Extrait des Annales de l'Académie d'Archéologie de Belgique, 21, 2e série, part I). Brussels, 1865, pp. 56-86.

present, the archdukes also showed themselves in all their glory to their subjects.[85] Often, though, Albert and Isabella did not follow the religious service from behind the *cortina* but from a tribune situated higher, which gave access to their personal quarters and from which they had a view of the main altar via a small window. In that way they could attend the celebration of the mass discreetly, without having to expose themselves to the spying glances of the churchgoers.

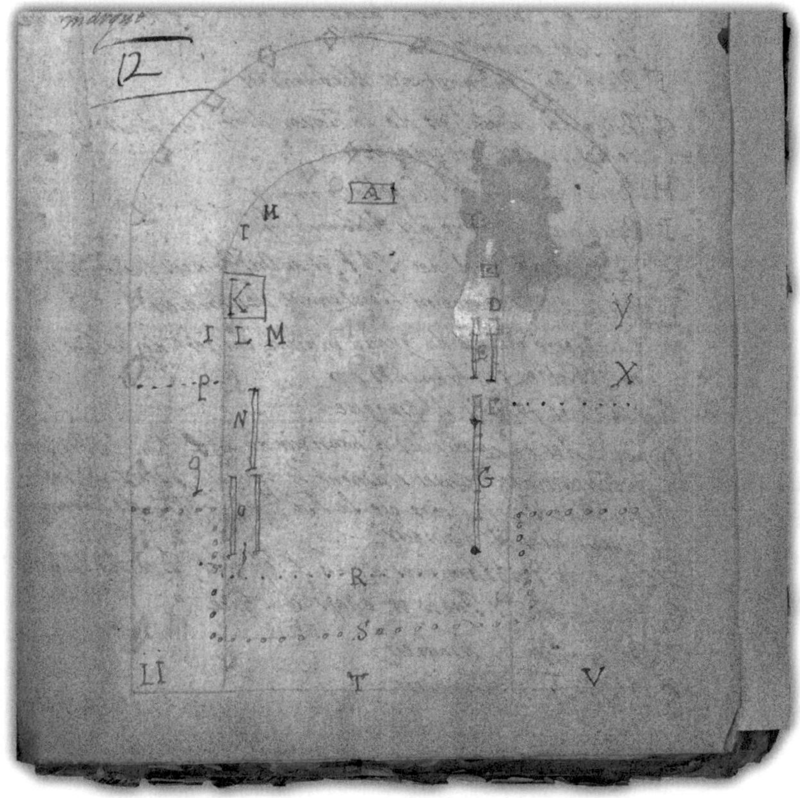

Illustration 1 – Ground plan of the palace chapel according to Lozano, with an overview of the ceremonial placement of the members of the archducal household during the religious service. (© ARA, Handschriftenverzameling 821, ff. 110-111.)

Legend: A= main altar; B= credence table; C= pew of the celebrant and the mass servers; D= place of the *mayordomo* on duty; E= pews and prie-dieux of the ambassadors; F= place of the lieutenant of the halberdiers; G= pew of the knights of the Golden Fleece; H= pew of the *capellán mayor*; I= place of the captain of the halberdiers; K = the *cortina*; L= place of the captain or the lieutenant of the *Hartschiere*; M= folding chair of the *mayordomo mayor*; N= pew of the *Grandes*; O= pew of the honorary chaplains, the father confessors, the preachers, the *sumiller de cortina* and the master of ceremonies; P= place of the *gentilhombres de la Cámara*, the *gentilhombres de la Boca* and the *caballerizos*; Q= place of the pages and the heads of the court departments; R= places of the *Hartschiere*; S= places of the halberdiers; T= rood screen; V= entry portal; X= door to the tribune with access to the princely apartments Y= window of the tribune with view of the main altar.

[85] Redworth & Checa, 'The Courts of the Spanish Habsburgs,' 60.

At the court of the archdukes the function of grand chaplain and grand almoner was exercised successively by Pedro de Alarcón (ca. 1595-1596), George of Austria (1596-1598), Pedro de Toledo (1598-1620), and François de Rye (1620-1637). Pedro de Alarcón belonged to the family of the lords of Valverde, a *señorío* in Cuenca, Spain, and received the position of *capellán mayor* shortly before Albert's journey to the Netherlands in 1595.[86] Even so, once arrived in Brussels he appeared not to be able to get used to his new environs, for after a few months he already asked for leave to be allowed to return to Spain.[87] He was succeeded by George of Austria, a bastard son of the prince-bishop of Liège with the same name and, as such, a distant family member of the archduke. George had been serving in Albert's household already since 1571, more specifically as *camarero*, a function that only occurred in the entourage of ecclesiastical princes and would logically cease to exist in Brussels after the archduke had ceded his cardinal's hat.[88] Just like his predecessor, George too would not hold the office of grand chaplain for long. Two years after his appointment he made it known that he did not wish to accompany Albert on his journey to Spain (where the wedding with the infanta would take place). Rather, he wanted to stay behind in the Southern Netherlands to pass away his final days there, as dean of the Saint Peter's Church in Leuven.[89] He was relieved in turn by Pedro de Toledo, a relative of the duke of Alba, who just like George had already served for a long time in the archducal household as *camarero* and *sumiller de cortina*. This prestigious duty consisted of opening and closing the ceremonial curtain in the Court Chapel during the consecration. Toledo would keep the position of *capellán mayor* until his death in September 1620, yet exercised other responsibilities in the meantime. So, for example, he was administrator-general of the military hospital in the Southern Netherlands, and he stayed in Rome from 1603 to 1605 as the archducal emissary to the Holy See.[90] During his absence he was replaced by Karel Maes, a scion of an influential Antwerp family, whose brother Engelbert would make it in 1614 to presiding head of the Privy Council.[91] Out of

---

86 Roco de Campofrío, J. *España en Flandes. Trece años de gobierno del archiduque Alberto (1595-1608).* Madrid, 1973. Op. cit. p. 7.

87 Hortal, 'The Household of Archduke Albert,' in press.

88 See Martínez Millán, J. 'El archiduque Alberto en la corte de Felipe II (1570-1580),' in: Thomas & Duerloo, *Essays*, pp. 27-37.

89 RAH, *SyC* A-61: *Representación del Almirante de Aragón al Archiduque Alberto siendo su Maiordomo Maior*. Op. cit. f. 8.

90 Goemans, L.V. *Het Belgische Gezantschap te Rome onder de regeering der aartshertogen Albrecht en Isabella (1600-1633), naar onuitgegeven diplomatische bronnen*. Ekeren-Donk, s.d. See also ASV, *Borghese* II 106, f. 162: Bentivoglio to Cardinal Borghese, March 14, 1615.

91 Concerning Karel and Engelbert Maes, see the relevant articles in the *Biographie Nationale*: Piot, C. 'Maes (Charles),' in: *Biographie Nationale*, vol. XIII (1894-1895) pp. 130-131 and Lefèvre, J. 'Maes (Engelbert),' in *Biographie Nationale*, vol. XXXVII (1971-1972) pp. 566-569. Their brothers Philip and Jan-Baptist Maes also made careers for themselves. Jan-Baptist was a councilor in the Council of Brabant, and for a long time Philip was the archducal emissary to the Holy See. After that he presided over the Treasury of Lille.

thanks for proven services Karel was appointed bishop of Ypres in 1607, and three years later bishop of Ghent (1610-1612). In 1620, finally, Pedro de Toledo was succeeded as grand chaplain by *sumiller de cortina* François de Rye, lord of Balançon in Franche-Comté, who would later be consecrated titular bishop of Cesarea as well as archbishop of Besançon.[92]

These successive appointments demonstrate that the assignment of the highest office in the Court Chapel was least of all devoid of political interests. Only scions of noble or influential families came under consideration. Inversely, the long career of a man like Pedro de Toledo illustrates that the *capellán mayor* could still be a politician of great weight. In addition to being grand chaplain and grand almoner, Toledo was a dyed-in-the-wool diplomat. He carried out various foreign missions commissioned by Albert and Isabella and represented the archducal regime at the Holy See.[93] Both commissions presupposed a fundamental knowledge not only of the political situation in the Netherlands and Europe, but also of the customs of early modern diplomacy in form and content alike. Even more than in the grand chaplain, this interaction between religious and profane areas is recovered in Iñigo de Brizuela and Andrés de Soto, the father confessors of Albert and Isabella.

It has already been convincingly argued among historians that the spiritual guides of princes were not only occupied with the individual care of the soul but just as well put their stamp on the princes' administration.[94] Their proximity to the monarch provided them great personal authority, which clearly brought political consequences along with it. That was no different at the time of the archducal regime. In 1924, Joseph Lefèvre already posited that the Dominican priest Brizuela, who was appointed father confessor to Albert in 1596, 'was not only a guide of conscience, but also one of the advisors most listened to.'[95] Over more than two decades Brizuela would actively interfere in the domestic and foreign policies of the archdukes. He played a prominent role in the negotiations that led to the conclusion of the Twelve Years' Truce, among other things, as well as in the discussions conducted with an eye to the provincial States' swearing an oath to Philip III in 1616. In addition he had a seat on the Council of State, and he functioned as point person for the archducal government

---

92 ASV, *Borghese* II 109, f. 155: Nuncio Lucio Sanseverino to Cardinal Borghese, October 24, 1620.

93 Brants, V. 'Pedro de Tolède,' in: *Biographie Nationale*, vol. XVI (1901) pp. 801-803.

94 Concerning the influential role of the father confessors in the princely entourage, see Minois, G. *Le confesseur du roi. Les directeurs de conscience sous la monarchie française*. Paris, 1988; Lamet, P.M. *Yo te absuelvo, Majestad. Confesores de reyes y reinas de España*. Madrid, 1991; Sánchez, M.S. 'Confession and Complicity: Margarita de Austria, Richard Haller, S.J. and the Court of Philip III.' *Cuadernos de Historia Moderna*, 14 (1993) 133-150; and Birely, R. *The Jesuits and the Thirty Years' War: Kings, Courts, and Confessors*. Cambridge U.P., 2003.

95 '*(...) fut non seulement le directeur de conscience, mais un des conseillers les plus écoutés.*' Lefèvre, J. 'Le ministère espagnol de l'archiduc Albert, 1598-1621.' *Bulletin de l'Académie Royale d'Archéologie de Belgique*, 1 (1924) 202-224.

in almost all political and ecclesiastical questions.[96] Contemporaries praised Brizuela for his professional way of tackling matters and for the seriousness and prescience with which he served the interests of the archduke. The Spanish ambassador Balthasar de Zúñiga described him as a 'great cleric and a good intellectual, quite discreet and prescient.'[97] The nuncio Bentivoglio called him 'a very serious and cautious person,' and the French geographer Pierre Bergeron wrote that Brizuela 'strongly administered the court.'[98] In 1621, the Holy See admonished the nuncio in Brussels, Guidi di Bagno, to maintain good contacts with the father confessor because the latter 'as concerns affairs of Church and state [was] more powerful than whoever else.'[99] That the value of Brizuela's services were even esteemed at court in Madrid is obvious from the fact that after Albert's death Brizuela was rewarded with the episcopal see of Segovia, and even later with an appointment as head of the High Council for the Netherlands.[100]

Although less pronounced than in Brizuela's case, the influence exercised by the Franciscan Andrés de Soto at court was surely no less veritable.[101] The father confessor of Archduchess Isabella enjoyed the reputation of being a distinctly devout and religious man, whose ascetic lifestyle contrasted with his hot-tempered personality.[102] He wrote erudite tracts and was a convinced adherent of the *Recollectio Vilacreciana*, a fifteenth-century reform movement that had been put through within the Franciscan order and that preached absolute obedience to the Rule of Saint Francis. The emphasis lay on prayer and on the observance of silence and poverty. As a fervent Recollect, Soto lived therefore not in the Coudenberg palace but in the monastery of the Observant Friars Minor in Brussels, and he declined even invitations to dine at court.[103] His duties consisted of hearing the confession of the infanta and advising her about religious matters. The confidence that Isabella placed in her father confessor was

[96] *Ibidem*, pp. 205-209.

[97] '*(…) gran religioso, de buenas letras, de mucha discreción y prudencia (…)*' BL, *Egerton* ms. 2079, ff. 236-246: *Relación de las cosas de Flandes y de las personas de importancia que sirven a Su Magestad.* Op. cit. f. 246.

[98] '*(…) persona molto grave et prudente (…).*' ASV, *Borghese* II 110, f. 83: Bentivoglio to Cardinal Borghese, November 8, 1614; '*(...) gouverne fort en la court (...).*' Michelant, *Voyage de Pierre Bergeron*, 346.

[99] De Meester de Ravestein, B., ed. *Correspondance du Nonce Giovanni-Francesco Guidi di Bagno (1621-1627).* Analecta Vaticano-Belgica, 2e série, section A: Nonciature de Flandre, VI. Rome-Brussels-Paris, 1938. Op. cit. vol. I, letter no. 2: Account concerning the nunciature in the Netherlands, directed to Guidi di Bagno at the start of his term of office.

[100] Lefèvre, 'Le ministère espagnol,' 205-209.

[101] Biographical data in Van Wyhe, C. 'Court and Convent: The Infanta Isabella and her Franciscan Confessor Andrés de Soto.' *Sixteenth Century Journal*, 35 (2004) 411-445 and De Troeyer, B., O.M.F. 'Bio-bibliografie van de minderbroeders in de Nederlanden. Voorstudies 6: Andreas de Soto.' *Franciscana*, 37 (1982) 69-96.

[102] De Meester de Ravestein, *Correspondance du Nonce Giovanni-Francesco Guidi di Bagno*, vol. I, letter no. 2.

[103] Van Wyhe, 'Court and Convent,' 415 and De Troeyer, 'Bio-bibliografie,' 72.

so great that their relationship was once compared to the bond between a daughter and her spiritual father.[104] Indeed there is no doubt that Andrés de Soto was one of Isabella's most important confidants. That position of confidence came in good use to him in his other occupations. After all, Soto was also commissioner-general of the German nation [i.e. the Netherlands, Germany, England, Ireland] within the Franciscan order, and in that capacity one of the driving forces behind the spread of post-Tridentine religious norms and practices among the regular religious orders in the Southern Netherlands. In that respect the figure of Isabella's father confessor can be seen as the ultimate personification of the fruitful collaboration between the archducal regime and religion.

The importance of the Court Chapel, however, is expressed not only in the activities of the grand chaplain and the father confessors; it is also shown in the presence of two to three court preachers and eight to nine *capellanes de Oratorio*, who theologically underpinned the religious doctrine propagated by the court by way of their tracts and sermons.[105] One of them was Richard Stanyhurst, an Irish historiographer who settled around 1580 in the Netherlands and converted to Catholicism. After the death of his wife he became a priest and a chaplain at the archducal court, where in 1607 he finished off the *Hebdomada Mariana*, a tract that was dedicated to the infanta and in which Stanyhurst related the seven stages of the Blessed Virgin's life to the seven days of the week.[106] Even so, the members of the Court Chapel did not limit themselves to the theoretical description of their ideas but also kept themselves occupied with the spread and application of them in practice. They were supported in this practice by the archdukes, who spared neither costs nor effort to install their chaplains and preachers in important ecclesiastical functions, so as to strengthen their grip on the Catholic revival in that way. The *capellán mayor* Karel Maes was already referred to above, who for his services was rewarded with the episcopal sees of Ypres and Ghent. In addition there was the court chaplain Antoon Triest, who was consecrated bishop of Bruges in 1616 and bishop of Ghent in 1622, and in that capacity proved to be a great reformer.[107] The same applies to the court preacher Paul Boudot, the archdeacon of Cambrai, who was appointed bishop of Saint-Omer in 1618 and eight years later

[104] According to Philippe Chifflet, court chaplain at the archducal court, Isabella was Soto's '*fille spirituelle*,' while he, inversely, was '*père spirituel de son âme*.' See Van Wyhe, 'Court and Convent,' 418.

[105] See concerning this, Hildebrand [Father O.M.F. Cap.]. 'Capucins belges et comtois, prédicateurs de la cour de Bruxelles sous Albert et Isabelle (1617-1633).' *Études franciscaines*, 49 (1937) 333-341.

[106] Stanyhurst, R. *Hebdomada Mariana, ex orthodoxis Catholicae Romanae Ecclesiae patribus collecta: in memoriam septem festorum Beatissimae Virginis Mariae, per singulos dies hebdomadae distributa*. Antwerp, 1609.

[107] Concerning these appointments, see ASV, *Borghese* II 102, f. 370: Nuncio Ascanio Gesualdo to Cardinal Borghese, November 26, 1616. See also De Schrevel, A.-C. 'Triest (Antoine),' in: *Biographie Nationale*, vol. XXV (1930-1932), pp. 614-624 and BAV, *BaL* 6812, f. 236: Nuncio Giovanni-Francesco Guidi di Bagno to Cardinal Ludovisi, February 12, 1622.

bishop of Arras;[108] to his colleague Claude du Vivier, who was the provincial-superior of the Order of the Minims;[109] and to Cesar Clemens, who in addition to being court chaplain was also vicar-general of the army and dean of the cathedral of Saint Gudula in Brussels.[110] The most well-known example, however, concerns Bernard de Montgaillard, the court preacher originally from France who on account of the religious troubles in his homeland had sought asylum in the Netherlands. In 1605, he was appointed by the archdukes as abbot of the Cistercian abbey of Orval, where he put through a rigorous reform of the regimen.[111]

In other words the influence of the archducal Court Chapel was comparable to that of the *Capilla Real* in Madrid. It was not limited to the spiritual support of the court but played an active role in the archdukes' politics of confessionalization. In that sense it contributed to an important extent to the reconstruction of the frayed Catholic fabric as well as the creation of a homogeneous religious landscape in the Southern Netherlands. In addition the *Capilla* had yet a second, more secular function: it was responsible for the musical embellishment of the religious services and other ceremonies and festivities at court. There is no doubt that the archducal chapel of musicians enjoyed an excellent international reputation.[112] Not coincidentally the Netherlands were known for their talented composers and choristers, witness in this the establishment of the famous *Capilla Flamenca* at the court of Philip II, where the renowned choirmaster Philippe Rogier was director and all the choristers had come from the Low Countries.[113] All the same, the archducal chapel of musicians scarcely had to feel inferior to its counterpart in Madrid. Only the best musicians – such as chapel master Gery de Ghersem, a student of Rogier – had the chance at

[108] In 1618, the papal nuncio Lucio Morra reported that the news of Boudot's appointment as bishop of Saint-Omer was received well by everyone. See ASV, *Borghese* II 112, ff. 254-256: Nuncio Lucio Morra to Cardinal Borghese, May 12, 1618. For a comparable letter, see f. 377, in which Morra Boudot praises him on account of '*la sua bontà, dottrina, e merito*' (July 28, 1618).

[109] Concerning Claude du Vivier, see Van Meerbeeck, L., ed. *Correspondance du Nonce Fabio de Lagonissa, archevêque de Conza (1627-1634).* Analecta Vaticano-Belgica, 2e série, section A: Nonciature de Flandre, XI. Brussels-Rome, 1966. Op. cit. letter no. 322: The Congregation of Regulars to Nuncio Fabio de Lagonissa, February 16, 1629.

[110] ASV, *Borghese* III 98, ff. 33-35: Nuncio Ottavio Mirto Frangipani to Cardinal Aldobrandini, February 10, 1601.

[111] Nuncio Bentivoglio maintained that Montgaillard was the most important preacher at the court in Brussels: '*I suoi meriti sono grandi, per dottrina e somma eruditione di varie lingue, e per singolar talento e gratia di predicare.*' BAV, *BaL* 6807, f. 47: Bentivoglio to Cardinal Borghese, August 4, 1612.

[112] See concerning this Proesmans, K. 'Muziek aan het hof van Albrecht en Isabella 1598-1621.' *Musica antiqua*, 6 (1989 no. 1) 4-8; 6 (1989 no. 2), 82-86 and 6 (1989 no. 3), 123-127; Proesmans, K. *Het muziekleven aan het hof van Albrecht en Isabella.* Unpublished master's thesis, Katholieke Universiteit Leuven, 1988; Clerckx, S. 'La chapelle royale de Bruxelles sous l'Ancien Régime.' *Annuaire du Conservatoire de musique de Bruxelles*, 65 (1942) 159-179; and Wangermee, R. 'La musique à la Chapelle royale des Pays-Bas,' in: Wangermee, R. & Mercier, P., eds. *La musique en Wallonie et à Bruxelles.* 2 vols. Brussels, 1980-1982, pp. 201-211.

[113] Becquart, P. *Musiciens néerlandais à la cour de Madrid. Philippe Rogier et son école (1560-1647).* Brussels, 1967.

a position. They were recruited from both inside as well as outside the borders.[114] 'The Archduke,' Charles Somerset noted in his travel journal, 'hath most excellent musike in his Chappell both for voice and instrument; he had some English at my being there, which were accounted the best of all his musike.'[115] With this comment Somerset was referring to the presence of the well-known English organists John Bull and Peter Philips, who had fled their homeland for religious reasons and – if their hefty salary at court may be an indication – were received in Brussels with open arms.[116] Furthermore the chapel of musicians was also populated by a few Spaniards (such as the famous composer Pedro Rimonte, who was maestro of music of the *Cámara*) and Italians (such as Giralomo Piccinini, a lutenist who had come to Brussels in the quarters of the nuncio Bentivoglio).[117] Those kinds of international influences created a stimulating climate for musicians at the court and saw to it that the Court Chapel in Brussels would play a forerunner's role in the spread of new music styles in the Netherlands.[118]

The *Casa*[119]

The core of the archducal household was constituted by the *Casa*, the overarching division that was responsible for the logistical support of the palace and its inhabitants. In the course of years the *Casa* came under the direction of three different high stewards successively. The first *mayordomo mayor* was Francisco de Mendoza, the Admiral of Aragon, who would hold the office beginning in 1595 with Albert's departure for Brussels, through to 1602.[120] Among historians the Admiral is better known on account of his position as general of the cavalry and the *de facto* supreme commander of the *Ejército de Flandes*, the Spanish army in the Netherlands. All the same, as a military leader Mendoza was not especially successful. In any case, the various field campaigns under his direction did not achieve many results. In 1599, a campaign led by Mendoza even brought about a storm of international indignation

---

[114] For an overview of the musicians and the choristers at court, see Thieffry, S. 'La Chapelle royale de Bruxelles de 1612 à 1618 d'après les Libros de la Razón de l'archiduc Albert.' *Belgisch Tijdschrift voor Muziekwetenschap*, 55 (2001) 103-126.

[115] Brennan, *The Travel Diary*, 287.

[116] See Hoppe, H.R. 'John Bull in the Archduke Albert's Service.' *Music & Letters*, 35 (1954) 114-115 and Grattan Flood, W.H. 'New Light on Late Tudor Composers: XL. Peter Philips.' *The Musical Times*, 70 (1929) 312-314.

[117] Russell, E. 'Pedro Rimonte in Brussels (C. 1600-1614).' *Anuario Musical*, 28-29 (1973-1974) 181-194.

[118] Proesmans, K. 'The Key Role of the Archducal Court in Spreading a New Musical Style in the Low Countries,' in: Thomas & Duerloo, *Essays*, pp. 129-135.

[119] In the main this section is based on Mayoral López, *La Casa Real de Felipe III*, 214-601; on Hofmann, *Das Spanische Hofzeremoniell*; on ARA, *Handschriftenverzameling* 821; on the *libros de razón* and on the various court indices of the archducal household.

[120] Concerning Mendoza, see Rodríguez Villa, A. *Don Francisco de Mendoza, almirante de Aragón*. Madrid, 1899. Part of his correspondence with Albert was published in CODOIN, vol. XLII.

when it turned out that his troops had left a path of destruction through Westphalia in their wake. Even in Brussels the often coarse and idiosyncratic appearance of the Admiral garnered the requisite criticism.[121] The archduke did what he could to provide cover for him, but Albert was not in the position to quash the negative comments.[122] In 1600, Mendoza's reputation worsened even more on the occasion of the Battle of Nieuwpoort, where the archducal troops came out on bottom and the Admiral himself was led away to prison. For a period of almost two years he would remain a hostage in the Dutch Republic. It cost Albert a fortune to buy his high steward's freedom, and although Mendoza rapidly took up his earlier functions again, confidence in his capacities was clearly damaged.[123] During the following months the Admiral's inability to turn the military tide would inevitably lead to his demise.[124] He did not succeed in setting free the besieged bulwark of Grave and, to make matters worse, had to deal with mutinies in the army. The archduke could no longer passively look on. Shortly afterward Mendoza fell into disgrace, and at the end of 1602, he was called back to Spain at Albert's asking to give an accounting to the king there.[125]

For reasons that will be discussed further on in this book, the position of *mayordomo mayor* remained vacant for ten years after Mendoza's departure (cf. Chapter III). Perhaps his function was taken over during this time period by the four subordinate *mayordomos*, who changed off with each other every week, or by the *sumiller de corps*. Not until 1612 was the office of high steward awarded anew to Rodrigo Niño y Lasso, the count of Añover, who had already been Albert's *sumiller de corps* and after that had also been appointed *caballerizo mayor*.[126] As such, beginning in 1615, Niño y Lasso combined the three most important offices in the archducal household; doing so, he was one of the most powerful nobles in the archducal entourage until his death in 1620. His role as Albert's *gran privado* will be delved into further in Chapter VI. In 1621, finally, Añover was succeeded as *mayordomo mayor* by the famous marquis Ambrogio Spínola, the orginally Genoese field commander who in the end saw his military career of many years in the Netherlands crowned with the highest possible

[121] Commentaries about this are to be found in the correspondence of nuncio Ottavio Mirto Frangipani. See ASV, *NF* 11, ff. 649-652: Frangipani to Cardinal Aldobrandini, April 22, 1599; and further ff. 657-659 (May 4, 1599), ff. 663-664 (May 31, 1599) and ff. 677-678 (July 8, 1599). See also the introduction to Volume III of Van der Essen, L. & Louant, A., eds. *Correspondance d'Ottavio Mirto Frangipani, premier nonce de Flandre (1596-1606)*. Analecta Vaticano-Belgica, 2e série, section A: Nonciature de Flandre, I-II-III. 3 parts in 4 vols. Rome-Brussels-Paris, 1924-1942.

[122] CODOIN, vol. XLII, p. 333: Albert to the duke of Lerma, February 6, 1600; *Ibidem*, p. 356: Albert to Lerma, August 17, 1600. See also CCE, vol. I, p. 43: Albert to Philip III, April 9, 1600.

[123] CODOIN, vol. XLII, p. 372: Albert to the duke of Lerma, October 27, 1600.

[124] BNF, *MsF* 16125: Antoine le Fèvre de la Boderie to Secretary of State Villeroy, August 19, 1602.

[125] Roco de Campofrío, *España en Flandes*, 282-283.

[126] BAV, *BaL* 6807, f. 8: Bentivoglio to Cardinal Borghese, July 7, 1612.

court office.[127] He would keep the function up until his departure for Spain in 1627, long after the death of Archduke Albert.

As head of the archducal household the high steward held a literally key position at court.[128] Each evening, after closing the gatehouse, the gatekeepers provided him with the palace keys. The ritual may be seen as a metaphor for his authorization to control the access to the archducal residence (and to the princes themselves). He himself possessed the freedom to go and be wherever he wanted, even into the personal quarters of Albert and Isabella. He consulted with the archdukes concerning their daily agenda, passed on their commands to the lower divisions of their household, and advised them about a number of administrative questions. His close bond with the princes was reflected on top of that in his right to spend time in their physical proximity at all times. In that way, the high steward was, for example, one of the few courtiers who had at his disposal an apartment of his own in the palace. During public processions, audiences, religious services and meals he was always to be found immediately behind or next to the archduke, but also in private circumstances he enjoyed absolute precedence over the others present. It would be wrong, though, to evaluate this ceremonial precedence as merely a matter of protocol. In a political constellation based on negotiation and reciprocity, everyone knew all too well what it meant to spend time as you please in the proximity of the prince, as well as to be able to deny the same possibility to others (cf. Chapter IV).

Assisted by the *mayordomos*, it was the responsibility of the high steward to steer day-to-day life at court in the right direction and to see to it that the various court departments functioned as was appropriate. So, for example, he kept an eye among other things on the provision of food and the maintenance of the palace, on the acquisition of new servants, on the transparency of the bookkeeping, on the payment of remunerations and honoraria, on the behavior of the courtiers, on the correct compliance with the court ceremonial, on the preparation of festivities and banquets, and on the security of the archducal residence.[129] Yet the office of *mayordomo mayor* may not be seen in any way as a purely domestic function. Rather than an ennobled housekeeper, the high steward of the court was one of the most important advisors and confidants of the prince. In Lozano's manuscript is to be read therefore that

---

[127] Concerning Spínola, there is quite a lot of literature. A sample from the offerings: Casoni, F. *Vita del Marchese Ambrogio Spinola, l'espugnatore delle piazze*. Genua, 1691; Rodríguez Villa, A. *Ambrosio Spínola, primer Marqués de los Balbases*. Madrid, 1904; Brants, V. 'Ambroise Spinola, 1569-1630, généralissime des armes de Flandre.' *Revue Générale Belge*, 1 (1915) 172-202; Lefèvre, J. *Spinola et la Belgique 1601-1627*. Brussels, 1947; Esteban Estríngana, A. *Guerra y finanzas en los Países Bajos católicos. De Farnesio a Spinola (1592-1630)*. Madrid, 2002.

[128] Concerning the functions of the *mayordomo mayor*, see Mayoral López, *La Casa Real de Felipe III*, 223-235 and ARA, *Handschriftenverzameling* 821, ff. 27-29.

[129] Mayoral López, *La Casa Real de Felipe III*, 223-235.

he 'is usually the prime minister of the Prince, the eye witness of his virtues, his confidant, and the one who participates the most in his glorious actions as well as in his misfortune and disgrace.'[130] As the chapters following will show, the function of *mayordomo mayor* illustrates once more that the presupposed distinction between the princely household and the princely administration is little more than an anachronistic construction.

The *Casa*

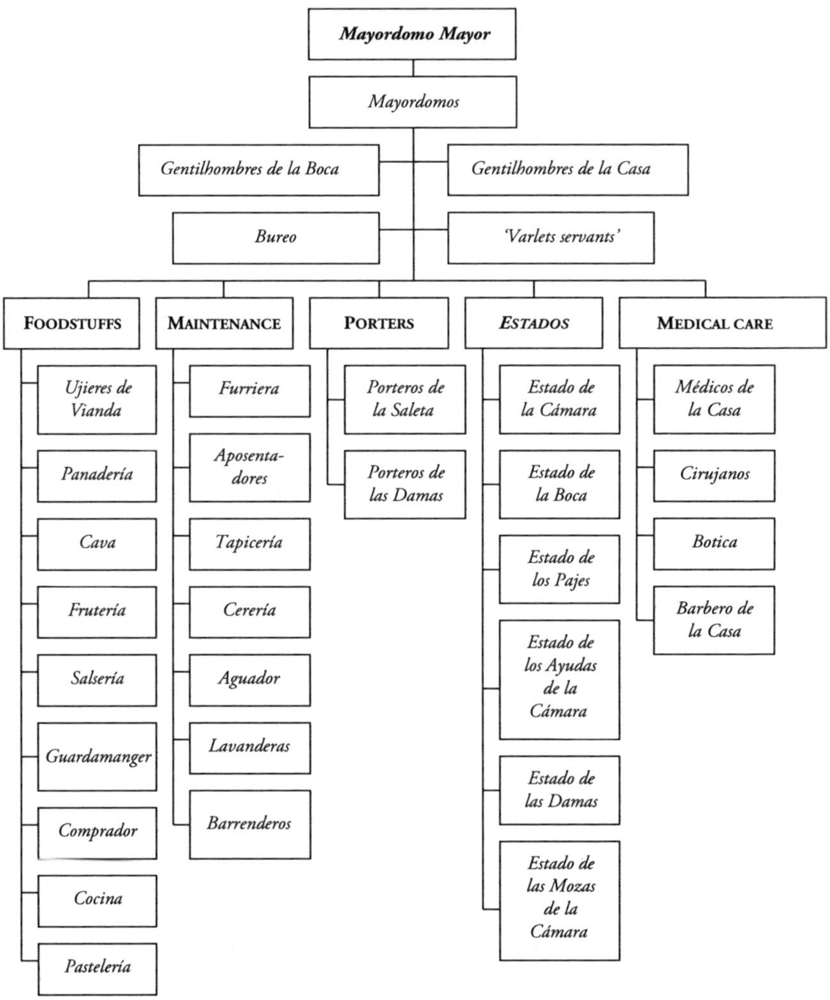

[130] *'(...) le Grand Maistre est ordinairement le premier ministre du Prince, le témoin oculaire de ses vertus, son confident et ce qui at plus de part dans ses plus glorieuses actions, aussi que dans ses infortunes et ses desgraces.'* ARA, *Handschriftenverzameling* 821, f. 27v.

As already said, the *mayordomo mayor* was directly responsible for the administration of the *Casa*. The organigram on the previous page offers a simplified presentation of the various departments making up part of it.

Just like the *Casa* itself, its various subdivisions were also organized according to a hierarchically built internal structure.[131] Most departments came under the command of a department head, who in turn was assisted by a number of master servants (*ayudas*) and grooms (*mozos*). So, for instance, the team that worked in the *Cava*, or wine and beer cellar, consisted in 1615 of sommelier Francisco Rodríguez Agraz, of his *ayudas* Valeriano Rama and Andrés Obrero de Benesa, and of the *mozo* Miguel de Solrivas.[132] Together they saw to the purchase and distribution of wine and beer at court. In the same way the *Salsería*, or saucery, consisted in 1615 of a *salsier* (Miguel de Pianca), two master servants (Tomás de la Riva and Francisco de Andrada), and two helpers (Domingo de Villarroel and Juan de Campuzano). Other divisions responsible for the provision of foodstuffs, like the *Panadería*, the *Pastelería* and the *Frutería*, were organized in a comparable manner. Respectively, they were responsible for making and distributing bread and cheese, for baking pies and pastries, and for the preparation of fruits and preserves. In the *Cocina*, or palace kitchen, head chef Juan de Terramunda held sway. In 1615 he led a team of eight cooks, six kitchen assistants, and two *portadores* who had to carry the dishes to the dining halls. Terramunda was assisted by the *comprador* Pasqual Navarro, whose duties consisted of purchasing the necessary ingredients at suppliers in town; by the *guardamanger* Martin Ruíz de Ezquerecocha, who concerned himself with the distribution of foodstuffs to the staff; and by Christoval de Arze and Juan Cortes, the so-called *ujieres de vianda*, who took upon themselves the practical organization of the public dining ritual of the archdukes.

In addition to the food supply the *Casa* also was responsible for the material support of the palace. In the *Cerería* great quantities of wax were processed into candles and torches, meant for lighting the rooms and hallways, by the *cerero* Martin Pérez de Morales and his servants. In the *Tapicería* the tapestry master Herman Vermeren and his team concerned themselves with the maintenance of the wall tapestries decorating the many walls in the princely residence and, presumably, also the beds and the baldachins. *Aguador* Juan de Salas saw to the supply of fresh water, which was used for the preparation of food as well as for hygiene and perhaps also by the various *lavanderas* who washed the table and bed linens as well as the clothing.

[131] An especially extensive overview of the responsibilities of the *Casa* can be found in Mayoral López, *La Casa Real de Felipe III*, 214-601.

[132] The overview of personnel of the archducal household in the second trimester of 1615 can be found in ARA, *RK* 1838, ff. 39-53.

The cleaning of the quarters, then again, was the responsibility of the five *barrenderos*, or floor sweepers.

Technical support was offered by the *Furriera* of the palace. Quartermaster Gil de Rey doled out the commands and together with his *aposentadores de Palacio* saw to the maintenance of the rooms and the furniture. They provided the different halls with firewood, lighted the fireplaces and the candles, prepared the rooms for receiving guests, repaired and moved tables and chairs, and so forth. In addition there were the *aposentadores de la Casa* or quartermasters of the court, who occupied themselves with housing personnel in town. In spite of the impressive dimensions of the Coudenberg palace, the building could not shelter all the servants of the archdukes. Except for a limited entourage most of them were quartered in private residences in Brussels. As opposed to what had been the case before then, during the reign of Albert and Isabella that no longer happened on an arbitrary basis. Whereas Brussels citizens were previously obliged to cede their rooms and houses to staff members of the court, that obligation was bought off by the city in the archducal period. In exchange the archduke enacted an edict in which the citizens were left to 'the free enjoyment of their houses and furniture'[133] In concrete terms this order meant that thenceforth members of the archducal household had to buy or rent their residence at a price that was calculated by the quartermasters of the court (cf. Chapter II).

It speaks for itself that the daily workings of the archducal household also presupposed shrewd financial policy. In practice the bureau (*Bureo*) had these finances at heart, which in addition to the *mayordomo mayor* and the *mayordomos* consisted of three persons. In the time period 1612-1618 they were the treasurer Antonio de Rovelasca, the court controller Charles de Hertoghe, and the clerk Pedro de Mendoza. They occupied themselves with the payment of remunerations and honoraria and with the distribution of the budgets in the different court departments. The porters too must be counted among the archducal household. The various doors leading to the personal quarters of the archdukes were watched by six *porteros de Saleta* and – in the case of the infanta's dwelling – by three *porteros de las Damas*. Furthermore, the *Casa* monitored the physical well-being of the court personnel, who in case of illness could go to the doctor Pedro Ricardo and his colleague Enrique Verlario. In addition they could call on a surgeon, a barber, and an apothecary (*Botica*), where medications were dispensed. Finally, the *Casa* also counted various *Estados*. These were the personnel divisions responsible for the table service of noble court dignitaries who had a right to dine at court, such as the *gentilhombres* of the *Cámara* and the *Boca*, the *ayudas de la*

[133] '*(...) la libre jouyssance de leurs maisons et meubles.*' ARA, *Aud* 1259: *Documents relatifs au logement des troupes: 1. Logement des gens de cour et ordements de la ville de Bruxelles de 1600 à 1619.*

Cámara, the pages, and the ladies-in-waiting. During mealtimes each of these groups was served by its own *mayordomo de Estado* and his *ayudas* and *mozos*.

After the *mayordomo mayor* and the four *mayordomos*, the highest position in the *Casa* was set aside for the *gentilhombres de la Boca*, closely followed by the *gentilhombres de la Casa*, and the honorary office of the *varlet servant*. As cited earlier, the original Burgundian court model was characterized by great participation from the nobility. The presence of nobles in the archducal household was seen as an affirmation of the bonds that existed for ages between the prince and the social elites. Although the noble *écuyers* in the course of years did evolve into *gentilhombres*, that objective of affirmation continued to be preserved even in later years. In that way the functions of the *gentilhombres de la Casa* and those of the *Boca* in the 1545 report of Jean Sigoney mentioned earlier, for instance, were still associated with a distinctly military-feudal background: officially their responsibilities were to assist the prince in time of war and to rally together on the battlefield with horse and weapons behind the royal banner. As far as the rest was concerned, they were by turns expected to make their way to court and to serve the prince.[134] In practice the official description of their duties was watered down in the course of years to a ceremonial function, which in many cases was aspired to on account of the prestige connected to it. In the case of the *gentilhombres de la Boca* that prestige was expressed in their prominent role during the dining ritual, where the nobles functioned as meat-carver or cup-bearer. In addition it was their responsibility to accompany the prince during public processions and appearances, where together with the *gentilhombres de la Casa* they displayed themselves richly attired to the spectators. As such, to an important extent both groups contributed to the visual spectacle as well as to the pomp and pageantry with which the princely regime manifested itself. Yet their role may not be reduced altogether to the *representatio maiestatis*. In certain cases the political influence of the *gentilhombres* could be very tangible. A number of them held influential offices in regional and municipal institutions, and many possessed domains in the countryside. Others exercised functions in diplomacy or in the army or, by way of family members, could boast of good contacts with the clergy. In that way the archducal household branched off toward other echelons in society, whereby *gentilhombres* could emerge as ideal intermediaries, top-down as well as bottom-up (cf. Chapter V).

In his article about the structure and the composition of the archducal household, Diederik Lanoye posits that the presence of noble *gentilhombres* in the princely entourage was an important instrument for consolidating the authority of the Habsburgs in the Spanish Netherlands:

[134] Mayoral López, *La Casa Real de Felipe III*, 245.

> 'Like other rulers of the seventeenth century, [Albert and Isabella] obliged the nobility to their court by offering them these mainly ceremonial functions. In the Spanish Netherlands, this was very important because the local nobility had shown during the Revolt of the second half of the sixteenth century that without their support, the Archdukes would not be able to govern their territories in peace or defend them against the North. To gain their loyalty and support, the Archdukes honoured these noblemen by giving them positions at court.'[135]

Lanoye thus connects this politics of acquisition with the ambition of Albert and Isabella to bind the local nobility to each other, underpinning his line of argumentation with an analysis of the origins of the *gentilhombres* in their household. That aspect comes up for detailed discussion in the third chapter of this book. For now it suffices to indicate that the archdukes did indeed have the intention of bringing large groups of nobles to their court. Whereas upon his departure in 1595 Albert still had thirteen *gentilhombres de la Boca* and eight *gentilhombres de la Casa* at his disposal, these numbers had risen in the first trimester of 1612 for both groups to 24, and in the first trimester of 1618 to 28 and 32, respectively (cf. Chart 1).

Chart 1 – Development of the number of *gentilhombres de la Boca and de la Casa*

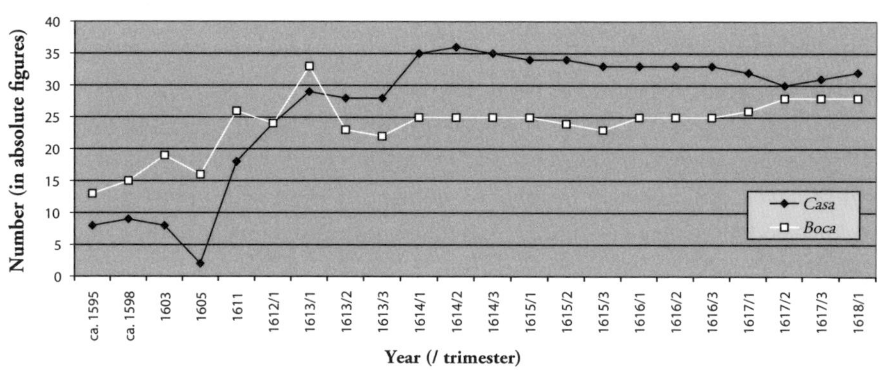

Data on the basis of ARA, *Aud* 23/10 (1595); ASV, *Borghese* I 913, ff. 339-344 (1598); SAA, *Privilegekamer* 1627 (1603); ARA, *Aud* 33/3 (1605); ARA, *Aud* 33/4, ff. 66-72 (1605); ARA, *RvS* 157 (1611) and ARA, *RK* 1837 and 1838 (1612-1618).

[135] Lanoye, 'Structure and Composition,' 112.

For the first decade of the seventeenth century the figures in the chart must be taken with a substantial grain of salt, in view of the fact that they are based on lists in which perhaps not all members of the archducal household were recorded (cf. Chapter II). According to a court index from 1605, only two *gentilhombres de la Casa* served in that year, for example, which is quite unlikely. Perhaps the low number is to be blamed on the fact that this list was drawn up on the occasion of the archducal visit to the city of Ghent: possibly not all *gentilhombres* took part in this.[136] For the period 1612-1618 the figures are more trustworthy. These data derive from the *libros de razón*, the accounting ledgers of the archducal household, which give a complete overview of the personnel force per trimester.[137] They demonstrate that the number of *gentilhombres* in this time period gradually increased and subsequently more or less stabilized, with an average of 25 *gentilhombres de la Boca* and 33 *gentilhombres de la Casa*. In this it needs to be noted that the figures offer an overview of names yet not of those present. Only a few *gentilhombres* stayed at court from day to day: most of them served on rotation and were paid, then, according to the number of days in which they in effect had 'worked' at the court. That applied mainly to those who combined their function with a position in the army, and who were to be found now in Brussels, then with their companies again in the countryside. Many spent time only sporadically at court, others seldom, some absolutely never. For this last group the title of *gentilhombre* was clearly little more than an honorary title. Nevertheless the rise in the official number of nobles in the archducal household is significant: it demonstrates that there was an active policy to integrate the nobility into that household. The reasons for this will be discussed in the following chapters.

The *Cámara*[138]

As a physical space, the *Cámara* enclosed the personal quarters of Albert and Isabella, consisting of the bedchamber, the *Retrete*, and the *Guardaropa*.[139] Here, in this hermetically screened-off part of the palace, the day-to-day life of the princes was for the large part played out. As mentioned earlier the chamber service was for obvious reasons split up into a male and a female division.

[136] ARA, *Aud* 33/3 (1605).

[137] ARA, *RK* 1837 and 1838.

[138] In the main this section is based on Mayoral López, *La Casa Real de Felipe III*, 214-601; on Hofmann, *Das Spanische Hofzeremoniell*; on ARA, *Handschriftenverzameling* 821; on the *libros de razón* and on the various court indices of the archducal household.

[139] Concerning the *Cámara*, see Martínez Millán & Fernández Conti, *La Monarquía de Felipe II*, vol. I, pp. 568-574.

a) The Cámara *of Albert*

In the *Cámara* of Albert the *sumiller de corps* held the scepter. A bastardization of the French *sommelier de corps*, the term recalls its Burgundian origins. According to the ordinances structuring life at court in Madrid, the grand chamberlain was responsible for the personal service of the prince.[140] Consequently, he took the oath of all staff members put to work in the *Cámara*. In addition it was his duty to assist the prince during the morning and evening ritual and to help him with dressing and undressing. For that reason he generally slept in a separate bed in the princely bedchamber, although he also had an apartment of his own in the palace at his disposal. Of the four highest dignitaries in the archducal court, the *sumiller de corps* was the only one who almost continually spent time in the immediate proximity of the prince. The position presupposed, then, a great intimacy with the sovereign, which explains at once why it was especially desired and only offered to courtiers who enjoyed the fullest confidence.

THE *CÁMARA* OF ALBERT

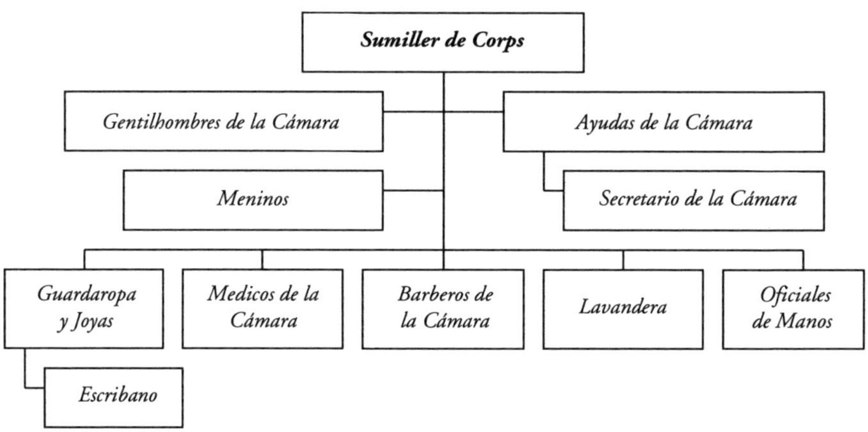

In Albert's household the function of *sumiller de corps* was assigned in 1595 to the Carinthian nobleman Maximilian von Dietrichstein.[141] The history of the Von Dietrichstein family is interwoven with that of the Austrian-Habsburg dynasty, in whose service they were able to work their way up to one of the most prominent families in the Holy Roman Empire. Maximilian's father, Adam von Dietrichstein,

[140] Concerning the function of the *sumiller de corps*, see Mayoral López, *La Casa Real de Felipe III*, 215-222.
[141] Roco de Campofrío, *España en Flandes*, 7.

was the imperial ambassador in Madrid for a long time, where he also held the office of *mayordomo mayor* in the households of the archdukes Rudolf and Ernst.[142] Maximilian's mother, Margarita Folch de Cardona, was of Spanish origin and had for a long time served as lady-in-waiting for Albert's mother, Empress Maria.[143] Maximilian himself began his career at the court of Emperor Rudolf II in Prague, where he was one of the chamberlains. After that he was promoted to *Oberststallmeister* [master of the horse] of Archduke Ernst, who in 1593 was appointed governor of the Netherlands. After the death of Ernst, finally, he was employed by Albert as *sumiller de corps*. Even so, Dietrichstein would not hold the office for long. During the archduke's journey of 1598-1599 he chose to remain behind in Spain. His function was taken over by Rodrigo Niño y Lasso, mentioned already, who at that moment was Albert's *gentilhombre de la Cámara* as well as captain of his mounted guard (cf. Chapter VI). Niño y Lasso would keep the office until his death in 1620, and was in turn succeeded by Charles-Emmanuel de Gorrevod, the marquis of Marnay.[144]

Just like Dietrichstein, Gorrevod had a prior history as courtier in the service of the Habsburgs. The marquis belonged to the high Burgundian nobility and as a child was called to the court in Madrid to become the *menino* or 'playmate' of the later Philip III.[145] He completed his upbringing and traveled subsequently to Savoy in the entourage of the infanta Catalina Micaela, where the latter would marry Duke Carlo Emanuele I. After that Gorrevod journeyed to the Low Countries, where he served in the *Ejército de Flandes* and was active as captain in the cavalry for seventeen years. During this time period he moved back and forth between the Netherlands and Savoy. In the end he returned to Spain to become a member of the household of the cardinal-archduke. The intention was for him to accompany Albert on his journey to Brussels in 1595, but circumstances caused Gorrevod to postpone his departure until a later point in time. That proved to be an unfortunate decision. The boat upon which he embarked suffered shipwreck and stranded on what – in Gorrevod's own words – was 'a coast of heretics,' supposedly, then, in England or Ireland. The adventure cost him a ransom of 25,000 *escudos*.[146] Yet in the end he did land in the Southern Netherlands, where he was received with open arms as *gentilhombre de la Cámara*.

142 Edelmayer, F. 'Honor y dinero. Adam de Dietrichstein al servicio de la Casa de Austria.' *Studia Histórica. Historia Moderna*, 10/11 (1992/93) 89-116.

143 de la Cruz Medina, V. 'La educación de las meninas en la corte de Felipe II: algunos aspectos a través de las cartas de Ana de Dietrichstein a su madre, Margarita de Cardona,' in: Jiménez Eguizábal, A. et al., eds. *Etnohistoria de la escuela. XII Coloquio nacional de historia de la educación. Burgos...* 2003. Burgos, 2003, pp. 523-534.

144 BNF, *MsF* 16133, f. 116: Jean Péricard to Secretary of State Puisieux, December 18, 1620.

145 For an abbreviated biography, see Anselme [Père]. *Histoire généalogique et chronologique de la maison royale de France*, vol. V. Paris, 1730, p. 670.

146 AGS, *Estado* 2294, s.f.: Charles-Emmanuel de Gorrevod to the duke of Lerma, December 24, 1612.

As head of the *Cámara*, the *sumiller de corps* kept an eye on the workings of the chamber service. To this service belonged all courtiers and employees who were directly occupied with personally serving the prince. One of the most important figures in that context was Joachim Denzenhear, the archduke's *Guardaropa y Joyas*, who together with three *ayudas* and two *mozos* was responsible for the purchase and preservation of Albert's clothing and jewels. In addition he also concerned himself with the silverware, the golden ornaments used in the palace chapel, and the maintenance of the paintings and artworks decorating the palace gallery. For taking inventory of all these pieces of clothing and objects, Denzenhear was assisted by Miguel de Olivares, the *escribano de la Cámara*. Furthermore the archduke had a few so-called *oficiales de manos* at his disposal, among them a *sastre* (clothier), a *calzetero* (hosier), a *zapatero* (shoemaker) and a *bordador* (embroiderer). Albert's clothes were washed by Francisca Vázquez, the *lavandera de la ropa de la Persona*. The physical well-being of the archduke was anxiously watched over by no less than three personal physicians. That was surely no superfluous precautionary measure: in the early modern period the stability of the regime stood or fell with the health of the prince. On top of that the doctors Francisco de Paz, Andreas Trevisius, and Henri Mastelein had their hands full with Albert, who like many of his contemporaries suffered from a serious form of gout and as a result of this often had to keep to his bed. Finally, the archduke had a personal barber, who shaved him, trimmed his hair and beard, and took care of his nails.

One of the most prominent ceremonial functions in the archducal household was set aside for the *gentilhombres de la Cámara*, whose duties consisted of making up the archduke's bed and serving him at table whenever he dined in the seclusion of his quarters. They served on a weekly rotation. Of the three large categories of *gentilhombres* in the household, these of the *Cámara* were the highest in rank, and consequently they were pretty much exclusively recruited from the top stratum of the aristocracy. Among them, then, representatives are found from illustrious families like those of Arenberg, Croÿ, Ligne, Merode and Noyelles. Their dignity was symbolically expressed by means of a golden key, which they received upon their employment and indicated that they belonged to the intimate entourage of the prince. Just as was the case with the nobles of the *Boca* and the *Casa*, the number of *gentilhombres de la Cámara* rose perceptibly through the years (cf. Chart 2). Upon his departure from Madrid, Albert had only six *gentilhombres* at his disposal, but immediately after his arrival in Brussels the group was expanded to include the princely count of Arenberg, the count of Ligne and the count of Egmont – a clear signal that the archduke still wanted to involve the indigenous nobility actively in his policy-making. The Milanese nobleman Octavio Visconti also got a golden key, and the marquis of Marnay, mentioned already, followed in 1597. After that a step-by-step increase followed. In the first trimester of 1612 the number of *gentilhombres de la Cámara* had already risen to 23, and from then on it would remain more or less constant.

Chart 2 – Development of the number of *gentilhombres de la Cámara*

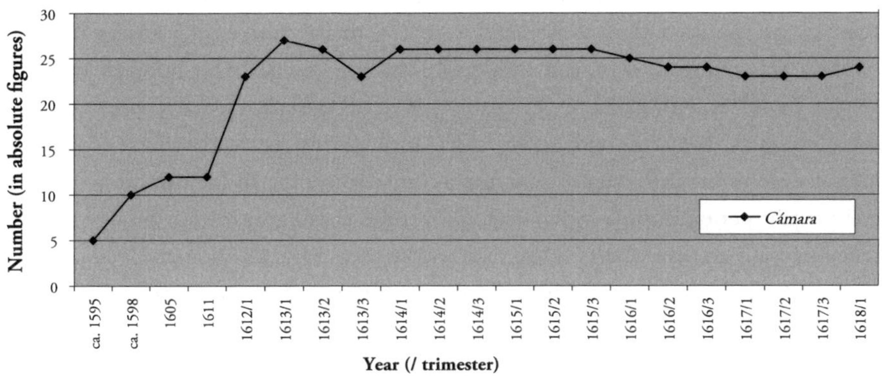

Data on the basis of ARA, *Aud* 23/10 (1595); ASV, *Borghese* I 913, ff. 339-344 (1598); SAA, *Privilegekamer* 1627 (1603); ARA, *Aud* 33/3 (1605); ARA, *Aud* 33/4, ff. 66-72 (1605); ARA, *RvS* 157 (1611) and ARA, *RK* 1837 and 1838 (1612-1618).

A rung lower on the hierarchical ladder stood the archduke's *ayudas de la Cámara* or chamberlains. There were usually ten members and they were generally of the lower nobility, or in any case came from families of means. They too changed off with each other weekly. The *ayudas* were responsible for the silverware, the linen, the clothing chests, and the lighting in the quarters of the *Cámara*, and furthermore they made up the bed of the *sumiller de corps* whenever the latter spent the night in Albert's bedchamber. In case the *gentilhombres* were absent, the *ayudas* took over their duties. A special *ayuda de la Cámara* was Antonio Suárez de Arguello, the private secretary of Albert, who came into his service already in 1586 and would remain in that function for 35 years.[147] The *meninos*, finally, were young men whose duties consisted of keeping the archdukes company. Generally they were the children of the high nobility who were taken up into the archducal household on account of the accomplishments of their fathers. That was the case for, among others, Jacinto and Felipe Alberto de Velasco, both the sons of Luis de Velasco, count of Salazar and general of the cavalry in the Spanish army, and for Felipe and Cristóval de Cardona, the sons of the Spanish ambassador in Brussels.

[147] ARA, *SSO* 185, f. 295: Albert to Philip IV, July 9, 1621.

b) The Cámara *of Isabella*

In the historiography of the nineteenth and the early twentieth century, the political regime of the archdukes was generally treated as a pretty much exclusively male matter. The only woman who got a political role of significance allotted, was the infanta herself, but even in this case the interest went in the main to the manner in which her share in the administration was related to that of the archduke. In that way Isabella's position was reduced to that of loyal and laughing spouse, who mingled with the general populace with pleasure. She gladly left affairs of state to Albert, whose policies she constantly defended with fervor. Not until during her widowhood would the infanta enter more into the political foreground. According to the historiography she grew in this period in time into a wise and good-hearted governess, who nevertheless relied strongly on the advice of the men in her entourage. In the same way her own vigorous initiatives were explained from the thinking that the princess had at her disposal 'typically male' characteristics like courage and resolve.[148] For a large part this traditional vision can be traced back to the image that Isabella presented and cultivated of herself. The actions and statements attributed to her in the historical sources leave no doubt about it that the infanta perceived very well what was expected of her as well as how she needed to comport herself as a married princess. She knew which position she was expected to take according to the norms and values of her times, and she played her role radiantly.

That Isabella was aware of the limitations of her status – and that she seemed altogether to accept it – does not mean, though, that she did not lament the limited freedom of movement that went with it hand in hand. So, for example, she admitted in a letter to the duke of Lerma to being jealous of Rodrigo Niño y Lasso, who regularly traveled to Spain as messenger of the archdukes. Aggrieved, Isabella wrote how sorry she was 'that it is not the custom in this world that women transport the mail and are able to come and go as men.'[149] Yet it would be incorrect to postulate that the limitations of Isabella's position as married princess hindered her from playing a role in policy-making.[150] Her correspondence with the duke of Lerma shows that she was perfectly informed of the situation in the country and that she did not sweep her opinion about it under the carpet. On top of that it is known that Albert frequently consulted with her about day-to-day politics.[151] In that sense the political role of

[148] See e.g. Hennequin de Villermont, M. *L'Infante Isabelle, gouvernante des Pays-Bas.* 2 vols. Paris-Tamines, 1912 and Klingenstein, L. *The Great Infanta: Isabel, Sovereign of the Netherlands.* London, 1910.

[149] '*Es muy malo que no se use en el mundo que las mugeres corran la posta y puedan ir y venir como los hombres.*' Rodríguez Villa, *Correspondencia*, letter no. 70: Isabella to Lerma, February 18, 1604.

[150] For an interesting discussion concerning this, see Sánchez, M.S. 'Sword and Wimple. Isabel Clara Eugenia and Power,' in: Cruz, A.J. & Suzuki, M., eds. *The Rule of Women in Early Modern Europe.* University of Illinois Press, 2009, pp. 64-79.

[151] *Ibidem*, p. 71.

Isabella during her marriage cannot be minimalized. Though clearly less pronounced and often indirect, the infanta did indeed really put pressure on policy. For that reason it is important to know with which people Isabella had herself surrounded. All too often her immediate entourage – which except for the father confessor pretty much exclusively consisted of women – has had to want for necessary scholarly attention. In the best case the female archducal household is described as a group of ladies who kept company with the infanta and had little better to do than embroider, pray, gossip, and take walks in the park. That their presence could also bring political consequences along with it has until today never been acknowledged. Nonetheless it is clear that the ladies-in-waiting in most cases also spent time as prominent representatives of their families at court. In that sense their proximity to the princess was a strategic benefit of which they were all too well aware. [152]

THE *CÁMARA* OF ISABELLA

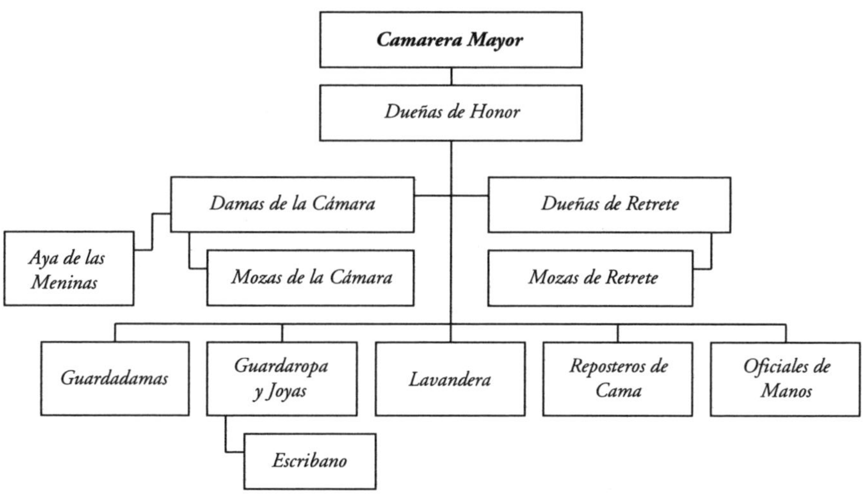

In the Spanish-Burgundian court ceremonial the responsibility for serving the princess fell to the *camarera mayor* or mistress of the household.[153] She was the female equivalent of the *sumiller de corps*, in the sense that she accompanied the princess at all times and slept in her bedchamber (or in adjacent quarters when the prince paid his respects there). She helped the princess with the morning and evening ritual,

[152] See Houben, B. & Raeymaekers, D. 'Women and the Politics of Access at the Court of Brussels. The Infanta Isabella's Camareras Mayores (1598-1633),' in: Akkerman, N. & Houben, B., eds. *The Politics of Female Households: Ladies-in-Waiting across Early Modern Europe*. Leiden, 2013, pp. 123-145.

[153] Concerning this function, see López-Cordón Cortezo, M.V. 'Entre damas anda el juego: las camareras mayores de Palacio en la edad moderna,' in: Gómez-Centurión Jiménez, C., ed. *Monarquía y Corte en la España Moderna*. Cuadernos de Historia Moderna, 2003 (Anejo II), pp. 123-152.

assisted her during audiences, and was responsible for the smooth flow of affairs in her *Cámara*. On top of that, together with the *aya de las meninas* she watched over the chaste behavior and the correct appearance of the ladies-in-waiting.[154] In Brussels the function of mistress of the household was exercised until 1614 by Jeanne de Chassincourt, a lady of French descent. She had traveled to Spain as a young woman in the retinue of Queen Elisabeth of Valois, and after the death of the latter remained connected to the household of the infantas Isabella and Catalina Micaela.[155] As thanks for proven services she was promoted in 1598 by Philip III to Isabella's *camarera mayor*, whereby she ultimately ended up in the Southern Netherlands. On account of Chassincourt's advanced age however many of her responsibilities were taken over in practice by her niece Catalina Livia, one of the archduchess' ladies-in-waiting.[156] Chassincourt died in January 1614. Not until two years later, in December 1615, was she succeeded by Antoinette-Guillemette of Arenberg, a sister of the duke of Aarschot and widow of Salentin, count of Isenburg-Grenzau. She would keep the office until her death in 1626.[157]

In many respects the infanta's *Cámara* was comparable to that of the archduke, in the sense that Isabella also had at her disposal her own *guardaropa y joyas*, an *escribano*, and the requisite *oficiales de manos*. In addition there were seven *reposteros de cama*, male servants who among other things were charged with making up the bed. The role of the *gentilhombres* and the *ayudas de la Cámara* was taken over, though, by the *dueñas de honor* (ladies of honor), the *damas* and *mozas de la Cámara* (ladies-in-waiting and attendants), and finally the *dueñas* and *mozas de Retrete*, who served the infanta in her most private quarters. The ladies of honor were two to three widows from the high nobility, who after the death of their spouses were offered a place of honor in the archducal household. That applied for example to Marguerite de Lille, the dowager countess of Buquoy, and to Antoinette de Ravenel, countess of La Fère.[158]

---

[154] In 1615 a document was sent from the court to the Arenberg family, in which the responsibilities of the *camarera mayor* were summed up. See ACA, 36-17: *Lo que toca a la Camarera Mayor.*

[155] In Spanish historiography this lady is generally referred to as 'Juana de Jacincurt.' See Rodríguez-Salgado, M.J. ' 'Una perfecta princesa.' Casa y vida de la reina Isabel de Valois (1559-1568). Primera parte,' in: Gómez-Centurión Jiménez, C., ed. *Monarquía y Corte en la España Moderna.* Cuadernos de Historia Moderna, 2003 (Anejo II), pp. 39-96.

[156] Bentivoglio, *Relationi*, 160.

[157] In the *libros de razón* of the archducal household, a certain 'Condesa de San Vitres' was always referred to under the heading *camarera mayor*. All the same, it is not clear whether Antoinette-Guillemette of Arenberg is denoted here, or another unknown lady instead. In any case, the appellation does not occur in other sources. It is striking, though, that the date of her appointment corresponds with that of the appointment of Antoinette-Guillemette.

[158] Marguerite de Lille was the mother of Charles-Bonaventure de Longueval, count of Buquoy. Antoinette de Ravenel was the spouse of Jacques Colas, marshal of Montélimar and count of La Fère, a leading member of the *Ligue.*

The ten to fifteen *damas*, on the contrary, were generally unmarried noblewomen, who were sent by their families to the court in order to receive an upbringing there.

An important function in the female *Cámara* was set aside for Juan Fernández de Eizaguirre, who as the *guardadamas* was responsible for monitoring the ladies-in-waiting. 'The protection of the chastity of the infanta's court ladies was definitely one of the prime concerns of the archducal household,' posits Cordula Van Wyhe in that context.[159] When the court chaplain Aubertus Miraeus described the strict religious court of the archdukes as a monastery, he was denoting among other things the separation of the sexes as well as the strict isolation of ladies and maidens who stayed there. The French poet Jean Puget de la Serre noted in that context that the ladies-in-waiting 'lived as they would in a convent.'[160] The Franciscan and theologian Franciscus Caprionius, who wrote a necrology of the infanta, compared the court to a '*pietatis asylum*' and a '*castitatis ac religionis sacrarium*,' where even the slightest suspicion of a lack of chastity dissipated all hope for a position or a promotion.[161] The women's dwellings indeed exhibited very striking similarity to a cloisters, where the inhabitants were admonished to chastity and anxiously screened off from the temptations of the external world. Not coincidentally their introduction at court displayed much similarity with a nun's entering into a convent. In his travel journal Charles Somerset noted,

> '[The infanta's] ladies are kept up as if they were in a Nunnerie (...). And upon their admittance at the first time, they are brought in, in the evening, attended by their Parents and kinred, and all the other nobilitie of the Courte with as great sollemnitie as if they were to be married, and are accompanied with 2 or 3 hundred white waxe torches, which the nobilitie & other of their friends doe for the greater honour sende to light them in. Then when they are brought into the Dutchesses [= Isabella's] presence and have kissed her hands, they be delivered to the keeping of the Ladie high Chamberlaine, and to the mother of the maydes, and then their lodging is appointed as well for themselves as for their wayting women; and after they be once admitted to the Dutchesse her service, they may not talk with anie one, not with their verie parents without the Ladie Chamberlaines leave or in her presence, and ever some olde woman is present, and when upon anie occasion anie of them doe ride abroad, they must goe in one of the Archdukes Coches with an olde matrone to accompanie

[159] Van Wyhe, C. 'Between Chastity and Passion. The Impact of the French Exiles on the Cult of Courtly Love at the Brussels Court in the 1630s,' in: *Passion, Affekt un Leidenschaft in der Frühen Neuzeit. Wolfenbütteler Arbeitungen zur Barockforschung*, vol. 11. Wiesbaden, 2005, pp. 951-980. Op. cit. p. 956.

[160] '*(...) vivoient comme dans un Cloistre.*' Cited in Van Wyhe, 'Between Chastity and Passion,' 957-958.

[161] *Ibidem.*

> them, and a manguardian called a Guardadamas, to keepe that they converse with no others but those which it concernes to deale with all.'[162]

Under these kinds of circumstances it need not surprise that the *guardadamas* carried a large key with him as a symbol of his function. The ladies-in-waiting found themselves to be literally and figuratively under lock and key, and it was not permitted them to have contact with male courtiers without approval from the *camarera mayor*. Infractions of this rule were taken very seriously. Luis Lasso de la Vega, one of Albert's *gentilhombres de la Cámara*, was able to experience that in the flesh in 1608. In his travel journal Charles Somerset recounted all the sights and smells of how Luis was passionately in love with Marie de Licques, a lady-in-waiting to the infanta, and how this passion came to cost him dearly.[163]

> '(…) Knowing that her chamber looked towards the streetes, he hired a chamber in the Cittie just opposite to her windowe, and from thence what with billets and other signes and tokens he continued his love so long to her, as having gotten her good will, if he could find the commoditie, and facilitate other impediments, he corrupted one of the Ladie Chamberlaines women, and wonne her to give him the printe of the maister keye of the doores of the ladies quarter in waxe, wherewithall he caused a key to be made, and used such meanes as he gott within the pallace and had accesse to his mistrisse, and did accommodate her.'[164]

The consequence can be guessed. Not much later the physicians at court discovered that Marie's sudden weight gain could not be blamed on a mysterious illness but on a pregnancy. The news provided the requisite consternation. Albert and Isabella were furious. It speaks for itself that they could not let stand that kind of grave infraction on the virtuous reputation of the court. The archduke obliged the young couple to marry so as to rub out the scandal, and after that condemned Luis Lasso to the death penalty 'for the dishonour that he had donne his Courte.'[165] The mediation of both the papal nuncio as well as the Spanish ambassador was required to cause Albert to think otherwise. In the end the penalty was converted to banishment from the court, and not much later the couple would depart without fanfare for Spain.

---

162 Brennan, *The Travel Diary*, 288.

163 Marie de Licques was a daughter of Gabriel de Recourt, baron of Licques, and his spouse Hélène de Merode.

164 Brennan, *The Travel Diary*, 292.

165 *Ibidem*, p. 293.

Even so, scandals like that of Luis Lasso and Marie de Licques seldom occurred. In general the court enjoyed a reputation of extreme virtue and piety. Inspired by the religious atmosphere at court and the personal piety of the infanta, then, many ladies-in-waiting chose to live their lives as monastics. More than twenty ladies-in-waiting would leave the archducal household for that reason.[166] They usually entered into religious orders that – in accordance with Habsburg tradition – were patronized by the archdukes, such as the Poor Clares, the Discalced Carmelites, and the Sisters of the Annunciation. Their decision to exchange the luxury of the court for the sobriety of the convent was seen by contemporaries as a sacrifice that testified to exceptional devotion. The ladies were supported in this by Isabella's father confessor Andrés de Soto, who established himself as a spiritual father who sent his daughters out to embrace the religious life. In that respect their entry into monasticism was not unconditional. The noble monastics were repeatedly reminded that they were expected to pray for the well-being of their princes and their country. In that context, Cordula van Wyhe speaks of 'the infanta's personal, elite force of nuns, who fought heresy with their prayers.'[167]

The *Caballeriza*[168]

In the organigram of the archducal household the *Caballeriza* occupies a somewhat peculiar though certainly not unimportant position. In practice this division occupied itself with the day-to-day care of riding animals as well as beasts of burden, with maintenance of the stables, and with support for the court in the areas of transportation and communications. In addition, though, the *Caballeriza* also had a representative function, in the sense that it was responsible for the organization of relocating and public appearances of the princes and, consequently, for the visual manifestation of the princely *maiestas* in public space.[169] In other words it was responsible for the external image of the court and the spread of this image to the public at large. In that respect it was the counterpart of the *Cámara*, where the private life of the archdukes played itself out in the seclusion of a few heavily monitored quarters.

---

166 Van Wyhe, 'Court and Convent,' 412.

167 *Ibidem*, p. 426.

168 In the main this section is based on Mayoral López, *La Casa Real de Felipe III*, 214-601; on Hofmann, *Das Spanische Hofzeremoniell*; on ARA, *Handschriftenverzameling* 821; on the *libros de razón* and on the various court indices of the archducal household.

169 See López Álvarez, A. 'Organización y evolución de la caballeriza,' in: Martínez Millán & Fernández Conti, *La Monarquía de Felipe II*, vol. I, pp. 293-339.

The *Caballeriza*

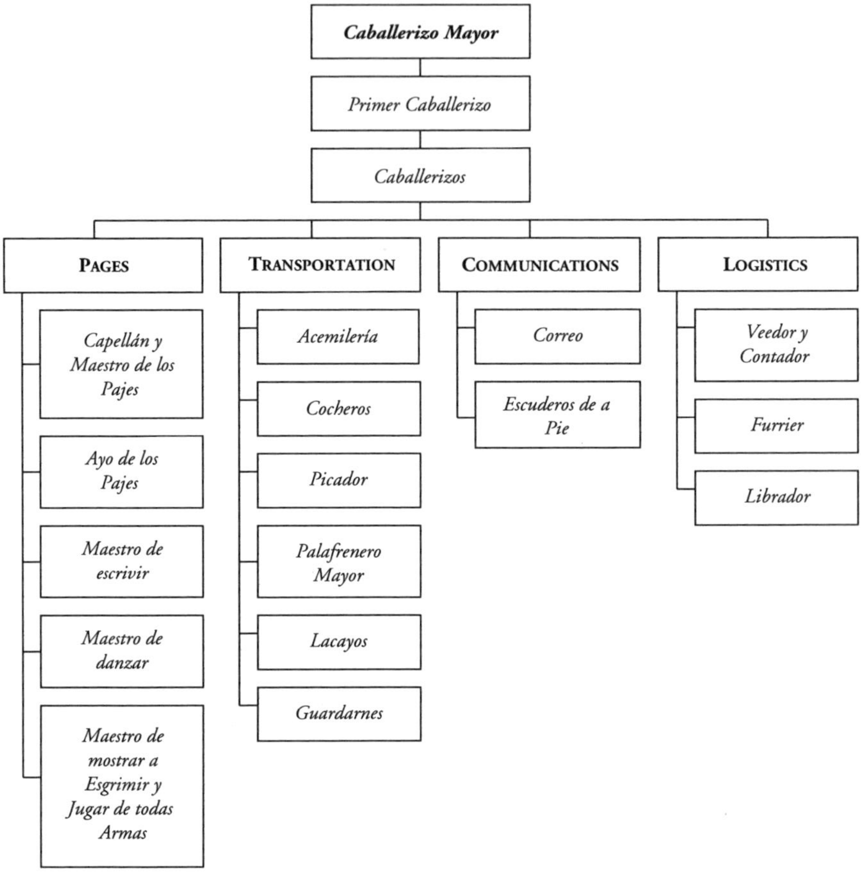

Each time Albert and Isabella made their way outside the gates of the palace – be it on foot, by horse or by coach; during long journeys, short jaunts, or ceremonial processions – the *caballerizo mayor*, or master of the horse, took over the general direction of the archducal retinue from the *mayordomo mayor*. He was also responsible for the budget of the *Caballeriza* and took the oaths of the servants who worked there. In 1595 this office was entrusted to Philippe de Croÿ, count of Solre – mentioned already – who would keep the function until his death in 1612. As member of one of the most prominent families in the Netherlands, Solre was no unfamiliar figure.[170] He had begun his career in the service of Alexander Farnese and traveled in 1588 to Spain to become captain of Philip II's personal guard there. Once returned to the

[170] Concerning Philippe de Croÿ, see Brants, V. 'Solre (Philippe de Croÿ, Comte de),' in: *Biographie Nationale*, vol. XXIII (1921-1924) pp. 126-129.

Low Countries, he functioned repeatedly as a diplomat for the successive (interim-) governors, after which Albert appointed him in 1595 as head of his *Caballeriza*. He was a member of the Council of State, knight of the Golden Fleece and governor of Tournai, and in that capacity a man of great political weight. After Solre's death in 1612 the function of *caballerizo mayor* remained vacant for a few years, until in 1615 it was awarded to Rodrigo Niño y Lasso. With that appointment, the count of Añover saw his powerful position as *mayordomo mayor* and *sumiller de corps* confirmed (cf. Chapter VI). In 1620, finally, Niño y Lasso was succeeded by Octavio Visconti. This Milanese nobleman had begun his career as chamberlain of Archduke Ernst, but after the latter's death transferred to the household of Albert, who appointed him *gentilhombre de la Cámara*.[171] During the decades following, Visconti grew into one of the most prominent courtiers in Brussels. He carried out various diplomatic commissions in the Holy Roman Empire and seems to have enjoyed the fullest confidence of the archduke.[172] His appointment as *caballerizo mayor* can be seen, then, as a reward for his years of loyal service.

During his absence the master of the horse was usually replaced by a lieutenant, the so-called *primer caballerizo*. Starting with 1597 this function was exercised by the originally Sicilian nobleman Gaston Spínola, who had already been Albert's *gentilhombre de la Cámara* and whose domain Bruay in Artois was elevated to a county in 1603.[173] Spínola died in December 1614, after which his office was entrusted to Diego Mexía, the subsequent marquis of Leganés.[174] He was a nephew of the count-duke of Olivares and a son of the countess of Uceda, one of Isabella's most beloved ladies-in-waiting (cf. Chapter IV). Thanks in part to these relatives, beginning in the 1620s Mexía would make a career for himself in the service of Spain both in the military as well as in politics. In addition to the *caballerizo mayor* and the *primer caballerizo*, the Mews also numbered four ordinary *caballerizos*, who stood in-between the *gentilhombres de la Boca* and the *gentilhombres de la Casa* in rank. Their duties consisted of accompanying the princes during official jaunts and journeys, during which they were placed behind the horse or the coach of the archduke.

171 Hortal Muñoz, 'The Household of Archduke Albert,' in press.

172 Visconti's correspondence with Albert can be found in ARA, *DuiS* 437.

173 Concerning Gaston Spínola, see Vander Linden, H. 'Spinola (Gaston de),' in: *Biographie Nationale*, vol. XXIII (1921-1924) pp. 426-428.

174 Concerning Diego Mexía, see Arroyo Martín, F. 'El marqués de Leganés. Apuntes biográficos.' *Espacio, Tiempo y Forma, Serie IV, Historia Moderna*, 15 (2002) 145-185; Corella Suárez, M.P. 'Orígenes históricos del marquesado de Leganés y su primer titular: Don Diego Messía de Guzmán.' *Anales del Instituto de Estudios Madrileños*, 18 (1981) 131-136 and Crawford Volk, M. 'New Light on a Seventeenth-Century Collector: The Marquis of Leganés.' *The Art Bulletin*, 62 (1980) 256-268.

The hands-on occupations of the *Caballeriza* were situated roughly in three major areas.[175] In the first place it was responsible for training the pages. These were sons from the high nobility sent to the court at Brussels to receive their upbringing there as well as to become acquainted with the customs of life at court. In 1595 already the count of Solre advised Archduke Albert to take 24 or 30 pages into his household, for the purpose of tightening the bonds between the local aristocracy and the archducal regime:

> 'Such a number of pages is of greater importance than can be imagined, and will be even more than that when they are brought up at the least possible cost to their parents (...), and this with an eye toward the fruit that can be picked from them. For [these pages] will become a true seedbed of virtue for the entire nobility, which at the moment quite deviates from the path and has little affection for its prince, and is full of flaws, and is far removed from every form of virtue.'[176]

According to Solre, the pages had to be trained in the proficiencies that any self-respecting courtier was presupposed to possess: handling weapons, horse riding, dancing, making music, as well as reading and writing in different languages. In addition they needed to be instructed in '*la virtud, piedad y cristiandad*,' and for this they could go to the Jesuit college in Brussels. In order to make the usefulness of this multifaceted upbringing clear, the count used a quite elucidating metaphor. He posited that the schooling of the pages would function 'as a hook for fishing them up and growing them into loyal subjects in the service of His Majesty.'[177] Subsequently the archduke would be able to utilize them in the army or in the clergy, where they would undoubtedly prove a great service to the dynasty.

As opposed to courtiers and servants, the pages of Archduke Albert were never systematically mentioned in the accounting ledgers of his household. Their names only pop up sporadically, every time when one of them 'graduated' and received fl. 375 for the purchase of a cloak, a dagger, and a horse. Consequently, it cannot be derived precisely from the *libros de razón* how many pages the archducal household numbered. A few court indices offer more consolation. According to a list from ca. 1595, the archduke had thirteen pages, and that number was confirmed in an overview from 1605.[178] During Albert's funeral cortege in 1622, twelve pages walked

[175] Mayoral López, *La Casa Real de Felipe III*, 627-690.
[176] IVDJ, envío 47, caja 63, doc. 506: *Autoridad absoluta sin ecesion alguna* (unpaginated).
[177] '*I este servira de anzuelo para pescarlos i criarlos mui sujectos al servicio de Su Majestad.*' *Ibidem.*
[178] See ARA, *Aud* 23/10 and ARA, *Aud* 33/3, respectively.

along, which indicates that the number perhaps remained more or less constant.[179] During their upbringing they were guided by an *ayo* or governor, and furthermore by a fencing master, a dancing master, and a writing master. The *capellán y maestro de los pajes* watched over their spiritual well-being.

A second area for which the *Caballeriza* carried hands-on responsibility was the transportation for the archdukes and their household. Depending on the nature of the relocation, this aspect of life at court could turn into an organizational *tour de force*. When in 1598 it was announced that the archduke would journey to Spain to marry the infanta there, it was calculated that no less than 110 coaches and wagons were necessary to transport the complete trappings of Albert's retinue.[180] In view of the fact that this proved to be financially unattainable, Albert was advised to have as much baggage as possible sent by ship to Spain, whereby 30 to 40 fewer wagons could be utilized. According to the same calculation there would be at least 250 horses necessary for the servants of the *Casa*, while the archducal stables had 'only' 140. The remaining number thus had to be purchased or hired, but on account of an acute lack of money that was not simple. The *gentilhombres* and the *camareros* generally possessed their own horses, but because the care of them was financed by the archducal household as well, it was proposed to limit the number of riding animals during the journey to four for the *gentilhombres de la Cámara*, three for the *gentilhombres de la Boca* and the *camareros*, and two for the *gentilhombres de la Casa*.[181]

Cochero mayor Juan de Torres and his *ayuda* Alonso de Novoa were responsible for the maintenance of the coaches and wagons.[182] Coachmen and wagon drivers were perhaps paid from a separate budget or only hired when necessary, for they are not mentioned in the accounting ledgers of the archducal household. According to a few court indices from 1605 and 1611, the horses of the archdukes were cared for by one or several *picadores*, yet in the *libros de razón* this appellation does not occur any longer.[183] In the time period 1612-1618 their function was taken over by the *palafrenero mayor* Simon Sterk and his *ayuda*, although it can be assumed that he was assisted in his duties by an entire team of stable boys, who are also not mentioned in the accounting ledgers, all the same. Perhaps they received only material compensation in the form of room and/or board, or their remuneration was settled by means of a separate budget. The gear of the horses and the coaches was maintained, then, by the *guardarnés* Sebastian de Binuelas and his *ayuda* Pedro de Mena. Furthermore the

---

179 See Puteanus & Francquart, *Pompa funebris*, notice LIIII.

180 RAH, *SyC* A-61, f. 15.

181 *Ibidem*.

182 Concerning the role of coaches and wagons in displaying princely *maiestas*, see López Álvarez, A. *Poder, lujo y conflicto en la Corte de los Austrias. Coches, carrozas y sillas de mano, 1550-1700*. Madrid, 2007.

183 ARA, *Aud* 33/3 and ARA, *RvS* 157 (1611).

archducal Mews also sheltered fifty mules and other beasts of burden, which were cared for by the *acemilero mayor* Francisco Enríquez de Caneda and both his *ayudas*. There is also mention of a supervisor of the workhorses [*sobrestante de los rocines*], a saddlemaker, and a quartermaster; the *acemileria* would clearly have counted yet other staff members, though these too are not mentioned. The duties of the twelve *lacayos*, finally, consisted of accompanying the coaches of the archducal retinue during short jaunts, and seeing to it that the route was free of obstacles and all too intrusive spectators.

The third and last area that came under hands-on responsibility of the *Caballeriza* was that of communications. The *correo* (courier) functioned as the messenger of the archdukes, although it is not at once clear precisely how large his orbit was. It could be that his commission was limited to conveying internal reports within the confines of the court, but it is possible just as well that he also provided for more informal contacts with the outside world. The eight to nine *escuderos de a pie* ('messenger boys') were occupied – in addition to other diverse duties – with conveying messages. *Veedor y contador* Antonio de Mendoza, then again, kept an eye on the bookkeeping and the payment of accounts. It speaks for itself that the diversified range of responsibilities of the *Caballeriza* required a large budget. Already in 1597 *mayordomo mayor* Francisco de Mendoza described the expenditures of the Mews as '*muy grande*,' and that need not come as a surprise.[184] Diego de Succa and Juan Sanders, quartermaster and supplier of the division, respectively, received enormous sums of money every month for the purchase of straw, hay, barley and other necessities for taking care of the animals. In that respect the *Caballeriza* was in its entirety one of the most expensive divisions of the archducal household (cf. Chapter II).

The *Guarda*

According to the nuncio Bentivoglio the personal guard of the archdukes consisted initially of three different corps.[185] In his capacity as supreme commander of the Spanish troops in the Netherlands, Albert had a mounted guard at his disposal, composed of lancers and harquebusiers. Since 1596 both these companies came under the command of Rodrigo Niño y Lasso and were abolished in 1613 on the occasion of a general reform in the army. In addition as sovereign prince the archduke had at his disposal a corps of one hundred *alabarderos* or halberdiers, who – in emulation of Philip II's *guarda tudesca* – were preponderantly of German origin. Finally there was a corps of *archeros* or *Hartschiere*, who were no archers, as opposed to what their

[184] RAH, *SyC* A-61, f. 1.
[185] Bentivoglio, *Relationi*, 159.

name would suppose, but who carried a traditional spear-shaped weapon that was originally used in the hunt for wild boar.[186] They stood at a higher rank than the halberdiers and came primarily from the Netherlands and Franche-Comté.[187] In 1596 the command over both these corps was assigned to Pierre de Hennin-Liétard, count of Boussu, and to his lieutenant Martin de Somoghy, a *gentilhombre de la Boca* of Hungarian descent. After the death of Boussu in 1598 it was decided that each corps would get its own captain. From then on the halberdiers were led by Robert de Ligne-Arenberg, baron and subsequent prince of Barbançon, and the *Hartschiere* by Guillaume de Bauffremont, baron of Scey and Sombernon in Franche-Comté.[188] After the death of the latter in 1599 the command over the *Hartschiere* would be taken over by Barbançon, who in turn left the halberdiers to Count Frederik van den Berg. In 1614, finally, Count Christoffel of Emden would succeed the late Barbançon as captain of the *Hartschiere*.

In the time period 1612-1618 the corps of halberdiers was composed of four squadrons of 18 soldiers each, led by a *cabo de escuadra*. In addition there were two officers, a quartermaster, a drummer, a piccolo player, and a serving boy. The corps of the *Hartschiere* was much less extensive and consisted of 41 to 42 soldiers, a lieutenant, a quartermaster, a trumpeter, and a serving boy. In practice the *Guarda* was responsible for the security of the archdukes, both inside as well as outside their residence. Furthermore they were responsible for the preservation of order at court. Just like the *Caballeriza*, though, the personal guard had above all a representative function. They accompanied the princes during their public appearances, and provided in that way for a visual spectacle. In that sense the positions of *albardero* and *archero* were quite prestigious, and consequently not simple to lay hold of. So, for example, the *archero* Jacques André was summoned in 1610 by a Brussels innkeeper in whose lodgings he had stayed various times 'during the time period in which he strived for the function of *archero*,' and where he – when his appointment finally was in the bag – organized a substantial debauch for 'his friends whom he had called together and engaged in order to get said function.'[189]

---

[186] Lanoye, 'Structure and Composition,' 116.

[187] Concerning the *Hartschiere*, see Hortal Muñoz, J.E. 'La Noble Guarda de Archeros de Corps en el contexto de la Casa Real de los monarcas Austrias Hispanos,' in: Vermeir, R., Fagel, R. & Ebben, M., eds. *Agentes e Identidades en Movimiento. España y los Países Bajos, siglos XV-XVIII*. Madrid, 2011, pp. 231-270 and Hortal Muñoz, J.E. 'Las guardas palatino-personales de los monarcas Austrias hispanos.' *Reales Sitios*, 179 (2009) 4-21.

[188] Guillaume II de Bauffremont, baron of Scey and Sombernon in Franche-Comté, was a *gentilhombre de la Boca* of Philip II. He died in Spain in 1599 and was buried in Clervaux.

[189] '*(...) durant le temps qu'il a poursuyvy l'estat d'archier (...) ses amys qu'il convegnoit et employoit pour obtenir ledit estat.*' ARA, *Hofrechtbank*, trial dossier no. 176.

Conclusion: the court ceremonial in its political context

The court of the archdukes,' Guido Bentivoglio wrote in his *Relationi*, 'can really compete with any other of the most flourishing and most splendid courts in the Christian world.'[190] With that the nuncio was one of the first to bear witness to the notable transformation that the court in Brussels had undergone since the coming of Albert and Isabella. In his travel journal Charles Somerset noted then again that '[the Archduke's] house is none of the fayrest, but the order of it, and the government of it both of the Archduke and his servants quarters, and also the Infanta and her Ladies in her quarter, both for vertue and pietie, is such that it may be the patterne for manie other princes to take example by it.'[191] These kinds of commentaries demonstrate that the revival of the court made a great impression on contemporaries. Clearly, the introduction of the new court ceremonial and the concomitant organization were of decisive importance. 'Of the utmost importance in projecting the imagery, splendour and pretensions of the court of the Archdukes, both to the people of the southern Netherlands and its nobility, and to the world beyond, was the elaborate ceremonial which broadcast and glorified the activities and projects of the court from its very inception,' posits Jonathan Israel in that context.[192] This statement asks for further clarification.

In her study concerning the court of the dukes of Savoy, Maria José del Río Barredo argues that the Spanish-Burgundian ceremonial was introduced there in 1585 on the occasion of the marriage of Duke Carlo Emanuele I to the infanta Catalina Micaela, the younger sister of Isabella.[193] According to the author it was a measure with conscious intentions, meant to breathe new life into the slackening life at court in Turin. Thanks to the introduction of the new court ceremonial they hoped to improve the radiance of the court and to accentuate the dynastic aspirations of the ducal family. Carlo Emanuele was an ambitious prince. His ardent attempts to have the strategically situated duchy of Savoy elevated to a kingdom would bring about many European headaches in subsequent years.[194] Consequently he grabbed with both hands at the chance to cultivate an image of sovereignty and royalty by

[190] Bentivoglio, *Relationi*, 160.

[191] Brennan, *The Travel Diary*, 287.

[192] Israel, J. 'Chapter 1: The Court of Albert and Isabella, 1598-1621,' in: Israel, J. *Conflicts of Empires. Spain, the Low Countries and the Struggle for World Supremacy 1585-1713*. London, 1997, pp. 1-21. Op. cit. p. 8.

[193] del Río Barredo, M.J. 'De Madrid a Turín: el ceremonial de las reinas españolas en la corte ducal de Catalina Micaela de Saboya,' in: Gómez-Centurión Jiménez, C., ed. *Monarquía y Corte en la España Moderna*. Cuadernos de Historia Moderna, 2003 (Anejo II), pp. 97-122.

[194] Oresko, R. 'The House of Savoy in Search for a Royal Crown in the Seventeenth Century,' in: Oresko, R., Gibbs, G.C. & Scott, H.M., eds. *Royal and Republican Sovereignty in Early Modern Europe: Essays in Memory of Ragnhild Hatton*. Cambridge U.P., 1997, pp. 272-350.

means of a splendid ducal household. At the same time Del Rio Barredo argues that the introduction of the new ceremonial was also especially advantageous for the father of the bride. The 'export' of his court model allowed Philip II to tighten the bonds with Savoy even more, to install a group of Spanish-oriented courtiers in the ducal household, and to firm up the prestige of Spanish culture in Italy. In that way the court ceremonial would contribute to strengthening the dependence of Turin with respect to Madrid as well as to expanding the political hegemony of Spain.[195]

It is tempting to compare the situation at the court of Savoy with circumstances at the archducal court. Both in Turin as well as in Brussels they had to deal with a regime that on the one hand invoked its political autonomy, yet on the other felt the hot breath of Spain down its neck.[196] At both courts they needed a refreshing élan after a period of troubles, and in both cases the shrewd marriage policy of Philip II saw to it that an infanta of Spain became the lady of the house. These are remarkable parallels, which may not lead to an oversimplification, all the same. In terms of politics, the situation in Savoy cannot possibly be compared with that in the Low Countries. Nevertheless Del Río Barredo's hypothesis gives cause for consideration. In any case it seems that Albert and Isabella also consciously opted for organizing their household after the example of the Spanish court. For that reason it was and is seen by some as a bastion of Spanish authority in the Netherlands.[197] The introduction of the Spanish-Burgundian court ceremonial would then indicate that the Brussels court was little more than a *subcourt*, a subdivision of its counterpart in Madrid. In that context it seems more than logical that one thing or another raises the requisite doubts about the political autonomy of the archducal regime. Yet these kinds of conclusions cannot be made too quickly. Undoubtedly the organization of the court in Brussels was also defined by political motivations. The question, though, is to what degree this reform can be seen as symptomatic of the presupposed dependence of the archdukes with respect to Spanish rule, or rather as conscious affirmation of the status of Albert and Isabella as independent, sovereign, Habsburg princes.

Just like in Turin, the court ceremonial in Brussels was adapted on the occasion of the wedding of the archdukes in 1598. The reforms were clearly inspired by the court model in vogue at the court in Madrid. In and of itself that need not surprise. Albert and Isabella had both grown up at the court of Philip II, which defined their frame of reference and on top of that enjoyed much prestige in Europe in this time

[195] *Ibidem*, pp. 112-122.

[196] See Oresko, R. 'The Sabaudian Court 1563-c. 1750,' in: Adamson, *The Princely Courts*, 232-253 and Osborne, T. *Dynasty and Diplomacy in the Court of Savoy. Political Culture and the Thirty Years' War.* Cambridge U.P., 2002.

[197] See e.g. Israel, J. 'Chapter 1: The Court of Albert and Isabella, 1598-1621' and García García, B.J. 'La Corte de los Archiduques en Bruselas.' *Torre de los Lujanes*, 44 (2001) 59-75.

period. Since their childhood their respective households were organized according to the Spanish-Burgundian court ceremonial. It seems consequently nothing more than logical that they wanted to keep the style familiar to them at their court in Brussels. But there was more going on. In terms of organization the archducal household was indeed a copy of its pendant portrait in Madrid. It could be posited just as well, though, that the court in Brussels did not seek so much to connect with the Spanish model as it did with the characteristic 'style of its dynastic house,' that which the August House of Austria employed and with which they wished to profile their household in Brussels. The specific religious practice that defined day-to-day life at court, to mention but one aspect, was to a greater or lesser extent a typical characteristic of all Habsburg courts. Profound devotion and spirituality made up part of the Habsburg identity, an identity with which the archdukes – whose marriage stood as a symbol for the unanimity and harmony between both dynastic branches – had been strongly diffused. As the following chapters will show, the archducal court was in the first place a Habsburg court, and in that sense the term *subcourt* simply does not apply. Its use implies a modern political interpretation of Habsburg rule, while in essence it was about a familial matter. All Habsburg courts rested on the same principles, and historians do well to take this dynastic component into account when evaluating specific cases.

One aspect that applies even more nuance to this complex material is the fact that the archducal marriage also went hand in hand with the transfer of sovereignty over the Netherlands to Albert and Isabella. Beginning with the arrival of the infanta in 1599, the court in Brussels was thus no longer the seat of a governor but of two sovereign princes of the blood. The meaning and impact of this change in status cannot be easily underestimated. It brought with it definite expectations which could and would not be ignored. In his authoritative essay *The Making of the Ancien-Régime Court* John Adamson argues that '(…) in the period between roughly 1550 and 1700 there was what might be termed a 'standardization of expectations' as to the features that a properly constituted court was expected to possess.'[198] According to Adamson every self-respecting sovereign court was expected to satisfy definite formal requirements. This was a matter not only of possessing a magnificent palace and displaying luxury and opulence, but also of patronizing the arts and sciences and of demonstrating a profound religiosity. In that sense there is mention of a pattern of expectations that entered into the foreground not only at Habsburg but at pretty much all Western and Central European courts. At the end of the sixteenth and the beginning of the seventeenth century, namely, this pattern would be very strongly applied, as Adamson posits:

[198] Adamson, J. 'The Making of the Ancien-Régime Court 1500-1700,' in: Adamson, *The Princely Courts*, pp. 7-41. Op. cit. p. 14.

> 'What is perhaps the most distinctive aspect of the late sixteenth- and early seventeenth-century court culture was the gradual acceptance of all, or almost all, of the items on this checklist as being virtually de rigueur for any sovereign court that aspired to be taken seriously by its peers. In this regard, studies of new courts are particularly revealing, whether they relate to newly elevated princes, such as the Medici or the Vasa, or to courts 'reinvented' after a relocation or period of abeyance, such as the Sabaudian court after its transference from Chambéry to Turin in 1563. The thoroughness with which these newcomers acquired the 'correct' courtly amenities reveals more than a pattern of copying and emulation. It effectively itemizes what contemporaries regarded as the defining features of a sovereign court.'[199]

In a certain sense the archducal court can be seen as a reinvented court. Since the departure of Philip II for Spain in 1559 the court in Brussels had been 'degraded' to a gubernatorial court. Under governess Margaret of Parma, it could still in a way maintain its glorious reputation, but in the turbulent years after that it lost much of its former luster.[200] When Albert and Isabella assumed their posts, it cast off its status as second-rung court and invented itself anew as an independent, autonomous, and above all else sovereign court. Through the introduction of the Spanish-Burgundian court ceremonial, which could be seen as the most prestigious in Europe, the archdukes breathed new life into the languishing court. Characterized by a deep-going ritualization of daily life, the new decorum accented their elevated and sacred status as princes of the blood – and consequently also the legitimacy of their reign. The archdukes were all too well aware of the political role their court could play. When the archdukes assumed their posts, the Netherlands found themselves to be in a situation of serious instability. For three decades the country had had to suffer from a civil war, with all its economic and social consequences. The wariness among the populace toward the new regime was great. A large number of members of the aristocracy had turned away from the Habsburg dynasty, and under the surface the fear reigned that even more would follow. In that kind of climate the archdukes opted to present their court as a beacon of political quiet and stability. The proliferation of offices and positions in their households made it possible – in combination with the system of *service par terme* – to attract large groups of nobles and to give them access to the renewed market of patronage which came to be developed there. In that way the court would play a defining role in rebuilding the much-plagued Habsburg regime in the Netherlands.

---

[199] *Ibidem.*

[200] Smolar-Meynart, *Het paleis van Brussel*, 95-101.

Adamson's argumentation recalls on top of that a hypothesis of John Elliott, who already in 1985 postulated that rulers of small principalities apparently made many more efforts to cultivate an image of pomp and grandeur than their counterparts in larger countries, for the simple reason that their legitimacy was called into question more.[201] Building further on this, Brian Weiser also concludes that 'the very smallness of these principalities encouraged rulers to concentrate on enhancing their image by splendor, distance, and decorum. (...) To counteract their questionable claims on the obedience of their subjects these princes emphasized their glory.'[202] Weiser refers to Milan and Burgundy to underpin his position, but perhaps the theory goes for the Archducal Netherlands as well. A few contemporaneous commentators were of the opinion in any case that the archdukes attached strikingly much importance to the image of their court, where 'glory precedes all other interests and affairs, which they would rather see ruined than to concede even one point.'[203] As the following chapters will also show, Albert and Isabella were especially sensitive, then, to infractions on the decorum and rules of precedence at court. In that context, the French ambassador Mathieu Brulart de Berny sighed, 'There were no princes in the world more jealous and punctual in these matters than they were.'[204] The English ambassador Lord Doncaster was also able to experience something similar in the flesh. When in 1619 he went for an audience with the archdukes, they refused to offer him a chair. Doncaster interpreted that to be a crude insult and made his complaint, upon which he got to hear drily that he was being given the same treatment as that which in turn had fallen to the count of Noyelles when the latter was received as the archducal emissary by King James I a few months before that. 'And this I have almost generally observed in my whole entertaynment here,' the aggrieved Doncaster wrote, 'that as in all thinges wherein [the archdukes] might sett forth the glory of their own magnificence, they have been desirous to exceede the pattern of their ambassador's usage in England (...), wherein I thinke his Majesty and all the world will judge there is a great overvaluation on their part.'[205]

In fact, with his complaint Doncaster hit the nail on the head. The court of the archdukes was, to be sure, a sovereign but not a royal court. Yet Albert and Isabella insisted on employing a court ceremonial that – following the model of the court at

[201] Elliott, J.H. 'Power and Propaganda in the Spain of Philip IV,' in: Wilentz, S., ed. *Rites of Power. Symbolism, Ritual and Politics Since the Middle Ages*. Philadelphia, 1985, pp. 145-173.

[202] Weiser, B. *Charles II and the Politics of Access*. Woodbridge, 2003. Op. cit. p. 10.

[203] '*(...) la gloire précède tous ces autres interests et affaires qu'ils aimeront mieux voir ruiner que d'en diminuer un poinct.*' BNF, *MsF* 16130, f. 274: Charles de l'Aubespinne de Chasteauneuf, abbot of Préaux, to Secretary of State Puisieux, May 28, 1614.

[204] '*Il ny avoit princes au monde plus jaloux et punctuelz en telles choses que ceulxcy.*' BNF, *MsF* 16129, f. 285: Mathieu Brulart de Berny to Secretary of State Puisieux, July 25, 1610.

[205] NA, *SP* 77/13, f. 267: Lord Doncaster to Secretary of State Robert Naunton, May 30, 1619.

Madrid – was cobbled from a royal model. Clearly, definite political ambitions were hidden behind this measure. There is indeed no doubt that the aspirations of Albert and Isabella reached further than dominion over the Netherlands. It says much, for example, that the archdukes at the beginning of their rule undertook ardent yet fruitless attempts to have themselves recognized by the pope and the international community as kings of Burgundy – a title that would have catapulted them at once to the top of the *pecking order* among European princes.[206] On top of that as the newly wed son of the emperor – with still good hopes for any possible birth of children around 1598 – the archduke was a candidate marked to succeed the childless Rudolf II on the imperial throne.[207] It was an option that the historiography of the archducal reign has dared to forget but one of which Albert himself was all too well aware. For a long time he saw himself as the future emperor of the Holy Roman Empire – or in any case as having a very great chance at this position (cf. Chapter V). Seen from that standpoint, the revitalization of the court in Brussels was nothing more than logical. With the introduction of the royal court ceremonial Albert and Isabella anticipated the splendid future that they saw set aside for themselves and their possible subsequent progeny. It could not be suspected in 1598 that none of those mentioned ambitions would in the end become the truth.

[206] See concerning this BFZ, *Altamira*, carpeta 39, grupo documental 13, doc. 61: Philip III to the duke of Sesa, Spanish ambassador in Rome, June 5, 1599.

[207] See Brants, V. *La Belgique au XVIIe siècle, Albert et Isabelle. Études d'histoire politique et sociale*. Leuven, 1910, pp. 18-19; Hennequin de Villermont, *L'Infante Isabelle*, pp. 217-223 and Sánchez, 'Sword and Wimple,' 65.

Chapter II
Household Scale & Finances

'One might perhaps reproach the archdukes for having maintained (...) such an expensive court even though they were always in want of money, but this was the custom at the time, and when the prince lacked resources, he did not pay his officials.'[1]

Marie Hennequin de Villermont
L'Infante Isabelle

During the summer of 1603, Albert and Isabella passed the time in Antwerp for a few weeks. Without a doubt, their stay saddled Antwerp's city magistrate with a great many logistical headaches. According to a contemporary source the archdukes arrived with a retinue of at least 382 persons, all of whom had to be housed and fed.[2] There were, among others, ten *gentilhombres de la Cámara*, nineteen *gentilhombres de la Boca*, nine *gentilhombres de la Casa*, twelve *ayudas de Cámara*, seven chaplains, thirteen footmen, two personal physicians, four washerwomen, seven violists, nineteen cooks and kitchen servants, thirteen coachmen, seven *escuderos de a pie*, nine trumpeters, and seven porters. In the princes' wake another sixty dignitaries went down to Antwerp, among them many who brought their own servants along with them. Finally, the archducal retinue was perhaps also accompanied by a contingent of *Hartschiere* and halberdiers. The entire undertaking had something to it of a mass exodus in miniature. Undoubtedly quite a lot of inhabitants of that city on the river Scheldt let loose a sigh of relief when the court departed again for Brussels in September.

That Albert and Isabella were accompanied by this kind of extensive entourage even during a relatively short relocation is not necessarily a surprise. In an essay concerning the court culture under the Stuarts in England, Malcolm Smuts writes about scholarship on visual representations of power and grandeur during the Ancien Régime. In it he argues that research is inclined to concentrate on the visual arts, while giving too little attention to the study of other, more classic methods that – as Peter

[1] '*On pourra peut-être faire ce reproche aux archiducs, d'avoir maintenu (...) une cour si dispendieuse alors que l'argent leur manquait toujours, mais c'était dans les mœurs du temps et quand le prince manquait de fonds, il ne payait pas ses officiers.*' Hennequin de Villermont, M. *L'Infante Isabelle, gouvernante des Pays-Bas*. 2 vols. Paris-Tamines, 1912. Volume II, p. 22.

[2] SAA, *Privilegekamer* 1627 (microfilm 392K): *Lyste van den Hove zoo Hunne Hoocheden hier waren gecomen 2 Augusti 1603 ende vertrocken 9 Septembris daernaer.*

Burke eloquently expressed it – had as their goal the 'fabrication' of a princely image.[3] Among other things Smuts points to the possession of an impressive entourage and to the exhibition of excessive pomp and pageantry as ways of expressing the *maiestas* of the prince. According to the author, contemporaries were impressed much more by the scale and the splendor of the princely household than by refined paintings and stately portraits. The latter were generally to be found in art chambers and galleries that were not accessible to the public at large. On top of that, the interpretation of those artworks demanded in many cases a thorough knowledge of mythology and history, which was given to few at that time. 'Traditional' expressions of luxury and luster were, consequently, much more appropriate for visualizing princely authority with respect to a large and heterogeneous public.[4] Smuts reminds his readers of

> 'the medieval principle that power and prestige must always be expressed through a large and impressive entourage, crowding into a great man's house and pursuing his favour. (...) Royal majesty became visible chiefly through massive assemblages of gorgeously dressed people and showy luxury objects. What needs emphasis is the scale of this display, the impression it must have made on spectators and the enormous expenditures required to sustain it.'[5]

The conviction has already been repeatedly argued among historians that the extent of the princely entourage during the Ancien Régime was expected to reflect the status and wealth of the prince.[6] In the perception of contemporaries the scale of the princely household functioned as a visual gauge for the range of princely power. Not coincidentally, all important princely courts of Europe experienced significant expansion over the course of centuries, with a peak in the period from 1650-1700.[7] In that context Jeroen Duindam is of the opinion that '[f]rom the thirteenth to the seventeenth or eighteenth centuries, rising numbers, a proliferation of honorary and administrative responsibilities, and an increasing sense of majesty changed the face

---

3 See the introduction in Smuts, M., ed. *The Stuart Court and Europe. Essays in Politics and Political Culture*. Cambridge U.P., 1996. The term 'fabrication' is borrowed from Burke, P. *The Fabrication of Louis XIV*. New Haven-London, 1992.

4 Smuts, *The Stuart Court and Europe*, 12.

5 Smuts, *The Stuart Court and Europe*, 88 and 96.

6 See e.g. Werner Paravicini, who in the context of the court of the Burgundian dukes argues that 'what impressed foreigners even more was quite simply the number of people who lived at the court at the Duke's expense.' Paravicini, W. 'The Court of the Dukes of Burgundy. A Model for Europe?' in: Asch, R.G. & Birke, A.M., eds. *Princes, Patronage and the Nobility: The Court at the Beginning of the Modern Age, c. 1450-1650*. Oxford U.P., 1991, pp. 69-102. Op. cit. p. 76.

7 Adamson, J. 'The Making of the Ancien-Régime Court, 1500-1700,' in: Adamson, J., ed. *The Princely Courts of Europe. Ritual, Politics and Culture under the Ancien Régime 1500-1750*. London, 1999, pp. 7-41.

of the court.'[8] That this kind of evolution also brought with it the requisite financial consequences requires no further line of argumentation. In light of the 'sovereignty debate' (cf. Introduction), then, the question arises as to whether and how this trend appeared at the court in Brussels, where the legitimacy and the precarious financial situation of the archdukes also provided for heated discussions already during their lifetimes.

The previous chapter showed how the archducal household was intentionally modeled on the example of a royal court.[9] In their attempts to affirm their authority and to make their dynastic ambitions known, Albert and Isabella made a particularly great deal of effort to restore to its honor the former luster of the court in Brussels. Yet did this strategy translate into a significant increase in scale? What was the archducal court like relative to other European courts? How large was their household, and how much did maintaining it cost? And – even more interesting – who actually paid for it? These seem like simple questions, but not one of them has produced an answer until now, in which there is no speculation involved. Traditionally it has been assumed that the court of Albert and Isabella was much larger than the courts of their predecessors and successors in the Netherlands, but in fact concrete data concerning this have never been studied. Statements – like this one from Jonathan Israel positing that 'the court of the archdukes [was] much larger and more ostentatious than that of any governor-general preceding or succeeding them' – are not based so much on figures, then, as on contemporaneous commentaries.[10] One of these formulated it as follows:

> 'There is no prince in our century more attentive than Albert, ruler of the Low Countries, to supporting and increasing the magnificence of his rank, filling up his court with a great number of nobles, ministers, and guards; convinced that as soon as the people cease to be struck by the splendor and power that make such an impression on their minds, they will easily come to disprove of sovereignty.'[11]

---

[8] Duindam, J. *Vienna and Versailles: The Courts of Europe's Dynastic Rivals, 1550-1780.* Cambridge U.P. Op. cit. p. 27.

[9] See in that context Elliott, J.H. 'La sociedad cortesana en la Europa del siglo XVII: Madrid, Bruselas, Londres,' in: Brown, J., ed. *Velázquez, Rubens y Van Dyck. Pintores cortesanos del siglo XVII.* Madrid, 1999, pp. 15-31.

[10] Israel, J. 'Het tijdperk van de Aartshertogen, 1598-1621,' in: Janssens, P., ed. *België in de Zeventiende Eeuw. De Spaanse Nederlanden en het prinsbisdom Luik.* 2 vols. Ghent, 2006, pp. 28-32. Volume I, p. 29.

[11] '*Il n'y a point de prince dans notre siècle plus attentif qu'Albert, prince des Pais-Bas, à soutenir l'éclat de son rang et à l'augmenter, en remplissant sa cour d'un grand nombre de la noblesse, de ministres et de gardes; persuadé qu'aussitôt que le peuple cesse d'être frappé par la splendeur et la puissance qui font tant d'impression sur son esprit, il passe aisément à mépriser la souveraineté.*' Butkens, C.F. *Supplément aux trophées tant sacrés que profanes du duché de Brabant de Mr.Butkens, Traduit et recueilli des meilleurs historiens de Brabant et tiré pour une grande partie des archives dudit pais.* 2 vols. The Hague, 1724-1726. Op. cit. vol. I, p. 358.

Commentaries like this one leave no doubt that the evolution of the extent of the archducal entourage cannot be seen separate from political motivations. With that thought in the back of the mind, this chapter gauges the scale of the archducal household and the financial cost that maintaining it produced. The answers to these questions link back to the broader theme of the representation of power, in which not so much the concrete creation of that household is of importance as is the motivation underlying that process.

Contours: the court and its household

It need not come as a surprise that the extent of the archducal court has to this day not ever been researched in detail. Gauging the dimensions of an early modern court is no simple exercise. Much depends on the definition employed: different interpretations of the concept of a 'court' lead of necessity to divergent opinions of its scale. In order to circumvent that problem, most historians satisfy themselves with an analysis of the extent of a princely household. Put another way: they count the number of courtiers and servants mentioned in the court indices and official remuneration lists.[12] Naturally this method is far from ideal. Thus, for example, it is clear that the actual household constituted only one component of a broad array of institutions and sectors that – in the perception of contemporaries – made up part of the princely court. The question arises as to what extent all these entities can be taken into account, and whether that is at all necessary. Given the lack of quantifiable data, estimates in the matter will always be arbitrary. On top of that, the fact needs to be taken into account that the court in many European principalities consisted of several households. Each member of the princely family thus had a more or less independent household at his or her disposal.[13] In the Archducal Netherlands that was not the case, but that still does not put the problems out of the way.

Whoever analyzes only the number of registered and paid staff members will have to overlook a significant 'dark number.' This kind of approach ignores a great number of persons who were not necessarily linked to the archducal household officially but who did indeed stay at court. So, for instance, an anonymous French spy announced around 1610 in a secret report that at the court in Brussels there were to be found 'always some governors-general, field marshals, colonels, governors of cities and places, captains, and others for the business of the Prince or their own,' and that the Spanish army in the Netherlands put to work many officers 'who are

[12] See the discussion concerning this in Duindam, *Vienna and Versailles*, pp. 47-51.

[13] Duindam, *Vienna and Versailles*, 48-49.

for the most part at Court during this [Twelve Years'] truce with the States.'[14] On top of that, the presence of a great number of members of the central administration and the *corps diplomatique*, who saw the Coudenberg palace as their biotope, has to be taken into account. Inversely, there were also nobles who officially belonged to the archducal household but who seldom or never stayed at court on account of military or diplomatic activities, or simply because their office was nothing more than an honorary function. Furthermore, an analysis of registered staff members ignores not only the families of courtiers and, in that case, their own households, but also other persons who were indirectly connected to the archducal household.[15] Here it is a matter of the employees of 'external' articulations like the division of the hunt, of a temporary workforce and hired day laborers, of painters and purveyors to the court, and so forth. On top of that, there were perhaps quite a lot of courtiers, clerks, and servants whose salary was disbursed by means of separate budgets, or who received only material compensation and, consequently, were not mentioned in the court indices. And what's to be thought of the undoubtedly numerous visitors who frequented the Coudenberg palace during balls, tournaments, and other events, or who came to the court to engage in politics or simply to schmooze with the others present there?[16]

It is perhaps clear that a ready-made solution for the problem with regard to the scale of the court is not just waiting there for the picking. In any event, for subsequently formulating careful hypotheses concerning the actual situation historians have to make do with the scarce information from court indices and personnel rosters (which are mostly limited to data concerning the number of paid employees). While these sources form an acceptable point of departure, in and of themselves they bring along several practical problems. For the entire archducal period, only a relatively small number of court indices are available, which can be seen more or less as representative.

[14] '*(…) tousjours aucuns gouverneurs-généraux, maistres de camp sur pied, colonelz, gouverneurs de villes et places, cappitaines et autres pour affaires du Prince ou pour leur particulier (…) qui sont pour la plus part en Court durant ceste trefve d'avec les Estats*.' [Anonymous]. *Relation de Flandres. État de la cour et maison des archiducs en 1610. Document inédit du temps enrichi de notes généalogiques et historiques.* In: *Souvenirs de la Flandre-Wallonne. Recherches historiques et choix de documents relatifs à Douai et au Nord de la France*, vol. VI. Paris-Douai, 1866, pp. 1-25. Op. cit. p. 7.

[15] Antoinette-Guillemette of Arenberg, *camarera mayor* of the infanta, had in her service, for example, '*une damoiselle vielle*', '*une damoiselle jeune*', '*deux femmes de chambre*', and '*une cuisinière*', as well as a certain Hauwach '*qui servira de maistre d'hôtel et de secrétaire*,' a certain Claude, a page, and, finally, Maternus, '*son laquay*.' ACA, 36-17: *Sensuyt tout ce que il fault pour Madame la Comtesse d'Isenbourgh*. The personal household of the count of Añover, *mayordomo mayor* of the archducal household, then again, would consist of at least 36 persons. IVDJ, ms. 26-I-11, ff. 43-50: *Relación de la enfermedad, muerte y entiero, honras y obsequias del Señor Conde de Añober que está en gloria*.

[16] Duindam, *Vienna and Versailles*, 49-51.

It concerns seven lists from 1595, 1598, 1603, 1605, 1611 and 1622.[17] In addition there is an overview from 1624, in which the names of servants are mentioned who received a pension after the death of Archduke Albert.[18] Depending on the reasons that gave occasion for their redaction, the different lists are often inaccurate or incomplete. In view of the fact that they employed a just as incoherent quantitative methodology, on top of that, it is not simple to define the evolution of the scale of the archducal household over time. So, for instance, quite a lot of categories of courtiers and servants seem to appear and disappear according to the authors' preference. In the same way names of staff members are bastardized, forgotten, or misspelled. Functions and offices are split up here, then combined again or deleted there. In some cases people appear to disappear into the void, only to pop up again suddenly a few years later. In interpreting the data carefulness is thus dictated. In a way, this problem can be compensated for with the aid of the archducal household's *libros de razón*, which reflect a more detailed picture.[19] These accounting ledgers contain trimester overviews of the remunerations handed out to the courtiers and servants in the period 1612-1618. Here, modifications and fluctuations in the personnel force can therefore be read in a systematic way. The following sections introduce the analysis of all these data.

The figures

On February 11, 1596, Cardinal-Archduke Albert held his festive entry into Brussels. According to a contemporaneous reporter, the new governor was accompanied by an entourage of more than 230 persons.[20] That number is more or less confirmed by a court index drawn up around 1595, which consequently reflects the situation right before or during Albert's coming to the Netherlands.[21] This document mentions 221 persons in total.[22] The difference with the number already named is negligible, and it

---

[17] They are, respectively, the ARA, *Aud* 23/10 (1595); ASV, *Borghese* I 913, ff. 339-344 (1598); SAA, *Privilegekamer* 1627 (1603); ARA, *Aud* 33/3 (1605); ARA, *Aud* 33/4, ff. 66-72 (1605); ARA, *RvS* 157 (1611) and ARA, *Aud* 20, ff. 16-26 (1622).

[18] ARA, *RvS* 157 (1624).

[19] ARA, *RK* 1837 and 1838.

[20] The number 230 is cited in a letter from A. Sarmiento de Valladares to the count of Gondomar, September 3, 1595. See Hortal Muñoz, J.E. 'The Household of Archduke Albert of Austria from his Election as Governor of Flanders until his Investiture as Sovereign Prince of the Low Countries: 1595-1598,' *Revue belge de Philologie et d'Histoire*, in press.

[21] ARA, *Aud* 23/10: *Relación de los Criados de Su Alteza el Archiduque Alberto*. Except for a few changes in the order of the names, this court index is pretty much identical to ARA, *Aud* 33/4, ff. 61-65.

[22] Of these, 18 are not mentioned by name. Thus, the father confessor of the cardinal-archduke, for example, is only designated as '*el padre confesor*,' which supposedly is to blame on the fact that Albert's father confessor, Juan Vicente, died right before the departure and would be replaced later by Iñigo de Brizuela. Furthermore, there were '*dos herradores*' (two ferriers), '*dos cocheros*' (two coachmen) and '*treze pajes*' (thirteen pages).

seems acceptable, then, that the core of Albert's household indeed numbered around 230 persons at the start of his reign – with the understanding that the members of the *Capella Maior* and the *Guarda* are not included here. The first subsequent preserved court index dates from 1598 and was drawn up on the occasion of Albert's journey to Spain in that year.[23] The list mentions only names of courtiers who accompanied him on his voyage and consequently reflects only a partial overview of the archducal household. As opposed to the previous court index, this document makes no mention, for example, of the archduke's pages. What is striking, though, is the presence of a few courtiers with origins in the Southern Netherlands and Burgundy, who were missing still in 1595 (cf. Chapter III). In total it concerns 215 individuals, in addition to fifteen '*personajes que vienen con el Archiduque demas de la Memoria de su Casa.*'[24]

In 1599, the archducal household underwent a fundamental transformation on the occasion of Albert's bride Isabella and her largely female entourage coming to Brussels. In view of the fact that the Coudenberg palace had sheltered a pretty much exclusively male company for many years, the introduction of this female household undoubtedly brought the requisite excitement along with it. In addition to ladies-in-waiting and chambermaids, Isabella was in need, on top of that, of extra staff to care for her wardrobe, to wash her clothing, to make up her bed, and to watch the entry to her quarters. There is no need to mention that these servants also had the right to a salary and – in a number of cases – to room and board: the financial impact of their coming was perhaps not to be underestimated. All the same, for lack of sources it is impossible to 'measure' the exact expansion of the archducal household around 1599. The first subsequent court index available dates only from 1603 and reflects an overview of the entourage of Albert and Isabella during their stay in the city of Antwerp (cf. above).[25] In view of the fact that it is an exceptional situation here, this list has its limitations as well. Thus, for instance, the court index mentions 382 persons in total (once again without the *Capella Maior* and the palace guard), among them 50 anonymous *azemileros*, or muleteers. Furthermore the document refers to an indefinite number of pages and sixty people who were not connected to the archducal household. Although this list includes a few functions not brought up in the court indices mentioned earlier (such as, e.g., nine *trompetas* and seven *musicos de violones*), nevertheless there is a noticeable rise with respect to the situation before 1599 (cf. Table 1).

This expansion is in its turn confirmed by two different court indices from 1605. The first was drawn up in preparation for the visit of the archdukes to the city of

[23] ASV, *Borghese* I 913, ff. 339-344.

[24] *Ibidem.*

[25] SAA, *Privilegekamer* 1627 (microfilm 392K): *Lyste van den Hove zoo Hunne Hoocheden hier waren gecomen 2 Augusti 1603 ende vertrocken 9 Septembris daernaer.*

Ghent and, consequently, shows only the staff members who would accompany the couple during this visit.[26] The document mentions 363 courtiers in total, in addition to a great number of '*Grandes y Señores que siguen la Corte*' and – for the first time – a hundred halberdiers. Furthermore, there are a number of functions without further description (such as the enigmatic *azemileros en la cabeza doro*) and, finally, it needs to be said that here, too, a few categories are included that are not mentioned in the remaining lists (such as, for example, the *libradores de casa*). The other court index from 1605 was drawn up by Pedro de Mendoza, Albert's clerk, and by Antonio de Mendoza, the *veedor y contador* of the *Caballeriza*.[27] It was perhaps meant to justify the number of courtiers who by the capacity of their office were exempted from paying taxes in the city of Brussels. The list mentions 307 staff members and 5 persons who are described as *pensionarios* (these last are consequently not taken into account in this analysis). To that have to be added 28 servants who were working in the stables of the mules, and 80 people who were paid separately from the account of the *Caballeriza*. Furthermore the list of the two Mendozas also contains the names of 37 members of the *Capella Maior* (*Capellanes de Altar, cantores y musicos de Capilla*), as well as 52 *Hartschiere*, and 101 halberdiers. During the five years after 1605 the sources in any language fall silent again. The first subsequent preserved court index dates only from 1611 and was drawn up with an eye to the purchase of mourning dress on the occasion of the death of Queen Margaret of Spain.[28] The document mentions 426 staff members, in addition to 49 members of the *Capella Maior*, 45 *Hartschiere* and 87 halberdiers, good for a total of 607 persons.

Table 1 – Extent of the archducal household in the period 1595-1611 on the basis of six court indices

	1595	**1598**	**1603**	**1605 (1)**	**1605 (2)**	**1611**
Household excluding the Capella Maior and Guarda	221	215	382	363	415	426
Capella Maior	?	?	?	?	37	49
Hartschiere	?	?	?	?	52	45
Halberdiers	?	?	?	99	101	87
TOTAL	**?**	**?**	**?**	**?**	**605**	**607**

Sources: ARA, *Aud* 23/10 (1595); ASV, *Borghese* I 913, ff. 339-344 (1598); SAA, *Privilegekamer* 1627 (1603); ARA, *Aud* 33/3 (1605 (1)); ARA, *Aud* 33/4, ff. 66-72 (1605 (2)) and ARA, *RvS* 157 (1611).

26 ARA, *Aud* 33/3.

27 ARA, *Aud* 33/4, ff. 66-72: *Relacion de los Criados de Sus Altezas Serenissimas que al presente sirven*.

28 ARA, *RvS* 157.

The inaccuracy and the incoherence of the different court indices do not make it simple to compare the data with one another in a trustworthy way. The numbers named therefore have to be taken with a substantial grain of salt. During the first decade of the seventeenth century, nevertheless, there seems clearly to be talk of a significant rise in numbers with respect to the situation before 1599. For the period 1612-1618, the *libros de razón* offer a more conclusive answer concerning the exact numbers. From these can be derived that the archducal household gradually grew from 344 staff members in the first trimester of 1612, to 390 in the first trimester of 1618. If counting up the members of the *Capella Maior* and the *Guarda* in the process, then it comes out to a total of 520 employees in 1612, and 566 in 1618 (cf. Table 2). The difference with the court indices of 1605 and 1611 seems significant, but it can be traced back in part to the fact that these lists implement categories that are not included in the *libros de razón*, like the 21 *palfreniers* and the 13 *varlets cochers* in 1611, or the 22 *azemileros* and 26 *mozos de cavallo* in 1605. Perhaps most of the lower servants from the *Caballeriza* and the *Acemilería* in the period 1612-1618 were noted in separate accounting ledgers, which unfortunately have not remained preserved.[29] Then, too, it can also be assumed that the *libros de razón* only contain data concerning the 'minimum minimorum' with regard to the number of members of the archducal household.

Table 2 – Extent of the archducal household in the period 1612-1618 on the basis of the *libros de razón*.

	1612	1613	1614	1615	1616	1617	1618
Household excluding the Capella Maior and Guarda	344	362	364	[309]*	376	374	390
Capella Maior	51	51	52	49	50	49	48
Hartschiere	45	45	45	45	45	46	46
Halberdiers	82	82	82	82	82	82	82
TOTAL	**522**	**540**	**543**	**[485]**	**553**	**551**	**566**

Sources: ARA, *RK* 1837 and 1838. Each time here they are the numbers during the first trimester of the year concerned. The remarkable decline in 1615 can be blamed on a few missing folios in the accounting ledgers, such that the number of servants of the Caballeriza could not be figured out.

[29] That these servants were indeed paid from a separate budget and therefore do not occur in the *libros de razón* is shown, among other things, in comments from the Admiral of Aragón, *mayordomo mayor* of the archducal household, around 1596: '*A la cavalleriza de los azemilos se han de librar 8400 reales para los raciones y sueldos de los oficiales, azemileros y mozos de cavallos que se pagan cada mes (sin los gajes y racion del azemilero mayor que se paga por la Casa quando y como a los demas criados de V[uestra] A[lteza]).*' RAH, *SyC* A-61, f. 1.

After the death of Archduke Albert in 1621, the household underwent a transformation anew. The sovereignty over the Netherlands again ended up in Spanish hands, and at the command of Philip IV the household budget of Isabella – whose status was reduced to governess – was drastically turned back. According to Giovanni-Francesco Guidi di Bagno, the papal nuncio at that time, Isabella accepted this decision without protest, however.[30] A few months after the death of her spouse she charged *mayordomo mayor* Ambrogio Spínola with the reorganization of her entourage. 'As concerns the reform of the archducal household,' the latter wrote to Philip IV, 'I believe that there is no one who will contend that it is not necessary to carry this out, nor that this is not very just.'[31] It speaks for itself that cutbacks were made above all among Albert's servants, who after his death had become redundant. In the court index of 1622, which contains only 251 names in total still (again, without the *Capella Maior* and the *Guarda*), various *gentilhombres de la Cámara* therefore no longer occur.[32] Even the *ayudas de Cámara* and the members of Albert's *Guardaropa* are wanting here – though, on the contrary, they are mentioned in the list of 1624, which offers an overview of 128 servants entitled to pensions.[33] As a consequence of one thing or another, after the death of the archduke the household in Brussels would be characterized by a new balance of power, in which the infanta's female entourage gained in influence.[34]

Discussion

How must the data above be interpreted? It speaks for itself that the numbers named are not unshakable: they only reflect an indication that is more or less trustworthy according to the source used. Nevertheless, the original entourage of Archduke Albert seems to have increased in a relatively short time after his marriage with Isabella. Thus, after the transition in status from a gubernatorial to a sovereign court, it went from around 230 employees to a princely retinue of 500 to 600 persons – an exponential rise, which after that assumed a more sluggish tempo. In view of the fact that the already mentioned 'dark number' still has to be added to this, the numbers in reality

---

30 The archducal household was allowed thenceforth to cost 200,000 *scudi* still (around fl. 514,000). BAV, *BaL* 6812, f. 102: Giovanni-Francesco Guidi di Bagno to Cardinal-Secretary of State Ludovisi, October 9, 1621.

31 ARA, *SSO* 127, s.f.: Ambrogio Spínola to Philip IV, August 31, 1621.

32 ARA, *Aud* 20, ff. 16-26.

33 ARA, *RvS* 157 (1624).

34 In her doctoral dissertation Birgit Houben demonstrates that this 'feminization' of the archducal household had an impact on existing networks and power relations at court that cannot be underestimated. See Houben, B. *Wisselende gedaanten. Het hof en de hofhouding van de landvoogden Isabella Clara Eugenia (1621-1633) en de kardinaal-infant don Fernando van Oostenrijk (1634-1641) te Brussel.* Unpublished doctoral dissertation, Universiteit Gent, 2009. See further also Jacobs, M. *Parateksten, netwerken en conventies in de Spaanse Nederlanden en Franche-Comté (1621-1678): de familie Chifflet uit Besançon.* Unpublished doctoral dissertation, Vrije Universiteit Brussel, 1998.

were much higher. Depending on the definition employed, a total of 800 to 900 persons – whether paid or not – for the complete court is not unrealistic, even if it is a question here of quite a tentative estimate which needs to be employed with the requisite caveats. If the central administration, the *corps diplomatique*, the courtiers' households, and the different persons present there 'without obligation' are also taken into account, then the number ran perhaps to around 1,500 persons, although here, too, any estimate is supremely arbitrary. On top of that, there is no saying that all these individuals actually stayed at court. Most of the more highly placed courtiers (such as the *gentilhombres*) served in accordance with a weekly, monthly, or varying rotation (*service par terme*), from which the turnover was quite great. The *libros de razón* mentioned, then, countless characters who are designated as '*ausente*' and who received no pay during this absence. On top of that, the court was often relocated to the smaller residences of Mariemont and Tervuren, where limited staffing sufficed.

How did the court of Albert and Isabella relate to other European courts? Naturally the answer to this question is dependent in large part on the quantitative methodology employed. In this section to the extent it is possible reference is made, then, to data concerning the actual princely household, which best lend themselves to a comparative approach. On top of that, in order to avoid much too large discrepancies, only the 'core household' (i.e. the courtiers and servants of the monarch himself, or herself – and excluding, thus, any possible households of his or her family members) is taken into account. Simon Adams estimates that the royal household of the English queen Elizabeth I (1558-1603) counted a permanent staff of 600 to 700 employees, not including the palace guard.[35] According to Ronald Asch, then again, the royal household of Charles I (1625-1640) numbered around 1,800 employees, even though there were usually not more than 700 to 800 staff members present full-time.[36] That was significantly less than the number of courtiers and servants of Henry IV of France (1598-1610), whose *maison* (i.e. the amalgam of divisions that were led by the *grand aumônier*, the *grand maître*, the *grand chambellan* and the *capitaine de la porte*) in this time period never put to work less than 1,000 staff members, in spite of attempts to keep the numbers within limits.[37] In that context, Olivier Chaline speaks of even more than 1,700 employees.[38] In Prague, the court of Rudolf II (1576-1612)

---

35 Adams, S. 'The Court as an Economic Institution. The Court of Elizabeth I of England (1558-1603),' in: Aymard, M. & Romani, M.A., eds. *La cour comme institution économique. Actes du douzième congrès international d'histoire économique, Séville-Madrid, 24-28 août 1998*. Paris, 1998, pp. 127-136.

36 Asch, R. 'The Court of Charles I. Some Reflections on the Social and Economic Role of the Court in Early Stuart England,' in: Aymard & Romani, *La cour comme institution économique*, pp. 139-148.

37 Duindam, *Vienna and Versailles*, 52.

38 Chaline, O. 'The Valois and Bourbon Courts c. 1515-1750,' in: Adamson, *The Princely Courts*, pp. 67-93.

experienced true inflation in his reign: the number of courtiers and servants there rose from around 700 in 1580, to 1,100 to 1,200 in 1611.[39] Under Emperor Matthias, the court index was reduced to around 785 persons, including the members of his advisory councils.[40] In Madrid, finally, the royal households of Philip IV (1598-1621) and his spouse numbered together around 1,700 permanent employees around 1623.[41] It speaks for itself that these data ought not be seen as sacrosanct. The actual extent of the four great European courts – including, thus, their 'external' articulations, which are difficult to estimate, as well as the households of princes and princesses – ran into the thousands in certain time periods.

In the Italian city-states and the principalities in the Holy Roman Empire, the princely households were generally smaller in their scope than in the royal and imperial courts, although the situation differed from region to region. So, for example, the household of the Gonzagas in Mantua numbered about 705 staff members around 1598, while that of the Estes in Ferrara put only about 430 to work in that same year. In 1609, then again, the household of Ferdinando I de' Medici in Florence numbered around 395 persons. The Farnese in Parma had around 226 people in their service in 1593, and the entourage of the dukes of Savoy in Turin consisted of around 200 employees in 1588.[42] Even so, it is not clear whether here it is a matter of 'core households,' or whether it is about the amalgam of households that made up part of the courts named. In Munich, the court of the Wittelsbachs – one of the most extensive princely courts in the Holy Roman Empire – was good for a court index with 866 persons around 1570, while that of the Hohenzollerns in Brandenburg numbered between 500 and 800 souls, according to cautious estimates.[43] Finally, at the court of the Vasas in Sweden the royal household consisted of around 400 employees at the beginning of the seventeenth century.[44]

On the basis of the figures reflected here – with the minimum named of around 600 courtiers and servants – the archducal court could be described as a player of average to above-average format, with the understanding that absolute numbers are perhaps neither the only nor the best indicators for evaluating how the different courts

[39] Duindam, *Vienna and Versailles*, 69-70.

[40] Duindam, *Vienna and Versailles*, 71.

[41] Elliott, J.H. 'The Court of the Spanish Habsburgs: A Peculiar Institution?' in: Mack, Ph. & Jacob, M.C., eds. *Politics and Culture in Early Modern Europe: Essays in Honour of H.G. Koenigsberger*. Cambridge University Press, 1987, pp. 5-24.

[42] The data are taken from the introduction in Aymard & Romani, *La cour comme institution économique*, p. 3. Even so, see also Fantoni, M. 'The Courts of the Medici 1532-1737,' in Adamson, *The Princely Courts*, pp. 255-273.

[43] See Babel, R. 'The Courts of the Wittelsbachs c. 1500-1750,' in: Adamson, *The Princely Courts*, pp. 189-209 and Völkel, M. 'The Hohenzollern Court,' in: Adamson, *The Princely Courts*, pp. 211-229.

[44] Persson, F. 'The Courts of the Vasas and Palatines,' in: Adamson, *The Princely Courts*, pp. 275-293.

related to one another. At courts counting several households the analysis of the 'core household' naturally gives a distorted picture. Furthermore, the question needs to be posed as to what extent the population figures of the principality influenced the scale of the court. England numbered around 4.2 million inhabitants in 1600, while the Spanish Netherlands numbered around 1.5 million. Yet the core household of Albert and Isabella was not that much smaller than that of Elizabeth I (even though the 'dark number' naturally remains guesswork). From this could be derived that the court of the archdukes, proportionally speaking, possessed more 'weight' than that of the English queen. Nonetheless, this reasoning, too, is not entirely conclusive: the Brussels household was, after all, responsible for serving two persons (Albert and Isabella), while its London counterpart served only one person.[45] On top of that, the English royal household counted primarily courtiers and servants of English origin, while the archducal household consisted of those from Spain, the Southern Netherlands, and Burgundy and thus recruited from 'beyond its borders.' Consequently, it remains difficult to evaluate the scale of the court and its importance, also because one thing or another depends on the proportional share of the aristocracy within the total population: the nobility was the most prominent social group from which court dignitaries were recruited, after all. Thus, Fabian Persson posits, for example, that the small scale of the Swedish court can be clarified in part by the low population figures of that country. Sweden numbered about 1.2 million inhabitants around 1600, of which only 450 were (adult, male) nobles. Yet the household of the Vasas always numbered around 100 noble courtiers in the course of the seventeenth century. Consequently, the royal household there was pretty small in absolute numbers but, then again, relatively speaking, pretty important because the nobility was present in large numbers there.[46]

It is perhaps clear that an objective comparison between the different European princely courts is quite problematic. In absolute numbers the court at Brussels seems to have not quite been at the top of the European charts. It was noticeably smaller than the royal courts of Paris and Madrid, which were to be found at lonely heights. Nor did it attain, at first glance, the level of the courts of Vienna and London, although these two were clearly smaller than their French and Spanish counterparts. On the other hand, the archducal court was in terms of scope at least equal to – and in many cases even greater than – most Italian and German princely courts. Even so, the question can be posed as to what extent these generally arbitrary numbers can

[45] In principle, even this comparison is incorrect, for although the archdukes did indeed share a joint household, they each had their own *Cámara* with their own servants available to them.

[46] Persson, 'The Courts of the Vasas and Palatines,' 279. Lacking trustworthy data about the nobility in this time period, a comparable analysis for the Netherlands is not possible.

serve as a yardstick, and whether contemporaneous perception does not form a more important indicator for defining the 'weight' of the court. Thus, it is striking, for instance, that the court at Brussels – regardless of its actual proportions – was seen by contemporaneous commentators as conspicuously large. That is shown, among other things, in an observation by the already mentioned anonymous French spy, who was of the opinion that the court of Albert and Isabella 'yields to no other in the quality and the diversity and quantity of persons of several nations who reside there. (...) The state of their household is grand.'[47] Even Guido Bentivoglio, the papal nuncio, was surprised by the great number of offices in the archducal household.[48] These and similar commentaries suggest that the Brussels court gave the impression of being an extensive court, in any case. One possible clarification for this could be that the court was not seen so much in comparison to other European courts as it was considered *disproportionally* large in relation to the status of the archdukes.

In the early modern political world the importance attached to status and reputation translated not only into an almost obsessive sensitivity to diplomatic precedence but also into a hierarchy of European princely courts, according to clearly distinct gradations of rank and standing. Just as sovereign princes enjoyed precedence over non-sovereign princes, sovereign courts were considered to be more important than non-sovereign courts, which put behind them in their turn the courts of viceroys, governors, and regents. As seen in the previous chapter, sovereign courts during the Ancien Régime were expected to satisfy definite formal requirements. In that context John Adamson points out that the 'new' or up-and-coming courts of the late sixteenth and early seventeenth century made many efforts to fashion for themselves a radiance that was seen by contemporaries as *de rigueur* – as indispensable, thus, for any sovereign court that wanted to be taken seriously by other courts.[49] Not coincidentally, the extent of the princely household also played a significant role in that process.

Although the archduke arrived with a noticeable entourage in Brussels already in 1596 (in that context Juan Roco de Campofrío, the court chaplain, spoke of 'a household that in its luster scarcely [had to] feel inferior to that of a king'[50]), the actual exponential growth of the archducal household seems to have only started

[47] '*(...) ne cedde-elle à aucune autre de sa quallité et la diversité et quantité de personnes qui y résident de plusieurs nations. (...) L'estat de leur maison est grand.*' [Anonymous], *Relation de Flandres*, 4-5.

[48] Bentivoglio, G. *Relationi del Cardinal Bentivoglio*. Brussels, 1632. Op. cit. p. 159 [Original edition: Bentivoglio, G. *Relationi fatte dall' illustrissimo, e reverendissimo signor cardinal Bentivoglio in tempo delle sue nuntiature di Fiandra, e di Francia. Date in luce da Erycio Puteano*. Antwerp, 1629].

[49] Adamson, 'The Making of the Ancien-Régime Court,' 14.

[50] Roco de Campofrío, J. *España en Flandes. Trece años de gobierno del archiduque Alberto (1595-1608)*. Madrid, 1973. Op. cit. p. 8.

after his marriage to the infanta – and thus after the transfer of sovereignty over the Netherlands to the bridal couple. It need not come as a surprise that the consciously conceived revitalization of the Brussels court went hand in hand not only with architectural and ceremonial adjustments but also with an enlargement sensitive toward scale, which served to mirror the renewed status of the court. Judging from contemporaneous commentaries and from the criticism that these reforms brought about (cf. Chapter I), it could be posited, rather, that the court of Albert and Isabella not only met the expectations proposed by Adamson, but also even exceeded these. Without a doubt the political aspirations of the archdukes exercised influence on their decision to keep a court that could withstand with verve comparison to those of most other European princes. At the same time the growth of the archducal household offered the possibility of taking on more and more nobles into their entourage. Not coincidentally, the expansion of their retinue was characterized above all by the gradual rise of the number of noble *gentilhombres* and *damas* (cf. Chapter III). Thanks to the system of *service par terme* large number of courtiers could offer their services on rotation to the princely couple. This active recruitment policy offered significant advantages. From the standpoint of the archdukes, their household functioned as an instrument with which the Habsburg dynasty could tighten the bonds with the local and European aristocracy anew. In exchange the chosen nobles enjoyed privileged access to the patronage market at court, which furnished them interesting political and financial perspectives and provided them the possibility to compete actively for princely favor. Both these aspects will be further elucidated in the following chapters.

Financial organization of the archducal household

In terms of prestige and grandeur, keeping a large princely household undoubtedly brought many advantages along with it. Early modern princes seemed to have much less interest in the other side of the medallion: the fact that an extensive entourage also demanded an extensive budget. Just like the question about the scale of keeping the archducal *house*, the analysis of keeping the archducal *books* is also an extremely complex problem. Once again the question arises as to the demarcation of the 'court' and its 'household' as well as to the presupposed partitioning between 'household' and 'administration.' The fact that these areas did not have clearly distinct budgets at their disposal already demonstrates in and of itself that the interweaving of both spheres was much greater than has been generally assumed. On top of that, the scarce and diffuse source material does not allow for disentangling this financial knot in a clear way. After all, the bookkeeping was not only a matter of balancing 'measurable' revenues and expenditures. 'The cost of maintaining the royal households and administration,' Mia Rodríguez-Salgado writes, in that context, 'is hard to estimate, not only because the documentation is disparate and dispersed, but also because remuneration was never solely a matter of a cash stipend.'[51] Many servants indeed received not only a salary but also material compensation in the form of food and drink, firewood, candles, liveries, and so forth. In addition, there was an extended (albeit primitive) pension system for former employees as well as widows and families of deceased staff members. On top of that, all manner of exceptional stipends and so-called *ayudas de costa* were handed out to courtiers and servants for their meritorious service in one way or another to the princes.

This chapter does not intend to dismember the financial situation of the archdukes down to the bone. That kind of approach presupposes especially time- and work-intensive research, which is neither necessary nor attainable within the dimensions of this study. What follows will indeed go more deeply into the *libros de razón*, in which expenditures were written down that actually tell something more about the functioning of the archducal household. For a number of reasons the analysis offered here remains of necessity tentative in nature. Thus, the accounting ledgers make no mention, for example, of the costs incurred by the repeated reconstruction of the Coudenberg palace, to mention but one example.[52] In general, however, studying the *libros de razón* suffices for getting a clear picture of the financial burden that accompanied the workings of the archducal household, and that is of great importance to this chapter. A closer look at the accounting ledgers makes it clear that Antonio de Rovelasca, Albert's treasurer, annually spent enormous amounts to have the archducal household function as was appropriate. In general the accounts contain information concerning three different expenditure lines. A significant part of the budget was allotted for payment toward remuneration of the courtiers and servants. Furthermore, the different heads of the household divisions were awarded monthly a specific amount with which they could cover the costs of the workings of their departments. Finally the *libros de razón* also contain – albeit to a lesser degree – data concerning extraordinary expenditures, among them the excessive sums spent on forms of conspicuous consumption. In what follows, these three categories are looked at more closely.

---

51 Rodríguez-Salgado, M.J. 'Honour and Profit in the Court of Philip II of Spain,' in: Aymard & Romani, *La cour comme institution économique*, pp. 67-86. Op. cit. p. 78.

52 Even so, information about this can be found by means of the inventory of the 'Hofwerken.' See De Bock-Doehaerd, R. *Inventaire des 'Ouvrages de la Cour'. Exemplaire annoté.* Algemeen Rijksarchief, Toegangen in Beperkte Oplage 95. Brussels, 1991.

Remuneration

The system of remuneration in effect at the archducal court is an intriguing phenomenon. While it was, on the one hand, characterized by the typical limitations issuing from the notorious financial instability of the early modern state (such as the irregularity of payments and the lack of transparency), on the other hand it exhibited a few characteristics that can be seen as strikingly 'modern.' So, for example, there is talk of a system of social security *avant la lettre* in the form of pensions and 'abbey bread' for sick and older employees, but also of the payment of lump-sum compensations for expenses, new year's bonuses, premiums, and so forth. All the same, this tense relationship to modernity must not be interpreted so much as an indication of increasing professionalization as rather a consequence of the traditional point of view that the prince was responsible for the well-being of his *familia* in the broadest sense of the word. The financial and material remuneration of the courtiers and servants constituted, then, one of the most important expenditure lines within the archducal household. The wages were calculated on the basis of fixed pay scales, and employees were compensated on the basis of the number of days worked. More than likely payment of these remunerations took place every trimester in open session in the *Aula Magna* of the palace, in the presence of the *contralor* who observed the proceedings very precisely.[53] The table on the following page demonstrates that Antonio de Rovelasca distributed nearly fl. 200,000 total per year in salaries, of which around fl. 150,000 went to the members of the *Casa*, the *Cámara* and the *Caballeriza*; around fl. 14,500 to the members of the *Capella Maior*; and around fl. 28,000 to the *Hartschiere* and the halberdiers (cf. Table 3).[54]

[53] It happened like this at least in the case of the palace guard: '*El pagam[ien]to destos gremios se hazia de la caxa del Principe y ara publicam[en]te en el salón de Palacio, con asistencia del controlar.*' ARA, *Handschriftenverzameling* 821, ff. 148-149.

[54] A list of equivalents for the different types of currency can be found at the beginning of this book.

Table 3 – Amounts spent on the payment of members of the archducal household, 1612-1618 (in fl.)

		Casa, Cámara* and *Caballeriza	***Capella Maior***	**Palace Guard**	**TOTAL**
	1st trimester	46,280	4,632	9,307	60,219
1612	2nd trimester	/	4,663	9,358	?
	3rd trimester	/	4,547	9,127	?
	Total	**?**	**13,842**	**27,792**	**?**
	1st trimester	49,505	4,697	8,988	63,190
1613	2nd trimester	51,663	4,961	9,451	66,075
	3rd trimester	50,812	5,038	9,368	65,218
	Total	**151,980**	**14,696**	**27,807**	**194,483**
	1st trimester	49,710	5,026	9,409	64,145
1614	2nd trimester	48,350	5,121	9,360	62,831
	3rd trimester	43,745	4,825	9,385	57,955
	Total	**141,805**	**14,972**	**28,154**	**184,931**
	1st trimester	/	4,555	9,357	?
1615	2nd trimester	48,019	4,829	9,369	62,217
	3rd trimester	49,259	4,886	9,271	63,416
	Total	**?**	**14,270**	**27,997**	**?**
	1st trimester	52,968	4,721	9,369	67,058
1616	2nd trimester	50,452	4,760	9,318	64,530
	3rd trimester	49,975	4,844	9,326	64,145
	Total	**153,395**	**14,325**	**28,013**	**195,733**
	1st trimester	53,653	4,862	9,375	67,890
1617	2nd trimester	50,283	4,942	9,385	64,610
	3rd trimester	50,726	4,878	9,407	65,011
	Total	**154,662**	**14,685**	**28,167**	**197,511**
	1st trimester	55,782	4,737	9,448	69,967
1618	2nd trimester	/	4,774	9,460	?
	3rd trimester	/	/	/	?
	Total	**?**	**?**	**?**	**?**

Sources: ARA, *RK* 1837 and 1838. The amounts were rounded off to whole numbers. A slash designates that the *libros de razón* contain no data or only partial data about the pay in the trimester concerned.

Parallel to the slight increase in the number of paid employees between 1612 and 1618 (cf. Table 2), the total amount spent on salaries also rose. The remarkable decline in 1614 can be blamed on the fact that during the third trimester many *gentilhombres* went on military campaigns occasioned by the conflict around the succession crisis in the duchies of Jülich and Cleves.[55] They were to be found only temporarily at court, or not at all, and therefore did not receive full pay. That seems to indicate that the archducal household was cheaper in times of war than in times of peace – an assessment that would benefit more, however, from a comparison between the time periods before and after the announcement of the Twelve Years' Truce in 1609. With the lack of sources, the latter is not possible, all the same. In any case, it would only be a question here of robbing Peter to pay Paul, for the amount saved in the archducal household was naturally recouped from the army budget.

It is also striking that the pay scales employed were not adjusted for financial inflation and possible market fluctuations: throughout the time period studied remunerations remained stable. Consequently, modifications in the salary awarded seldom occurred, unless there was talk of an internal promotion, which generally brought a significant raise in pay along with it. The differences between the individual wages were indeed great. Depending on the rank and function of a staff member, his or her salary could be up to several thousand guilders higher per year than that of less fortunate employees. This discrepancy is clearly expressed when looking at the wage scale that was employed in the archducal household (cf. Appendix 1 in the back of this book). While the lowest pay of all amounted to only a paltry 9,000 *maravedis* (approx. fl. 66) per year, on the other end of the spectrum employees annually earned up to 1 million *maravedis* (approx. fl. 7,353). Even so, a closer look teaches that between both these extremes great variety occurred in pay scales, mirroring the hierarchical structure of the archducal household. Thus it is clear, for example, that the lower staff members – the employees who were responsible for the day-to-day workings of the household – received a rather modest wage between around fl. 66 and around fl. 500 per year. Only the higher dignitaries, such as the *caballerizos*, the *gentilhombres*, and the *mayordomos*, earned more than fl. 500 annually. This artificial fault-line logically also coincided more or less with the distinction between the noble and non-noble members of the archducal household. On both sides of the pay scale, however, a further differentiation is found, which emphasizes the strict hierarchy between the different staff members.

On the basis of the table in Appendix 1, it can be roughly posited that the 'lowest' servants in the archducal household all earned between 10,000 and 30,000

[55] Concerning the succession crisis in Jülich and Cleves, see Anderson, A.D. *On the Verge of War: International Relations and the Jülich-Kleve Succession Crises (1609–1614)*. Boston, 1999.

maravedis (approx. fl. 74 - approx. fl. 221) per year. That was true for the servant boy of the halberdiers, among others; for the footmen; for the *mozos* and *ayudas* of the *Guardaropa*; and for the kitchen boys.[56] In this category are further found a number of members of the *Capella Maior*, such as the choirboys, the attendant of the organ bellows, and a few musicians.[57] The halberdiers, too – the lowest in rank in the palace guard – earned only fl. 180 per year. Surprisingly enough, the lowest remuneration of all was set aside for the noble *meninos* of the archduke, who received around fl. 66 per year. They enjoyed room and board at court, however, and their 'salary' must therefore be seen rather as a form of allowance. Striking, too, is the presence in this group of the majority of the ladies-in-waiting to the infanta, such as the *mozas* and *dueñas de Retrete* and the *mozas* and *damas de la Cámara*.[58] With few exceptions, most women in the archducal court were thus faced with a proverbial 'glass ceiling.' In the case of the ladies-in-waiting, the reason for their low salary is found close-at-hand: they were young, unmarried women who did not necessarily need to have an income at their disposal. On top of that Albert and Isabella had the habit of giving their ladies-in-waiting – who as a rule were expected to leave the archducal household after their wedding – a dowry of 1 million *maravedís*, plus another mrs. 327,000 extra for a bridal gown.[59] Converted into guilders, that came to a sum of fl. 9,757, approximately ten times the annual remuneration for a *gentilhombre de la Cámara*.

Further on in the list comes the archducal household's 'middle management': the accomplished employees who earned between 30,000 and 50,000 *maravedis* per year (approx. 221 fl. - approx. 368 fl.). To this category belonged, among others, the *mozos* and *ayudas* of the various departments of the *Casa*, such as those in the *Panadería*, the *Tapicería*, the *Cerería*, the *Furriera*, the *Cava*, the *Saltería*, the *Acemilería*, and so forth. Most *mozos* earned approximately fl. 235 per year. The more experienced *ayudas* were to be found somewhat higher up the hierarchical ladder and received annually around fl. 309. The assistant cooks and the concierges for the antechambers also earned the same amount. In addition, in this group come the *Hartschiere*, the *escuderos de a pie*, the *ayudas de Cámara*, and the chaplains of the altar.[60]

[56] The servant boy of the halberdiers earned around fl. 120 fl. per year, the footmen around fl. 149, the *mozos* and *ayudas* of the *Guardaropa* around fl. 154 and around fl. 199, respectively, and the kitchen boys around fl. 221.

[57] The choirboys earned around fl. 109 per year; the attendant of the organ bellows around fl. 91.

[58] The *mozas* and *dueñas de Retrete* earned around fl. 73 and around fl. 147, respectively, per year. The *mozas* and *damas de la Cámara* earned around fl. 110 and around fl. 199, respectively.

[59] See e.g. ARA, *RK* 1837, f. 152: Payment of fl. 9,757 to the count of Willerval in honor of his marriage to Maria Zapata, a lady-in-waiting to the infanta.

[60] The *Hartschiere* earned fl. 225 per year, the *escuderos de a pie* around fl. 235, the *ayudas de Cámara* around fl. 268 fl., and the chaplains of the altar around fl. 273.

A third category comprises the remunerations of various department heads and managerial functionaries, who generally earned between 50,000 and 70,000 *maravedis* per year (approx. 368 fl. - approx. 515 fl.). Here, among others, are the *sumiller de la Cava*, the *sumiller de la Panadería*, the *acemilero mayor*, the *tapicero mayor*, the *boticario*, the *cochero mayor*, the *cosinero mayor*, the *salsier*, the *guardamanger*, the *comprador*, the *ujieres de vianda*, and the *varlets servants*.[61] The *reposteros de camas* belonged to this group, too, just as the *mayordomos* of the different *Estados*.[62] Finally, the surgeon, the *medicos de la Casa*, the *ayo* or schoolmaster of the pages, the *lavandera de la ropa de la infanta*, and the *escribano de la Cámara* also come in here.[63]

As said before, truly top pay in the archducal household was set aside for only the highest dignitaries. To them belonged, among others, the *guardadamas*, the chaplains of the oratory, the *aposentador mayor*, and the *guardaropa y joyas*.[64] Furthermore, here also come the archduke's personal physicians, and – somewhat surprisingly – the washerwoman who was responsible for Albert's clothing.[65] Both of the archdukes' father confessors as well as Albert's personal secretary earned substantial remunerations, just as the *gentilhombres*, the *caballerizos*, the *mayordomos*, and the *capellán y limosnero mayor*.[66] Not coincidentally, the highest sums of all were set aside for the courtiers who were responsible for the personal security of the archdukes: the captains of the palace guard and both of their lieutenants.[67] It is also a surprise to determine that both the *dueñas de honor* of the infanta each earned around fl. 2,206 fl. Equally striking is the fact that Isabella's *camarera mayor*, the elderly Jeanne de Chassincourt, earned the highest pay within the archducal household with her 1 million *maravedis* (approx. 7.353 fl.) per year. With that she exceeded even Rodrigo Niño y Lasso, the count of Añover, who received a combined salary of around fl. 5,514 per year as *mayordomo mayor*, *sumiller de corps*, and *caballerizo mayor*.

[61] They all earned around fl. 441 per year.

[62] The *reposteros de camas* each earned around fl. 419 per year; the *mayordomos de los Estados* each around fl. 441.

[63] The surgeon earned around fl. 368 per year, the *medicos de la Casa* around fl. 414, the *ayo* around fl. 441, the *lavandera de la ropa de la infanta* around fl. 404, and the *escribano de la Cámara* around fl. 441.

[64] The *guardadamas* earned around 538 fl. per year, the chaplains of the oratory each around fl. 551, and the *aposentador mayor* around fl. 827. Juan de Elordi y Silva, the *guardaropa y joyas* of the infanta, earned around fl. 1,103 per year, and his colleague Joachim Denzenhear, the *guardaropa y joyas* of Albert, received around fl. 1.371.

[65] Francisco de Paz and Henri Mastelein each earned around fl. 827 per year; Andreas Trevisius received fl. 1,379, and the washerwoman got fl. 772 per year.

[66] Andrés de Soto, the father confessor of the infanta, earned fl. 750 per year. His colleague Iñigo de Brizuela, Albert's father confessor, got around fl. 1,379, just like Antonio Suárez de Arguello, Albert's secretary. The *gentilhombres de la Casa* each received around fl. 551, the *caballerizos* and *gentilhombres de la Boca* each around fl. 689, the *gentilhombres de la Cámara* each around fl. 965, the *mayordomos* each around fl. 1,379, and the *capellán y limosnero mayor* also around fl. 1,379.

[67] Both captains of the personal guard each earned around fl. 2,206 per year; their lieutenants each received fl. 1,500.

Discussion

That great differences existed among the individual wages of the courtiers and servants cannot be any surprise. The pay scale mirrored the diversity of the archducal entourage, which in essence consisted of a motley company in which pretty much all social ranks and standings were represented. In and of itself an internal comparison of the salaries therefore offers little added value. It is much more interesting to research whether the pay handed out in the archducal household was financially more attractive than that which was current elsewhere in the labor market. Put another way: what can be told about the courtiers' and servants' real income and the buying power issuing from it? Or, too: did the salary offered possibly form a stimulus for striving after a position in the archducal household?

If only the individual wage is taken into account, it can be roughly posited that the income of the lower servants of this household was in this time period comparable to that of unskilled laborers in the construction sector. For Brussels few data exist concerning this, but in Antwerp a bricklayer's helper earned about 12 stuivers per day around 1610.[68] Presupposing that bricklayers worked only 250 days per year on average, their pay on a yearly basis amounted to approximately fl. 150. The daily pay for the lowest servants in the archducal household generally was only between 6 and 12 stuivers, but in view of the fact that they were usually busy at work 365 days a year, their annual pay was indeed dozens of guilders higher than that of the bricklayer's helpers. In the case of 'middle management' in the archducal household, it perhaps makes more sense to broach the comparison from the pay of skilled laborers and master artisans. Around 1610 a typesetter in the famous printing-house of Plantin received an average weekly pay of 92 stuivers (or approx. fl. 239 per year),[69] while a master mason in Antwerp got 22 to 24 stuivers per day (which comes to an average yearly pay of fl. 275 to fl. 300).[70] These amounts are more or less comparable to the yearly pay of most *mozos* and *ayudas*, respectively, in the archducal household. The individual wages for the division heads of the different court departments, then again, were higher than the salary of a master mason. Instead, their pay probably has to be compared to that of a printer for Plantin, like Peeter Van Standonck, whose yearly pay in 1615 amounted to around fl. 480 (or on average 184 ½ stuivers per week, at a rate of 52 weeks per year) – although it needs to be noted that not all printers earned the same pay.[71]

---

[68] Verlinden, C. et al. *Dokumenten voor de geschiedenis van prijzen en lonen in Vlaanderen en Brabant. Deel II (14de-19de eeuw).* Bruges, 1965. Op. cit. p. 1022.

[69] *Ibidem*, p. 1228.

[70] *Ibidem*, p. 1020.

[71] *Ibidem*, p. 1138.

All in all, the remuneration of servants in the archducal household was thus rather modest in nature and certainly not higher than the wages that were current in the traditional labor market. For noble court dignitaries a position at court was in financial respects even less attractive still. In relation to their social status and lifestyle, the *gentilhombres de la Casa*, *Boca*, and *Cámara* – to which the majority of the male nobility belonged – earned distressingly little at around fl. 551, fl. 689, and fl. 965 per year, respectively.[72] For the courtiers from the high nobility, who generally had at their disposal expansive country estates and domains and, consequently, collected substantial domanial rents, the remuneration did not amount to more than a fraction of their total income. In their case, consequently, the wage represented little more than symbolic compensation for proven services.

The remunerations policy at the archducal court differed little from those at other European courts. In general the individual wages of court personnel in early modern Europe were – to cite Jeroen Duindam – 'depressingly low, increasingly so as they were only rarely adjusted for inflation.'[73] On top of that, as the author adds, the courtiers and servants were frequently paid late. At most courts late payment of wages was indeed an enormous problem, and at the archducal court it was no different. Its household's *libros de razón* are roiling with calculations for delinquent pay, which in many cases were not disbursed until months or even years afterwards. In the meantime many staff members were obliged to go deep into debt. On top of that, they often had to advance the expenses they incurred for their work themselves. Countless employees of the archducal household claimed, then, to find themselves in '*muy grande necesidad y pobreza*' and did not neglect to ask the archdukes for financial support.[74]

The circumstances sketched here suggest that the salary was seldom the only, let alone the most prominent stimulus for aspiring to a position in the archducal household. Yet, as mentioned earlier, not only individual pay can be taken into account in the analysis of the remuneration of household members. 'The regular wages for service at court were moderate at best,' as Duindam posits. Yet, as he adds, 'it is clear that ordinary wages did not constitute the prime reason for service at court (...).'[75] Most courtiers and servants could, after all, supplement or compensate their modest pay with all manner of extra reimbursements, honoraria in kind, and lucrative financial advantages. Even at the court in Brussels, this was the case. So, for example,

[72] Concerning the financial and economic situation of the nobility in the Southern Netherlands during the Ancien Régime, see Degryse, K. & Janssens, P. 'Le rôle économique de l'aristocratie belge aux XVIIe et XVIIIe siècles,' in: Núñez, C.E., ed. *Aristocracy, Patrimonial Management Strategies and Economic Development, 1450-1800*. Sevilla, 1998, pp. 43-53.

[73] Duindam, *Vienna and Versailles*, 306.

[74] RAH, *SyC* A-61, passim.

[75] Duindam, *Vienna and Versailles*, 110-111.

in addition to their official salary some employees got supplemental financial bonuses, like Christmas and New Year's premiums every year.[76] Then again, others received so-called *gajes extraordinarios* – an 'exceptional' wage that was distributed nevertheless every trimester. In certain cases, this exceptional wage made the real difference in the individual salaries. Thus, as father confessor, Iñigo de Brizuela officially earned around fl. 1,379 per year, with the understanding that he got another fl. 1,000 worth '*de gajes extraordinarios*' every trimester. The same was true for Francisco de Paz as personal physician (fl. 827), whose official pay was much lower than that of his colleague Andreas Trevisius (approx. fl. 1,379), but who earned much more in total than the latter with his exceptional wage of fl. 2,757. In addition to *gajes extraordinarios* some members of the archducal household could also call on a so-called *ayuda de costa ordinaria* – a kind of lump-sum compensation for expenses. This clarifies, for example, the remarkable fact that both of the *mozos de Capilla* earned at first sight the same annual pay (approx. 255 fl.) as their direct superior, the *maestro de Capilla* Gery de Ghersem. The chapel master, though, also received a fixed compensation for expenses of fl. 250 per year, whereby his real income was almost twice as high as that of both his assistants.

Ayudas de costa, moreover, could be *extraordinaria* too: in that case they were distributed on the occasion of certain accomplishments or on the basis of need (be it once only or recurring). The *libros de razón* are full of these kinds of exceptional compensations for expenses. Some employees received one of them as '*merced en consideración de sus servicios*,' that is, out of gratitude for their carrying out certain assignments, missions, or labors in the service of the archdukes. Others got an *ayuda de costa* for sending their sons to study or their children to monasteries; as a bit of support to purchase certain things, to pay off debts, or to reimburse travel costs; or simply because they were poor and in need of help. In certain cases this kind of compensation could acquire a permanent nature in the form of a pension or an *entretenimiento*. In that way sick or elderly staff members received the financial assistance necessary, and even widows of deceased employees were secure in their old age. Still other (former) employees could call on an alternative system of social security in the form of so-called 'abbey bread,' whereby certain abbeys and monasteries in the Southern Netherlands were obligated to distribute a part of their revenues among members of the archducal household or their family members (whether needy or not). As charged by the archduke, for example, the abbey of Saint Bertin in Saint-Omer doled out fl. 1,000 to five persons annually, among them the court chaplain

[76] In December, 1615, fl. 67 were distributed among the pages of Archduke Albert, as a Christmas gift. At the beginning of the new year, the members of the *Capella Maior* and the palace guard each received one month's pay extra.

Jehan Vilanus (fl. 250); the *ayuda de la Guardaropa* Louis Coudenhoven (fl. 200 fl.); a son of the *ayuda de Furriera* Pedro Viera (fl. 150); a son of the *acemilero mayor* Francisco Enriquez de Caneda (fl. 250); and Claude Rossel, a servant of the *camarera mayor* Jeanne de Chassincourt (fl. 150).[77]

In addition to financial compensations, there were all manner of honoraria in kind on top of that, which made a position in the archducal household worth the effort. On top of their pay most employees received a *ración* [ration] every day, intended to provide them with the requisite victuals. This tradition was adopted from the Spanish court, where a *ración ordinaria* traditionally consisted of two pounds of bread, a pound of mutton, a pound of beef, and a few other goods such as wine, firewood, and candles. The products mentioned were apparently purchased directly by the *comprador* for the court, at the value of two *reales* or fl. 0.50 per day and per person. In the Southern Netherlands this sum was sometimes increased to three *reales* or fl. 0.75 per day.[78] Still, there appear to have been differences among the rations. Thus, Beatrijs Omben, the *lavandera de la Ropa del Estado de los Ayudas y Pajes*, maintained around 1598, for instance, to have the right only to one *ración* at the value of one *real* per day, which according to her did not suffice to provide her with her daily needs. After that it was decided to increase her ration to two *reales* per day.[79] On the other hand, the count of Añover as *sumiller de corps* received annually around fl. 551 '*de la cera* [(bees)wax] *y demas provechos que los sumillers de corps suelen llevar (...) a la cassa de Borgoña a razon de 200 ducados al año.*'[80] Evidently the count thus received a monetary amount of 200 ducats per year for the purchase of goods to which he had a right in accordance with Spanish-Burgundian tradition.

For most courtiers and servants the *raciones* proved to be a nice supplement to their official salary. Generally, however, these honoraria were not noted in the accounting ledgers. Consequently, how many members of the archducal household got a *ración* is not known, and it is especially difficult to define its total financial cost. The *libros de razón* lift up the corner of the veil only very sporadically. So, for example, in March, 1616, the *comprador* of the court received an amount of fl. 4,371 '*para las raciones de los criados.*'[81] A month later he got fl. 5,294 for the same reason.[82] Assuming that the financial value of a ration did indeed amount to fl. 0.75 per day on average, this seems

---

77 See ARA, *Aud* 1413/1: *Documents relatifs aux pensions ecclésiastiques et pains d'abbaye (de 1598 à 1615).*

78 RAH, *SyC* A-61, f. 20: '*Cerca de las raciones que pretenden los criados de la casa se a bisto y hecho tanteo de lo que es una racion en España que es: dos libras de pan, una de carnero otra de vaca y otros adecentes que alla vale los dos reales que al presente se les da por dia y reduzida a la de estos payses montara tres reales que es lo que se les podra dar por una racion.*'

79 RAH, *SyC* A-61, f. 48.

80 ARA, *RK* 1837, f. 39r-39v.

81 ARA, *RK* 1838, f. 122v.

82 ARA, *RK* 1838, f. 139v.

to indicate that the number of those entitled to a ration in this time period fluctuated between 188 and 227 – somewhat more than half of the total number of members of the archducal household (excluding the *Capella Maior* and the palace guard).

Presupposing that a member of this household had the right to a *ración* on top of his or her pay (and assuming that this amount did indeed suffice for buying two pounds of bread and two pounds of meat per day), it can be assumed that most employees had sufficient means at their disposal to feed themselves and their families. Yet a position at court brought other advantages along with it too. In the first place all courtiers and servants of the archducal household enjoyed special legal status, which provided them with more legal security than normal citizens. In both criminal as well as civil matters they were subject to the jurisdiction of the court tribunal, which as a rule was presided over by *mayordomo mayor*, the *sumiller de corps*, or the *caballerizo mayor*, as well as the members of the *Bureo*.[83] On top of that they also enjoyed a few exceptional privileges. So, for instance, the members of the archducal household were exempted from paying taxes in Brussels (such as the levies on beer and wine), which surely provided them with financial advantages.[84] Furthermore, the court itself took on the responsibility for the physical well-being of the employees: 'His Alteza,' wrote the English nobleman Charles Somerset in his travel journal, 'doth also here allowe to all those that serve him both unto them and their whole families all things that be necessarie for them in their sicknesse, and for that purpose hath his Phisitians and Apothecaries to assist in the like exigents.'[85] Finally, the courtiers and servants did not have it bad in terms of housing. The previous chapter already touched upon how the employees of the archducal household were obligated to buy or rent their residence in Brussels at a price calculated by the *aposentadores* or quartermasters of the court. It seems that a few of the more prosperous servants chose the first option and in their turn turned that investment into money by renting their purchased premises to others. Thus, Miguel de Pianca, head of the *Salsería*, was the owner of a house in the center of town, which he rented for fl. 150 per year to Captain Diego de Texeda as well as to Geronima de Lizana, the widow of a former *gentilhombre de la Casa* of the archduke.[86] Lorenzo Vallon, one of the kitchen servants, did the same thing and

[83] See ARA, *Aud* 33/1-2, no. 21, doc. 52. See also Vanhemelryck, F. 'Hofrechtbanken (15de eeuw-1794),' in: Aerts, E., Baelde, M., Coppens, H. et al., eds. *De centrale overheidsinstellingen van de Habsburgse Nederlanden (1482-1795)*. 2 vols. Brussels, 1994. Op. cit. vol. I, pp. 180-187.

[84] '*Item qu'un Domesticque sera francq de touttes les impositions de vin et bière, assisses, maltotes, ou tel autre sorte de taelle, que les non francqz sont obligez de payer.*' ARA, *Aud* 33/1-2, no. 21, doc. 53: *Privilèges des Domesticques de Son Alteze, lesquels sont comme sensuit, se rapporte au livre des escrois, que les Courtisans, Conseil d'Estat, Privé, Finances son ambulatifz (1613).*

[85] Brennan, M.G., ed. *The Travel Diary (1611-1612) of an English Catholic Sir Charles Somerset, edited from the manuscript in the Brotherton Collection University of Leeds*. Leeds, 1993, p. 302.

[86] ARA, *Hofrechtbank*, trial dossier no. 179.

received fl. 110 annually for the rent of one (or a few) room(s) to Antoine Payen, a dwarf who belonged to the archducal household.[87] Although scarcely any sources exist concerning this practice, the question can be posed all the same as to what extent the price determined by the quartermasters approximated the real market value of these premises. That this was perhaps not always the case is shown from the legal proceedings that were initiated by the said Captain Texeda and the widow Lizana against the landlord Miguel de Pianca before the court tribunal in 1615. After a few vitally necessary repairs the latter had raised the rental price from fl. 150 to fl. 175 per year – an amount that his renters could not pay. Pianca claimed that the new price was realistic, however, and that for years he had rented the premises under the market rate because the *aposentador mayor* Manuel de Arinzano had requested he do this, as charged by the count of Añover. Supposedly Albert's *mayordomo mayor* had made this decision as a concession to the ill and needy widow Lizana, who had to make do with a meager pension after the death of her spouse.[88]

The preceding has shown that the average pay of courtiers and servants perhaps constituted no direct stimulus for aspiring to a position in the archducal court but that the many privileges, honoraria, and financial extras made these kinds of jobs nevertheless worth the effort. In the case of the more highly placed court dignitaries, the most prominent motivation for striving after a court office, though, has to be sought in an entirely different domain. In her essay *Honour and Profit in the Court of Philip II of Spain*, Mia Rodríguez-Salgado convincingly argues that 'household office was valued more in terms of honour and influence than money.'[89] With that she straightforwardly exposes the real motivation of the courtiers. The prestige and the influence that a position in the archducal household brought along with it were more important than the paltry pay that was connected to it. On top of that, by the capacity of their office courtiers had direct access to the princes, which provided a possibly crucial advantage in the rat race for power and wealth. These aspects of life at court will come up for discussion in the following chapters.

Departmental budgets

That the ordinary pay of court personnel was in general rather modest in nature also becomes clear when considering the pattern of expenditures for the archducal household. The share of wages in these expenditures is significantly smaller than the budgets that were necessary to ensure the day-to-day functioning of the household. In principle the various department heads received an amount every month, with which

[87] ARA, *RK* 1837, f. 324v.
[88] ARA, *Hofrechtbank*, trial dossier no. 179.
[89] Rodríguez-Salgado, 'Honour and Profit,' 77.

the fixed operating costs of their respective departments could be facilitated, such as those for the purchase of bread, meat, fish, fruit, wine, beer, firewood, candles, spices, and so forth. The maintenance of the many pieces of furniture, wall tapestries, and decorative objects cost fistfuls of money as well; the care for the horses and mules was also a line of expenditure not to be underestimated. On top of that, the costs rose to the extent the archducal household grew. In 1596, the *mayordomo mayor* Francisco de Mendoza calculated that the various *oficios* of the household still needed around fl. 10,625 every month to cover their operating costs:

> *'Conforme al gasto que de presente ay en la casa de V[uestra] A[lteza] y a los cavalleros y otras personas que comen en los Estados, sera necessario librar para el ordinario a los oficios cada mes de siguiente: Al comprador 33.000 reales [= fl. 8,250]; a la paneteria 1.000 reales [= fl. 250]; a la fruteria 1.400 reales [= fl. 350]; a la salseria 300 reales [= fl. 75]; a la potageria 800 reales [= fl. 200]; a la cava 1500 reales [= fl. 375]; al pastelero 1.200 reales [= fl. 300]; a la furriera 300 reales [= fl. 75]; a la cereria 3.000 reales [= fl. 750]. Monta todo a 42.500 reales [= fl. 10,625].'*[90]

As the following table can show, some – albeit not all – of these amounts had risen perceptibly twenty years later (cf. Table 4). The table offers an overview of the budgets employed in 1616, as reflected in the *libros de razón*. Whereas in 1596 the *comprador* still spent around fl. 8,260 every month, in 1616 that was on average fl. 12,697 per month. The same is true for the *Panadería*, where the expenses rose from fl. 250 per month in 1596 to on average fl. 1,868 per month in 1616, as well as for the *Cerería*, where they rose from fl. 750 to on average fl. 1,400 per month. The table shows as well that all *oficios* of the archducal household together spent on average fl. 25,000 per month, good for a total of around fl. 300,000 for the entire year – or around fl. 100,000 more than what was disbursed in salaries in 1616 (cf. Table 3).[91]

Of the various departments of the archducal household, only the *Pastelería*, the *Bótica*, and both of the *Guardaropas* always received the same amount per month – the remaining amounts varied according to the expenses incurred. The largest budget was allotted for the *comprador* Pasqual Navarro and his successor Lucas Hernández, who spent between fl. 9,000 and fl. 15,000 on victuals every month, of

[90] RAH, *SyC* A-61, ff. 1-6: *Lo que se me offrece que advertir a V.A. cerca del Estado en que quedan las cosas de su casa es lo siguiente* (around 1596).

[91] All the same, that the *oficios* spent on average fl. 25,000 in 1616, does not mean to say that the costs per month were more than doubled with respect to 1596. Note that in 1596, the expenditures of the *Caballeriza* and the *Acemilería* are not included, while on the other hand certain *oficios* are taken into account that no longer occur in 1616 (such as the *Potagería* and the *Frutería*). Perhaps these departments were combined with other *oficios* after 1596, whereby a comparison of the monthly expenses between them is difficult to carry out.

Table 4 – Monthly expenditures of the *oficios* of the archducal household in 1616, on the basis of the *libros de razón* (in fl.).

	Guardaropa del Archiduque	*Guardaropa de la Infanta*	*Furier y Aposentador de Palacio*	*Tapicería*	*Panadería*	*Cava*	*Cerería*	*Salsería*	*Comprador*	*Pastelería*	*Caballeriza*	*Acemilería*	*Bótica*	Total
Jan	250	250	249	10	1,295	1,226	1,605	51	12,502	142	3,044	2,785	500	**23,909**
Feb	250	250	392	425	1,568	1,130	2,096	83	9,943	142	4,199	2,532	500	**23,510**
Mar	250	250	367	13	2,162	1,154	2,289	83	10,001	142	3,802	2,878	500	**23,891**
Apr	250	250	776	13	1,248	1,255	824	82	13,063	142	4,278	2,660	500	**25,341**
May	250	250	316	142	1,776	1,465	1,234	82	13,621	142	3,435	3,579	500	**26,792**
June	250	250	276	134	1,623	1,541	1,055	73	14,356	142	3,801	2,899	500	**26,900**
July	250	250	492	77	1,641	1,470	1,639	82	13,781	142	3,491	3,103	500	**26,918**
Aug	250	250	359	15	1,284	1,396	1,125	100	12,371	142	3,772	2,462	500	**24,026**
Sept	250	250	422	112	1,843	1,230	1,083	70	13,614	142	3,030	2,962	500	**25,508**
Oct	250	250	483	46	1,908	1,297	1,129	73	14,423	142	4,115	2,704	500	**27,320**
Nov	250	250	373	9	1,813	1,234	1,252	79	13,171	142	3,211	2,790	500	**25,074**
Dec	250	250	452	8	1,854	1,146	1,480	49	11,517	142	3,596	2,633	500	**23,877**
Total	**3,000**	**3,000**	**4,957**	**1,004**	**20,015**	**15,544**	**16,811**	**907**	**152,363**	**1,704**	**43,774**	**33,987**	**6,000**	**303,066**

Sources: ARA, *RK* 1838, ff. 110r-111r (January); ff. 115r-116r (February); ff. 122r-122v (March); ff. 139r-140r (April); ff. 146r-147r (May); ff. 147v-149r (June); ff. 161v-162r (July); ff. 175v-176v (August); ff. 192r-193r (September); ff. 195r-196r (October); ff. 203r-204r (November); ff. 215v-216v (December). All amounts are rounded off to whole numbers.

which approximately one third was allotted for the *raciones* of the court personnel. Other money-devouring departments were the *Caballeriza* and the *Acemilería*, where the many horses and mules were fed, cared for, and trained, and where the coaches and wagons were maintained. In the *Panadería*, Pedro de Aguilera spent on average somewhat more than fl. 1,800 per month on bread, salads, sugar, fruit, and preserves; while in the *Cava*, Francisco Rodríguez Agraz spent approximately fl. 1,300 per month on wine and beer. In the *Cerería* white and yellow wax was bought at a value of around fl. 1,400 for the production of candles every month. The notable raises at the beginning of the year can be blamed on the Feast of the Purification of the Virgin on February 2, and on the celebration of the Holy Week in March. Other noticeable fluctuations are more difficult to clarify. Thus it is unclear, for instance, why the budgets of the *Tapicería* are scarcely worth mentioning here one time, then amount to a few hundred guilders the next – perhaps this had to do with specific purchases, maintenance rounds, or repairs.

Although expenses in some departments seem to spiral out of control, it is surely not the case that money was being thrown out the window. Attempts to save were indeed made, albeit without much success. In 1596, for instance, Francisco de Mendoza advised the archduke to diminish the number of horses and mules in the *Caballeriza* and the *Acemilería* to fifty or less, in order to keep down costs that way. He advised as well to reduce the number of *entretenidos* (i.e. the courtiers and servants who enjoyed no permanent appointment in the archducal household) to 25 to 30, whereby a third of the costs connected to them could be recouped.[92] In spite of these and other measures the expenditures remained astronomically high, certainly if it is assumed that the data discussed here only show the fixed expenses and, consequently, say nothing about the many exceptional expenditures. In 1611, for example, more than fl. 40,000 was spent on mourning dress for courtiers and servants on the occasion of the death of Margaret, the Spanish queen. The organization of the many tournaments, hunting parties, religious ceremonies, festivities, balls, and ballets at court also must have cost fistfuls of money, just like the maintenance of the residences in Mariemont and Tervuren, the many relocations of the court within the country, and the journey of Archduke Albert to Spain in 1598-1599. Even so, it is not clear to what extent these rather exceptional expenditures must be seen as belonging to the domain of the archducal household, or as recouped from other budgets instead.[93]

[92] *'El gasto desta cavalleriza es muy grande, como V[uestra] A[lteza] lo ha visto por los tanteos que se le han dado y conforme a ellos acabada esta campaña, se podria reformar, reduziendo el numero de las azemilas a cinquenta, y aunque alli me parescio que tambien se podia reduzir a menos el de los cavallos (...)'* RAH, *SyC* A-61, ff. 1-6.

[93] For a discussion concerning these problems, see Gómez-Centurión Jiménez, C. & Sánchez-Belén, J.A., eds. *La herencia de Borgoña: La hacienda de las Reales Casas durante el reinado de Felipe V.* Madrid, 1998. Op cit. pp. 13-14.

Conspicuous consumption

In September, 1614, Anne de Croÿ, duchess of Aarschot and spouse of Charles, princely count of Arenberg, wrote a scorching letter to her son.[94] The 21-year-old Antoine of Arenberg had been staying for some time at the court in Brussels, were he would be appointed *gentilhombre de la Cámara*. As the third surviving son of one of the most important and richest noble families in the Netherlands, the young man was fond of excessive luxury and diversions. He took enormous enjoyment in the many delights of court life then too. With great pleasure Antoine frequented the many festivities and banquets that were organized in the palatial Brussels townhouses, on the occasion of which he could dress himself up in grandiose fashion. Fistfuls of money were spent on jewels, necklaces, rings, decorative daggers, outfits, perfumes, and beauty products. Like clockwork, Antoine bought new furniture, paintings, wall tapestries, sculptures, and books for decorating his residence in Brussels.[95] None of that fell on fertile ground with Antoine's mother, however, who was faced not only with the mounting bills of her son but also with recurring laments concerning the difficulties he experienced covering the costs of his expensive lifestyle. After having received alarming reports from the caretaker of Antoine's house, Anne had had enough. The desperate majordomo warned her that in a year's time Antoine had spent no less than fl. 1,000 on the purchase of furniture and that he did not know how the young Arenberg was supposed to pay his creditors. The duchess, who watched over the well-being of her children as a true *mater familias*, was furious. She gave her son a substantial scolding and threatened to make good no longer on his mounting debts as long as the hole in his purse was not plugged. At the same time she gave Antoine good advice about ways in which he could save money. So, for example, she advised him to wear his expensive outfits longer and not to throw them away as soon as they displayed a trace of deterioration. Furthermore, her son needed to take better care of his many possessions and not leave them flung around. Antoine ceremoniously promised to better his life but clearly did not take that promise quite scrupulously. Not much later he fell back into his old pattern of buying and spending again, which furnished him time after time with reprimands from his mother. Not until 1616 did the young nobleman see the light: he decided to enter into the Capuchins and, so doing, took a vow of poverty.[96]

---

[94] Callaey, F. [= Fredegand of Antwerp, Father O.M.F. Cap.]. *La vie religieuse et familiale en Belgique au XVIIe siècle. Étude sur le Père Charles d'Arenberg, frère-mineur Capucin (1593-1669)*. Paris-Rome, 1919. Op. cit. pp. 85-87.

[95] *Ibidem*, pp. 97-109.

[96] *Ibidem*, pp. 85-87.

Antoine of Arenberg was not the only one who had a difficult time covering the costs of the lifestyle current in court circles. In that area, the archducal court appears to have enjoyed a substantial reputation. Already in 1597, the apostolic nuncio Ottavio Mirto Frangipani complained in a letter to his Italian banker about the lavish standard of living at the Brussels court, where according to him more money was spent in one day than during a whole week in the Holy Roman Empire.[97] That was perhaps exaggerated, but there is no denying that the court of Albert and Isabella was a place of luxury and excess. Even the Florentine prince Giovanni de' Medici, who was staying in the Low Countries in this time period, was surprised about the large amounts that were spent there. In his letters to Belisario Vinta, the secretary of the grand duke of Tuscany, he did not neglect to complain about the meager endowment he received from Florence. As opposed to other Italian courtiers in the Netherlands, Giovanni wrote testily, he had to make do with a stingy sum of barely a thousand *scudi* (approx. fl. 2,570) per month:

> 'And to tell the truth, Signore Vinta, what are 1,000 scudi a month? I haven't any more, and I've never had more. (...) And so that you, Sir, would have some notion of my situation, I will tell you, Sir, what the others whom you know very well do. Count Teodoro Trivulzio, the lieutenant-general in the cavalry, usually spends – without having a large household or acting extravagantly – 500 scudi per week (...). The prince of Palestrina[98] spends 2,000 scudi per month (...), apart from [the costs for] his wardrobe and exceptional necessities. That one from Caserta[99] spends 2,500 and, including extraordinaria, even he comes close to 3,000 scudi (though that is an aberration and will not last). By which you, Sir, can see how much this poor Don Giovanni can do with only 1,000 scudi a month, and 100 extra for extraordinary costs.'[100]

---

[97] Frangipani to the banker Albertinelli, January 12, 1597. See Van der Essen, L., ed. *Correspondance d'Ottavio Mirto Frangipani, premier nonce de Flandre (1596-1606)*. Analecta Vaticano-Belgica, 2e série, section A: Nonciature de Flandre, I-II-III. 3 parts in 4 vols. Rome-Brussels-Paris, 1924. Op. cit. vol. I, letter no. 117.

[98] Francesco Colonna, prince of Palestrina (+1636).

[99] Andrea Matteo Acquaviva, prince of Caserta (+1634).

[100] Archives of the Grand Dukes of Tuscany (Archivio di Stato, Florence): *Carteggi dei Principi, delle Granduchesse e delle Principesse / Giovanni di Cosimo I e di Eleonora degli Albizi / Lettere del principe ai granduchi e alla Segretaria*, volume 5157, f. 57: Giovanni de' Medici to Belisario di Francesco Vinta, March 4, 1604. To be found on the website for *The Medici Archive Project*, http://documents.medici.org, docID 8633 (last accessed: July 10, 2013).

In their attempts to answer to the high standards of life at court, the courtiers followed the example of Albert and Isabella, who seldom regarded a guilder when it was a matter of their personal comfort. Precious gems, articles of clothing, decorative daggers, drinking goblets, parade armor, hunting falcons, books, astrolabes, garden ornaments, songbirds, coaches, paintings, crucifixes ... the accounting ledgers leave no doubt that a significant percentage of the household budget was reserved for conspicuous consumption.[101] Joachim Denzenhear, Albert's *guardaropa y joyas*, can be referred to as an example: he spent thousands of guilders annually on the purchase of jewels and jewelry as commissioned by his master.[102] In many cases these were destined for the archducal wardrobe, but they were doled out more frequently still – in an ultimate demonstration of gift-giving – to meritorious courtiers and visitors. Thus, in December, 1615, for instance, the goldsmith Isaac Stilman received at least fl. 11,641 for making 27 golden chains and accompanying medallions for the '*cavalleros y criados*' of Albert's brother Maximilian, who was a guest in Brussels.[103] Taking into consideration that Denzenhear himself only earned fl. 1,371 per year in this time period – and with that he was still one of the better paid members of the archducal household – that jewelry order was an insanely high amount, demonstrating at once how great the importance of gifts was in the early modern political constellation.[104]

The archducal household budget

As seen already above, the different departments of the archducal household jointly spent approximately fl. 300,000 in the year 1616 (cf. Table 4). In the same year approximately fl. 200,000 was spent on pay for courtiers and servants (cf. Table 3). Added up, the fixed expenses in 1616 ran up to at least fl. 500,000, and it can be assumed that this amount was rapidly attained during other years too. The total expenditures of the archducal household (that is, including the sums spent on *ayudas de costa*, *entretenimientos*, pensions, exceptional compensations, festivities, religious ceremonies, tournaments, hunting parties, the maintenance of parks and buildings,

[101] ARA, *RK* 1837 and 1838, *passim*.

[102] Concerning the activities of Joachim Denzenhear, see ARA, *SSO* 518: *Registro de partes de las cosas tocantes a la casa de Su Alteza*.

[103] ARA, *RK* 1838, f. 61v.

[104] Concerning the importance of giving gifts in the early modern world, see Kettering S. 'Gift-Giving and Patronage in Early Modern France.' *French History*, 2 (1988) 131-151 and Krausman Ben-Amos, I. 'Gifts and Favors: Informal Support in Early Modern England.' *The Journal of Modern History*, 72 (2000) 295-338.

the care for animals, conspicuous consumption, and so forth) were much higher still on top of that – amounts between fl. 750,000 and fl. 1 million are surely not unthinkable in that context. It is perhaps clear that these kinds of astronomical sums put heavy pressure on the archducal treasury. The question arises as to how this burden was facilitated. Here too for the large part the answer remains shrouded in fog. As already touched upon above, the analysis of finances is hampered by the difficult situation with sources, which leave us in uncertainty concerning the precise origin of the budgets. One of the problems concerns the scarce information about the total treasury revenues in the archducal period and about the application and distribution of these resources. Roughly speaking, government finances in the Southern Netherlands were supported by five mainstays. In addition to the proceeds from their domains, the archdukes had at their disposal the receipts from petitions, toll levies, taxes, and the sale of licenses and passports. The anonymous French spy, mentioned already, declared that 'all the *deniers*, coming from the said five kinds of revenues and finances, amount to 1,200,000 *philippes* [= approx. fl. 3 million] per year. And that is all Their Highnesses get from the said Low Countries.'[105] According to calculations by Daniel Ghéret, the annual *recette* of the receiver-general in the period 1598-1621 exhibited especially great fluctuations all the same, with amounts that varied annually between around fl. 1 million and around fl. 3.5 million.[106] On average the total receipts in this time period amounted roughly to fl. 2.2 million per year.

The figures

In order to finance their households, in theory early modern princes in the main made use of the proceeds from their crown domains. The French spy estimated the domanial revenues of the archdukes around 1610 to be good for about fl. 900,000 per year – with the understanding that only a portion of that was actually at their disposal:

> 'The domain owned by Their Highnesses is worth around 900,000 florins per year, including that which falls under the sway of the States of the United

[105] '*(...) tous les deniers, provenans desdits cinq sortes de revenus et finances, montent par an au plus: douze cens mil philipes. Et est tout ce que Leurs Altesses ont desdits Pays-Bas.*' [Anonymous], *Relation de Flandres*, 13. In the archducal period the value of the *Filipsdaalder* amounted to around 50 stuivers. The mentioned amount of 1,200,000 *Filipsdaalders* consequently corresponded to around fl. 3 million.

[106] Ghéret, D. 'Le produit des licentes et autres impôts sur le commerce extérieur dans les Pays-Bas espagnols (1585-1621),' in: Arnould, M.-A., Despy, G., Ghéret, D. et al. *Acta Historica Bruxellensia. Recherches sur l'histoire des finances publiques en Belgique*, 3 vols. Brussels, 1968-1974. Volume II, pp. 43-122. Concerning the sale of licenses and passports, see also De Sturler, J. 'Un épisode de la politique douanière des Archiducs: L'expérience de Juan de Gauna (1603-1605).' *Revue de l'Université de Bruxelles*, 42 (1936-1937) 362-386.

> Provinces. Of these 900,000 livres, 500,000 have been engaged, which means that there are only 400,000 left for Their Highnesses.'[107]

The spy proved to be pretty well informed of the financial situation in the country: according to the calculations of Ghéret, in the period 1598-1621 the domanial revenues indeed fluctuated per year between fl. 200,000 at the minimum and fl. 500,000 at the maximum, with an average of around fl. 385,000.[108] These were considerable sums, but in practice these resources proved to suffice least of all in financing the household of the archdukes. For that reason alternative sources of money were diligently sought after. And as was so often the case when the treasury had to be larded, the subjects were prodded into – literally – giving their two cents. In 1600, the archdukes convoked the States-General in Brussels.[109] During the opening session on April 26, the president of the Privy Council, Jean Richardot, gave a fiery plea in which the provincial States were confronted, among other things, with the financial crisis of the princes. According to Richardot the proceeds from the patrimony did not in any way suffice in providing for the sustenance of Albert and Isabella:

> 'And moreover, you know that everyone has to live by his own means, and that holds for princes as well as individuals. The inheritance and patrimony of our princes is their domain, which in the past provided for the dukes of Burgundy, our princes, and their predecessors, who reserved it for the sustenance and maintenance of their households. However, ever since we have been united with Spain, our princes have been so powerful, and have obtained so many other lands and crowns, that they have not concerned themselves with taking their nourishment from here, but have liberally mortgaged and engaged their domain for the necessities of war and the tutelage and defense of the country: as a result it is barely sufficient [today] to pay the debtors. This, Milords, is something you should take into consideration; and you are by nature obliged to acquit those debts, which were made for your own benefit, so that our princes would have something to live by, without burdening and inconveniencing their subjects. And one hopes that this engagement will be made within a few years, either by the means which you yourselves suggest, or by those which will be advised to you on the part of Their Highnesses. And in

[107] '*Le domaine est le propre de Leurs Altesses (...), vallant environ neuf cens mil florins par an, comprins ce qui est soubz la puissance des Estatz des Provinces-Unies. Des 900.000 livres, il y en a d'engaigé cinq cens mil, de sorte qu'il n'en reste que quatre cens mil pour leursdites Altesses.*' [Anonymous], *Relation de Flandres*, 11. The spy is most likely calculating in pounds Artois, which had the same value as the guilder in this time period.

[108] Ghéret, 'Le produit des licentes,' 54.

[109] Gachard, L.-P., ed. *Actes des États-Généraux de 1600*. Brussels, 1849.

the meantime, they will require you to provide them with what they need to live, while they liquidate their debts.'[110]

To help the archdukes out of the crisis, the States-General were asked to contribute fl. 250,000 annually to sustain the princes.[111] As was to be expected, the States initially reacted to that proposal with little enthusiasm. The enormous amounts necessary for financing the archducal household – which according to one delegate was '*fort grande et excessive*' – aroused their dissatisfaction.[112] Even so, after several rounds of negotiations they declared themselves prepared to pay the requested sum, on the condition that the entourage of the archdukes would be drastically reduced in size:

> 'Milords prelates and nobles, for the first two Estates, and with the consent of the third Estate and the other provinces, hereby accord the sum of two hundred fifty thousand florins to Their Highnesses, for the period and term of one year only, on the condition, however, that they reform their household immediately and discharge all superfluous and useless persons, and keep it on the same footing as did the dukes of Burgundy.'[113]

The requested change in the scale of the archducal household was a demand that the archdukes – according to what they themselves said – wanted only too gladly to sanction, but that – as seen earlier – quickly landed in the oubliette after the receipt of the promised funds.[114] And although the sum of fl. 250,000 in principle was

---

[110] '*Et dadvantage, vous sçavez qu'ung chascun doibt vivre du sien, et que cela s'entend des princes comme des particuliers. L'héritage et patrimoine de noz princes est leur domaine, duquel vivoient, du passé, les ducqz de Bourgongne, noz princes, et leurs devanciers, qui se réservoient cela pour la nourriture et entretien de leur maison. Mais, depuis qu'avons esté uniz à l'Espagne, noz princes ont esté si puissans, et ont eu tant d'aultres Estatz et coronnes, qu'ilz ne se sont pas soucié de prendre leur nourriture d'icy, ains ont libéralement chargé et engagé leur domaine pour les nécessitez de la guerre, et la propre tuition et défense du païs: de sorte qu'à peine est-il suffisant pour payer les rentiers. À cela, messieurs, debvez-vous avoir considération; et estes naturellement obligez d'acquicter ces debtes, qui sont faictes pour vostre propre bénéfice, afin que noz princes ayent de quoy vivre, sans travailler et incommoder leurs subjects. Et l'on espère que ce désengaigement se pourra faire en peu d'années, soit par les moyens que vous-mesmes adviserez, soit par ceulx qui, de la part de Leurs Altèzes, vous pourront estre suggérez. Et cependant, elle vous requièrent leur subministrer de quoy vivre, pendant que le domaine s'ira deschargeant.*' Gachard, *Actes des États-Généraux*, 387-388.

[111] Gachard, *Actes des États-Généraux*, 237.

[112] Gachard, *Actes des États-Généraux*, 192.

[113] '*(...) accordent messieurs les prélatz et nobles, pour leurs deux premiers Estatz, et parmy le consentement du tiers Etat et des aultres provinces, la somme de deux centz cinquante mil florins demandez par Leurs Altèzes, pour le temps et terme d'ung an tant seullement, à condition, néantmoings, qu'ilz réformeront leur maison présentement de tous gens superfluz et inutils, la remectront et maintiendront au pied comme ont faict les ducqz de Bourgoigne.*' Gachard, *Actes des États-Généraux*, 152.

[114] The archdukes' answer to this demand went as follows: '*Ceste requisition se prend de bonne part; et auront Leurs Altèzes tout favorable esgard tant sur icelle, que sur toutes aultres semblables; se pouvans lesdicts Estatz asseurer qu'en tout ce que Leurs Altèzes pourront faire pour l'advancement de leurs bons vassaulx et subjectz, elles s'y rendront tousjours fort promptes et volontaires.*' Gachard, *Actes des États-Généraux*, 688.

only conditionally awarded, and just for one year, even this condition would silently disappear into the background. In 1605, the Spanish *Consejo de Estado* calculated that the different regions were still contributing 8,333 *escudos* (approx. fl. 21,415) per month for sustaining the princes.[115] On an annual basis that was around fl. 256,989. During the two subsequent decades the States-General would not be convoked any more – and, consequently, would also no longer get the chance to negotiate the petition anew.[116]

If the annual contribution of the States-General is added up with the estimated proceeds from the crown domain, then that comes to a total amount fluctuating between around fl. 450,000 and around fl. 750,000 per year. That was a fantastical sum, but assuming that around fl. 500,000 was already needed annually for everyday expenditures (= ordinary pay and operating resources), perhaps that amount did not always suffice in covering the many extraordinary costs of the archducal household as well. During the 'lean years' they undoubtedly had difficulty keeping their heads above water, which clarifies at once why the pay was sometimes disbursed after years of delay. The question then arises as to which other funds were addressed to facilitate costs. The shortfalls were possibly supplemented with proceeds from taxes, toll levies, and the sale of passports and licenses, even though there is no direct proof for this. Furthermore, those available financial resources described at present as 'personal funds' naturally need to be taken into account – although there is still the question as to what extent an early modern prince made a distinction between his 'private' budget and that of the state. Thus, Albert's last will and testament, for instance, contains an overview of his *hacienda*, from which it appears, among other things, that after the death of his father Maximilian II in 1576, the archduke made claim to an annuity of 45,000 German guldens (= approx. 33,000 ducats).[117] After the death of his brother Ernst in 1595, the return on this investment rose to fl. 56,250. All the same, the archduke never got to see one *kreutzer* of this promised money: they simply did not have the money to pay Albert.[118] In 1608, Rudolf II was already indebted to him for 1.2 million German guldens. Four years later the death of the emperor provided for quite a lot of financial tug-of-war between Albert and the other heirs, his own brother Matthias among them – a situation that only got cleared up when Emperor Ferdinand II promised to raise Albert's annuity to fl. 115,000. Yet the archduke would never

[115] AGS, *Estado* 2024, s.f.: *Relación particular de las ayudas que cada provincia obediente da a Sus Altezas desde la Junta de los Estados generales del año 1600 y en que se gastan* [1605].

[116] Ghéret, 'Le produit des licentes,' 55.

[117] ARA, *Papiers du Comté de Mercy-Argenteau* 125, s.f.: Last will and testament of Archduke Albert.

[118] Fischer, J. 'Die Erbteilung Rudolfs II. mit seinen fünf Brüdern vom. 10 April 1578. Nach bisher unbekannten Archivalien.' *Ferdinandeums-Zeitschrift*, III. Folge, 41. Heft. Innsbruck, 1897. Op. cit. pp. 5-14.

get anything from this sum in his hands, either.[119] The few 'private' funds that Albert did indeed have at his disposal were, consequently, rather modest in nature. So, for example, after the death of his mother in 1603, he inherited annual rents of 3,053 ducats (= approx. fl. 8,417) on a few areas in Naples.[120] It is quite possible that these and other 'personal' resources were used to supplement the financing of the archducal household, yet it is perhaps clear that they in essence had no more impact than a drop in a bucket.

On top of that, it is not unthinkable that the origin of the budgets remained consciously vague. After all, from the beginning of his reign, rumors popped up that Albert did not shrink back from misusing the funds that were sent monthly from Spain to the Southern Netherlands to finance the standing army. In the period 1599-1609 these shipments fluctuated between 750,000 and 4.75 million Spanish ducats per year.[121] In spite of that the military treasury was pretty much constantly in a monetary crisis. The soldiers' pay was seldom disbursed on time, with frequent mutinies as a consequence. In his book *Philip III and the Pax Hispánica* Paul Allen rightly wonders, then, where the Spanish money in reality ended up.[122] According to the author, the answer is found close-at-hand. Thus Allen argues that Albert used approximately one third of the 1599 shipment – which was good for 3 million ducats in total – to cover the costs of his jouney to Spain in 1598.[123] Various commentaries make it appear that these kinds of unannounced 'loans' from the military treasury were indeed not unusual. In 1599, the nuncio Frangipani wrote that mutinies were feared in the Southern Netherlands because the soldiers believed that their pay was being held back to get rid of the shortfalls in the archducal household.[124] Around 1602, the already mentioned Giovanni de' Medici was also of the judgment that 'the situation in this country [is] worse than ever' because the budgets for the army were being eaten up by the entourage of the archduke.[125] Albert and Isabella defended

[119] *Ibidem*.

[120] ARA, *Papiers du Comté de Mercy-Argenteau* 125.

[121] See the chart in Allen, P. *Philip III and the Pax Hispánica, 1598-1621. The Failure of Grand Strategy*. Yale U.P., 2000, p. 31.

[122] Allen, *Philip III and the Pax Hispanica*, 30.

[123] *Ibidem*, p. 31.

[124] '*Il nuestro exercito sta diviso per il Ducato de Gheldria et per le parti extreme di Brabanza su la Mosa, mal sodisfatto per il dinaro che se gli manca, onde se time un mottino generale, che se non segue, sara di honore et di gloria al Sr. Almirante, et à la mala sodisfattion tanto peggiore, quanto ch'il Serenissimo Arciduca sia in opinione appresso il soldate, ch'il dinaro delle sue paghe se converta da Sua Altezza in usa di sua persona et di sua casa*.' ASV, *NF* 11, f. 741: Ottavio Mirto Frangipani to Cardinal-Secretary of State Aldobrandini, 22 December 1599.

[125] Archives of the Grand Dukes of Tuscany (Archivio di Stato, Florence): *Carteggi dei Principi, delle Granduchesse e delle Principesse / Giovanni di Cosimo I e di Eleonora degli Albizi / Lettere del principe ai granduchi e alla Segretaria*, volume 5155, docID 9069: Giovanni de' Medici to Grand Duke Ferdinando de' Medici, October 16, 1602. Found on the website of *The Medici Archive Project* (http://documents.medici.org, last accessed: July 10, 2013).

themselves against these sorts of accusations constantly and emphatically. In 1606, the infanta expressed her indignation to the duke of Lerma, who had informed her of a few stubborn rumors on the matter. According to Isabella, Lerma was misled by informants who took pleasure in making known unfounded opinions. She claimed that the Spanish funds were always distributed with the requisite care, although she honestly admitted that the commands from Madrid were not always followed to the letter for the simple reason that these decisions were often already superseded when they arrived in the Southern Netherlands.[126]

Was Isabella's indignation right? In spite of her protests, commentaries concerning the improper use of the Spanish shipments would regularly pop up anew during the entire archducal time period. Thus, the French ambassador delicately noted in 1611, for instance, that his fellow Spanish official would do well to petition Albert for an across-the-board round of economizing. The archduke had too many people in his service, after all, and according to the ambassador, Madrid was of the opinion that the court in Brussels did not need to be financed by the Spanish treasury.[127] Indeed, attempts were repeatedly undertaken from Madrid to get more control over the budgets allotted for the *Ejército de Flandes*. When the Spanish army was reformed on the occasion of the signing of the Twelve Years' Truce in 1609, the *Consejo de Estado* explicitly put emphasis on the fact that the *entretenimientos* of the Brussels courtiers could no longer be recouped from the army budget, unless these courtiers actually held a military office.[128] Apparently, Albert went along with this decision, yet quickly enough it turned out that a number of exceptions were requested and awarded – with the support of the archduke.[129] In practice little came of financial reform with the members of the archducal household. Four years later, in any case, the problem proved to be still serious enough to venture an attempt at remedying the matter anew.[130] Once again Albert was commanded to set the situation right, but now too there was little follow-up given to it.[131] For the Spanish ambassador in Brussels it

[126] Rodríguez Villa, A., ed. *Correspondencia de la Infanta Doña Isabel Clara Eugenia de Austria con el Duque de Lerma y otros personajes*. Madrid, 1906. Letter no. 104: Isabella to Lerma, October 7, 1606.

[127] BNF, *MsF* 16129, f. 418: Mathieu Brulart sieur de Berny to Secretary of State Puisieux, September 28, 1611.

[128] Documents concerning this *reformación general* are to be found primarily in AGS, *Estado* 2025-2031 and 2291-2292. See AGS, *Estado* 2291, nos. 217-218: *Copia de la orden de S.A. para que se reformen todos sus criados, y Relación de los a quien desea que S.M. haga merced de los sueldos que solían tener, moderadas segun la reformación general* (August 8, 1609). See also no. 200: *Copia de la orden para los criados de Su Alteza* (December 22, 1609) and no. 173: The count of Añover to Philip III, August 28, 1609.

[129] AGS, *Estado* 2291, no. 201: Añover to Philip III, December 24, 1609. See also AGS, *Estado* 2292, s.f.: The count of Añover to Philip III, February 20, 1610.

[130] AGS, *Estado* 2027, s.f.: Consult of the *Consejo de Estado*, January 16, 1613.

[131] AGS, *Estado* 628, s.f.: Juan de Mancisidor to Philip III, November 15, 1613, and AGS, *Estado* 628, s.f.: Ambrogio Spínola to Philip III, February 1, 1614.

was painfully clear that the archduke quite simply concerned himself little with the protests that reached him from Spain.[132]

Discussion

In the historiography concerning early modern European courts, much attention is generally given to the question as to how the budget of the princely household was related in this time period to the total budgetary plan for the government. After all, these kinds of analyses say much about the relative weight of the court in the financial administration of the state, which, then again, can be an indication for the importance that the monarch attached to the political role of the court as a center of power within an expanding state apparatus, as well as to its symbolic role as a factor in externalizing and consolidating princely authority.[133] For the French court, Jeroen Duindam calculated that 'in Henry IV's reign, the aggregate of costs related to the court frequently represented around 25 per cent of the total ordinary and extraordinary expenditures; in 1618 it peaked at 38 per cent.'[134] In the same way, Carlos Javier Carlos Morales argues that the budget of the Spanish under Philip III – including all the royal households except for the *Casa de Castilla* – represented between 10% and 27% of the majority of annual government expenditures.[135] According to Fabian Persson, then again, the budget of the royal Swedish household amounted to between 10% and 20% of the total government budget.[136]

Lacking sufficient source material, a comparable analysis for the Archducal Netherlands is problematic. In the first place it is almost impossible to calculate how large the budget of the archducal household was. As said, there is relatively good information for the more or less fixed costs of the household (wages and operating resources), yet uncertainty remains concerning the total costs. As opposed to Duindam, Carlos Morales, and Persson, there are just as few sufficient data available with regard to the government budget in this time period. The calculations of Daniel Ghéret only offer information about the treasury *revenues* – not about the state *expenditures*. The lack of trustworthy figures, consequently, does not make it easy to make statements concerning the relative importance of the archducal 'household budget' within the

---

[132] AGS, *Estado* 2026, s.f.: Consult of the *Consejo de Estado*, October 16, 1612.

[133] Jurado Sanchez, J. 'La financiación de la Casa Real española y sus repercusiones sobre la Hacienda y la economía (1561-1808),' in: Aymard & Romani, *La cour comme institution économique*, pp. 57-64.

[134] Duindam, *Vienna and Versailles*, 65.

[135] Carlos Morales, C.J. *The Economic Foundations of the Royal Household of the Spanish Habsburgs, 1556-1621*. Paper presented at the colloquium *A Constellation of Courts: The Households of Habsburg Europe, 1555-1665*, organized by the universities of Antwerp and Ghent (Brussels, Paleis der Academiën, November 3-4, 2006).

[136] Persson, F. 'Splendour at a Price. The Economy of the Swedish Court in the Early Modern Period,' in: Aymard & Romani, *La cour comme institution économique*, pp. 151-159.

total scheme of government finances. Nevertheless, the scarce data lend themselves well to a cautious hypothesis, which is naturally susceptible to interpretation. The following constitutes an exercise for the year 1616.

According to the calculations of Ghéret, the *recette* of the receiver-general in 1616 amounted to approximately fl. 2 million. As seen above, in that same year there was around fl. 500,000 spent on pay and operating resources (cf. Tables 3 and 4). Presupposing that the expenditures of the archducal household were completely recouped from the money coffers of the state, it can be posited that the amount named represented already 25% of the resources available to the treasury in 1616.[137] Naturally, the representative nature of this percentage is dubious. In the first place only the 'fixed costs' of the household are taken into account here: in reality the expenditures of the archducal household ran much higher still. On top of that, the great fluctuations in government revenues in this time period need to be taken into account. So, for example, it appears that the general receipts in 1615 were good for around fl. 3.5 million, while in 1614 they amounted to only around fl. 1 million.[138] Presupposing – especially hypothetically – that the budget of the archducal household in this period only varied to a minor extent, the sum of pay and operating resources [fl. 500,000] thus represented between 14% and 50% of the amount that the treasury collected annually. Assuming that all manner of exceptional expenditures (for *ayudas de costa*, pensions, and *entretenimientos*; for countless festivities and religious ceremonies; for the maintenance of residences; for the reception of foreign guests; for conspicuous consumption ...) have to be added to this, it can be posited that the percentages were much higher in reality.

On the other hand, it needs to be noted that the revenues mentioned do not take the shipments from Spain into account, which raised the available government budget – at least in the period 1599-1609 – by an amount between 750,000 and 5 million ducats (= fl. 2,067,750 and fl. 13,785,000, respectively).[139] In principle, this money was supposed to finance Spanish troops and was not used for other purposes. Even so, as was indicated above, it is not impossible that a part of it was applied to sustain the archdukes. If that was indeed the case, entirely different proportions have to be taken into account. In 1605, for example, the Spanish shipment amounted to 4.5 million ducats (= fl. 12,406,500). Added up with the revenues from the treasury in that year, this resulted in a total amount of fl. 15 million. Logically, then, the share of the fixed archducal household costs sinks to around 3.33% of the available government budget in the process. If the exceptional expenses would be added to this, a percentage of 5%

[137] Ghéret, 'Le produit des licentes,' 112.
[138] *Ibidem.*
[139] Allen, *Philip III and the Pax Hispanica*, 31.

to 7% does not seem unrealistic for 1605. It must be said, though, that 1605 was an exceptional year for the Southern Netherlands: the *recette* of the receiver-general was higher than ever in this year, and the shipment from Spain was the second highest for the period 1599-1609. During other years the financial situation of the government was most likely much less rose-colored, whereby the percentage of the 'household budget' would again come out to be higher.

On account of the many nuances the analysis proposed here has to be taken with a substantial grain of salt. In any case, it is clear that the total budget of the archducal household (including all ordinary and extraordinary costs) ran especially high. Once again it is certain that in any case the court in Brussels did not have to feel inferior to other European courts in any way, and it even seems that Albert and Isabella spent more money proportionally than other European princes. That hypothesis would connect to the presupposition mentioned earlier that the archducal court exceeded posited expectations.

Conclusion

In her early twentieth-century biography of the infanta Isabella, Marie Hennequin de Villermont concluded that 'one might perhaps reproach the archdukes for having maintained (...) such an expensive court even though they were always in want of money.' Yet, as the author added, condoning in a way, 'this was the custom at the time and when the prince lacked resources, he did not pay his officials.'[140] There is indeed no doubt that Albert and Isabella kept an extensive and expensive court. In absolute numbers their entourage rivaled that of many other princes. Athough their court in Brussels perhaps could not withstand the comparison with the French and Spanish courts, which were at that time bursting at the seams, it is clear that it took a high position, in any case, on the rankings list of European princely courts. Just as the archducal court had been cobbled from a royal model in an organizational and ceremonial sense, it can be posited that it was calculated on a royal scale in terms of size. Albert and Isabella did not sweep their political and dynastic ambitions under the carpet, and they accented these aspirations with the aid of a magnificent princely household and lifestyle. The financial consequences of this were not to be underestimated, all the same. From the analysis of the *libros de razón*, it appears that the combination of an extensive archducal household and a lavish pattern of consumption demanded enormous sums annually, which represented more than a

[140] Hennequin de Villermont, M. *L'Infante Isabelle, gouvernante des Pays-Bas*. 2 vols. Paris-Tamines, 1912. Op. cit. vol. II, p. 22.

significant percentage of total government revenues. If the year 1616 may serve as a point of reference, that share amounted to at least 25% – at least, for only the fixed costs are recorded here.

'The custom at the time' may have been very demanding, then, in the early modern period; yet it seems that the court of the archdukes was proportionally too large and too expensive – and this in relation to both their purse as well as their status. Once again the Brussels court answers wonderfully well to the hypothesis of John Elliott that princes whose legitimacy was disputed would supposedly make more of an effort, relatively speaking, to emphasize the grandeur of their court, than would their powerful counterparts in larger principalities (cf. Chapter I). The many critical commentaries of contemporaries make it appear that the archdukes did everything to exceed the 'standard expectations' of a sovereign court, as proposed by John Adamson. Albert and Isabella simply lived above their standing. Their household cost an insanely large amount of money, and in times of scarcity it was most likely not simple to square its financial scheme.

That maintenance of the archducal household demanded an extremely large bite out of the available government budget is at once an indication of the relative weight of the archducal court within the state apparatus at that time. In financial respects it was, without any doubt, the most money-devouring institution in the Southern Netherlands. That need not come as a surprise: earlier it was argued that the court fulfilled a central function with regard to the representation of power. The archducal regime wanted to be seen, and to be seen with all the luster and *pompa* that a princely court could have at its disposal. Even more than by means of portraits and paintings by famous court painters like Pieter Paul Rubens, Jan Breughel the Elder, and Denis van Alsloot, in which scarcely concealed political messages were brought to expression, that happened by means of displaying unbridled luxury and organizing much talked-about Joyous Entries, public parades, and processions, where spectators could gape at the pomp and pageantry of the extensive princely entourage.

The archducal court naturally had not only a representative, but also – and above all – a political function. In that respect the doling out of positions in the archducal household to great numbers of *gentilhombres* and *damas* was a way not only to increase the luster of the court, but also to tighten the disrupted bonds between the Habsburg dynasty and the aristocracy in the Southern Netherlands again, as well as to involve the members of that aristocracy in the regime. As the following chapters will show, the nobility savored the proliferation of these prestigious functions, as it gave them anew the opportunity to make their way onto the patronage market at court as well as to gain princely favor – an opportunity that had been denied them for a long time by the persistent political troubles in the Low Countries. The third chapter goes into how the 'recruiting' of these courtiers went in practice and to which criteria they had to answer to have a chance at a position in the archducal household.

Chapter III
In the Service of the Dynasty*

'The selection of ministers is of no little importance to a prince; and they are good or not, according to the prince's prudence. The first thing one does to evaluate a ruler's prudence is to look at the men he has around him. When they are capable and loyal, one can always consider him wise, for he has known how to recognize their capacities and to keep them loyal; but when they are otherwise, one can always form a negative judgement of him, for the first error he makes is made in this selection.'[1]

Niccolò Machiavelli
Il Principe

That the choice of an entourage could be of crucial concern for a prince was a consideration that Archduke Albert was presumably very conscious of early on. Already at the age of ten he had been able to experience how the composition of his own household became the object of a tug-of-war between his father, the Habsburg Emperor Maximilian II, and his uncle, King Philip II of Spain. Maximilian had agreed with Philip's proposal to have the Catholic upbringing of Albert and his younger brother Wenceslas perfected at the court in Madrid beginning in 1570. Yet the emperor was in no way willing to give his sons up completely to his brother-in-law's sphere of influence. He was especially upset when it appeared that the entourage Philip had in mind for both boys consisted only of Castilians.[2] It was a sly and forward-looking move by the king, with which he honored his nickname of '*Rey Prudente*.' In spite of their young age Albert and Wenceslas were important pawns on the political chessboard of Europe. Both were Maximilian's legitimate children

* Throughout this chapter I have made grateful use of the doctoral dissertation of Dr. José Eloy Hortal Muñoz, which has been published as Hortal Muñoz, J.E. *El manejo de los asuntos de Flandes, 1585-1598. Las relaciones entre las cortes de la Monarquía Hispánica y de los Países Bajos durante el siglo XVI.* Saarbrücken, 2011. I am very appreciative to Dr. Hortal for his willingness to share his expertise with me.

1 Machiavelli, N. *Il Principe* (1532). English translation taken from Niccolò Machiavelli's *The Prince*, translated and edited by P. Bondanella. Oxford, 2008. Op. cit. p. 79.

2 Concerning the organization of the household of both archdukes, see Martínez Millán, J. 'El archiduque Alberto en la corte de Felipe II (1570-1580),' in: Thomas, W. & Duerloo, L., eds. *Albert & Isabella, 1598-1621: Essays*. Turnhout, 1998, pp. 27-37 and Hortal Muñoz, J.E. 'The Household of Archduke Albert of Austria from his Election as Governor of Flanders until his Investiture as Sovereign Prince of the Low Countries: 1595-1598.' *Revue belge de Philologie et d'Histoire*, in press.

and potential candidates to succeed their father as emperor of the Holy Roman Empire after his death. Philip's attempt to populate the household of the young archdukes with his own confidants was thus in no way free from self-interest. His strategy offered him the opportunity to monitor the conduct of his nephews from a young age and – even more strongly – to steer them in the direction he wished. The well-considered composition of their entourage was consequently no futile matter, but an affair in the interest of the state. As concerned Philip, it was a question of investing in the future. On his end, Maximilian perceived but all too well what his brother-in-law was planning. He showed himself to be appalled at the course of affairs and demanded that the household of Albert and Wenceslas also count a number of '*tudescos*' [Germans].[3] Officially the standpoint went that the emperor wished that his sons would not unlearn the German language during their stay in Spain.[4] In reality, though, Maximilian feared that in the end they would not only disown their mother tongue but also their fatherland.

The coming of the young archdukes could count on much interest in Madrid. The news had scarcely been announced when the royal administration became overwhelmed with letters and memoranda from persons who aspired to a position in the household that would be organized for the brothers.[5] The stay of Albert and Wenceslas – even before it had gotten well and truly started – thus became entangled in the dire disputes that had thoroughly leavened social life in Spain for quite some time, and not the least of which manifested themselves in the court at Madrid. Without going too deeply into this disputed history, it can be posited that the frictions in essence arose from two opposed ideological standpoints with regard to the political, military, and religious policy that needed to be conducted in the 'composite monarchy' of Philip II. In view of the fact that these contrasting visions – and their adherents – were represented by prominent courtiers, among others, like Ruy Gómez de Silva, the prince of Éboli, and Fernando Álvarez de Toledo, the infamous duke of Alba, this conflict of interests is described traditionally in Spanish historiography

---

[3] See the letter from Empress Maria, spouse of Maximilian II, to her brother Philip II, May 29, 1570: '*El Emperador me paresçe que determina enviar dos hijos como vos mandáis. Pienso que serán los medianos de los que están acá, aunque no lo sé çierto (...). El Emperador pasó bien por todo lo que de parte de vos se le dijo sobre esto, pero después vi que le pareçía estrano que no uviesen de tener tudescos. Yo pongo la culpa a otros y pienso que como tengan algunos porque no se les holvide la lengua, quen esto tiene razón, estará muy contento de toda la merced que vos le aze y a ellos.*' Published in: Galende Díaz, J.C. & Salamanca López, M., eds. *Epistolario de la emperatriz María de Austria. Textos inéditos del Archivo de la Casa de Alba*. Madrid, 2004, pp. 181-182.

[4] Galende Díaz & Salamanca López, *Epistolario de la emperatriz*, pp. 220-221: Empress Maria to Philip II, July 31, 1571.

[5] Martínez Millán, 'El archiduque Alberto en la corte de Felipe II,' 28.

as a factional conflict between the so-called *partido ebolista* and the *partido albista*.[6] During the 1560s the heated feelings between these parties flared high, whereby the rather measured attitude of the *ebolistas* and the very repressive attitude of the *albistas* with respect to the Dutch Revolt are seen as illustrative for their ideological positions.[7] Both groups tried to push through their vision on policy and, in the process, sought and received the requisite support of highly-placed secular and religious functionaries. Via a network of patrons they succeeded in expanding their political influence to almost all the echelons abounding in the state apparatus. As the environment *par excellence* in which the prince could be approached, the royal household constituted a desired target.

According to José Martínez Millán, the faction of the prince of Éboli enjoyed a clear preponderance in the Spanish court at the beginning of the 1570s. The fact that Don Juan de Ayala, one of its most prominent members, was appointed to head the household of Albert and Wenceslas seems to indicate that the party was able to get their way here as well.[8] As *mayordomo mayor*, Ayala not only would hold sway over the archducal household but also would exercise control over the conduct of his pupils. On top of that, the further selection of court personnel was entrusted to the secretary Martín de Gaztelu, a notorious *ebolista* and perhaps not coincidentally a good friend of Juan de Ayala.[9] The installation of them both was, then, of great importance for the Éboli party. With Ayala at the rudder and Gaztelu as his second-in-command the *ebolistas* would be able to put the household of Albert and Wenceslas completely to their own purpose. With an eye to the future political role that the king had in mind for both archdukes, that circumstance produced possibly interesting advantages.

It is doubtful whether young Albert even then grasped in full what kinds of machinations were at play in the choice of his retinue. One thing is certain: he would face these sorts of tricky questions again at various times for the rest of his life. The anecdote illustrates that the composition of Albert's entourage was never – and could not possibly ever be – a matter that could be disposed of separate from the reality of day-to-day politics. For a Habsburg prince of the blood the choice of his retinue was by definition a political question. A number of conflicting interests had to be taken into account, like religious and aristocratic sensitivities, claims for inclusion (whether right or not), and recommendations (both well-intentioned and less so) – all of which

[6] Martínez Millán, J. 'Grupos de poder en la corte durante el reinado de Felipe II: la facción ebolista, 1554–1573,' in: Martínez Millán, J., ed. *Instituciones y élites de poder en la Monarquía Hispana durante el siglo XVI.* Madrid, 1992, pp. 183–197.

[7] For an analysis, see Lagomarsino, D. *Court Factions and the Formulation of Spanish Policy towards the Netherlands (1559-1567).* Unpublished doctoral dissertation, Cambridge University, 1973.

[8] Martínez Millán, 'El archiduque Alberto en la corte de Felipe II,' 29.

[9] *Ibidem.*

could influence the selection of courtiers and servants. Even so, there was no lack of candidates. The prestige and the advantages that a position at court brought along with it, much as the possibility for spending time in the proximity of the prince, saw to it that court offices were the object of fierce competition. Inversely, it was just as important for the prince to surround himself with trustworthy and competent employees, who had at their disposal the requisite qualities, capacities, and contacts to assist him in the administration. This situation tosses up an interesting question. As sovereign princes, the archdukes were obliged by their status to keep an extensive retinue (cf. Chapter II). Whom did they select to make up part of it, and why? Or – even more interesting – who did not succeed in laying hold of a position in their household, and why not?

This chapter tries to expose the mechanisms that were the basis for the formation of the entourage of Albert and Isabella. The question as to who was appointed or not, and for what reason, can teach much about the expectations that were placed on the courtiers – and, in that way, about the role that the archducal household was expected to play in the early modern political constellation. Whereas the 'recruiting process' in most princely households at that time was a delicate matter anyway, those intricacies applied to the archducal household possibly even more. Although the archdukes enjoyed a sovereign status, their principality was and remained connected to the Spanish-Habsburg monarchy in several respects. The question, then, can be posed as to how this situation influenced the organigram of the archducal household in Brussels, and to what extent Madrid made (joint) decisions about it. To the degree the reign of Albert and Isabella advanced, their childlessness came to hang more and more like a sword of Damocles over the Southern Netherlands. From around 1610 it was clear to everyone that the infanta would bear no more children and that in the end the territory would fall into Spanish hands anew. Did this prospect – for some a welcome turn-around, for others a vision of doom – have consequences for the composition of the archducal entourage? On top of that, it is often forgotten that the Southern Netherlands constituted a small but substantial component of the great Habsburg imperium. Was this connection mirrored in the personnel force of the archducal household in Brussels?

In addition to dynastic perils, Albert and Isabella had a revolt in their own country to take into account, one that seriously threatened the stability of their regime. The political radicalization of recent decades had seen to it that the relationship with the nobility in the Low Countries was troubled at the very least. In the North, most nobles had already definitively turned away from Brussels. In the South, the aristocracy had remained loyal, yet even here mutual wariness was great. Was the prospect of a position in the archducal household a possible solution for facing up to this problem?

And to what degree did the origins and religious convictions of the candidates play a role in the process?

The creation of the archducal household

In order to be able to grasp in full the composition of the archducal household, it is necessary to return to Albert's youth, in which were sown the first seeds of his later household in Brussels. As already said, Albert and his brother Wenceslas had had since their arrival in Spain a joint princely household at their disposal, which entered into effect May 1, 1571.[10] It consisted of seventy or so persons and was composed partly of newly acquired staff members, and partly of servants who had been transferred from the former households of the deceased crown prince Don Carlos and Queen Elisabeth of Valois. In addition it also counted a number of courtiers who came from the Holy Roman Empire and who, as charged by Maximilian II, were taken up into the entourage of his sons.[11] To the extent the brothers became older, the necessity for splitting up their princely household grew. The premature death of Wenceslas in 1578 made that plan superfluous, yet it did give occasion to reform the entourage, which now came to be fully in the service of Albert.[12] The young archduke, who was appointed as cardinal one year earlier by Pope Gregory XIII, now had a personal household at his disposal under the leadership of the *mayordomo mayor* Juan de Ayala. Already in this early stage the first names of persons pop up who twenty years later would journey to the Netherlands in Albert's wake, among them the *camarero* George of Austria, who would be appointed grand chaplain in 1596, and Cosme de Meneses, a *gentilhombre de la Cámara* who was promoted to *mayordomo* in 1595.[13]

In January, 1583, Albert was installed by Philip II as viceroy of Portugal, a function that he would exercise for ten years.[14] To this day, documents concerning the structure and the organization of his household in Lisbon have not come to light, yet it is certain that in the end this household evolved into a fully-fledged princely entourage, with its own *Capilla*, *Caballeriza*, personal guard, and division of the hunt.[15] According to Hans Khevenhüller, who held the office of imperial ambassador in Madrid

[10] Hortal Muñoz, *El manejo de los asuntos de Flandes*, 189.
[11] *Ibidem*, p. 401.
[12] Martínez Millán, 'El archiduque Alberto en la corte de Felipe II,' 33-35.
[13] Martínez Millán, 'El archiduque Alberto en la corte de Felipe II,' 35.
[14] Concerning Albert's stay in Portugal, see Jordan Gschwend, A. 'In the Shadow of Philip II, *El Rey Lusitano*: Archduke Albert of Austria as Viceroy of Portugal (1583-1593),' in: Duerloo & Thomas, *Essays*, pp. 39-46 and Caeiro, F. *O Arquiduque Alberto de Austria. Vice-rei e inquisidor-mor de Portugal, cardeal legado do papa, governador e depois soberano dos Países Bajos*. Lisbon, 1961.
[15] Hortal Muñoz, *El manejo de los asuntos de Flandes*, 401-402.

between 1574 and 1606, the cardinal-archduke initially planned to take up Castilians exclusively into his household, but the decision was revoked by Philip II, who needed the support of the Portuguese aristocracy and did not want to incite the belligerence of its members against him.[16] For that reason the household was organized according to the Portuguese model and various local nobles were taken up into Albert's retinue. Most of them would remain behind in Portugal after his mandate had run its course in 1593, but a few decided to follow their master on his journey back to Madrid. One of them was Antonio Suárez de Arguello, who had entered into service in 1586, as private secretary of the archduke.[17] He would continue to exercise the function until the death of Albert in 1621.

An important new phase in the development of the archducal household presented itself in 1595, the year in which Albert was appointed governor of the Netherlands. That the cardinal-archduke would take his own courtiers and servants along with him to Brussels need not come as a surprise. Many among them had been in his service for years already and had distinguished themselves in the meantime through their trustworthiness and competence. On top of that, a princely court at the time of the Ancien Régime was by definition bound and determined by the persons in it. In principle its members were appointed for life, and in many cases positions were even passed on from generation to generation. Not coincidentally, Albert had written down in his last will and testament that he saw his *criados* as his children.[18] The courtiers belonged to the *familia* of the prince, in whose hands they had taken an oath of obedience and loyalty. In exchange the prince promised to be responsible for their sustenance and well-being. It was an especially intense form of reciprocity, which implied a high degree of loyalty. Consequently, it spoke for itself that the courtiers were presumed to go where their master went. Yet Albert's household underwent a fundamental reorganization in 1595, in which many staff members were replaced and others first came into his service.[19] The reasons for this change were both pragmatic as well as political in nature.

---

16 Veronelli, S., & Labrador Arroyo, F., eds. *Diario de Hans Khevenhüller, embajador imperial en la corte de Felipe II* (Sociedad Estatal para la Conmemoración de los Centenarios de Felipe II y Carlos V). Madrid, 2001. Op. cit. p. 270.

17 ARA, *SSO* 185, f. 295: Archduke Albert to Philip IV, July 9, 1621.

18 '*A todos mis criados, a los quales he tenido e tengo como por hijos (…)*' ARA, *Papiers du Comté de Mercy-Argenteau* 125: Last will and testament of Archduke Albert.

19 For a detailed overview of the composition of Albert's entourage in this time period, I gladly refer the interested reader on to Hortal Muñoz, J.E. 'The Household of Archduke Albert of Austria from his Election as Governor of Flanders until his Investiture as Sovereign Prince of the Low Countries: 1595-1598,' *Revue belge de Philologie et d'Histoire*, in press. Dr. Hortal Muñoz bases his study, among other things, on the proceedings of the *Bureo*, which – under the direction of Francisco de Mendoza – watched over the organization of the household of the cardinal-archduke. These proceedings can be consulted in RAH, *SyC*, manuscript A-61: *Representación del Almirante de Aragón al Archiduque Alberto siendo su Maiordomo Maior* (1595-1603).

In the first place, not all courtiers and servants were excited at the prospect of having to leave the Iberian peninsula. On account of the many troubles there, faraway *Flandes* enjoyed a less than inviting reputation, and the journey was long and dangerous on top of that. Many did not want to leave their families in the lurch, or maintained to be too poor, too old, or too sick to be able to start that kind of undertaking.[20] They asked permission to remain behind in Madrid, and out of thanks for their proven services were rewarded with financial compensation or with a position in one of the other princely households of the royal house. That was the case for, among others, Albert's *caballerizo mayor* Luis Enríquez, who on account of his advanced age got leave to stay and out of appreciation was appointed Philip II's *mayordomo*.[21] The courtiers and servants who indeed did journey along to the Netherlands were perhaps not sorry about the discharge of those who stayed behind. They saw their chance to be promoted or – if desired – to be transferred to another division within the archducal household.[22] The outflow, however, not only gave occasion for a series of internal shifts but also necessitated the recruitment of new staff members to fill in the vacant positions. Among the new staff were also to be found a few from the Southern Netherlands who had served for years in Philip's royal household, and who now grabbed the chance to return to the land of their birth in Albert's retinue.[23]

In addition to being simply necessary, the reform of 1595 was also politically motivated, in the sense that it was seized upon in order to prepare the archducal household for Albert's future as administrator of the Netherlands. As the governor in Brussels, the cardinal-archduke would occupy a crucial post within the Spanish-Habsburg monarchy. That the composition of his entourage was followed with much interest speaks, then, for itself. In a memorandum Philippe de Croÿ, count of Solre, emphasized that the selection of the archducal retinue had to be handled with care:

> 'Your Highness may not permit that servants of your Chamber and House would bring the administration into difficulties by keeping their gaze directed at their own profit and their private interests, which are harmful to the service of God and His Majesty, and in particular for the reputation of Your Highness, for it is these sorts of affairs that have done disgrace to the rule of

20 RAH, *SyC* A-61, passim.

21 Roco de Campofrío, J. *España en Flandes: Trece años de gobierno del archiduque Alberto (1595-1608)*. Madrid, 1973. Op. cit. p. 7.

22 RAH, *SyC* A-61, passim.

23 It was, among other things, a question of a few of Philip II's *archeros* from the Southern Netherlands, among them Wallerand Morel, Denis de la Forge, Bertrand Le Saige, Jehan van Oostendorp, and Jacques de Hamis. See Hortal Muñoz, *El manejo de los asuntos de Flandes*, 446, 450, 465, 469 and 485.

your predecessors in this country and, even more, are responsible in large part for the ravages dominating there.'[24]

As cited earlier, Philippe de Croÿ was a seasoned politician (cf. Chapter I). He knew the political situation in the Low Countries like the back of his hand and seldom hesitated to make his ideas about it known.[25] According to Solre, Albert needed to surround himself with competent and experienced courtiers, who were familiar with the situation on the ground, could advise him concerning policy, and would not allow themselves to be led by individual self-interest. Whether Solre's memorandum was ultimately decisive is difficult to say, but it is indeed a fact that the complete top-level of the cardinal-archduke's household was replaced with new functionaries in 1595.[26] One of them was Solre himself, who succeeded the afore-mentioned Luis Enríquez as Albert's *caballerizo mayor*. The function of the *sumiller de corps* went to Baron Maximilian von Dietrichstein, who as the former *Oberststallmeister* of Archduke Ernst was well familiar with the Netherlands.[27] The most disputed appointment, rather, was that of Francisco de Mendoza, the Admiral of Aragon, as *mayordomo mayor*.

In 1594, the elderly Juan de Ayala, who had exercised the function of high steward in Albert's household since 1570, was carried to his grave. And just as it had been the case in 1570, the choice of the new *mayordomo mayor* now, too, led to fierce competition, which was advanced even within the royal family. Shortly after Albert's return from Lisbon, Philip II had commissioned his own *sumiller de corps* and favorite, the powerful Cristóbal de Moura, to assist the cardinal-archduke with his political responsibilities.[28] In view of the fact that the king had lost control over his nephew's entourage since his stay in Portugal, Philip asked Moura also to keep an eye on the organization of Albert's household. That was, however, not to the liking of Albert's mother, Empress Maria, who after the death of Maximilian II had returned to Madrid to pass away her final days there in the convent of the *Descalzas Reales*. Cristóbal de Moura was known to adhere to a political/religious ideology that above all looked out

[24] '*(...) no permita V.A. que los domesticos de su Camara i Casa se empachen en el govierno llevando el ojo a solos sus provechos intereses o pasiones particulares tan acosta i perjuicio del servicio de Dios, de S.M. i particularmente de la reputacion de V.A. porque es casa que a escandalizado mucho en aquellos Estados en el govierno de los predesesores de V.A i digo gran parte i ocasion del mal que alli ai (...).*' IVDJ, envío 47, caja 63, doc. 506: *Autoridad absoluta sin ecesion alguna.*

[25] See in that context also Brants, V., ed. *Avis sur les affaires des Pays-Bas, adressés à l'archiduc Albert par Philippe de Croy, comte de Solre.* In: *Bulletin de la Commission Royale d'Histoire*, 83 (1914) 254-279.

[26] Roco de Campofrío, *España en Flandes*, 7. See also Veronelli & Labrador Arroyo, *Diario de Hans Khevenhüller*, 437.

[27] Concerning the household of Archduke Ernst, see Hortal Muñoz, J.E. 'La casa del Archiduque Ernesto durante su gobierno en los Países Bajos (1593-1595),' in: Álvarez-Ossorio Alvariño, A. & García García, B.J., eds. *La Monarquía de las Naciones. Patria, nación y naturaleza en la Monarquía de España.* Madrid, 2004, pp. 193-205.

[28] Hortal Muñoz, *El manejo de los asuntos de Flandes*, 195.

for Castilian interests and opposed the influence of the Holy See. The empress did not plan in the least to expose her son to Moura's sphere of influence and that of his political allies.[29] She succeeded in having her own confidant – the already mentioned imperial ambassador Hans Khevenhüller – appointed as Albert's *mayordomo mayor* and *sumiller de corps*, in order to involve the cardinal-archduke in a political trajectory that was oriented, rather, internationally, as well as to the pope.[30] Maria's triumph was of short duration, however. Once it became known that Albert would succeed his brother Ernst as governor in Brussels, Moura and his adherents grabbed at the chance to push Khevenhüller to the sidelines and to go in search of a *mayordomo mayor* who would serve their interests better. After a long selection process Khevenhüller was – to his great aggravation – replaced by Francisco de Mendoza.[31]

In light of the foregoing, the appointment of the Admiral of Aragon as *mayordomo mayor* seems in a way remarkable. Mendoza stemmed from an old and prominent Castilian lineage, but he held a vision of religion that was rather papally oriented and was not in keeping in the least with the ideological position of Cristóbal de Moura.[32] By circumstance the Admiral was much indebted to Moura's party, all the same. At the end of the 1580s Mendoza became entangled in an event that would come to cost him dearly. Believing that his family would benefit from a stronger bond with the family of the duke of Alba, he tried to have his niece Mencía, a daughter of the duke of Infantado, married to Antonio Álvarez de Toledo, Alba's grandson.[33] That, however, was not to Philip II's liking, who judged that that kind of union would produce an all too large position of power for both families. In spite of Philip's prohibition, Mendoza allowed the marriage to go through. This flagrant expression of disobedience to the will of the king could not remain unpunished. Not much later the Admiral was arrested and locked up in the castle of Turégano. Having meanwhile become a widower, Mendoza tried to gain back his freedom by striking up marriage negotiations with Mencía de la Cerda, a lady-in-waiting to the infanta

[29] Concerning the role of Empress Maria at the court of Philip II, see Martínez Millán, J. 'La Emperatriz Maria y las pugnas cortesanas en tiempos de Felipe II,' in: Belenguer Cebriá, E., ed. *Felipe II y el Mediterráneo. Vol. III: La Monarquía y los reinos (I).* Madrid, 1999, pp. 143-162; Sánchez, M.S. *The Empress, the Queen and the Nun: Women and Power at the Court of Philip III of Spain.* Johns Hopkins U.P., 1998, and Sánchez, M.S. 'Empress Maria and the Making of Political Policy in the Early Years of Philip III's reign,' in: Saint-Saëns, A., ed. *Religion, Body and Gender in Early Modern Spain.* San Francisco, 1991, pp. 139-147.

[30] Veronelli, & Labrador Arroyo, *Diario de Hans Khevenhüller,* 24-25.

[31] '*Llevó mal el conde de Franquenburg que estando ya tan cansado y debilitado de la mucha edad y negocios de la corte y del grave peso de la embajada, quedarse agora con el mismo trabajo, tubo algún sentimiento en renunciar en el almirante y barón de Dietrichstein sus oficios (...).*' *Ibidem,* p. 437.

[32] Concerning Francisco de Mendoza, see Rodríguez Villa, A. 'Don Francisco de Mendoza, almirante de Aragón (1547-1623),' in: Valera, J., ed. *Homenaje a Menéndez y Pelayo en el año vigésimo de su profesorado. Estudios de erudición española.* 2 vols. Madrid, 1899, volume II, pp. 486-610.

[33] *Ibidem,* pp. 580 f.

Isabella. Mencía was a sister of the powerful count of Chinchón, who possessed much influence at the court in Madrid and was an ally of Moura. In exchange for this marriage, Chinchón promised to persuade Philip II to restore his future brother-in-law to honor with a position in one of the princely households of the royal house. Although the marriage ultimately did not go through, the count kept his promise. Shortly after, Mendoza was appointed as *mayordomo mayor* of Cardinal-Archduke Albert. The appointment provided the restoration of honor ardently desired by the Admiral, but also an enormous moral obligation toward his benefactors Chinchón and Moura, which can possibly explain the at times quite hard political line he would follow in the Netherlands.[34]

In addition to political concerns, the divergent origins of Mendoza, Dietrichstein, and Solre suggest that still other motivations lay at the basis of their appointments. The Admiral of Aragon was born and raised in Castile, the heartland of the Spanish monarchy. The family of Maximilian von Dietrichstein stemmed from Carinthia, and Philippe de Croÿ grew up in the Netherlands. Consequently, Albert's *mayordomo mayor*, his *sumiller de corps*, and his *caballerizo mayor* came from three different centers of power in the Habsburg imperium. In that capacity the trio mirrored in a symbolic way the heterogeneous character of the court in Brussels, which united in itself the Spanish, Austrian, and Burgundian traditions like no other. At the same time, however, it can be posited that opting for figures like Dietrichstein and Solre was playing it safe. After all, both nobles had been amply exposed in the past to Spain's sphere of influence. Maximilian was a son of Baron Adam von Dietrichstein, the former imperial ambassador in Madrid, and of Margarita Folch de Cardona, a Spanish lady-in-waiting to Empress Maria (cf. Chapter I).[35] In that sense he was even related to the Admiral of Aragon, whose deceased spouse was a member of the Cardona family as well.[36] Philippe de Croÿ, then again, was appointed captain of the royal guard in Madrid in 1588, a function he would exercise for four years.[37] His loyalty to the Spanish-Habsburg dynasty was, consequently, already considerably put to the test and found suitable. The choice of Dietrichstein and Solre, then, raises the question to what degree a criterion like origin played out, too, in the awarding of functions in Albert's household, and in the process how 'nationality' – to use an anachronistic term for the moment – was related to (expectations of) political loyalty.

[34] Hortal Muñoz, *El manejo de los asuntos de Flandes*, 266.

[35] See Edelmayer, F. *Söldner und Pensionäre. Das Netzwerk Philipps II. im Heiligen Römischen Reich.* München, 2002. Op. cit. p. 100.

[36] In 1584, Francisco de Mendoza married María Ruíz de Liori Colón y Cardona, daughter of Sancho de Cardona, Admiral of Aragon, and of María Colon, marquise of Guadaleste.

[37] See the brief biography in Martínez Millán, J. & Fernández Conti, S., eds. *La Monarquía de Felipe II: La Casa del Rey.* 2 vols. Madrid, 2005. Op. cit. vol. II, pp. 125-126.

Nation and loyalty

In February, 1596, Cardinal-Archduke Albert installed himself in the Coudenberg palace with a noble retinue that – except for Maximilian von Dietrichstein and Philippe de Croÿ – consisted in the main of courtiers of Spanish (and, in most cases, Castilian) origin. That was true of both the Admiral of Aragon as well as the *mayordomos* Cosme de Meneses, Luis Dávalos, and Diego de Ibarra. Save for one rare exception, the five *gentilhombres de la Cámara*, the thirteen *gentilhombres de la Boca*, and the eight *gentilhombres de la Casa* were all of Spanish origin as well.[38] Even so, shortly after his arrival the cardinal-archduke already installed three new *gentilhombres de la Cámara*. The title was awarded to Charles, count of Egmont; to Lamoral, count (and later prince) of Ligne; and to Charles, princely count of Arenberg.[39] There is no doubt that the appointment of the three most prominent nobles in the country may be seen as a symbolic expression both of Albert's determination to restore to honor the disrupted relationship between the local aristocracy and the Habsburg dynasty, and of his resolution to involve them in policy making. That was a reasonable choice. If the cardinal-archduke wanted to see his authority affirmed as governor of the Netherlands and Franche-Comté, then he needed to be assured of the support of the local populace. Tightening the bonds with the local social elites was a priority, and the distribution of court offices constituted an efficient aid to that process. It is not improbable that Albert acted here on the advice of Philip II, who – as seen above – was very conscious of the importance of integrating local nobles into the princely entourage. For that same reason the king would advise him in June, 1598, to send six noble ladies from the Netherlands to Spain, where they would be added to the retinue of the infanta – Albert's future bride:

> 'It seems indicated to me that you, Sir, have six highly-placed women (of which two widows and four ladies) come from the Netherlands (...) to serve my daughter the infanta and in the end to return with her [to Brussels] (...). I leave their choice to you, Sir, as one who is present in that place and shall

[38] For the *gentilhombres de la Cámara*, they were Rodrigo Niño y Lasso, Bernardino de Ayala, Alonso de Cárdenas, Gutierres de Fonseca, and Luis de Venegas. The *gentilhombres de la Boca* were Francisco de Córdoba, Garcia Sarmiento de Mendoza, Alonso de Guzmán, Antonio de Toledo y Meneses, Juan de Toledo y del Aguila, Juan Maldonado y Vargas, Vicente Serrano Zapata, Beltrán de la Cueva, Francisco de la Cerda, Onofre Escrivá, Pedro Rodríguez de Ovalle, and the count of Valdemarino. Only Count Ferdinando Spínola was of Genoese descent. Further, the *Cámara* initially also counted a nobleman of German origin, a certain 'Enrique' Berg, but this man died during the journey to the Netherlands in 1595. The *gentilhombres de la Casa* were García Muriel de Valdivieso, Francisco Campi, Juan Prieto de Posada, Diego Velázquez de la Canal, Pedro Hurtado Barrades, Agustín de Samaniego, Francisco de Anaya Pereira, and the famous historiographer and author Lupercio Leonardo de Argensola. See the court index in ARA, *Aud* 23/10.

[39] Hortal Muñoz, *El manejo de los asuntos de Flandes*, 269.

most certainly be in the position to find persons who have the requisite capacities for this responsibility at their disposal.'[40]

Albert did not throw Philip's counsel to the wind and selected seven noble ladies to serve his future bride. Shortly after that, the countess of Buquoy and the noble ladies of Trazegnies, Montmorency, Croix, Bours, Merode, and Selles departed for Spain.[41] Their melodious names demonstrate that it clearly was not a question of the least among the local noblewomen.[42]

In his essay concerning the structure of the archducal household Diederik Lanoye argues that the appointment of 'autochthonous' nobles (understood by Lanoye as those from the Southern Netherlands and Burgundy) in the course of years would grow into a strategy of Albert and Isabella with conscious intentions.[43] An analysis of the origin of the *gentilhombres* over time seems to support that proposition. As was demonstrated in a prior chapter, the number of *gentilhombres de la Cámara* rose gradually from 5 in 1595, to 24 in 1618. An overview of the distribution of the different nations teaches that the balance clearly tilted to the advantage of the nobility from the Southern Netherlands and Burgundy (cf. Chart 3).

In view of the fact that this development ran more or less analogously in the cases of the *gentilhombres de la Boca*, the *gentilhombres de la Casa*, and the ladies-in-waiting, these data seem to indicate that an active policy for appointments indeed made up part of a broader plan to advance the integration of the indigenous aristocracy into the archducal household. Whereas the numerical preponderance initially lay clearly with the Spaniards, twenty years later there was little left of it to notice. That need not come as a surprise: it is clear that Albert and Isabella benefited from binding their vassals to them as firmly as possible, and to apply all means available to them for this end. Thus, they not only doled out positions in their household, for instance, but also made strikingly frequent use of their sovereign right to award noble titles: in the period 1600-1621 no less than 34 elevations to the nobility took place (cf. below).[44]

---

40 AGS, *Estado* 2224, f. 155: Philip II to Albert, June 3, 1598.

41 Gachard, L.-P. & Piot, C., eds. *Voyage de l'archiduc Albert en Espagne*. In: Gachard, L.-P. & Piot, C., eds. *Collection des voyages des souverains des Pays-Bas*. 4 vols. Brussels, 1876-1882. Volume IV, pp. 457-562. Op. cit. p. 458. See also AGS, *Estado* 603, s.f.: Philippe de Croÿ to Philip II, s.d.

42 According to Louis-Prosper Gachard, Albert was quite amused, by the way, concerning the prospect of seeing French ladies communicate with Isabella's Spanish ladies-in-waiting and with Queen Margaret's German ladies. In a letter the archduke wrote that '*Las damas que yo llevo no saven mas que su francés, que sera buena comedia verlas entre Españolas y Alemanas; sin que las unas se entiendan con las otras.*' Gachard, L.-P., ed. *Actes des États-Généraux de 1600*. Brussels, 1849. Op. cit. p. iii.

43 Lanoye, D. 'Structure and Composition of the Household of the Archdukes,' in: Thomas & Duerloo, *Essays*, pp. 107-119. Op. cit. p. 118.

44 See Duerloo, L. & Janssens, P. *Wapenboek van de Belgische adel van de 15de tot de 20ste eeuw*. 4 vols. Brussels, 1992-1994.

Chart 3 – Development of the number of *gentilhombres de la Cámara* and their origins

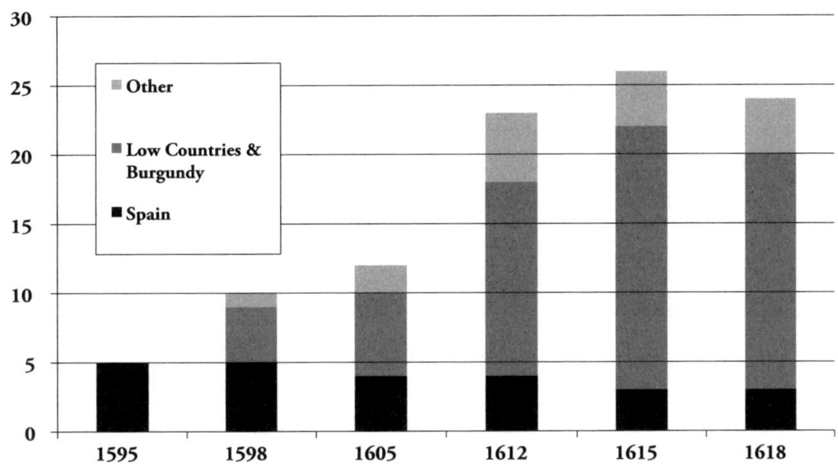

Data based on ARA, *Aud* 23/10 (1595); ASV, *Borghese* I 913, ff. 339-344 (1598); ARA, *Aud* 33/4, ff. 66-72 (1605) and ARA, *RK* 1837 and 1838 (*libros de razón*, 1612-1618).

In light of the historiographical debate concerning the political autonomy of the archdukes, the question arises as to whether the shift in the composition of their entourage also translated into a shift in the balance of power at court. It is perhaps clear that the chart here produces a distorted image. A merely quantitative analysis of the number of *gentilhombres* of this or that origin by definition passes over qualitative factors that can influence the correct interpretation of the figures enormously. Put another way: the archducal household may well have predominantly counted nobles originating from the Southern Netherlands and Burgundy in absolute numbers. Still, this does not necessarily imply that they had the final say at court, of which the historiography on the matter was and is still unconvinced. So, for example, in his monumental *History of Belgium*, Henri Pirenne already pointed out that the most prominent courtiers in the archducal household always proved to be of Spanish origin:

> 'Indeed, the palace of the archdukes resembles much more that of Madrid than that of the dukes of Burgundy. There one finds a *mayordomo mayor*, young noblemen and noblewomen. The father confessors of Albertus and of Isabella, their chaplains and their preachers are Spaniards. Among the noblemen of the chamber as among the ladies-in-waiting, the Spaniards held the primary

> positions. Appearances here answer at once to the truth. Obviously the prince, in this country, is only the representative of Spain.'[45]

Pirenne's judgment dates from the first half of the twentieth century, yet echoes of it resound even today still in the historical sciences. During a recent colloquium, Werner Thomas argued that the numerical preponderance of indigenous nobility in the archducal entourage was neutralized in practice by the fact that key positions always remained in Spanish hands.[46] Although the three groups of *gentilhombres* indeed counted many local nobles, the most intimate entourage of Albert and Isabella (i.e. those who were able and allowed to spend time in the proximity of the princes on a daily basis) would have consisted in the main of Spaniards, according to Thomas. In that way, as the underlying reasoning goes, the court of Albert and Isabella always remained a bastion of Spanish authority in the Netherlands. Although this course of thought rightly tries to apply nuance in all too premature conclusions concerning numerical proportions at the court in Brussels, it in fact calls forth a larger problem. From a certain optic, after all, the question about courtiers' origins is not innocent. In the nineteenth and early twentieth century the political history of the archducal period was traditionally studied from the dichotomy of 'Spanish versus indigenous'.[47] In the same way the court of Albert and Isabella was described as the result of a forced balancing act, in which attention in the main went to the partitioning between those there present from Spain and the Southern Netherlands.[48] The archducal entourage was seen in that case as a bipolar entity, consisting of a monarchist Spanish party on the one hand and a rather recalcitrant indigenous party on the other. This kind of paradigm, however, not only ignores the complex diversity of collective and individual interests that contributed to political developments in this time period, but it suggests, on top of that, that the courtiers' origins were coupled to their political affinity. In essence the concepts of 'nation' and 'faction' were seen here as mutually interchangeable with each other. From a certain angle that approach is not inconceivable. Even in the historical sources, the rivalry between Spaniards and locals pops up frequently, and there is no doubt that both in Spain as well as in the Netherlands quite a lot of prejudices were harbored with respect to each other's populace. In the army, namely,

---

45 Pirenne, H. *Geschiedenis van België*. 7 vols. Ghent, 1902-1933. Op. cit. vol. IV, p. 391 (Accessed via the Digitale Bibliotheek voor de Nederlandse Letteren ['Digital Library for Dutch Humanities'], http://www.dbnl.nl/).

46 Thomas, W. *The Court of the Archdukes and the Spanish Faction.* Paper presented at the colloquium *A Constellation of Courts: The Households of Habsburg Europe, 1555-1665*, organized by the universities of Antwerp and Ghent (Brussels, Paleis der Academiën, November 3-4, 2006).

47 A classic example is Gossart, E. *La domination espagnole dans les Pays-Bas à la fin du règne de Philippe II.* Brussels, 1906.

48 In the process, the Burgundian vassals of the archdukes were conveniently forgotten.

the suspicion between the different nations was great, frequently leading to conflicts.[49] On top of that there is no denying that the wariness toward *los Señores del Pais* – as the nobles from the Southern Netherlands were frequently called in the sources – also played a role in the matter of appointment policy in the case of the top-levels of the military and in the administration. It is known that the government in Madrid was reluctant vis-à-vis installing indigenous officers and functionaries, and that they had a preference for Spanish *cabezas* at the head of the troops.[50] Inversely, in Brussels there was a fair amount of irritation toward the power of the Spaniards in decision-making. So, for instance, the papal nuncio Frangipani complained in 1604 that 'all the misfortune' arose from the fact that Albert was being advised by foreigners, while the counsels of the local populace were not heard.[51] These and similar commentaries are undoubtedly what led Joseph Lefèvre to introduce his concept of the *ministère espagnol* in 1924, further building upon an historiographical tradition in which the rivalry between the Spanish and the 'autochthonous' nation dominated the debate.[52]

Even so, it is a scholarly conviction that contemporaneous prejudices toward 'foreign' nations ought not to be confused with facts – a principle which among historians indeed risks being lost in the background. The assessment that 'national' arguments above all were played out whenever that turned out well in political respects provokes wariness concerning the extent to which this rivalry was decisive. During the Ancien Régime 'nation' and 'loyalty' were not necessarily coupled to each other, even though the historical sources frequently seem to suggest this.[53] When Charles-Bonaventure de Longueval, count of Buquoy, was appointed as general field commander of the Habsburg army by Emperor Matthias in 1613, the French ambassador announced that the Spaniards at court in Brussels were quite satisfied about this decision. After all, they had worked hard for a long time for 'one of them' to get an executive military position in the Holy Roman Empire, and Buquoy – who in their eyes was '*alleman de naisanse*' but '*espaignol d'effect*' – was seen as the person cut out to strengthen the Spanish grasp on the imperial army.[54] The fact that the count in reality had been

[49] Parker, G. *The Army of Flanders and the Spanish Road 1567-1659*. Cambridge U.P., 2004 [Orig. ed.: 1972]. Op. cit. pp. 25-27.

[50] See in that context Esteban Estríngana, A. *Guerra y finanzas en los Países Bajos católicos. De Farnesio a Spinola (1592-1630)*. Madrid, 2002.

[51] '*Tutt' il male viene, ch' il conseglio di Sua Altezza è straniero, quel del paese non s'intende (...)*' ASV, *Borghese* III 110, f. 136: Frangipani to Cardinal Aldobrandini, May 8, 1604.

[52] Lefèvre, J. 'Le ministère espagnol de l'archiduc Albert, 1598-1621.' *Bulletin de l'Académie Royale d'Archéologie de Belgique*, 1 (1924) 202-224.

[53] Concerning the concept 'nation,' see the various contributions in Álvarez-Ossorio Alvariño, A. & García García, B.J., eds. *La Monarquía de las naciones. Patria, nación y naturaleza en la Monarquía de España*. Madrid, 2004 and van Sas, N.C.F., ed. *Vaderland. Een geschiedenis van de vijftiende eeuw tot 1940*. Amsterdam, 1999.

[54] BNF, *MsF* 16130, f. 178: Charles de l'Aubespinne-Chasteauneuf, abbot of Préaux, to Secretary of State Puisieux, September 27, 1613.

born in Arras and that the Longueval family stemmed from Artois, did not appear to occur to them (or was in any case not seen as relevant).[55] The anecdote illustrates that the correlation between nation and loyalty in the early modern period was perceived in an entirely different way than is the case at present. Both concepts could overlap but were not necessarily interchangeable. As opposed to what is frequently assumed, loyalty to the prince during the Ancien Régime was not automatically bound to place of birth. This vision relies all too strongly on an interpretation of nationality and nation-building that came into being in the nineteenth century, and is in that sense anachronistic. Loyalty had to do with being of service to the prince and to the dynasty, and was supported both on notions of identity and sense of honor that crossed boundary lines, as well as on wide-branching personal and familial interests. By means of noble marriage policies, which were bothered just as little by 'national' boundary lines, various aristocratic families acquired titles, possessions, and seigniorial rights in principalities that were sometimes miles and miles away from their original homeland. These kinds of unions naturally brought new obligations along with them. In that sense they frequently led to a redefinition of family concerns, and not seldom to a reorientation of the political affiliation of these families. Loyalty rested in other words on grounds that far transcended the rationale of the modern concept of nation. Consequently, concerning the relationships of political power at the court in Brussels, few statements can be made merely on the basis of an analysis of the courtiers' origins – in any case not without taking other factors also into consideration.

On top of that, the focus on the presence of those from Spain and the Southern Netherlands at court threatens to distort any impression of reality. Although both groups were indeed the most numerous, this 'bipolar' vision stands in sharp contrast to the way in which the court was perceived by its contemporaries. In his *Relationi* the nuncio Bentivoglio wrote that the archducal court 'can seem more joyful and pleasant than [the court at Madrid], on account of the freedom of the country and the mishmash ['*mescolanza*'] of so many nations that one usually sees in Brussels on account of the army. In that respect the court in the Netherlands can be seen without a doubt as superior to any other in Europe.'[56] The nuncio was joined in this view by an anonymous French spy, who – as seen in a previous chapter – concluded that the archducal court 'cedes to no other in the quality and the diversity and quantity

[55] Concerning the Longueval family, see de Vegiano, J.-C.-J. & de Herckenrode, J.S.F.J.L. *Nobiliaire des Pays-Bas et du Comté de Bourgogne*. 4 vols. Ghent, 1862-1868. Op. cit. p. 1250-1255.

[56] Bentivoglio, G. *Relationi del Cardinal Bentivoglio*. Brussels, 1632 [Original edition: *Relationi fatte dall' illustrissimo, e reverendissimo signor cardinal Bentivoglio in tempo delle sue nuntiature di Fiandra, e di Francia. Date in luce da Erycio Puteano*. Antwerp, 1629]. Op. cit. p. 161.

of persons of several nations who reside there (…).'[57] The English earl of Hertford, who was fulfilling a diplomatic assignment at the court in Brussels in 1605, was also quite impressed by the cosmopolitan atmosphere that dominated there.[58] Much more than an arena of two groupings diametrically positioned with respect to each other, contemporaries appear to have seen the court of the archdukes as a melting pot of diverse nations. In addition to those from Spain (in this case an overarching term for those from Castile, Aragon, and other peoples from the Iberian peninsula), from the Southern Netherlands (peoples from Brabant, Flanders, Hainault, and Artois, etc.), and from Franche-Comté, the court sheltered courtiers from Habsburg hereditary lands, from the Holy Roman Empire, from Italy, Portugal, Bohemia, and Hungary. Additionally, there were quite a lot of Catholic refugees from England, Ireland, France, and the Northern Netherlands, who came to Brussels in search of asylum, and who were generally received with open arms.

On top of that, it seems that a mixed composition of the archducal household was also actively strived for. Already around 1595, the count of Solre wrote that the archducal entourage ideally needed to mirror the variety of the Spanish-Habsburg monarchy:

> 'I very much desire that the household of Your Highness would consist of different nations, vassals of His Majesty, so as to preserve the benevolence of all. In particular it should be more Spaniards, Flemings, and Burgundians, as well as a few Italian vassals of His Majesty, and Germans, all Catholic and meritorious persons (…).'[59]

Solre assumed that mutual relations between nations would benefit from a balanced composition in the archducal household. His plea suggests, though, that it was not so much a question of searching for balance between those from Spain on the one hand and those from the Southern Netherlands on the other, but instead for a harmonious composition in which even subjects from other regions of the Spanish-Habsburg imperium had their place. In that sense the selection process of courtiers in this early stage perhaps has to be interpreted instead in the context of the composite monarchy of Philip II, in which the court in Brussels functioned as a subcourt of the court in Madrid and, consequently, put vassals from diverse regions to work.

---

[57] '*(…) ne cedde à aucune autre de sa quallité en la diversité et quantité de personnes qui y résident de plusieurs nations.*' [Anonymous]. 'Relation de Flandres. La Court et Maison des Archiducs en Flandres en 1610,' in: *Souvenirs de la Flandre-Wallonne. Recherches historiques et choix de documents relatifs à Douai et au Nord de la France*, vol. VI. Douai-Paris, 1866, pp. 1-25.

[58] NA, *SP* 77/7, no. 149: The earl of Hertford to the *Privy Council*, May 13, 1605.

[59] IVDJ, envío 47, caja 63, doc. 506: *Autoridad absoluta sin ecesion alguna.*

After the transfer of sovereignty to the archdukes, too, policy remained oriented to an eclectic composition of the entourage, albeit with different accents in a way. Whereas on the one hand the emphasis came to lie more and more on the appointment of their own vassals, on the other hand Albert and Isabella also sought to attract courtiers from all far corners of Habsburg Europe (cf. below). In many respects, after signing the Act of Cession the court in Brussels came to be on the cutting edge of two worlds, with the Spanish branch of the Habsburg dynasty on the one side and the Austrian branch on the other. One of the positions of this book is that the court of the archdukes in the period 1598-1621 has to be seen as a Habsburg court *par excellence*. Naturally it owed much accountability to the court in Madrid, which stood as a model for its organization, but it sought to connect just as well with the imperial court in Prague and later in Vienna. On top of that it is frequently forgotten that the August House of Austria was not only based in these classic centers but also branched out over all Europe via possessions of the younger members of the dynasty. The court in Brussels consequently made up part of an extended network of Habsburg courts and princely households in cities like Innsbruck, Graz, Saverne, and Hall, which jointly constituted an especially large and lucrative source of patronage and employment for the European aristocracy. Preliminary research seems to indicate that these courts shared a common organizational structure and that the course of courtiers' careers could lead them from one court to the other, in the service of the dynasty.[60] Although the research into this phenomenon is still in its infancy, there is perhaps in this respect instead talk of a Habsburg corporate culture that crosses boundary lines, in which the reciprocal exchange of human resources had an important place.

In evaluating the process of selecting courtiers, thus, caution is dictated. Research into the composition of the archducal household benefits little from a premise that postulates the rivalry between Spaniards and locals as predominating everything. That kind of vision takes the dynastic position of the archducal court, as well as the interaction between service and loyalty, too little into account. On top of that it passes over the individual and familial concerns of the courtiers. Yet this book does not mean to refute in any way that origins played a role in awarding positions in the archducal household. So, for instance, it is clear that Spanish wariness with respect to courtiers from the Southern Netherlands could be quite great. Their trustworthiness was continually called into question, and in essence that was understandable. The bottom line was that many among them had once flirted with the side of the Dutch

---

60 The Von Dietrichstein family offers a good example of this (cf. below). See in that context Edelmayer, F. 'Honor y dinero. Adam de Dietrichstein al servicio de la Casa de Austria.' *Studia Histórica. Historia Moderna*, 10-11 (1992/93) 89-116.

rebels in one way or another. Frequently forgotten, however, is that this Spanish suspicion was not automatically correct for that reason.

Although origin indeed could be an important factor, a nuanced analysis of the selection process teaches that where the courtiers originated from was frequently subordinate to other criteria, and in some cases constituted nothing more than a theoretical concern. When Archduke Albert sought a new *primer caballerizo* to assist his premier master of the horses and the mews in 1597, Francisco de Mendoza advised him to choose a Spaniard:

> 'Your Highness has not yet awarded the office of *primer caballerizo*, and although the count of Solre – who holds the function of *caballerizo mayor* – is from the Southern Netherlands ['*flamenco*'], it seems indicated that the *primer caballerizo* would be a Spaniard, because most of the servants of the *Caballeriza* – with whom he needs to associate – are of Spanish origin.'[61]

In this case it is not at once clear whether Mendoza's advice intended to preserve the balance between both nations or, on the contrary, was motivated by purely pragmatic considerations. The Admiral seems to suggest that the appointment of the Spanish *primer caballerizo* would possibly lead to the *Caballeriza*'s more efficient operation, yet does not go into the matter further. In any case the problem was certainly not situated in the area of communication, for the count of Solre spoke fluent Spanish. Whatever the case may be: it seems that Mendoza's concern in practice ultimately mattered little. Albert appears, to be sure, to have had his eye on the Spanish nobleman Francisco de Córdoba, but he did not come under consideration for the function on account of being absent from the court for too long.[62] Mendoza consequently proposed an alternative candidate, who remarkably enough proved to be not even of Spanish origin. It was Gaston Spínola, a nobleman who came from Palermo and in that sense was a Sicilian subject of Philip II.[63] Originally, though, his family stemmed from Genoa, and Spínola himself had lived for years already in the Netherlands, where he was married to Marie de Renty, heiress to the domain Bruay in Artois.[64] He was known as a man 'of quality, competence, dedication, and intelligence,' which according to Mendoza made him the person cut out for the job.[65] If the archduke did

[61] '*El officio de primer cavallerizo no ha provehido V.A. y aunque siendo el conde de Solre que tiene el de cavallerizo mayor flamenco paresce que fuera conveniente ser español el primer cavallerizo por serlo los mas officiales de la Cavalleriza con que se ha de tratar (...)*' RAH, *SyC* A-61, ff. 11r-11v.

[62] *Ibidem.*

[63] *Ibidem.* In 1603, the domain Bruay was elevated to county, with the granting of the title (transferable to the first-born) to Gaston Spínola.

[64] Vander Linden, H. 'Spinola (Gaston de),' in: *Biographie Nationale*, vol. XXIII (1921-1924) pp. 426-428.

[65] RAH, *SyC* A-61, f. 11v.

not accord with the choice, however, or if Spínola would decline the offer, then Albert could also opt for the Genoese nobleman Ferdinando Spínola, who was a distant relative of Gaston. Ferdinando was already *gentilhombre de la Boca* of Albert and was seen just as well as a competent and virtuous man. On top of that, his father and uncle had long worked in the service of the emperor, and they had urged the latter to have the archduke appoint Ferdinando as *gentilhombre de la Cámara*. That Ferdinando was not a subject of the Spanish king, technically speaking, evidently did not make a difference. If his origin played a role at all, it was because as a Genoese he was presumed to have an understanding of bookkeeping ['*save de cuentas como ginovés*'].[66]

The archduke followed Mendoza's advice and awarded the function to Gaston Spínola. The anecdote illustrates that origin was indeed taken into consideration in theory, but in practice it constituted in no way the only, let alone always the decisive, criterion, on the basis of which an office in the archducal household was awarded. In addition to origin, the selection of courtiers was generally dependent on a delicate combination of factors, such as religious and political affinity, lineage and reputation, and competence and experience. In addition, the influence and advocacy of third parties also played an important role. These criteria are discussed in the following sections.

The selection process

As seen above, shortly after taking office as governor, Albert began work on appointing nobles from the Southern Netherlands and Burgundy to his household. The Spanish Habsburgs had enough experience with regional revolts to realize that the recognition of the different regions of their composite monarchy was crucial to keeping their regime intact. As the most prominent power base of the Habsburg dynasty in the Netherlands, the court in Brussels, then, had an important integrative and reconciliatory function. In that sense the factor of 'origin' was naturally of great importance. That does not mean, however, that just any nobleman from the Southern Netherlands or Burgundy came under consideration for a position in the archducal household. Candidates were expected to answer to the strict requirements of the ethos current at the court in Brussels, which surely did not make the search for persons well-suited to it easy. In that context, Albert's court chaplain Aubertus Miraeus wrote:

> 'For Services at his court [the archduke] selected from the Nobility those who stood out through the rectitude of their Lives, wisdom, decency, and other Virtues. People of evil nature, and young men given over to excess and lust,

[66] *Ibidem.*

> he turned out of his Household at once. For that reason he had the activities of everyone investigated in secret by competent and loyal Men, before he took anyone into any Service in his Court. And if anyone did not satisfy the expectation one had of him, or changed his morals, he was at first instance put out of his Office, to the end that he should not through his Evil, like a Plague, infect his Court, which was otherwise Holy.'[67]

That Miraeus had it right is shown by the proceedings of the *Bureo*, which was charged, among other things, with the selection of the new *mayordomos* and the *gentilhombres de la Boca* in the period 1596-1598.[68] Already there was no lack of candidates. The *Bureo* – under the direction of the Admiral of Aragon – got dozens of letters and memoranda to process from nobles from the Southern Netherlands and Burgundy who aspired to a position in the archducal household. In its proceedings the pros and cons for each of them are nicely weighed out against each other. The document explicitly posited that applicants needed to answer to various conditions:

> 'As concerns the choice of servants from these countries whom His Majesty shall have to take into his household, it is such that many matters must be taken into consideration, to wit, their steadfastness and unshakability in the Catholic Religion and in the service of His Majesty [Philip II]; the virtuousness and quality of their person; experience and their [financial] capability and their social proficiencies; so that they who have all these qualities at their disposal would be selected above others, and so that – if not all the mentioned qualities and virtues are found in one person – the best and the one with the fewest wants would be selected from among those who present themselves.'[69]

The instructions were followed precisely. For the position of *mayordomo* more than twenty candidates presented themselves, who were all thoroughly 'screened' by the *Bureo*.[70] The evaluation of the applicants left little to the imagination. Thus, for instance, Robert de Ligne-Arenberg, baron and later prince of Barbançon, got merciless criticism to swallow: 'This knight is a legitimate brother of the count of

---

67 After Miraeus, A. *De vita Alberti Pii, sapientis, prudentis Belgarum Principis commentarius*. Antwerp, 1622, p. 106.

68 RAH, *SyC* A-61, ff. 20-31: *Relacion de las personas del Pays que pretenden servir a Su Alteza de Mayordomos*. For the *gentilhombres de la Boca*, see ff. 24-26.

69 '*Prosupuesto que para las ellectiones de los criados destos Payses de S[u] A[lteza] ha de meter en su casa se han de considerar muchas cosas, es a saber la firmeza y seguridad en la Religion Catholica y en el servicio de S[u] M[ajestad], la virtud y qualidad de la persona, la experiencia y hazienda y la apacibilidad de la condicion, paraque hallandose todos se prefieran los que les tuvieren a los demas, y faltando algunas se elixe lo mejor de lo que se offreciere y que menos inconvenientes tenga.*' RAH, *SyC* A-61, f. 30r.

70 RAH, *SyC* A-61, ff. 20-31: *Relacion de las personas del Pays que pretenden servir a Su Alteza de Mayordomos*.

Arenberg, [he is] noble and rich and [member] of a house that has always loyally served His Majesty. He is a young man who knows little and drinks a lot, and who has an unruly life behind him.'[71] Another candidate, the lord of Willerval, was '[member of] the House of Ongnies, old and quite social, lacking caution, and tempestuous.' On top of that it was known that in the past he 'had chosen the side of the rebels against His Majesty.' [72] The lord of Vendegies, then again, was a member of the prominent Montmorency family. He was quite devout and was seen as a loyal servant of the king, but the fact that 'his health was bad this year,' and that he was recovering from an illness, had to be taken into account.[73] In his turn, the count of Ligne was a rich and prominent nobleman, but he was 'a boy with few proficiencies, and there are people who doubt his suitability for this kind of office in the service of His Highness, and others who say that there is no objection.'[74] Among the candidates who did receive a positive evaluation was Maximilien de Noircarmes, count of Sainte-Aldegonde:

> 'He is approximately 36 years old and a son of the deceased lord of Noircarmes, who was the *sumiller de corps* of Emperor Charles V and member of his Council of State, head of Finances and governor of Hainault. He is a virtuous man, grasps matters quickly, and is in good condition. He has been to Spain and speaks Spanish, and enjoys rents of fl. 20,000 per year.'[75]

Despite the positive comments, Noircarmes was not installed as *mayordomo* during this round of appointments – that would not happen until a few years later.

The integration of nobles from the Southern Netherlands and Burgundy at court was, to be sure, a factor that was indeed taken into account, yet that is not to say that candidates from other areas were not taken into consideration. For the function of *mayordomo*, Francisco de Mendoza could announce that three 'foreign' applicants had presented themselves ['*pretenden ansimismos ser mayordomos de Su Alteza demas de los del Pays*'].[76] It was the Sicilian nobleman mentioned earlier, Gaston Spínola, 'governor and captain-general of the province of Limburg, member of the *Consejo de Guerra* of His Majesty and *primer caballerizo* of Your Highness. He is 45 years old and enjoys rents of 8,000 to 9,000 ducats, and wears the vestments of [the military order of] Santiago. He has the intellect and the remaining qualities [which are necessary] for this office.'[77] Furthermore, the Spaniard Domingo de Orbea also came under

[71] RAH, *SyC* A-61, f. 30r.
[72] *Ibidem*, f. 30v.
[73] *Ibidem*, f. 30r.
[74] *Ibidem*.
[75] *Ibidem*, f. 27r.
[76] *Ibidem*, f. 26r.
[77] *Ibidem*.

consideration for the position. His candidacy was found to be problematic, though, in a way. According to Mendoza, Orbea was a 'very honorable *hidalgo*,' a knight in the order of Santiago, and owner of lands that brought in annual rents of 3,000 ducats, and yet he was lower in prestige than his fellow countryman Diego de Ibarra, who already was *mayordomo*.[78] On top of that, the archduke had to take into consideration that Orbea, whose father did not belong to the high nobility, was 'of lesser quality' than the other Spaniards to whom Albert had given the function of *mayordomo*.[79] Finally, the French nobleman Jacques Colas, count of La Fère and member of the Catholic League, also laid claim to the position. Mendoza, however, harbored the requisite suspicion in the case of Colas' candidacy: 'Your Highness could accept as well the count of La Fère for this office (although he is a Frenchman, and does not belong to a great family).'[80] The question needed to be considered, though, 'whether it is desirable that His Highness (…) would make use of the services of the count, in a function so close to his Person.'[81] Despite the fact that Colas was seen as a meritorious and competent man, the idea that a French nobleman would serve in the immediate proximity of the archduke was a bridge too far. It seems, then, that prepossession toward 'foreign' nations came to expression above all whenever it was a question of potential courtiers who were not vassals of the Habsburgs. Yet one needs to realize that this suspicion was not justified for that reason. Jacques Colas was not necessarily less trustworthy than other candidates. The count was a convinced *Ligueur* who had sought refuge at the court in Brussels and clearly committed himself there to the Habsburg cause.[82] Thus, for example, he fought on the side of the archducal troops during the Battle of Nieuwpoort in 1600, where he became fatally wounded.[83] After that, out of appreciation for his services, his widow Antoinette de Ravenel, countess of La Fère, was installed as *dueña de honor* to the infanta. Over the course of years she would grow to become one of Isabella's dearest ladies-in-waiting.[84]

Ultimately the *Bureo*'s choice fell upon Jacques-Philippe de Gand-Vilain, count of Izegem – 'who is a prominent man, virtuous, and grasps matters quickly, although he

---

78 *Ibidem*, f. 26v.

79 *Ibidem*.

80 *Ibidem*, f. 26r.

81 *Ibidem*.

82 Concerning Jacques Colas, see Colas de la Noue, E. *Un Ligueur: le comte de la Fère*. Paris, 1892 and Descimon, R. & Ruiz Ibánez, J.J. *Les Ligueurs de l'exil. Le refuge catholique français après 1594*. Seyssel, 2005.

83 According to Colas' nineteenth-century biographer Colas de la Noue, the count of La Fère fought '*avec une vaillante furie à côté de son prince*.' See Colas de la Noue, *Un Ligueur*, 148.

84 Beginning in 1627, Antoinette de Ravenel would even unofficially take over the duties of the deceased *camarera mayor* Antoinette-Guillemette of Arenberg, although she did not get the title of mistress of the household. See ASV, *NF* 21 A, f. 546: Nuncio Giovanni-Francesco Guidi di Bagno to Cardinal Spada, February 27, 1627. See also Hennequin de Villermont, M. *L'Infante Isabelle, gouvernante des Pays-Bas*. 2 vols. Paris-Tamines, 1912. Op. cit. vol. II, p. 469-471.

is a cripple and has few possessions' – and upon Gerard de Croÿ, lord of Crecque – who '[is] a brother of the count of Roeulx, a virtuous Catholic and quite a good Christian. He is poor, withdrawn, and timid rather than meddlesome.'[85] In comparison with some of the others, the judgment concerning both men was mild, yet not especially enthusiastic. Perhaps Izegem and Crecque had their appointment as *mayordomo* above all thanks to the fact that their fathers – as opposed to many other nobles – had always proved themselves loyal servants of the Habsburg dynasty. Izegem's father Maximilien de Gand-Vilain (+1583), baron of Rassegem, had distinguished himself in the service of Philip II as sovereign-bailiff of Aalst, governor of Lille, Douai, and Orchies, member of the Council of State, and president of the Council of Finances. In addition, he was commander of a company of 1,200 soldiers in the *Ejército de Flandes*.[86] Crecques' father Adrien de Croÿ was a knight of the Golden Fleece and for a long time the chamberlain, grand marshal, and *mayordomo mayor* of Charles V, who had elevated him to count of Roeulx out of thanks for proven services. He was captain of a company in the imperial army as well and successively held the governorships of Flanders, Artois, Lille, Douai, and Orchies.[87]

Information concerning appointments of the *gentilhombres de la Boca* is also found in the proceedings of the *Bureo.* Francisco de Mendoza made it known that these positions were strived for, namely, by 'sons and brothers of the most prominent nobles of these countries.'[88] The Admiral at once proposed a few well-suited candidates:

> 'The lord of Bredam is a member of the prominent House of Burgundy, and of good standing ['*de buen talle*'] (...), and has not one want, albeit that he is a cripple in a way. The lord of Staden is a son of the lord of Noyelles, governor of Bapaume, and is a very prominent man of very good standing (...). Both knights are brothers-in-law and nephews of the count of Solre and of the count of Arenberg. Monseigneur de Fresin, too, is a prominent man with quite good proficiencies ['*de muy buen arte*'] and requests the office of *mayordomo* but will be satisfied with that of the *Boca.*'[89]

---

[85] RAH, *SyC* A-61, f. 24r and 30v. In their edition of the report of Archduke Albert's journey to Spain in 1598-1599, L.-P. Gachard and C. Piot maintain incorrectly that this would be a question of Claude de Croÿ, lord of Crecque and later count of Roeulx. This Claude was indeed *mayordomo* of the archducal household, but only beginning March 9, 1614 (see ARA, *RK* 1837, f. 268v). Naturally, Gerard and Claude were indeed related to each other. Gachard, L.-P. & Piot, C., eds. *Voyage de l'archiduc Albert en Espagne*. In: Gachard, L.-P. & Piot, C., eds. *Collection des voyages des souverains des Pays-Bas*. 4 vols. Brussels, 1876-1882. Volume IV, pp. 457-562 and Vegiano & Herckenrode, *Nobiliaire*, 579-580.

[86] Vegiano & Herckenrode, *Nobiliaire*, 782-783.

[87] Vegiano & Herckenrode, *Nobiliaire*, 579.

[88] RAH, *SyC* A-61, f. 24r.

[89] *Ibidem.*

According to Mendoza, the three men were the best-suited for the position, although many other candidates had presented themselves who, all the same, were not of such a good house as the persons mentioned ['*y otros naturales que no son de tanta qualidad como los dichos*'].[90] In any case, Archduke Albert seems to have gone along in agreement here in part: not much later Charles de Bourgogne, lord of Bredam, and Hugues de Noyelles, lord of Staden, were both appointed as *gentilhombre de la Boca*. Bredam's installation came perhaps thanks to the fact that he could pride himself on an illustrious ancestry. After all, he was a great-grandson of Anthony, nicknamed the '*Grand Bâtard*,' a natural son of Philip the Good.[91] Of course Charles was not the only issue of the dukes of Burgundy who made his career in the service of the archdukes. His nephew Herman de Bourgogne was elevated by Albert and Isabella to count of Fallais in 1614, while Charles, lord of Wakken – the relative of both Anthony and Herman – was promoted in that same year to baron.[92] Knowing that two of Herman's daughters and one of his sons also made up part of the archducal household, it can be safely posited that this side-tracked bastard branch of the dukes of Burgundy was 'fished up' by the archdukes and placed prominently in the foreground again.[93] Hugues de Noyelles, then again, was a scion of a family from the high nobility, whose members had worked their way up in service to the Habsburg dynasty. His father Paul was appointed governor and captain of Bapaume in 1609, and his grandfather François had been governor and grand-bailiff of Hesdin for a long time.[94] That the House of Noyelles enjoyed great trust ever since is shown by the fact that various members from it would fulfill a function in the archducal household. Hugues' niece Alexandrine de Noyelles, lady of Bours, was a lady-in-waiting to the infanta and in 1600 would marry the afore-mentioned Maximilien de Noircarmes, count of Sainte-Aldegonde, who would later be appointed *mayordomo*.[95] Her sister Roberte, then again, wed Francesco Bernardino de Cassina, an Antwerp merchant of Milanese origin who bought the barony of Boelare from the prince of Orange and became *gentilhombre de la Boca* of

---

90 *Ibidem*.

91 See Vegiano & Herckenrode, *Nobiliaire*, 283-284. For a complete genealogical overview of the De Bourgogne family, see Bergé, M. 'Les bâtards de la Maison de Bourgogne et leur descendance,' in: *L'intermédiaire des Généalogistes. Bulletin du Service de Centralisation des Etudes Généalogiques et Démographiques de Belgique*, 60 (1955) 316-408.

92 Vegiano & Herckenrode, *Nobiliaire*, 283 and Bergé, 'Les bâtards,' 376 and 388-389.

93 Herman de Bourgogne had several children, but in view of the fact that his sons Philippe and Felix (who was a former page of Albert) entered into the Jesuit order, the title passed on to his daughter Marguerite de Bourgogne, countess of Fallais. She was a lady-in-waiting to the infanta and in 1620 married Count Hugues de Noyelles, *mayordomo* in the archducal household. Her sister Isabelle de Bourgogne also made up part of the retinue of the infanta. In 1621, she married Charles-Emmanuel de Gorrevod, marquis of Marnay and *sumiller de corps* of Albert beginning in 1620. See Vegiano & Herckenrode, *Nobiliaire*, 281-282 and Bergé, 'Les bâtards,' 389-390.

94 Vegiano & Herckenrode, *Nobiliaire*, 1458-1461.

95 *Ibidem*, p. 1459.

the archdukes.[96] Another relative, Adrien de Noyelles, was *mayordomo* as well in the archducal household and was elevated by Albert and Isabella to count of Marles in 1621. His son Florent, baron of Rossignol, was in his turn a *gentilhombre de la Cámara* and married his distant niece Françoise de Noyelles, a lady-in-waiting to the infanta and heiress of the county of Croix and the marquisate of Lisbourg.[97] Hugues himself got the title of count of Noyelles in 1614 and was appointed *mayordomo* another two years later. In his turn he married the lady-in-waiting Marguerite de Bourgogne, the oldest daughter of the afore-mentioned count of Fallais.[98]

The criteria

Although the proceedings of the *Bureo* only contain data concerning the selection of the *mayordomos* and the *gentilhombres de la Boca* in the period 1596-1598, various criteria come to the surface from the commentaries on the candidates that would lie at the foundation of the recruitment policy in the household during the entire archducal reign. These factors are discussed briefly in what follows by means of a few specific examples.

Religious and political affinity

The different factors were certainly not all similarly equal. Two criteria stand out head and shoulders above the rest. In order to come under consideration for a position, applicants had to be both convinced Catholics as well as loyal adherents to the Habsburg dynasty. Both conditions were coupled to each other in essence. The August House of Austria was inseparably connected with the princely virtue of *Pietas*. Whoever wanted to have a chance at a position in the archducal household was consequently expected to adhere to the Catholic faith. Here it was a matter of a constant requirement in the policy of the archdukes, which was recorded, on top of that, in the list of clauses added to the Act of Cession in 1598.[99] The archducal court profiled itself as a bastion of the Catholic religion and would consequently never admit persons with other religious convictions. On top of that, that rule applied not only to members of the archducal household but also to the servants of the courtiers. When Antoinette-Guillemette of Arenberg was appointed *camarera mayor* of the

[96] *Ibidem*. Concerning the Cassina family, see Jodogne, P. *Entre Italie et Pays-Bas méridionaux: le 'libro de memoria' de la famille Cassina*. Brussels, 2002.

[97] Vegiano & Herckenrode, *Nobiliaire*, 1458.

[98] *Ibidem*, pp. 1459-1460.

[99] The text of the Act of Cession can be found in Brants, V., ed. *Recueil des Ordonnances des Pays-Bas. Règne d'Albert et d'Isabelle*. 2 vols. Brussels, 1909.

infanta in 1615, Albert's secretary at once informed the Arenberg family that the new mistress of the household was expected to dismiss all non-Catholic ladies from her personal retinue, 'and that she was not in any way [allowed] to bring anyone with her who [was] not entirely Catholic.'[100] At the same time the strict religious reputation of the court in Brussels saw to it that it became an important place of refuge for Catholic nobles from England, Ireland, France, and the Dutch Republic. Albert and Isabella usually received these exiles with open arms. That was the case, among others, for the Irish Catholic Dermot O'Mallun, baron of Glean-O'Mallun, whose possessions in Ireland had been declared forfeited.[101] Thereupon he had fled to Brussels, where he was appointed by the archdukes as *gentilhombre de la Casa*. The same was true for Jan Mulert, a Catholic who came from the province of Overijssel in the Northern Netherlands. After the death of his father Ernest, who was governor of Lingen, Mulert fled to Brussels, where he became *gentilhombre de la Boca* in the household of Archduke Ernst and after that was appointed by Albert to lieutenant of the *Hartschiere*.[102] As a convinced *Ligueur*, the French nobleman Charles de Lorraine, duke of Aumale, would also seek asylum at the court in Brussels.[103] Even so, as opposed to O'Mallun and Mulert, Aumale never held a position in the archducal household, which does not take away from the fact that he pretty much always stayed at court.

The second condition was just as much logic personified. Ever since the Dutch Revolt had broken out, great numbers of nobles had turned away from the Habsburg regime. The chance that others would follow their example was still especially real at the beginning of the seventeenth century. It need not come as a surprise then either, that positions in the archducal household were awarded in the first place to aristocrats, such as Arenberg and Ligne, whose families during those times of trouble had given proof of irreproachable loyalty to the Spanish regime. As seen above, the distribution of offices in the archducal household constituted an important strategy for tightening the ages-old bonds between the Habsburg dynasty and the aristocracy from the Southern Netherlands anew. Not coincidentally, this tactic would be applied above all during crucial moments in the life cycle of the archducal regime. That was the case, for example, in the period 1613-1614, in which Albert was seriously ill for a time and the future of the Southern Netherlands was experienced as especially

[100] ACA, 36/17, s.f.: Antonio Suárez de Arguello to Charles of Arenberg, November 19, 1615.

[101] AHN, *OOMM*, expediente 1828 (Dermicio de Omallun, 1617). See also BAV, *BaL* 6810, s.f.: Nuncio Sanseverino to Cardinal Ludovisi, May 8, 1621 and AGS, *Estado* 2305, s.f.: Archduke Albert to Philip III, May 24, 1618.

[102] AHN, *OOMM*, expediente 1745 (Juan Mulert y Vandencamp, 1617); ARA, *SSO* 177, f. 15: Archduke Albert to Philip III, March 8, 1610 and ARA, *SSO* 201, f. 341: The infanta Isabella to Philip IV, October 22, 1621.

[103] Extensive information concerning Charles de Lorraine can be found in Descimon & Ruiz Ibánez, *Les Ligueurs de l'exil*, passim.

uncertain.[104] In view of the fact that the archdukes had no progeny, after the death of either the sovereignty would return to the Spanish crown. That kind of scenario contained great risks for the political stability in the Low Countries. And although, contrary to all expectations, the archduke did pull through, it was clear to everyone that he did not have much longer to live. Seen from that optic, it was a reasonable move of Albert to embark upon the appointment of a great number of new *gentilhombres* during this time period.[105] During the early months of 1614, on top of that, he handed out no less than ten noble titles, eight of which on one day alone.[106] In that way he tried to assuage flared-up feelings and to assure himself of the continuing support of the aristocracy.

Although an irreproachable prior history constituted an important criterion in awarding positions in their household, the archdukes would also act forgivingly in certain cases, with respect to the family members of former rebels. Among others, that was the case for Charles, count of Egmont and prince of Gavere.[107] He was a son of the infamous Lamoral of Egmont, who together with the count of Horn was executed on accusations of high treason in 1568. Approximately thirty years later, Cardinal-Archduke Albert showed himself to be ready to expunge the past, for Charles was one of the first nobles from the Low Countries to be appointed *gentilhombre de la Cámara* in 1596. Not much later he was installed as governor of Namur and in 1599, Philip III gave him the title of knight in the Order of the Golden Fleece.[108] In spite of Charles' dubious descent, there was thus clearly room for reconciliation, and that is not

[104] AGS, *Estado* 628, s.f.: Consult of the *Consejo de Estado*, January 16, 1614.

[105] For the *gentilhombres de la Cámara*, they were Antoine de Lalaing, count of Hoogstraten (appointed on March 16, 1613), Florent de Ligne, marquis of Roubaix (March 16, 1613), Florent de Noyelles, baron of Rossignol (March 16, 1613), Maximilian von Dietrichstein, nephew of the *sumiller de corps* of the same name (February 1, 1614) and Philippe-Lamoral de Gand-Vilain, count of Izegem (March 7, 1614). For the *gentilhombres de la Boca*, they were Francisco de Acuña (August 21, 1613), a certain 'Monseigneur de Lagni' (August 21, 1613) and François van der Gracht, lord of Schardau and Bavikhove (February 18, 1614). For the *gentilhombres de la Casa*, they were Charles de Hannedouche, lord of Le Fay (January 6, 1614), Henri de Waha known as Baillonville (January 12, 1614), and François van den Hecke, lord of Aponlieu (February 1, 1614).

[106] On February 8, 1614: elevation to principality of the barony Barbançon in Hainault and granting of this title to Robert de Ligne, princely count of Arenberg; elevation to marquisate of the barony Trazegnies in Brabant and granting of this title to Baron Charles de Trazegnies et de Silly; elevation to county of the domain Vertaing in Cambrai and granting of this title to Philippe de Rubempré; elevation to county of the domain Bailleul in Artois and granting of this title to Maximilien de Bailleul; elevation to county of the domain Gommegnies (Le Quesnoy) in Hainault and granting of this title to Baron Guillaume de Hamal, Monceaux et Gommegnies; elevation to county of the domain Moerbeke in Flanders and granting of this title to Robert de Saint-Omer; elevation to county of the domain Fallais in Brabant and granting of this title to Herman de Bourgogne, baron of Fallais; elevation to barony of the domain Wakken (Dentergem) in Flanders and granting of this title to Charles de Bourgogne. On March 5, 1614: elevation to county of the domain Noyelles in Artois and granting of this title to Hugues de Noyelles, lord of Staden. On March 10, 1614: elevation to viscountcy of the domain La Thieuloye in Artois and granting of this title to Charles de Bernemicourt.

[107] Vegiano & Herckenrode, *Nobiliaire*, 712.

[108] ASV, *NF* 11, f. 705-706: Nuncio Frangipani to Cardinal Aldobrandini, September 18, 1599.

necessarily surprising. After all, the count of Egmont profiled himself not only as a loyal subject of the Habsburg dynasty but also as a very devout Catholic and as a passionate patron of the Catholic community in the Northern Netherlands. In view of the fact that most of his possessions were situated in the North, he frequently stayed in The Hague, where he owned a house that he opened up for Catholic religious services.[109] No need to say that for that reason he especially fell into favor with the archdukes. Balthasar de Zúñiga, the Spanish ambassador, called Charles a fairly weak figure, yet indeed a very courteous man with genuine intentions. According to Zúñiga, Charles, then, had deserved to receive the favor of the archdukes and the Spanish king.[110] When Charles died in 1620, the wariness toward his family had clearly disappeared entirely. One year later, they were restored all the rights and dignities they had lost in 1568.[111] Out of gratitude for Charles' services, his son Louis received the prestigious title of *grande* of Spain, by which he entered into the select group of nobles who enjoyed the prestigious privilege of being allowed to keep their hats on in the presence of the prince. In his turn, Louis thanked the king by naming his newborn son after Philip IV and by offering that the latter become his godfather. In his accompanying letter he posited that his family was one of the 'most loyal and obedient of all the vassals and subjects of Your Majesty.'[112] With that, the reconciliation between the House of Egmont and the Habsburg dynasty was sealed.

A comparable case is that of the noble Melun family. Pierre de Melun, prince of Épinoy, was until his death in 1594, one of the most notorious opponents of the Spanish regime in the Netherlands.[113] Yet at the beginning of the seventeenth century, his son Guillaume was installed as *gentilhombre de la Cámara* in the archducal household. Guillaume and his sister Anne were both brought up at the French court but returned some time after the death of their father back to Brussels. They were received at the court of the archdukes with open arms, and they were restored to pretty much all their earlier rights in 1602.[114] The reconciliation between the archdukes and the Melun family proved to be a successful move for both parties. Albert and Isabella got another prominent adherent in the process, while Guillaume acquired the positions of viscount of Ghent, constable of Flanders, and seneschal, governor and grand bailiff of Hainault. In 1621, on top of that, he became knight in the Order

[109] ASV, *Borghese* II 98, f. 243: Nuncio Lucio Sanseverino to Cardinal Borghese, January 25, 1620.

[110] BL, *Egerton* ms. 2079, f. 237.

[111] AGS, *Estado* 2310, s.f.: The marquis of Bedmar to Philip III, February 24, 1621.

[112] '*(...) plus fidelles et obeissantes d'entre celles des vassauts et subiects de Vostre Majesté.*' AGS, *Estado* 2312, s.f.: Louis of Egmont to Philip IV, September 29, 1622.

[113] Piot, C. 'Melun (Pierre de),' in: *Biographie Nationale*, volume XIV (Brussels, 1897), p. 332.

[114] See Marini, M. *Anna van Croÿ (1564-1635), hertogin van Aarschot en prinses-gravin van Arenberg. Vermogen en onvermogen van een hoogadellijke dame in het begin van de zeventiende eeuw*. Unpublished master's thesis, Katholieke Universiteit Leuven, 2006. Op cit. p. 118.

of the Golden Fleece – the highest possible recognition that was handed out in the Spanish-Habsburg imperium.[115]

Lineage and reputation

One aspect that most certainly would have contributed to the rehabilitation of Guillaume de Melun is the fact that his family belonged to the most prominent noble houses in the Netherlands. Albert and Isabella were indeed conscious of the fact that the presence of high nobility in their household could contribute not only to restoring the bonds between the Habsburg dynasty and the local aristocracy but also to the splendid radiance and prestige of their court in general. In that sense the social status of the candidates seems to have been an important factor in the choice of courtiers – whether their origins were in the Southern Netherlands, Spain, or anywhere else. Members from families of the high nobility (such as Arenberg, Croÿ, Ligne, Noyelles, Gorrevod, Melun, Ibarra, Dietrichstein, and Visconti) clearly had a mark in their favor. Inversely, the archdukes were rather reluctant vis-à-vis persons who did not have the requisite noble *qualidad* at their disposal. In that area Archduke Albert seldom proved to be ready to make concessions – and that was true just as well for Spanish lords. In 1615, Balthasar de Zúñiga (who was now ambassador in Prague) wrote the archduke a letter in which Zúñiga asked him to take into consideration the promotion of Iñigo de Brizuela, a nephew of the father confessor of the same name. Iñigo was already *gentilhombre de la Boca* in the archducal household, yet gladly wanted to climb up the ladder to *gentilhombre de la Cámara*.[116] The archduke, however, proved to find nothing in favor of that, because according to him Iñigo did not have the required *qualidad* at his disposal. Zúñiga disagreed with that and complained that Albert was going too much on rules that were current in the Holy Roman Empire, where nobles who wanted to make claims on a position as chamberlain evidently had to satisfy much stricter conditions:

> 'The House of Brizuela is one of the oldest and most noble in (…) Burgos, and if the ears of Your Highness would not be so purely German, one would be able to say to You, Sir, that this family carries in it the blood of the royal House of Castile, for according to my information the mistress of King Alonso XI (from whom the Kings descend) was a daughter of Teresa de Brizuela. And although that is no matter valued for its worth in Germany, it is quite worthwhile in Castile and other countries.'[117]

---

[115] Vegiano & Herckenrode, *Nobiliaire*, 1332-1333.
[116] Concerning Iñigo de Brizuela, see AHN, *OOMM*, expediente 1259 (Iñigo de Brizuela y Urbina, 1609).
[117] ARA, *SSO* 516, s.f.: Balthasar de Zúñiga to Archduke Albert, October 17, 1615.

Zúñiga's arguments seem to have made little impression on the archduke, all the same. In any case, Albert did not allow himself to be mollified: Iñigo de Brizuela would never be promoted to *gentilhombre de la Cámara*.

In view of the fact that descent from high nobility was so important, some families appear to have assumed that their presence in the archducal household spoke for itself, as though it concerned an innate right instead of a privilege. In March, 1613, Philippe-Charles of Arenberg, the oldest son of Charles, princely count of Arenberg and duke of Aarschot, let his father know that the archduke had appointed three new *gentilhombres de la Cámara*. They were Antoine de Lalaing, count of Hoogstraten; Florent de Ligne, marquis of Roubaix; and the already mentioned Florent de Noyelles, baron of Rossignol. Philippe-Charles, who himself had been a *gentilhombre* for five years, was of the opinion that his brother Alexandre of Arenberg also could make a claim on this position and insisted that his father should address the archdukes about this. According to Philippe-Charles, no one had more right to the golden key than Alexandre, 'to whom they will be unable to refuse it.'[118] He pointed out that the archducal household already had two brothers and an uncle from another noble family – sadly enough not described in greater detail, but presumable that of Croÿ – despite the fact that the accomplishments of his father 'are greater than theirs.' The Arenberg family could not remain behind like that, 'as there may well be one father and two sons where there are already two brothers and one uncle, that is how the world is governed.'[119] It was a somewhat puzzling argument, in which Philippe-Charles clearly assumed that his family ought to be *incontournable* at court. All the same, whether the princely count of Arenberg went along in accord with the proposal of his son is not known. In any case, Alexandre would never be appointed *gentilhombre de la Cámara*.

That honor was in fact set aside for Alexandre's younger brother Antoine of Arenberg, count of Zenegem, who received the golden key on March 19, 1615.[120] Here is clearly shown how a position in the archducal household frequently passed from generation to generation. Antoine received the title out of thanks for the good services of his father, who had been appointed *gentilhombre de la Cámara* already in 1596 and would give it up twenty years later for health reasons.[121] In a letter to the princely count, a proud Antoine describes all the sights and smells of how he was

---

[118] '*(...) auquel l'on ne le pouldra refuser.*' ACA, 38/3, file 72, no. 122: Philippe-Charles of Arenberg to Charles of Arenberg, s.d. [March, 1613].

[119] '*(...) sont plus grands que les leurs (...) car il y peult bien avoir un père et deulx filz puis qu'il y a deulx frères et un oncle, voyla comme le monde se gouverne.*' *Ibidem.*

[120] Concerning Antoine of Arenberg, see Callaey, F. [= Fredegand of Antwerp, Father O.M.F. Cap.]. *La vie religieuse et familiale en Belgique au XVIIe siècle. Étude sur le Père Charles d'Arenberg, frère-mineur Capucin (1593-1669).* Paris-Rome, 1919.

[121] *Ibidem*, pp. 90-92.

received at court.[122] In the morning he had taken the oath of obedience in the hands of *mayordomo mayor* Rodrigo Niño y Lasso, count of Añover, who handed the golden key over to him. Around noontime he was brought to the archduke, accompanied by a large number of nobles, where he listened on his knees to Albert's address concerning the obligations of the *gentilhombre* and concerning the good services of his father Charles of Arenberg:

> '[While I was] still on one knee, he took the sword (which is considered a great favor) that was hanging from my side and gave me three taps on the shoulder, and made me kiss the hilt and embraced me, saying that I would be a good knight and that he hoped that the memory of my sword having come from such a prince [= Charles of Arenberg] would give occasion to wield it even better in his service, and plenty of other beautiful things.'[123]

Subsequently, Antoine was brought to the quarters of the infanta, where Isabella congratulated him in the presence of all the ladies-in-waiting and handed over a pair of gloves to him as a gift.

The pronounced preference for reputable candidates from the high nobility is very clearly expressed when examining the list of *gentilhombres de la Cámara*. In 1615, for example, the Chamber numbered no less than 26 members. Among them were to be found three Spaniards (Diego Mexía, Francisco de Ibarra, and Juan Niño de Tavora), one Italian (Felipe Pallavicino), and two nobles who had come from the Holy Roman Empire (Wratislas von Fürstenberg and Maximilian von Dietrichstein, a nephew of the *sumiller de corps* of the same name). The nineteen remaining members belonged to prominent noble houses from the Southern Netherlands and Franche-Comté. They were the princely count of Arenberg, the princes of Ligne and Épinoy, the marquises of Marnay, Havré and Roubaix, the counts of Egmont, Solre, Buquoy, Hoogstraten, Bruay, Vertaing, Cantecroix, Hénin, Megem, Izegem, and Zenegem, and the barons of Zevenbergen and Rossignol.[124] Jointly these *gentilhombres* represented twenty noble houses, with the Arenberg and Croÿ families (three *gentilhombres* each) as well as the Ligne family (two *gentilhombres*) as the most important members. This impressive total demonstrates as well that the archdukes' tactic to tighten anew the disrupted bonds between the Habsburg dynasty and the nobility from the Southern

[122] ACA, 38/1, file 32, f. 29: Antoine of Arenberg to Charles of Arenberg, s.d.

[123] '*Estant encore à genou, il me tira (quy est extraordinaire estimé à faveur) l'espée que javoy au costé et me donna trois coups sur l'espaule et me donna à baiser le poncau et me donna l'abbrase, disant que je serois bon cavalier et quil esperoit que la souvenance que mon espée venoit d'ung tel prince seroit occasion de la tant mieulx gouverner à son service et beaucoup d'aultre belle chose.' Ibidem.*

[124] ARA, *RK* 1838, ff. 41v-43r.

Netherlands was able to be fully unfurled toward the end of their reign. Around 1615, pretty much all prominent aristocratic houses from the Southern Netherlands had one or more representatives at their disposal in the archducal *Cámara*, while their sisters and daughters received a position as lady-in-waiting to the infanta.[125] In their turn, members of the lower nobility got a lesser position allotted as *gentilhombre de la Boca* or *de la Casa.*[126] To the degree that they climbed up the ladder at court, many *gentilhombres* gradually acquired a function in the army or in the administration, or they were installed as governor or bailiff in one of the provinces. In that way the court fulfilled an important patronage function: a shrewd nobleman could quickly make his career there. Handing out a great number of noble titles also contributed to this large-scale strategy of reconciliation.

In other words, at the court in Brussels a genuine court aristocracy was constituted anew, consisting in the main of courtiers from the Southern Netherlands, yet also from Burgundy, Spain, Italy, and Germany. The presence of exiles from the Northern Netherlands, Ireland, and France made the court into a quite cosmopolitan environment.

Experience and competence

Another criterion that is often overlooked in the historiography concerning courts and courtiers, yet nevertheless played a role of importance in the selection of courtiers, was simply their suitability for the position for which they presented themselves. An office in the princely household may have well been prestigious, yet it is forgotten all too frequently that the courtiers were presumed to carry out their diplomatic and representative duties as appropriate. Competence and experience were consequently yardsticks that were also constantly taken under observation when inspecting the

[125] The ladies-in-waiting are frequently quite difficult to identify. In 1615, they were certainly Marie de Montmorency, Marguerite de Bourgogne, Ernestine of Arenberg, and Madeleine de Conflans. Further found among the ladies-in-waiting in that year are also 'Marquesa de Bergas' (= perhaps Marie-Mencie of Witthem, marquise of Berghes), Madame d'Ava (= possibly Marie of Barbançon, viscountess of Dave and spouse of Albert de Ligne-Arenberg, prince of Barbançon), Mademoiselle Merquen (= perhaps Marie of Halewyn, a daughter of Frans of Halewyn, lord of Merkem), Madame de Vertaing (= perhaps Jacqueline de Recourt de Licques, spouse of Philippe de Rubempré, count of Vertaing), Mademoiselle de Frentz (= perhaps a daughter of Philippe de Merode, count of Middelburg and *mayordomo* of the archdukes), Mademoiselle de Pallant (= perhaps a daughter of Florent of Pallant, count of Culemborg), Mademoiselle de Balançon (= perhaps a member of De Rye family), Madame Vasini (= Basigny?), Mademoiselle de Feller (?), and Mademoiselle Rongi (?). See ARA, *RK* 1838, ff. 40r-40v.

[126] In the *Boca* they were, among others, Jean-François de Barwitz, lord of Fernelmont; Charles-Philippe de Liedekercke, lord of Akeren; Charles d'Ydeghem, baron of Boesbeke; François van der Gracht, lord of Schardau and Bavikhove; Charles de Bernemicourt, lord of La Thieuloye; and François of Halewyn, lord of Merkem. For the *gentilhombres de la Casa* are found, among others, members like Justiniaan Triest, lord of Riddershoven; Philippe du Bosch, lord of Maesdam; Louis de Landas, lord of Wamehain; Charles de Courteville, lord of Sasbroek; Charles de Hannedouche, lord of Le Fay; and Jean-Baptiste Bulteel, lord of Reningelst. ARA, *RK* 1838, ff. 44v-47v.

candidates. That was undoubtedly of importance in the appointment of figures like Maximilian von Dietrichstein and Octavio Visconti, who thanks to their prior history in the household of Archduke Ernst were sufficiently familiar with life at the court in Brussels.[127] Visconti spoke fluent German, on top of that, so that in later years he could be utilized as a negotiator for Albert in the Holy Roman Empire (cf. Chapter V).[128] Yet also in a purely domestic sense candidates had to have the requisite capacities at their disposal. That was the case, for example, for the position of *mayordomo*, which required great organizational talent. When in 1597 part of the archducal household made ready to accompany the archduke on his journey to Spain, Francisco de Mendoza expressed his concern over the fact that only two *mayordomos* would be traveling with him so as to keep everything going in the right direction.[129] That was too few according to Mendoza, also because the newly appointed count of Izegem still had too little experience in this function. Consequently, Mendoza proposed to take four new *mayordomos* into service, and explicitly put the emphasis on the capacities of candidates whom he had in mind:

> 'The custom [that is kept] in France of having many [*mayordomos*] does not seem bad, both for their service to the prince as well as for the peace and quiet of the *mayordomos* themselves, and for being able to make use of their services in other assignments. For that reason I am of the opinion that Your Highness should take on four of them, namely Alonso de Cárdenas, Juan Bautista [de Tassis], Don Gaston [Spínola], and Gerónimo Walter Zapata.'[130]

Alonso de Cárdenas was already *gentilhombre de la Cámara* and, according to Mendoza, 'a man of great quality and quite a good intellect, and more careful than he seems because he is not meddlesome, but I hold him to be a man who will accomplish any task whatsoever quite well.'[131] Gaston Spínola was already a candidate earlier for the function of *mayordomo* (cf. above), but still had 'the ardent desire to serve His Highness.' According to Mendoza, he also had the requisite competence ['*sufficiencia*'] for the job and, on top of that, because of his great accomplishments in the army, 'suppressing him in a corner' was not indicated ['*no dexarle arrincondado*'].[132] Juan Bautista de Tassis, too, thanks to his activities as a diplomat, had already picked up

[127] Hortal Muñoz, J.E. 'La casa del Archiduque Ernesto durante su gobierno en los Países Bajos (1593-1595),' pp. 193-205.
[128] Visconti's correspondence with Archduke Albert can be found in ARA, *DuiS* 437.
[129] RAH, *SyC* A-61, ff. 9-10.
[130] RAH, *SyC* A-61, f. 10r.
[131] *Ibidem*, ff. 9r-9v.
[132] *Ibidem*, f. 9v.

the necessary experience in the service of the Habsburg dynasty, whereby he – despite his advanced age – 'was qualified in all areas' ['*le ha qualificado en todas partes*'].[133] Gerónimo Walter Zapata, finally, was the *pagador general* (paymaster) of the *Ejército de Flandes* and had at his disposal 'intellect, virtue, diligence, and competence in all matters' ['*entendimiento, virtud, diligencia y buena maña para todas la cosas*']. According to Mendoza, he would also be quite suited for guiding the journey to Spain, in view of the fact that he 'is quite careful and intelligent and will serve Your Highness well.'[134] The commentaries illustrate that competence clearly was a trump card for candidates who aspired to a position in the archducal household. Yet not all of the four candidates were taken on. The function of *mayordomo* ultimately went to Zapata, who was not only especially suited for the job but was also of descent from the very high nobility and, on top of that, enjoyed splendid rents of more than 8,000 ducats per year. It was perhaps the combination of these factors that was decisive in his appointment.

Advocacy and appreciation

That the selection of courtiers was subject to certain criteria, however, did not hinder awarding an office in practice on more pragmatic grounds also. In some cases handing out the title of *mayordomo* or *gentilhombre* clearly was not more than a prestigious token of appreciation toward persons who had committed themselves in one way or another to the service of the Habsburg dynasty. That was the case for the Spanish nobleman Don García de Pareja, among others, who as Philip III's extraordinary ambassador came to the Southern Netherlands in 1617, to thank the provincial States for their willingness to recognize the Spanish king as their future sovereign.[135] The archdukes gave Pareja the title of *mayordomo* – a function that he would never take up in practice, all the same – as an expression of respect.[136] A similar motivation can perhaps clarify the presence, too, of a few illustrious figures from the Holy Roman Empire in the archducal *Cámara*. Thus, for example, the *libros de razón* make mention of *gentilhombres* Zdenko Popel von Lobkowitz and Ulrich Desiderius Proskowski, baron of Proskau.[137] Lobkowitz was the grand chancellor of the kingdom of Bohemia,

[133] *Ibidem*, f. 10r.

[134] *Ibidem.*

[135] See in that context Lonchay, H. 'Le serment de fidélité prêté par les Belges à Philippe III en 1616,' in: *Mélanges Paul Fréderica. Hommage de la Société pour le progrès des études philologiques et historiques.* Brussels, 1904, pp. 311-317.

[136] ASV, *Borghese* III 110, f. 144: Nuncio Ascanio Gesualdo to Cardinal Borghese, June 24, 1617.

[137] Lobkowitz is mentioned in 1612 and 1613. ARA, *RK* 1837, f. 40r, f. 105r. and f. 161r. Proskowski is mentioned during the first two trimesters of 1614. ARA, *RK* 1837, f. 270r. and 306v.

while Proskowski was the former *Oberstkämmerer* of Emperor Rudolf II.[138] Both are only mentioned a few times in the accounting ledgers, and always with the comments '*ausente*,' indicating that the title of *gentilhombre* in these cases was little more than a title of honor, only awarded to tighten the bonds with the Viennese aristocracy.

Just as striking is the fact that also many children of prominent figures were devised a position out of appreciation – whether genuine or not – toward their parents. That was the case, for example, when Diego de Ibarra (Albert's former *mayordomo*) was sent by Philip III to the Netherlands in 1607, to defend Spanish interests in peace negotiations with the Dutch Republic (cf. Chapter V).[139] To show their good will, Albert and Isabella received Ibarra with every possible token of honor. One of these was appointing Ibarra's son Francisco to *gentilhombre de la Cámara* of the archduke, while his daughter became *menina* of the infanta.[140] Handing out the title *menino* or *menina* to children of meritorious nobles was an oft-used and effective method to tighten the bonds between their families and the archducal court. In that way, for instance, Jacinto and Felipe Alberto, the sons of Luis de Velasco (the general of the cavalry in the *Ejército de Flandes*) were both appointed as *menino*.[141] The same was true for Felipe and Cristóval de Cardona, the sons of the Spanish ambassador in Brussels; for Pedro and Alberto, the sons of *veedor general* Francisco Vaca de Benavides; and for Sean and Philip O'Neill, the sons of the earl of Tyrone, who as an Irish Catholic had broached a union with the Spanish Habsburgs.[142]

In a political constellation that for the large part rested on granting and acquiring favors, the advocacy of third parties could also influence the recruiting process enormously. Not coincidentally, the preserved correspondence of the archdukes contains a large number of letters of recommendation in which highly-placed persons asked them to take this or that man or woman into their household. In many cases it was a matter of recommendations from princes on behalf of their family members or vassals. The afore-mentioned Francesco Bernardino de Cassina, baron of Boelare, was installed as *gentilhombre de la Boca* based on the advocacy of Elector Ernst of Bavaria, for example.[143] And when the elector of Mainz let Albert know in 1615, that his nephew Adam Philipp von Cronberg would be coming to Brussels to study, the latter was promptly appointed *menino* and, not much later, *gentilhombre de la Cámara*.[144] Even the elector of Trier in his turn asked Albert to take one of his grand-nephews

[138] Menčík, F. 'Beiträge zur Geschichte der Kaiserlichen Hofämter.' *Archiv für Österreichische Geschichte*, vol. 86. Vienna, 1899, pp. 449-563. Op. cit. p. 474.
[139] BNF, *MsF* 16128, f. 114: Mathieu Brulart de Berny to Puisieux, June 5, 1607.
[140] BNF, *MsF* 16128, f. 127: Mathieu Brulart de Berny to Puisieux, June 23, 1607.
[141] ARA, *RvS* 157 (1611) and ARA, *RK* 1837, passim.
[142] *Ibidem*.
[143] ARA, *DuiS* 392, f. 181: Ernst of Bavaria to Archduke Albert, September 25, 1610.
[144] ARA, *DuiS* 400, f. 174: The elector of Mainz to Archduke Albert, June 29, 1615.

into service as a page.[145] Recommendations from other princes were not always but usually received with a positive response – in part because some correspondents just could not be ignored, in part because awarding these kinds of favors also contained an expectation of reciprocity, which could always come in good use. The archdukes were also quick to respond, after all, when it came to recommending their own vassals to other princes. Thus, in 1608 for instance, Albert asked Archduke Maximilian of Austria to take Ernst de Croÿ, a brother of the marquis of Havré, into his service as *Kämmerer*.[146]

Naturally, it was not only princes who wanted to help their family members, friends, or clientele with a position in the archducal household. The former Spanish ambassador in Brussels, Balthasar de Zúñiga, indicated above, maintained good contacts with the archduke and did not neglect to use them in order to recommend certain figures for court office. So, in 1613 for instance, he wrote a letter from his new station in the Holy Roman Empire in favor of one of his clients, '*un gentilhombre flamenco que se llama Renegels*.'[147] It was Jean-Baptiste Bulteel, lord of Reningelst, who had been *caballerizo* in Zúñiga's household for a time, and who now aspired to the position of *gentilhombre de la Casa* in the archducal household.[148] More than likely Archduke Albert did not immediately get involved in this: the *libros de razón* make no mention of Bulteel in any case. Not until 1621, during the funeral cortege of Albert, does he pop up for the first time as *gentilhombre de la Casa*.[149] Zúñiga was surely not the only one who utilized his good relationship with the archduke to help certain persons with a position in the archducal household. It is probably no coincidence that the *gentilhombre de la Cámara* Juan Niño de Tavora was a nephew of Rodrigo Niño y Lasso, Albert's powerful *sumiller de corps*, or that the lady-in-waiting Catalina Livia and the *gentilhombre de la Boca* Louis de Chamborant, lord of Droux, were both related to the *camarera mayor* Jeanne de Chassincourt.[150] As will be seen in the following chapters, Niño y Lasso and Chassincourt enjoyed the special favor of Albert and Isabella, and it can be safely assumed that their advocacy was an important factor in the installations of the three characters mentioned (cf. Chapters IV and VI). Even Albert's secretary Antonio Suárez de Arguello was quick to respond in that area: his relative Bartolome de Arguello was appointed *ayuda de la Cámara* in 1613.[151]

[145] ARA, *DuiS* 408, f. 93: The elector of Trier to Archduke Albert, January 9, 1602.

[146] ARA, *DuiS* 39, f. 18: Archduke Albert to Maximilian of Austria, February 13, 1608.

[147] ARA, *SSO* 516, s.f.: Balthasar de Zúñiga to Archduke Albert, October 25, 1613.

[148] Concerning the Bulteel family, see Allen, V. *The Bulteels. The Story of a Huguenot Family*. London, 2004.

[149] See Puteanus, E. & Francquart, J. *Pompa funebris (...) Alberti Pii, archiducis Austriae...* Brussels, 1622.

[150] Juan Niño de Tavora was a son of Rodrigo's uncle Gabriel Niño. Catalinia Livia was a niece of Jeanne de Chassincourt; Louis de Chamborant was her nephew. See for more infomation Chapter IV in this book.

[151] See in that context a few letters from Antonio Suárez de Arguello to Balthasar de Zúñiga in ARA, *SSO* 516, s.f.

Subsequent chapters will show of course that the secretary indeed had his hand more frequently in those kinds of appointments. Thus, for example in 1615, he would be one of the mediators who at the request of the princely count of Arenberg saw to it that Antoinette-Guillemette of Arenberg would succeed the elderly Chassincourt as the infanta's mistress of the household.

Influence from Madrid?

As the preceding sections show, the selection of courtiers was tackled in most cases in a very thought-out way. That need not come as a surprise. As opposed to what has been all too frequently assumed in the past, the courtiers not only kept themselves occupied with 'household' duties. As will become clear in subsequent chapters, their function was in the first place a political function. The courtiers were expected to be the archdukes' confidants, who could assist them in word and deed with policy making, and who could function as their eyes and ears beyond the protection of the court. In that sense, their appointment was a matter of the greatest importance. At the same time, thanks to their free access to the princes, the courtiers were excellently positioned to exercise their influence on policy making (cf. Chapter IV). In light of the scholarly debate over the political autonomy of Albert and Isabella, the question arises, then, whether and to what extent the Spanish government had a finger in the pie when composing the archducal entourage.

In principle, the answer to this question is relatively simple. Albert and Isabella were sovereign princes and thus enjoyed the right to decide about the organization of their household with complete independence. Madrid was consequently not authorized to intervene directly here. When Octavio Visconti was appointed *caballerizo mayor* in 1621, the marquis of Bedmar, the Spanish ambassador in Brussels at that time, wrote that he had only heard this news after the decision had already been made.[152] The ambassador was clearly annoyed by the issue: 'I believe positively that one should have avoided this appointment, because it is so important to look at the quality and the nation of those who should remain in the service of the infanta.'[153] Bedmar most likely realized that Albert did not have much longer to live, and he was of the opinion that in the future Isabella had to be surrounded by trustworthy – and therefore: Spanish – advisers. As a nobleman of Italian descent, Visconti did not fit into that picture. The appointment clearly rubbed Bedmar the wrong way, but he did not see what he could do about it. On top of that, the ambassador feared that Visconti would now

[152] AGS, *Estado* 2310, s.f.: The marquis of Bedmar to Philip III, February 11, 1621.
[153] *Ibidem.*

also make claim to a position in the Council of War, '*lo qual no conviene por muchas razones*.'[154] Bedmar did not want the Council to be opened up to '*estrangeros*,' and Visconti '*no es español ni flamenco, que son aquí las naciones propriamente naturales*.'[155] The ambassador therefore requested that the king should address Albert about this, but a reply failed to arrive.

The anecdote may count as an example of the fact that in principle the opinion of Madrid was not asked in appointing courtiers. That does not take away from the fact, though, that the Spanish government could sometimes indeed put on the requisite pressure, and that in any case attempts were undertaken to get a grip on the household of Albert and Isabella. Not coincidentally they tried above all to exercise their influence on the appointment of the high steward of the household, who was by definition one of the most important political advisers of the archdukes. As seen in Chapter I already, *mayordomo mayor* Francisco de Mendoza fell into disgrace in October, 1602, and upon Albert's request was recalled to Madrid. Although the Admiral would still be mentioned in the *libros de razón* until 1612 – albeit with the designation '*ausente*' – in practice his office became vacant as a result.[156] The archduke, however, did not take that vacancy sitting down and installed *mayordomo* Gerónimo Walter Zapata as Mendoza's temporary replacement. This decision was received with jubilation in Madrid least of all. A few years before that, Zapata, who was *pagador general* (paymaster) in the *Ejército de Flandes*, had also got the function of *veedor general* (controller-general) on Albert's recommendation.[157] In other words, Zapata kept an eye on the finances in the army and, although he only owed responsibility to the Spanish king in that capacity, he profiled himself more and more as a confidant of the archduke. The *Consejo de Estado* watched that happen with regret. The *consejeros* were of the judgment that Zapata's function in the army was impossible to combine with his duties in the archducal household, and they made it understood that it would be better for him to give up the post of *veedor*.[158] The archduke, however, wiped this criticism quickly off the table, saying that precisely the *veedoría* functioned better under the direction of Zapata, who as member of the archducal household enjoyed free access to the court and consequently could consult more quickly and efficiently with Albert and his councilors.[159] Although the archduke undoubtedly had a valid argument, he handily forgot to mention that by means of his frequent contact with Zapata, he was also in the position to keep an eye on the budgets of the

154 *Ibidem*.
155 *Ibidem*.
156 ARA, *RK* 1837, f. 39r.
157 CODOIN, vol. XLII, p. 300: Archduke Albert to the duke of Lerma, s.d. [1599].
158 CCE I, p. 40: Juan Carillo to Archduke Albert, December 6, 1600.
159 CCE I, p. 42: Archduke Albert to Juan Carillo, January 10, 1600.

Ejército – which naturally was the precise reason for great concern from the *Consejo de Estado*. In Madrid they clearly did not go along with Albert's explanation. When, after Mendoza's departure, Zapata became replacement *mayordomo mayor* as well, the *Consejo* had enough. Scarcely a few months later, the *veedor general* was accused of misuse of finances and called back to Madrid to answer for himself to the king.[160] Both Albert as well as Isabella protested against this decision heavily, but without results.[161] Even during the years after that, the archdukes would continue to defend their former *mayordomo* – who in his own words remained completely destitute from the affair.[162] For that reason, both of his daughters Maria and Teresa Zapata received a position as *menina* and after that as lady-in-waiting in the *Cámara* of Isabella.[163]

The entire incident resulted in a situation where the appointment of a new *mayordomo mayor* would prove especially sensitive for years after that. In 1603, it was whispered that Don Sancho de la Cerda, marquis of La Laguna, would be sent to the Netherlands to succeed Mendoza, but that proved to be an empty rumor.[164] The marquis came to Brussels in the first place to offer his condolences to the archduke on the death of Empress Maria, and in the end would stay to replace Balthasar de Zúñiga as Spanish ambassador.[165] Even so, as a diplomat Don Sancho turned out to be anything but a highflyer. In 1923, Joseph Lefèvre would maintain that the political influence of the ambassador '*fut véritablement nul*' – a judgment that summarized the opinion of many contemporaries right on target.[166] When the *Consejo de Estado* recalled him to Madrid in 1606, the archdukes were noticeably happy to be rid of him.[167] It comes, then, as no surprise that the infanta Isabella was anything but happy when the duke of Lerma requested that she still appoint Don Sancho as *mayordomo*

[160] CODOIN, vol. XLII, p. 447: Archduke Albert to the duke of Lerma, April 16, 1603.

[161] *Ibidem*, p. 455: Archduke Albert to the duke of Lerma, May 31, 1603 and Rodríguez Villa, A., ed. *Correspondencia de la Infanta Doña Isabel Clara Eugenia de Austria con el Duque de Lerma y otros personajes*. Madrid, 1906, letter no. 59: The infanta Isabella to the duke of Lerma, June 1, 1603.

[162] For the letters from Albert, see CODOIN, vol. XLII, p. 568: Albert to Lerma, June 26, 1606 and CODOIN, vol. XLIII, p. 7 (August 30, 1606), p. 22 (November 11, 1606) and p. 74 (September 7, 1607). For the letters from Isabella, see Rodríguez Villa, *Correspondencia*, letter no. 59: The infanta Isabella to the duke of Lerma, June 1, 1603, and letter no. 169: Isabella to Lerma, March 12, 1610. See also ARA, *SSO* 100, s.f.: Gerónimo Walter Zapata to Archduke Albert, April 12, 1609.

[163] ARA, *SSO* 100, s.f.: Gerónimo Walter Zapata to Archduke Albert, February 7, 1605.

[164] '*Arrivo qui la sera delli xi come scrissi a V. S. Ill. et Rev. per l'ordinario partito la matina, il Sr. Marchese di Laguna mandato dal Re di Spagna a questi Ser. Principi per condolerse publicamente con lor A.A. in nome di S.M. della morte dell' Imperatrice. Fù incontrato da molti gentilhomi del paese, et condott' in carrozza alla Ser. Infante, et da palazzo a casa del Sr. Marchese d'Havré, dove se spesa a nome di lor A.A. in quest' essenza del Ser. Sr. Arciduca. La sua venuta non tien' altro titolo che dell' officio sudetto; con tutto ciò se crede che sia per fermasse con la carica di sopremo maggiordomo, ch' haveva il Sr. Almirante d'Aragona.*' ASV, *Borghese* III 110, ff. 17-19: Nuncio Frangipani to Cardinal Aldobrandini, October 25, 1603.

[165] ASV, *Borghese* III 110, f. 59: Frangipani to Aldobrandini, December 20, 1603.

[166] Lefèvre, J. 'Les ambassadeurs d'Espagne à Bruxelles sous le règne de l'archiduc Albert (1598-1621).' *Revue belge de Philologie et d'Histoire*, 2 (1923) 61-80. Op. cit. p. 69.

[167] CODOIN, vol. XLII, pp. 572-574: Archduke Albert to the duke of Lerma, August 24, 1606.

mayor of the archducal household. In a letter to the duke, Isabella explained amicably yet adamantly that she could not possibly answer this request, for the simple reason that the highest positions in the court were, according to her, traditionally reserved for those from the Southern Netherlands: 'We have promised to the people here that we shall make use of their services in the most prominent offices of the household, for that is the custom in these countries. And I, as mistress of the house, am the first to hold to [this promise].'[168] The infanta knew all too well, though, that her argument was not water-tight, but nevertheless she used it quite consciously. Not coincidentally, Sancho de la Cerda was a brother-in-law of Lerma, and the archdukes were anything but ready to give the duke the chance at installing one of his faithful in their household – certainly not in such an important function.[169] By pretending that she was bound to local tradition in the matter of appointment policy, Isabella succeeded in conveying her message without affronting the duke all too much. Lerma perceived that he would be better striking his attempt and directed his arrows at another target. Not much later Don Sancho returned to Madrid, where he became *mayordomo mayor* in the household of Queen Margaret.[170]

In Brussels, the function of the high steward would remain vacant until 1612. Perhaps his duties were adopted in this time period by the four *mayordomos*, who changed off with each other every week, or by Rodrigo Niño y Lasso, who as *sumiller de corps* was a rising star in the archducal household (cf. Chapter VI). Yet rumors would repeatedly continue to pop up concerning the appointment of a new *mayordomo mayor*. One of the candidates speculated about was Charles de Croÿ, who as duke of Aarschot was the most prominent nobleman in the Southern Netherlands. His candidacy was to be found problematic for various reasons, all the same. In the first place, there was confusion concerning the question as to whether the Admiral of Aragon would yet return to Brussels. In August, 1605, Archduke Albert wrote to Lerma that the king urgently had to make a decision concerning the future of Francisco de Mendoza, 'because, in order to guarantee Aarschot [in our service] and to oblige him [to us] anew, it has proven necessary to promise him the office [of *mayordomo mayor*] in case the Admiral gives it up, and it is certain that [the Admiral] is needed here.'[171] In the second place, not everyone proved to be convinced of the suitability of Charles de Croÿ. Already in January, 1605, the nuncio Frangipani announced that 'the duke

[168] Rodríguez Villa, *Correspondencia*, letter no. 100: The infanta Isabella to the duke of Lerma, Ascension Sunday, 1606.

[169] Lerma was married to Doña Catalina de la Cerda, a sister of Don Sancho.

[170] See Feros, A. *Kingship and Favoritism in the Spain of Philip III, 1598-1621*, Cambridge U.P., 2000, p. 97.

[171] '*No puedo dejar de acordar a V[uestra] S[eñoría] procure se tome resolución con el Almirante de Aragón; porque por asegurar y obligar de nuevo a el [Duca] de Ariscote, ha sido fuerza prometerle el oficio en caso que el Almirante le deje, y cierto que hace falta en él.*' CODOIN, vol. XLII, p. 539: Archduke Albert to the duke of Lerma, August 26, 1605.

of Aarschot has arrived [here], accompanied by a rumor that he has a good chance of becoming general in the Netherlands, and one is of the opinion that he cannot be a *mayordomo mayor* of His Highness.'[172] More than likely, the reticence toward the duke had to do with the fact that he did not enjoy an irreproachable reputation. In the early 1580s Charles – perhaps under the influence of his Calvinist spouse Marie de Brimeu – had abjured the Catholic faith.[173] In that time period, he had also banded with the side of the rebels for a few years, which was taken badly by Philip II. Even so, in 1585, the duke changed his gun to the other shoulder. He separated from his spouse and reconciled with the Catholic Church and the king of Spain.[174] Twenty years later, the duke was still a loyal adherent of the Habsburg dynasty, yet it seems that his prior history continued to cause him trouble. In any case he was never appointed *mayordomo mayor*. In spite of that, Albert's promise was perhaps one of the hindrances that saw to it that the office of the high steward would not be awarded anew until 1612 – not coincidentally shortly after the death of Charles de Croÿ. The fortunate appointee was – just as uncoincidentally – Rodrigo Niño y Lasso (cf. Chapter VI).

A 'Spanish bastion'?

In 1595, the *Cámara* of Cardinal-Archduke Albert consisted of five *gentilhombres* of Spanish origin. In 1621, there was still little of this Spanish presence to note. A comparable development arose with the *gentilhombres de la Boca* and *de la Casa* as well as with the ladies-in-waiting of the infanta. The resolution of the archdukes to attract more and more courtiers originating from the Southern Netherlands and Burgundy was clearly being applied. As already mentioned, it was and is assumed among historians that key positions in the archducal household always stayed in Spanish hands – and that the court of the archdukes was consequently always a bulwark of Spanish authority in the Netherlands. Disregarding the question as to whether the origins of the courtiers may be coupled to a certain political affinity, this conclusion seems in a way premature. The following table offers an overview of the functionaries who successively held the five highest offices in the archducal household in the period 1595-1621, whereby each of their (original) native lands is designated:

[172] '*Arrivo qui il Duca d'Arschot accompagnato d'una voce populare dove è ben voluto, ch'andaria per General in Fiandra, et Maggiordomo Maggiore di S[u] A[ltezza] se giudica non poter essere (…).*' ASV, *Borghese* III 110, f. 252-255: [Ottavio Mirto Frangipani to Cardinal Aldobrandini], January 22, 1605.

[173] Guillaume, G. 'Croy (Charles de),' in: *Biographie Nationale*, volume IV, pp. 544-552. See also de Reiffenberg, F.A.F., ed. *Une existence de grand seigneur au seizième siècle. Mémoires autographes du Duc Charles de Croy*. Brussels, 1845.

[174] *Ibidem.*

Table 5 – Leading functionaries in the archducal household, 1595-1621

<table>
<tr><th></th><th>Mayordomo mayor</th><th>Sumiller de corps</th><th>Caballerizo mayor</th><th>Capellán mayor</th><th>Camarera mayor</th></tr>
<tr><td>1595</td><td rowspan="7">Francisco de Mendoza (1595-1602) Spain (Castile)</td><td rowspan="4">Maximilian von Dietrichstein (1595-1599) HRE (Carinthia)</td><td rowspan="17">Philippe de Croÿ (1595-1612) South. Neth.</td><td>Pedro de Alarcón (1595-1596) Spain (Castile)</td><td rowspan="3"></td></tr>
<tr><td>1596</td><td rowspan="2">George of Austria (1596-1598) Prince-bishopric of Liège</td></tr>
<tr><td>1597</td></tr>
<tr><td>1598</td><td rowspan="5">Pedro de Toledo (1598-1603) Spain (Castile)</td><td rowspan="14">Jeanne de Chassincourt (1598-1612) France</td></tr>
<tr><td>1599</td><td rowspan="21">Rodrigo Niño y Lasso (1599-1620) Spain (Castile)</td></tr>
<tr><td>1600</td></tr>
<tr><td>1601</td></tr>
<tr><td>1602</td><td rowspan="10">vacant (1602-1612)</td></tr>
<tr><td>1603</td><td rowspan="2">Karel Maes (interim) (1603-1605) South. Neth.</td></tr>
<tr><td>1604</td></tr>
<tr><td>1605</td><td rowspan="15">Pedro de Toledo (1605-1620) Spain (Castile)</td></tr>
<tr><td>1606</td></tr>
<tr><td>1607</td></tr>
<tr><td>1608</td></tr>
<tr><td>1609</td></tr>
<tr><td>1610</td></tr>
<tr><td>1611</td></tr>
<tr><td>1612</td><td rowspan="9">Rodrigo Niño y Lasso (1612-1620) Spain (Castile)</td><td rowspan="3">vacant (1612-1615)</td><td rowspan="3">vacant (1612-1615)</td></tr>
<tr><td>1613</td></tr>
<tr><td>1614</td></tr>
<tr><td>1615</td><td rowspan="5">Rodrigo Niño y Lasso (1615-1620) Spain (Castile)</td><td rowspan="7">Antoinette-Guillemette of Arenberg (1615-1626) South. Neth./ HRE</td></tr>
<tr><td>1616</td></tr>
<tr><td>1617</td></tr>
<tr><td>1618</td></tr>
<tr><td>1619</td></tr>
<tr><td>1620</td><td rowspan="2">Charles-Emmanuel de Gorrevod (1620-1621) Franche-Comté</td><td rowspan="2">Octavio Visconti (1620-1632) Italy (Milan)</td><td rowspan="2">François de Rye (1620-1637) Franche-Comté</td></tr>
<tr><td>1621</td><td>Ambrogio Spínola (1621-1627) Italy (Genoa)</td></tr>
</table>

As opposed to what would be expected on the basis of the dominant image in historiography, the table shows a surprisingly rich palette of names and origins. Nevertheless, four of the five leading functions were for the majority of the time indeed in Spanish hands – the nuance being that it is for the large part a question of one pair of hands. The fact that Rodrigo Niño y Lasso was able to accumulate the three most prominent offices in the archducal household, already suggests that his Castilian origin was not the only factor playing a role in this process. On the other hand it turns out that Niño y Lasso's functions were passed on after his death to two courtiers from Italy and one from Burgundy. The office of grand chaplain, too, was for the majority of the time in the hands of a Spaniard, but would be exercised by a Burgundian beginning in 1620. In the *Cámara* of Isabella, the function of *camarera mayor* was exercised successively by Jeanne de Chassincourt, a lady of French descent, and by Antoinette-Guillemette of Arenberg, the sister of the princely count of Arenberg. In that sense it could be posited, then again, that Spanish preponderance had to make room for other nations at the end of Albert's life.

It speaks for itself that the functions introduced here are not the only ones that can be seen as key positions in the archducal household. Whenever we descend the hierarchical ladder, we meet a great number of figures who belonged to the intimate entourage of the archdukes and who, consequently, must be taken into consideration. Iñigo de Brizuela and Andrés de Soto, the influential father confessors of the archdukes, were both of Spanish origin, just like the captain of the mounted guard – once again Rodrigo Niño y Lasso. The captains of the *Hartschiere* and the halberdiers, on the contrary, were always nobles who came from the (Southern as well as Northern) Netherlands and from Franche-Comté.[175] Their lieutenants Jan Mulert and Martin de Somoghy were from the Northern Netherlands and Hungary, respectively. Albert's private secretary Antonio Suárez de Arguello was from Portugal, while his *guardaropa* Joachim Denzenhear came from the Holy Roman Empire.[176] Except for the Spanish countess of Uceda and the French countess of La Fère, the infanta's *dueñas de honor* were usually ladies from the Southern Netherlands.[177] From around 1610, pretty much all *mayordomos* had their origins in the Southern Netherlands or Burgundy. Inasmuch as they can be identified, there is an entire array of nations in the *ayudas de la Cámara*, such as Spain, the Southern Netherlands, Burgundy, Germany, and

[175] It was a question of Pierre de Hénin-Liétard, count of Boussu; Robert de Ligne-Arenberg, prince of Barbançon; Guillaume de Bauffremont, baron of Scey and Sombernon; Count Frederik van den Berg; and Count Christoffel of Emden. Cf. Chapter I.

[176] See ARA, *SSO* 185, f. 295: Archduke Albert to Philip IV, July 9, 1621, and HHStA, Belgische Korrespondenz, Schachtel 29: recommendation in favor of Joachim Denzenhear for an appointment in the Teutonic Order, April 9, 1612.

[177] It was a question of Marguerite de Lille, countess of Buquoy; 'Madame de Pallant' (= perhaps Catharina van den Berg, spouse of Florent of Pallant, count of Culemborg); and 'Madame de Roisin' (= possibly Eleonore de Hénin-Liétard, spouse of (Baudoin?) Baudry de Roisin and daughter of Jean de Hénin-Liétard, count of Boussu, and of Anne de Bourgogne).

Portugal.[178] The three personal physicians of the archduke had their origins in Spain, Italy, and (perhaps) the Southern Netherlands.[179] The treasurer Joseph Hartelieb (also known as Hertevliet) presumably came from the Netherlands or the Holy Roman Empire; his successor Antonio de Rovelasca was of Italian origin.[180] The clerk Pedro de Mendoza was a Spaniard; the court controller Charles de Hertoghe was from the Southern Netherlands.

Undoubtedly, the list of key figures is even longer. Even so, the tendency may perhaps be clear. Throughout the period 1595-1621, the household of the archdukes was characterized by a great variety of nations. Some key positions were indeed taken by courtiers from Spain, others by those from the Southern Netherlands, Burgundy, Italy, Portugal, Hungary, and even France. On top of that, in the case of *mayordomos*, *gentilhombres*, and ladies-in-waiting, the balance would tilt toward a preponderance of 'indigenous' members during the second decade of the seventeenth century. The question remains, however, as to whether and to what extent these kinds of lists are relevant when the political affinity of the courtiers is gauged. It was already argued above that nation and loyalty were not necessarily coupled to each other during the Ancien Régime. At the early modern court, loyalty to the prince or the dynasty was no innate characteristic but a well- or ill-considered choice determined by a multiplicity of factors – not least of which were personal and familial interests. Research into the political affinity of the courtiers, then again, profits little from an analysis that is based merely on data like origins. Loyalty went hand in hand with being of service to the prince and – in a broader context – to the dynasty. Its touchstone, consequently, is not that of origin but instead the quality and standing of a person and his family and forbears. That can be shown in the case of the Von Dietrichstein family, among others.

As already seen in Chapter I, this family worked its way up in the service of the Habsburg dynasty. Baron Siegmund von Dietrichstein, the grandfather of Albert's *sumiller de corps*, was the *Obersthofmeister* of Queen Anna, the spouse of Ferdinand I.[181] His son Adam began his career at the court of Maximilian II, yet later moved

---

[178] In the period, 1595-1621, the following *ayudas de la Cámara* are found (in order of seniority): Cataño Mola, Joachim Denzenhear, Juan de Ribera, Diego Daça, Antonio Suárez de Arguello, Jean Laynez, Diego Woislawski, Pedro Castellanos, Blaise Hütter, Bartolome Salinas, Juan Diego Fleckhamer, Juan Jacomo, Juan de Verdugo, Attanasio de Cegaspy, Francisco de Lordat y Cardona, Pedro de Bodens, Bernardo Cornelio, Antoine de Funes, Juan de Maturana, Sebastian de Eizaguirre, Guillén de Loquinguien, Sebastian de Rey, Albert Knoff, Enrique Vermeren, Antoine Laynez, Lorenzo de Arze, Pedro Martínez, Bartolome de Arguello, Albert Laynez, Jean Baptiste de Contreras, Jean Baptiste de Lonzon van Eelen, and Guillaume Martini.

[179] Francisco de Paz, Andreas Trevisius (Andrea Trevigi), and Henri Mastelein, cf. Chapter I.

[180] The De Rovelasca family was an Italian merchant family with ties in Antwerp. See Ghys, I. *De Antwerpse magistraat in een laat-humanistische en contra-reformatorische periode: 1585-1621. Een institutionele, sociaal-economische en culturele analyse*. Unpublished master's thesis, Katholieke Universiteit Leuven, 1988. Op. cit. p. 155.

[181] Menčík, 'Beiträge zur Geschichte der Kaiserlichen Hofämter,' 451.

to Madrid, where he – in addition to being imperial ambassador – was *ayo* in the household of the archdukes Rudolf and Ernest.[182] Adam's spouse Margarita Folch de Cardona had made the opposite move earlier and had traveled in the retinue of the future Empress Maria to the Holy Roman Empire. Their sons Maximilian, Franz, and Siegmund were born in Madrid. Once grown, Maximilian became *Kämmerer* at the court of Rudolf II in Prague. After that he journeyed to Brussels, where he successively became the *Oberststallmeister* of Archduke Ernst and the *sumiller de corps* of Albert. He would return to the Holy Roman Empire in 1599.[183] Meanwhile, his brother Franz succeeded in his career as a cleric. He established himself as a dedicated protagonist of the Counter-Reformation and was appointed cardinal and bishop of Olmütz in 1599. In that capacity he would grow into one of the mightiest princes of the Church in the Holy Roman Empire, and into a prominent adviser of the emperors Rudolf II, Matthias, and Ferdinand II. From the correspondence of the cardinal is clearly shown that the Von Dietrichstein family saw Archduke Albert as one of its most important patrons.[184] The letters contain various examples of characteristic language of patronage as employed in the early modern period.[185] In 1611, the cardinal informed the archduke of the news that Maximilian von Dietrichstein had died. The cardinal indicated that he now became head of the family, as well as 'the heir of the (...) obligations' of his brother.[186] According to Franz, the most important of those obligations was 'the service to your Highness, of whom [Maximilian] was always a loyal *criado*.'[187] For that reason, Franz offered Albert his services, and he asked that the latter would take the House of Dietrichstein into his protection. The archduke did not neglect supporting the family of his former *sumiller de corps*. He proposed appointing Franz's nephew – also called Maximilian – as *menino* and in that way provide the young man with an upbringing at the court in Brussels. The cardinal was clearly quite satisfied with that offer: 'The token of honor and expression of thanks ['*merced*'] that Your Highness has provided me with his letter (...), have added especially strong links to the chain of obligations which I am indebted to Your Highness ['*an añidido eslavenes muy fuertes a la cadena de las obligaciones que yo tengo con V.A.*'].'[188] The young Maximilian was received at court on March 12, 1612, and evidently treated quite well there.[189] A year later the cardinal wrote that

[182] *Ibidem*, pp. 454-456 and Edelmayer, 'Honor y dinero,' 89-116.

[183] Hortal Muñoz, *El manejo de los asuntos de Flandes*, 440.

[184] His correspondence with Archduke Albert can be found in ARA, *SSO* 494.

[185] See in that context Herman, A.L. 'The Language of Fidelity in Early Modern France.' *The Journal of Modern History*, 67 (1995) 1-24.

[186] ARA, *SSO* 494, s.f.: Franz von Dietrichstein to Archduke Albert, April 9, 1611.

[187] *Ibidem*.

[188] *Ibidem*: Dietrichstein to Albert, January 6, 1612.

[189] ARA, *RK* 1837, f. 40v.

> 'my family is so truly dedicated to the Illustrious House of Austria that every day we make claims on new *mercedes* of Your Highness based on rights of inheritance [*'por derecho de herencia'*]. And I am especially appreciative for [the *merced*] that the count my nephew has received from Your Highness, and wish to increase this even more (...). And therefore I most humbly ask that it should please Your Highness to appoint [Maximilian] as *gentilhombre de la Cámara* from the moment he gets the dagger [= 'completes his studies' as page].'[190]

This time, too, the archduke did not disappoint: on February 1, 1614, the young Maximilian was indeed appointed *gentilhombre de la Cámara.*[191]

The history of the Von Dietrichstein family makes clear that loyalty frequently passed down from generation to generation and was in no way disturbed by borderlines of countries or otherwise. In the first place, loyalty to the prince and the dynasty was shown as a very intense form of being of service. That was true for pretty much all persons of significance in the archducal household. A few examples may suffice. The Portuguese Antonio Suárez de Arguello was Albert's private secretary for 35 years. In the end, according to the French ambassador, he evolved into 'one of the most favored ministers of his master.'[192] Suárez's parents and grandparents had also made their careers in the service of the Spanish crown. In former times, his grandfather had been captain in the Spanish army; his father was the *aposentador mayor* of Empress Maria; and his mother was the *azafata* (wet-nurse) of the later Philip IV.[193] The Frenchwoman Jeanne de Chassincourt, the elderly *camarera mayor* of the infanta, traveled to Spain in the retinue of Elisabeth of Valois in 1559, and after the death of the queen remained in the service of the infantas Isabella and Catalina Micaela.[194] In 1598, she was appointed mistress of the household *'en consideracion de sus meritos y por la mucha confiança y satisfacción.'*[195] The Spaniard Diego Mexía, the later marquis of Leganés, was the son of Leonor de Guzmán, one of the most beloved *dueñas de honor* of the infanta.[196] He was *menino* in the archducal household

---

[190] ARA, *SSO* 494, s.f.: Dietrichstein to Albert, February 13, 1613.

[191] ARA, *RK* 1837, f. 270r.

[192] BNF, *MsF*, f. 27: Charles de l'Aubespinne de Chasteauneuf, abbot of Préaux, to Puisieux, March 17, 1612.

[193] '*(...) un des plus favorisez ministres de son maître.*' ARA, *SSO* 185, f. 295: Archduke Albert to Philip IV, July 9, 1621.

[194] See López-Cordón Cortezo, M.V. 'Entre damas anda el juego: las camareras mayores de Palacio en la edad moderna,' in: Gómez-Centurión Jiménéz, C., ed. *Monarquía y Corte en la España Moderna.* Cuadernos de Historia Moderna, 2003 (Anejo II), pp. 123-152.

[195] AGPR, *Sección Personal* 588, expediente 32: Appointment of Jeanne de Chassincourt ['Juana de Jacincurt'] as *camarera mayor* of the infanta Isabella, October 16, 1598.

[196] AHN, *OOMM*, expediente 5274 (Diego de Mesía y Guzmán, 1614).

and after that was appointed *gentilhombre de la Cámara*. In 1600, he saved the life of the archduke during the Battle of Nieuwpoort, and the latter would always remain appreciative to him for this.[197] In 1615, Mexía was installed as *primer caballerizo*, and was one of the few explicitly mentioned in Albert's last will and testament in 1621 – very much to the disliking of other candidates, by the way.[198] Regardless of their origins, all the characters mentioned could pride themselves on the irreproachable standing of their service. Much more than an innate characteristic, with respect to the Habsburg dynasty their loyalty was a slowly shaped acquisition.

Conclusion

The composition of the archducal entourage was determined by a multiplicity of factors and was surely not left to chance. The carefulness with which candidates were 'screened' for their suitability and trustworthiness demonstrates already in and of itself that the archducal household was more than a princely 'household.' It was a political body, the members of which had to be chosen with the requisite circumspection. For the archdukes it was extremely important to be surrounded by courtiers who would not only fulfill their domestic duties appropriately, but who could also – and above all – provide a useful contribution to the regime. As opposed to what frequently is assumed uncritically by historians, the origins of the candidates were not of decisive importance in the process. That the relationship between the courtiers from Spain and the Southern Netherlands did not always run spotlessly is sufficiently known. That the distribution of court offices was a useful instrument to attune the local nobility favorably speaks for itself just as well. However, it is of no use to interpret these observations so as to imagine the archducal household as a 'bipolar' entity in which only those from Spain or the Southern Netherlands counted. Similarly, the recruiting policy may not be imagined as a process that was fully dominated by 'national' considerations. That kind of anachronistic vision mistakes the characteristic identity of the early modern court, where nation and political loyalty were not necessarily coupled to each other. On top of that, this approach neglects the cosmopolitan character of the archducal court, which attracted courtiers from all the far corners of Europe.

---

[197] Esteban Estríngana, A. *Madrid y Bruselas. Relaciones de gobierno en la etapa postarchiducal (1621-1634).* Leuven, 2005, p. 71.

[198] '*(...) Supplico a la infanta mi señora que de los bienes que cumplido mi testamento sobrara como dicho es haya en primer lugar merced a don Diego Mesia dandole lo que a su aviso pareziere y en caso que no sobre nada la supplico que por el [... ?] que pudiere le haga merced o procure que se la haga Su Magestad.*' ARA, *Papiers du Comté de Mercy-Argenteau* 125: Last will and testament of Archduke Albert. See also BNF, *MsF* 16133, f. 344: Jean Péricard, French ambassador in Brussels, to Secretary of State Puisieux, July 16, 1621.

The recruiting policy in the archducal household was consequently eclectic in nature. Various criteria played a role in awarding a court function. In certain cases the origins of an applicant were also taken into consideration – certainly when it was a question of persons who were not vassals of the Habsburg dynasty. Frequently they were categorized automatically as 'less trustworthy,' which was naturally not necessarily correct. Then again, in other cases origin played no role and merely the capacities and the standing of the service of a candidate and his or her family were looked at. That assessment implies that it makes little sense to situate the candidates on this side or that of the political spectrum merely based upon their origin. What matters much more is to evaluate each of them individually based on their political activities, the networks they formed, the marriages they entered into, and the interests they wished to defend. Only then can their role inside the archducal household be solidly analyzed. The second part of this book goes deeper into these aspects.

Part II

The Political Role of the Courtiers

Chapter IV
'Une Liberté Absolue d'Entrer'

'(...) Porque además de tener siempre un pie en palacio para muchas cosas que han menester las casas grandes como la de Vuestra Excellencia, se continuarian los servicios y tener cerca la Infanta nuestra Señora tal accogado será muy aproposito (...)'[1]

Gaston Spínola to Charles of Arenberg
March 16, 1613

On November 9, 1619, the French ambassador in Brussels, Jean Péricard, informed his superiors of a rumor that was making the rounds at the archducal court.[2] He reported that Count Wratislas von Fürstenberg, one of Albert's *gentilhombres de la Cámara*, had returned to the Southern Netherlands after a long stay in the Holy Roman Empire and that he was going to pay his respects to the archduke, who lay sick in bed, later that week. Fürstenberg, a scion from a lineage of the German high nobility, had made up part of the archducal entourage for many years, yet was connected to the imperial court in Vienna as well. At that moment the count was in transit to Paris, where he would undertake diplomatic deliberations in the name of the emperor with Louis XIII.[3] According to Péricard there were whispers in the corridors that the archdukes would receive Fürstenberg in his capacity as imperial emissary, and thus with the ceremonial pomp and pageantry that properly went hand in hand with that kind of status. The ambassador, however, attached little faith to that rumor. After all, Fürstenberg belonged to the archducal household, he wrote, and 'can, as a member of the household [*domestique*], obtain an audience in private and without ceremony.'[4] Péricard, who was a keen observer, had got it right. For most visitors, the ceremonial in the matter of gaining access and having audiences at the court in Brussels was quite cumbersome, though in principle the *gentilhombres de la Cámara* could walk in and

1 ACA, 38/4, file 133, f. 5: Gaston Spínola, count of Bruay, to Charles of Arenberg, princely count of Arenberg and duke of Aarschot, March 16, 1613.

2 BNF, *MsF* 16132, f. 264: Jean Péricard to Secretary of State Pierre Brulart, marquis of Puisieux, November 9, 1619.

3 Concerning this mission, see Kettering, S. *Power and Reputation at the Court of Louis XIII. The Career of Charles d'Albert, Duc de Luynes (1578-1621)*. Manchester U.P., 2008, p. 174.

4 '*(...) pourra comme domestique avoir audience dans le lieu privément et sans cérémonie.*' BNF, *MsF* 16132, f. 264: Péricard to Puisieux, November 9, 1619.

out freely. A few days later the ambassador announced, then, that the count had been received simply at Albert's sickbed, '*comme domestique*.'[5]

In the past historians were inclined to overlook these kinds of comments, perhaps presupposing that their presence can merely be traced back to an early modern passion for hierarchy and protocol. They were mistaken. That these and similar observations have to be interpreted much more as contemporaneous estimations of power and influence is a conviction that is still fully dawning in the historiography concerning the archducal regime. In the perception of the seventeenth-century diplomat, however, nothing was held to be more self-evident. Foreign ambassadors and agents realized all too well that politics was practiced not only within the fold of administrative institutions, advisory councils, and *juntas*, but also – and above all – in the private quarters of the prince, where the so-called 'politics of intimacy' had free range. Since the 1980s numerous studies have demonstrated that there was no mention of an absolute separation between the public and the private sphere in politics during the Ancien Régime.[6] The formal and informal foyers of power did not function separately from one another but in reciprocal interaction among themselves.[7] They flowed over into each other, as it were. One of those foyers was the princely *Cámara*, where the intimate entourage of the monarch made up the staff. As John Adamson writes,

> 'This was a place where the mere fact of access to, and intimacy with, the sovereign could result in political influence far greater than that of any noble grandee; and where courtiers became adept of detecting swings of mood or favour in the slightest change of the monarch's visage. It was this rarefied world that was the political hub of the court, the point where matters of state were decided, and where the fortunes of the courtiers were made and unmade.'[8]

Contemporaneous diplomats were conscious of the fact that clear insight into the mechanisms of decision-making presupposed not only a fundamental knowledge of the conversations that took place within these walls, but also of the comings and goings of persons who enjoyed free and unlimited access there.

---

5 BNF, *MsF* 16132, f. 266: Péricard to Puisieux, November 13, 1619.

6 To name but a few examples: Rodríguez-Salgado, M.J. 'Honour and Profit in the Court of Philip II of Spain,' in: Aymard, M. & Romani, M.A., eds. *La cour comme institution économique. Actes du douzième congrès international d'histoire économique, Séville-Madrid, 24-28 août 1998*. Paris, 1998, pp. 67-86; Adamson, J. 'The Making of the Ancien-Régime Court, 1500-1700,' in: Adamson, J., ed. *The Princely Courts of Europe. Ritual, Politics and Culture under the Ancien Régime 1500-1750*. London, 1999, pp. 7-41; and Duindam, J. *Vienna and Versailles. The Courts of Europe's Dynastic Rivals, 1550-1780*. Cambridge U.P., 2003.

7 The expression 'foyers of power' comes from Adamson, 'The Making of the Ancien-Régime Court,' p. 17.

8 Adamson, J. 'The Tudor and Stuart Courts, 1509-1714,' in: Adamson, *The Princely Courts*, pp. 95-117. Op. cit. p. 108.

For a few decades now the concept of 'access' has been getting a lot of attention in scholarly research into early modern courts and their households. Pioneers like David Starkey and Neil Cuddy have argued convincingly that the right of access to the prince (and the familiarity and/or intimacy that could go hand in hand with it) constituted an essential component in the acquisition and exercise of power during the Ancien Régime.[9] In political constellations largely dependent on the authority of one single ruler, this kind of proximity offered inestimable added value in the rat race for individual and familial promotion and – in many cases – political influence. Inversely, a lack of access could bring disastrous consequences along with it. Although this hypothesis has led to refreshing results in studying early modern politics in countries like England, Spain, or France, until today its value for the situation in the Archducal Netherlands has never been researched.[10] Nevertheless it could be argued that the *Cámara* of Albert and Isabella was in many ways a political entity and has to be studied as such.

By now the notion of access has grown into a dominant factor in the study of early modern decision-making.[11] Yet the concept has not been spared critical objections. Without wanting to deny its importance, various historians point out that access can in no way be made one and the same with political power in every circumstance. John Adamson notes that 'access and intimacy did not always equate with political power' and is of the opinion that the impact of both concepts on policy was always relative, for example, inasmuch as the actual range of princely authority itself was varying.[12] Jeroen Duindam, too, argues that access and political influence were not necessarily exactly in proportion, let alone mutually interchangeable.[13] Both authors rightly posit

[9] Starkey, D. *The Development of the Privy Chamber, 1485-1547*. Unpublished doctoral dissertation, Cambridge University, 1973; and Cuddy, N. 'The Revival of the Entourage: The Bedchamber of James I, 1603-1625,' in: Starkey, D. et al. *The English Court from the Wars of the Roses to the Civil War*. London-New York, 1987, pp. 173-225.

[10] For England, see e.g. Loades, D. *The Tudor Court*. London, 1986, pp. 85-95; Gunn, S.J. 'The Courtiers of Henry VII.' *The English Historical Review*, 108 (1993) 23-49; and Asch, R.G. ' 'The Politics of Access.' Hofstruktur und Herrschaft in England unter den frühen Stuarts 1603-1642,' in: Paravicini, W., ed. *Alltag bei Hofe* (3. Symposium der Residenzen-Kommission der Akademie der Wissenschaften in Göttingen. Residenzenforschung 3). Sigmaringen, 1995, pp. 243-266. For an interesting theoretical discussion with regard to the 'political body' versus the 'natural body' of the prince, see Garganigo, A. ' 'Coriolanus', the Union Controversy, and Access to the Royal Person.' *Studies in English Literature, 1500-1900*, 42 (2002) 335-359. For Spain, see e.g. Gómez-Centurión Jiménez, C. 'Etiqueta y ceremonial palatino durante el reinado de Felipe V: el reglamento de entradas de 1709 y el acceso a la persona del rey.' *Hispania*, LVI/3, 194 (1996) 965-1005. For France, see e.g. Kettering, S. 'Brokerage at the Court of Louis XIV.' *The Historical Journal*, 36 (1993) 69-87; and Le Roux, N. *La faveur du roi. Mignons et courtisans au temps des derniers Valois (vers 1547-1564)*. Paris, 2000.

[11] A few recent examples: Weiser, B. *Charles II and the Politics of Access*. Woodbridge, 2003; and Whitelock, A. & MacCulloch, D. 'Princess Mary's Household and the Succession Crisis, July 1553.' *The Historical Journal*, 50 (2007) 265-287.

[12] Adamson, 'The Tudor and Stuart Courts,' 109.

[13] Duindam, *Vienna and Versailles*, 234. See also the discussion on pp. 161-180.

that access is only one aspect in a broad array of factors that have to be taken into account. Nevertheless, both Adamson and Duindam alike share the opinion that the acquisition of access was without a doubt one of the most important and efficient ways of acquiring power and, for that reason, deserves the requisite scholarly attention.

With that thought in the back of the mind, the chapter at hand puts the 'distribution' and the importance of access at the archducal court under the magnifying lens.[14] In the first place it means to demonstrate that prominent members of the archducal household – as opposed to outsiders – were able to lay claim to free and unlimited access to the princely couple, and that, precisely for that reason, they could count on the requisite interest in terms of the *corps diplomatique* in Brussels. At pretty much all early modern princely courts, access to the prince was subjected to detailed regulation. In this, the archducal court constituted no exception: Albert and Isabella were anxiously screened off from the outside world. The anecdote about the count of Fürstenberg illustrates, though, that the members of the *Cámara* were entitled to circumvent the strict restrictions in the matter of access. As opposed to most contemporaries (for whom the right of access was only conditionally applicable), they enjoyed guaranteed access (which was to a certain degree enforceable or, in any case, not questioned). In other words, members of the Bedchamber could enter into contact with the princes immediately, directly, and on their own initiative. In a socio-political context fundamentally based on negotiation and reciprocity, this fiercely fought for privilege offered significant added value. On top of that it will be shown that an all too frugal distribution of access could bring along with it ponderous political consequences. So, for instance, some courtiers were in the position to control and even monopolize access to the archdukes, whereby other candidates were literally and figuratively cut off from power.

In the second place this chapter means to go deeper into the connection between access and granting favor at the archducal court. After all, the right to access was not an end in and of itself, but a means. It was seen by contemporaries as a strategic advantage – sometimes even as a precondition – for being able to maintain and to improve their position in society (i.e. socially, financially, and/or politically). Consequently, the goal of access was situated first and foremost in the possibility of acquiring princely favor. During the past decades various historians have gone in detail into the role of the prince as the source from which all sorts of material (money, estates, gifts...) and immaterial (military and political offices, titles of nobility, power, influence,

[14] See in that context also Raeymaekers, D. 'The Power of Proximity: The Cámara of Albert and Isabel at their Court in Brussels,' in: Van Wyhe, C., ed. *Isabel Clara Eugenia. Female Sovereignty in the Courts of Madrid and Brussels*. London, 2011, pp. 258-279.

information…) favors issued forth.[15] Several studies have demonstrated that access indeed constituted an important factor in its acquisition and (re-)distribution.[16] It speaks for itself that the members of the princely entourage had a mark in their favor here. Their multiple contacts with the monarch frequently resulted in mutual affinity, fondness, affection, and even intimacy. These kinds of profound emotions could have a great impact on the unequal distribution of princely favor and, consequently, on the political system in its entirety. It was no different at the archducal court. It need not come as a surprise, therefore, that positions in the archducal household were quite desired. The acquisition of a court office was seen by contemporaries as a way to build up, strengthen, and make an emotional relationship with the princes operational. In that sense, access and granting favor were closely connected with favoritism, a topic that is treated elsewhere in this book (cf. Chapter VI).

Access in the spatial and ceremonial sense

In order to make their vision of access clear, some authors employ a graphic model in which the early modern court is visualized as a system of concentric circles.[17] The expanding rings, then, represent the different gradations of proximity to the prince (X), who was to be found in the center:

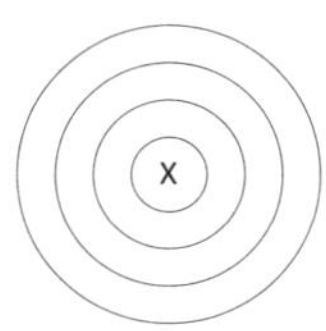

In the optic presented here, access to the prince is mostly studied from the question concerning accessibility of the princely residence in the spatial and ceremonial sense. Jeroen Duindam posits that

> '[court] ordinances invariably attempted to structure access on the basis of rank or function, using the ruler's timetable as well as the spatial arrangements

[15] The literature concerning this topic is far from scarce. In addition to the works already cited, well-known examples are Le Roux, N. *La faveur du roi. Mignons et courtisans au temps des derniers Valois (vers 1547-1564)*. Paris, 2000; Kettering, S. 'Brokerage at the Court of Louis XIV.' *The Historical Journal*, 36 (1993) 69-87; and Jouanna, A. 'Faveur et favoris: l'exemple des mignons de Henri III,' in: Sauzet, R., ed. *Henri III et son temps*. Paris, 1992, pp. 155-165.

[16] For an interesting discussion, see Le Roux, N. 'Courtisans et favoris: l'entourage du prince et les mécanismes du pouvoir dans la France des guerres de religion.' *Histoire, Économie et Société*, 17 (1998) 377-387. See also Duindam, *Vienna and Versailles*, 234-242.

[17] See e.g. Bertelli, S. *The Courts of the Italian Renaissance*. Milan, 1985, pp. 26-27.

> of the palace as their main devices. Spatial and temporal thresholds were set up to prevent outsiders from intruding; guards and ushers barred the way, checking the status of unknown visitors before letting them pass.'[18]

The entry gates of the palace, the various interior doors, and the customs of the court ceremonial formed artificial barriers, in other words, with which the physical distance between the monarch and his subjects was maintained. The private quarters of the prince are seen, then, as the space most screened-off in the residence. Is this kind of situation found at the archducal court as well?

As opposed to what would perhaps be expected, the Coudenberg palace was not a massive bastion. Just like most of the princely residences from the time period studied here, the building was hermetically closed off from the outside world least of all. From various written and iconographic sources an entirely different image arises in every sense. In contemporaneous paintings and drawings the palace is shown to be a microcosm of busyness, in which courtiers as well as visitors and coincidental passersby took part.[19] The palace complex needs to be imagined as a place where hustle and bustle ruled every day. Nobles, councilors, and servants all crossed paths on the inner square, while around them coaches rode up and off. Shops and market stalls were set up in the *Aula Magna* and on the Place des Bailles, where various merchants brought their wares to the man on the street.[20] In the maze of corridors, stairways, and antechambers visitors met to schmooze with each other or to exchange bits of political news with the courtiers present. The palace gardens were also opened to the public at set times.[21] In these sorts of circumstances it was pretty much impossible to keep all entrances and passages of the princely residence under surveillance 24 hours a day. In addition, balls, parties, ceremonies, parades, tournaments, and other festivities for the masses presumably attracted great throngs of not only desired but also undesired spectators to the palace. Although there is scarcely any proof for it, it can be assumed that gatekeepers and porters were not averse to bribery.[22] In that context, even the most closed-off parts of the residence proved to be not entirely safe from unauthorized persons. So, for example, the papal nuncio reported in 1624, that a certain Nicolas Anaia, a former page of Ambrogio Spínola, had succeeded – perhaps with the aid of

---

[18] Duindam, *Vienna and Versailles*, 161.

[19] See as an example Plate 3 in the color section of this book.

[20] Smolar-Meynart, A., Vanrie, A., Soenen, M. et al. *Het paleis van Brussel. Acht eeuwen kunst en geschiedenis*. Exhibition catalogue. Brussels, 1991, p. 122.

[21] *Ibidem*, p. 116.

[22] Loades, *The Tudor Court*, 86. See in that context also the anecdote concerning Luis Lasso de la Vega, who thanks to bribing a lady-in-waiting was able to copy the key that gave entry to the women's quarters in the Coudenberg palace (cf. Chapter I).

an insider – in making off with the keys of the archducal wardrobe and subsequently stealing Isabella's jewels.[23]

That the palace walls were not as impenetrable as might be thought in the first instance is a consideration that cannot be lost sight of.[24] The question arises, though, to what extent the 'infiltration' described here – in which various persons, wanted or not, could enter or penetrate the archducal residence – was significant. Undoubtedly many (un-)invited guests hoped to catch a glimpse of the archdukes, draw their attention, perhaps even be addressed by them during their visit.[25] That chance existed yet was extremely small. Having access to the residence was not the same as acquiring access to the princes, and even if one succeeded in approaching them, they could in no way just simply be addressed. In his study about Charles II of England, Brian Weiser puts forward that 'historians [tend to view] access in a binary manner: rulers are seen under the simple rubric as being either strict or easy of access. (…) But (…) in the sense of the ability to come into contact with the king, [it] was a more nuanced phenomenon.'[26] Weiser rightly argues that the importance of access was not so much in physical proximity *per se* as in the possibility for interacting with the prince. In an era in which long-distance communication was limited to correspondence – an efficient yet vulnerable medium and, on top of that, subject to lags in time – physical proximity proved to be an enormous advantage, though naturally only useful if communicating with the prince was possible (and permitted). More than finding the prince, access was a question of finding the prince's ear. Consequently, it is not so much a matter of researching how accessible the princely residence was shown to be, but of investigating in what way access to the prince himself was controlled, as well as whether and how entering into contact with him was possible. The latter proved to be least self-evident of all. The Ancien Régime stood as a time period in which the prince increasingly isolated himself in a physical as well as psychological sense from his subjects.[27] Physically because the right of access to his private quarters was restrained, and psychologically because the interaction with the monarch was ritualized more

---

23 De Meester de Ravestein, B., ed. *Correspondance du Nonce Giovanni-Francesco Guidi di Bagno (1621-1627).* Analecta Vaticano-Belgica, 2e série, section A: Nonciature de Flandre, VI. Rome-Brussels-Paris, 1938. Op. cit. vol. I, letter no. 974: Giovanni-Francesco Guidi di Bagno to Domenico Marini, archbishop of Genoa, May 4, 1624.

24 Duindam, J. 'Palace, City, Dominions: The Spatial Dimension of Habsburg Rule.' Lecture held at the colloquium *The Politics of Space: Courts in Europe and the Mediterranean, ca. 1500-1750* (The Huntington Library, San Marino, California, January 26-27, 2007). See also the discussion in Duindam, *Vienna and Versailles*, 209-210.

25 Adamson, 'The Tudor and Stuart Courts,' 96.

26 Weiser, *Charles II and the Politics of Access*, 13-15.

27 This point has been demonstrated by several authors. See e.g. the different contributions in Adamson, *The Princely Courts*; and in Asch, R.G. & Birke, A.M., eds. *Princes, Patronage and the Nobility: The Court at the Beginning of the Modern Age, c. 1450-1650.* Oxford U.P., 1991.

and more strongly, whereby conversations seldom ran openly and comfortably. Both of these aspects are put under the magnifying lens in the following sections.

Access to the archducal *Cámara*

In his book about the Tudor court David Loades determines that 'there were no strict rules as to who might, or might not, be admitted to any palace or residence where the court was situated; a presentable appearance, a show of legitimate business, and a supply of ready cash, were all that was required.'[28] Yet, the author adds, 'to obtain access to the Privy Chamber was a different matter; there the ushers were given the strictest instructions that no one should be allowed to pass who was not either a known officer or servant, or a person who had been specifically summoned to the royal presence.'[29] As opposed to the rest of the palace complex, access to the princely apartments was thus strictly monitored. That need not come as a surprise. The bottom line was that these were the quarters in which the monarch spent the majority of his time, in which he ate, slept, worked, read reports, wrote letters, signed documents, and drew up laws. Here, in the seclusion of the scarce, personal space made available to him, the prince was anxiously screened off from the outside world. At the court of the archdukes it was no different.

Around 1598, shortly before his marriage with the infanta, Archduke Albert decided to embark upon the full renovation of the residential wing of his palace.[30] Whereas this part of his residence had previously always consisted of a simple *enfilade* of suites, through the addition of a second series of rooms the wing was split in two (cf. Illustration 2). By doing this, the internal route leading to the princely bedchamber became approximately half again as long as previously. In this strictly monitored sequence of chambers and antechambers visitors were literally 'pre-sorted' according to rank, function, and/or social status. The spatial arrangement of the residential wing mirrored, as it were, a social hierarchy: the higher on the social ladder you stood, the closer you were allowed to approach the *sanctum sanctorum* of the palace – the archducal *Cámara*. After having climbed the grand processional staircase to the second floor, visitors traversed in succession the entrance hall (6); the porters' room (9) (flanked by the room of the *Hartschiere* (10)); the dining room in which the archdukes took their meals under a baldachin on public occasions (11); the first antechamber, or the room of the *grandes* (12); the second antechamber, or the room

[28] Loades, *The Tudor Court*, 86.
[29] *Ibidem.*
[30] De Jonge, K. ' ' 't Hof van Brabant' als symbool van de Spaanse hofhouding in de Lage Landen.' *Bulletin van de Nederlandse Oudheidkundige Bond*, 98 (1999) 183-197.

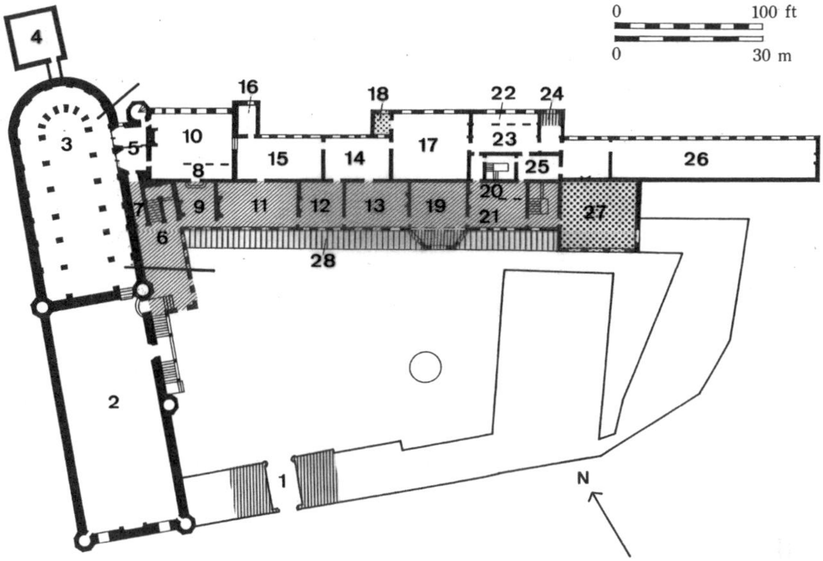

Illustration 2 – Ground plan of the princely apartments in the Coudenberg palace at the time of the archdukes (main floor). The arcaded space was added to the residential wing in the period 1598-1603 by the architects Hieronymo Hardouin and Mathieu Bollin.
(Reconstruction: Krista De Jonge)

(1) Main entrance of the palace complex
(2) *Aula Magna*
(3) Chapel
(4) Sacristy
(5) Tribune where religious services were attended
(6) Entrance hall and staircase
(7) Corridor
(8) Corridor
(9) Porters' room
(10) Room of the *Hartschiere*
(11) Room in which public meals took place
(12) First antechamber (room of the *grandes*)
(13) Second antechamber (room of the *gentilhombres*)
(14) Audience hall
(15) Private dining room and withdrawing room
(16) Cabinet
(17) *Chambre de parade*
(18) Wardrobe
(19) Private oratory
(20-21) Withdrawing chamber
(22) Corridor
(23) Study
(24) Cabinet
(25) Chamber
(26) Long gallery
(27) Apartment of the *sumiller de corps*
(28) Balcony

of the *gentilhombres de la Cámara* (13); to land finally in the audience hall (14). For most of those invited this suite constituted the terminus of their visit. The space for audiences marked the borderline between the public and the private section of the princely apartments. From here on out, only the happy few pushed on through into the *Cámara*, which encompassed Albert's bedchamber and adjoining rooms (17-25).[31]

[31] On account of the many successive renovations the precise functions of the various spaces remain especially unclear. The order of chambers proposed here is perhaps the most accurate. For more information, see De Jonge, ' ' 't Hof van Brabant',' 192-193; and De Jonge, K. et al. 'Building Policy and Urbanisation during the Reign of the Archdukes: The Court and its Architects,' in: Thomas, W. & Duerloo, L., eds. *Albert & Isabella, 1598-1621: Essays*. Turnhout, 1998, pp. 191-219.

Originally the principle of a shrewd spatial arrangement for the princely dwelling stemmed from the Burgundian court ceremonial, in which the creation of distance between the sovereign and his subjects constituted an essential objective (cf. Chapter I). Its finer points were worked out by the Habsburgs, however, with Philip II as the undisputed champion. It is probable, then, that as an architect Albert was inspired by the example of his uncle, whose palaces in Madrid and San Lorenzo exhibited an especially complex spatial organization with an eye to secluding the prince. It is not for nothing that the Spanish-Habsburg monarchy is denoted by some historians as a hidden monarchy, a kingship that was characterized by the splendid isolation of the monarch.[32] With that, the Spanish court stood in sharp contrast to its French counterpart, which for ages enjoyed a reputation of openness and accessibility – even though this image is also in need of nuance.[33]

In the 1960s it was already convincingly argued that the architectural planning of princely residences during the early modern period not only contributed to the splendor of the court but also had a concrete regulating function.[34] To the degree that the separation between the public and private spheres of the prince's life began to manifest itself more and more clearly in the course of time, the manner in which the prince structured the space around him became increasingly loaded politically. 'Of all the influences on the conduct of politics, none impinged more directly than the allocation and control of space within the palace,' Adamson concludes.[35] By literally distancing himself from the spying glance of his subjects and denying them access to his chambers, the monarch strengthened the inviolability and the mystique surrounding the princely *persona*. On a more secular level his physical withdrawal necessitated a reorientation of the patronage networks at court, which became more and more independent of the few persons who were authorized to approach the prince. This kind of pattern of increasing isolation was introduced in the course of the early modern period at pretty much all European princely courts – albeit in different

---

[32] See e.g. Redworth, G. & Checa, F. 'The Courts of the Spanish Habsburgs 1500-1700,' in: Adamson, *The Princely Courts*, pp. 43-65.

[33] Duindam, *Vienna and Versailles*, 22. See also Justus, K.L. 'Gilded Palace, Gilded Playpen: Louis XV's Use of Palatial Space to Control his Rebellious Children and Their Politics.' *The Journal of Family History*, 21 (1996) 470-495. See also Chatenet, M. *La Cour de France au XVIe siècle: vie sociale et architecture*. Paris, 2002; and Spangler, J. 'Aulic Spaces Transplanted: The Design and Layout of a Franco-Burgundian Court in a Scottish Palace.' *The Court Historian*, 14 (2009) 49-62.

[34] The standard work concerning this topic is still Baillie, H.M. 'Etiquette and the Planning of the State Apartments in Baroque Palaces.' *Archaeologia*, 101 (1967) 169-199. In emulating Baillie's article, numerous studies concerning palace architecture and spatial arrangement of the princely residence in the early modern time period have appeared in the meantime. Well-known examples are Thurley, S. *The Royal Palaces of Tudor England. Architecture and Court Life 1460-1547*. London-New Haven, 1993; Newton, W.R. *L'Espace du roi. La cour de France au château de Versailles 1682-1789*. Paris, 2000; and Brown, J. & Elliott, J.H. *A Palace for a King: The Buen Retiro and the Court of Philip IV*. Yale U.P., 2003.

[35] Adamson, 'The Tudor and Stuart Courts,' 108.

gradations. In that sense it could be posited that the shrewd spatial organization of the princely residence went on to make up part of the 'formal requirements,' cited in a prior chapter, to which any self-respecting sovereign court was expected to answer (cf. Chapter I).

In emulating these theories recent research has connected the architectural operations in the Coudenberg palace with the political aspirations of the archdukes, whose sovereign status was even a subject of discussion during their lives. The well-considered spatial arrangement of the palace, identical to that of the royal residences in Spain, is interpreted in that case as symbolic legitimization of the authority of Albert and Isabella as sovereign Habsburg princes.[36] In addition, the architectural adjustments can also be seen as an externalization of the dynastic ambitions of the archdukes, who in this time period repeatedly undertook attempts to have themselves recognized by the pope and the international community as kings of Burgundy.[37] This proposition gains in force when taking into consideration that the reorganization of that space went hand in hand with the introduction of a new court ceremonial, which was based on the Spanish example as well. As seen earlier, this measure could count on much criticism from the indigenous nobles in Brussels (cf. Chapter I). They accused the archduke of wanting to organize his court '(...) like that of the king of Spain, with distinctions between chambers, locked doors, and porters at each entrance (...),' which was seen as excessive and inappropriate in view of the fact that Albert was not a king.[38] Even so, it can be supposed that the dissatisfaction of the nobles not only had to do with the archduke's aspirations – in their eyes unfounded – but also with the fact that suddenly their right of access to the prince was brusquely truncated.

Norms and practices

Although various sources suggest that access to the archducal *Cámara* was regulated in a meticulous way – as was the case at other early modern European courts – no court ordinances about this have come to light.[39] That is unfortunate, for although those kinds of orders are normative in nature, they would nevertheless be able to render

36 De Jonge, ' ''t Hof van Brabant',' passim.

37 See e.g. BFZ, *Altamira*, carpeta 39, grupo documental 13, doc. 61: Philip III to the duke of Sesa, Spanish ambassador to Rome, June 5, 1599.

38 ASV, *NF* 11, ff. 705-706: Ottavio Mirto Frangipani to Cardinal-Secretary of State Aldobrandini, September 19, 1599.

39 At least not for the period 1598-1633. The Algemeen Rijksarchief in Brussels [National Archives of Belgium, Brussels] does preserve a *Mémoire touchant les entrées en les sales et antichambres de la Cour* from 1594 (ARA *Aud* 33/1, no. 6). These regulations were in force during the governorship of Archduke Ernst and are based on the Austrian-Burgundian ceremonial that was in effect at the imperial court.

more clarity concerning the way in which access at the archducal court was perceived and 'distributed.' Even so, in view of the fact that the court ceremonial in Brussels was modeled after the Spanish example, it is probable that the rules of access were comparable with the regulations in effect at the royal court in Madrid. In the Spanish system access to the *Cámara* of the prince was channeled with the aid of a number of strict restrictions.[40] Save for a few exceptions the right to free access there was reserved for the leading members of the royal household, among them the *mayordomo mayor*, the *sumiller de corps*, the *mayordomos*, the *gentilhombres de la Cámara*, the *gentilhombres de la Boca*, and the *ayudas de la Cámara* – albeit all of them according to different gradations and under well-defined conditions.[41] Given observation of the requisite decorum, the *grandes*, the knights of the Order of the Golden Fleece, as well as the most important councilors and secretaries of State were also allowed to enter the private quarters of the prince. It speaks for itself that, if circumstances demanded it, then other courtiers and staff members were allowed (e.g., the barber, the personal physician, the floor sweepers, etc.), although never without express approval of the *mayordomo mayor* or the *sumiller de corps*.[42] Although etiquette presupposed that the prince was not left alone at any one moment, a series of unbending rules made it in principle impossible to approach or address him without being invited to do so. According to Yves Bottineau, these kinds of rigid measures had only one goal:

> 'They betray an untoward tendency of Spanish etiquette: to limit the contacts – those of conversation or even of mere presence – that the King can have with a limited number of privileged persons; excepting the latter, the people he can see tend to be no more than shadows charged with subordinate duties.'[43]

For want of court ordinances, whether the situation in Brussels was indeed comparable to that in Madrid can only be derived from indirect information. That does not need to be as problematic as it seems. Orders concerning access reflected hypothetical intentions, to be sure, but were not always strictly observed for that reason. In that context Aloys Winterling already pointed to the possibility of a discrepancy between

---

40 See e.g. IVDJ, envío 114, caja 163, doc. 170: '*Las personas que los porteros de Cámara y Capilla Real de Su Majestad an de dexar entrar en San Lorenzo son las siguientes.*'

41 On the basis of Bottineau, Y. 'Aspects de la Cour d'Espagne au XVIIe siècle.' *Bulletin Hispanique*, 74 (1972) 138-157.

42 For more information, see Mayoral López, R. *La Casa Real de Felipe III (1598-1621). Ordenanzas y Etiquetas.* Unpublished doctoral dissertation, Universidad Autónoma de Madrid, 2007.

43 '*Ils laissent (...) deviner une tendance fâcheuse de l'etiquette espagnole: limiter les contacts – ceux de la conversation ou même de la simple présence – que peut avoir le Roi à un nombre restreint de privilégiés; en dehors de ceux-ci, les hommes qu'il peut voir tendent à n'être plus que des ombres chargées d'un service subalterne précis.*' Bottineau, 'Aspects de la Cour,' 148.

norms and practices – a problem that is all too frequently underestimated in studies concerning the early modern court ceremonial.[44] That does not pose a problem in the research into access at the archducal court for the simple reason that the regulations on the matter are no longer at hand. Consequently, it is necessary to hearken back to indications from different types of sources, such as private correspondence and diplomatic reports, which tell something more about the situation in practice. Generally, this is a question of short anecdotes, which are often wrongly overlooked because they – seemingly – contain little to no concrete information. An historian who goes in search of hard political facts will seldom be inclined to dwell on commentaries concerning ceremonial questions. Nonetheless, in these small observations hides a treasure trove of data concerning the nature and workings of early modern politics. They produce a less clear-cut complete picture, to be sure, but nevertheless carry great significance.

Whoever reads over the correspondence of ambassadors and foreign representatives for these practices discovers pretty much at once that the *Cámara* of Archduke Albert held a central, ceremonial status, and that physical proximity to the prince was seen as a precious commodity. Thus, it is striking, for instance, that the importance and status of visitors reported about is measured, among other things, by the precise distance that Albert covered from his private quarters to go to meet them. Just like the Spanish princes, who distinguished themselves by their 'statuesque immobility' according to Glyn Redworth and Fernando Checa, the archduke seldom condescended to come out of his bedchamber to receive guests.[45] Whenever he did indeed do that, this was seen as an exceptional honor. When the Spanish nobleman Rodrigo Calderón – the famed favorite of Lerma – got an audience at court in June, 1612, according to the papal nuncio he was collected by Ambrogio Spínola and by '*tutti cavalieri della Camara*.' Once arrived at the palace he was awaited by the archduke at the door of his Bedchamber.[46] That was already less a great honor than that which in turn fell to the prince of Condé when he was received by the archdukes in December, 1609. The prince – as the French ambassador reported – was collected by Albert himself, already halfway to the antechamber.[47] An even greater display of honor was set aside for the duke of Neuburg, who in 1614 was not only collected by Albert in the antechamber,

[44] Winterling, A. *Der Hof der Kurfürsten von Köln, 1688-1794. Eine Fallstudie zur Bedeutung 'absolutistischer' Hofhaltung*. Bonn, 1986. Op. cit. p. 156. See also Adamson, 'The Making of the Ancien-Régime Court,' 28; and Duindam, *Vienna and Versailles*, 161-180.

[45] Redworth & Checa, 'The Courts of the Spanish Habsburgs,' 57.

[46] BAV, *BaL* 6806, f. 281: Guido Bentivoglio to Cardinal-Secretary of State Borghese, June 16, 1612.

[47] *MsF* 16129, f. 204: Berruyer, secretary of the French ambassador Mathieu Brulart de Berny, to Puisieux, December 27, 1609.

but was also taken back again to the stairway to the ground floor.[48] The duke of Vaudemont, then again, was awaited by the court in full attendance, half a mile away from Brussels, and subsequently accompanied to the palace, where Albert stood waiting for him at the top of the processional staircase.[49] Finally, for the reception of the elector of Mainz in 1612, Albert himself rode to outside the city walls – a greater expression of honor could not be imagined.[50]

There was also brisk correspondence concerning the actual access to the princely quarters. Once again the rules appear to have been comparable with those at the court in Madrid. In June, 1597, the Frisian noble Frederik van Vervou, court steward of William Louis of Nassau, was in Brussels to visit the prince of Orange. In his memoirs Vervou noted that he had attended the public meal of the (at that moment still) cardinal-archduke in the Coudenberg palace.[51] Albert was waited on with ritual respect by his *gentilhombres de la Boca*, who served him food and drink while on their knees. The residential wing of the palace had not yet been rebuilt in 1597, so that it is impossible to say in which quarters this meal took place precisely. With certainty, though, after the renovation of 1598-1603, the public meals continued in the '*salette où leurs Altesses mangent en publicq*,' which was outfitted with a podium and a baldachin (cf. number 11 on the ground plan).[52] It was very clearly the intention that the archdukes could be looked at here in all their princely majesty.[53] For that reason, the room was accessible to outsiders – albeit perhaps not for everyone. The English nobleman Charles Somerset was one of the lucky ones. In 1612, he gave a description of the dining ritual in his travel diary:

> 'When the Duke and Dutchesse doe eate publikely, the Dutchesse is served by 3 ladies, which attende on her with comelie grace; the one serves her bread, the other her wine, and the third playes the Carver; the rest of the ladies stand along by the walles side, and be Courted by those Noblemen that are their servitours, which speake alowde unto them all dinner time with their hatts on, which priviledge is only allowed them at that time. And upon such daies the Infante her messe is served up by young Noblemens sonnes called Meninos or

---

[48] NA, *SP* 77/11, f. 209: William Trumbull to James I, December 18, 1614.

[49] BNF, *MsF* 16130, f. 108: Berruyer to Puisieux, February 9, 1613.

[50] AGS, *Estado* 2294, s.f.: The marquis of Guadaleste to Philip III, s.d. [August, 1612].

[51] van Vervou, F. *Enige gedenckvveerdige geschiedenissen, tot nachrichtinge der nakomelingen, sommarischer wijze beschreven deur Jr. Fredrich van Vervou, dewelcke hij eensdeels gesien, om ende over geweest, anderdeels deur loffweerdige mannen gehoort ende verstaan heeft; dit alles na den ouden stijl.* Leeuwarden, 1841. Op. cit. p. 69. I thank Erik Swart for this reference.

[52] De Jonge, 'Building Policy and Urbanisation,' 195.

[53] Hennequin de Villermont, M. *L'Infante Isabelle, gouvernante des Pays-Bas.* 2 vols. Paris-Tamines, 1912. Op. cit. vol. II, p. 35.

> little Minions, and are in estimation much more noble in their calling, then the state of the Pages.'[54]

Although the dining room was freely accessible to visitors on these public occasions, that was certainly not the case for Albert's *Cámara.* Somerset stated that

> 'there is great Ceremonies kept in [the Archduke's] Chambers of state; in the first Chamber all Captaines and ordinarie Gentlemen come in, and passe no further; in the second come Coronels and Noblemen of the Countrie; and the thirde is the Chamber where none come but those that are the Grandoes of Spayne, that are alwaies covered before the king, and those of the Order of the Golden Fleece, and also princes of the Countrie, and such princes as shall come unto his Courte, and the Chamber adjoyning next unto the third Chamber, is the Chamber, where the Archduke according unto his accustomed manner everie weeke giveth audience unto any that will come unto him: he sitteth in a chayre, where everie one in his turne hath accesse unto him according as they have given their names up unto the Chamberlan.'[55]

Somerset's description is confirmed by a report, among others, from the French ambassador Péricard, who was obliged to take his place behind a curtain during the ceremonial appointment of the count of Emden as knight of the Golden Fleece – a ceremony that proceeded in Albert's private quarters – because only knights of the Order were allowed to be present in this space.[56] The papal nuncio, too, had to follow the ceremony from behind the curtain, and even the infanta was only allowed to look on from an opening in the doorway. It had been arranged that way by Rodrigo Niño y Lasso, count of Añover, who as *sumiller de corps* of the archducal household decided with quasi-sovereignty over the question who was allowed into the *Cámara,* and who was not. These strict rules applied also to Isabella's quarters, by the way, where the *camarera mayor* monitored the arrangement for access: 'The Infanta her Chamberlan is a woman, and none come within her quarter but women,' Somerset wrote.[57] When this function was entrusted to Antoinette-Guillemette of Arenberg in 1615, the necessary instructions concerning it were sent to her.[58] The new mistress of the household had to see to it, among other things, that none of the ladies-in-

[54] Brennan, M.G., ed. *The Travel Diary (1611-1612) of an English Catholic Sir Charles Somerset, edited from the manuscript in the Brotherton Collection University of Leeds.* Leeds, 1993. Op. cit. p. 289.
[55] *Ibidem,* pp. 287-288.
[56] BNF, *MsF* 16131, f. 274: Péricard to Puisieux, April 20, 1618.
[57] Brennan, *The Travel Diary,* 288.
[58] ACA, 36/17: *Lo que toca a la Camarera Mayor.*

waiting remain behind after services were finished in the infanta's chamber, without having explicitly received permission to do so. The key to the antechamber that led to Isabella's sleeping quarters was kept by one of the *dueñas de Retrete* and was only given to the *reposteros de cama* when the infanta went away to dine. After the *reposteros* had made up the bed of the princess, the key was given up anew to the *camarera mayor*, who kept it until the following morning.[59] A letter from Antoinette-Guillemette to her sister-in-law Anne de Croÿ, duchess of Aarschot, shows that here, too, the count of Añover had a substantial finger in the pie. In 1616 she wrote that the infanta wanted to grant the duchess access to her *Cámara*. Yet Antoinette-Guillemette advised her sister-in-law that she always ask the approval of the *sumiller de corps* beforehand: 'The infanta says that you can enter via the antechamber and the gatehouse whenever it pleases you. Nevertheless it would be good to speak about it to the count of Añover, because even though the infanta permits it, he always wants to be asked for permission as well.'[60] This last example demonstrates that access was anxiously monitored not only to Albert's *Cámara* but also to Isabella's. In any case, it was seen as an especially great honor to get free access here. When the princesses of Condé paid their respects to the archducal court in 1611, the French ambassador reported that they were received with much courtesy, and that Isabella gave them the fiercely fought-for right 'to be able to see the infanta in private in her chamber at all times.'[61]

The examples cited illustrate that when they were to be found in their private quarters, getting to see or speak to the archdukes was in practice least of all self-evident. The right of free access to the *Cámara* was only set aside for the happy few. Others did not get in or, in any case, not without prior permission. In most cases requesting an audience, and hoping for a favorable answer, was required. In his memoirs the papal nuncio Bentivoglio noted that Albert had the custom of holding audiences in the morning as well as in the evening, doing so for several hours as well.[62] In view of the fact that Isabella shared sovereignty over the Netherlands with her spouse, she

---

59 *Ibidem.*

60 '*L'Infante dit (...) que porés antrer par l'anteschambre et porterÿe quant il vous plerat. Touttefois il serat bon que an fisiés parler au Conte d'Añovere, car quant bien l'Infante l'acorde sy veut il touiour que l'on ly demande le syne.*' ACA, 38/11, file 464, s.f.: Antoinette-Guillemette of Arenberg to Anne de Croÿ, July 14, 1616. For a similar citation, see ACA, 38/2, file 48, no. 9: Antoinette-Guillemette of Arenberg to Charles of Arenberg, s.d.: '*(...) Madame vostre fame, laquelle Son Altesse dit avoir pouvoir de venir quant il s'y plerat par la porterie ou par l'anteschambre.*'

61 '*(...) de pouvoir voir l'infante en particulier à touttes heures dedans sa chambre.*' BNF, *MsF* 16125, f. 259: Charles de l'Aubespinne-Chasteauneuf, abbot of Préaux, to Secretary of State Villeroy, October 9, 1611.

62 Bentivoglio, G. *Relationi del Cardinal Bentivoglio*. Brussels, 1632. Op. cit. p. 142 [Original edition: Bentivoglio, G. *Relationi fatte dall' illustrissimo, e reverendissimo signor cardinal Bentivoglio in tempo delle sue nuntiature di Fiandra, e di Francia. Date in luce da Erycio Puteano*. Antwerp, 1629]. Based on the writings of Jules Chifflet, Marie Hennequin de Villermont posits that the archduke's evening audience usually started at 6:30 p.m. and ended at 8:00 p.m. Hennequin de Villermont, *L'Infante Isabelle*, volume II, 30.

also regularly held audiences with visitors received. Important guests usually went for conversations with the infanta as well as the archduke, and – interestingly enough – always in that order, too (cf. Chapter I).[63] On these occasions visitors were permitted to express their respect, to discuss political questions, to voice complaints, and to plead requests. In addition, the audience offered a forum to foreign representatives and agents for tightening diplomatic bonds with the archdukes. Even so, on account of the official character of these conversations (*and* because they seldom were devoid of political or personal interests), audiences were subject to various limitations. In the first place obtaining an audience was not easy: a request to be received by the archdukes could simply be declined. Even if the petition was approved, you usually had to wait a little while before the conversation actually could take place. Depending on the circumstances, this could last from a few days to even weeks. In that manner, above all, the archduke's frequent attacks of gout provided for postponement or cancellation.[64] In these moments Albert kept to his bed and sometimes did not come out of the *Cámara* for weeks.[65] The political impact of this cannot be underestimated: time and again whenever Albert was chained to his sickbed, diplomatic intercourse went completely quiet. Lord Doncaster, the English ambassador, wrote in 1619,

> 'I sent a gentleman to Mariemont to enquire of his Highnes health, and to solicit the Comte d'Anover, that, through his favor, I might be admitted to an audience, as soone as his Highnes indisposition would permitt. From whome I receyved answere that his Highnes was upon amendment, and that, by the ordinary course of his fittes, he made confident reckoning that within foure or five dayes at the farthest his Highnes would be in a state to give me accesse.'[66]

Further, it appears to have been difficult to get permission for a visit when Albert and Isabella were to be found in the hunting palace of Tervuren. So, for instance, Isabella's *camarera mayor* announced that 'this place [is] not proper enough' for receiving guests, although the latter did indeed occur now and then.[67] Ceremonial procedures could provide for delays, too. When the Spanish nobleman Garcia de Pareja arrived

[63] See e.g. ASV, *Borghese* III 113, f. 184: Nuncio Lucio Morra to Borghese, August 19, 1617.

[64] See e.g. AGS, *Estado* 2307, s.f.: The marquis of Bedmar to Philip III, November 10, 1619; and ASV, *Borghese* II 98, f. 240: Nuncio Lucio Sanseverino to Borghese, January 11, 1620.

[65] BNF, *MsF* 16132, f. 19: Péricard to Puisieux, January 18, 1619; f. 31: Péricard to Puisieux, February 5, 1619; and f. 36: Péricard to Puisieux, February 6, 1619.

[66] NA, *SP* 77/13, f. 267: Lord Doncaster to Secretary of State Robert Naunton, May 30, 1619. In June, 1621, the English ambassador William Trumbull reported that he had got an audience with the infanta, '*but could not have accesse to the archeduke (...), by reason of his weaknes.*' See NA, *SP* 77/14, f. 345: William Trumbull to Secretary of State Robert Naunton, June 24, 1621.

[67] '*(...) le lieu n'estoit icy assez propre (...)*' ACA, 38/11, file 465, s.f.: Antoinette-Guillemette of Arenberg to Anne de Croÿ, November 6, 1616.

in Brussels in 1617, his audience was postponed because the archduke did not know whether he had to receive Pareja as an ambassador extraordinary of the Spanish king (and thus with the appropriate pomp and pageantry), or as an ordinary emissary.[68] In the same way the new papal nuncio had to wait for his first conversation in July, 1621, with the infanta, who had – as was the custom at that time – secluded herself for forty days from the outside world after the death of her spouse.[69]

Even if the audience could proceed, the difficulties were not out of the way. Often the conversations experienced hindrance from the strict protocol that visitors needed to respect. Meetings with the archdukes ran according to a choreography drawn out in minute detail, which frequently led to disputes about precedence and decorum. So as to avoid that the latter would grow into genuine diplomatic conflicts, the conversations had to be tackled with great circumspection. That was not always conducive to smooth communication.[70] Further, it needs to be assumed that you could seldom speak freely during audiences. Generally the conversations ran in public and were attended by a large crowd.[71] In theory prominent visitors could be received in a private audience, but even in this case conversations seldom took place heart-to-heart. The Spanish court ceremonial prescribed that the *mayordomo mayor* and – if possible – a number of *gentilhombres de la Cámara* were expected to attend the archduke's audiences at all times.[72] During her audiences, too, the infanta was always accompanied by a few ladies-in-waiting and by her mistress of the household. In a letter to Anne de Croÿ, therefore, the *camarera mayor* Antoinette-Guillemette of Arenberg excused herself for the fact that she had so little time to write, 'because of the audiences that I have to attend so as to be near Her Highness at all times.'[73]

For outsiders the audience constituted one of the few possibilities for having personal, direct, and lasting contact with the princes. On account of the aforementioned limitations, though, a successful conversation was not always guaranteed. On top of that, the fact that visitors had to request a discussion beforehand was a great disadvantage: in the diplomatic world delays and hold-ups were powerful weapons. This shows that access for most contemporaries was a *conditional* right. It was granted with the greatest possible frugality: the physical access to the archdukes as well as the possibility for interaction was bound to a number of strict conditions. As cited earlier, however, that was not the case for the prominent members of the archducal household.

68 ASV, *Borghese* III 113, f. 60: Nuncio Ascanio Gesualdo to Borghese, March 11, 1617.

69 BAV, *BaL* 6812, f. 4: Nuncio Giovanni-Francesco Guidi di Bagno to Cardinal Ludovisi, July 24, 1621.

70 See e.g. NA, *SP* 77/13, f. 267: Lord Doncaster to the secretary of State, May 30, 1619.

71 BAV, *BaL* 6807, f. 65: Bentivoglio to Borghese, August 4, 1612.

72 Bottineau, 'Aspects de la cour,' 144.

73 '*(…) pour autant que j'ay en sy peu de loisir tant pour les audiances ou y me faut toujour estre auprès de Son Altesse.*' ACA, 38/11, file 465, s.f.: Antoinette-Guillemette of Arenberg to Anne de Croÿ, December 26, 1616.

By the capacity of their offices, staff and members of the *Cámara* enjoyed free access to the private quarters of the prince. The anecdote about the count of Fürstenberg, with which this chapter began, illustrates, on top of that, that they did not have to request an audience in order to get to speak with the archdukes. That is not to say that the courtiers were allowed to put aside the required decorum and the prescribed etiquette. It means that they had the right to circumvent standard procedures in the matter of access and audiences, and that this right was not questioned. Not for nothing did the *gentilhombres de la Cámara* receive a golden key at their installation. More than a prestigious accessory, the key was a symbol of their status as members of the archducal inner circle. Access to the princes was guaranteed to them, and to a certain degree even enforceable. As the following sections will show, this privilege brought with it important advantages.

The golden key

As *gentilhombre de la Cámara* and *primer caballerizo*, Gaston Spínola, count of Bruay, was a leading member of the archducal household. Although the count did not live in the palace, the letters he exchanged show that he saw the archducal residence as his workplace.[74] Just like commuters nowadays, he traveled back and forth between the court and where he lived on pretty much a daily basis. As such, he was excellently informed of everything that was playing out within the palace walls. His correspondence contains a veritable treasure trove of information concerning life at court in Brussels. Bruay not only told of special occasions like hunting parties, wedding feasts, and balls, but he was also able to report all manner of relevant and less relevant bits of news concerning the experiences of the courtiers. In addition, he expanded in detail upon the comings and goings of visitors as well as the agenda of the archdukes. In some ways his familiarity with life at court is even expressed in the development of a vocabulary that strongly recalls work-related jargon. Whereas most Spanish-speaking contemporaries would refer to Albert as *Su Alteza* ('His Highness'), Bruay used the term *nuestro Amo* ('our master').[75] His detailed descriptions of the state of the archduke's health further point out that Bruay's orbit extended into Albert's *Cámara*, even when the latter was chained to his bed with gout. This free access put Bruay in the position of staying informed about all manner of political questions, about which he then made a detailed report in his letters. Even more important was that fact that Bruay enjoyed the right of seeking out Albert whenever he wanted. As

[74] Spínola's letters to Charles of Arenberg can be found in ACA, 38/3 and 38/4.
[75] ACA, 38/3 and 38/4, passim.

opposed to many others, he was entitled to approach the archduke on his own initiative and at any moment. That occurred in 1612, among other times, when his friend and confederate Charles, princely count of Arenberg, asked Bruay to recommend one of his clients for a position in the Great Council of Mechelen. Bruay did not hesitate and sought out the archduke at once. Scarcely one day later he reported, in a way triumphantly, that he 'had spoken with the master about this matter for more than a quarter of an hour yesterday,' whereby he had pointed out to Albert the qualities and accomplishments of the client in question.[76]

The Bruay case offers a good illustration of the usefulness and significance of guaranteed access. In the case of Bruay, the privilege offered him the possibility of gathering first-hand information, and subsequently distributing this among third parties. At a time in which the court constituted the epicenter of power and the least whim of the prince could bring the political equilibrium out of balance, this was especially interesting. In addition, Bruay had at his disposal the possibility of approaching the archduke personally and directly, without having to ask for an audience in advance. These kinds of opportunities proved to be ideal for bringing up his concerns and those of his political allies immediately and directly to Albert. It need not come as a surprise, then, that Albert's *gentilhombres* could count on the requisite interest from foreign ambassadors in Brussels. Although the *corps diplomatique* gave attention now and then to the lesser gods of the archducal court (such as the *gentilhombres de la Boca* and the *gentilhombres de la Casa*), it is clear that it was above all the officials in the *Cámara* who stirred up the most dust in diplomatic correspondence. Just like today's paparazzi the foreign emissaries reported about the comings and goings of Albert's *gentilhombres* with indefatigable zeal. Time and again whenever a new courtier received the golden key, they set to sharpening their pens. The ink flowed just as richly whenever the archduke handed out titles of nobility to them, or whenever they received special favors. In the incessant flow of reports the diplomats sent to the home front, they seldom forgot to make mention of the exact position of a courtier, or in which way the latter was related to another member of Albert's entourage. A returning subject was the treatment the *gentilhombres* received at court. How were they addressed? Were they permitted to keep on their hats in the presence of the princes? In which pew did they take their place in the Court Chapel? Much more than insignificant details giving proof of a bizarre sense of protocol and hierarchy, these were commentaries intended to convey information concerning the degree of access a courtier enjoyed, and concerning his status in terms of (political) power and influence.

[76] ACA, 38/3, file 108, no. 4: Gaston Spínola to Charles of Arenberg, January 11, 1612.

On April 30, 1621, a few months before the death of the archduke, the ambassador Jean Péricard reported that Albert and Isabella had appointed the Genoese field commander Ambrogio Spínola as the *mayordomo mayor* of their household. According to the ambassador, that position had not coincidentally fallen in turn to Spínola. Péricard supposed that the decision was motivated by a sly balancing act: 'Their Highnesses have given him the position of grand master of the household, which is called *mayordomo mayor* (...). The said office of grand master provides an absolute liberty to enter the quarter of the infanta at all times and to speak with her (...).'[77] On July 16, 1621, three days after Albert's death, Péricard came back to his earlier observation once more: 'This office of *mayordomo mayor*, which has been given to the marquis [Spínola] solely to give him liberty to enter the Bedchamber of the infanta at all times, without having to ask for an audience like he used to, and to speak with her about all occurrences, being the only and unique one to enjoy this privilege (...).'[78] Péricard was convinced that Spínola had only got the most important office in the archducal household so that he would have free and unlimited access to the infanta, who as the future governess would hold sway in the Habsburg Netherlands. The ambassador did not expand upon the question further, but there is no doubt that what he noted provided for the requisite consternation in Paris. By emphasizing the connection between the office of *mayordomo mayor* and the concomitant privilege of guaranteed access, Péricard was notifying his superiors that Spínola had now become one of the infanta's most prominent advisors, and that, if possible, he would acquire even more influence than he already had before that.[79]

Contemporaries realized all too well, though, that the right to free access brought great political consequences along with it. Inversely, a lack of access could have far-reaching consequences as well. In November, 1612, the Spanish ambassador Felipe de Cardona, marquis of Guadaleste, informed Philip III about the archduke's weak health. Although Guadaleste succeeded in giving the prince a detailed report about Albert's worrisome situation, the marquis emphasized that his report was necessarily based on rumors, in view of the fact that the count of Añover had forbidden that he visit the archduke more frequently than was necessary.[80] What the ambassador

[77] '*Leurs Altesses (...) luy ont donné l'estat de grand maistre d'hostel, que l'on nomme mayordomo mayor (...). Ladite charge de grand maistre donne une liberté absolue d'entrer à toute heure au quartier de l'infante et de parler à elle (...).*' BNF, *MsF* 16133, f. 271: Péricard to Puisieux, April 30, 1621.

[78] '*Cette charge de mayordomo mayor, qui n'a esté déférée audict marquis [Spínola] que pour luy donner liberté d'entrer en la chambre de l'infante à toute heure, sans demander audience comme il faisoyt auparavant, et conférer avec elle sur toutes occurrences, estant seul et unique en ce privilège (...).*' BNF, *MsF* 16133, f. 344: Péricard to Puisieux, July 16, 1621.

[79] Nuncio Bentivoglio also wrote in his memoirs that the *mayordomo mayor* of the archducal household 'enjoyed free access to the archduke and the infanta at any moment and in the most privy places.' Bentivoglio, *Relationi*, 158.

[80] AGS, *Estado* 2294, s.f.: The marquis of Guadaleste to Philip III, November 15, 1612.

noted snappishly was only one of several complaints about the way in which Añover sabotaged his attempts to have contact with the archduke. Already in August, 1612, Guadaleste had written the following about this: 'Since his appointment as *mayordomo mayor*, the count of Añover has twice neglected to notify me when Their Highnesses left the palace.'[81] The first time that happened was during the visit from the elector of Mainz, who was awaited a few miles outside the city walls. The second time was when the archduke went outside the city for the reception of the duke of Mantua. On that occasion Añover had commanded the ambassador to stay at home, in view of the fact that 'His Highness wanted to ride out only in the company of his servants.'[82]

Guadaleste was furious. According to him, this kind of negligence clashed with the right of ambassadors to be kept informed of the doings of the princes. The marquis realized all too well, though, that attempts were undertaken to undermine his authority, and accused Añover of wanting to monopolize the access to the archdukes. He asked Philip III to reprimand the count on account of his unwillingness to treat the official representative of the Spanish crown with the requisite respect, and it seems that his lament struck the right chord. Shortly after that, the king asked Añover for an explanation. The latter had seen the storm approaching, all the same, and was well prepared. In a letter to Philip's secretary Juan de Ciriza, he answered the following:

> 'His Majesty has taken note that in former times it was the custom that the resident ambassador was informed of the comings and goings of Their Highnesses, and demands to know why this is no longer the case. I say that it is right that the resident ambassador generally accompanied Their Highnesses on their journeys, but not because it belonged to the duties of his office, but because they gave him the permission for it and appreciated it, which today is no longer the case, because every day His Highness experiences more hindrance from his gout and his attacks and, with the exception of his servants, would rather be left alone, which is his most prominent motivation in this question, and in this way he has also explained that to the marquis of Guadaleste. For the rest, as previously [the ambassador] is notified beforehand about all public activities, and also about private matters and dinners, and he rightly has full access to the chambers of Their Highnesses, and is respected by all servants in the appropriate manner. And I shall take special care that all this continues to go in this way with his work (…)'[83]

[81] AGS, *Estado* 2294, s.f.: The marquis of Guadaleste to Philip III, s.d. [August, 1612].
[82] *Ibidem*.
[83] AGS, *Estado* 2294, s.f.: Rodrigo Niño y Lasso to Juan de Ciriza, November 14, 1612.

The answer left little to the imagination. By indicating that he was only following up on the orders of the archduke, Añover tossed the ball back to the king. Philip was now obliged to enter into discussion with Albert, who was not exactly known for making concessions in matters of ceremonial questions. The king wisely chose not to allow the conflict to escalate and threw the towel in the ring. He notified his advisors in the *Consejo de Estado* that 'it seems harmful to go into this further' and commanded Guadaleste to let the matter rest.[84] As far as Philip was concerned, the problem was out of the way. In reality, though, little to nothing had changed. Scarcely a month later the ambassador reported that he had wanted to greet Albert and Isabella immediately after their return from their stay in the country, but was held back by Añover, who had commanded him to come back the following day.[85] A few days after that a similar incident took place, when Guadaleste left for the palace to attend mass and upon arrival was given to understand that – on account of an adjustment in the court ceremonial – he was no longer permitted to accompany the archdukes on their way from the *Cámara* to the Court Chapel and back.[86] Again, Guadaleste requested the king's help: 'I entreat Your Majesty not to see this kind of situation as negligible, but to put order to the matter as quickly as possible.'[87] He pointed out how much harm the reputation of the king would suffer if the local populace in the Southern Netherlands would find out that the right to precedence and access of important Spaniards was being restricted, 'for the local populace only respects us because it sees that His Highness reserves more access [*más entrada*] for those among us who are serving here [= in the Southern Netherlands].'[88] This time, however, Philip did not allow himself to be seduced into reacting, and Guadaleste found himself obliged to swallowing his injured pride.

Although it is not clear whether the count of Añover did or did not act on the orders of the archduke, this anecdote demonstrates that a lack of access to the prince was disastrous for the contemporaneous diplomat. Through Añover's conscious neglect to inform Guadaleste about Albert's comings and goings, and by his refusal to grant Guadaleste access, the ambassador was literally cut off from power. In that way the count limited Guadaleste's possibilities for gathering information, and he hampered him in the execution of his diplomatic commission. No wonder the marquis showed himself to be appalled about the course of affairs.

[84] See the marginalia in the afore-mentioned letter from Rodrigo Niño y Lasso to Juan de Ciriza.

[85] AGS, *Estado* 2294, s.f.: The marquis of Guadaleste to Philip III, December 14, 1612.

[86] *Ibidem.*

[87] *Ibidem.*

[88] *Ibidem.*

Access and favor

The examples of Spínola and Guadaleste demonstrate that an unequal 'distribution' of access could have far-reaching political consequences, and that members of the archducal household could count on the requisite interest precisely on account of their guaranteed access. Yet with that, the story is not finished. In the preceding sections access was studied, namely, from the question of a) physical access to the princes and b) the possibility for interaction. Both notions are important but do not suffice for fully exposing the complex stratification of the concept. Although the symbolic representation of the early modern court as a system of concentric circles can indeed create more clarity concerning the general idea, it risks misleading the spectator by way of suggesting that access in essence was a static phenomenon. If only grasped in this way, the concentric pattern does not succeed in capturing the variability of the concept. As opposed to how the model makes it appear, the orbit of the prince did not remain limited to the seclusion of the *Cámara*. He moved around, and the court moved along with him: '*Hof wird genennet, wo sich der Fürst aufhält* ['It is called the court wherever the prince resides'],' Johann Heinrich Zedler wrote already in his *Universal-Lexicon*.[89] Consequently, the court made itself manifest in various ways and under various circumstances, in the main within the palace walls yet frequently also on location. Access was thus necessarily dynamic in nature. The concept was not only subject to dimensions of space, but also to dimensions of time and motion. Seen from that standpoint, it becomes pretty much impossible to take all gradations of access into account. Here, the historian unavoidably runs into the limitations of the written source. The question, though, is not how all these gradations are to be taken into account; the question, rather, is whether the correct angle is employed here.

Until now access had been studied in the main from a 'quantitative' aspect (i.e. the conditionality or even the guarantee of access; the rapidity with which the prince could be reached; the duration of the interaction; etc.). The question arises whether research would not benefit more with an analysis that also takes the qualitative aspect into consideration (i.e. the durability of the contact; the nature of the relationship with the prince; etc.). The approach takes as its point of departure the idea that access – much more than an objectively measurable criterion – was a complex and widely encompassing *process*, in which the emotional relationship with the prince also played a role. In that case, the importance of access lies not so much in the possibility of entering into contact with the prince (be it in person or 'from a distance'), but

[89] Cited in Duindam, *Vienna and Versailles*, 3. See Zedler, J.H. *Grosses vollständiges Universal-Lexicon aller Wissenschafften und Künste*... Vol. XIII (1739) 405. A digital version of the complete encyclopedia (68 vols., 1731-1754) can be consulted at http://www.zedler-lexikon.de (last accessed on July 10, 2013).

rather in the guaranteed, day-to-day proximity that made it possible to build up a solid bond of trust, and that could lead in certain cases to friendship, affection, and even intimacy. The 'proximity' was, then, not so much physical as psychological in nature. These kinds of emotional bonds could be of decisive importance in striving for princely favor. In this way Nicolas Le Roux argues that early modern politics cannot be grasped without solid insight into the way in which proximity and granting of favor stood in reciprocal correlation to each other:

> 'It is thus a matter of studying not only the concept of favor, its theory and usage, but also the signs of favor; in other words, the representations and the political, economic, symbolic and discursive manifestations outlining or acknowledging the relationship of proximity with the prince.'[90]

In the first place, according to Le Roux, granting favor had to do with creating and keeping intact an emotional connection between the prince and the members of his entourage: 'Favor appears to be (...) a situation of informal power, resting neither on social status nor on official positions, but on an emotional link outlining a voluntary and affective relationship with a selection of people.'[91] At the court of the archdukes various examples of this are to be found.

In December, 1620, Jean Péricard informed his superiors in Paris about the rising star of one of Albert's courtiers. Earlier that year, the court in Brussels had been immersed in mourning on the occasion of the death of the count of Añover, Albert's *sumiller de corps*. The ambassador wrote that after his death the count had been succeeded by Charles-Emmanuel de Gorrevod, marquis of Marnay and count of Pont-de-Vaux. As was mentioned in a previous chapter, the marquis stemmed from the Burgundian aristocracy and served in the archducal court for more than twenty years as the *gentilhombre de la Cámara* (cf. Chapter I).[92] During this time period Gorrevod had evidently succeeded in making himself especially beloved with the archduke. Thus in 1618, for instance, the papal nuncio reported that Albert had given the marquis a fantastical monetary sum of not less than 4000 *scudi* (approx. fl.

[90] *'Il s'agit donc d'étudier non seulement le concept de faveur, sa théorisation et son utilisation, mais aussi les signes de la faveur, autrement dit les représentations et les manifestations politiques, économiques, symboliques et discursives traduisant ou reconnaissant la relation de proximité avec le prince.'* Le Roux, N. 'Courtisans et favoris: l'entourage du prince et les mécanismes du pouvoir dans la France des guerres de religion.' *Histoire, Économie et Société*, 17 (1998) 377-387. Op. cit. p. 378.

[91] *'La faveur apparaît (...) comme une situation de pouvoir informel, ne reposant ni sur le statut social ni sur les charges officielles, mais sur un lien dilectif traduisant une relation volontaire et affective des personnages choisis.'* Le Roux, 'Courtisans et favoris,' 381.

[92] An overview of his career in AGS, *Estado* 2294, s.f.: Charles-Emmanuel de Gorrevod to the duke of Lerma, April 24, 1612.

10,000).[93] The reason for that, according to the nuncio, was not far to be found: 'This knight shows himself to be quite dedicated and fervent in the personal service of the archduke, whereby His Highness quite loves him, and grants him new favors ['*nuove gratie*'] every day.'[94] The latter was certainly no lie. Various sources show that Albert made quite a lot of effort over the years to help advance Gorrevod's career. So in 1602, for instance, the barony of Marnay was elevated to marquisate, and in 1613, at the recommendation of the archduke, Gorrevod was taken into the Order of the Golden Fleece.[95] In 1616, Albert gave him a regiment in the army, and he was appointed governor of Limburg in 1620.[96]

Gorrevod was clearly favored by the archduke, and his installation as *sumiller de corps* did not remain unnoticed at court. Shortly after his appointment Marnay took up his residence in the chamber of his predecessor, which was situated next to Albert's apartments. Péricard noted that the marquis was 'greatly loved and favored by the archduke, sleeping in his Bedchamber and having gained such familiarity with His Highness that the latter can suffer no other touch when getting dressed, moving around, or being carried from one place to another.'[97] As the *sumiller de corps* Gorrevod assumed the custom of spending the night in Albert's bedchamber. On top of that, the marquis was the only one whose touch the archduke still endured when he was plagued by attacks of gout. The bright ambassador needed no further indications to let the importance of this situation sink in. He went off immediately to congratulate Gorrevod on his appointment and informed his superiors of the fact that the marquis now spoke with great authority.[98] It did not take long before Péricard's words proved to be prophetic. As the head of the *Cámara*, Gorrevod became the official intermediary between the archduke and the outside world. Thenceforth he arranged the audiences, and he managed the agenda of the princely couple. A few weeks later the ambassador reported that Gorrevod was still the only one who was allowed to speak with the archduke when the latter had to keep to his bed on account of attacks of gout.[99] From that moment on, the marquis acquired the monopoly over access to Albert. For Péricard, that provided the occasion to insist with Louis XIII

---

[93] ASV, *Borghese* II 112, ff. 254-256: Lucio Morra to Cardinal Borghese, May 12, 1618.

[94] *Ibidem.*

[95] Cf. the article 'Gorrevod (de)' in Duerloo, L. & Janssens, P. *Wapenboek van de Belgische adel, van de 15de tot de 20ste eeuw.* 4 vols. Brussel, 1992-1994; and AGS, *Estado* 2027, s.f.: Consult of the *Consejo de Estado*, January 16, 1613.

[96] AGS, *Estado* 2296, s.f.: The marquis of Guadaleste to Philip III, January 26, 1615; and AGS, *Estado* 2308, s.f.: The marquis of Bedmar to Philip III, February 7, 1620.

[97] '*(...) grandement aymé et favorisé de l'archiduc, couchant en sa chambre et ayant gaigné une telle habitude auprès de Son Altesse quelle ne peut souffrir qu'aultre la touche de luy en son habillé, mouvoir et porter de lieu à aultre.*' BNF, *MsF* 16133, f. 116: Péricard to Puisieux, December 18, 1620.

[98] *Ibidem.*

[99] BNF, *MsF* 16133, f. 161: Péricard to Puisieux, January 8, 1621.

that Gorrevod's county Pont-de-Vaux, which was a French fiefdom, be elevated to duchy as soon as possible – a favor the marquis had already been fishing for more than a while.[100] The French king did not hesitate to follow up on the advice of his ambassador and awarded Gorrevod the title of duke in March, 1621.[101]

The diplomatic reporting concerning the marquis of Marnay demonstrates that the unequal distribution of access could have a dramatic impact on power relations at court. At the same time his story makes it clear that the assured right to access frequently went hand in hand with a certain emotional affinity. It seems that the archduke harbored a great fondness for Gorrevod. For the marquis this privileged status produced not only all manner of tangible advantages, among them money, titles of nobility, and political and military offices, but also notable political influence. Historiography has already excessively pointed to the importance of the study of interpersonal relationships at the early modern court and their interwoven nature with the granting and the acquiring of princely favor.[102] That was no different at the archducal court. It is thus inconceivable that historians until now have seldom stopped to dwell on the exceptional position of the count of Añover, who was clearly Albert's favorite (cf. Chapter VI). After Añover's death in 1620, it seems that Gorrevod was very well on his way to taking over that role of favorite – a rising star that unexpectedly went out when the archduke died in 1621.

Various historical sources suggest that both Albert as well as Isabella harbored genuine feelings of affinity and affection for certain members of their household. These kinds of emotions developed above all with respect to courtiers – like Añover and Gorrevod – whose service was long-standing and who through the years had proven to be worthy of the princes' trust.[103] That was true, for example, for Isabella's *dueña de honor* Leonor de Guzmán, countess of Uceda, who had made up part of the infanta's entourage already before her marriage.[104] This lady is repeatedly mentioned in the correspondence of the archduchess and clearly was gladly seen by her mistress. These letters show that Isabella regularly conducted long and intimate conversations with her companion, who perhaps was one of the few ladies-in-waiting with whom she

[100] BNF, *MsF* 16133, f. 174: Charles-Emmanuel de Gorrevod to [Puisieux ?], January 23, 1621; and f. 195: Péricard to Puisieux, February 25, 1621.

[101] BNF, *MsF* 16133, f. 226: Péricard to Puisieux, March 26, 1621.

[102] See the many references in the preceding footnotes.

[103] For an interesting sociological look at this theory, see Schutte, J.G. & Light, J.M. 'The Relative Importance of Proximity and Status for Friendship Choices in Social Hierarchies.' *Social Psychology*, 41 (1978) 260-264.

[104] Leonor de Guzmán – an aunt of the count-duke of Olivares – came from Seville. She was the widow of Diego Mexía, count of Uceda, who was a *mayordomo* in the household of the queen before his death. See García Carraffa, A. & García Caraffa, A. *Diccionario Heráldico y Genealógico de apellidos españoles y americanos*. 86 vols. Madrid, 1920-1963. Op. cit. vol. LVII, p. 24. See also AHN, *OOMM*, expediente 5274.

could smoothly converse in her mother tongue. Thus, for example, Uceda confided to her during one exchange of thoughts about the horrors of war that during her youth she had always found it to be a pity to be a woman, but was now glad not to be a man, because otherwise she would have had to take part in the siege of Ostend.[105] Another very telling example is the fact that the countess secretly got in touch with the Florentine prince Giovanni de' Medici in 1603, in order to ask him '*con molta familiarità et secretezza*' whether he knew anyone in Italy who could provide her with a remedy for infertility.[106] In view of the fact that the countess herself had children, there is little doubt that she was acting as commissioned by Isabella, who at the age of 37 desperately desired an heir.

The countess of Uceda was clearly a confidante of the infanta. Even so, that did not prevent her from using her influence with Isabella to look out for her own interests – as witnessed in the numerous letters of recommendation the infanta sent to the duke of Lerma on her behalf. In so doing, Uceda's children were not forgotten, either. In 1600, Isabella wrote that the countess 'is such a mother to her sons that she always asks me to favor them, and she serves me so well that I cannot neglect to give them that help.'[107] That turns out not to be exaggerated. It was perhaps at Isabella's insistence that Albert wrote a letter to the pope in 1599, in which he requested that the latter give Uceda's sons Pedro and Francisco Mexía – who were both studying in Salamanca – an ecclesiastical benefice to be able to cover the costs of their studies.[108] Even after that the archdukes continued to support Uceda's sons. In March, 1604, Pedro Mexía had to struggle with a further unspecified problem. The matter proved to be so serious that Uceda found herself obliged to journey to Spain to plead the question with Philip III. In her letters, the infanta repeatedly asked Lerma and the king to help Pedro as much as possible. She felt herself morally obliged to do that: 'Because his mother serves me so well, I shall keep to giving her a form of consolation in this matter.'[109] Apparently Isabella's intervention was successful. A few months later she announced that Uceda was quite satisfied with the *merced* that the king had given her son, and Isabella expressed her hope that the countess would now rapidly return to Brussels.[110] With that thought in the back of the mind, it can be called surprising

[105] Rodríguez Villa, A., ed. *Correspondencia de la Infanta Doña Isabel Clara Eugenia de Austria con el Duque de Lerma y otros personajes*. Madrid, 1906. See letter no. 32: Isabella to Lerma, August 11, 1601.

[106] Archivio di Stato, Florence: *Carteggi dei Principi, delle Granduchesse e delle Principesse / Giovanni di Cosimo I e di Eleonora degli Albizi / Lettere del principe ai granduchi e alla Segretaria*, volume 5155, f. 408: Giovanni de' Medici to Ferdinando de' Medici, May 30, 1603. It can be found at the website of *The Medici Archive Project*, http://documents.medici.org, docID 9195 (last accessed: July 10, 2013).

[107] Rodríguez Villa, *Correspondencia*, letter no. 21: Isabella to Lerma, October 27, 1600.

[108] ASV, *Borghese* III 105 ABC, f. 42: Albert to Clement VIII, June 28, 1599 [from Genoa].

[109] Rodríguez Villa, *Correspondencia*, letter no. 73: Isabella to Lerma, s.d. [March, 1604]. See also no. 74: Isabella to Lerma, April 2, 1604.

[110] Rodríguez Villa, *Correspondencia*, letter no. 87: Isabella to Lerma, December 7, 1604.

that Uceda's position of trust has until now never been connected with the rise of her son Diego Mexía, the later marquis of Leganés.[111] As a young man, Diego served in the household of Archduke Albert, but from the 1620s forward he would play an important role as cavalry general in the *Ejército de Flandes* and as president of the High Council for the Netherlands and Burgundy in Madrid. Historiography generally explains Leganés' meteoric career exclusively from his being related to the influential count-duke of Olivares (who was a cousin of Diego), but perhaps one would do well to look at the privileged position of his mother as an important factor too.[112]

In any case, the influence of the countess of Uceda did not remain unnoticed. In 1606, the *audiencier* Louis Verreycken let the archduke know that in Madrid there were rumors being spread concerning the supposed wealth of the archdukes, who would 'fatten up' their courtiers with *mercedes* to such a degree that even the king could not equal their generosity. The countess of Uceda was pointed to as an example, who evidently received more financial favors than any other courtier whatsoever.[113] Albert defended himself by positing that the countess had actually earned these *mercedes*, which Verreycken knew but all too well, according to Albert.[114] With that, the conversation was ended for the archduke, but it is clear that in Madrid Uceda's growing influence was followed Argus-eyed. That she had the requisite authority at her disposal is also shown in a comment from the papal nuncio Frangipani. In 1600, the countess submitted a petition for the Holy See to award a privileged altar to the chapel of San Tomaso de Ávila, the Dominican monastery patronized by her in Spain. The nuncio supported that petition and did not neglect to point out to his superiors that Uceda 'has come from Spain with the infanta, with whom she enjoys great authority and, consequently, at the entire court as well.'[115] All the same, the pope declined to go into the question, saying that he was not a proponent of these kinds of concessions.[116] Frangipani promptly sent him a second letter in which he emphasized that the countess was a '*persona di molta [e]stima, di molte credito, e di auttorità presso questi Serenissimi Altezze*,' and, consequently, that it would not be

[111] Concerning Leganés, see Corella Suárez, M.P. 'Orígenes históricos del marquesado de Leganés y su primer titular: Don Diego Messía de Guzmán.' *Anales del Instituto de Estudios Madrileños*, 18 (1981) 131-136; and Vermeir, R. *In staat van oorlog. Filips IV en de Zuidelijke Nederlanden, 1629-1648.* Maastricht, 2001. Op. cit. p. 23.

[112] See e.g. Volk, M.C. 'New Light on a Seventeenth-Century Collector: The Marquis of Leganés.' *The Art Bulletin*, 62 (1980) 256-268.

[113] CCE, vol. VI, p. 106: Louis Verreycken to Albert, February 20, 1606.

[114] CCE, vol. VI, p. 111: Albert to Louis Verreycken, May 3, 1606.

[115] ASV, *Borghese* III 98 C1, f. 22: Frangipani to Aldobrandini, January 15, 1600.

[116] Van der Essen, L. & Louant, A., eds. *Correspondance d'Ottavio Mirto Frangipani, premier Nonce de Flandre (1596-1606).* Analecta Vaticano-Belgica, 2e série, section A: Nonciature de Flandre, I-II-III. Brussels-Rome-Paris, 1924-1942. Op. cit. vol. III, p. 657 and p. 664.

reasonable to cast her request to the wind.[117] The pope proved not to be mollified, even so, yet promised to award the countess an indulgence as consolation.[118] A few months later the nuncio sent him a third letter in which he made known that both Uceda as well as the archdukes were quite amazed about his declining.[119] Whether the petition was approved after all is unknown, but there is no doubt that Frangipani felt quite uneasy with the entire situation.

As cited earlier, the female entourage of the infanta has until now gotten little attention among historians (cf. Chapter I). It is clear that the political role of the ladies-in-waiting was rather minor in comparison to that of the male courtiers, yet that does not mean that their influence was non-existent.[120] The example of the countess of Uceda demonstrates that physical proximity and the distribution of favors could be closely interwoven with each other. Another lady for whom Albert and Isabella harbored a special affinity was Jeanne de Chassincourt, the infanta's elderly *camarera mayor*, who since Isabella's earliest youth already had made up part of her entourage. As seen in a previous chapter, this Frenchwoman had left for Spain in the retinue of Queen Elisabeth of Valois in 1559. She was there at the births of the infantas Isabella and Catalina Micaela and after the death of Elisabeth was assigned to the household of Queen Anna.[121] She was appointed as Isabella's mistress of the household '*en consideracion de sus meritos y por la mucha confiança y satisfacción*' in 1598, and she journeyed along to the Netherlands as one of the few 'Spanish' ladies in the archducal retinue.[122] Chassincourt would not have lamented it. As *camarera mayor* she received a salary of 1 million *maravedis* per year (approx. fl. 7,353), with which she easily earned the highest remuneration in the archducal household.[123] Even so, that did not prevent her from getting herself deep into debt, whereby the infanta found herself obliged to provide her aged lady-in-waiting with all manner of extra financial favors.[124] On top of that, the infanta did not neglect to recommend Chassincourt repeatedly to her half-brother Philip III.[125] When the mistress of the household ran

[117] ASV, *Borghese* III 98 C1, f. 67-68: Frangipani to Aldobrandini, April 22, 1600.

[118] ARA, *SSO* 494 ter, f. 53: Cardinal Aldobrandini to Albert, August 19, 1600.

[119] ASV, *Borghese* III 98 C1, f. 195-196: Frangipani to Aldobrandini, September 22, 1600.

[120] See in that context also Houben, B. & Raeymaekers, D. 'Women and the Politics of Access at the Court of Brussels. The Infanta Isabella's Camareras Mayores (1598-1633),' in: Akkerman, N. & Houben, B., eds. *The Politics of Female Households: Ladies-in-Waiting across Early Modern Europe*. Leiden, 2013, pp. 123-145.

[121] See López-Cordón Cortezo, M.V. 'Entre damas anda el juego: las camareras mayores de Palacio en la edad moderna,' in: Gómez-Centurión Jiménez, C., ed. *Monarquía y Corte en la España Moderna*. Cuadernos de Historia Moderna, 2003 (Anejo II), pp. 123-152.

[122] AGPR, *Sección Personal* 588, expediente 32: Appointment of Jeanne de Chassincourt ['Juana de Jacincurt'] as *camarera mayor* of the infanta Isabella, October 16, 1598.

[123] See e.g. ARA, *RK* 1837, f. 38.

[124] See e.g. ACA, 38/24, file 1249, no. 144: Chassincourt to Anne de Croÿ, November 6, 1613.

[125] See e.g. Rodríguez Villa, *Correspondencia*, letter no. 78 (July 8, 1604), no. 87 (December 7, 1604), no. 91 (February 28, 1605), no. 127 (September 7, 1607).

the risk of being evicted from her rental home in Brussels in 1611, because the owner wished to sell it, Isabella tried to convince the king to buy the premises and give it to Chassincourt as a gift. According to the infanta, Philip could not imagine how many problems the courtiers' housing in Brussels produced and, on top of that, the house was not so expensive that Philip would lose much on it.[126] Apparently the infanta had substantial powers of persuasion at her disposal. Scarcely two months later the purchase of the home was a fact.[127] The anecdote is very telling. Thanks to Isabella, the elderly Chassincourt could enjoy her old age in peace.[128] When the elderly lady died on January 25, 1614, the total value of her estate was a 'shabby' 200,000 *escudos* (approx. fl. 514,000), according to the Spanish ambassador.[129] A magnificent mass was held for her in the church of the Friars Minor in Brussels, after which at the request of her family her body was transported to and interred in a monastery in La Châtre in Le Berry, the region where she had been born.[130]

Chassincourt may not have been among the youngest any longer, yet even she did not shrink back from engaging her proximity to the infanta for the promotion of the interests of her relatives and confederates. She had no children herself, yet it cannot be a coincidence that two of her closest family members got a position in the archducal household. Chassincourt's nephew Louis de Chamborant, lord of Droux, received the title of *gentilhombre de la Boca*, while her niece Catalina Livia was taken on as a lady-in-waiting. Both were also her most prominent heirs.[131] Chassincourt saw to it, on top of that, that Catalina Livia was allowed to take over the hardest duties from her in the *Cámara* – and thus was put to work in the environs closest to the infanta.[132] The position did no harm to her niece. According to the nuncio Bentivoglio, Catalina Livia already became '*molto favorita da Su Altezza*' rapidly and, consequently, also '*molto stimata in Palazzo*.'[133] When Chassincourt died in 1614, Catalina, then, did not have to fear for her future. Thanks to the princely legacy from her aunt, she already could rapidly tie down one of Albert's most prominent courtiers as a marriage candidate: in 1615, Catalina wed no one less than the count of Fürstenberg.[134]

---

[126] Rodríguez Villa, *Correspondencia*, letter no. 185: Isabella to Lerma, March 3, 1611.

[127] Rodríguez Villa, *Correspondencia*, letter no. 190: Isabella to Lerma, May 19, 1611.

[128] In 1614, she was more than 70 years old according to the nuncio Bentivoglio. ASV, *Borghese* II 99, f. 64: Bentivoglio to Borghese, January 25, 1614.

[129] AGS, *Estado* 2296, s.f.: Guadaleste to Philip III, February 1, 1614. See also ASV, *Borghese* II 99, f. 79: Bentivoglio to Borghese, February 1, 1614.

[130] ASV, *Borghese* II 99, f. 79: Bentivoglio to Borghese, February 1, 1614. See also the entry on Chamborant in the *Armorial Général de France* (*Armorial Général, ou Registres de la Noblesse de France. Registre troisième, première partie* (Paris: Pierre Prault, 1752)), p. 54.

[131] ASV, *Borghese* II 99, f. 79: Bentivoglio to Borghese, February 1, 1614.

[132] Bentivoglio, *Relationi*, 160.

[133] ASV, *Borghese* II 99, f. 79: Bentivoglio to Borghese, February 1, 1614.

[134] ASV, *Borghese* II 106, f. 163: Bentivoglio to Borghese, March 14, 1615.

That Chassincourt used her influence with Isabella also in favor of her confederates can be shown in the letters she exchanged with Anne de Croÿ, the countess of Arenberg (cf. Plate 4 in the color section of this book).[135] There is no doubt that Chassincourt harbored a special affection for Anne. So, for instance, it is notable that she addressed the countess as 'my daughter,' and signed her letters with '*Su madre de Vuestra Señoría y que la quiere más que así, Juana de Jasincurt.*'[136] When the court was away in Nieuwpoort during the siege of Ostend, Chassincourt wrote repeatedly how terribly she missed her dear 'daughter': 'Since you went away, Madame, I have stayed behind with the greatest pain and loneliness in the world, and nothing can even captivate me now.'[137] Even Anne's family was close to the heart of the *camarera mayor*: 'I love all your children, Madame, as if they were my grandchildren, and they say that [grandparents] generally love their grandchildren more than their own children, but that is not true for [me and] my daughter [Anne], whom I love even more than myself.'[138] It need not come as a surprise, then, that Chassincourt did everything to look out for the interests of the Arenbergs at court. In countless letters she wrote that she would not hesitate to recommend Anne's many *negocios* to the infanta, so that the latter would speak about her with the archduke:

> '(...) and in everything that presents itself in your Service, Madame, I shall not hesitate to act just as you, Madame, commission me, and I shall ask it of Her Highness and remind her of it...'[139] 'There is for me no greater reward than that you commission me with something, Madame, so that I can act on it, and in the meantime I shall do everything necessary to bring up the affairs of the count [of Arenberg] to Her Highness...'[140] 'My daughter may be sure of it that I will not hesitate to put her affairs before Her Highness.'[141]

In view of the fact that Anne's own letters to Chassincourt have not remained preserved, the nature of her many *negocios* is not always clear. Yet in a few cases it is known precisely what these *negocios* are about. So, for example, among other things Anne asked that Chassincourt convince the infanta to take on one of her daughters as a lady-in-waiting. 'From as soon as Her Highness needs more ladies here, [your

[135] This correspondence can be found in ACA, 38/24.
[136] ACA, 38/24, file 1245, no. 2: Chassincourt to Anne de Croÿ, s.d. [September 12].
[137] ACA, 38/24, file 1245, no. 1: Chassincourt to Anne de Croÿ, October 11, 1601.
[138] ACA, 38/24, file 1245, no. 15: Chassincourt to Anne de Croÿ, s.d. [August 9].
[139] ACA, 38/24, file 1247, no. 59: Chassincourt to Anne de Croÿ, s.d.
[140] ACA, 38/24, file 1247, no. 53: Chassincourt to Anne de Croÿ, s.d.
[141] ACA, 38/24, file 1250, no. 154: Chassincourt to Anne de Croÿ, s.d. [1613]. For similar commentaries and promises, see file 1245 (no. 4 en no. 13); file 1246 (no. 31, no. 34, no. 48); file 1247 (no. 73); file 1249 (no. 106); file 1250 (no. 156).

daughter, Madame,] shall be the first that I shall advise to her; of that my daughter and granddaughter may be certain,' the *camarera mayor* answered.[142] And Chassincourt kept her word: all Anne's daughters would be ladies-in-waiting in the archducal household for a while. Another time Anne wanted Chassincourt to recommend a certain candidate for the vacant bishop's seat in Antwerp ['*la provycion del ovispado de Anvers que está vaco*'], and although it is not at once clear here, either, whom it is precisely about, Chassincourt answered that she would not hesitate to bring up the question with the infanta, 'whereby there will be occasion to give your son, Madame, a *merced*.'[143] Was it Anne's intention that her son Charles, who was predestined for life as a cleric, should get the bishop's crosier?[144] Even the claims of the Arenberg family to the fiercely fought-for inheritance of the duchy of Aarschot came up for discussion ('I have shown the letter from my daughter to Her Highness, and she has answered me that my daughter may be sure of it that Their Highnesses shall do everything that is reasonable for my daughter ['*que se aga con my hyja lo que es razón*']').[145] In these and other matters Chassincourt promised to do what was necessary, and evidently the Arenbergs assumed that her influence at court was quite great. When Anne's son Philippe-Charles was up for a position as commandant of a Walloon regiment in the army, he asked explicitly that his mother bring up the matter with Chassincourt, for 'this will further the matter greatly.'[146] In exchange for her help, by the way, Anne did not neglect to reward the elderly noblewoman with different services in return. Thus, she gave Chassincourt a number of precious relics, for instance, and saw to it that the aforementioned nephew Louis de Chamborant repeatedly got a solid sum of money, to the great joy of his aunt.[147]

The Arenberg family realized but all too well how important it was to have family members, friends, and allies who had access to the archdukes directly and frequently (cf. Plate 5 in the color section of this book). In March, 1613, the above-mentioned Gaston Spínola, count of Bruay, wrote a letter to Charles, princely count

[142] ACA, 38/24, file 1251, no. 194: Chassincourt to Anne de Croÿ, s.d.

[143] ACA, 38/24, file 1245, no. 5: Chassincourt to Anne de Croÿ, s.d. During the period of the archducal regime the bishop's seat in Antwerp was vacant twice (the first time between 1601 and 1603 and once more in 1611). Chassincourt's letter bears no date but was sent from Nieuwpoort, where the archdukes frequently stayed during the siege of Ostend (1600-1604). So perhaps the letter dates from the period 1601-1603.

[144] If this was indeed the case, Chassincourt clearly did not succeed in convincing the infanta: Johannes Miraeus was consecrated bishop of Antwerp in 1603.

[145] ACA, 38/24, file 1250, no. 160: Chassincourt to Anne de Croÿ, June 8, 1612. Anne's brother Charles de Croÿ was duke of Aarschot and lay dying. He would die on June 12, 1612.

[146] '*(...) ce fera pousser fort à l'ouvrage.*' ACA, 38/3, file 72, no. 137: Philippe-Charles of Arenberg to Charles of Arenberg, s.d.

[147] ACA, 31/25, no. 66; ACA, 38/24, file 1249, no. 150: Chassincourt to Anne de Croÿ, July 3, 1613; and ACA, 38/24, file 1251, no. 190: Chassincourt to Anne de Croÿ, October 23, 1609.

of Arenberg and spouse of Anne de Croÿ (cf. Plate 6).[148] Both lords were good friends and, on top of that, were related to each other by marriage: Gaston's son Bertin was married to Charles' daughter Claire. In his letter, Bruay proposed that the princely count undertake steps to have his sister Antoinette-Guillemette of Arenberg, widow of the count of Isenburg-Grenzau, appointed as the infanta's *dueña de honor* as a replacement for the only just deceased countess of Uceda (cf. Plate 7). According to Bruay, Antoinette-Guillemette was the ideal candidate to succeed Uceda: '(...) for, on account of the many matters needed by illustrious families like that of Your Excellency, it is advantageous not only to have one foot always in the palace ['*tener siempre un pie en palacio*'], but also to continue our services in the environs of the infanta our princess (...).'[149] Bruay proved to be quite a prescient man. According to him it was clear that Jeanne de Chassincourt did not have much longer to live, either, and consequently it was not impossible that Antoinette-Guillemette in the end would be appointed *camarera mayor*, which would naturally be even more advantageous.[150] Bruay did not need any more arguments to convince the princely count of the importance of this question. When Chassincourt did die ten months later, Charles carefully began to engage his contacts at court to give force to the candidacy of Antoinette-Guillemette as her successor.[151] One of those contacts was Antonio Suárez de Arguello, Albert's private secretary, with whom Charles maintained an extensive correspondence, and who in his letters not coincidentally used to call himself '*su menor criado de Vuestra Excellencia.*'[152]

Although Suárez had seemingly nothing to do with the Arenberg family, he appears nevertheless to have been a good friend of the princely count. Both lords were fervent lovers of landscape architecture and kept each other informed about their mutual projects. So, for instance, Charles regularly sent Antonio young trees for the garden the latter was having laid out just outside Halle.[153] Antonio showed himself also to be a steadfast and loyal confederate of the Arenbergs: 'Your Excellency may be very certain of it,' he wrote in one of his letters, 'that each favor His Highness has provided me and will yet provide me in the future shall always be used to commit myself even better to the service of Your Excellency, whose affairs I wish to look out

148 ACA, 38/4 file 122, f. 5: Bruay to Charles of Arenberg, March 30, 1613.

149 *Ibidem.*

150 *Ibidem.*

151 See the dossier in ACA, 36/17: *Charles d'Arenberg: Son intervention dans la nomination de sa soeur Antoinette Guillemette d'Arenberg, Comtesse d'Isenburg, comme camarera mayor à la cour de l'infante Isabelle, 1614-1615.*

152 The correspondence between Charles of Arenberg and Antonio Suárez de Arguello can be found in ACA, 38/3, files 73 to 77 (1604-1612).

153 See e.g. ACA, 36/17, s.f.: Antonio Suárez de Arguello to Charles of Arenberg, August 25, 1614.

for very earnestly.'[154] Charles did not hesitate to make use of this offer as well as to ask Antonio to recommend the candidacy of Antoinette-Guillemette to the archdukes.[155] Evidently the secretary accomplished this task with much verve, for in October, 1615, Charles' son Antoine – who himself was Albert's *gentilhombre de la Cámara* – wrote that his father could be at ease with the good outcome: 'Your Excellency can rest assured in this matter. It will conclude favorably and all the world will see that His Highness looks to distant countries [in order to hire] the kinsmen of Your Excellency and his House.'[156] Antoine proved to be right. Scarcely a month later Charles' sister was indeed appointed as the infanta's *camarera mayor*. In a letter to Philip III, the marquis of Guadaleste wrote that it did not look like she would be able to be of service to Isabella, both on account of her advanced age as well as on account of the fact that she had little to no knowledge of the ceremonial that was in effect at court.[157] Yet with that the infanta herself evidently had no bone to pick:

> 'I have installed a sister of the duke of Aarschot [= Charles of Arenberg] as *camarera mayor*. She is a very good woman who will do everything that is commissioned her without complaining (...) Some of those who did not want that I should appoint a *camarera mayor* attribute many faults to her, but I cannot make do without [a mistress of the household] and thus I have taken on the best one of those they have here.'[158]

The Arenberg family, too, did not take the negative commentaries to heart. In terms of proximity, the function of *camarera mayor* was the most attractive position that a noblewoman could wish for herself. Charles would not lament it. The correspondence of Antoinette-Guillemette shows that she never hesitated to use her informal contacts

[154] ACA, 38/3, file 76, no. 1: Antonio to Charles, January 23, 1610.

[155] '*Aviendo entendido que por muerte de la Camarera Mayor avia prepuesto a V[uestra] S[eñoría] Ill[ustrissima] el Conde de Bruay (...) a mi hermana la Condesa de Issemburg para este puesto, y aviendo me venido a ver, he querido saver della su voluntad y hallando en ella la misma que he tenido siempre que es que yo y los mios nos empliemos todos en el servicio de Sus Altezas. He querido suplicar a V.S. Ill. por esta que en mi nombre lo quiera pedir y supplicar a Sus Altezas, para que honrren a mi hermana con el puesto de la Camarera Mayor y mandar encaminar esto como espero lo hara V.S.Ill. haciendomela en avisarme si he de haver alguna otra diligencia que todo lo estimare como guiado de mano de V.S.Ill. que guarde nuestro Señor como desseo.*' ACA, 36/17, s.f.: Charles of Arenberg to Antonio Suárez de Arguello, s.d.

[156] '*Vostre Excellence se mette a repose de ceste afaire. Elle en sortirat heureusement et tout le monde voyrat comme Son Altesse vat chercher en des pays eslognés les parens de Vostre Execellence et ceulx de sa maison.*' ACA, 38/1, file 31, no. 11: Antoine of Arenberg to Charles of Arenberg, October 21, 1615.

[157] AGS, *Estado* 2299, s.f.: Guadaleste to Philip III, November 28, 1615.

[158] Isabella to the marquis of Velada, November 24, 1615. See Martínez Hernández, S. 'Significación y trascendencia del género epistolar en la política cortesana: la correspondencia inédita entre la infanta Isabel Clara Eugenia y el marques de Velada.' *Hispania*, 64/2, no. 217 (2004), 467-514. Op. cit. p. 506.

with the infanta to support the interests of her family actively.[159] In that sense she showed herself to be a worthy successor of Chassincourt.

Conclusion

Around 1613, at the request of Albert and Isabella, Jan Breughel the Elder completed the painting 'Wedding Banquet Presided Over by the Archduke and Infanta', which at the moment can be viewed in the Museo del Prado (cf. Plate 8). The painting shows the princes while they are taking part in a lively wedding banquet in the country. Albert and Isabella sit together with the bridal couple at the richly filled table, surrounded by a whole multitude of invitees and partygoers. The peaceful tableau bathes in an atmosphere of conviviality and solidarity. The archdukes are profiling themselves here as good and benevolent princes who gladly go out among their people, and who harbor a harmonious relationship with their subjects.[160] A comparable political message is encountered in a canvas attributed to Anthonis Sallaert. It depicts the so-called 'Procession of the Maidens' in Brussels' Sablon/Zavel district – an event in which both the princes as well as the courtiers and the inhabitants of the city used to take part in reciprocal harmony with each other (cf. Illustration 3). In the middle of thick throngs of spectators the archdukes stroll through the streets of Brussels. Both paintings support the idea that the gulf between court and country in the Archducal Netherlands was not in the least unbridgeable. They suggest a degree of openness and accessibility that is seldom encountered in early modern princes. In reality, though, the question remains as to what extent this political ideal actually manifested itself in daily life. Whoever takes a better look at the 'Peasant Wedding' sees how the festival is being closely observed by a company of halberdiers, who screen off the members of the court from the partygoers, standing ready to intervene at the slightest irregularity. In the 'Procession of the Maidens,' too, the archdukes are literally surrounded by a living wall of bodyguards, who keep the spectators at a safe distance.

---

[159] See the correspondence of Antoinette-Guillemette with Charles of Arenberg (ACA, 38/2) and Anne de Croÿ (ACA, 38/11) for countless examples. See also Houben & Raeymaekers, 'Women and the Politics of Access at the Court of Brussels,' in press.

[160] See in that context Van Wyhe, C. 'Court, City and Countryside: Jan Brueghel's Peasant Weddings as Images of Social Unity under Archducal Sovereignty,' in: Thomas & Duerloo, *Essays*, pp. 151-160; and Duerloo, L. 'Boerenbruiloft met Infante: Breughels genrestukken tussen belegering en propaganda,' in: Blondé, B., De Munck, B. & Vermeylen, F. eds. *Doodgewoon. Mensen en hun dagelijks leven in de geschiedenis. Liber Amicorum Alfons K.L. Thijs* (published in *Bijdragen tot de Geschiedenis*, 87 (2004) 255-267).

Illustration 3 – Albert and Isabella at the *Procession of the Maidens* in Brussels' Sablon/Zavel district in 1615 (detail). Attributed to ANTHONIS SALLAERT.
(Brussels, Royal Museums of Fine Arts of Belgium. © Brussels, KIK-IRPA.)

Both paintings can be seen as exemplary for the subject discussed in this chapter. Although the archdukes wished to profile themselves as accessible and approachable princes, in reality they were well screened-off from the outside world. Even when relocating they were to be found in a strictly monitored 'virtual' *Cámara*. Getting access to the princes was not impossible, to be sure, but it was especially difficult. Acquiring regular and lasting access, if possible, was even less self-evident, and even in this case most of the candidates had to ask *and* receive permission beforehand. At the same time, however, there were a few for whom right to access was by definition unlimited, guaranteed, and to a certain extent enforceable. This was first and foremost the privilege of the members of the *Cámara*, who by the capacity of their office were in the position to approach and address the archdukes on their own initiative and at any moment. Those members are, not coincidentally, portrayed in the painting by Sallaert *inside* the living barrier formed by the halberdiers. This kind of literal proximity was a privilege to which only a few could make claim. It offered them the chance to gain the favor of the princes, to build up a relationship of trust with them, to discuss personal questions, to make advantageous recommendations, to defend political standpoints, and to influence important decisions. That was at once also the reason for their prominent presence in the diplomatic correspondence from that time. It was not the contemporaneous preference for hierarchy and status that incited foreign diplomats to give comments about the members of the archducal *Cámara*, but rather the realization that the unlimited access of the latter made them into politically relevant figures. In the following chapters the political role of the courtiers will be further elucidated.

Chapter V
Eyes & Ears*

'In the Courts of Kings and Princes one knows that many Bootlickers are found who, as they say, sweet-talk them, obscure the truth, and despise those whom they have come to hate; and there is nothing to be found in this World that is not subject to any risk.'[1]

Aubertus Miraeus
De vita Alberti Pii

In December, 1617, Lucio Morra, the papal nuncio in Brussels, informed his superiors in Rome of a remarkable incident that had drawn his attention. In the aftermath of the death of Don Juan de Meneses, *maestre de campo* in the *Ejército de Flandes*, Archduke Albert had devised a new command for no less than three army officers. Don Diego Mexía succeeded Meneses as the leader of a *tercio* in the infantry. The company of lancers Mexía had already commanded was awarded to Don Juan Niño de Tavora, whose own company of cuirassiers was in turn passed on to a son of the marquis of Belveder.[2] At first sight the content of Morra's letter seems somewhat peculiar. In the daily flow of news reports concerning ecclesiastical and diplomatic questions issuing from the nunciature in Brussels to the Holy See, an anecdote concerning a military matter is the odd one out. Why did the nuncio find it necessary to make mention of this seemingly unsensational round of appointments?

A closer look clears things up. Morra's zealous notations show that Diego Mexía was not only a *gentilhombre de la Cámara* of Archduke Albert but also his *primer caballerizo*. Juan Niño de Tavora was a *gentilhombre de la Cámara* as well and on top of that – as the nuncio delicately notes – a nephew of Albert's *mayordomo mayor* and

* Throughout this chapter I make multiple use of the recently published, magisterial study by Luc Duerloo, *Dynasty and Piety. Archduke Albert (1598-1621) and Habsburg Political Culture in an Age of Religious Wars* (Farnham, 2012). I want to thank Luc Duerloo explicitly for his willingness to put the manuscript of his study at my disposal while writing this book as well as for his comments on the chapter at hand.

1 After Miraeus, A. *De vita Alberti Pii, sapientis, prudentis Belgarum Principis commentarius*. Antwerp, 1622, p. 105.

2 '*È morto Don Giovanni di Meneses, ch'era Maestro di Campo d'un terzo d'Infanteria Spagnuola di questo essercito, il qual terzo è stato dato al Signore Don Diego di Messia, Cavaliere Spagnuolo, Primo Cavallerizo di Su Altezza, e la Compagnia di lance, ch'egli haveva, è stata data al Signore Giovanni Nigno, nepote del Conte d'Agnover, e quella, ch'esso haveva di corazze, Su Altezza ne ha fatto gratia al figliuolo del Signore Marchese di Belvedere.*' ASV, *Borghese* III 113, f. 319: Nuncio Lucio Morra to Cardinal Borghese, December 23, 1617.

favorite, the count of Añover. The third candidate was Jacinto de Velasco, a *menino* of the archdukes. He was the oldest son of Luis de Velasco, marquis of Belveder, who in his capacity as general of the cavalry frequently spent time at court. Consequently, all the newly appointed officers had close ties to the household of Albert and Isabella in one way or another. The motive behind Morra's report comes floating to the surface at once. By subtly pointing out that the archduke had distributed the vacated posts among the members of his personal entourage, the nuncio wanted to make clear that Albert had been able to strengthen his grip on the army's leadership. On top of that, Lucio Morra was not the only one who had noted this dance of musical chairs in the army. A few weeks later Philip III received a letter from Juan de Mancisidor, the secretary of State and War in the Netherlands, in which the round of appointments in question was reported on. It is clear that Mancisidor, too, had his questions about the flagrant way in which the archduke was trying to put the officer corps to his own purpose.[3]

Mexía, Niño de Tavora, and Velasco were exceptions least of all. In the time period before the announcement of the Twelve Years' Truce – and the reduction of troops subsequent to this – strikingly many courtiers held a military function. Until his fall in 1602, Francisco de Mendoza was not only Albert's *mayordomo mayor* but also general of the cavalry and *de facto* supreme commander of the army.[4] *Sumiller de corps* Rodrigo Niño y Lasso commanded a company of lancers as well as a company of harquebusiers in the cavalry, and the *caballerizo mayor* Philippe de Croÿ was captain-general of the so-called '*bandes d'ordonnance*' in the army.[5] *Mayordomo* Gerónimo Walter Zapata succeeded his colleague Diego de Ibarra as *veedor general* or financial controller-general of the *Ejército de Flandes*.[6] Robert de Ligne-Arenberg and Frederik van den Berg, captains of the *Hartschiere* and the halberdiers, respectively, were both commandants of a regiment in the infantry.[7] Even among the *gentilhombres*, a large number of lords can be found who held a military office. Count Charles of Arenberg was appointed admiral of the fleet in 1599.[8] Charles-Bonaventure de Longueval, count of Buquoy, became general of the artillery in 1603.[9] Gaston Spínola, count of

3 ARA, *SSO* 182, f. 3: Juan de Mancisidor to Philip III, January 12, 1618.
4 Rodríguez Villa, A. 'Don Francisco de Mendoza, almirante de Aragón (1547-1623),' in: Valera, J., ed. *Homenaje a Menéndez y Pelayo en el año vigésimo de su profesorado. Estudios de erudición española.* 2 vols. Madrid, 1899, volume II, pp. 486-610.
5 Roco de Campofrío, J. *España en Flandes. Trece años de gobierno del archiduque Alberto (1595-1608).* Madrid, 1973, p. 161.
6 CODOIN, vol. XLII, p. 300: Archduke Albert to the duke of Lerma, s.d. [1599].
7 AGS, *Estado* 2290, s.f.: *Relación de la Infanteria y Cavalleria de todas naciones que ay en este exercito de Su Magestad y lo que monta una paga y mes de sueldo.*
8 Cf. Pollentier, F. *De Admiraliteit en de oorlog ter zee onder de Aartshertogen (1596-1609).* Brussels, 1972.
9 Rahlenbeek, C. 'Longueval (Charles-Bonaventure de),' in: *Biographie Nationale*, vol. XII (1892-1893) pp. 359-368.

Bruay, was the *maestre de campo* of a *tercio* for a long time, and a significant number of his colleagues – among them Alexandre de Bournonville and Charles-Alexandre de Croÿ, count of Fontenoy – led a company in the army.[10] In the Court Chapel, the grand chaplain Pedro de Toledo was the administrator-general of the military hospital in Mechelen, and the court chaplain Juan Roco de Campofrío and his successor Cesar Clemens were charged with the function of vicar-general of the armed forces.[11] Even the medical personnel of the *Cámara*, like the doctors Francisco de Paz and Andreas Trevisius and the surgeon San Juan de Beraça, were connected to the army by way of their activities in the military hospital.[12]

The tendency is clear. The connections between the archducal household and the *Ejército de Flandes* were especially numerous. It was a situation with which they were anything but happy in Spain. Already in 1603, the *Consejo de Estado* made known that Philip III was of the judgment that the *criados* of Albert and Isabella should not be allowed to combine their function in the household with a function in the army.[13] On top of that, a year later the king decided that Albert was no longer allowed to have supreme command over the army.[14] The measure did not have the desired effect, all the same. The *Consejo de Estado* realized but all too well that the archduke continued to exercise influence on military policy and did everything to prevent the intertwining of both spheres. For that reason, as seen already in Chapter III, Gerónimo Walter Zapata had been pushed aside.

The situation sketched here can stand as an example for the proposition defended in this chapter, namely, that the members of the archducal household – and those of the *Cámara* in particular – could play an important role as representatives of the archdukes in different strategic domains, such as the army, the administration, and the diplomatic corps. Their free access to the princes made them into ideal mouthpieces of archducal authority, and in a certain sense they functioned as the 'eyes and ears' of Albert and Isabella outside the walls of the court. Although this conception has stood as self-evident for several decades in the international literature concerning early modern courts and their households, the entourage of Albert and Isabella has never been studied from this kind of angle before. Nevertheless, a thorough study of its

[10] AGS, *Estado* 2291, no. 201: Rodrigo Niño y Lasso to Philip III, December 24, 1609. See also Vander Linden, H. 'Spinola (Gaston de),' in: *Biographie Nationale*, vol. XXIII (1921-1924) pp. 426-428; Guillaume, G. 'Croy (Charles-Alexandre de),' in: *Biographie Nationale*, vol. IV (1873) pp. 555-558; and Rahlenbeek, C. 'Bournonville (Alexandre de),' in: *Biographie Nationale*, vol. II (1868) pp. 860-862.

[11] ASV, *Borghese* II 106, f. 162: Nuncio Bentivoglio to Cardinal Borghese, March 14, 1615; Roco de Campofrío, *España en Flandes*, 8; and BAV, *BaL* 6812, f. 167: Nuncio Giovanni-Francesco Guidi di Bagno to Cardinal Ludovisi, December 11, 1621.

[12] AGS, *Estado* 2291, no. 200: *Copia de la orden para los criados de Su Alteza*, December 22, 1609.

[13] AGS, *Estado* 2023, no. 60: Consult of the *Consejo de Estado*, January 18,1603.

[14] AGS, *Estado* 634, s.f.: Philip III to Rodrigo Niño y Lasso, s.d. [May 3, 1604].

activities can produce important new insights with regard to political relationships at court. As seen already in Chapter III, research into the archducal regime was dominated for a long time by excessive attention to the rivalry at court between those from Spain and the Southern Netherlands. The rivalry between these two nations did indeed exist and was certainly not unimportant. Yet historians have pointed it out all too frequently so as to reduce the history of the archducal period to a story of simplistic opposites, whereby a Spanish faction at all times stood positioned over against an 'indigenous' faction, and whereby the archducal and Spanish governments were continually at each other's necks. That the situation was much more complex in reality is by now clear. Before going into the political and diplomatic role of the archducal household, the following section will mount a more nuanced image of the 'factional conflict' at the court of Albert and Isabella.

Faction vs. nation

As to be expected, the political disputes at the archducal court manifested themselves above all during moments of crisis. Namely, during the run-up to the announcement of the Twelve Years' Truce in 1609, feelings flared high. The disunity was a question of how the archducal regime ought to react to the Dutch Revolt, which not only constituted a threat to the reign of Albert and Isabella but also – in the worst-case scenario – could bring the stability of the entire Spanish-Habsburg monarchy into jeopardy. Various diplomats mentioned that there was talk of two different factions at the court in Brussels.[15] The members of the first group were generally described as 'the Spaniards.' Of the opinion that Spanish hegemony in the Netherlands had to be safeguarded at all costs, they argued for powerful military action against the rebels. The other group was designated as that of 'the Flemings' ('*flamencos*' or '*naturales del País*'), who held a more pacifist conviction and promoted negotiating peace with the Republic.[16]

In the traditional historiography of the late nineteenth and the first half of the twentieth century, national labels have been but all too gladly adopted in order to explain the political frictions in the archducal period. That these categories were not taken all that precisely is shown by the fact that Ambrogio Spínola and Antonio Suárez de Arguello – of Genoese and Portuguese origin, respectively – were assigned without question to the camp of 'the Spaniards,' while the Burgundian Jean Richardot, the

[15] See e.g. ASV, *NF* 11, f. 718: Nuncio Ottavio Mirto Frangipani to Cardinal Aldobrandini, October 23, 1599.

[16] See ASV, *Borghese* III 110 BCDG, f. 236: Nuncio Frangipani to Borghese, November 24, 1604.

president of the Privy Council, was marked as being from the Southern Netherlands.[17] Yet even apart from this nuance, the question arises as to what extent the labels employed in the sources were in keeping with the political reality. All too frequently it is assumed that the fault lines cutting through the archducal regime always ran parallel to the gulf that separated the two contending nations from each other. In that way those from Spain automatically become one and the same as the intractable 'hawks' at court, and those from the Southern Netherlands as the peace-loving 'doves.' That this kind of linkage of political and 'national' interests does not necessarily reflect an accurate picture of the oppositions at that time has already been brought up in Chapter III. The discord between the nations at court was present yet certainly not the only factor in the story. Other, more pragmatic considerations contributed to the political frictions, too. That is suggested in every sense in the exchange of diplomatic letters being sent during the negotiations concerning the Twelve Years' Truce.

The French ambassador wrote in 1609, that the ratification of the Truce by the Spanish government was being delayed because the *grandes* in the *Consejo de Estado* sided against negotiating a solution, 'all of them having an interest in prolonging the war in order to employ their kinsmen, friends, and confidants, who all return rich from it.'[18] With that the ambassador exposed a motivation that is not to be underestimated in this story. For a great number of members of the Castilian aristocracy the *Ejército de Flandes* constituted an important source of income and career opportunities. Between 1607 and 1609, the army numbered approximately 6,500 soldiers of Spanish origin, whose combat pay came from the royal treasury.[19] So, for example, the three Spanish *tercios* of the infantry jointly numbered 4,054 military personnel (368 officers among them) in 1608, who in total received not less than 35,137 *escudos* (= approx. fl. 90,302) per month.[20] On average that came down to a salary of approximately 8 *escudos* per person per month. Yet in view of the fact that a common foot soldier never earned more than 3 *escudos* in this time period, it is clear that the vast portion of the money ended up with the officers, who as a rule were from the nobility.[21] On top of that, the animosities also brought forth the requisite spoils of war by way of pillage and

[17] Lefèvre, J. 'Le ministère espagnol de l'Archiduc Albert, 1598-1621.' *Bulletin de l'Académie Royale d'Archéologie de Bruxelles*, 1 (1924) pp. 202-224.

[18] '*(...) estans tous interessez à y faire entretenir la guerre pour y faire employer leurs parents, amys et confidents qui s'en retournent riches.*' BNF, *MsF* 16125, f. 177: Mathieu Brulart de Berny to Villeroy, January 2, 1609.

[19] Parker, G. *The Army of Flanders and the Spanish Road 1567-1659*. Cambridge U.P., 2004 [2nd edition]. Op. cit. p. 231.

[20] The three Spanish *tercios* were led by *maestres de campo* Iñigo de Borja, Juan de Meneses, and Simon Antunez. AGS, *Estado* 2290, s.f.: *Relación de la Infanteria y Cavalleria de todas naciones que ay en este exercito de Su Magestad y lo que monta una paga y mes de sueldo.*

[21] Parker, *The Army of Flanders*, 133. Presupposing that the 3,686 regular soldiers of the *tercios* did indeed each get 3 *escudos* per month, then the 368 officers got on average a wage of 65 *escudos* (= approx. fl. 167) per person per month.

plunder. Geoffrey Parker determined that an infantryman who was able to withstand the horror of the war and was bright enough to profit from the opportunities that presented themselves could return to Spain as a relatively rich man despite his low wages.[22] That was true, naturally, even more for the officers.

Seen from this angle, it need not come as a surprise that in May, 1607, the infanta Isabella expressed unconcealed criticism of Juan Fernández de Velasco, better known as the Constable of Castile, who as a prominent member of the *Consejo de Estado* had heavily opposed the ceasefire that was announced earlier that year. In a letter to the duke of Lerma, the infanta wrote that the Constable had allowed himself to be led in his judgment by deceptive information from his family and friends in the Netherlands, who had an interest in the war with the Republic not being stopped 'because they are living from it.'[23] Isabella did not name names, but there is no doubt that she was alluding to Luis de Velasco and Iñigo de Borja, who were both closely related to the Constable and who, not coincidentally, both held a prominent function in the *Ejército de Flandes*.[24] As indicated above, Velasco was the general of the cavalry in the army. He was described by the *corps diplomatique* in Brussels as one of the most ardent proponents of assertive military action against the rebels.[25] Iñigo de Borja was the commandant of the citadel of Antwerp and was not only a family member but also a good friend of Velasco. He, too, was described as belonging to the faction of nobles who sided against negotiating peace.[26] In addition to Velasco and Borja, this group was represented, among others, by Diego de Ibarra, the former *mayordomo* of the archdukes, who as the representative of the Spanish government took part in the talks, as well as by Rodrigo Niño y Lasso, Albert's *sumiller de corps*.[27] According to the

---

22 Parker, *The Army of Flanders*, 156.

23 '(...) *de parientes y amigos que todos son interesados en la guerra, porque viven della, y asi están peor que con el demonio con todos cuantos tratan de la pax.*' Rodríguez Villa, A., ed. *Correspondencia de la Infanta Doña Isabel Clara Eugenia con el Duque de Lerma y otros personajes.* Madrid, 1906, letter no. 117: Isabella to Lerma, May 19, 1607.

24 Luis de Velasco belonged to a bastard branch of the family of the Constable of Castile. Iñigo de Borja, then again, was a grandson of the Constable.

25 ASV, *Borghese* II 100, f. 167: Bentivoglio to Borghese, August 18, 1607. See also NA, *SP* 77/8, f. 118: Thomas Edmondes to Cecil, August 5, 1607.

26 AGS, *Estado* 2289, s.f.: Diego de Ibarra to Philip III, June 24, 1607 (in code).

27 '*Los pocos del Pays que me han hablado hasta agora lloran como pudieramos nosotros la forma en que se ha entablado este negocio, mostrando que en él no se lleba otra mira que al beneficio de los Rebeldes sin mirar por los catholicos que allí ay (reparan es este el mayor dolor y de mayor nota), ni por el bien de los Estados obedientes de V[uestra] M[ajestad] y quando no huviera tantas causas y tan importantes para no tener acertado proseguir debaxo de tan mal titulo y condicion, bastanta prueba desello es juzgallo assi los naturales yendoles tanto en conseguir reposo y paz, y otros criados que aqui tiene V.M. como don Luys de Velasco, don Ynigo de Borja, don Rodrigo Laso y el Governador de Cambray Juan de Ribas y otros muchos lo entienden de la misma manera y algunos dellos tienen por mas cierto que se aventuraran estos Estados obedientes.*' AGS, *Estado* 2289, s.f.: Diego de Ibarra to Philip III, June 24, 1607 (in code). See also NA, *SP* 77/8, f. 118: Thomas Edmondes to Cecil, August 5, 1607; and ASV, *Borghese* II 111, f. 191: Bentivoglio to Borghese, December 13, 1608.

papal nuncio in Brussels, their vision stood at odds with that of Archduke Albert, who was a proponent of negotiating a solution and was supported by figures like Ambrogio Spínola, Juan de Mancisidor, and Jean Richardot.[28]

It need not come as a surprise that Luis de Velasco and Ambrogio Spínola figured prominently in contemporaneous reporting concerning the factional conflict. When Velasco died at the age of 77 in 1625, he was described by the papal emissary Chrisogono Flacchio as a fervent rival ('*emule acerrimo*') of Spínola.[29] That was certainly not exaggerated: the displeasure between both men stemmed from the beginning years of the seventeenth century already, when Spínola got offered command over the siege of Ostend in exchange for his financial support.[30] The arrival of the new field marshal could count on little enthusiasm with the Spanish army officers. In a note to the duke of Lerma, an indignant critic wondered, 'What can a Genoese merchant, who has left his family in the lurch, know of war, and what can he offer, except the way for getting at money?'[31] The observation typifies the reactions of the leaders in the *Ejército de Flandes*, who clearly felt themselves to have been passed over by Spínola's appointment and did not plan to give the new commander much credit. Velasco, above all, showed himself in those terms to be the least accommodating of all. In May, 1604, for instance, he declined to follow Spínola's order in time so as to call a halt to the sudden invasion of Stadtholder Maurice of Nassau in the province of Zeeland.[32] When in the end he did swing into action, it was already too late. Maurice's troops were laying siege to the city of Sluis, which a few months later – and in spite of a final attempt by Spínola to liberate it – capitulated.[33] The archduke was enraged on account of Velasco's insubordination and had him promptly placed under house arrest.[34] The incident, though, still could not move Velasco to adjust his opinion about Spínola.

[28] '*In questo stato sono hora le prattiche intanto qie nella divisione de gli animi si sono divise ancora le persona e si sono veduute nascere due fattioni. L'una è quella dell'arciduca e del Marchese Spinola, co i quali va unito en el senso e nella trattatione del negotio il presidente Ricciardotto e Mancisidor, secretario di guerra per SM e per SA, ch'é ministro principalísimo. L'altra è quella di Don Diego d'Ibarra, che si tira dietro tuttli gli altri Spagnuoli e principalmente il Duca de Ossuna, e Don Luigi di Velasco, generale della cavalleria.*' ASV, *Borghese* II 100, f. 167: Nuncio Bentivoglio to Cardinal Borghese, August 18, 1607.

[29] ASV, *NF* 14 C, ff. 417-418: Chrisogono Flacchio to Cardinal Antonio Barberini, September 20, 1625.

[30] Cf. Esteban Estríngana, A. *Guerra y finanzas en los Países Bajos católicos. De Farnesio a Spínola (1592-1630)*. Madrid, 2002, p. 97.

[31] CCE, vol. I, p. 100: Note marked for the duke of Lerma, s.d.

[32] '*Al dubio di perdere o non perdere detto forte s'aggiugne il male delle solite discordie nel nostro campo, ch'il Sr. Don Loisi di Velasco come Generale della Cavalleria, pretendendo comandar' esso in assenza del Sr. Arciduca, s'oppose al Sr. Marchese Spinola, quale, et per la commission che tiene da S.A. su la impresa d'Ostenda (...), non douta cedere al detto Sr. Don Luisi, et cosa parmi, che sia stato giudicato de S.A. con l'haverlo fatto arrestar in Bruges nella sua casa assignatagli per carcere.*' ASV, *Borghese* III 110 BCDG, ff. 129-132: Nuncio Frangipani to Cardinal Aldobrandini, May 3, 1604. See also ASV, *Borghese* III 110 BCDG, f. 189: Frangipani to Aldobrandini, August 27, 1604.

[33] Thomas, W., ed. *De val van het Nieuwe Troje. Het beleg van Oostende, 1601-1604*. Exhibition catalogue. Leuven, 2004, p. 98.

[34] ASV, *Borghese* III 110 BCDG, ff. 129-132: Nuncio Frangipani to Cardinal Aldobrandini, May 3, 1604.

The mutual relationship between both men did not get any better when, in 1605, Spínola was appointed *maestre de campo general* of the *Ejército de Flandes*, a position that Velasco according to his own words was striving for.[35]

The developments sketched here suggest that the political fault lines at the archducal court in this time period were not based so much upon displeasure between the different nations as upon a complex interwoven nature of political, personal, and material interests. Nobles who in a financial sense depended on an income from the military treasury looked at the suspension of animosities teary-eyed. Those who possessed estates (and the concomitant glorious rents) in the Netherlands, on the contrary, had every interest that a swift and more stable peace should come. On top of that, there was also talk of mutual rivalry between the protagonists in the archducal entourage. One thing or another indicates that the 'Spanish faction' cannot be identified with the 'Spanish nation' at the court in Brussels without reservation. Not all Spaniards were proponents of a military solution for the conflict. The sources clearly show that a figure like Juan de Mancisidor disagreed with the vision of Ibarra and Velasco, and that was also true, for example, for Iñigo de Brizuela, Albert's father confessor, who was sent to the Spanish court to defend the standpoint of the archdukes.[36] Inversely, certainly not all nobles from the Southern Netherlands were excited about the conditions that were attached to the ceasefire. In July, 1607, Andrés de Prada, secretary of the *Consejo de Estado*, received a letter from Nicolas de Montmorency, baron of Vendegies and Haveskerke and president of the Council of Finance, in which the latter declared that

> 'already voices and lamentations are being heard from the majority of our people, who cannot suffer the despicable conditions of this treaty, and who attribute them in part to cowardness, in part to treason or ignorance of those who have advised the Princes, in such a way that they have lost much respect for the Prince, and from now on will stand firmer with regard to the punctual preservation of their privileges, and less willing to assist the Prince in his necessities.'[37]

---

[35] Esteban Estríngana, *Guerra y finanzas*, 151-152. See also NA, *SP* 77/8: Thomas Edmondes to Cecil, December 10, 1606; and AGS, *Estado* 2292, s.f.: Luis de Velasco to Philip III, August 10, 1610.

[36] CODOIN, vol. XLIII, p. 144: Albert to Lerma, November 29, 1608; and p. 146: Albert to Lerma, November 30, 1608. See also ASV, *Borghese* II 114, f. 48: Bentivoglio to Borghese, February 14, 1609.

[37] '*Desià s'entendent des voix et lamentations de la pluspart de nostre peuple, qui ne peuvent souffrir ces conditions gouteuses de ce traicté, et l'attribuent partie à lascheté, partie à trahison ou ignorance de ceux qui l'ont conseillé aux Princes, de façon que par là ils en perderont beaucoup de respect du Prince, et se tiendront desormais plus fermes à la conservation punctuelle de leurs privileges, et moins volontaires d'assister le Prince en ses necessitez.*' AGS, *Estado* 2289, s.f.: Nicolas de Montmorency to Andrés de Prada, July 17, 1607.

It is perhaps no coincidence that this letter was accompanied by a letter of recommendation from Diego de Ibarra, who asked that Montmorency be awarded an *ayuda de costa* of 2,000 or 3,000 *escudos* as pension for life.[38]

That the ceasefire ran into opposition with a number of courtiers from the Southern Netherlands had to do above all with the fact that even local nobles had established interests in the *Ejército de Flandes*. One of them was Maximilien de Hennin-Liétard, count of Boussu and later the archdukes' *mayordomo*, who, as captain of a regiment, received a hefty wage from the military treasury.[39] Even so, Boussu's affiliation with the 'hawks' at court did not rest only on material motives but also on familial bonds: his sister Anne was married to Luis de Velasco. According to several diplomats at the court of Brussels, this kinship at once offered the explanation for the fact that in July, 1607 – at the height of the factional conflict – Ambrogio Spínola saw to it that Boussu's regiment in the army was suddenly disbanded.[40] The fact that the protests of the 'hawks' against this decision had little effect was, according to the English ambassador, a sign of the impotence of Diego de Ibarra and his allies.[41] The ambassador's words proved to be prophetic, for a few months later Ibarra was called back to Spain.[42] His dishonorable retreat demonstrates how little influence the 'Spanish faction' was able to exercise on the peace negotiations. The fact that Ibarra's son Francisco was allowed to remain as the archduke's *gentilhombre de la Cámara* in Brussels was only small consolation in that context.[43]

With Ibarra's departure, the 'Spanish faction' found itself suddenly deprived of its most important representative. Evidently this caused frustration among those who stayed behind. In October, 1607, a stream of reports left Brussels for all the great courts of Europe when it turned out that Luis de Velasco and Iñigo de Borja had flown at each other in a fight. According to the French ambassador, both nobles were 'first cousins and very good friends, staying in the same lodgings,' but that did not prevent Borja from abusing Velasco's hospitality.[44] He succeeded in copying the keys to the room of Velasco's sister-in-law Hélène de Hennin-Liétard and – at least according to the rumors – spent the night with her. When Velasco heard about this, he accused Borja of besmirching the honor of his house. Thereupon followed a fight

[38] *Ibidem*: Diego de Ibarra to Andrés de Prada, July 17, 1607.

[39] Boussu entered into service as *mayordomo* of the archducal household on May 20, 1613. ARA, *RK* 1837, f. 160v.

[40] BNF, *MsF* 16125, f. 167: Mathieu Brulart de Berny to Villeroy, June 26, 1607; NA, *SP* 77/8, f. 104: Thomas Edmondes to Cecil, July 8, 1607; and f. 114: Edmondes to Cecil, July 29, 1607.

[41] *Ibidem*, f. 104.

[42] NA, *SP* 77/8, f. 127: Edmondes to Cecil, September 9, 1607.

[43] *Ibidem*.

[44] '*(...) cousins germains et trèsgrans amys logez en mesme logis (...)*.' BNF, *MsF* 16128, f. 178: Mathieu Brulart de Berny to Puisieux, October 21, 1607.

in which Velasco drew his dagger and wounded Borja in the head.[45] The incident caused much disruption at the court in Brussels. Archduke Albert had both men immediately locked up in the *castillos* of Antwerp and Ghent.[46] The French ambassador reported that the news of their arrest was received by Spínola with satisfaction: 'No one doubts that he [Spínola] would like it very much if this could give cause for their removal from here. For him, it would mean a marvelous thorn out of his foot.'[47] Velasco and Borja were, all the same, not called back to Spain. Instead of that, the Spanish ambassador got the commission to reconcile both men with each other. His intervention led to a marriage between Borja and Hélène de Hennin-Liétard, whereby the bonds between the leaders of the 'Spanish faction' and the family of the count of Boussu were tightened even more strongly.[48]

The reconciliation between Velasco and Borja, however, could not hinder negotiations with the Republic resulting in a compromise. With the signing of the Twelve Years' Truce in 1609, a provisional end came to the factional conflict that had dominated the political life at the archducal court for the first decade of the seventeenth century. Albert had got his way and the 'Spanish faction' had to satisfy itself with the outcome, which consolidated the political influence of Spínola and his allies as well. After 1609, Spínola, Juan de Mancisidor, and Iñigo de Brizuela would increasingly profile themselves as the strong men of the regime. Next to them Rodrigo Niño y Lasso took his place, who – as will be seen in the following chapter – was reasonable enough to turn his cart around and seek out connections with the moderate faction at court. Yet as general of the cavalry Luis de Velasco also remained a prominent figure. Although the wrinkles were never fully ironed out, his relationship with Spínola in a way improved in the course of years.[49] That does not take away from the fact, though, that feelings regularly flared high during the Twelve Years' Truce too. So, for example, the French ambassador wrote in 1614, that the military conflict surrounding the succession in the nearby duchies of Jülich and Cleves – one of the

[45] AGS, *Estado* 2289, s.f.: The marquis of Guadaleste to Philip III, November 2, 1607. See also ASV, *Borghese* II 100, f. 248: Bentivoglio to Borghese, October 20, 1607.

[46] AGS, *Estado* 2289, s.f.: Guadaleste to Philip III, November 8, 1607.

[47] '*On ne doubte point qu'il [Spinola] voudroit bien que celà peust estre cause de les tirer tous deulx dicy. Ce luy seroit une merveilleuse espine hors du pied.*' BNF, *MsF* 16128, f. 178: Mathieu Brulart de Berny to Puisieux, October 21, 1607.

[48] ASV, *Borghese* II 100, f. 255: Bentivoglio to Borghese, October 27, 1607.

[49] In August, 1614, Spínola supported his old rival when the latter submitted a request to be elevated to marquis. See AGS, *Estado* 2028, s.f.: Consult of the *Consejo de Estado*, August 8, 1614. All the same, see also ASV, *Borghese* II 112, f. 369: Nuncio Lucio Morra to Cardinal Borghese, July 28, 1618: '*Co'l Sr. Conte di Bucquoi andera il Cesati Commissario generale della Cavalleria. Perilche s'intende sia passato qualche disgusto tra'l Sr. Marchese Spinola e'l Sr. Marchese di Belvedere, Generale della Cavalleria, perche il Marchese Spinola l'ha fatto senza darne parte a quel di Belvedere il quale, come Generale della Cavalleria non havrebbe voluto, che si partisse o havendosi da partire fosse stato con participatione sua; Ma è cosa di pochissima consideratione, già che stanno amici, et amorevoli, come prima.*'

most touchy moments of crisis in the run-up to the Thirty Years' War (cf. below) – raised the fear of a flare-up of the old factional conflict at the court in Brussels.[50] All the same, this time it quickly turned out that the 'Spanish faction' – now led by the Spanish ambassador, the marquis of Guadaleste – could exercise only a little pressure. Not much later the English ambassador communicated that

> 'the Archduke's peaceable inclination and his power in Spaine hath so overswayed the relations of the Spanishe ambassador here – who is the captain and ringleader of the faction against these princes and the Marquis Spínola – as all things are referred to his definition notwithstanding the oppositions and remonstrance of Don Luis de Velasco and Don Yñigo de Borja to the contrary.'[51]

In 1616, the papal nuncio contended that the conflict concerning Jülich and Cleves had caused all hope for a stable peace with the United Provinces to be lost. Despite that, the archduke did not want to break the Truce, and that was also the thinking of Spínola and Mancisidor, 'upon whom every decision in military matters depends, and upon no one else.'[52] With that, peace and quiet seemed to return. After Albert's death, which more or less coincided with the Twelve Years' Truce having run its course, the old disputes turned out to raise their heads anew, however. The papal nuncio reported that Luis de Velasco and Andrés de Soto, Isabella's father confessor, were promoting a new military operation against the Republic, while Spínola and Brizuela were rather reticent and wanted to wait to see whether there were means enough to be able to maintain the army for a long time.[53]

The evolution described here demonstrates that the classic interpretation of the factional conflict at the court in Brussels gives too much attention to the disunity between the nations, and too little to other factors that also gave shape to the political discord. On top of that, an all too modern interpretation of the term 'factional conflict' needs to be guarded against, one in which factions are seen as organized parties with an agenda resting merely on political/ideological bases as well as a great degree of internal cohesion. Without a doubt, there were serious differences of opinion concerning the way in which the policies of the archdukes had to be conducted. It

[50] BNF, *MsF* 16130, f. 357: Charles de l'Aubespinne de Chasteauneuf, abbot of Préaux, to Puisieux, December 6, 1614.

[51] NA, *SP*, 77/11/2, f. 245: William Trumbull to Sir Ralph Winwood, February 10, 1615.

[52] '*(...) da quali dipende ogni risolutione in materia d'armi, e non da alteri.*' ASV, *Borghese* II 102, f. 86: Nuncio Ascanio Gesualdo to Borghese, March 12, 1603.

[53] BAV, *BaL* 6812, ff. 8-10: Nuncio Giovanni-Francesco Guidi di Bagno to Cardinal Ludovisi, July 31, 1621.

would be wrong, however, to see this divisiveness among opinions as something static, as if it had functioned independently of the changing political circumstances and had remained almost insensitive to dynamism. Even a factional conflict had a life cycle.

On top of that, the classic approach looks over an important nuance. In August, 1607, the French ambassador Mathieu Brulart de Berny reported that the peace process was hanging by a silk thread in the Netherlands.[54] According to Brulart, Diego de Ibarra was doing everything to work against Spínola and his people. The ambassador wrote that Ibarra was an adherent of the Constable of Castile, who had shown himself to be a fervent opponent of the duke of Lerma at the Spanish court.[55] On top of that, the Constable was an opponent of Spínola as well, who, then again, could get along excellently with Lerma.[56] In that sense the frictions in Brussels seem to have mirrored the internal struggle for power at the court of Philip III, where the policies of Lerma had to deal with criticism more and more frequently.[57] All too often the historiography concerning the archducal regime assumed and assumes that the Spanish government unanimously sided against negotiating a peace with the Republic. Nevertheless, various diplomats contended that Lerma was in fact a proponent of a pacifist solution instead and that it was, above all, the *Consejo de Estado*, as populated by Castilian aristocrats, which opted for military action.[58] Thus, in November, 1607, for instance, Mathieu Brulart wrote that the treaty concerning the ceasefire could only be approved thanks to the omnipotence of Lerma.[59] It becomes clear here that the so-called 'Spanish' faction in Brussels did not so much underwrite the policy line of the duke of Lerma as did, rather, the opposition in the *Consejo de Estado*. At the Spanish court, consequently, they were just as divided about how to tackle the Dutch Revolt as was the court in Brussels.

This chapter does not intend to dismember relations between Brussels and Madrid down to the bone. It simply means to make clear that an all too simplistic look at the relationship between the archducal and royal courts does not do right by the complexity of the political relationships in this time period. The political frictions in Brussels issued forth from a multiplicity of motivations and factors and, consequently,

---

54 BNF, *MsF* 16128, f. 157: Mathieu Brulart de Berny to Puisieux, August 22, 1607.

55 *Ibidem.*

56 *Ibidem.*

57 Concerning the competition between Lerma and the Constable of Castile, see Williams, P. *The Great Favourite. The Duke of Lerma and the Court and Government of Philip III of Spain, 1598-1621.* Manchester U.P., 2006, pp. 92-93. See also Feros, A. *Kingship and Favoritism in the Spain of Philip III, 1598-1621.* Cambridge U.P., 2000, pp. 224-225.

58 ASV, *Borghese* II 100, f. 173: Nuncio Bentivoglio to Cardinal Borghese, August 24, 1607; and f. 197: Bentivoglio to Borghese, September 8, 1607. See also BNF, *MsF* 16128, f. 178: Mathieu Brulart de Berny to Puisieux, October 21, 1607; and BNF, *MsF* 16125, f. 177: Mathieu Brulart de Berny to Villeroy, January 2, 1609.

59 BNF, *MsF* 16128, f. 194: Mathieu Brulart de Berny to Puisieux, November 23, 1607.

cannot be clarified exclusively by the conflict between the conservative Spanish government on the one hand and, on the other hand, an archducal regime striving for autonomy. That approach elucidates only one part of the story and has need of nuance in any case. The relations between both courts were complicated. They rested not so much on disunity concerning the nature of the political objectives as they did on the differences of opinion concerning the manner in which those objectives had to be realized. In the case of the peace process it was clear to both courts that the Dutch Revolt constituted a threat. That the situation demanded an urgent solution was as plain as day. Yet in both Brussels as well as Madrid unanimity over the best solution was far to be found. The fact that the financial situation was anything but rose-colored and that the troops turned to mutiny time after time naturally contributed to the discord among them. That does not take away from the fact, however, that Philip III as well as Albert and Isabella in essence departed from the same standpoint. Their most prominent goal was first and foremost to safeguard Habsburg authority in the Low Countries. This commission overruled all other political objectives and determined to a great degree the policy line that was kept to inside the entire Habsburg imperium. It is one of the propositions of this book that the reign of the archdukes was determined in the first place by *dynastic* interests, and that it also has to be studied in that way. And, as the following sections will show, it was precisely in this area that the members of the archducal household would play a crucial role.

The swearing of oaths in 1616

In December, 1613, Archduke Albert became seriously ill. By now he was 54 years old, and his health left him more and more in the lurch. During the initial months of 1614, his condition was so precarious that the doctors considered it advisable to prescribe him a diet of ass's milk.[60] It speaks for itself that the physical well-being of the archduke was of great importance for the political stability in the Habsburg Netherlands. In Madrid the alarm bells rang upon hearing the news. The *Consejo de Estado* advised to take immediate action and have the provinces of the Southern Netherlands swear their loyalty to Philip III as the rightful heir and successor of the archdukes. In that way the king would be able to take possession of his territories on the North Sea '*con mucha más facilidad*' in case of Albert's death.[61] Ambrogio Spínola – Lerma's ally in Brussels – got the commission to feel out Albert's opinion in

[60] ASV, *Borghese* II 99, f. 90: Bentivoglio to Borghese, February 8, 1614; and f. 114: Bentivoglio to Borghese, February 15, 1614.

[61] AGS, *Estado* 2027, s.f.: Consult of the *Consejo de Estado*, December 20, 1613.

secret and to convince him of the importance of this question.[62] In February, 1614, Spínola announced that he had called in the help of the father confessor Iñigo de Brizuela, who used his influence with the archduke to plead for the necessity of a swearing of oaths.[63] According to the father confessor, Albert thought it 'a good idea and it [seemed] time to him to do this.'[64] And yet the archduke – who against all expectations was getting better again in the meantime – did not seem inclined to put his words into deeds at once. In March, Spínola reported that Albert still had made no decision concerning the matter.[65] Not until April did the archduke give his approval for the plan, even though he proposed that Philip III perhaps had better send one of his younger sons to the Southern Netherlands to claim the succession. Even so, that suggestion was swiftly cast away in Madrid, and, according to Spínola, the archduke did not come back to it any more after that.[66] In August, Albert as well as Spínola and Brizuela made it known that they would do everything to speed up the swearing of oaths.[67] Juan de Mancisidor, too, pledged his whole-hearted collaboration.[68] The task proved to be anything but simple, however.

As was to be expected, the provinces in the Southern Netherlands were initially not quite enthusiastic about the plan. To prevent that the swearing of oaths would be misused in order to get certain political demands on the table, Spínola suggested that it would be wise to circumvent the States-General and approach each province separately.[69] It cost a lot of time and effort, all the same, to persuade the provincial States to recognize Philip III as their future sovereign.[70] The different representative bodies of the estates came up with all manner of objections.[71] In the provinces of Brabant and Flanders, namely, where the say of the cities was quite large, they kept the plan at bay.[72] On top of that, the entanglements in Jülich and Cleves provided for delay.[73] Not until during the springtime of 1616 did things finally get moving in the matter. In May of that year the different provinces each sent a delegation to the castle

62 *Ibidem.*
63 AGS, *Estado* 2028, s.f.: Spínola to Philip III, February 1, 1614.
64 *Ibidem.*
65 AGS, *Estado* 2296, s.f.: Spínola to Philip III, March 9, 1614.
66 CCE 1, p. 426: Philip III to Spínola, June 16, 1614; and p. 428: Spínola to Philip III, August 9, 1614.
67 AGS, *Estado* 2028, s.f.: Consult of the *Consejo de Estado*, August 28, 1614. See also CCE 1, p. 430: Philip III to Spínola, September 18, 1614.
68 AGS, *Estado* 2296, s.f.: Juan de Mancisidor to Philip III, December 1, 1614.
69 AGS, *Estado* 2030, s.f. Consult of the *Consejo de Estado*, May 21, 1616.
70 Concerning the negotiations, see Lonchay, H. 'Le serment de fidélité prêté par les Belges à Philippe III en 1616,' in: *Mélanges Paul Fréderica. Hommage de la Société pour le progrès des études philologiques et historiques.* Brussels, 1904, pp. 311-317.
71 NA, *SP* 77/12, f. 76: William Trumbull to the secretary of State, April 27, 1616; and f. 91: Trumbull to the secretary of State, May 19, 1616.
72 NA, *SP* 77/12, f. 112: Trumbull to the secretary of State, May 22, 1616.
73 AGS, *Estado* 2299, s.f.: Spínola to Philip III, January 15, 1616.

of Mariemont, where the delegates would swear the oath of loyalty at the hands of Albert, who acted as Philip III's deputy. Only the Estates of Brabant demanded that the ceremony proceed within the borders of their province.[74] On May 22, the deputies of Hainault, Valenciennes, Namur, Tournai and the Tournaisis, and Cambrai swore the oath.[75] A few days later came the turn for Limburg, Luxembourg, Gelderland, Artois, and Mechelen, '*con mucho demostración de contento*.'[76] Flanders and the castellanies of Lille, Douai, and Orchies followed on June 19, Brabant on July 18.[77]

Various sources show that the agreement of the different provinces had come about not without the requisite external pressure. On May 5, 1616, the marquis of Guadaleste wrote a letter to Philip III, in which he called upon the king to reward various nobles in the provinces of the Southern Netherlands.[78] They were, among others, the count of Hoogstraten, governor of Tournai; the prince of Ligne, governor of Artois; and the count of Sainte-Aldegonde, governor of Limburg. In Flanders and Brabant there was no governor, though here the king had to give satisfaction to the count of Estaires and the chancellor Peter Peckius. Then again, in Hainault, where the governor Charles-Bonaventure de Longueval was absent, the duke of Aarschot earned a reward. Finally, in Cambrai, Namur, and Gelderland, the count of Roeulx, the count of Marles, and François de Berghes, respectively, had to be thanked.[79] Naturally, Guadaleste wrote his letter not without reason. It seems that each of these men had executed good services with an eye to the approval of the swearing of oaths in the provinces named. The way in which they did that is less clear, but in any case their actions did produce the desired result. During that same month the king received a letter from Ambrogio Spínola, who announced that Philippe-Charles of Arenberg, duke of Aarschot, had presented the proposal of the oath to the States of Hainault.[80] According to Spínola, his mediation had been decisive, for Hainault was the first province that agreed to declare its loyalty. For that reason Spínola had asked Philippe-Charles also to use his influence with the obstructive States of Brabant, where the duke enjoyed much authority.[81] Spínola directed a similar question to Charles de Lalaing, the count of Hoogstraten. He was the governor of Tournai and the Tournaisis, but

---

[74] AGS, *Estado* 2299, s.f.: Spínola to Philip III, July 5, 1616.
[75] AGS, *Estado* 2299, s.f.: Spínola to Philip III, May 28, 1616.
[76] AGS, *Estado* 2299, s.f.: The marquis of Guadaleste to Philip III, May 29, 1616.
[77] AGS, *Estado* 2299, s.f.: Spínola to Philip III, July 5, 1616; and AGS, *Estado* 2300, s.f.: Report of the swearing of oaths by the States of Brabant, July 18, 1616.
[78] CCE 1, p. 469: The marquis of Guadaleste to Philip III, May 1, 1616.
[79] *Ibidem.*
[80] AGS, *Estado* 2299, s.f.: Spínola to Philip III, s.d.
[81] *Ibidem.*

according to Spínola his intervention in Brabant would also be of great importance.[82] Finally, the Genoese field commander reported that the prince of Ligne, governor of Artois, was doing his best to get the oath through.[83]

Whoever reads closely the letters of Guadaleste and Spínola rapidly makes a notable observation. With few exceptions, all persons named were in one way or another connected to the archducal household. Aarschot, Ligne, Hoogstraten, and Marles bore the title of *gentilhombre de la Cámara*, while both Roeulx and Sainte-Aldegonde were *mayordomo*. On top of that, three of them were also provincial governors. Here an interesting question arises. Was it coincidence that courtiers like Ligne, Hoogstraten, and Sainte-Aldegonde were appointed governor by Archduke Albert? In a certain sense, their appointments need not come as a surprise: it could be argued that it is not abnormal that precisely the most prominent nobles in the country also got the function of governor, in recognition of their status. Yet that argument is not entirely watertight. There were more important nobles who stood as candidates for a governorship than there were provinces, so in essence the archduke had abundant choice. Still, in pretty much all provinces governors were systematically installed who also held a function in the archducal household.[84] In that way it is striking, for example, that when the papal nuncio reported on awarding the governorship of Tournai to the count of Bruay in 1612, he explicitly mentions that Bruay was a '*cavaliere italiano della Camera di S[u] A[ltezza]*.'[85] It is striking as well that he described the count of Sainte-Aldegonde – who replaced Bruay as governor of Limburg – as '*il primo de i maggiordomi delle Sue Altezze*.'[86] In the same way the nuncio announces in 1615, that the governorship of Tournai was awarded after the death of Bruay to the count of Hoogstraten, '*della camera dell Archiduca*.'[87]

---

[82] Cf. Lebrecht, F. *Les Lalaing, une famille au service des archiducs*. Paper presented at the colloquium *Les 'Trente Glorieuses' (ca. 1600 – ca. 1630) dans les Pays-Bas méridionaux et la France septentrionale*, organized by the Université Charles-de-Gaulle – Lille 3 (Lille, Maison des Sciences de l'Homme, March 22-23, 2007). I thank Fréderick Lebrecht for his willingness to put the text of his paper at my disposal.

[83] AGS, *Estado* 2299, s.f.: Spínola to Philip III, s.d.

[84] A few examples may suffice. In Limburg, the governorship was awarded, successively, to the count of Bruay (1601-1614), the count of Sint-Aldegonde (1614-1620), and the marquis of Marnay (1620-1625), all members of the archducal household. In Tournai, they were the count of Solre (1592?-1612), the count of Bruay (1612-1614), and the count of Hoogstraten (1614-1624). In Hainault, it was the duke of Aarschot (Charles de Croÿ) (-1612), the count of Buquoy (1613-1621), and the prince of Épinoy (1621-). In Artois, it was the count of Berlaymont, the prince of Ligne (1610-), and the count of Hoogstraten (1624-). In Namur, it was the count of Egmont (1599-1620) and the count of Sainte-Aldegonde (1620-). A notorious exception is Cambrai, where the governorship was awarded, successively, to Don Sancho de Leiva (1598-), Don Juan de Rivas (-1616), and Don Carlos Coloma (1617-). Cf. Poullet, E. 'Les gouverneurs de province dans les anciens Pays-Bas Catholiques.' *Bulletin de l'Académie Royale de Belgique*, 2de reeks, 35 (1873) pp. 362-436 and 810-921.

[85] BAV, *BaL* 6806, f. 146: Bentivoglio to Borghese, March 31, 1612.

[86] *Ibidem*.

[87] ASV, *Borghese* II 106, f. 60: Bentivoglio to Borghese, January 24, 1615.

The commentaries of the nuncio carry a deeper meaning in them. By emphasizing their connection with the archducal *Cámara*, Bentivoglio indicated that the new governors made up part of Albert's small circle of intimates. And that need not come as a surprise. The governors were expected to be the representatives of the archduke in the different provinces. Consequently, they had to be trustworthy persons, who were perfectly informed of Albert's political standpoints and motivations, and who could defend these to the outside world. Thanks to their position in the *Cámara* – and the accompanying right of free access to Albert – the *gentilhombres* were ideally placed for functioning as provincial governors. They served the interests of their master and functioned in that way as 'extensions' of Albert's authority outside the court. In that sense it is least of all a surprise that figures like the prince of Ligne and the count of Hoogstraten put their best foot forward to accelerate the process for the swearing of oaths. That was also true for the *gentilhombres de la Cámara* who were not provincial governors, but who did hold other top functions in the provinces, such as the count of Marles, who was the grand bailiff of Hainault.[88] Still – and this is important – even without an official function the courtiers could apply much influence in the provinces, such as the duke of Aarschot, who would not be appointed governor of Namur until 1626, yet who as *pair* of Hainault and the most important, landowning nobleman in Brabant also enjoyed much authority already before that. In exchange for their help the *gentilhombres* could count on the support of the archduke in striving for their personal interests. So, for instance, Philippe-Charles of Arenberg was appointed knight in the Order of the Golden Fleece by proxy of Albert, Spínola, and Brizuela in 1616, out of thanks for his proven services in the swearing of oaths and on account of '*la calidad y fidelidad de su cassa*.'[89] The count of Hoogstraten was put forward as well but would not receive the Fleece until 1621.[90]

The role of the courtiers in the provinces, all the same, was not limited to a one-way street. There are strong indications that Albert's *gentilhombres* were also seen by the provinces themselves as persons of political importance, and were selected precisely on account of their good contacts with the court to represent the provincial States to the archduke. Thus, it is striking, for instance, that most delegations charged by the States to swear the oath of loyalty numbered one or more delegates who were directly connected to the archducal household. For Brabant it was, among others, the count of

[88] de Vegiano, J.-C.-J. & de Herckenrode, J.S.F.J.L. *Nobiliaire des Pays-Bas et du Comté de Bourgogne*. 4 vols. Ghent, 1862-1868. Op. cit. p. 1458.

[89] AGS, *Estado* 2299, s.f.: Spínola to Philip III, s.d.; CCE vol. I, p. 478, s.f.: Consult of the *Consejo de Estado*, 19 July 1607; AGS, *Estado* 2030, s.f.: Consult of the *Consejo de Estado*, November 30, 1616; and AGS, *Estado* 2030, s.f.: Memorandum of Iñigo de Brizuela to the *Consejo de Estado*, s.d. [1616]. For the citation: ARA, *SSO* 180, f. 184: Philip III to Albert, October 24, 1616.

[90] AGS, *Estado* 2299, s.f.: Albert to Philip III, March 8, 1616.

Hoogstraten who took the task upon himself.[91] For Flanders it was, among others, the gentilhombre *de la Cámara* Philippe-Lamoral de Gand-Vilain, count of Izegem, and of the *gentilhombre de la Casa* Justiniaan Triest, lord of Ruddervoorde.[92] Lille sent Jean of Montmorency, baron of Wastines, who was *gentilhombre de la Boca* and would later be appointed *mayordomo*.[93] Artois was represented by Guillaume de Melun, prince of Epinoy and *gentilhombre de la Cámara*, and by Charles de Bernemicourt, lord of La Thieuloye and *gentilhombre de la Boca*.[94] Luxembourg sent, among others, the court preacher Bernard de Montgaillard to the swearing of oaths.[95] Hainault, finally, wanted to delegate the marquis of Havré, but he sent his cat because he did not get any precedence over the prince of Chimay, a brother of the duke of Aarschot.[96]

The prominent presence of members of the archducal household in the different delegations makes it seem that the courtiers enjoyed much political authority in the provinces themselves. This shows that they could function as intermediaries between the court and the other political strata of society. In this case they constituted the connection between the court and the representative bodies of the estates. The swearing of oaths in 1616, then, may count as an example of a political process in which the courtiers played a central role. The archduke, Ambrogio Spínola, and Iñigo de Brizuela all had a hand in it, and Albert's *gentilhombres* used their influence in the provinces to bring the plan to its execution. Here it becomes clear that the decision-making in the Archducal Netherlands not only ran via the established institutional channels, but was also directed just as well from the archducal *Cámara*. At present there would be talk of an interwoven nature of the formal and informal paths of power, with the understanding that the discrepancy between both spheres was not perceived as such by contemporaries. As was argued in the Introduction to this book, household and government in the early modern period were as yet inseparably connected with each other. Contemporaries saw the political actions of the members of the *Cámara*, therefore, not as an unallowed circumvention of the 'standard' channels but as a valid and complementary component of the decision-making process.

---

91 The other delegates for the nobility from Brabant were the abbot of Gembloers, the baron of Grimbergen, the baron of Wezemaal, and the baron of Jauche. AGS, *Estado* 2300, s.f.: Report of the swearing of oaths of the States of Brabant, July 18, 1616.

92 The other delegates for the nobility from Flanders were the count of Estaires, the baron of Wakken, and Nicolas Triest. AGS, *Estado* 2299, s.f.: Report of the swearing of oaths of June 19, 1616.

93 *Ibidem*.

94 AGS, *Estado* 2299, s.f.: Report of the swearing of oaths of May 26, 1616.

95 *Ibidem*. The other representative of Luxembourg was the lord of Frischbach.

96 AGS, *Estado* 2299, s.f.: The marquis of Guadaleste to Philip III, May 29, 1616.

Dynastic perils

It need not come as a surprise that Archduke Albert engaged his own courtiers to speed up the swearing of oaths. With an eye to political stability in the Archducal Netherlands, the recognition of Philip III as the future sovereign was of crucial importance. Albert and Isabella were childless and consequently would not be able to further the dynastic line. The archduke was on top of that a man at an advanced age and clearly not in good health. Nobody knew what would occur when the Twelve Years' Truce would run its course in 1621. Consequently it was necessary to arrange the succession of the archdukes as swiftly as possible, now that the political climate was still favorable. The fact that Albert went relatively rapidly along with having the provinces in the Southern Netherlands swear their loyalty to the Spanish prince demonstrates once again that Brussels and Madrid were not always on different wavelengths. The archduke realized but all too well how matters stood and resigned himself to the awareness that his personal interests as sovereign prince had to make room for a higher goal: the preservation of Habsburg rule in the Netherlands.

As indicated above, the reign of Albert and Isabella was seldom or never illuminated by historians from the dynastic aspect. They until now had above all an eye for the way in which the complex of Burgundian lands developed in the course of centuries into a modern nation-state. Centralization, professionalization, and bureaucratization constituted the core terms in that process. This excessive attention to the process of state-building saw to it, all the same, that the presupposed early modern *raison d'état* was seldom connected with dynastic interests. Yet here is precisely where the key lies to being able to understand decision-making in this time period better. That the administration of the state during the Ancien Régime for the large part coincided with the administration of the dynastic patrimony is a conclusion that has yet to dawn in the historiography concerning the archducal regime. The historiographical debate concerning the political autonomy of Albert and Isabella has led to the attention going in the main to the Dutch Revolt and its consequences for the relationship between the courts in Brussels and Spain. Seldom has there been the insight that the archdukes always kept half an eye directed at the situation in the Holy Roman Empire, where the internal political and religious conflicts succeeded one another in rapid tempo and the mental condition of Emperor Rudolf II gave ever more reason for being worried.[97] The fact that Albert for years was an important candidate to

[97] The run-up to the Thirty Years' War has already been extensively described by historians. A standard work remains Parker, G., ed. *The Thirty Years' War*. London, 1984. Concerning Rudolf II, see the splendid study of Robert Evans: Evans, R.J.W. *Rudolf II and his World. A Study in Intellectual History, 1576-1612*. Oxford, 1973.

succeed his brother on the imperial throne nevertheless seems reason enough to study the archducal regime from this angle too.

As seen in previous chapters already, at the beginning of their reign Albert and Isabella were in no way devoid of dynastic aspirations. They not only consciously organized their court according to the royal model, but they also actively strived for the title of kings of Burgundy.[98] During the negotiations concerning the Act of Cession the archduke had put this suggestion on the table once already, though without result. Shortly after his marriage, however, he began a new, international campaign to lay hold of the title of king after all. As opposed to what would be expected, Philip III was in no way disinclined toward this proposal.[99] The king asked the duke of Sesa, his ambassador in Rome, to plead the question with the pope, who had to give his approval to restore the medieval kingdom of Burgundy to its honor. The negotiations needed to be conducted in the greatest secrecy, though, so that they would not give ideas to other possible pretenders to a royal title – such as the duke of Savoy.[100] For that reason, Sesa had to impress heartily upon the pope that it was a question of reintroducing a title that had fallen into disuse, not one of creating a new title.[101] Philip commissioned his ambassador to carry out the advice of the archduke in this regard punctually and well, and if Albert should send anyone to set the negotiations in motion, then the ambassador had to support this person, though while observing the strictest secrecy.[102]

The idea to claim the title of kings of Burgundy naturally did not come about without reason.[103] What was already pretty much clear at the signing of the Act of Cession, though frequently overlooked by historians, is the assessment that Albert did not see dominion over the Netherlands as his ultimate goal. In reality his ambitions lay elsewhere. Since the death of his elder brother Ernst in 1595, Albert was more than ever in the running to succeed Rudolf II as emperor of the Holy Roman Empire. Rudolf had no legitimate children and had to fight more and more frequently with what was

[98] See in that context Bonenfant, P. 'Les projets d'érection des Pays-Bas en royaume du XVe au XVIIIe siècle. Aperçu sur l'évolution de ce concept politique.' *Revue de l'Université de Bruxelles*, 41 (1935-1936) 151-169.

[99] BFZ, *Altamira*, carpeta 39, grupo documental 13, doc. 61: Philip III to the duke of Sesa, June 5, 1599.

[100] See Oresko, R. 'The House of Savoy in Search for a Royal Crown in the Seventeenth Century,' in: Oresko, R., Gibbs, G.C. & Scott, H.M., eds. *Royal and Republican Sovereignty in Early Modern Europe: Essays in Memory of Ragnhild Hatton*. Cambridge U.P., 1997, pp. 272-350.

[101] '*El secreto es summamente necessario y assi os lo encargo mucho y quede mi parte le pidays a S[u] S[antidad] (...) Tambien importa infinito que junto con negociar este titulo vays desviando las pretensiones de otros en materias semejantes y assegurando con S.S. que no admita tal cosa, pues demas de las otras causas que aqui singularmente concurren que son muchas, es unica qualidad tratar de titulo antiguo y no instituyr le de nuevo sino revivir el viejo, con que no se abre puerta a las nuevas pretensiones que despues podrian acudir*.' BFZ, *Altamira*, carpeta 39, grupo documental 13, doc. 61: Philip III to the duke of Sesa, June 5, 1599.

[102] *Ibidem*.

[103] The following paragraphs are based in particular on Duerloo, *Dynasty and Piety*, 257-282.

described in contemporaneous sources as 'melancholy' moods.[104] Of all his brothers still living, Albert was the one who in principle came most under consideration for being elected the King of the Romans. To be sure, he was younger than the archdukes Matthias and Maximilian, but he could call upon the fact that the election of the emperor – at least in the legal sense – was not bound to primogeniture. On top of that, he had his own sovereign principality at his disposal, had the requisite political and military experience, and was the only one of his brothers who was married – and, more than that, to a Spanish infanta, which could be of crucial importance with an eye to furthering the dynastic line. As if that were not enough, his candidacy enjoyed the support of Philip III.[105] The only thing lacking to make the picture complete was a royal title. In that sense the possible reestablishment of the kingdom of Burgundy offered the ideal solution. The prestigious title would have catapulted Albert to the top of the European pecking order among kings and would have strongly increased his chances at the imperial throne. Consequently it need not come as a surprise that the archduke did everything to lay hold of the title of king. In the meantime he began to negotiate quietly about Rudolf's succession. And here, too, the members of the *Cámara* were engaged to give their two cents.

Already in 1596, Albert had sent his *mayordomo mayor* Francisco de Mendoza on a mission to the Habsburg courts of Prague, Vienna, Graz, and Linz. Officially, the Admiral of Aragon had to inform the emperor and the Austrian archdukes of Albert's appointment as governor of the Netherlands. Behind the scenes, however, they were busily meeting about Albert's approaching marriage to the infanta Isabella and about his candidacy as a possible successor to Rudolf's throne. It speaks for itself that not all family members were equally enthusiastic concerning this development. The archdukes Matthias and Maximilian did not want just simply to give up their own claims to the throne, and Rudolf limited himself to a few empty responses. Two years later, during his trip to Spain, the archduke made use of the occasion, then, to plead his case in person with the emperor and Pope Clement VIII. His plea left nothing to be desired in terms of clarity. Albert asked them to take the reestablishment of the former kingdom of Burgundy under consideration and, on top of that, wanted to be elected King of the Romans as swiftly as possible. Yet both Rudolf as well as Clement took on a rather wait-and-see attitude, and for the time being it did not look like Albert's request would be rapidly granted.[106]

---

[104] Midelfort, H.C.E. 'A Melancholy Emperor and His Mad Son,' in: Midelfort, H.C.E., ed. *Mad Princes of Renaissance Germany*. Virginia U.P., 1996, pp. 125-143.
[105] CCE, vol. I, p. 229 and AGS, *Estado* 2298, s.f.: Spínola to Philip III, June 30, 1613.
[106] Duerloo, *Dynasty and Piety*, 251.

Within the set-up of this chapter it is impossible to explain all the political entanglements that preceded the final election of the new King of the Romans. A short sketch of the negotiations – which would drag on for more than ten years – may suffice to offer the reader the requisite background knowledge. During the years after 1600 the contacts between Rudolf and his brothers would run ever more roughly.[107] Above all, Archduke Matthias showed himself to be indefatigable in his zeal to claim the succession and seemed willing to go to extremes for it. Rudolf himself, then again, seemed to decline into complete inertia and withdrew more and more frequently into the seclusion of his *Cámara*, where he engrossed himself in astrology and alchemy in an almost obsessional way. All attempts to move him to a decision about the succession ran into a wall of unwillingness and paranoia. As a consequence of this, the *Bruderzwist* became increasingly dire, to the extent even that Matthias raised an army in April, 1608, and prepared to push aside Rudolf, whether he wanted or not. On top of that, the flare-up of the struggle against the Ottoman Turks as well as the internal unrest in Hungary and the neighboring principalities of Moldavia, Transylvania, and Walachia also contributed to the political impasse. The Holy Roman Empire was in danger of descending into a completely dead-end situation.[108] Alarmed by the seriousness of this crisis, Archduke Albert sent Octavio Visconti, one of his most trusted *gentilhombres de la Cámara*, to Prague to mediate, albeit according to the Spanish ambassador 'with little to no certainty that this mission would produce something.'[109] The papal nuncio Bentivoglio had more confidence in a good outcome: he reported that the Italian nobleman was a '*cavaliere de più principali e più estimati della sua Camera*,' and a man with '*molta (…) prudenza*.'[110] Visconti had already served since the reign of Archduke Ernst in the Netherlands, spoke fluent Spanish and German, and knew the character of Rudolf and Matthias.[111] As such he was the ideal intermediary to reconcile both brothers with each other and to work out a solution for the disunity surrounding the succession. On top of that, as a Milanese he was a relative outsider in the conflict: that unconnectedness could also speak in his favor.

Albert commissioned Visconti to offer his services as intermediary to Rudolf and Matthias and to tell them that their behavior was bringing harm to the dynasty and imperial dignity.[112] In the meantime he had to work together with other prominent figures like the Spanish ambassador Guillén de San Clemente and Cardinal Franz von

[107] See in that context Vocelka, K. 'Matthias contra Rudolf. Zur politischen Propaganda in der Zeit des Bruderzwistes.' *Zeitschrift für Historische Forschung*, 10 (1983) 341–351.
[108] Duerloo, *Dynasty and Piety*, 257-267.
[109] AGS, *Estado* 2290, s.f.: The marquis of Guadaleste to Philip III, May 14, 1608. See also ACA, 38/3, file 100, f. 21: Gaston Spínola to Charles of Arenberg, May 20, 1608.
[110] ASV, *Borghese* II 115, f. 183: Bentivoglio to Borghese, May 10, 1608.
[111] *Ibidem*.
[112] Duerloo, *Dynasty and Piety*, 265.

Dietrichstein, who – as seen in a previous chapter – was favorably disposed toward Albert. Visconti and his allies evidently accomplished their task especially well, for the negotiations between Rudolf and Matthias ended in a provisional compromise in June, 1608. Rudolf kept the imperial crown and Matthias was declared king of Hungary and heir to the kingdom of Bohemia, which strongly increased his chances at the succession.[113] Even so, nothing concrete was arranged concerning the succession itself. Both Matthias as well as Albert stayed in the running, and the latter clearly did not plan to throw the towel into the ring. In March, 1609, he sent the marquis of Marnay to Rome in a final attempt to convince the pope after all of the necessity for elevating him to king of Burgundy.[114] As seen in Chapter IV already, Marnay was one of Albert's most beloved courtiers. It need not come as a surprise, then, that precisely this nobleman was selected to carry out this kind of important and top-secret mission. Even Herman van Ortenberg, the archducal emissary to the Holy See, was not informed of Marnay's instructions. He reported that the marquis had got two audiences with the pope and three with the cardinal-nephew, yet did not appear to know what precisely was discussed.[115] Not until May did he discover the true story, when the pope told him that the international political situation was to delicate too be able to give Albert the title of king.[116]

It was the umpteenth setback for the archduke. Albert enjoyed the support of a few electors, to be sure, yet he did not succeed in acquiring a kingdom. On top of that, he realized that the Holy Roman Empire stood at the edge of a civil war. The compromise between Rudolf and Matthias had only made matters worse. The emperor had also gathered troops together in the meantime. Everywhere in the Holy Roman Empire sides were being taken for this party or that – not least of all on the basis of religious interests. More than his own defeat, Albert feared that the Habsburg dynasty would lose the imperial crown. In 1610, he sent Octavio Visconti to a specially convened convocation of princes, where the electoral princes as well as the archdukes Maximilian and Ferdinand were present to discuss the crisis. Visconti's secret instructions read that Albert would support the succession of Rudolf by Matthias if no unanimity were reached concerning a possible solution. For the time being, however, Visconti was not supposed to make this concession public. After months of negotiations the convention ended with symbolic recognition of Rudolf's authority and his promise to withdraw his troops. The problem of succession was still hanging in the air, to be sure, but would be cleared up not long after that.[117]

[113] *Ibidem.*
[114] Duerloo, *Dynasty and Piety*, 269.
[115] ARA, *Aud* 444, f. 72: Herman van Ortenberg to Filips Prats, May 15, 1609.
[116] ARA, *Aud* 444, f. 96: Herman van Ortenberg to Filips Prats, May 30, 1609.
[117] Duerloo, *Dynasty and Piety*, 272-273.

In May, 1611, Matthias was crowned king of Bohemia, and in December he married his niece Anna, a daughter of Ferdinand of Tyrol. These were the last feats necessary to secure his position as successor to the throne. In pretty much all respects Matthias had kept up with Albert and even surpassed him. The archduke finally resigned himself to the situation. He sent the count of Solre to the wedding banquet to congratulate the bridal couple. During the political negotiations following the wedding, Solre conveyed that Albert had agreed to give up his claim on the imperial crown.[118] Thenceforth the archduke would support Matthias' candidacy. When Rudolf died on January 20, 1612, the electoral college proved to be divided, all the same. Some electors opted for Matthias, yet others continued to see Albert as the better choice. Bizarrely enough, Albert had to use all his powers of persuasion to convince the electors *not* to vote for him.[119] That came from the lips of Count Wratislas von Fürstenberg, again a *gentilhombre de la Cámara*, who was visiting the electors of Mainz, Trier, Saxony, and the Palatinate.[120] His mission consisted of getting the doubters to toe the line and admonishing them to support Matthias' candidacy fully. This intervention appears to have been decisive. On June 13, 1612, Matthias was elected emperor of the Holy Roman Empire.

The story concerning the succession of Rudolf II knows many nuances and deserves more attention than it can get within the set-up of this chapter. Yet this short sketch is necessary, if only to demonstrate that Albert's courtiers played a central role in this process. It is decidedly no coincidence that the archduke engaged his own *gentilhombres* to represent himself to the pope, the emperor, the Austrian archdukes, and the electors. More than with any other political objective whatsoever, Albert was committed to the maintenance of Habsburg authority. He had his personal ambitions, to be sure, but when push came to shove, dynastic interests came first. Precisely in order to defend these interests, he made use of a few of his most trustworthy courtiers: Francisco de Mendoza, Octavio Visconti, the count of Fürstenberg, the count of Solre, and the marquis of Marnay. Their diplomatic and as a rule secret missions can stand as examples for a bold proposition. The archduke had a large number of diplomats and jurists at his disposal who could represent him outside the walls of the court, to be sure, yet the really crucial missions – such as these in which his dynastic position or the preservation of the August House of Austria was at risk – were pretty much always carried out by the *gentilhombres de la Cámara*. They enjoyed Albert's fullest confidence and were expected to defend his interests as well as possible. The instructions that the archduke had drawn up on the occasion of the princes' convention in 1610,

[118] Correspondence concerning Solre's mission can be found in ARA, *DuiS* 434.
[119] Duerloo, *Dynasty and Piety*, 279-280.
[120] AGS, *Estado* 2294, s.f.: The marquis of Guadaleste to Philip III, April 5, 1612.

not coincidentally, read that Octavio Visconti was supposed to speak in the name of Albert as if the latter were present there in person.[121] The *gentilhombres* were expected to act, in other words, as Albert's deputies – they functioned almost literally as his mouthpiece.

Courtiers in diplomacy

That many courtiers of Albert and Isabella fulfilled an important function as diplomats is a fact that only seldom comes up for discussion among historians. Still, their contribution to the regime can be underestimated only with difficulty. A character like Octavio Visconti, for example, has never been studied before in detail, while he nevertheless must be seen as one of the top diplomats of the archdukes. He was quite active, above all, in the Holy Roman Empire and in the negotiations with the electors. So, for instance, he traveled in the name of Albert to Wesel in 1614, where a conference was convened by the United Provinces and the elector of Cologne in the hope of solving the succession crisis in the duchies of Jülich and Cleves.[122] Once again, it would lead too far afield to expose this especially complex historical episode down to the details. Suffice it to say that the crisis, which turned on the fiercely fought-for possession of the strategically situated duchies, constituted a serious threat to political and religious stability in the Rhineland and, by refraction, to the entire Habsburg imperium – including the Southern Netherlands.[123] When Visconti's mediation proved to be fruitless and it looked more and more like the bickering parties would reach for their arms, he was sent to Madrid in all haste to inform Philip III about the conditions on the ground, '*como persona de tanta experiencia y platica de las cosas de por acá*.'[124] He got the commission to convince the king to provide 200,000 *escudos* and to send at least 13,300 infantry soldiers in order to defuse the crisis, and to do so as swiftly as possible.[125]

Visconti was one of the most important, yet certainly not the only *gentilhombre* who accomplished his diplomatic tasks excellently. A few examples may suffice. Already pointed to above was Philippe de Croÿ, count of Solre, who showed himself to be especially active in the area of foreign relations. Thus, for example, he was sent

[121] ARA, *DuiS* 437, s.f.: Albert to Octavio Visconti, February 24, 1610.

[122] AGS, *Estado* 2296, s.f.: Ambrogio Spínola to Philip III, July 11, 1614; *Ibidem*, s.f.: The marquis of Guadaleste to Philip III, July 11, 1614. For the correspondence between Albert and Visconti, see ARA, *DuiS* 437.

[123] For a recent overview, see Anderson, A.D. *On the Verge of War: International Relations and the Jülich-Kleve Succession Crises (1609–1614)*. Boston, 1999.

[124] AGS, *Estado* 2296, s.f.: Albert to Philip III, July 9, 1614.

[125] *Ibidem*.

by Albert to the Spanish court in 1604, in order to render an explanation to the king and Lerma concerning the touchy situation which the Netherlands were in, 'of which you [= Solre] are so well informed that, without any other instruction, you could give such a particular account of it that nothing would have to be added.'[126] Indeed, Solre was quick to respond and presented the king with an extensive document that summed up a number of points which, according to him, could lead to a solution to the political impasse in the Low Countries.[127] The count, however, did not shrink back from letting his own political standpoints shine through. In addition to more money and a punctual disbursement of the combat pay, in his opinion there was need, above all, for a more balanced appointment policy in the army. According to Solre, too many Spanish captains were being sent to the Netherlands, and local nobles had too little opportunity for promotion. Should the king want to preserve the support of the aristocracy in the Southern Netherlands, then he needed to see to it that they, too, got positions in the top ranks of the army.[128] Although the *Consejo de Estado* went along with most of Solre's observations, the councilors were, not coincidentally, hardly excited with his comments concerning the surfeit of Spanish captains.[129] Here again it turns out that, according to the members of the *Consejo*, the interests of the Castilian aristocracy in the *Ejército de Flandes* had to be safeguarded, whatever it might cost.

Another *gentilhombre* who carried out an important diplomatic mission was nobody less than Charles, princely count of Arenberg. He was sent to London in 1603 to put the peace negotiations with England on the right track – a commission in which much was at risk as well.[130] The death of Queen Elizabeth I in 1603 and her succession by James I Stuart gave occasion for a slow thaw in the relations between the courts in Brussels and London. During the past decades England had pretty much always taken the side of the United Provinces, yet when James took up office, the time seemed ripe for new talks.[131] Charles of Arenberg got the commission to cross the Channel and congratulate the king on his accession to the throne. In view of the fact that Spain dallied for a long time in sending an official emissary, the count

[126] '*(...) dont vous [= Solre] estes si bien informé que, sans aultre instruction, vous pourriez de vous mesme en donner compte si particulier qu'il n'y auroit rien à y adjouster.*' Cf. Brants, V., ed. *Une mission à Madrid de Philippe de Croy, comte de Solre, envoyé des archiducs en 1604*. In: *Bulletin de la Commission Royale d'Histoire*, 77 (1908) 185-203. Op. cit. p. 193. See also CODOIN, vol. XLII, p. 519: Albert to Lerma, October 11, 1604.

[127] AGS, *Estado* 2024, s.f.: The count of Solre to Philip III, s.d. [1605].

[128] *Ibidem*.

[129] AGS, *Estado* 2023, no. 132: Consult of the *Consejo de Estado*, March 5, 1605.

[130] Cuvelier, J. 'Les préliminaires du traité de Londres (29 août 1604).' *Revue belge de Philologie et d'Histoire*, 2 (1923) 279-304 and 485-508.

[131] Croft, P. 'Brussels and London: The Archdukes, Robert Cecil and James I,' in: Thomas, W. & Duerloo, L., eds. *Albert & Isabella, 1598-1621: Essays*. Turnhout, 1998, pp. 79-86.

was the only representative of the Spanish-Habsburg dynasty in London for several months.[132] That meant that the negotiations for a possible peace on the Habsburg side were pretty much exclusively directed from the archducal court, and not from Spain. The archdukes could not lay as much money and bribes on the table as the representatives of the Republic, to be sure, but they did know how to compensate amply for this lack by way of a tactic that the latter could not touch: the exchange of gifts between sovereign princes. And precisely in this area Arenberg played a central role. After all, he was the archdukes' grand falconer and in the name of Albert and Isabella gave James a few splendid birds of prey – a gift that James as an ardent hunter could appreciate to the utmost.[133] James' spouse, Anne of Denmark was not forgotten either: she received two portraits of Albert and Isabella.[134] The importance of these kinds of gifts is all too frequently overlooked in the historiography concerning the archducal regime. Even so, it is precisely these exquisite shows of benevolence that contributed to a slow normalization of the relationship between the Stuarts and the Habsburgs. Asked what Anne could do in exchange, Arenberg said that he hoped the queen would commit herself to effecting peace and to putting a stop to the financial support from England to the United Provinces.[135]

The list of courtiers who carried out diplomatic missions is much longer still. In 1613, the archduke sent Count Frederik van den Berg, captain of the halberdiers, to the Holy Roman Empire to represent him at the Imperial Diet in Regensburg. According to the papal nuncio, the count was able to have this commission, above all, thanks to 'the quality of his family,' which had many relatives in the German empire, and to the fact that he spoke the German language – two conditions '*che non sono di picciol momento per far credere ch'egli debba essar ben venduto, e che sia per haver miglioro mezzi alla introduttione di tutti le cose occorenti.*'[136] In 1606, the count of Sainte-Aldegonde, *mayordomo* of the archdukes, was sent to London to congratulate James I on his escape from the so-called Gun Powder Plot. At the same time Sainte-Aldegonde was supposed to plead that James not take out his rage on the Catholics.[137] In 1616, Francisco de Ibarra, *gentilhombre de la Cámara* and son of Diego de Ibarra, went on a mission to the grand duke of Tuscany, where he should strike up talks, as charged by Albert, concerning the Catholic League in the Holy Roman Empire.[138] Gilles du

[132] *Ibidem.*
[133] HHStA, *Belgien*, PC 44: Charles of Arenberg to Albert, August 1, 1603.
[134] HHStA, *Belgien*, PC 44: Charles of Arenberg to Albert, September 24, 1603.
[135] *Ibidem.*
[136] BAV, *BaL* 6808, f. 164: Bentivoglio to Borghese, April 20, 1613.
[137] ASV, *Borghese* II 108, f. 72: Frangipani to Borghese, April 15, 1606.
[138] NA, *SP* 77/12, f. 24: William Trumbull to the secretary of State, March 14, 1616.

Faing, one of Albert's *gentilhombres de la Boca*, was quite an active diplomat as well.[139] When Philip III had sought someone to go to negotiate with King Christian IV in Denmark in 1612, Albert proposed sending du Faing. According to the archduke, the nobleman of Luxembourg descent had at his disposal 'the characteristics that are necessary' for that kind of commission.[140] On top of that, du Faing had journeyed to Denmark once already as commissioned by Albert, '*empleado por mi en cosas de importancia*,' and at that time had accomplished his task quite well.[141] Consequently it was not du Faing's first commission as a diplomat, nor would it be his last.[142] When Ambrogio Spínola wrote him a recommendation in 1616, according to du Faing himself he had not less than 23 diplomatic missions behind him.[143]

The tendency is clear. Albert's *gentilhombres* were no ennobled chamber servants but were actively utilized in international diplomacy. As representatives and emissaries they played a decisive role in the foreign policy of the archduke. As even seen in certain cases, the courtiers entered first in order to break the ice and discuss the most prominent points, after which the jurists and technocrats appeared on the stage to work out the details. That was the case, for example, during the peace negotiations with England in 1603-1604, where Charles of Arenberg laid out the agreement in principle, and Jean Richardot and the *audiencier* Louis Verreycken joined him afterward to discuss the concrete conditions.[144] In the same way, the negotiations with the pope concerning the title of king were not left to Herman van Ortenberg, the archducal emissary to the Holy See, but to the marquis of Marnay, who specially journeyed to Rome for this. Only afterward – when it turned out that the pope would not concede – was Ortenberg allowed to know what the talks were precisely about. It speaks for itself that not all the diplomatic missions of the *gentilhombres* were as important as those that are summed up here. The courtiers were also sent out whenever condolences or congratulations had to be passed on to friendly courts. Thus, in 1616 for instance, the prince of Ligne departed for Paris to congratulate Louis XIII on his marriage.[145] And in 1612, the count of Megem went to Lorraine to give condolences

[139] Gilles du Faing was also the author of the report that was written up on the occasion of Albert's journey to Spain in 1598-1599. This report was published in in Gachard, L.-P. & Piot, C., eds. *Voyage de l'archiduc Albert en Espagne*. In: Gachard, L.-P. & Piot, C., eds. *Collection des voyages des souverains des Pays-Bas*. 4 vols. Brussels, 1876-1882. Volume IV, pp. 457-562; and in de Reiffenberg, F.A.F., ed. *Itinéraire de l'archiduc Albert, de la reine d'Espagne Marguérite d'Autriche et de l'infante Isabelle, en 1599 et 1600, tiré d'une relation contemporaine et manuscrite*. In: *Nouveaux Mémoires de l'Académie Royale des Sciences et Belles-Lettres de Bruxelles*, 14 (1841) 3-33.

[140] AGS, *Estado* 2026, s.f.: Albert to Philip III, March 23, 1612.

[141] *Ibidem*.

[142] AGS, *Estado* 2296, s.f.: Albert to Philip III, July 9, 1614.

[143] AGS, *Estado* 2300, s.f.: Spínola to Philip III, August 13, 1616.

[144] Croft, P. 'Brussels and London,' 81-82.

[145] ASV, *Borghese* II 102, f. 340: Nuncio Ascanio Gesualdo to Borghese, October 29, 1616.

to the duchess on the death of her father, the duke of Mantua.[146] It is clear that these kinds of procedures did not immediately carry the highest political priority – even though the importance of them may not be underestimated, either. They contributed to the maintenance of good relations with the other European princes and in that sense belonged to the customs of early modern diplomacy. Nevertheless it is clear that the most weighty missions were left only to the most trustworthy persons. In these kinds of cases the importance of the message could already be 'read from' the political status of its bearer. So, for example, no one less than Peter Paul Rubens could announce in 1627, that Ambrogio Spínola was just about to depart for Spain, and although the artist did not know what Spínola's mission entailed precisely, according to him it could be not be other than extremely important, '*secondo la qualità del messagiero*.'[147]

Conclusion

In 1617, the English ambassador William Trumbull sent a list of important persons in the Archducal Netherlands to London. He began his overview with the military commanders in the *Ejército de Flandes*, subsequently mentioned the members of the Collateral Councils and the Council of Brabant, after that summed up the most prominent courtiers, and ended with the provincial governors and the commandants of the fortified citadels.[148] The self-evident nature with which Trumbull placed the different groups next to one another may stand as characteristic of the fact that the archducal household in this time period was seen not as a separate political sphere but as one of the established structures of power that an early modern principality had at its disposal. Yet historians of the archducal regime have always exhibited the inclination to assign the courtiers to a separate category, as if their contribution to decision-making would have deviated too much from the 'standard' *modus operandi* of early modern politics. After all, the activities of the archducal household were not

[146] BAV, *BaL* 6806, f. 195: Bentivoglio to Borghese, April 28, 1612.

[147] Rooses, M. & Ruelens, C., eds. *Codex Diplomaticus Rubenianus. Correspondance de Rubens et documents épistolaires concernant sa vie et ses œuvres.* 6 vols. Antwerp, 1887-1909. Op. cit. vol. IV, p. 332: Rubens to Pierre Dupuy, December 3, 1627.

[148] For the most important courtiers, Trumbull mentions, successively, the count of Añover, the duke of Aarschot, the marquis of Havré, the prince of Chimay, the prince of Épinoy, the duke of Aumale, the count of Cantecroix, the prince of Ligne, the marquis of Roubaix, the prince of Barbançon, Diego Mexía, the count of Sainte-Aldegonde, Ferdinand d'Andelot, Adrien de Noyelles, the baron of Frenz, the duke of Boussu, and the count of Izegem. Further, he mentions also the court controller Charles de Hertoghe, the treasurer Antonio de Rovelasca, the secretaries Antonio Suárez de Arguello and Theodore Piespord, and both of the *guardaropa y joyas* of the archdukes. NA, *SP* 77/12, f. 447: William Trumbull to the secretary of State, s.d. [1617].

in keeping with a vision in which the early modern state was treated as the harbinger of the modern bureaucratic state, and in which politics was neatly practiced in the institutions and channels provided for that purpose.

That this kind of anachronistic vision cannot suffice for unraveling the complexity of decision-making in the Archducal Netherlands is clear. Just as in other European principalities, the intertwining of *domus* and *res publica* was even much greater than is generally assumed. As was the custom with early modern princes, the archduke had himself surrounded by an entourage of intimates who advised him in his policy decisions and who could represent him outside the walls of the court. In doing so, it was not only about Ambrogio Spínola, Iñigo de Brizuela, and Juan de Mancisidor – figures who already have been able to count on the requisite attention in the historiography – but also about the *gentilhombres de la Cámara* – whose political role was symbolized by the golden key. Members of the archducal household fully participated in the business of politics and were consciously engaged in military and administrative domains. Even more, they belonged to the most important diplomats whom Albert could send out so as to defend his interests and those of the Habsburg dynasty.

The developments sketched in this chapter with regard to the factional conflict at court demonstrate, on top of that, that political oppositions during the archducal regime are all too frequently – and in general implicitly – connected with the presupposed 'national struggle for emancipation,' while on the contrary they were defined by a complex whole of political, personal, and financial interests. In the same way the swearing of oaths in 1616 is generally seen as the final defeat for the archdukes with respect to Philip III, while it concerned much more a collaboration for making the continued existence of the Habsburg regime in the Southern Netherlands secure. In that sense it would do well to study the policies of Albert and Isabella from the aspect of dynasty, much more than that of striving for political autonomy. After all, the excessive attention to the relationship between the archducal and Spanish courts has led to the fact that other important topics have become snowed under. Thus, it is clear, for instance, that the political motivations of the archdukes have seldom or never been connected with events happening in the Holy Roman Empire. In the same way, the Eighty Years' and Thirty Years' War are studied as separate conflicts, while the connection between both phenomena was much more important than is presupposed.

The case studies discussed in this chapter, on top of that, can show that the origins of the *gentilhombres* scarcely played a role when it was a matter of representing the archduke in the outside world. As opposed to what would perhaps be expected, the messengers whom Albert sent to the Spanish court were sometimes from Spain (such as Brizuela, e.g.), or sometimes from the Southern Netherlands (Solre), or sometimes from Italy (Visconti). In the negotiations concerning the election of the emperor, to be sure, the archduke made use of the services of the count of Fürstenberg – whose family came from the Holy Roman Empire – yet just as well of those services of Mendoza, Solre, Visconti, and Marnay. In other words, it was a question of sending courtiers who had already proven their loyalty repeatedly with respect to Albert and the Habsburg dynasty, and who for that reason enjoyed the fullest confidence. How this exceptional form of trust in one well-defined case resulted in exceptional political power and influence is shown in the sixth and final chapter.

Chapter VI
The Archduke's *Gran Privado*

'Above all [Albert] took care that no one claimed so much Authority for himself, that he would steer even a portion of the common weal, much less the entire State, according to his own caprice. Formerly Spain had its Alvarez Luna, and recently a Calderon; France, a Concini; England, an Essex; and Germany, a Klesl; other Regions at other times had brought their own Sejanuses as objects of mockery onto the World-stage. And while rumors of these kinds of things have indeed been abided in the Netherlands, still they have never seen examples of them in their own Bosom. It was [Albert] alone who did everything befitting a great Prince.'[1]

Aubertus Miraeus
De vita Alberti Pii

In February, 1619, the court in Brussels was making ready for the reception of the Spanish nobleman Don García de Pareja.[2] Three years earlier Pareja – who had the reputation of being one of the duke of Lerma's creatures – had journeyed once already to the Southern Netherlands to steer the swearing of oaths by the provincial States to Philip III in the right direction.[3] On that occasion he had been appointed by Albert and Isabella to *mayordomo* in the archducal household, an honorary function that he now – perhaps not coincidentally shortly after the fall of Lerma – wanted to take up effectively. Through Pareja's own fault, however, the reception that fell to him in turn at court was anything but cordial. Shortly after his arrival in Brussels, the local courtiers had gone to greet him.[4] The delegation was led by Rodrigo Niño y Lasso (ca. 1560-1620), count of Añover, who as the *mayordomo mayor, sumiller de corps*, and *caballerizo mayor* exercised supervision over pretty much all members of the archducal household. Añover's visit was intended as a show of courtesy toward Pareja, yet evidently the latter was not quite impressed. In a burst of recklessness he dared to address the count with '*Vuestra Merced*' instead of the more respectful '*Vuestra*

[1] After Miraeus, A. *De vita Alberti Pii, sapientis, prudentis Belgarum Principis commentarius*. Antwerp, 1622, p. 105.

[2] ASV, *Borghese* II 105, f. 41: Nuncio Lucio Morra to Cardinal-Secretary of State Borghese, February 9, 1619.

[3] Concerning this swearing of oaths, see Chapter V and Lonchay, H. 'Le serment de fidélité prêté par les Belges à Philippe III en 1616,' in: *Mélanges Paul Fréderica. Hommage de la Société pour le progrès des études philologiques et historiques*. Brussels, 1904, pp. 311-317.

[4] ASV, *Borghese* II 105, f. 52: Morra to Borghese, February15, 1619.

Señoría Illustrissima,' which in the eyes of contemporaries was a grave infraction of etiquette and, consequently, a crude insult.[5] Severely indignant, Añover went to the archduke to make his complaint, who did not hesitate to give his *mayordomo mayor* satisfaction. Even within the hour Pareja got to hear that his services were no longer desired at court. He got the commission to leave the country on the spot. Pareja was confounded. His request to speak with the archduke was bluntly rejected. A few days later he was already on his way back to Spain. His stay in Brussels had not lasted a week.[6]

The incident did not go by unnoticed at court. It gave the members of the *corps diplomatique* something to gnaw on. The French ambassador Jean Péricard noted that it was highly unusual for the archduke to make these kinds of ponderous decisions in such a short period of time, 'in less than an hour without further consideration.'[7] Albert's fierce reaction can indeed be called surprising. Although conflicts of protocol were seldom taken up airily in early modern society, the impression is that the nature of the punishment in this case was inversely proportional to the nature of the crime. That notwithstanding, the nuncio Lucio Morra reported that the archduke's strict verdict could count on much agreement from the courtiers and, according to him, that was nothing more than logical.[8] Morra declared that Añover was a man of great importance at court, who could not be hurt without repercussions. After all, the count was '*amatissimo da tutta la Corte*' and, on top of that, '*amato e stimato grandemente*' by both Albert as well as Isabella, with whom he was '*in grandissima privanza*.'[9]

Nuncio Morra was certainly not the only one who was convinced of the privileged status that the count of Añover enjoyed at court. Already in 1604, his predecessor Frangipani noted that Rodrigo Niño y Lasso was an '*intimo del Señor Arciduca*.'[10] In 1612, Charles Somerset described him in his travel journal as '*the Counte of Añaver* [sic], *one of the Archdukes greatest favourites*.'[11] In that same year the English ambassador Thomas Edmondes kept it to '*a man of great account among the Spaniards*.'[12] Two years later the nuncio Bentivoglio noted that the count was '*di grandissima auttorità in questa Corte*.'[13] In 1617, then again, Bentivoglio's successor Morra described him

5 *Ibidem*.

6 *Ibidem*.

7 '*(...) au bout d'une heure sans plus longue considération*.' BNF, *MsF* 16132: Jean Péricard to the secretary of State Pierre Brulart, marquis of Puisieux, February 15, 1619.

8 ASV, *Borghese* II 105, f. 52: Morra to Borghese, February 15, 1619.

9 *Ibidem*.

10 ASV, *Borghese* III 110 BCDG, f. 87: Ottavio Mirto Frangipani to Cardinal Aldobrandini, February 14, 1604.

11 Brennan, M.G., ed. *The Travel Diary (1611-1612) of an English Catholic Sir Charles Somerset, edited from the manuscript in the Brotherton Collection University of Leeds*. Leeds, 1993, p. 292.

12 NA, *SP* 77/10, f. 193: Thomas Edmondes to the count of Salisbury, July 10, 1612.

13 ASV, *Borghese* II 99, f. 324: Guido Bentivoglio to Cardinal Borghese, May 17, 1614.

as a '*cavaliero di tanto merito et auttorità, che non può esser maggiore en esta corte.*'[14] A few months later Morra referred to the count as the archducal '*primo ministro, e'l più potente in questa Corte,*' and as a man '*di gran valore, e di gran credito.*'[15] Again, in another letter the nuncio posited that Añover was a '*ministro di tanta auttorità,*' who certainly had to be kept as a friend by the Holy See because 'his authority here is greater than that of the duke of Lerma in Spain.'[16] In 1619, the French geographer Pierre Bergeron determined that 'the one who is the favorite of the archduke and who governs and deals with all sorts of matters under him, is a count of Ognavel or Agnovel, a Spaniard of a great house.'[17] In 1620, finally, the English ambassador William Trumbull referred explicitly to Añover as the archduke's 'grand *privado.*'[18]

These and similar commentaries leave little doubt that Rodrigo Niño y Lasso was seen by his contemporaries as one of the most beloved and powerful courtiers in Brussels, *and* as a special favorite of Archduke Albert. Their word choice leaves little to the imagination. Not coincidentally, the Spanish term *privado* (or also *valido*) referred in the late sixteenth and the seventeenth century to persons who enjoyed the exceptional favor and/or affection of the prince, and who for that reason were in the position to climb to the highest spheres of power. In modern historiography the overarching yet vague term 'princely favorites' is generally employed to describe this phenomenon. Its definition is necessarily problematic. On account of the fickle character of princely favor there were different types of favorites, who clearly cannot all be painted with the same brush. In that context John Adamson argues,

> 'Though contemporaries used terminology promiscuously – referring to the 'favourite', *valido*, or *privado*, almost synonymously – the phenomenon occurred in a variety of distinct types: from 'minister-favourites' such as Richelieu or Olivares; sexual favourites who also exercised ministerial power, such as James I's erstwhile lover, the Duke of Buckingham; even kinsman-favourites, such as the *nipoti* of Renaissance popes.'[19]

---

14 ASV, *Borghese* II 137, f. 43: Lucio Morra to Borghese, September 1, 1617.

15 ASV, *Borghese* II 112, f. 115: Morra to Borghese, 24 February 1618 and f. 133: Morra to Borghese, March 10, 1618.

16 ASV, *Borghese* II 112, f. 162: Morra to Borghese, March 17, 1618.

17 '*Celuy qui est le favory de l'archiduc et qui gouverne et traicte toutes sortes d'affaires sous luy, c'est un comte d'Ognavel ou Agnovel, espagnol de grande maison.*' Michelant, H., ed. *Voyage de Pierre Bergeron ès Ardennes, Liège et Pays-Bas en 1619.* Liège, 1875. Op. cit. p. 345.

18 NA, *SP* 77/14, f. 224: William Trumbull to Dudley Carleton, October 15, 1620.

19 See the discussion in Adamson, J. 'The Making of the Ancien-Régime Court, 1500-1700,' in: Adamson, J., ed. *The Princely Courts of Europe. Ritual, Politics and Culture under the Ancien Régime 1500-1750.* London, 1999, pp. 7-41. Op. cit. pp. 19-20.

Nevertheless a consensus dominates in the literature on the matter, which posits that favorites generally exhibited a number of specific characteristics, such as the ability to usurp high positions in the princely household and to control access to the prince. Frequently, too, they held the patronage of the prince firmly in their hands. Doing so, they were in the position of building up an extended network of clients, who in their turn had an interest in supporting their patrons in their positions of power. The result was that these *validos* could gather together immeasurable riches as well as keep a quasi-princely lifestyle.[20]

Scholarly research into favoritism in early modern politics has been causing some commotion in very recent years. After a long time of being stuck in a paradigm in which the appearance of the *valido* was seen as symptomatic for the weak policies of the so-called *rois fainéants*, since the 1990s the phenomenon has been approached from a more structural angle.[21] In 1999, John H. Elliott and Laurence Brockliss published the influential collection *The World of the Favourite*, compiling essays about the development of the so-called *valimiento* (i.e. the 'reign' of a *valido*) in the period 1550-1650.[22] Based on an older hypothesis by Jean Bérenger, the authors aimed to demonstrate that a) the spectacular rise of prominent minister-favorites like Cardinal Richelieu, the count-duke of Olivares, and the duke of Buckingham points to the existence of a time-bound phenomenon that arose in several European principalities in the first half of the seventeenth century, and b) that this phenomenon can be seen as a specific phase in the early modern process of state-building.[23] Briefly summarized, their theory consisted of the notion that the rise of the *valido* offered an answer to the growing complexity of the state apparatus. The *valimiento*, according to these authors, was therefore an unavoidable and even necessary stage in the transition from the medieval principality to the modern state. Although this theory has experienced much emulation in the meantime, it has not remained spared from criticism.[24] In 2004, the conference proceedings for *Der Fall des Günstlings* ['The Fall of the Favorite'] appeared, in which the standpoint was taken that favorites are of every era and occurred in a sixteenth- or seventeenth-century context in no way exclusively:

---

[20] See Kettering, S. *Power and Reputation at the Court of Louis XIII. The Career of Charles d'Albert, Duc de Luynes (1578-1621).* Manchester U.P., 2008.

[21] Wirth Marvick, E. 'Favorites in Early Modern Europe: A Recurring Psychopolitical Role.' *The Journal of Psychohistory*, 10 (1983) 463-489; Adams, S. 'Favourites and Factions at the Elizabethan Court,' in: Asch, R.G. & Birke, A.M., eds. *Princes, Patronage, and the Nobility: The Court at the Beginning of the Modern Age, c.1450-1650.* Oxford U.P., 1991, pp. 265-287; Jouanna, A. 'Faveur et favoris: l'exemple des mignons de Henri III,' in: Sauzet, R., ed. *Henri III et son temps*. Paris, 1992, pp. 155-165; Benigno, F. *La sombra del Rey. Validos y lucha politica en la España del siglo XVII.* Madrid, 1994.

[22] Elliott, J.H. & Brockliss, L.W.B., eds. *The World of the Favourite*. London-New Haven, 1999.

[23] Bérenger, J. 'Pour une enquête européenne: le problème du ministériat au XVIIe siècle,' in: *Annales. Economies, Sociétés, Civilisations*, 29 (1974) 166-192.

[24] See e.g. Escudero López, J.A., ed. *Los validos*. Madrid, 2005.

'Every regime that rests on favor [will] produce favorites over and over, whether in Antiquity, the Middle Ages, or Modernity,' Werner Paravicini argued in that regard.[25]

The discussion sketched here – about which more to follow – is only one example of the fundamental problems with which research into favoritism in the early modern period is confronted. In addition to the debate over the presupposed uniqueness of the phenomenon in the sixteenth and seventeenth centuries, its correct definition also remains especially problematic ('in times of political stability, we speak of 'ministers', in times of instability, we speak of 'favorites' ').[26] On top of that, the research is directed all too frequently toward the most famous and powerful figures, who generally are not very representative for the topic as a whole.[27] The Spanish *valimiento* is seen as typical as well for the phenomenon in all its forms, while it is entirely unknown how this quasi-institutionalized favoritism was exactly related to the rise of favorites in other European countries – and in particular at smaller princely courts.[28] The few attempts at a comparative approach therefore seldom succeed in making true on their expectations.[29] That is lamentable, for fundamental research into the rise of the *valimiento* in less than obvious principalities would bring more clarity not only to the functioning and importance of favoritism in and of itself, but also to the current theories surrounding politics and state-building in the early modern period. In recent years, in order to come closer to this approach, more and more studies are popping up, which are trying to give the scholarly debate a new turn – albeit with varying success.[30] They concentrate above all on the lesser-known *validos* of the sixteenth and seventeenth centuries and, in so doing, employ a very broad definition of the concept.

---

25 Hirschbiegel, J. & Paravicini, W., eds. *Der Fall des Günstlings. Hofparteien in Europa vom 13. bis zum 17. Jahrhundert* (Residenzenforschung 17). Ostfildern, 2004. Op. cit. p. 16.

26 '*(...) en temps de stabilité politique, on parle de 'ministres', en temps d'instabilité, on parle de 'favoris'.*' Lewis, P.S. 'Être au Conseil au XVe siècle,' in: Paviot, J. & Verger, J., eds. *Guerre, pouvoir et noblesse au Moyen Age. Mélanges en l'honneur de Philippe Contamine*. Paris, 2000, pp. 461-469.

27 See e.g., Elliott, J.H. *The Count-Duke of Olivares. The Statesman in an Age of Decline*. New Haven-London, 1986; Feros, A. *Kingship and Favoritism in the Spain of Philip III 1598-1621*. Cambridge U.P., 2000; Williams, P. *The Great Favourite. The Duke of Lerma and the Court and Government of Philip III of Spain, 1598-1621*. Manchester U.P., 2006.

28 Feros, A. 'Lerma y Olivares. La práctica del valimiento en la primera mitad del seiscientos,' in: Elliott, J.H. & García Sanz, A., eds. *La España del Conde-Duque de Olivares*. Valladolid, 1990, pp. 195-224; Feros, A. 'Twin Souls: Monarchs and Favourites in Early Seventeenth-Century Spain,' in: Kagan, R.L. & Parker, G., eds. *Spain, Europe and the Atlantic World*. Cambridge U.P., 1995, pp. 27-47.

29 Watanabe-O'Kelly, H. 'Der Fall des Günstlings. Hofparteien in Europa vom 13. bis zum 17. Jahrhundert (book review).' *The English Historical Review*, 121 (2006) 1529-1530.

30 See e.g. Kaiser, M. & Pečar, A., eds. *Der Zweite Mann im Staat. Oberste Amtsträger und Favoriten im Umkreis der Reichsfürsten in der Frühen Neuzeit* (Zeitschrift für Historische Forschung, Beiheft 32). Berlin, 2003; Onnekink, D. *The Anglo-Dutch Favourite: The Career of Hans Willem Bentinck, 1st Earl of Portland (1649-1709)*. Aldershot, 2007; and the afore-mentioned Kettering, S. *Power and Reputation at the Court of Louis XIII. The Career of Charles d'Albert, Duc de Luynes (1578-1621)*. Manchester U.P., 2008.

The chapter at hand consciously seeks to connect with this new movement in research, which desires to study early modern favoritism from a more holistic approach.

That Rodrigo Niño y Lasso can be seen as the 'minister-favorite' of Albert and Isabella is a conviction shared by many contemporaries. It is, then, remarkable that the count of Añover has never got a lot of attention from historians. The fact that his authority in historical sources was not only compared to but was even estimated as *higher* than that of the duke of Lerma – the all-powerful favorite of Philip III – might have aroused at least some interest.[31] As the following sections will show, Añover's prominent position not only offered him the possibility for exercising significant political influence, but it generated enormous riches for him as well. Yet his role has never been the subject of any profound scholarly analysis until today. On the one hand, that has to do with the fact that only a few fractions of his correspondence – spread across different European archives and libraries – have been preserved, which makes the research anything but simple.[32] On the other hand, it turns out, here again, that historiography regarding the reign of Albert and Isabella has concentrated on the traditional and well-circumscribed power structures (i.e. the government institutions that have left behind copious written remains of their meetings), while a rather elusive center of power like the princely household was never seen as politically relevant. As a consequence of this, characters like the count of Añover remained for the large part – and wrongly so – outside the field of vision.

This chapter sets for itself the goal of hauling Rodrigo Niño y Lasso out of the proverbial oubliette and subjecting his long career at the court in Brussels to a thorough study.[33] There is no doubt, after all, that the story of the count of Añover can have important consequences for today's scholarly interpretation of the reign of Albert and Isabella, in which until now little to no attention was given to the impact of favoritism and the so-called politics of intimacy on policy. The chapter consists of four parts. The first section sketches the biographical background and the count's *cursus honorum*. The second section goes deeper into Añover's role as a politician,

[31] Concerning the role of the duke of Lerma as favorite of Philip III, see the mentioned works by Feros, *Kingship and Favoritism in the Spain of Philip III,* and Williams, *The Great Favourite.*

[32] It is here, namely, a matter of Añover's political and diplomatic correspondence. Despite the requisite efforts my search for the private correspondence of Rodrigo Niño y Lasso produced no result. The Algemeen Rijksarchief [National Archives of Belgium] in Brussels possesses few documents by his hand, and inquiry to various Spanish archival institutions and to the current count of Añover produced just as little. Even so, the Instituto Valencia de Don Juan in Madrid preserves a few interesting manuscripts, among them ms. 26-I-11, which contains Rodrigo's last will and testament as well as an extensive household inventory, and ms. 26-I-9, which deals with the establishment of the *Capilla de las Santas Reliquias* in Cuerva by Rodrigo and his brother Pedro.

[33] See in that context also my introductory study Raeymaekers, D. 'The 'Gran Privado' of Archduke Albert: Rodrigo Niño y Lasso, Count of Añover (c. 1560-1620),' in: Vermeir, R., Fagel, R. & Ebben, M., eds. *Agentes e Identidades en Movimiento. España y los Países Bajos, siglos XV-XVIII.* Madrid, 2011, pp. 129-149.

whereby the focus lies on the importance of access and proximity as well as on the way in which the count used (or abused) his exceptional status to look out for his interests and those of his confederates. The third section will demonstrate that Añover – just like most other favorites – was no stranger to the temptations of power and financial profit issuing from this status. Finally, the fourth section looks at how the case presented here can be harmonized with current scholarly theories surrounding favoritism in early modern politics.

The long path to power

Rodrigo Niño y Lasso was born around 1560, and grew up in Cuerva, a small city in the vicinity of Toledo. Both his parents belonged to the Castilian aristocracy and had made their careers in the service of the Spanish crown.[34] Rodrigo's father, Don Garci Lasso de la Vega y Guzmán – a nephew and namesake of the famous Renaissance poet Garcilaso de la Vega – held various offices under Charles V as well as under Philip II, and out of thanks received the title of knight in the military order of Alcántara. He died around 1567.[35] Rodrigo's mother, Doña Aldonza Niño, was a sister of Cardinal Fernando Niño de Guevara, the archbishop of Seville, and was appointed *guardamayor de las damas* in the household of Queen Anna around 1580. She appears to have been quite a devout woman, who founded the Convento de Nuestra Señora de la Encarnación in Cuerva, on the behalf of the order of the Discalced Carmelites. Doña Aldonza died in 1604.[36] Rodrigo's older brother Pedro Lasso de la Vega (1559-1637), who inherited the familial *señoríos* Cuerva, Arcos and Batres after the death of their father, received his upbringing at the court of Philip II and was subsequently appointed *mayordomo* in the household of Queen Margaret. After the installation of his uncle Fernando as Grand Inquisitor of Spain in 1599, Pedro was elevated to count of Los Arcos. In 1606, the king offered him the position of Spanish ambassador to the imperial court but, surprisingly enough, he declined this offer. In its stead Pedro became *mayordomo* in the household of the crown prince Philip – later Philip IV – an office that he likely kept until his death in 1637.[37]

[34] The history of the Lasso de la Vega family is treated briefly in Martín-Peñato Lázaro, M.J. 'Los Laso de la Vega y su vinculación con la ceca de Toledo,' in: *Numisma*, 250 (2006) 525-535; and Kagan, R.L. 'The Count of Los Arcos as Collector and Patron of El Greco,' in: *Anuario del Departamento de Historia y Teoría del Arte*, IV (1992) 151-159.

[35] Kagan, 'The Count of Los Arcos,' 152.

[36] *Ibidem.*

[37] Kagan, 'The Count of Los Arcos,' 151-153. See also Martínez Millán, J. & Fernández Conti, S., eds. *La Monarquía de Felipe II: La Casa del Rey*. 2 vols. Madrid, 2005. Op. cit. vol. II, p. 241.

Little to nothing is known concerning Rodrigo's childhood. Just like his older brother he was brought up at the royal court in Madrid, where he was *menino* in the household of Queen Anna.[38] As the second son in the Lasso de la Vega family, Rodrigo was obliged to seek out his own path. He was quite a devout young man and appears – perhaps upon his mother's advice – to have played for a time with the idea of entering into the Discalced Carmelites. For unknown reasons, however, he ultimately chose a career in the army. In 1588, he, along with many other Spanish nobles, mustered in on the *Gran Armada* of Philip II.[39] According to Bernardino de Mendoza, the Spanish ambassador in London, Rodrigo went on board the Venetian merchantman *La Trinidad Valencera*, one of the largest ships in the fleet.[40] It transported, among others, a regiment of Neapolitan soldiers led by Colonel Alonso de Luzón. During the passage to England the ship became cut off from the rest of the Armada. In the end it was shipwrecked in Kinnagoe Bay, on the northern coast of Ireland, where it would be recovered by nautical archeologists in 1972. Rodrigo and his fellow officers succeeded in reaching the shore but were lured into an ambush by English troops who robbed them of their possessions. A large number of Spanish soldiers were murdered on the spot. After a march of 100 miles under miserable circumstances, the survivors were locked up in the Irish town of Drogheda.[41] A few weeks later Rodrigo and his companions were brought over to London, where they were placed in custody of Sir Horatio Pallavicini. The latter promised to let them go in exchange for the release of Odet de la Noue, lord of Téligny, a son of the famous military man and author François de la Noue.[42] In view of the fact that Téligny was being held captive at that moment in the Netherlands, Rodrigo got leave to cross the Channel and to strike up negotiations about this with Alexander Farnese, the governor at that time. In the end, the exchange of hostages took place in December, 1589.[43]

After this adventure, Rodrigo served for a time in the *Ejército de Flandes*, the Spanish army in the Netherlands.[44] He made up part of the company of Antonio de Mosquera, which in turn belonged to the regiment of the *maestro de campo* Manuel de

---

[38] Martínez Millán & Fernández Conti, *La Monarquía de Felipe II*, vol. II, p. 694.

[39] Kagan, 'The Count of Los Arcos,' 152.

[40] Mendoza's letters concerning this were published in Hume, M.A.S., ed. *Calendar of State Papers, Spain (Simancas)*, vol. IV (1587-1603). London, 1899. Concerning the discovery of *La Trinidad Valencera* in 1972, see Martin, C. 'La Trinidad Valencera: An Armada Invasion Transport Lost off Donegal,' in: *International Journal of Nautical Archeology*, 8 (1979) 13-38.

[41] The story of the survivors from *La Trinidad Valencera* is given in Martin, C. & Parker, G. *The Spanish Armada*. London, 1988.

[42] Ungerer, G. *A Spaniard in Elizabethan England: The Correspondence of Antonio Pérez's Exile*. 2 vols. London, 1975-1976. Op. cit. vol. I, p. 126, note 14.

[43] Hume, *Calendar of State Papers* (December 1589).

[44] Kagan, 'The Count of Los Arcos,' 154.

Vega.[45] It was said this company was the only one that did not turn to mutiny in this time period on account of the late payment of the combat pay: the Spanish historian Herardo García Rey emphasized that '*siempre esta compañía estuvo firme y constante en el servicio del Rey.*'[46] As the captain *cerca de la persona* ('attached to the person') of Farnese, Rodrigo appears to have taken part in a great number of military campaigns. It is not known precisely when (or why) he returned to the Iberian peninsula, but that occurred likely around the early 1590s. In 1595, after all, he was installed as *gentilhombre de la Cámara* in the household of (at that time still) Cardinal-Archduke Albert.[47] The exact circumstances of this appointment are unclear, but it could be that Rodrigo simply took over the position from his uncle Gabriel Niño, who had held the office for more than ten years and perhaps felt too old to accompany Albert to his new station in Brussels.[48] Whatever it may have been, it seems that the cardinal-archduke could get along well with his new *gentilhombre* from the outset. When Albert and his retinue journeyed later that year to the Low Countries, he gave Rodrigo command over a company of mounted soldiers, with the title of captain of the archducal guard.[49] Scarcely a few years later Rodrigo was already promoted to *sumiller de corps*, whereby he came to stand at the head of Albert's *Cámara*. This position provided him not only unlimited access to the archduke but also the opportunity to control the access of others.[50] The appointment indicates that at this moment he was one of Albert's most prominent – and likely most trusted – courtiers. As *sumiller de corps*, Rodrigo was expected to follow and to serve his master everywhere, even during the latter's most private moments.[51] He had his own apartment at his disposal but usually slept in a separate bed in the archducal bedchamber.[52] It was his duty to help the archduke dress

---

45 García Rey, H. 'Alonso Vázquez, soldado e historiador.' *Boletín de la Real Academia de Bellas Artes y Ciencias Históricas de Toledo*, 11 (1919) 1-25.

46 *Ibidem*, p. 25.

47 See Hortal Muñoz, J.E. 'The Household of Archduke Albert of Austria from his Election as Governor of Flanders until his Investiture as Sovereign Prince of the Low Countries: 1595-1598,' *Revue belge de Philologie et d'Histoire*, in press.

48 Concerning Gabriel Niño, see García Rey, 'Alonso Vázquez,' pp. 22-23; and Martínez Millán, J. 'El Archiduque Alberto en la corte de Felipe II (1570-1580),' in: Thomas, W. & Duerloo, L., eds. *Albert & Isabella, 1598-1621: Essays*. Turnhout, 1998, pp. 27-35. See also Martínez Millán & Fernández Conti, *La Monarquía de Felipe II*, vol. II, pp. 325-236.

49 Roco de Campofrío, J. *España en Flandes. Trece años de gobierno del archiduque Alberto (1598-1608)*. Madrid, 1973. Op. cit. p. 74.

50 The exact date of his appointment is not known. Perhaps Rodrigo took over the position from Maximilian von Dietrichstein, when the latter left the archducal household in 1598. See Hortal, 'The Household of Archduke Albert, in press.

51 Concerning the duties of the *sumiller de corps*, see Mayoral López, R. *La Casa Real de Felipe III (1598-1621). Ordenanzas y Etiquetas*. Unpublished doctoral dissertation, Universidad Autónoma de Madrid, 2007, pp. 215-223. See also Martínez Millán & Fernández Conti, *La Monarquía de Felipe II*, volume I, 569-571.

52 See the travel journal of Johann Wilhelm Neumeir von Ramssla, published as Schayes, A.G.B., ed. *Voyage de Jean-Ernest duc de Saxe en France, en Angleterre et en Belgique*. Trésor national, Receuil historique, littéraire, scientifique, artistique, commercial et industriel, 2e série, III, 1843, pp. 168-254.

in the morning and undress in the evening, as well as to assist him during public and private audiences. The office presupposed consequently a high degree of intimacy, which would only become greater with the years.

One possible reason for Rodrigo's rapid advance at court could possibly consist of the fact that he always showed himself to be an ardent supporter of the Habsburg cause in the Dutch Revolt. So, for example in 1600, he fought side by side with Albert in the famous Battle of Nieuwpoort, which would later acquire renown as one of the bloodiest land battles of the Eighty Years' War. Albert himself could only narrowly escape certain death, and Rodrigo – who as captain of the archduke's personal guard likely was to be found close to the vicinity of his master – was gravely wounded in the neck. According to one source, he was 'found between the dead, so seriously wounded that one supposed all life had flowed out of him.'[53] Three days later it was still thought that he 'would never again answer his letters, for he is so fiercely wounded by an harquebus shot in his throat that there is little hope of recovery.'[54] Yet, wonder of wonders, Rodrigo survived the incident, and it is quite possible that the feat made him rise even more in the archduke's esteem.

In the course of the following years Albert confirmed his confidence in Rodrigo by sending him on important diplomatic missions. So, for instance, he journeyed various times back and forth between the Netherlands and Spain to negotiate disputed political decisions and financial quandaries. That was the case in 1601, among others, when the Spanish troops turned to mutiny on account of their outstanding combat pay.[55] The archduke, feeling the hot breath of the rebels on his neck, sent Rodrigo post-haste to journey to Spain to ask Philip III for additional funds. Although Rodrigo was received with many honors and his message was genuinely listened to, his mission was not quite successful. Financial means were simply scarce. Rodrigo was sent back with what little money could be scraped together in a short time and with the announcement that the king was doing everything to solve the problem.[56] Nevertheless it seems that his careful diplomatic approach went down well in Brussels and in Madrid alike, and he would not wait long for new missions.

In 1604, Rodrigo traveled to Spain anew in order to discuss the financial implications of the persistent war.[57] As opposed to the previous time, the discussions ran anything but smoothly. Once returned to Brussels, he found himself obliged

[53] Roco de Campofrío, *España en Flandes*, 271.
[54] ARA, *Aud* 363, f. 186: Louis Verreycken to the commissioners of Boulogne, July 5, 1600.
[55] AGS, *Estado* 2023, no. 42: Consult of the *Consejo de Estado*, August 18, 1601. See also CODOIN, vol. XLII, pp. 402-403. For more information concerning this mission, see Allen, P.C. *Philip III and the Pax Hispanica, 1598-1621: The Failure of Grand Strategy*. Yale U.P., 2000. Op. cit. pp. 63-64.
[56] Allen, *Philip III and the Pax Hispanica*, 71.
[57] ASV, *Borghese* III 110 BCDG, f. 87: Ottavio Mirto Frangipani to Cardinal Aldobrandini, February 14, 1604.

to announce to his master that the Spanish crown would provide no extra funds, and – even worse – that Philip III desired that Albert should step down as supreme commander of the army.[58] Upon hearing this news Albert and Isabella were gravely taken aback.[59] They declined to believe that the king would saddle them with this kind of scandal and sent Rodrigo immediately back to Madrid to plead their case.[60] The conflict would sicken the atmosphere between both governments for quite some time, yet ultimately a compromise was found. Although Albert was compelled to transfer the actual supreme command to the field commander Ambrogio Spínola, he remained titular captain-general of the army in the Netherlands. With that, his reputation was wiped clean of the blot of incompetence.[61]

In spite of the frequently difficult relationship between Brussels and Madrid, Rodrigo appears to have carried out his diplomatic duties with much care and efficiency. At least that was the opinion of the archdukes, who did not neglect to thank him at length for his commitment. In her letters to the duke of Lerma, the infanta calls Rodrigo a man of great achievement, and she praised him on every occasion that arose. 'He is such a good servant [*criado*], that I cannot do otherwise than to recommend him to you, Sir,' Isabella maintained.[62] If the number of letters that she wrote together with her spouse in support of Rodrigo's affairs may be any indication, it does seem that the infanta meant it. In the period 1599-1608, the archdukes sent Lerma no less that 21 letters of recommendation on behalf of Rodrigo.[63] Albert and Isabella lauded his many virtues and even went so far as to ask for him the title of councilor of the Spanish *Consejo de Guerra*, which indeed was likely awarded to him shortly thereafter.[64] In addition they also asked that Rodrigo should be appointed as

---

[58] AGS, *Estado* 634, s.f.: Philip III to Rodrigo Niño y Lasso, s.d. [May 3, 1604].

[59] Rodríguez Villa, A., ed. *Correspondencia de la Infanta Doña Isabel Clara Eugenia con el Duque de Lerma y otros personajes*. Madrid, 1906, letter no. 77: Archduchess Isabella to the duke of Lerma, June 20, 1604. See also CODOIN, vol. XLII, pp. 488-489.

[60] AGS, *Estado* 634, s.f.: Archduke Albert to Rodrigo Niño y Lasso, June 18, 1604.

[61] Allen, *Philip III and the Pax Hispanica*, 143-144.

[62] Rodríguez Villa, *Correspondencia*, letter no. 70: Isabella to Lerma, February 18, 1604.

[63] For the letters of recommendation from Isabella, see Rodríguez Villa, *Correspondencia*, letter no. 11 (May 28, 1600), no. 31 (June 22, 1601), no. 32 (August 11, 1601), no. 42 (April 23, 1602), no. 65 (December 10, 1603), no. 70 (February 18, 1604), no. 106 (November 10, 1606), and no. 147 (September 15, 1608). For the letters from Albert, see CODOIN, vol. XLII, p. 312 (September 28, 1599), p. 319 (November 15, 1599), p. 356 (August 17, 1600), p. 397 (May 11, 1601), p. 403 (August 9, 1601), p. 413 (January 19, 1602), p. 417 (April 21, 1602), p. 473 (February 17, 1604) and CODOIN, vol. XLIII, p. 7 (August 30, 1606), p. 19 (November 10, 1606), p. 46 (April 18, 1607), and p. 130 (September 23, 1608). This last letter is accompanied by a comparable letter from Isabella: see p. 131, Isabella to Lerma, September 25, 1608.

[64] The exact date of the appointment is unknown. Rodríguez Villa, *Correspondencia*, letter no. 42: Isabella to Lerma, April 23, 1602; and CODOIN, vol. XLII, p. 417: Albert to Lerma, April 21, 1602. For more information concerning the *Consejo de Guerra*, see Domínguez Nafría, J.C. *El Real y Supremo Consejo de Guerra (siglos XVI-XVIII)*. Colección Historia de la Sociedad Política. Madrid, 2001.

gentilhombre de la Cámara of the king.[65] This request was apparently rejected, though Rodrigo's star continued to rise nevertheless. In the course of the following years he would grow into one of the archduke's most prominent political advisors. He advised Albert in domestic as well as foreign affairs, occupied himself with financial and political questions, and established himself as an important intermediary between Brussels and Madrid. As the following sections will show, he conducted himself in certain respects as Albert's prime minister, which in this case must be understood as a political jack-of-all-trades who had a finger in the pie in just about every aspect of daily decision-making. At the same time, however, Rodrigo also succeeded in building up a good relationship with the king of Spain. Philip III sought and welcomed his help in certain political affairs, and he recognized Rodrigo's importance by giving him the commandry of Montiel and La Osa in the military order of Santiago.[66]

In 1609, Rodrigo inherited the title of count of Añover from his uncle Juan Niño de Guevara. The English ambassador William Trumbull noted, in a way slighting, that '[he] is made an Earl (...) to have some sauce to season his dignity.'[67] Three years later, in July, 1612, Rodrigo was appointed *mayordomo mayor* of the archducal household.[68] Since the scandalous retreat of Francisco de Mendoza, this function had been vacant for approximately ten years, and without a doubt it was the most important position a courtier could wish for himself. Combined with the office of *sumiller de corps* (which he kept), it offered Rodrigo the chance to monopolize the access to the archdukes. Yet his career had still not reached its zenith. In February, 1615, Albert and Isabella surprised friend and foe alike by awarding the position of *caballerizo mayor*, which had been vacant for a time, to Rodrigo, who with this position now also laid hold of the last of the three top functions in the archducal household.[69] It was a striking example of a display of power. Even the duke of Lerma had never succeeded in laying hold of more than two top functions in the household of Philip III.[70] According to the Spanish ambassador, Rodrigo's appointment ran into quite a lot of criticism from the nobility in the Southern Netherlands: 'One says that the lords of this country, who themselves had been candidates for this position,

[65] Rodríguez Villa, *Correspondencia*, letter no. 32: Isabella to Lerma, August 11, 1601; and CODOIN, vol. XLII, p. 403: Albert to Lerma, August 9, 1601.

[66] The document can be found in ARA, *SSO* 315, s.f.

[67] Purnell, E.K. & Hinds, A.B., eds. *Report on the Manuscripts of the Marquess of Downshire preserved at Easthampstead Park, Berkshire. Volume II: Papers of William Trumbull the Elder, 1605-1610.* London, 1936. Op. cit. p. 106.

[68] Martín-Peñato Lázaro, 'Los Laso de la Vega,' 531; and BAV, *BaL* 6807, f. 8: Bentivoglio to Borghese, July 7, 1612.

[69] ASV, *Borghese* II 106, f. 112: Bentivoglio to Borghese, February 21, 1615.

[70] Lerma was *sumiller de corps* and *caballerizo mayor* of the royal household, but was never appointed *mayordomo mayor*.

lament this decision, though it is just, for the count of Añover deserves it.'[71] The papal nuncio agreed with that, saying that the office was given to Rodrigo out of thanks for his many services, 'concerning which the archdukes are quite satisfied.'[72] His appointment as ***caballerizo mayor*** marked the zenith of Rodrigo's fame. As cited earlier, the foreign diplomats and agents in Brussels were but all too well aware of the special status that he enjoyed at court. Even the archducal diplomats abroad found it important to maintain a separate exchange of letters with him, so as to ascertain his 'favor and friendship.'[73] The anecdote about García de Pareja, with which this chapter began, shows that Rodrigo had become pretty much untouchable at court around 1619. Everything indicated that he had succeeded in establishing himself as the archduke's unequaled favorite, and indeed, as his *gran privado*.

The minister-favorite

There is no doubt that Rodrigo Niño y Lasso – during the second half of the archducal regime, in any case – became generally recognized as the 'minister-favorite' of Archduke Albert, and it is one of the endeavors of this book to demonstrate that he was indeed one of the most influential politicians in the Netherlands. As opposed to many other contemporaneous protagonists, though, Rodrigo did not derive his power from an official position in one of the government councils or in the administration. The count never made up part of the established institutions that generally are associated with the archducal regime, such as the Council of State or the Council of Finance. His authority issued forth from his unofficial position as the archduke's right-hand man. Just like most *validos*, he did not operate *via*, but rather *alongside* the traditional channels of power.[74] Añover was, to be sure, a member of the royal *Consejo de Guerra*, but it is not at once clear how this advisory council precisely functioned in the time period concerned.[75] The Council of War convened a few times each month in Madrid, in order to meet about military and political affairs, but in view of the fact that Añover was not in the position to attend these meetings, his appointment as *consejero* – which he had got, after all, only by Albert's proxy – perhaps has to be seen instead as recognition of his role as point person for the Spanish government in

[71] AGS, *Estado* 2297, s.f.: The marquis of Guadaleste to Philip III, February 19, 1615.
[72] ASV, *Borghese* II 106, f. 112: Bentivoglio to Borghese, February 21, 1615.
[73] HHStA, *Belgien*, PC 53, s.f.: Jan Baptist van Male to Charles della Faille, April 27, 1617.
[74] Thompson, I.A.A. 'The Institutional Background to the Rise of the Minister-Favourite,' in: Elliott & Brockliss, *The World of the Favourite*, pp. 13-25.
[75] Domínguez Nafría, *El Real y Supremo Consejo de Guerra*, 101-118.

the Netherlands. In that sense, his installation was in fact little more than the official confirmation of an existing situation.

Departing from a nineteenth-century interpretation of the early modern state apparatus, historiography concerning the archducal regime was plagued for a long time by the idea that political power manifested itself in the main in official political offices – ministers, secretaries of state, diplomats, etc. Seen from that standpoint, the count of Añover was a figure of little interest. The only official political function he seems to have had was that of interim-ambassador of Philip III in Brussels, and that for a period of two years only. In 1609, the marquis of Guadaleste, Philip's resident ambassador, returned temporarily to Spain to take care of a few personal matters. It seems that Añover replaced the marquis during his absence.[76] Although no official document of this appointment has been recovered, it is confirmed by the papal nuncio Bentivoglio, who reported that Añover fulfilled the function of ambassador '*per modo di provisione*,'[77] and also by the French ambassador, who wrote that the count '*faict la charge d'ambassadeur d'Espagne*.'[78] Yet even in this case it seems that Añover only got the position because he was already functioning as the liaison between Brussels and Madrid. Guadaleste returned to take up the ambassadorship in 1611, which was perhaps one of the reasons for the cool relationship that would always exist between the two men (cf. Chapter IV).

In spite of the fact that he held no official political office for the majority of the time, Rodrigo Niño y Lasso was actively involved in archducal policy-making. That his role has never been studied in detail until now can simply be blamed on the fact that the office of *mayordomo mayor* was never seen as politically relevant in the historiography on the matter. All the same, it was already touched upon in Chapter I that this function entails much more than is generally presupposed. The *mayordomo mayor* not only directed the household of the prince but was also just as occupied with the 'management' of his position as prince. Both spheres were inseparably bound to each other. In that sense, the *mayordomo mayor* was the right hand of the monarch. In Añover's case, this meant that he was one of the most important political and military advisors of Albert and Isabella, and the head of what for want of a better word could be called the archduke's 'core cabinet.' Just like most early modern princes, in his policies Albert relied on a permanent group of intimates who functioned as his councilors. In addition to Añover, illustrious characters also belonged to this group, such as Jean Richardot (the presiding head of the Privy Council), Peter Peckius (the chancellor of

[76] As mentioned in Allen, *Philip III and the Pax Hispanica*, p. 265, note 35.

[77] BAV, *BaL* 6804, f. 211: Bentivoglio to Borghese, June 25, 1611.

[78] BNF, *MsF* 16125, f. 240: Charles de l'Aubespinne-Chasteaneuf, abbot of Préaux, to Villeroy, June 29, 1611.

Brabant), Ambrogio Spínola (the *maestro de campo general* of the army), the father confessor Iñigo de Brizuela, and the secretary of State and War Juan de Mancisidor.[79] Not coincidentally, two of them (Añover and Brizuela) made up part of the archducal household for many years – and Spínola would be appointed *mayordomo mayor* after Añover's death in 1620. The fact that Albert used members of his personal entourage to advise him and to maintain his diplomatic relations with the Spanish government supports the thesis that the services of the courtiers in no sense remained limited to the domestic domain. On the contrary, members of the archducal household were actively employed in policy and diplomacy. Here the limitations of the modern definition of political office are confronted, which reasons only from formal statutes and which consequently does not take into account the complex interwoven nature of the princely household and princely administration in the early modern period. The case of Rodrigo Niño y Lasso offers a textbook example of this.

As the right-hand man of Archduke Albert, the count of Añover seems to have occupied himself in the first place with financial questions. Not coincidentally, the marquis of Guadaleste wrote in 1610, that it was the responsibility of the Spanish ambassador in Brussels to supervise the financial administration in the Southern Netherlands, which in his view was only possible by combining the office of ambassador with that of the *superintendente de la hacienda* or – if the latter was not vacant – with the function of the archduke's *mayordomo mayor*.[80] Evidently this last office presupposed a firmer finger in the pie for managing the treasury. In that sense it need not come as a surprise that the *mayordomía mayor* was entrusted to a man like Añover in 1612, who as Albert's confidant had occupied himself with the financial quandaries of the archduke for years already. In the period before 1609, he not only journeyed regularly to Madrid to convince the king and Lerma of the need of resources for the army, but he also tried to recruit additional funds in the Netherlands themselves to cover costs for the persistent war. So, for example in 1606, by commission of Albert, he went in search of money to finance the military campaign in Friesland, and he succeeded in coming off with a loan worth 53,666 *escudos* (fl. 137,921) from a few

[79] For a general introduction concerning these characters, see Lefèvre, J. 'Le ministère espagnol de l'archiduc Albert, 1598-1621.' *Bulletin de l'Académie Royale d'Archéologie de Belgique*, 1 (1924) 202-224.

[80] '*Y quando no se le pueda dar la superintendencia se le podría dar la mayordomía mayor de S.A., juntamente con rubrica en la distribucion de la hazienda lo uno o lo otro para que tenga el embaxador mano y autoridad para yr ganando las voluntades que tanto importan y tener subordinados y a la deboción de V[uestra] M[ajestad] la gente de aquellos Estados para el caso que puede tan facilmente suceder de bolverse a incorporar a la Corona Real de V[uestra] M[ajestad].*' AGS, *Estado* 2026, s.f.: Memorandum from the marquis of Guadaleste to Philip III, s.d. [1610].

Portuguese *hombres de negocios* in Antwerp.[81] Even so, Añover emerged as not only a successful financial negotiator; as a bookkeeper, the count also proved to be worth his weight in gold. So, for instance in 1611, he threw himself at the complete financial inspection of the crown domains of Albert and Isabella, most likely to the benefit of the archducal treasury.[82] At his death in 1620, the French ambassador would report that the archdukes '*ont perdu un serviteur très util et grand oeconome qui avoys restably leur maison ylustre (...).*'[83] The English ambassador agreed with that, saying that Añover's 'severity towards [the Archdukes'] servants was as much grudged at by somme, as his justice (in paying their wages duly) was commended by others.'[84] The latter is also visible in the accounting ledgers of the archducal household, which show that delinquent wages were paid at set times from 1612 forward.[85]

Even so, Añover's duties were in no way limited to scraping together and managing budgets. Another domain in which the count played a striking role concerns diplomatic contacts with the court in Madrid. Just quickly leafing through the correspondence between the archducal and the royal courts establishes that Añover – in addition to the Spanish ambassador, Ambrogio Spínola, and Albert himself – was one of the most important point persons for the Spanish *Consejo de Estado*.[86] The count was frequently consulted about the political situation in the Netherlands and advised the *Consejo* not only concerning military matters and the condition of the treasury but also concerning tricky questions like the peace negotiations with the United Provinces and the question of succession in the duchies of Jülich and Cleves. In addition, Añover commented at length on the political circumstances in France, on the economic situation in the Netherlands, and even on ecclesiastical topics. In his reports he seldom hesitated in venting his own thoughts and opinions. So, for instance, he repeatedly spurred the *Consejo* into sending more Spanish troops to the Netherlands in order to face up to the rebels.[87] The situation of the *Ejército de Flandes*, then, appears to have been one of Añover's most prominent points of attention.

[81] AGS, *Estado* 2290, s.f.: *Relacion de las partidas a que esta obligado don Rodrigo Laso, a los de la nacion Portuguesa y Ferrante Balbani*, s.d. Concerning the role of the Portuguese in Antwerp in financing the war, see Ebben, M. 'Portuguese Merchant Bankers and the Court of the Archdukes, 1596-1633,' in: Thomas & Duerloo, *Essays*, pp. 303-307.

[82] Documents concerning this can be found in AGS, *Estado* 2026, passim.

[83] BNF, *MsF* 16133, f. 58: Péricard to Puisieux, October 8, 1620.

[84] NA, *SP* 77/14, f. 220: William Trumbull to the secretary of State, September 28, 1620 (old style).

[85] Cf. ARA, *RK* 1837 and 1838.

[86] This bold postulation is based on analysis of the correspondence preserved in the Fondo *Estado* of the Archivo General de Simancas, in particular *legajos* 2288-2312 (*Cartas de Flandes*) and – to a lesser degree – *legajos* 2023-2036 (*Negociaciones de Flandes*). For an introduction to these sources, see Van Durme, M. *Les Archives générales de Simancas et l'histoire de la Belgique (IXe-XIXe siècles)*. Commission Royale d'Histoire: Collection de chroniques belges inédites et de documents inédits relatifs à l'histoire de la Belgique. 4 vols. Brussels, 1964-1990.

[87] AGS *Estado* 2026, s.f.: Consult of the *Consejo de Estado*, March 3, 1611.

Consequently, it need not come as a surprise that after the signing of the Twelve Years' Truce in 1609, he was asked by Madrid to carry through reform in the army, for the purpose of restraining its financial cost.[88] The count got the command to visit various *castillos* in the Southern Netherlands and to report over the number of soldiers that could be discharged. He was also required to write up lists of courtiers who wrongly got paid an *entretenimiento* at the cost of the military treasury.[89] In view of the fact that this reform was quite sensitive for the soldiers and the aristocracy in the Southern Netherlands, it was an undertaking of the very highest importance. It was clearly no commission that could be entrusted to a political lightweight.

Añover's interest, all the same, did not remain limited to the situation in the Netherlands. Various historical sources show that he was remarkably well informed of the political conditions in other parts of Europe. Various diplomatic sources make it seem like the count not only received a lot of information concerning this but that he also distributed this information to third parties. More than likely he was in the position to do so thanks to his position as *mayordomo mayor* and *sumiller de corps*, which allowed him to follow all the audiences with foreign diplomats from close-by. So, for instance, the French ambassador noted that he had discussed in secret the progress of the negotiations concerning the politically sensitive marriage of the daughter of the duke of Aumale with both the archdukes and with Añover, 'who as the only one among their ministers deserved to hear about it.'[90] Further, it is striking that the count constantly appears to be one of the first informed of news from abroad. The papal nuncio Bentivoglio wrote in 1611, that in the capacity of his function as interim-ambassador, Añover '[has access] to the correspondence of all of His Majesty's ambassadors' and allowed the nuncio to read a letter from the Spanish ambassador in London.[91] What is more, the reports of the French ambassador Péricard show that Añover was his most prominent source of information in many cases. The count not only informed the ambassador concerning the political situation in the Southern Netherlands but also shared, for example, his knowledge about the progress of the negotiations regarding the election of Emperor Ferdinand II in the Holy Roman Empire.[92] Añover himself received these bits of news first-hand from the count of

[88] ASV, *NF* 12 A, f. 92: Nuncio Bentivoglio to Cardinal-Secretary of State Borghese, August 8, 1609. Documents concerning this reform can be found in AGS, *Estado* 2025, 2026, 2291, and 2292.

[89] AGS, *Estado* 2291, nos. 216-217: *Copia de la orden de S.A. para que se reformen todos sus criados, y Relacion de los a quien desea que S.M. haga merced de los sueldos que solian tener, moderadas segun la reformacion general* (August 8, 1609).

[90] '*(...) qui seul entre leurs ministres en méritoit la communication.*' BNF, *MsF* 16133, f. 270: Jean Péricard to Louis XIII, March 15, 1618.

[91] BAV, *BaL* 6804, f. 211: Bentivoglio to Borghese, June 25, 1611.

[92] BNF, *MsF* 16132, f. 205: Péricard to Puisieux, August 31, 1619; and f. 207: Rodrigo Niño y Lasso to Péricard, August 31, 1619.

Oñate, the Spanish ambassador in Vienna.[93] In that context it seems opportune to point to the fact that Añover was both a relative and a friend of Oñate. When the son of the latter was accused of having committed a murder in Vienna, he fled to the Southern Netherlands, where Añover provided him shelter at once, '*come suo parente et amico*.'[94]

Various examples demonstrate that Añover was a leading actor in just about all political questions that concerned the archducal regime, both in domestic as well as foreign affairs. When the so-called 'Nine Nations' of Brussels – a collection of the most important guilds – refused to pay the required taxes on comestibles like beer, wine, bread, and meat in 1619, and the archduke found himself obliged to have his troops occupy the city, it turned out that many citizens of Brussels were convinced that Añover was one of the councilors who had spurred Albert into this tough approach.[95] And in 1610, when the Condé affair blew up – in which the prince of Condé sought asylum in Brussels, after it turned out the French king Henry IV had fallen in love with his wife and had shown himself to be literally ready to unleash a war for her – the French ambassador wrote that no one knew where precisely the prince was staying, except for Albert, Añover, and Spínola, who were able to keep the secret well.[96] The ambassador reported that the provincial States let their dissatisfaction show concerning the threat of war but that Añover and Spínola held the strings taught in their hands – on instruction from Spain.[97] At a later stage he wrote that the archduke consulted exclusively with Añover, Spínola, and Juan de Mancisidor concerning this affair.[98]

Whereas Añover's involvement in archducal policy-making can in a number of respects still be compared to that of figures like Spínola and Mancisidor, he had two crucial trump cards at his disposal, the combination of which produced a significant advantage for him. In the first place, as the head of the archducal household, he

93 A few examples in AGS, *Estado* 2307, s.f.: Rodrigo Niño y Lasso to Juan de Ciriza, July 22, 1619; AGS, *Estado* 2309, s.f.: Rodrigo Niño y Lasso to Juan de Ciriza, August 2, 1620; and AGS, *Estado* 2309, s.f.: Rodrigo Niño y Lasso to Juan de Ciriza, August 16, 1620.

94 ASV, *Borghese* II 112, f. 183: Morra to Borghese, April 7, 1618.

95 NA, *SP* 77/14, f. 220: William Trumbull to the secretary of State, September 28, 1620 (old style). Concerning this affair, see Van Honacker, K. 'Reorganisatie in Brussel of de strijd om de privileges. Het conflict tussen de ambachten en de aartshertogen van 1619.' *Bijdragen tot de geschiedenis*, 73 (1990) 299-312; and Van Honacker, K. *Lokaal verzet en oproer in de 17de en 18de eeuw. Collectieve acties tegen het centraal gezag in Brussel, Antwerpen en Leuven*. Standen en Landen, 98. Kortijk-Heule, 1994, in particular pp. 97-101. See also Galesloot, L., ed. *Troubles de Bruxelles de 1619. Justification apologétique pour l'advocat Rombaut van Uden*. Brussels, 1868.

96 BNF, *MsF* 16129, f. 218: Mathieu Brulart de Berny to Puisieux, March 2, 1610. Concerning the Condé affair, see Henrard, P. *Henri IV et la princesse de Condé*. Brussels, 1885.

97 BNF, *MsF* 16129, f. 247: Brulart de Berny to Puisieux, April 19, 1610.

98 BNF, *MsF* 16129, f. 256: Brulart de Berny to Puisieux, May 2, 1610.

enjoyed absolute and free access to the archdukes. That privilege offered him the opportunity to discuss certain questions with the princes as he pleased, and in a very direct and informal manner. As seen in a previous chapter, he never shrank back, on top of that, from denying others access to the princes and in that way cutting them off from power (cf. Chapter IV). In the second place, Añover was especially beloved both by Albert as well as by Isabella, whereby they were inclined to take his interests and those of his relatives and confederates personally to heart. This clarifies not only the abundance of recommendation letters that were sent on his behalf to the Spanish court, but likely also the fact that his nephew Juan Niño de Tavora was appointed *gentilhombre de la Cámara* of Archduke Albert.[99] The competition for these prestigious positions was quite heavy, and it can be easily assumed that Añover's advocacy played a decisive role here. What is more, it even seems that Añover thought that he had every right to direct the appointments in the archducal household.

As seen in Chapter IV, Charles, princely count of Arenberg, engaged his contacts at court to have his sister Antoinette-Guillemette, countess of Isenburg, appointed the infanta's *camarera mayor*. Doing so, he counted above all on the help of Albert's private secretary Antonio Suárez de Arguello, who indeed did what was necessary in order to give force to the candidacy of Antoinette-Guillemette. Even so, when the matter was almost clinched, Antonio wrote a letter to Charles in which he advised the latter to involve the count of Añover in the question and to ask him to recommend Antoinette-Guillemette to the archduke.[100] According to Antonio, he was writing this letter in the name of Albert and Isabella, who wished that their *mayordomo mayor* would have a good relationship with the new *camarera mayor* and for that reason had to be involved with her appointment.[101] Charles' son Antoine of Arenberg supposed, however, that Antonio Suárez was not acting entirely on the command of the archdukes and advised his father to be cautious.[102] According to Antoine, the secretary feared the rage of Añover, should the latter notice that the appointment of Antoinette-Guillemette had been negotiated behind his back, without recognizing his authority in the process:

[99] Juan Niño de Tavora was a son of Rodrigo's uncle Gabriel Niño. He served in the archducal household at least from 1611 forward, and certainly until 1618 (see the personnel lists in ARA, *RvS* 157; and ARA, *RK* 1837 and 1838). Later he would even be appointed viceroy in the Philippines.

[100] ACA, 36/17, s.f.: Antonio Suárez de Arguello to Charles of Arenberg, October 19, 1615.

[101] '*S[u] A[lteza] quedó muy satisfecho de la buena voluntad de mi Señora la Condesa [=Antoinette-Guillemette of Arenberg] y dela de V[uestra] E[xcellencia]. Atra me ha mandado S[u] A]lteza] escriva a V.E. esta y le diga que como Sus Altezas dessean que aya buena correspondencia entre mi señora la Condessa y el Conde de Añover que holgarian Sus Altezas que V.E. escriviesse de su parte al Conde de Añover pidiendole quiera hablar a Sus Altezas en nombre de V.E. pidiendoles el cargo de Camarera Mayor para mi Señora la Condesa de Isemburg y que esta carta la embie V.E. al Señor Conde de Senegem o a mi para darla al dicho Conde de Añover.*' *Ibidem.*

[102] ACA, 38/1, file 31, no. 10: Antoine of Arenberg to Charles of Arenberg, October 19, 1615.

> 'And so I fear that, having been warned of it, [Añover] will stymie this affair so as to maintain the authority he has now or to augment that which they will let him have, and so I leave it to Your Excellency to consider whether making haste with this letter [of recommendation] would be good or not. If it pleases you, Your Excellency could well find an excuse to stall and, in that way, see whether His Highness has commanded it or if it comes from the said Antonio Suares.'[103]

Even so, various indications suggest that Añover's influence on archducal appointment policy did not remain limited to positions in their household. The correspondence of Charles of Arenberg demonstrates in every sense that time and again whenever the Arenberg family wanted to lay hold of certain public offices (be they for their own family members or for one of their many clients), Añover's support was seen as indispensable. That was the case, among others, when Philippe-Charles of Arenberg – the oldest son of Charles – made a bid for the vacant position of extraordinary commissioner of the county of Flanders, a function which, according to him, 'is not at all one of the most difficult to exercise, and it is a start towards being chosen for higher things.'[104] He asked his father to send the letters of recommendation necessary for this to the archduke and the count of Añover, as well as to Albert's father confessor Iñigo de Brizuela, who was accused by some of being an '*Arembergiste*,' and who indeed conceded to being '*muy afficionado*' to the House of Arenberg.[105] Philippe-Charles heartily impressed upon his father to send the letters as quickly as possible and, most preferably, to antedate them by one month, without mentioning the precise date, all the same.[106] In that way, Charles' letters would end up first on the desks of those to whom they were addressed and, consequently, would be read before the other candidates could invoke the support of Añover and the father confessor:

> 'Everyone starts to perform his duties [= write letters] in the month of January, which is why, if it pleases Your Excellency, it would be necessary for me to have

[103] '*(...) de façon que je crains qu'en estant adverti il ne le brouille cest affaire pour maintenir l'hautorité quil at asteur ou pour augmenter celle qu'on luy laisserat, de façon que je laisse a V[ostre] E[xcellence] de considérer sy la precipitation de ceste lettre seroit bonne ou non. V.E. sy elle le trouve bon pourrat bien trouver une excuse pour prolonger et voir par là sy S[on] A[ltesse] l'at commandé ou sy cela vient dudit Antonio Suares.*' *Ibidem.*

[104] '*(...) n'est point des plus mal aysées à exercer et que c'est un commencement pour estre enhemis par après à choses plus grandes.*' ACA, 38/3, file 72, no. 158: Philippe-Charles of Arenberg to Charles of Arenberg, s.d. Philippe-Charles of Arenberg (1587-1640), baron of Zevenbergen and from 1616 forward princely count of Arenberg and duke of Aarschot.

[105] ACA, 38/2, file 70, no. 13: Philippe-Charles of Arenberg to Charles of Arenberg, s.d.

[106] ACA, 38/3, file 72, no. 158: Philippe-Charles of Arenberg to Charles of Arenberg, s.d.

the letters of recommendation from Your Excellency for the Count of Añover and for the father confessor before Wednesday when I leave for Beuvrages[107] so that in my absence they will not be preceded by others [and so that] His Highness can still address them.'[108]

It proved to be a successful strategy. Some time later, an extremely happy Philippe-Charles wrote that Albert had decided to appoint him commissioner of Flanders, and that he would do his best to exercise the function as was appropriate.[109]

Whether Añover's recommendation was decisive in this case is difficult to say, but the fact is that the Arenbergs constantly called on his support whenever they were interested in certain offices. That was also the case in 1612, when Philippe-Charles, as charged by his father, asked Añover to nominate a certain Pierre Cuvelier for the position of councilor in the Grand Council of Mechelen.[110] This particular Cuvelier was a client of the Arenbergs, and Añover – who according to one source saw himself as a '*gran amigo y buen servidor*' of Charles of Arenberg – did not hesitate to go in on the request.[111] '[The count] has asked me to remind him of [Cuvelier's] name and has promised me to do his duties [*debvoirs*],' Philippe-Charles wrote to his father.[112] To be certain of the affair's good outcome, he also went to talk with Antonio Suárez de Arguello after that, who promised him to make the requisite '*debvoirs*' with Albert as well, and with a certain Joachim (perhaps Joachim Denzenhear, the archduke's *guardaropa y joyas*). According to Philippe-Charles, the latter turned out initially to have a slight preference for another candidate, but 'after having talked to him about it, he has promised me to [support] Cuvelier.'[113] Finally, the help of Gaston Spínola, count of Bruay, was also called in, so as to help advance the matter (cf. Chapter IV).[114] Once again the result of these efforts turned out to be successful. Not much later Philippe-Charles announced triumphantly that 'it has pleased His Highness to give

[107] The domain of Beuvrages belonged to the legacy of Pierre-Hippolyte Anne de Melun, baroness of Caumont, with whom Philippe-Charles entered into marriage in 1610. She was a daughter of Pierre de Melun, prince of Épinoy, and of Hippolyte of Montmorency-Horn.

[108] '*Tout le monde commence à fayre ses debvoirs au moys de Janvier, c'est pourquoy s'il plairoit à V[ostre] E[xcellence] il seroit bien necessaire que i'eusse les lettres de recomandation de V.E. pour le Comte d'Añover et pour le père confesseur avant mercredy que ie parte pour Beuuranges affin qu'en mon absence il ne soyent prevenu d'aultres pour S[on] A[ltesse] l'on pouldra encor bien attendre.*' ACA, 38/2, file 70, no. 29: Philippe-Charles of Arenberg to Charles of Arenberg, s.d.

[109] ACA, 38/3, file 72, no. 171: Philippe-Charles of Arenberg to Charles of Arenberg, s.d.

[110] ACA, 38/2, file 70, no. 32: Philippe-Charles of Arenberg to Charles of Arenberg, s.d. [1612].

[111] ACA, 38/4, file 125, no. 3: Gaston Spínola to Charles of Arenberg, June 15, 1603.

[112] '*[Le comte] m'a faict donner par memoyre son nom et m'a promis de fayre tous debvoirs.*' ACA, 38/2, file 70, no. 32: Philippe-Charles of Arenberg to Charles of Arenberg, s.d. [1612].

[113] '*(...) après luy en avoir parlé, il m'a promis de fayre pour Cuvelier.*' *Ibidem*.

[114] ACA, 38/3, file 108, no. 4: Gaston Spínola to Charles of Arenberg, January 11, 1612.

the position of councilor in Mechelen to Cuvelier, there being no doubt that you will be extremely happy because he is your creature.'[115]

The commentaries from Philippe-Charles of Arenberg suggest that sending recommendation letters to the archduke's intimates was a current – and perhaps even necessary – practice whenever certain positions in the central administration were preferably laid hold of. When the governorship of Tournai came open in 1612, Philippe-Charles wrote that if the count of Arenberg wished his son to be a candidate for this, then he would have to send letters of recommendation as quickly as possible to Albert, Añover, Mancisidor, Brizuela, Suárez de Arguello, and 'Joachim,' in that order.[116] Not coincidentally, all the characters mentioned turned out to belong to the immediate entourage of the archduke. Evidently they were seen as the most influential figures at court. Añover was thus one of the most important, to be sure, but certainly not the only person whose support was actively sought. Despite this, the count's reputation was known far and wide. With regard to ecclesiastical questions Añover's long arm seems even to have extended itself to the papal court in Rome. In March, 1618, the nuncio Morra wrote that Añover had asked him to insist with the pope that the main altar in the parish church of his hometown receive the status of a privileged altar, on behalf of the Lasso de la Vega family.[117] Morra declared that Añover and his brother Pedro had a special bond with this church – which they saw as their future resting place – and he spurred his superiors in Rome to award the requested indult. The papal nuncio argued that he had much to thank Añover for, who had helped the Papal See with many matters already, '*esser egli qui ministro di tanta auttorità, et tanto bene affetto a [questa] Santa Sede*.'[118] That proved to be a convincing argument: the indult was awarded in June, 1618.[119]

Even the papal nuncio Bentivoglio contended that Añover was quite inclined toward the Church. In 1614, he let his superiors in Rome know that the count had nominated a certain Alonso de Castillo for a position as canon in the collegiate Church of St. Peter in Lille. Bentivoglio posited that it was better to enter into this question, for Añover was the '*maggiordomo maggiore di queste Altezze, di grandissima*

[115] '*(...) il a pleu à S.A. de donner l'estat de Conseiller de Malines à Cuvelier, ne doubtant que vous en recevez un extreme contentement pour estre luy vostre créature.*' ACA, 38/2, file 71, no. 85: Philippe-Charles of Arenberg to Charles of Arenberg, s.d. [1612]. Pierre Cuvelier was indeed appointed councilor in the Great Council of Mechelen in 1612. Cf. Leyder, D. *Les archives du Grand Conseil des Pays-Bas à Malines (vers 1445-1797)*. Brussels, Algemeen Rijksarchief, Guides 73, 2010. Op. cit. p. 95. I thank Harald Deceulaer for this reference.

[116] ACA, 38/2, file 70, no. 6: Philippe-Charles of Arenberg to Charles of Arenberg, s.d. [1612].

[117] ASV, *Borghese* II 112, f. 162: Morra to Borghese, March 17, 1618.

[118] *Ibidem.*

[119] ASV, *Borghese* II 112, f. 310: Morra to Borghese, June 30, 1618.

auttorita in questa corte, e che sempre si è mostranto favorenole alle cose ecclesiastiche.'[120] A similar incident took place in December, 1617, when the nuncio Morra informed the pope of a problem that had arisen in connection with the appointment of a new canon in the collegiate church of Tongeren, in the prince-bishopric of Liège. Three years earlier, Emperor Matthias – who on the basis of the so-called *Preces Imperiales* had the prerogative to award certain ecclesiastical offices to clerics of his choice – had awarded this beneficence to a certain Francisco Loget. The nuncio explained that the emperor had done so at the insistence of the count of Añover, who was Loget's patron.[121] In view of the fact that at that moment Loget was still too young for such an office, technically speaking, Añover had at once requested dispensation from the pope.[122] Now, however, Loget's appointment was being disputed by the University of Leuven, which posited that the emperor did not have the right to meddle in this affair, legally speaking. Morra admonished his superiors to settle the question as quickly as possible, yet warned that Loget was a client of Añover, '*della casa del quale e molto favorito è questo Loget*' and who had recommended the affair to him '*molto caldo et affettuoso.*'[123] The nuncio needed no more arguments to convince the Holy See. Two months later the pope confirmed Loget's appointment. Morra showed himself to be extraordinarily relieved and posited that the matter was quite important to Añover, who, according to him, was '*il primo ministro e'l più potente in questa Corte.*'[124]

Even so, Añover did not always get his way. In 1617, a position came open in the cathedral chapter of Ghent. The count tried anew to see to it that the beneficence would be given to one of his clients, a certain Charles Boccabella, who, according to the papal nuncio Morra, was '*una persona amorevole del [...] Signor Conte.*'[125] The nuncio was a fervent proponent of Boccabella's candidacy and reminded his superiors in Rome that Añover was a '*cavaliero di tanto merito et auttorità,*' and '*che non puo esser maggiore in questa Corte.*'[126] Yet although the pope wanted to confirm Boccabella's appointment, it was disputed by the bishop of Ghent. The latter argued that this specific canonate was coupled to the office of the dean and therefore subjected to the jurisdiction of the chapter, which opted for another candidate. The pope could not

---

120 ASV, *Borghese* II 99, f. 324: Bentivoglio to Borghese, May 17, 1614.

121 Not coincidentally, Francisco Loget was also one of the beneficiaries in the last will and testament of Añover. See IVDJ, ms. 26-I-11: *Antonio Vedell su cuenta de los effectos que el Sr. don Rodrigo dejo en Flandes desde el año 1620 à 1625.*

122 ASV, *Borghese* II 116, f. 277: Bentivoglio to Borghese, October 3, 1615

123 ASV, *Borghese* III 113, f. 320: Morra to Borghese, December 23, 1617.

124 ASV, *Borghese* II 112, f. 115: Morra to Borghese, March 3, 1618.

125 ASV, *Borghese* II 137, f. 44: Morra to Borghese, September 1, 1617. This letter was accompanied by a personal letter from Añover to the Holy See.

126 *Ibidem.*

introduce anything to counter this, but compensated Añover's defeat amply after that by installing Boccabella as canon in Lille.[127]

The courtiers in Brussels realized but all too well that the count of Añover was a man whom they had to keep as a friend. His prominent position, therefore, was difficult to ignore. Countless sources indicate that he was in pretty much all respects *incontournable* at court. When the English emissary John Bennet went for an audience with the infanta in 1617, Añover took a seat next to the baldachin under which Isabella was seated. Ambrogio Spínola and the papal nuncio had to place themselves a few meters further apart.[128] During the wedding of the duke of Nemours with a daughter of the duke of Aumale – which was celebrated by proxy – Añover played the role of Nemours and was led into the *Aula Magna* by Albert.[129] When a courtier from Brussels was dubbed knight in the military order of Santiago in 1613, Añover extended the vestments to him in the name of the king.[130] During the wedding banquet of the marquis of Guadaleste with a daughter of the prince of Ligne, Añover sat together with Albert in the first coach of the wedding procession, and he opened the dance.[131] These and similar examples leave no doubt that Rodrigo Niño y Lasso took in a visible position at court. Not coincidentally, the other courtiers prided themselves on their good relationship with the count. In his letters to Charles of Arenberg, Gaston Spínola did not neglect to boast about his friendship with Añover. In June, 1613, both men visited the healing springs in Spa together, and although they were the only guests there, they had an excellent time of it, according to Spínola: 'even though there is no one else in Spa, we are not lonely for the extreme comradeship between us.'[132] He made it known that Añover's company was the best to be possibly wished for, although he hastened to mention that the count was a '*grande amigo y servidor de Vuestra Excellencia*' also, 'and esteems him like he should.'[133] Charles' son Antoine of Arenberg, who resided at court as *gentilhombre de la Cámara*, did his very best 'to caress the Count of Añover,' and not without success: the count declared 'that he wants to keep the young knight as his son and that he will serve him in any way he

[127] Van Meerbeeck, L., ed. *Correspondance des Nonces Gesualdo, Morra, Sanseverino avec la Secrétairie d'Etat pontificale (1615-1621)*. Analecta Vaticano-Belgica, 2e série, section A: Nonciature de Flandre, IV. Rome-Brussels, 1937. Op. cit. p. 568: Morra to Borghese, November 11, 1617.

[128] NA, *SP* 77/12, f. 333: Report by William Trumbull concerning the mission of Bennet, s.d. [1617].

[129] BNF, *MsF* 16131, f. 299: Péricard to Puisieux, April 25, 1618.

[130] ACA, 38/1, file 30, no. 13: Antoine of Arenberg to Charles of Arenberg, December 26, 1613.

[131] ACA, 38/1, file 30, nos. 8-9: Antoine of Arenberg to Charles of Arenberg, November 14, 1613.

[132] '*(...) aunque no hay aun persona a Spa, no passamos soledad por ser estremada la camaradería que tenemos.*' ACA, 38/4, file 125, f. 1: Gaston Spínola to Charles of Arenberg, June 6, 1613.

[133] '*(...) y le estima como es razón.*' ACA, 38/4, file 125, f. 3: Gaston Spínola to Charles of Arenberg, June 15, 1613.

can.'[134] Finally, Charles' daughter Albertine, who was a lady-in-waiting to the infanta, was proud to be able to announce to her father that she stood in Añover's good graces:

> 'I cannot wait to tell you, Mylord, that I am very much in the good graces of the count of Añover: he says many good things about me and [says] that I please him very much. Yesterday in Anderlecht, he came to me and made a big *reverence*, and told me '[I am] your most humble servant, Mademoiselle.' Is that not a great honor for me?'[135]

The count of Arenberg likely must have been quite elated with the fact that his oldest daughter had been able to please the count of Añover. Undoubtedly a connection between the Arenberg family and the most influential man at court would have been quite advantageous. All the same, unfortunately for Charles, Añover's interest in Albertine did not go further than a friendly word. The count would never marry, even though around 1613, it was whispered that he would become engaged to Dorothée de Croÿ – the young, extremely rich and, consequently, quite desirable widow of the duke of Aarschot.[136]

Añover's power had reached an absolute zenith around 1618. An umpteenth indication of that is the fact that the count was appointed member of the newly established War Council in the Netherlands. After the death of Juan de Mancisidor in March, 1618, Albert opted for establishing an advisory council that would – now that the end of the Twelve Years' Truce was approaching – advise him on political and military questions.[137] In addition to Añover the council consisted of four other councilors who, not coincidentally, all had a lot of military experience at their disposal. They were Ambrogio Spínola, Luis de Velasco (marquis of Belveder and general of the cavalry), Charles-Bonaventure de Longueval (count of Buquoy and general of the artillery), and Fernando Girón (former *maestre de campo* and Spanish ambassador in Paris). Henceforth they would meet twice a week in Añover's apartment in the palace – once again a striking confirmation of the central position the count had taken in archducal policy-making.[138] It can be argued, by the way, that Añover's private quarters

[134] '*(...) pour carresser le Conte de Añover (...) quil veut tenir ce jeun cavalier pour son filz et quil le servirat en tout ce que luy serat posible.*' ACA, 38/7, file 343, s.f.: Nicolas Scorsa, authorized agent of the Arenberg family, to Charles of Arenberg, March 19, 1615; and *Ibidem*, Scorsa to Charles, March 22, 1615.

[135] '*Je ne puis laiser de vous dire, Monsieur, que je suis tant au bone grâce du conte d'Agnovere; il dict tant de bien de moi et que je lui contente fort. Hier à Anderlec il vint auprès de moi et me fit une grande reverense et me dict « Votre serviteur trèshumble, mademoiselle ». N'ès-se pas beaucoup d'honeur pour moi?*' ACA, 38/1, file 24, f. 17: Albertine of Arenberg to Charles of Arenberg, s.d.

[136] ACA, 38/1, file 30, no. 16: Antoine of Arenberg to Charles of Arenberg, December 24, 1613.

[137] ASV, *Borghese* II 112, f. 133: Morra to Borghese, March 10, 1618.

[138] AGS, *Estado* 2032, s.f.: Ambrogio Spínola to Philip III, April 3, 1618.

also had been a *locus* of power before that already. The correspondence of Gaston Spínola shows that Añover frequently invited prominent politicians and nobles for informal meals in his apartment. So, for instance, Spínola wrote on September 10, 1614: 'Today [the secretary Mancisidor] and I will dine in the bedchamber of the count of Añover. Tomorrow we will dine together anew, before we go to the *comedia* in the secretary's house.'[139] On September 14, 1614: 'The count of Añover and I have eaten together today.'[140] On November 24, 1614: 'Yesterday I dined together with the duke of Aumale in the bedchamber of the count of Añover. Today we will dine with the count of Estaires, the papal nuncio, the [Spanish] ambassador, [the duke of] Aumale, Añover, [the marquis of] Marnay, and I do not know who else.'[141] Ambassadors and diplomats also were invited '*chez* Añover' like clockwork.[142] Although as a rule it is not known what topics of conversation were taken up during these informal meetings, it can easily be assumed that day-to-day politics stood high on the agenda. Here the limitations of written sources are confronted, which seldom allow finding out more about what precisely played out in the many suites and backrooms of the Coudenberg palace.

Favorites and fortunes

One of the characteristics generally associated with favorites is their presupposed inclination toward avarice and self-aggrandizement. If this feature can indeed be seen as characteristic for the early modern favorite, then Rodrigo Niño y Lasso would certainly come under consideration. At the end of his life the count of Añover had an immense fortune at his disposal. At his death in October, 1620, an inventory was made up of all the movable goods he possessed at that moment.[143] The document numbers no less than 80 pages and mentions a fantastical quantity of jewels (rings, diamonds, necklaces, medallions,...), gold- and silverwork (plates, platters, utensils), furniture (beds, desks, cabinets, wardrobes, chairs,...), clothing and fabric (tunics, uniforms, gloves, silk stockings, shoes, sheets,...), tapestries, paintings, portraits, books, relics, ceramics, and much, much more, everything of excellent quality. In view of the fact that the count had no children, his complete estate went to his family

[139] ACA, 38/4, file 140, f. 23: Gaston Spínola to Charles of Arenberg, September 10, 1614.

[140] *Ibidem*, f. 31: Gaston Spínola to Charles of Arenberg, September 14, 1614.

[141] ACA, 38/4, file 142, f. 21: Gaston Spínola to Charles of Arenberg, November 24, 1614.

[142] See e.g. ASV, *Borghese* II 105, ff. 202-203: Morra to Borghese, June 8, 1619; BAV, *BaL* 6804, f. 93: Bentivoglio to Borghese, April 2, 1611; and NA, *SP* 77/13: William Trumbull to the secretary of State, June 20, 1619.

[143] IVDJ, ms. 26-I-11, ff. 53-92: *Inbentario de los bienes y hazienda que quedaron por fin y muerte del Sr. Conde de Añover en los Estados de Flandes.*

in Spain, with his brother Pedro and Pedro's son Luis Lasso de la Vega (who would succeed him as the third count of Añover) as the most important heirs. Pedro and Luis decided to dispose of the majority of Rodrigo's possessions. According to the executor of Añover's last will and testament, *contador* Antonio Vedell, the public sale produced an amount of fl. 65,222.[144] In addition, the count left behind a sum of 332,514 *reales* (or fl. 83,128) in cash, of which approximately half was saved in a few treasure chests in the convent of the Discalced Carmelites in Brussels.[145] After adding in a number of smaller sums and settling up outstanding debts, Vedell could announce that Añover's total estate was financially worth no less than fl. 117,958.[146] It was an astronomical amount for that time.

The question arises as to how Rodrigo Niño y Lasso succeeded in gathering together a fortune like this. For want of information, that problem is especially difficult to solve. So, for example, pretty much nothing is known about the sources of income Rodrigo had at his disposal in Spain. It was already mentioned above that the *señoríos* Cuerva, Arcos, and Batres were inherited by Rodrigo's brother Pedro after the death of Garci Lasso de la Vega in 1567. These small domains generated perhaps rather modest proceeds. Rodrigo himself inherited no country estates from his father but did take over his office of treasurer of the Mint of Toledo. This office – which Rodrigo would hold until his death in 1620, and which was taken over by Pedro for years during Rodrigo's absence – was presumable quite lucrative, but it is not known precisely how much the function produced for him.[147] Even so, this dark number in and of itself does not need to carry any weight in the analysis: even if the most lucrative scenario is taken into account, Rodrigo's joint incomes in Spain are likely unable to suffice as a clarification for the immeasurable wealth he had been able to gather together at the end of his life. It is much more probable that he – as the second son of a high-born, yet not exceptionally rich family – had his fortune thanks to the favors of his patron and the various financial advantages that his status as favorite brought along with it.

Archduke Albert indeed did not neglect to reward his favorite richly for services delivered. As *sumiller de corps* of the archducal household, Rodrigo earned 1000 ducats (fl. 2,757) per year (cf. Chapter II). With this it needs to be noted that he enjoyed both room and board at court, by which his expenditures in that area were limited in any case. Further, by the capacity of his office he had the right to a number of honoraria in support of his own household (which according to one source numbered at least 36 servants), among these a monthly quantity of bread, meat, wine, firewood,

[144] IVDJ, ms. 26-I-11, ff. 103-123: *Relación de lo bendido y que resta por bender dela Almoneda que se hizo en Flandes de los bienes del Sr. Conde de Añover.*
[145] IVDJ, ms. 26-I-11, f. 92 and f. 165v°.
[146] *Ibidem.*
[147] Martín-Peñato Lázaro, M.J. 'Los Laso de la Vega y su vinculación con la ceca de Toledo,' 531-532.

beeswax, and other products, together financially worth 200 ducats (fl. 551) per year.[148] When Rodrigo was appointed *mayordomo mayor* in 1612, his annual salary was doubled, on top of that, to 2,000 ducats (fl. 5,514) – the second-highest wage in the archducal household.[149] This amount was four times the wage of a normal *mayordomo*, approximately six times that of a *gentilhombre de la Cámara*, and ten times that of a *gentilhombre de la Casa*.

In addition to his salary at court, Rodrigo received several remunerations as an officer in the *Ejército de Flandes* – for posts that for the most part he had thanks to Albert. In this it needs to be realized that this combat pay came from the royal treasury, which is to say that the count was dependent on Madrid for a large part of his income. According to his own calculations, Rodrigo earned an annual wage of 2,000 *escudos* (approx. fl. 5,000) as captain of a company in the archducal guard, and yet another 1,200 *escudos* (approx. fl. 3,000) as captain of a company of lancers, thus fl. 8,000 in total.[150] When he got the commission to steer the army reform in the right direction in 1609, Rodrigo decided to disband his company in the archduke's personal guard to demonstrate that the economizing had to be taken seriously. What he easily forgot to mention is the fact that, as a member of the Spanish *Consejo de Guerra*, he was able to persuade the Spanish government to convert this lucrative command into a pension of no less than 300 *escudos* (fl. 750) per month (or approx. fl. 9,000 per year).[151] Through this, his income from the military treasury rose to a shabby fl. 12,000 per year. Realizing well that this was perhaps somewhat exaggerated, Rodrigo proposed to drop his remuneration as captain of the lancers, so that his yearly income again fell to fl. 9,000.[152] Yet this was still fl. 1,000 more than his earlier annual wage, whereby, strikingly enough, Rodrigo was one of the few courtiers who benefitted from the army reform.

Yet it did not end with this high compensation. Now and then the archduke saw to it that his favorite got lavish *ayudas de costa*, varying from fl. 845 – which Rodrigo got 'for secret expenditures in my service'[153] – to 7,000 ducats (fl. 19,299)[154] to no less than 12,000 ducats (fl. 33,084).[155] On top of that, Albert's many recommendations saw to it that even Philip III was quick to respond whenever it came to rewarding Rodrigo for proven services. In that way he received an *ayuda de costa* of 10,000

[148] IVDJ, ms. 26-I-11, ff. 43-50: *Relación de la enfermedad, muerte y entiero, honras y obsequias del Señor Conde de Añober que está en gloria.*
[149] ARA, *RK* 1837, f. 104v°.
[150] ARA, *Estado* 2027, s.f.: Consult of the *Consejo de Estado*, January 16, 1613.
[151] *Ibidem.*
[152] *Ibidem.*
[153] ARA, *RK* 1837, f. 331.
[154] AGS, *Estado* 2024, s.f.: Consult of the *Consejo de Estado*, January 31, 1606.
[155] IVDJ, ms. 26-I-11, ff. 27-41.

ducats (fl. 27,570) in 1606.[156] The commandry of Montiel and La Osa, which Philip III gave to Rodrigo in 1614, brought in fl. 7,500 yearly.[157] In addition, according to his last will and testament, he enjoyed rents of 2,000 ducats (fl. 5,514) on property in Sicily – a gift from the Spanish king as well.[158] In 1619, finally, Rodrigo received a *merced* from Philip in the form of a pension worth 8,000 ducats (fl. 22,065).[159]

Rodrigo's status as favorite clearly did him no harm, and that did not stay unnoticed at court. Already in 1602, complaints were expressed concerning his luxurious lifestyle. The Florentine prince Giovanni de' Medici, who was residing in the Netherlands at that moment, described how a few Spanish nobles in Brussels seemed to be throwing the money allotted for the army out the window:

> 'They possess not a cent, and yet they want not only to live in a splendid manner, but they also want to advance [in life], and everything is done for them. And they are the ambassador of Spain, who despite his poverty dwells and lives like a prince and betters himself as if he is a talented merchant, and Don Rodrigo, who does the same, and each of them both receives compensation in addition to his wages, under the guise of having to go on military campaigns.'[160]

Madrid, too, was well informed of Rodrigo's greed. In 1613, when he made his complaint concerning the outstanding sum of 2,000 ducats on delinquent wages, the *Consejo de Estado* hesitated to give that to him because 'everyone knows that he already enjoys many favors.'[161] And in 1619, when Rodrigo showed himself to be unsatisfied with the *merced* of 8,000 ducats mentioned earlier, the *Consejo* protested that 'he is now already the richest man who exists, both here [in Spain] as well as there [in the Southern Netherlands], and that while he has no single other duty than to serve the archduke.'[162]

---

[156] AGS, *Estado* 2024, s.f.: Consult of the *Consejo de Estado*, January 31, 1606.

[157] Gómez Centurión, J. 'Jovellanos y las Ordenes Militares, VI,' in: *Boletín de la Real Academia de la Historia*, 61 (1912) 370-431.

[158] This is mentioned in IVDJ, ms. 26-I-11, ff. 27-41: *Copia authorizada que el señor Don Rodrigo Niño y Lasso Conde de Añover otorgó en los Estados de Flandes.*

[159] AGS, *Estado* 2033, f. 88: Consult of the *Consejo de Estado*, April 20, 1619.

[160] Archive of the Granddukes of Tuscany (Archivio di Stato, Florence): *Carteggi dei Principi, delle Granduchesse e delle Principesse / Giovanni di Cosimo I e di Eleonora degli Albizi / Lettere del principe ai granduchi e alla Segretaria*, volume 5155, f. 237: Giovanni de' Medici to Ferdinando I de' Medici, October 16, 1602. To be found on the website of *The Medici Archive Project*, http://documents.medici.org, docID 9069 (last accessed: July 10, 2013).

[161] AGS, *Estado* 2027, s.f.: Consult of the *Consejo de Estado*, July 26, 1613.

[162] AGS, *Estado* 2033, f. 88: Consult of the *Consejo de Estado*, April 20, 1619.

A *valimiento* in the Archducal Netherlands?

The preceding sections show that Rodrigo Niño y Lasso united in himself a large number of characteristics that allow him to be described as Archduke Albert's *gran privado*. He had more than significant political power at his disposal; exercised influence on the appointment policy in the archducal household, in the central institutions, and in the Church; and succeeded in converting his privileged status at court into a remarkable fortune. Yet the question arises as to how the role of the count of Añover relates to that of other *validos* of his time. According to the papal nuncio Morra, Añover's authority in the Southern Netherlands was greater than that of the all-powerful duke of Lerma in Spain. If that was indeed so, it can be assumed that the historiography concerning the archducal period has to be drastically rewritten. Yet was the nuncio right? How powerful was the count of Añover in reality, and how does his story fit into the broader framework of the *valimiento*? This question poses a problem, for its answer presupposes a clear description of what precisely the *valimiento* entailed. As seen already in the introduction to this chapter, the scholarly discussion concerning this is far from settled. Some authors situate the *valido*'s ascent and florescence, respectively, in the sixteenth and seventeenth century, and see in it a response to the increasing complexity of the early modern state. Others indicate that favorites were particular to any regime that was based on the extension and acquisition of princely favor and, consequently, already occurred much earlier.

There is indeed no doubt that some rulers in Classical Antiquity and in the Middle Ages already had personal favorites at their disposal, who exercised a certain degree of influence on decision-making. For that matter, the question can be raised as to what extent that is still the case in contemporary politics. Yet most historians support the vision that the seventeenth-century *validos* distinguished themselves in one way or another from favorites in other time periods. Laurence Brockliss posits,

> 'In the long and ongoing history of the favourite as a political phenomenon, [the period 1550-1650] cannot but attract especial attention, for it witnessed the rise and then rapid decline of a particularly interesting species of the genus (...); the temporary blooming of an entirely new type of favourite (...). This was a new and singular variety that took root in virtually all the large courts of Europe and many of the small ones too.'[163]

[163] Brockliss, 'Concluding Remarks: The Anatomy of the Minister-Favourite,' 280.

His colleague I.A.A. Thompson goes in accord with this, yet posits that 'part of the difficulty is definitional. The language of 'favouritism' is both imprecise and protean, covering different relationships and roles.'[164] Still, Thompson recalls that it can be no coincidence that in the late sixteenth and early seventeenth century a new terminology came into being to denote the phenomenon of 'favoritism,' which indicates, according to the author, that contemporaries had the feeling that the seventeenth-century *valido* 'was in some way different from the *privados* of the past.'[165]

This argument does not sound illogical. Although the early modern conceptions concerning favoritism are plagued by vagueness and ambiguity, it seems that awareness about the phenomenon – and its impact on the political system – increased perceptibly from the end of the seventeenth century forward. In a letter to his French friend Pierre Dupuy, no one less than Peter Paul Rubens noted that the increasing influence of Cardinal Richelieu reminded him of an incident that took place during his stay at the Spanish court.[166] Rubens told how Philip III got a visit one day from an Italian nobleman, who came to plead a question, one not described in greater detail. To Philip's question why the nobleman had not put this matter before the duke of Lerma, the Italian answered: 'If I could have got an interview with the duke, I would not have come to Your Majesty.'[167] Rubens shook his head compassionately about this kind of state of affairs, saying that 'it must be difficult to arrange one's affairs in a country where only one person has the power and the king is only there for appearances (...). That situation cannot last long like that.'[168] This and similar anecdotes make it seem like the notion of favoritism – in the words of John H. Elliott – 'impinged itself upon the collective consciousness' during the first decades of the seventeenth century.[169] In that context Ronald Asch noted,

> 'In this epoch at least the perception of the role of the favorite changed. The role of an extremely powerful personal confidant naturally becomes especially conspicuous where there is already an administrative system with fixed, permanent responsibilities and where the ad hoc transfer of tasks to individuals is no longer the rule and where, on top of that, the court is still the

---

[164] Thompson, I.A.A. 'The Institutional Background to the Rise of the Minister-Favourite,' in: Elliott & Brockliss, *The World of the Favourite*, pp. 13-25. Op. cit. p. 14.

[165] *Ibidem.*

[166] Rooses, M. & Ruelens, C., eds. *Codex Diplomaticus Rubenianus. Correspondance de Rubens et documents épistolaires concernant sa vie et ses œuvres.* 6 vols. Antwerp, 1887-1909. Op. cit. vol. III, p. 479: Pieter Paul Rubens to Pierre Dupuy, October 22, 1626.

[167] *Ibidem.*

[168] *Ibidem.*

[169] Elliott, J.H. 'Introduction,' in: Elliott & Brockliss, *The World of the Favourite*, pp. 1-10. Op. cit. p. 2.

> center of politics and patronage but not any more in the same way as in the past it was the center of the entire central administration.'[170]

Contemporaries were thus more and more aware of the presence of favorites in politics. That, however, is not to say that the seventeenth-century *valido* also actually differed from his antecedents in one way or another.

Various authors have tried to investigate the criteria that would have made the seventeenth-century favorite 'unique in his class.'[171] So, for instance, Thompson argues that the *valido* in this time period is typified by four characteristic and interrelated features:

> 'First, they were operating in the areas of both power and patronage (…) and they were predominant, if not monopolists, in both (...). Second, they operated outside (or alongside) established institutional channels, and indeed often without any formal ministerial status. (…) Third, they stood at the centre of a national network of clientage (…) which was the means of integrating court and country on a broad front. (…) Fourth, (…) they were using influence for a political rather than for just a private purpose, promoting a policy (…) designed to reinforce the authority and reputation of the state.'[172]

Thompson concedes that not every seventeenth-century *valido* met each of these conditions, and that not all favorites fit into the picture. Even so, this nonetheless correct caveat prevents the author from constructing his further argumentation on the basis of the characteristics mentioned, which brings him, not coincidentally, to the conclusion that famous favorites like the duke of Lerma, the count-duke of Olivares, and the cardinals Richelieu and Mazarin did indeed really distinguish themselves from their predecessors. This conclusion, which seems to depart from circuitous reasoning, naturally calls forth the requisite questions. Thus, it is questionable to what extent the figures named are representative for 'the seventeenth-century *valido*,' and to what extent less powerful favorites can be seen as 'deviating' from this. Thompson seems to start out from the position that the *valimiento* carried an inherent objective in it, that is, the establishment of a monopoly on power. *Validos* who acquired pretty much absolute authority in their principality, however, can be counted on the fingers of one

---

[170] Asch, R.G. 'Schlussbetrachtung. Höfische Gunst und höfische Günstlinge zwischen Mittelalter und Neuzeit. 18 Thesen,' in: Hirschbiegel & Paravicini, *Der Fall des Günstlings*, pp. 515-531. Op. cit. p. 530.

[171] See e.g. Brockliss, 'Concluding Remarks: The Anatomy of the Minister-Favourite,' 280-285; and Asch, 'Höfische Gunst und höfische Günstlinge,' passim.

[172] Thompson, 'The Institutional Background,' 14-15.

hand. In that respect, figures like Lerma and Olivares were the exception rather than the rule. How does Rodrigo Niño y Lasso fit into this lineup?

On the surface the count of Añover gave every appearance of being an all-powerful *valido*: he accumulated the three highest positions in the archducal household, exercised pressure on the appointment policy of the archdukes outside the standard channels, and in the meantime gathered together an enormous fortune. Courtiers tried to come into favor with him, and foreign diplomats indeed took his influential position into account. That the count was one of the most authoritative protagonists in the archducal government is, on top of that, beyond dispute. And yet, Añover was no second Lerma. As opposed to Philip III's *valido*, he never succeeded in acquiring a monopoly on power. His control over princely patronage was significant, yet not absolute. Nor was he at the head of a network of clients in the princely administration and in the provinces, either. On top of that, his authority was not the only one that was applied at the archducal court: prominent figures like Spínola, Mancisidor, and Brizuela were also influential. Finally, he was in no sense in a position to take over the policy-making of the prince fully. As opposed to Philip III, the archduke would never permit that his favorite at court would comport himself like a 'surrogate-sovereign.'[173] Then, too, Albert had little in common with Philip. In some instances the archduke stood out in indecisiveness, to be sure, yet he was nevertheless a shrewd politician. He mirrored himself on his uncle Philip II, who – conforming to the last will and testament of his father Charles V – took care never to rely on one councilor fully, and who kept the control over his government firmly in his hands. Albert's own position, on top of that, was not stable enough at all to hand over the policy-making to members of his entourage just like that. Delegating power is only indicated if the actual possessor of it is not questioned by anyone. In the Archducal Netherlands that was least of all the case. Albert's court chaplain and biographer Aubertus Miraeus, in any case, was convinced that the archduke took care that

> 'no one claimed so much Authority for himself, that he would steer even a portion of the common weal, much less the entire State, according to his own caprice. Formerly Spain had its Alvarez Luna, and recently a Calderon; France, a Concini; England, an Essex; and Germany, a Klesl; other Regions at other times had brought their own Sejanuses as objects of mockery onto the World-stage. And while rumors of these kinds of things have indeed been abided

[173] I borrow this term from Brockliss, L.W.B. 'Concluding Remarks: The Anatomy of the Minister-Favourite,' in: Elliott & Brockliss, *The World of the Favourite*, pp. 279-309. Op. cit. p. 283.

in the Netherlands, still they have never seen examples of them in their own Bosom. It was [Albert] alone who did everything befitting a great Prince.'[174]

Miraeus' comments, no matter how subjective, give something to think about concerning the role that a favorite could play in the Archducal Netherlands. The preceding shows, in any case, that the count of Añover does not belong in the lineup of all-powerful *validos* like Lerma, Olivares, or Richelieu. And yet he was like a '*gran privado*' just as well. How, then, must his role as favorite be interpreted?

An initial aspect that has to be taken under observation is the nature of the relationship between Añover and Albert. All too frequently the importance of emotions like friendship and affection in early modern politics is underestimated.[175] Contemporaries realized but all too well, though, that the emotional relationship between the prince and the members of his entourage could have a crucial influence on the decision-making process.[176] That Rodrigo Niño y Lasso enjoyed the archduke's special favor is clear by now. It is more difficult to track down why that was so. Gauging the emotional connections between princes and their favorites is problematic anyway: frequently these kinds of studies risk losing themselves in the controversial approach of psychoanalytic historiography, in which it is not seldom that vague assumptions are proposed as well-established facts. So, for example, Elizabeth Wirth Marvick distinguished two 'prototypes' of favoritism in 1983: a 'paternal affective link,' in which the relationship between the favorite and the prince is compared to the affective relationship between father and son (the author refers here, among others, to Richelieu and Louis XIII, and to Olivares and Philip IV), and a 'sibling affective link,' in which it is instead a question of a relationship comparable to that between brothers and/or sisters (e.g., Louis XIII and the duke of Luynes).[177] There is no arguing that this interpretation is susceptible to much debate. And yet, there is no need to throw out the baby with the bathwater: as long as the pitfalls of Freudian thinking are avoided, research into the emotional bonds between the prince and his favorite can produce much relevant information – think of the duke of Buckingham, whose rising star at

[174] After Miraeus, A. *De vita Alberti Pii, sapientis, prudentis Belgarum Principis commentarius*. Antwerp, 1622, p. 105.

[175] Concerning the function of friendship in the early modern period, see Kettering, S. 'Friendship and Clientage in Early Modern France.' *French History*, 6 (1992) 139-158; Swett, K.W. ' 'The Account Between Us': Honor, Reciprocity and Companionship in Male Friendship in the Later Seventeenth Century.' *Albion*, 31 (1999) 1-30; and Miller, P.N. 'Friendship and Conversation in Seventeenth-Century Venice.' *The Journal of Modern History*, 73 (2001) 1-31.

[176] See in that context Wirth Marvick, E. 'Favorites in Early Modern Europe: A Recurring Psychopolitical Role.' *The Journal of Psychohistory*, 10 (1983) 463-489; and Wirth Marvick, E. 'Psychobiography and the Early Modern French Court: Notes on Method with Some Examples.' *French Historical Studies*, 19 (1996) 943-965.

[177] Wirth Marvick, E. 'Favorites in Early Modern Europe,' 466-467 f.

the English court reportedly went hand in hand with a sexual liaison with James I. In the case of Albert and Añover, all the same, it is quite difficult to research how and why the count succeeded in becoming *and* remaining the archduke's favorite. For want of sources there is in principle little to say concerning the nature and evolution of their relationship with each other. Yet it seems opportune to formulate a few suggestions about this.

As already seen above, Rodrigo Niño y Lasso came into Albert's service around 1595. It is, however, quite possible that they already knew each other much longer than that. Both men were approximately as old as each other (Albert was born in 1559; Rodrigo around 1560), and it is not unthinkable that they had met each other at the court of Philip II. Perhaps they were even playmates, or they went hunting together in their youth. In any case the presence of Rodrigo's uncle Gabriel Niño in the household of the cardinal-archduke suggests that Albert maintained good relations with the Niño y Lasso family – albeit not necessarily with Rodrigo himself. Whatever the case may be, Rodrigo succeeded his uncle as *gentilhombre de la Cámara* in 1595, and there is no doubt that he was able to win the archduke's trust rather rapidly. Scarcely a few months later Albert gave him the command of his mounted guard, and three years later he was appointed *sumiller de corps*. Both positions presupposed a sincere belief in Rodrigo's capacities and loyalty, and that need not come as a surprise. Rodrigo had always showed himself to be a loyal adherent of the Habsburg dynasty and had never hesitated to put his life at risk for it.

As head of the *Cámara*, Rodrigo's responsibility was to be in Albert's vicinity almost 24 hours out of 24. It is difficult to imagine that this kind of intense physical proximity did not bring emotional closeness along with it, even though the strict upbringing of an early modern prince certainly cannot be underestimated in that context. The office of *sumiller de corps* presupposed a high degree of intimacy and trust, but it would be a bridge too far to posit that Albert and Rodrigo were close friends, at least not in the 21st-century sense of the word. For that, the hierarchical distinction between both of them was simply too great. However, it is not unthinkable that with time a certain degree of affection arose between both men. As an unmarried nobleman, on top of that, Rodrigo had few familial obligations and, consequently, much time to dedicate almost exclusively to the service of his master. Further, it is quite possible that Albert and Rodrigo shared certain interests that brought them closer together. They were both ardent art collectors, and – going from the sums that they both spent on their appearance – also lovers of expensive clothing. Even so, their greatest shared passion was their religious zeal. Not for nothing, Archduke Albert was known as Albertus the Pious, and it seems that Rodrigo was no less god-fearing. As a young man he considered entering into the Discalced Carmelites, and although he still opted for a secular life, he would nevertheless emerge as a fervent patron of this religious order, which was also favored by the archdukes.[178] On top of that, Rodrigo's devotion seems to have been genuine. According to the French ambassador, he carried around his neck a relic of Saint Teresa of Jesus [Teresa de Ávila], for whom he harbored a special reverence. It was said that Rodrigo supposedly even had done a miraculous deed by predicting that he would die on the feast day of Saint Teresa – which indeed would be the case.[179] A kind of profound religiosity like that likely made much of an impression on Albert.

All these hypotheses are naturally most highly speculative. There is not a single proof for postulating that Albert and Añover talked with each other about religion, let alone about fashion or art. Only a few letters from their correspondence with each other remain preserved, and these treat merely political and military matters. Consequently, it will never be known why Rodrigo Niño y Lasso of all people became Albert's *gran privado*. Perhaps his privileged status can best be clarified from the simple observation that Añover always showed himself to be a reliable advisor, a competent politician, *and* a loyal protagonist of the Habsburg dynasty. Taking into consideration the political circumstances at that time in the Low Countries, a combination of those kinds of qualities was rare in any case. On top of that, Añover profiled himself pretty much always as one of Albert's most loyal supporters, and this, namely, in questions close to the archduke's heart. A characteristic example of that is found in the correspondence of the French ambassador Mathieu Brulart de Berny. In 1610, when the archduke became angry about the address with which he was regarded in the letters from the French king and, with that, unchained a long-persistent diplomatic disturbance, Añover was the only one, according to Brulart, who continued to support his master all down the line.[180] In Albert's eyes, Añover must have been a grateful pillar of support.

Even so, in all of this it cannot be forgotten that the count of Añover enjoyed much trust not only in the Southern Netherlands but also in Spain. During the first decade of the seventeenth century he was the one who time after time ironed out the wrinkles between Brussels and Madrid. Evidently he succeeded in doing this without blatantly taking sides for this party or that one, for his diplomatic services

[178] See e.g. the print series *Vitae Beatae Virginis Teresiae a Iesu* concerning the life of Saint Teresa of Ávila, published in 1613 and dedicated to the count of Añover. Cf. Duerloo, L. & Thomas, W., eds. *Albrecht & Isabella, 1598-1621: Catalogus*. Turnhout, 1998, pp. 267–268 and Diels, A. 'De familie Colaert (ca. 1555-1630) en de prentkunst in Antwerpen.' *Archives et bibliothèques de Belgique*, extra issue 88. Brussels, 2010, p. 193, note 784.

[179] '*Ledit conte portoyt sur luy par dévotion une petite piece du vray cœur de la mère Thérèse, et avoyt souvent ez la bouche, qu'il mourroyt le jour de sa feste comme il arriva audit jour à neuf heures du soyr.*' BNF, *MsF* 16133, f. 58: Péricard to Puisieux, October 8, 1620.

[180] BNF, *MsF* 16129, f. 293: Mathieu Brulart de Berny to Puisieux, August 6, 1610.

were especially valued on both sides. Just like Albert, Philip III saw the count as a political confederate, and the latter took care to profile himself as such as well. That turned out to be the case, among others, in 1610, when Philip gave the marquis of Guadaleste the command to hinder the distribution of the book *Tractatus Septem* – in which the Jesuit Juan de Mariana took aim at Spain's monetary policy, among other things – in the Southern Netherlands.[181] In view of the fact that Guadaleste was no longer working in Brussels at that moment, Añover wrote that he would gladly take over his commission and would see to it in quiet that the book would be taken off the market.[182] During the Condé affair, too, Añover kept the king systematically informed of developments.[183] Consequently, Philip had no reasons to doubt the loyalty of the count, and the latter was reasonable enough to keep it that way. As was touched upon above, Añover had a significant portion of his wealth thanks to the Spanish monarch. He was clearly not planning to bite the hand that fed him.

The count of Añover served in essence not one but two different princes. That he, like no other, succeeded in keeping himself upright in that kind of complex situation argues for his political shrewdness. In the turbulent diplomatic relationship between Brussels and Madrid, the count, as one of few courtiers, moved like a fish in water. However, that in no way means that he never ended up in a dangerous current. Namely, during the first decade of the seventeenth century, Añover did not sweep his political conviction under the carpet, and that was not always taken well. As seen already in the previous chapter, the count was ranked by some observers among the so-called 'Spanish faction' at court.

That these observers had it right is shown, among other things, from the fact that a few years later Añover would get involved with an obscure and one-sided initiative to break the Twelve Years' Truce. Archduke Albert discovered in 1611, that without his knowledge Luis de Velasco had set up a plan to invade the city of Sluis, and this on the advice of the Spanish spy Diego López Sueyro.[184] The latter maintained secret contacts with a few rebels in the North and acted in his own words on the commission of the king – something that Philip III would later adamantly deny, but which nonetheless proved to be the truth.[185] Already in July, 1610, Philip had commissioned the count of Añover to seek out what the offers of López Sueyro precisely were worth.[186] Añover went in on this and saw to it, among other things, that the spy got fl. 600 at his

[181] Concerning Mariana, see Braun, H.E. *Juan de Mariana and Early Modern Spanish Political Thought*. Aldershot, 2007.
[182] AGS, *Estado* 2292, s.f.: The count of Añover to Philip III, February 18, 1610.
[183] See e.g. AGS, *Estado* 2292, s.f.: Añover to Philip III, February 20, 1602.
[184] AGS, *Estado* 2026, s.f.: Consult of the *Consejo de Estado*, March 3, 1611.
[185] AGS, *Estado* 2293, s.f.: Albert to Philip III, April 7, 1611.
[186] AGS, *Estado* 2227, s.f.: Philip III to Añover, July 3, 1610.

disposal to cover his costs and to continue his secret negotiations.[187] Via an informant from Holland, however, the archduke got wind of the affair. Albert was confounded concerning the developments that had played out behind his back. He refused to believe that the king would want to put the ceasefire obtained with much effort at risk, and had López Sueyro promptly arrested.[188] To argue his innocence the spy sent one of his sons to Añover. The latter turned out not to be informed of the arrest, all the same. When he went to ask the archduke for an explanation, to his great surprise Albert snapped at him 'with much acrimony that this was an affair that did not concern him.'[189] Displeased, Añover wrote to Philip III that he did not grasp why, in spite of their good relationship, the archduke had not informed him about this matter.[190]

The case of López Sueyro is one of the few instances that shows that the trust Albert put in the count of Añover was great, to be sure, though it was not unconditional. Yet the affair does not seem to have influenced his faith in Añover's competence: a year later the count would be appointed *mayordomo mayor* of the archducal household. There are indeed vague indications that Añover would take a more cautious position after this affair. He remained good friends with Luis de Velasco, yet sought and found connections with Spínola and Mancisidor, who more and more frequently entered into the foreground at the court in Brussels. Jointly they would profile themselves during the Twelve Years' Truce as the strong men of the regime. Nevertheless the story gives something to think about concerning the specific circumstances with which a minister-favorite was confronted at the archducal court. It seems that Aubertus Miraeus had it right: Albert was not the kind of man to rely fully on one member of his entourage. The archduke kept a *gran privado*, to be sure, but he was in no sense willing to have Añover exercise power in his stead. Perhaps, then, Añover's privileged position needs to be judged not so much on content as on form.[191] At a time in which pretty much all great princes kept a favorite, as a self-respecting sovereign Albert could naturally not stay behind. Seen from that standpoint, the remarkable proliferation of favorites in the seventeenth century is perhaps much more a question of imitation and emulation. Housing a favorite was, then, *de rigueur* for every splendid court that considered itself worthy of that name. In that respect it can be posited that the

---

[187] AGS, *Estado* 627, s.f.: Diego López Sueyro to Añover, September 20, 1610.

[188] AGS, *Estado* 626, s.f.: Albert to Philip III, February 2, 1611.

[189] '*El Conde [de Añover] añada que aviendo mostrado sentimiento al Señor Archidque de que no se le hubiese dado parte deste negocio saviendo S.A. que tratava el con Diego Lopez de algunos avisos de Olanda, le respondió con mucha sequedad que no eran cosas que tocavan al Conde el saverlas (…).*' AGS, *Estado* 2026, s.f.: Consult of the *Consejo de Estado*, March 3, 1611. See also AGS, *Estado* 626, s.f.: Añover to Philip III, February 3, 1611.

[190] AGS, *Estado* 626, s.f.: Añover to Philip III, February 3, 1611.

[191] I thank Luc Duerloo for this suggestion.

archduke 'copied' the standard model of the *valido* from other princes, but did give it his own supplement that would hinder his favorite from appropriating too much power for himself. The political circumstances in the Southern Netherlands, on top of that, were not of such nature that the *valimiento* could thrive there undisturbed. In a political climate in which two different sovereigns and two contrasting policy lines had to be taken into account, it was pretty much impossible for one man to strive for an absolute concentration of power. In order to hold his own Añover needed to gain and keep not only the favor of Albert but also that of Philip III. In that capacity he was always balancing on a slack rope. That the count – despite a few small blemishes – succeeded like no other in keeping the balance testifies to great political insight.

Conclusion

Rodrigo Niño y Lasso would keep his prominent position at the court of the archdukes until the end of his life. He died on October 5, 1620, after a lingering illness.[192] According to the Spanish ambassador, the archdukes were stricken by sorrow:

> 'On the fifth of this [month] the count of Añover died, with great sadness of the archduke and the infanta as a result, because he was a man who enjoyed so much prestige and was so important to their service, as is well known. And I can and must affirm that he was no less [important] to the service of Your Majesty, to which he dedicated himself with the appropriate zeal and care.'[193]

In a last show of appreciation Archduke Albert had given the count an annuity of fl. 5,000 'for the benefit of [Añover's] servants.'[194] The French ambassador reported that 'the offices of grand master, grand chamberlain and grand marshall which he alone exercised with absolute power in this household, are greatly sought after and will no doubt only be given to those who deserve it.'[195] Albert and Isabella took leave of their

[192] A contemporaneous report of Añover's illness, death, and burial can be found in IVDJ, ms. 26-I-11, ff. 43-50: *Relación de la enfermedad, muerte y entiero, honras y obsequias del Señor Conde de Añober que está en gloria.*

[193] '*A 5 deste murió el conde de Añover con mucho sentimiento del señor archiduque y de la señora infanta, por ser persona de tanta estima y tan importante en su servicio, como es notorio y yo puedo y devo affirmar que no lo era menos en el de VM porque acudía a el en todo lo que se offrecía con la affición y cuydado que devia a quien era.*' AGS, *Estado* 2309, s.f.: The marquis of Bedmar to Philip III, October 11, 1620.

[194] '*(...) pour en bénéficier ses serviteurs.*' HHStA, Belgien PC 27, s.f.: Charles della Faille to Ferdinand van Booischot, October 10, 1620.

[195] '*(...) les charges de grand maistre, grand chambelan et grand écuyer quil tenoyt seul avec pouvoir absolu en cette maison sont fort recherchées et sans doute ne seront deferées qu'au mérite.*' BNF, *MsF* 16133, f. 58: Péricard to Puisieux, October 8, 1620.

Illustration 4 – Tombstone of Rodrigo Niño y Lasso, count of Añover, in the *Capilla de las Santas Reliquias* in the parish church of Cuerva.
(Photo: author.)

The epitaph reads:

D.O.M.
Aqvi iace D. Rodrigo Niño
y Lasso Conde de Añover
Maiordomo Maior Svmiller
de Corps y Cavallerico
Maior de los Serenissimos
Archidvque Alberto y In-
fanta de España D. Isabel
Fvlgebit post nvbila serena dies
Exibit spiritvs eivs et revertetvr in
terram svam. Psal. 145

favorite with a magnificent mass in the collegiate church of Saint Gudula, in the presence of the complete court. The sermon was held by Añover's father confessor, who was also prior of the monastery of the Discalced Carmelites in Brussels. According to one source, it was 'one of the most magnificent and harmonious masses that was ever organized in this country.'[196] After that, Añover's body was conveyed to Spain, where – in accordance with the stipulations of his last will and testament – it was interred in the parish church of Cuerva (cf. Illustration 4).[197]

The case of Rodrigo Niño y Lasso raises various questions about the manner in which the reign of Albert and Isabella has been described in the past by historians. Until now research on the matter has concentrated in the main on established political institutions and structures. Although this approach has produced many useful insights, it does not suffice for unraveling the full complexity of the decision-making process in this time period. Attention has seldom been paid to the less visible structures of power, nor to the influential role of access, proximity, and favoritism. Nevertheless a thorough analysis of these aspects can create more clarity concerning the workings of archducal policy-making. Añover's remarkable career, his personal influence at court, and his talent for converting his privileged status into immense financial gain indicate that the role of courtiers has wrongly been overlooked.

[196] IVDJ, ms. 26-I-11, f. 49r°.

[197] IVDJ, ms. 26-I-11, ff. 27-41: *Copia authorizada del testamento que el Señor Rodrigo Niño y Lasso Conde de Añober otorgó en los Estados de Flandes*. Añover was interred in a side chapel of the church, the construction of which chapel he had arranged himself. See Ríos de Balmaseda, A. 'La Capilla de Reliquias de Cuerva y el cuadro de la Sagrada Cena de Tristan,' in: *Toletum: Boletín de la Real Academia de Bellas Artes y Ciencias Históricas de Toledo*, 27 (1991) 129-143.

Conclusion

'In general, however, if you want to last long at the Court, acquire the following two qualities: Endurance (...) and Caution: for there are many traps waiting for you, and Deceit rules amidst the greatness of the court. At that place, everyone is burning with desire to find fault with another one's words and deeds. They have hardly opened their mouths before their tongues seem to be ready. There you will meet with ambushes and enemies; who try to disgrace you by secret accusations while you are unaware of it, and while they praise you in public, in order to catch you more easily.'[1]

Justus Lipsius
Monita et Exempla Politica

In his tractatus *Monita et Exempla Politica*, published in 1605, Justus Lipsius sketched an anything but exhilarating picture of the early modern court. According to the famous humanist, the splendid façade of the princely residence masked a world of mendacity, treachery, and defamation. The question can be asked as to what extent Archduke Albert, to whom the work was dedicated, felt himself to be addressed by Lipsius' comments. Did he recognize his own court in the description? Did it perhaps make him think of the court of his father Maximilian II, where he first saw the light of day in 1559? Or did it remind him instead of Philip II's court in Madrid, where he had spent the greatest part of his youth? It will most likely never be known. For that matter, it is quite possible that the archduke did not dwell at all on Lipsius' remark. In the end, Albert was born at an early modern court, and he knew like no other how things happened in that kind of environment. From his childhood he had seen how the palaces where he had grown up were not only opulent places of luxury but also hotbeds of political conflict. In that sense, the archduke did not need Lipsius' *Monita et Exempla Politica* to become aware of the many dangers lurking at court. He knew them but all too well.

For the modern reader, Lipsius' critical observation is much more sensational than it must have been for Albert. In today's political landscape, after all, the princely court no longer takes in a place of significance. In constitutional monarchy, policy is laid

[1] Lipsius, J. *Monita et Exempla Politica, libri duo, qui virtutes et vitia principum spectant* (1605). Citation taken from the modern edition by Waszink, J., ed. *Politica: six books of politics or political instruction.* Assen, 2004. Op.cit. p. 379.

out by the parliament and carried out by the government. The prince plays only a symbolic role in what has become, as far as the rest is concerned, a professional and bureaucratic state apparatus. In principle, his signature is his only relevant trump card left. The decision-making itself has been relocated to the chamber of public representatives and to the cabinets of ministerial excellencies. In a sense, the court has been left behind like an orphan. Little more than a morose remnant of a past long since flown away, it is associated in the media with special speeches at Christmastime and romantic scenes on cookie tins. The greatest danger still to threaten the court lies in the activities of *paparazzi* who pop up, rightly or wrongly, to violate the privacy of the royal family.

Once upon a time, it was different. During the Ancien Régime the court was not only the residence of the prince but also the seat of the government. It was the forum *par excellence* where political power was negotiated, favor acquired, and conflicting interests fought out. As such, it formed the nexus of political and diplomatic busyness, with the prince as the pivotal figure and the courtiers as councilors, policymakers, and lobbyists. Despite this, the early modern court was treated like a stepchild for decades among historians. The court and its household simply did not fit into the success story of the triumphant modern state, which was, not coincidentally, typified by the uncoupling of the princely household from the princely administration. Politics, as it went, was supposed to play out in the institutions and advisory councils provided for it, not in the corridors and backrooms of one royal residence or the other. Not until the 1970s and 1980s did that vision have to make room for an approach that no longer postulated the state-building process as dominating over everything, and that awarded the court a central position anew as the most prominent *locus* of power. Since then, the advance of court studies is not to be stopped.

In emulating this new tendency in historical studies, this book went in search of the political significance of the court of Brussels during the reign of Albert and Isabella. 'The court of the archdukes,' Jonathan Israel wrote in the recently published survey *België in de Zeventiende Eeuw* ['Belgium in the Seventeenth Century'], 'was much grander and more in love with pomp than that of any other governor-general whatsoever preceding or following it. It grew into one of the most important diplomatic and cultural nerve centers of Europe.'[2] It can be called surprising, then, that the archducal court has never before been the subject of an in-depth study. The surprise is that much greater, knowing that the reign itself of Albert and Isabella did get relatively much attention from historians. Namely, during the late nineteenth

[2] Israel, J. 'Het tijdperk van de Aartshertogen, 1598-1621,' in: Janssens, P., ed. *België in de Zeventiende Eeuw. De Spaanse Nederlanden en het prinsbisdom Luik*. 2 vols. Ghent, 2006, volume I, pp. 28-32. Op. cit. p. 28.

and early twentieth century, scholarly debate concerning the political autonomy of the archdukes scaled great heights. That the role of the court and its household seldom or never was taken into consideration in the process says much about the manner in which historians at that time thought early modern decision-making had to be studied. Entirely in accordance with the historiographical norms of their time, they concentrated in the first place on the political institutions and structures that constituted a foreshadowing of what in the nineteenth century would come to belong to the standard trappings of the modern state. It was not recognized as such that political power manifested itself during the Ancien Régime also – and even above all – in entirely different, less tangible ways. On top of that, these historians elucidated the archducal period from a strongly nationalistic paradigm, in which the Southern Netherlands, aching for political emancipation, moaned and groaned under the yoke of Spanish tyranny.

In later decades this institutionalistic and polarizing vision made way for a more nuanced approach. The sharp edges were, as it were, filed away. Nonetheless, even today the traditional impression still exercises much influence on the historiography concerning this period, albeit rather under the surface and sometimes even unconsciously – which makes it that much more dangerous. In the main the archducal regime is still elucidated from the established and traditional powers of structure, and the rivalry between Spain and the Southern Netherlands is still a dominant factor in the story. Up to a certain level that is conceivable: being able to contend that politics was *not* practiced in traditional administrative institutions, or that no wariness existed in Brussels between those from Spain and the Southern Netherlands, is difficult. All the same, it is clear that this all too one-sided impression cannot possibly suffice for getting to the bottom of the complexity of political relationships in the archducal period. Although international research with regard to early modern decision-making has for a few decades enthusiastically been making use of new and refreshing theories concerning politics and political culture, historiography concerning the archducal regime seems to want to hold stubbornly onto an historiographical agenda that was drawn up in the second half of the nineteenth and first half of the twentieth century.[3] As a result, until now the court and household of Albert and Isabella have for the large part remained out of historians' field of vision. Above all, attention has gone out

[3] In that context it is in no sense exaggerated to posit that Belgian historiography concerning the archducal period – and by expansion concerning the entire Eighty Years' War – still relies to a great degree on the monumental but strongly tinted editions of primary sources, published in the late nineteenth and early twentieth century by archivists like Louis-Prosper Gachard and Henri Lonchay. Cf. Gachard, L.-P., ed. *Correspondance de Philippe II sur les affaires des Pays-Bas publiée d'après les originaux conservés dans les Archives royales de Simancas*. 6 vols. Brussels, 1848-1936; and Lonchay, H., Cuvelier, J. & Lefèvre, J., eds. *Correspondance de la Cour d'Espagne sur les affaires des Pays-Bas au XVIIe siècle*. 6 vols. Brussels, 1923-1937.

to the role of the court as a catalyst of cultural, artistic, and religious patronage. Its household came up for discussion much less and, on top of that, was seldom seen as a politically relevant body.

Building further on the insights that the historical discipline of court studies has brought forth in recent years, the political significance of the court and household of the archdukes was studied in the book from the conviction that *domus* and *res publica* were bound inseparably to each other during the Ancien Régime. That coupling expressed itself very concretely not only in the political and diplomatic activities of the courtiers but also in the function of the early modern court as the environment *par excellence* in which princely authority was evoked and displayed. In the twentieth-century debate over the political autonomy of Albert and Isabella, these kinds of elements were never taken into consideration. Nevertheless it is clear that the knowledge of these mechanisms is indispensable for being able to make a balanced judgment about the nature and workings of the archducal regime.

An interesting observation in that context is the fact that in 1598-1599, Albert and Isabella introduced a new court ceremonial at the court in Brussels. The introduction of this court paradigm cobbled from the Spanish-Burgundian model went hand-in-hand not only with a number of architectural operations in the residential wing of the Coudenberg palace but also with new regulations concerning access to the princes' private quarters. The fact that the archdukes consciously opted for organizing their court after the model of the Spanish court was seized upon by some historians as an argument for the proposition that the court of Albert and Isabella was a bastion of Spanish authority in the Netherlands. With that, they overlooked a few important matters, all the same.

It is decidedly no coincidence that the introduction of the new court ceremonial and the concomitant rules went hand-in-hand with the transfer of sovereignty over the Netherlands to the archdukes. From 1598 forward, the court in Brussels was no longer the court of a governor of the blood but of two sovereign princes. The significance of this revaluation cannot be underestimated. The change in status presupposed an adjustment to the 'formal requirements' to which every self-respecting sovereign court in this time period was expected to answer. If the court in Brussels – which in the second half of the sixteenth century had lost much of its earlier luster – wanted to be taken seriously by its peers and to play a role of significance within the international community, it needed to shake the reputation of regional subcourt off itself. Thenceforth it would have to present itself as a self-aware, independent, and above all sovereign court. The introduction of the Spanish-Burgundian court ceremonial, which in this time period was held to be the most prestigious in Europe, played into this. Albert and Isabella consciously chose to breathe new life into the languishing court in Brussels. On top of that, the new ceremonial contributed to their political and dynastic aspirations in a very tangible way. Thus, for example, the adjusted rules of access would play an important role in the splendid isolation of the archdukes, whereby their sublimity as sovereign princes was emphasized even more. The fact that Albert and Isabella were in the habit of taking their place in the Court Chapel behind the *cortina* can be held to be illustrative as well for the almost sacred status they took on for themselves. It speaks for itself that many of these novelties did not fall on fertile ground with everyone. The nobility from the Southern Netherlands reproached the archduke for wanting to organize his court 'as if he was a king.' Albert was not that as yet in 1599, but he did indeed harbor the ardent ambition to lay hold of the title of king. In that sense, with the introduction of the new ceremonial he anticipated the future he saw set aside for himself – a future that never would become the truth, all the same.

The consciously conceived revitalization of the court in Brussels did not only go hand-in-hand with an adjustment of the court ceremonial. The religious practices that were introduced would contribute to the new image also. Only a few matters would influence life at the archducal court in such an intrusive manner as the strict Catholic ethos in effect there. The court of Albert and Isabella profiled itself as a beacon of light for Christian devotion and piety and, in the process, was inspired by the princely virtue of *Pietas* – one of the ideological pillars of the Habsburg dynasty. All too frequently, however, this militant religious zeal was elucidated by historians from a too one-sided angle, as if its importance could be reduced to mere cultural/religious scope. Only thanks to recent research has it become clear that the ethos cultivated at the court in Brussels made up part of a conscious strategy to give the requisite force to Habsburg authority in the Netherlands and was, in that sense, in no way devoid of a political/ideological dimension. The far-reaching religious experience at court constituted a component of an inventive program of princely exhibition, in which the perpetuation of dynastic power – with Albert and Isabella as representatives – constituted the underlying motivation. The way in which this princely exhibition was fleshed out by the archdukes was characteristic for the Habsburg dynasty. In a very visual, almost tangible manner, the court externalized the three fundamental values on which the identity of the Habsburgs had rested: House, State, and Religion. By engaging themselves in an unmistakable Habsburg tradition the archdukes demarcated the mental borderlines of their rule.

Religious practices were an important, though not the only element that contributed to the *representatio maiestatis*. One aspect that is often overlooked by historians, but that nonetheless played an important role in the 'fabrication' of a princely image, was the extent of the household. During the Ancien Régime the scale of the court functioned as a gauge for the scope of princely authority – or in any case for the ambitions that the prince harbored in that area. Although the incoherent nature of the sources necessitates some caveats, it can be posited that in comparison to other European princes Albert and Isabella kept an entourage of above-average size. It speaks for itself that their household could not measure up to the seemingly always expanding households in Madrid, Paris, Vienna, or London. Yet it seems to have kept pace with the larger households in the Holy Roman Empire and in Italian principalities. More important, though, than precise quantitative data concerning this question is the assessment that the archducal court was judged by contemporaries as excessively large. It was seen as *disproportionally* large not so much in comparison to other courts as it was in comparison to the status of Albert and Isabella. Just as the archducal court in an organizational and ceremonial sense had been cobbled from a royal model, it can be posited that in terms of size it was calculated on a royal scale. It exceeded expectations as a consequence. That conclusion gains in force when considering that the archdukes also lived above their standing in financial respects. Already for the fixed costs of the household alone (i.e. wages and operating resources) enormous sums of money were necessary, which – based on a tentative estimate – amounted yearly to between 14 % and 50 % of the total treasury revenues. On average the share likely fluctuated around 25 %. In the knowledge that all manner of exceptional expenditures must be added to this, it can easily be assumed that the archducal court – at least as concerns the financial picture – certainly did not have to feel inferior to other European courts. It seems that relatively speaking the archdukes spent even more money on their household than their counterparts in other principalities, although this proposition would also benefit from more, and clearer, data. In any case it is clear that the archducal court – together with the *Ejército de Flandes* – was the most money-devouring institution in the Southern Netherlands, which in and of itself is already an indicator for its political importance.

One of the largest expenditure lines within the archducal household comprised the trimester payments of personnel remunerations. Still, the individual wages of the courtiers and servants were in and of themselves not very attractive. In the case of the 'lower' servants, the salary was still more or less comparable to wages that were current elsewhere in the labor market, but for the noble courtiers – who often enjoyed splendid rents – it was clearly a matter of mere symbolic compensation. On top of that, the remunerations were frequently paid late. In other words, the salary offered was not at once a stimulus for aspiring to a position in the archducal household. In spite of that, these functions were especially desired: many contemporaries gladly wanted to lay hold of a post in the archducal entourage. That means that in addition to the remuneration there were other factors that made a position in the archducal household worth the effort. The lower functions were interesting on account of the many honoraria and financial extras connected with them. A job in the household offered the right to shelter, legal assistance, medical care, favorable tax status, a (primitive) system of social security, and a daily ration. In times of crisis and uncertainty these kinds of things were naturally a bonus. Even so, for noble courtiers there was yet another reason that encouraged them to strive for a position in the archducal household. In addition to the requisite prestige, a court office offered them the possibility to spend time in the proximity of the prince on a daily basis. That this kind of privilege could bring important advantages along with it is clear by now.

Positions in the archducal household were desired, yet they were certainly not simple to lay hold of. The awarding of court offices was bound to a number of strict conditions. The question of who was or was not appointed (and for what reason) can teach much about the expectations that were placed on courtiers – and thus about the role the household was expected to play in the early modern political constellation. In classical historiography this intriguing question has constantly had to make room, though, for an approach that made the rivalry there between those present from Spain and the Southern Netherlands central to this question. That research into the origins of the courtiers can in principle bring forth interesting results needs no argument. So, for instance, it appears clear that the archdukes made many efforts to integrate the nobility from the Southern Netherlands and Burgundy into their household. The question remains, however, as to what extent a quantitative analysis of the number of courtiers of this or that origin has something to say about political relationships at court. Historians do dare sometimes to pass by the fact that nation – in any case an especially elastic concept in an early modern context – and loyalty were not necessarily mutually interchangeable concepts during the Ancien Régime. The early modern court was still cosmopolitan enough to allow that a courtier could be born as a subject of one prince yet could swear loyalty to another. It makes little sense, then, to assign members of the household to this or that side of the political spectrum on the basis of their origins. In the same way an analysis of the recruitment policy in the archducal household does not benefit from a premise that postulates the competition between the courtiers from Spain and the Southern Netherlands as dominating over everything. The origins of the candidates were, to be sure, taken into consideration in awarding a court function but were certainly not the only, and also not always the decisive, factor in the final decision. In addition to origin, the selection of courtiers was dependent on a combination of factors, such as religious and political affinity, lineage and reputation, competence and experience, and the influence and advocacy of third parties. Above all, though, the trustworthiness of a candidate was looked at. That trustworthiness was not tested so much against his or her origin but rather against the standing of his or her service. Loyalty, after all, went hand-in-hand with being of service to the prince and – in a broader context – to the dynasty. In that sense it was also a phenomenon that crossed boundary lines. Within the Habsburg imperium the course of courtiers' careers could lead them from one Habsburg court to the other, in the service of the dynasty. The Dietrichstein family, whose members were spread across the courts of Vienna, Prague, Madrid, and Brussels, offers in that context an excellent example of the exchange of human resources in Habsburg Europe.

That the selection of courtiers was bound to strict criteria need not come as a surprise. The opportunity to spend time in the proximity of the archdukes proved to be of inestimable importance, after all, in the rat race for the acquisition of favor and political influence. Although Albert and Isabella cultivated an image of accessibility and approachability, they were in actuality well screened-off from the outside world. To be sure, the old palace on the Coudenberg hill was no impenetrable bulwark, but the access to the archducal *Cámara* was always strictly monitored. Unauthorized persons did not enter into it without prior permission, and that was not simple to get. As a result, the right to access became a fiercely fought-for privilege. It could be both monopolized as well as constrained and, in that sense, brought political consequences along with it. Politics, after all, did not come into being only in the traditional administrative institutions and advisory councils encircling the palace of Brussels but just as well in the private quarters of Albert, where the politics of intimacy had free range. It was not for nothing that the *gentilhombres de la Cámara* bore a golden key as a sign of their dignity. For them, the right of access to the archduke was by definition unlimited, guaranteed, and even to a certain extent enforceable. In essence, the key stood as a symbol for the fact that the bearer made up part of Albert's small circle of intimates. It need not come as a surprise, then, that these *gentilhombres* usually figured prominently in the stream of diplomatic correspondence flowing from the court in Brussels to the other princely courts of Europe. It was not contemporaneous preference for hierarchy and status that encouraged foreign diplomats to give comments concerning the members of the archducal *Cámara* but, rather, the realization that the assured access of the latter made them politically relevant figures.

At the same time, however, it needs to be noted that access at the early modern court must be researched not only from a 'quantitative,' but also from a 'qualitative' standpoint. Much more than an objectively measurable criterion, access was a complex and widely encompassing *process* in which, above all, the emotional relationship with the prince played a role. The importance of access did not lie so much in the possibility of entering into contact with the archdukes as it did in the guaranteed, day-to-day proximity that made it possible to build up a solid bond of trust, and that in certain cases could lead to friendship, affection, and even intimacy. In that case the 'proximity' was not so much physical as it was psychological in nature. A good example is the relationship between Archduke Albert and the marquis of Marnay. The marquis made up part of the archducal household already since its early beginning and, as a *gentilhombre de la Cámara*, was able to gain the trust and favor of Albert. It need not come as a surprise, then, that the archduke dared to charge him with an extremely important and ultra-secret mission in 1609: Marnay was sent to Rome, where he had to negotiate with the pope concerning the awarding of the title of king to Albert. The fact that the marquis was appointed *sumiller de corps* in 1620 indicates that he enjoyed an exceptional status at court. According to the French ambassador, Marnay was the only one who was still allowed to approach, address, and touch Albert during his attacks of gout. These and similar commentaries are overlooked in the historiography concerning the archducal regime, yet they are nevertheless of crucial importance for getting to the bottom of decision-making in this time period. They demonstrate that Albert's *Cámara* was a political entity in the first place, and must be studied as such.

That the *gentilhombres* could exercise influence on policy thanks to their free access to Albert is an assessment that is never recognized as such in the historiography concerning the archducal regime. For that reason much attention has never been given to the role of courtiers as intermediaries between the court and other strata of society. Still, their contribution to the regime is not to be underestimated. The courtiers were fully engaged in the military, administrative, and diplomatic domains and functioned there as representatives of the archdukes. In a certain sense they were the 'eyes and ears' of Albert and Isabella outside the walls of the court. It need not come as a surprise, then, that the royal *Consejo de Estado* did everything to keep the members of the archducal household out of the army leadership – albeit without much result. Striking as well is the fact that pretty much all provincial governors in one way or another were connected to the household and, inversely, that the representative bodies of the estates in the provinces were represented by nobles who held a court function with the archduke. Not coincidentally, the interventions of these *gentilhombres* proved to be of decisive importance in 1616, when the provincial States had to be convinced to recognize Philip III as their future sovereign. It turns out to be clear here that the interwoven nature between the princely household and the princely administration in this time period is much greater that has been generally presupposed. The process of the swearing of oaths was almost fully directed from the archducal *Cámara*, with figures like Ambrogio Spínola – who, not coincidentally, would later be appointed *mayordomo mayor* – and the father confessor Iñigo de Brizuela at the helm. In essence, here the most prominent function of the courtiers comes floating to the surface: they were expected to serve the interests of the archdukes and the Habsburg dynasty as well as possible. The fact that various *gentilhombres* were engaged as diplomats to represent Albert to foreign princes shows this as well. It cannot be any coincidence that the really crucial diplomatic missions – like those in which Albert's dynastic position or the preservation of the August House of Austria was at risk – were pretty much always carried out by *gentilhombres de la Cámara.*

The assessment that the courtiers served in different sectors as representatives of Albert and Isabella indicates that in archducal policy-making there was no talk of an absolute separation between public and private domains. The interwoven nature of both spheres was much greater than is generally assumed. Nowhere was that intertwining better expressed than in the archducal *Cámara*, where the *gentilhombres* occupied themselves with the administration of the household as well as with the management of the state. The example *par excellence* is Rodrigo Niño y Lasso, the count of Añover, who as *mayordomo mayor*, *sumiller de corps*, and *caballerizo mayor* combined the three most important functions in the archducal household and at the same time was one of the most influential politicians of the archducal regime. That Añover must be seen as the minister-favorite or *valido* of Archduke Albert is a conviction that was shared by many contemporaries but that has never dawned on historians. And yet just quickly leafing through the political and diplomatic correspondence of that time is all that is necessary to determine that Niño y Lasso enjoyed the exceptional favor of the archduke and, precisely for that reason, was able to climb to the highest reaches of power. The fact that his authority in the Southern Netherlands was compared to that of the duke of Lerma in Spain says quite a lot in that context. Yet the count of Añover has never been able to count on any interest from historians. Undoubtedly, this lack of interest has to do with the fact that Añover could not be connected to the established administrative institutions of the time period. As a member of the archducal household, the count did not operate by way of the traditional channels of power, after all. That was also not necessary: Añover's political influence was based on his personal relationship with the archduke, in whose immediate proximity he spent time for more than twenty years.

Although the different chapters in this book treat quite divergent topics, they in fact all point in the direction of one overarching conclusion: the current impression concerning the archducal regime is in need of fundamental revision. Building further on an historiographical agenda that was drawn up in the late nineteenth and early twentieth century, the government of Albert and Isabella was elucidated until now from a paradigm in which the process of state-building stood front and center. In so doing, politics was seen as the resultant of policy actions and perspectives that – if not exclusive, then in the main still – came into being within the established institutions of the state apparatus. In that sense the historiography concerning the archducal regime is running miles behind international research concerning early modern politics and early modern political culture. On top of that, the excessive attention to the sovereign status of Albert and Isabella as well as to the Spanish presence in the Netherlands has led to a lack of scholarly interest in other topics, the study of which is nevertheless crucial for arriving at a good grasp of the archducal regime. In that sense, a reorientation of historiographical priorities is urgent.

As opposed to what is frequently uncritically assumed by historians, the archducal court was no bastion of Spanish authority. It was, however, just as little a bulwark of those from the Southern Netherlands. The court of Albert and Isabella was in the first place a power base of the Habsburg dynasty. All too frequently historians have neglected to study the history of the Archducal Netherlands from a dynastic context. It needs to be realized, though, that the *raison d'état* during the Ancien Régime was never uncoupled from the dynastic interests of the prince. In his eyes the administration of the early modern state coincided with the administration of the familial patrimony. In the case of the Habsburg dynasty, naturally, it was a matter of an especially extended patrimony, which precisely on account of this large scale was split up between different branches of the princely family. Still, that does not take away from the fact that the whole always was seen as a family possession that had to be safeguarded at all times. All members of the dynasty were expected to take responsibility in that context – with much disunity with each other as a consequence.

Seen from this angle, it becomes clear that the archducal regime cannot be evaluated without paying attention to the political entanglements in the Spanish-Habsburg monarchy, yet also to those in the Holy Roman Empire. And in that last area, above all, the historiography has remained tremendously lacking. The fact that Albert was for years an excellently positioned candidate to succeed his brother Rudolf II on the imperial throne suggests nevertheless that his political priorities did not lie only in the Netherlands. There is no doubt, then, that many of his political decisions can be placed in a new light provided they are connected to the frictions surrounding the succession of Rudolf at that time. On top of that, the dynastic approach can cast a new light on the relationship between Brussels and Madrid. As opposed to what is frequently assumed, the archducal and royal governments were not always on different wavelengths. When it came down to defending the interests of the House of Habsburg, their relationship was not so much determined by confrontation as it was by cooperation. In that context, the swearing of oaths in 1616 is a good example. Both courts worked together to effect a common goal: the continued existence of the Habsburg dynasty in the Low Countries.

Another aspect that deserves more scholarly attention is the relationship between political influence and the acquisition of favor in the Archducal Netherlands. Until now the focus has lain on institutions and individuals making up part of traditional power structures. By this point it is clear that this kind of vision cannot suffice to tease out the different knots in the decision-making process at that time. In the entourage of Albert and Isabella were to be found various characters who succeeded in gaining the ear of the princes and laying hold of their favor. That this unique position brought the requisite political consequences along with it is a proposition that was demonstrated in different ways in this book. So, for example, the privilege of (assured) access proves to play an important role in this story. Still, more research is necessary to be able to assess the precise impact of phenomena like 'favor' and 'favoritism' on policy-making. That is true, for that matter, not only for the archducal regime but by extension for the entire early modern period.

Finally, the classic opposition between the public and private domains as well as between the formal and informal spheres in archducal policy-making needs to be taken under the magnifying lens anew. The question needs to be asked as to whether and to what extent these categories can still be of use in research into the early modern decision-making process. Contemporaries appear to be unaware, in any case, of these kinds of discrepancies. In their eyes decision-making ran via different channels, which operated partly alongside one another and were partly interwoven with each other. These channels were complementary to one another and converged in the central focal point of power: the princely court. There were, to be sure, a few tendencies toward a gradual professionalization and formalization present already, but these were still much less pronounced in the time period discussed here than is generally assumed. So, for instance, Charles of Arenberg saw absolutely no bone to pick when it came to engaging his contacts at court to bring up to the archduke the candidacy of his sister Antoinette-Guillemette for the position of *camarera mayor*. In the same way he regularly sent letters of recommendation to influential persons at court to look out for the interests of his family. Even so, his actions must not be interpreted as a tactical move to circumvent the so-called 'legitimate' channels of power, but simply as a generally accepted *modus operandi* in decision-making of that time. In the early modern context it is inappropriate, consequently, to speak about 'formal' and 'informal' paths of power, at least not if that is meant to suggest a contradiction between a 'legitimate' or 'correct' form of conducting policy and an uncontrollable method opposed to it that makes use of cronyism and nepotism in a sinister manner so as to get certain things done. That kind of vision reasons too much from a modern perspective on decision-making and, consequently, mistakes the characteristic identity of early modern politics.

This book has in no sense solved all the questions that could be posed concerning the court and household of Albert and Isabella. Perhaps it calls forth even more questions than it answers. Nonetheless, one thing is clear: the historian who goes in search of the nature and workings of the archducal regime does well always to keep one foot in the palace.

Appendix

Annual wages of the paid members of the archducal household based on the *libros de razón*. 1612-1618 (in *maravedis*, ducats, and guilders)[1]

Function	Number	mrs./year	dct./year	fl./year
Menino	15 to 30	9000	24	66.18
Moza de Retrete	3 to 4	10000	26.66	73.53
Ayuda del Portero de las Damas	1	12000	32	88.24
Levantador de los Fuelles de los Organos	1	12410	33.09	91.25
Muchacho de Coro	6 to 10	14892	39.71	109.50
Aya de las Meninas	1	15000	40	110.29
Moza de Cámara	4 to 8	15000	40	110.29
Mozo de los Alabarderos	1	16320	43.52	120
Zapatero	1	17500	46.66	128.68
Mozo de los Archeros	1	19584	52.22	144
Ayuda del Portero de Cocina	1	20000	53.33	147.06
Bordador del Archiduque	1	20000	53.33	147.06
Dueña de Retrete	4 to 5	20000	53.33	147.06
Peluquero	1	20000	53.33	147.06
Sastre del Archiduque	1	20000	53.33	147.06
Lacayo	12	20250	54	148.90
Mozo de la Guardaropa y Joyas de la Infanta	2	20880	55.68	153.53
Mozo de la Guardaropa y Joyas del Archiduque	2	20880	55.68	153.53
Bajo (Christophe de Robles)	1	22338	59.75	164.25
Cantor	4	22338	59.75	164.25
Instrumentalista (Philippe Vermeulen)	1	22338	59.75	164.25
Ministril (Hans Vermeulen)	1	22338	59.75	164.25
Organista (Peter Philips)	1	22338	59.57	164.25
Alabardero	72	24480	65.28	180
Furrier de la Capilla	1	24820	66.19	182.50

[1] A list of equivalents for the different types of currency can be found at the beginning of this book.

Function	Number	mrs./year	dct./year	fl./year
Instrumentalista (Laurent Van der Linden)	1	24820	66.19	182.50
Barbero de la Casa	1	25000	66.66	183.82
Prevoste de la Casa	1	25000	66.66	183.82
Ayuda de la Guardaropa y Joyas de la Infanta	2	27000	72	198.53
Ayuda de la Guardaropa y Joyas del Archiduque	3 to 4	27000	72	198.53
Ayuda de la Sala de las Damas	2	27000	72	198.53
Ayuda del Barbero de Cámara (Cosme Calvo)	1	27000	72	198.53
Dama de la Infanta	10 to 16	27000	72	198.53
Escribano de la Cámara de la Infanta	1	28000	74.66	205.88
Cazador y Ballestero	1	29376	78.34	216
Pífano de los Alabarderos	1	29376	78.34	216
Tambor de los Alabarderos	1	29376	78.34	216
Ministril (Jean Cocquiel and Nicolas de Robles)	2	29784	79.42	219
Mozo de Cocina	6 to 9	30000	80	220.59
Mozo de la Pastelería	1	30000	80	220.59
Mozo de Officio de Aguador	1	30000	80	220.59
Labrandera	1	30000	80	220.59
Lavandera de la Ropa de la Boca	1	30000	80	220.59
Archero	41 to 42	30600	81.60	225
Furrier de los Archeros	1	30600	81.60	225
Trompeta de los Archeros	1	30600	81.60	225
Barrendero de la Casa	4 to 5	32000	85.33	235.29
Correo de la Caballeriza	1	32000	85.33	235.29
Escudero de a Pie	8 to 9	32000	85.33	235.29
Mozo de la Cava	1 to 3	32000	85.33	235.29
Mozo de la Cerería	1 to 2	32000	85.33	235.29
Mozo de la Furriera	3	32000	85.33	235.29
Mozo de la Panadería	2	32000	85.33	235.29
Mozo de la Salsería	3 to 6	32000	85.33	235.29
Mozo de la Tapicería	1 to 2	32000	85.33	235.29
Mozo de Retrete	2	32000	85.33	235.29

Function	Number	mrs./year	dct./year	fl./year
Mozo del Estado de los Gentileshombres de la Cámara	1 to 3	32000	85.33	235.29
Mozo del Guardarnes	1	32000	85.33	235.29
Cantor (Abraham De Vos)	1	32266	86.04	237.25
Pintor y Illuminador	1	34000	90.66	250.00
Maestro de Capilla	1	34748	92.66	255.50
Ministril	3	34748	92.66	255.50
Mozo de Capilla	2	34748	92.66	255.50
Calzetero	1	35000	93.33	257.35
Sastre de la Infanta	1	35000	93.33	257.35
Ayuda de Cámara	9 to 12	36500	97.33	268.38
Ayuda del Barbero de Cámara (Juan Merlin)	1	36500	97.33	268.38
Ministril (Jean Volcart)	1	37026	98.74	272.25
Organista (Pedro Cornet)	1	37026	98.74	272.25
Preceptor de la Lengua Latina de los Muchachos de Coro	1	37026	98.74	272.25
Cantor (Alonso Rodriguez)	1	37230	99.28	273.75
Capellán de Altar	9 to 12	37230	99.28	273.75
Maestro de Organo	1	37230	99.28	273.75
Lavandera de la Ropa de los Estados de los Pajes y Ayudas de Cámara	1	37500	100	275.74
Portador de Cocina	2	37500	100	275.74
Cabo de Escuadra de los Alabarderos	4	37536	100.10	276
Pintor	1	40800	108.80	300.00
Predicador	3	40800	108.80	300.00
Maestro de la Sala de las Damas de la Infanta	1 to 2	41000	109.33	301.47
Aposentador de la Casa	2	42000	112	308.82
Ayuda de la Azemilería	2	42000	112	308.82
Ayuda de la Botica	2	42000	112	308.82
Ayuda de la Cava	1 to 2	42000	112	308.82
Ayuda de la Cerería	1 to 2	42000	112	308.82
Ayuda de la Furriera	2	42000	112	308.82
Ayuda de la Panadería	2	42000	112	308.82
Ayuda de la Pastelería	1	42000	112	308.82

Function	Number	mrs./year	dct./year	fl./year
Ayuda de la Salsería	1 to 2	42000	112	308.82
Ayuda de la Tapicería	2	42000	112	308.82
Ayuda del Cochero Mayor	1	42000	112	308.82
Ayuda del Comprador	1 to 2	42000	112	308.82
Ayuda del Furrier de la Caballeriza	1	42000	112	308.82
Ayuda del Guardamanger	2	42000	112	308.82
Ayuda del Guardarnes	1	42000	112	308.82
Ayuda del Palafrenero Mayor	1	42000	112	308.82
Ayuda del Tesorero	1	42000	112	308.82
Cocinero	8 to 9	42000	112	308.82
Librador de la Caballeriza	1	42000	112	308.82
Mayordomo del Estado de los Ayudas de Cámara	1	42000	112	308.82
Mayordomo del Estado de los Pajes	1	42000	112	308.82
Mozo de Oratorio	1	42000	112	308.82
Pastelero	1	42000	112	308.82
Portero de Cocina	1	42000	112	308.82
Portero de Saleta	6 to 8	42000	112	308.82
Sobrestante de los Rocines de la Acemilería	1	42000	112	308.82
Teniente del Ayo de los Pajes	1	42000	112	308.82
Ministril (Philippe van Ranst)	1	44608	118.95	328.50
Lavandera de la Ropa de los Estados de los Gentilhombres de la Boca y Cámara	1	45000	120	330.88
Furrier de los Alabarderos	1	48960	130.56	360
Sargento de los Alabarderos	1	48960	130.56	360
Organista (Juan Zacarias)	1	49640	132.37	365
Bordador de la Infanta	1	50000	133.33	367.65
Capellán y Maestro de los Pajes	1	50000	133.33	367.65
Cirujano	1	50000	133.33	367.65
Palafrenero Mayor	1	52000	138.66	382.35
Lavandera de la Ropa de la Persona de la Infanta	1	55000	146.66	404.41
Médico de la Casa (Pedro Ricardo)	1	56250	150	413.60
Portero de las Damas de la Infanta	2	57000	152	419.12
Repostero de Camas	6	57000	152	419.12

Function	Number	mrs./year	dct./year	fl./year
Acemilero Mayor	1	60000	160	441.18
Ayo de los Pajes	1	60000	160	441.18
Boticario	1	60000	160	441.18
Cerero y Busier	1	60000	160	441.18
Cochero Mayor	1	60000	160	441.18
Cocinero Mayor	1	60000	160	441.18
Comprador	1	60000	160	441.18
Escribano de la Cámara	1	60000	160	441.18
Furrier de la Caballeriza	1	60000	160	441.18
Guardamanger	1	60000	160	441.18
Guardarnes	1	60000	160	441.18
Mayordomo del Estado de los Gentileshombres de la Cámara	1	60000	160	441.18
Salsier y Mayordomo del Estado de los Gentileshombres de la Boca	1	60000	160	441.18
Sumiller de la Cava	1	60000	160	441.18
Sumiller de la Panadería	1	60000	160	441.18
Tapicero Mayor	1	60000	160	441.18
Ujier de Vianda	2	60000	160	441.18
Varlet Servant	2	60000	160	441.18
Veedor y Contador de la Caballeriza	1	60000	160	441.18
Ayuda de Cámara (Diego Woislawski)	1	61200	163.20	450.00
Maestro de Danzar de los Pajes	1	61200	163.20	450.00
Cantor (Juan Belmonte)	1	68000	181.36	500.00
Cornet (Antonio Chambers)	1	68000	181.36	500.00
Reloxero	1	68250	182	501.84
Furrier y Aposentador de Palacio	1	73000	194.66	536.76
Guardadamas y Aposentador de Palacio	1	73000	194.66	536.76
Capellán de Altar (Pedro Campis and Juan Stefano)	2	75000	200	551.47
Capellán de Oratorio	7 to 11	75000	200	551.47
Gentilhombre de la Casa	24 to 36	75000	200	551.47
Maestro de los Pajes	1	75000	200	551.47
Médico de la Casa (Enrique Verlario)	2	75000	200	551.47
Platero de Oro	1	81600	217.60	600.00
Caballerizo	3 to 4	93750	250	689.34

Function	**Number**	**mrs./year**	**dct./year**	**fl./year**
Gentilhombre de la Boca	22 to 33	93750	250	689.34
Confesor de la Infanta	1	102000	272	750.00
Ministril (Daniel Norcam)	1	102000	272	750.00
Lavandera de la Ropa de la Persona del Archiduque	1	105000	280	772.06
Ayuda de Cámara (Juan Laynez)	1	111500	297.33	819.85
Aposentador Mayor	1	112500	300	827.21
Capellán y Receptor de la Capilla	1	112500	300	827.21
Despensero Mayor	1	112500	300	827.21
Médico de la Cámara (Francisco de Paz and Henri Mastelein)	2	112500	300	827.21
Primer Caballerizo	1	112500	300	827.21
Gentilhombre de la Cámara	23 to 27	131250	350	965.07
Sumiller de Cortina	1	131250	350	965.07
Contralor	1	150000	400	1102.94
Greffier	1	150000	400	1102.94
Guardaropa y Joyas de la Infanta	1	150000	400	1102.94
Tesorero y Maestro de la Cámara	1	150000	400	1102.94
Guardaropa y Joyas del Archiduque	1	186500	497.33	1371.32
Confesor del Archiduque	1	187500	500	1378.68
Mayordomo	8 to 10	187500	500	1378.68
Médico de la Cámara (Andreas Trevisius)	1	187500	500	1378.68
Secretario de la Cámara	1	187500	500	1378.68
Capellán y Limosnero Mayor	1	187500	500	1378.68
Teniente de los Alabarderos	1	204000	544	1500
Teniente de los Archeros	1	204000	544	1500
Capitán de los Alabarderos	1	300000	800	2205.88
Capitán de los Archeros	1	300000	800	2205.88
Dueña de Honor	2	300000	800	2205.88
Mayordomo Mayor, Sumiller de Corps y Caballerizo Mayor	1	750000	2000	5514.71
Camarera Mayor	1	1000000	2666.66	7352.94

Bibliography

Archival Sources

Algemeen Rijksarchief, Brussels [National Archives of Belgium] [ARA]

- *Audiëntie* [*Aud*]: 20, 23/10, 33/1, 33/2, 33/3, 33/4, 363, 444, 640, 1259, 1413/1, 1469/1, 1469/2.
- *Duitse Staatssecretarie* [*DuiS*]: 39, 392, 400, 408, 434, 437.
- *Geheime Raad - Papieren Roose en De Paepe*: 1591.
- *Handschriftenverzameling*: 821, 822.
- *Hofrechtbank*: trial dossiers 176, 179.
- *Papiers du Comté de Mercy-Argenteau*: 125.
- *Raad van State* [*RvS*]: 157, 158.
- *Rekenkamer* [*RK*]: 1837, 1838.
- *Secretarie van Staat en Oorlog* [*SSO*]: 100, 127, 177, 180, 182, 185, 201, 315, 494, 516, 518, 666.

Arenberg Archives and Cultural Centre, Enghien [ACA]

- Correspondence of Anne de Croÿ: 38/11, 38/24.
- Correspondence of Charles of Arenberg: 38/1, 38/2, 38/3, 38/4.
- Files: 36/17.
- *Honneurs*: 31/25.

Archivio di Stato, Florence [accessed via the website of *The Medici Archive Project* (http://documents.medici.org)]

- Archives of the Grand Dukes of Tuscany: *Carteggi dei Principi, delle Granduchesse e delle Principesse / Giovanni di Cosimo I e di Eleonora degli Albizi / Lettere del principe ai granduchi e alla Segretaria*: volumes 5155 and 5157.

Archivio Segreto Vaticano, Vatican City [ASV]

- *Borghese* I: 913.
- *Borghese* II: 98, 99, 100, 102, 105, 106, 108, 109, 110, 111, 112, 114, 115, 116, 137.
- *Borghese* III: 40, 98, 98 C 1, 105 ABC, 110, 110 BCDG, 113.
- *Nunziatura di Fiandra* [*NF*]: 11, 12 A, 14 C, 21 A.

Archivo General del Palacio Real, Madrid [AGPR]

- *Sección Administrativa: Viajes y Jornadas* 788.
- *Sección Personal*: 588.

Archivo General de Simancas, Valladolid [AGS]

- *Estado*: 603, 626, 627, 628, 634, 2023, 2024, 2025, 2026, 2027, 2028, 2029, 2030, 2031, 2032, 2033, 2034, 2224, 2227, 2289, 2290, 2291, 2292, 2293, 2294, 2296, 2297, 2299, 2300, 2305, 2307, 2308, 2309, 2310, 2312.

Archivo Histórico Nacional, Madrid [AHN]
- *Órdenes Militares* [*OOMM*]: expedientes 199, 1259, 1745, 5217, 1828, 4048, 5274.

Biblioteca Apostolica Vaticana, Vatican City [BAV]
- *Barberini Latini* [*BaL*]: 6804, 6806, 6807, 6808, 6810, 6812.

Biblioteca Francisco de Zabálburu, Madrid [BFZ]
- *Altamira*: 39, 212.

Bibliothèque Nationale de France, Paris [BNF]
- *Manuscrits Français* [*MsF*]: 16125, 16128, 16129, 16130, 16131, 16132, 16133.

British Library, London [BL]
- *Egerton*: ms. 2079.

Haus-, Hof- und Staatsarchiv, Vienna [HHStA]
- *Repertorium P, Abteilung C*: 44, 53.
- *Repertorium P, Belgische Korrespondenz*: 29.

Instituto Valencia de Don Juan, Madrid [IVDJ]
- *Envíos*: 47 (*caja* 63), 114 (*caja* 163).
- *Manuscritos*: 26-I-9, 26-I-10, 26-I-11.

National Archives, Kew [NA]
- *State Papers* [*SP*]: 77/7, 77/8, 77/10, 77/11, 77/12, 77/13, 77/14.

Real Academia de la Historia, Madrid [RAH]
- *Colección Salazar y Castro* [*SyC*]: ms. A-61 (9-61).

Rijksarchief in Brussels (site Anderlecht), Anderlecht [National Archives of Belgium – Anderlecht site] [RA]
- *Kerkelijk Archief van Brabant*: 6915 [= microfilm 1647].

Stadsarchief, Antwerp [City Archives of Antwerp] [SAA]
- *Privilegekamer*: 1627 [= microfilm 392 K].

Printed Primary Sources

[Anonymous]. *Relation de Flandres. État de la cour et maison des archiducs en 1610. Document inédit du temps enrichi de notes généalogiques et historiques.* In: *Souvenirs de la Flandre-Wallonne. Recherches historiques et choix de documents relatifs à Douai et au Nord de la France*, vol. VI. Paris-Douai, 1866, pp. 1-25.

Bentivoglio, G. *Relationi del Cardinal Bentivoglio*. Brussels, 1632. [Original edition: Bentivoglio, G. *Relationi fatte dall' illustrissimo, e reverendissimo signor cardinal Bentivoglio in tempo delle sue nuntiature di Fiandra, e di Francia. Date in luce da Erycio Puteano*. Antwerp, 1629.]

Brants, V., ed. *Avis sur les affaires des Pays-Bas, adressés à l'archiduc Albert par Philippe de Croy, comte de Solre*. In: *Bulletin de la Commission Royale d'Histoire*, 83 (1914) 254-279.

Brants, V., ed. *Recueil des Ordonnances des Pays-Bas. Règne d'Albert et d'Isabelle.* 2 vols. Brussels, 1909.

Brants, V., ed. *Une mission à Madrid de Philippe de Croy, comte de Solre, envoyé des archiducs en 1604*. In: *Bulletin de la Commission Royale d'Histoire*, 77 (1908) 185-203.

Brennan, M.G., ed. *The Travel Diary (1611-1612) of an English Catholic Sir Charles Somerset, Edited from the Manuscript in the Brotherton Collection University of Leeds.* Leeds, 1993.

Butkens, C.F. *Supplément aux trophées tant sacrés que profanes du duché de Brabant de Mr. Butkens, traduit et recueilli des meilleurs historiens de Brabant et tiré pour une grande partie des archives dudit pais.* 2 vols. The Hague, 1724-1726.

Casoni, F. *Vita del marchese Ambrogio Spinola, l'espugnatore delle piazze.* Genoa, 1691.

Chifflet, J. *Aula Sacra Principum Belgii; sive commentarius historicus de Capellae Regiae in Belgio, Principiis, Ministris, Ritibus atque universo apparatu.* Antwerp, 1650.

Colección de Documentos Inéditos para la Historia de España, 112 vols. Madrid, 1842-1895.

Courvoisier, J.J. *Le sacré Mausolée ou les parfums exhalant le tombeau de la sérénissime princesse Isabelle...* Brussels, 1634.

de Beer, E.S., ed. *The Diary of John Evelyn.* 6 vols. Oxford, 1955.

de la Marche, O. 'Sensuyt l'estat de la maison du duc Charles de Bourgogne, dit le Hardy,' in Beaune, H. & d'Arbaumont, J., eds. *Mémoires d'Olivier de la Marche, maitre d'hôtel et capitaine des gardes de Charles le Téméraire,* IV. Paris, 1888, pp. 1-94.

de Meester de Ravestein, B., ed. *Correspondance du Nonce Giovanni-Francesco Guidi di Bagno (1621-1627).* Analecta Vaticano-Belgica, 2e série, section A: Nonciature de Flandre, VI. Rome-Brussels-Paris, 1938.

de Montgaillard, B. *Le Soleil Eclipsé, ou Discours sur la vie et mort du Sérénissime Archiduc Albert Prince Souverain des Pais bas et de Bourgogne.* Brussels, 1622.

de Reiffenberg, F.A.F., ed. *Itinéraire de l'archiduc Albert, de la reine d'Espagne Marguérite d'Autriche et de l'infante Isabelle, en 1599 et 1600, tiré d'une relation contemporaine et manuscrite.* In: *Nouveaux Mémoires de l'Académie Royale des Sciences et Belles-Lettres de Bruxelles,* 14 (1841) 3-33.

de Reiffenberg, F.A.F., ed. *Une existence de grand seigneur au seizième siècle. Mémoires autographes du Duc Charles de Croy.* Brussels, 1845.

De Ridder, A., ed. *Les règlements de la Cour de Charles Quint.* In: *Messager des sciences historiques* (1893) pp. 392-418 and (1894) pp. 36-52, pp. 180-201 and pp. 280-291.

de Seur, J., ed. *Rolle des noms, gages et pensions des conseilliers, ministres et autres officiers de leurs altesses sérénissimes...fait en l'an 1609.* In: de Seur, J. *La Flandre illustrée par l'Institution de la Chambre du Roi à Lille.* Lille, 1713.

Gachard, L.-P. & Piot, C., eds. *Voyage de l'archiduc Albert en Espagne.* In: Gachard, L.-P. & Piot, C., eds. *Collection des voyages des souverains des Pays-Bas.* 4 vols. Brussels, 1876-1882. Volume IV, pp. 457-562.

Gachard, L.-P., ed. *Actes des États-Généraux de 1600.* Brussels, 1849.

Gachard, L.-P., ed. *Correspondance de Philippe II sur les affaires des Pays-Bas publiée d'après les originaux conservés dans les Archives royales de Simancas.* 6 vols. Brussels, 1848-1936.

Galende Díaz, J.C. & Salamanca López, M., eds. *Epistolario de la emperatriz María de Austria. Textos inéditos del Archivo de la Casa de Alba.* Madrid, 2004.

Hagemans, G., ed. *Voyage par la France, la Flandre et l'Allemagne rapporté par l'Excellentissime Giorgio Justiniani, à son retour à Venise de son ambassade ordinaire en Angleterre, 1605.* In: Hagemans, G., ed. *Relations inédites d'ambassadeurs Vénitiens dans les Pays-Bas sous Philippe II et Albert et Isabelle* (Extrait des Annales de l'Académie d'Archéologie de Belgique, 21, 2e série, vol. I). Brussels, 1865, pp. 56-86.

Hume, M.A.S., ed. *Calendar of State Papers, Spain (Simancas)*, vol. IV (1587-1603). London, 1899.

Jodogne, P., ed. *Entre Italie et Pays-Bas méridionaux: le 'libro de memoria' de la famille Cassina.* Brussels, 2002.

Lipsius, J. *Monita et Exempla Politica, libri duo, qui virtutes et vitia principum spectant.* Edited by J. Waszink, *Politica: six books of politics or political instruction.* Assen, 2004.

Lonchay, H., Cuvelier, J. & Lefèvre, J., eds. *Correspondance de la Cour d'Espagne sur les affaires des Pays-Bas au XVIIe siècle.* 6 vols. Brussels, 1923-1937.

Macchiavelli, N. *Il Principe* (1532). [English edition: Macchiavelli, N. *The Prince.* Translated and edited by P. Bondanella. Oxford, 2008.]

Michelant, H., ed. *Voyage de Pierre Bergeron ès Ardennes, Liège et Pays-Bas en 1619.* Liège, 1875.

Miraeus, A. *De vita Alberti Pii, sapientis, prudentis Belgarum Principis commentarius.* Antwerp, 1622.

Purnell, E.K. & Hinds, A.B., eds. *Report on the Manuscripts of the Marquess of Downshire preserved at Easthampstead Park, Berkshire. Volume II: Papers of William Trumbull the Elder, 1605-1610.* London, 1936.

Puteanus, E. & Francquart, J. *Pompa funebris (...) Alberti Pii, archiducis Austriae, (...) verus imaginibus expressa a Jacobo Francquart (...) Eiusdem principis morientis vita, scriptore E. Puteanu.* Brussels, 1622.

Roco de Campofrío, J. *España en Flandes. Trece años de gobierno del archiduque Alberto (1595-1608).* Madrid, 1973.

Rodríguez Villa, A., ed. *Correspondencia de la Infanta Doña Isabel Clara Eugenia de Austria con el Duque de Lerma y otros personajes.* Madrid, 1906.

Rodríguez Villa, A., ed. *Etiquetas de la Casa de Austria.* Madrid, 1913.

Rooses, M. & Ruelens, C., eds. *Codex Diplomaticus Rubenianus. Correspondance de Rubens et documents épistolaires concernant sa vie et ses œuvres.* 6 vols. Antwerp, 1887-1909.

Schayes, A.G.B., ed. *Voyage de Jean-Ernest duc de Saxe en France, en Angleterre et en Belgique.* Trésor national, Recueil historique, littéraire, scientifique, artistique, commercial et industriel, 2e série, III, 1843, pp. 168-254.

Stanyhurst, R. *Hebdomada Mariana, ex orthodoxis Catholicae Romanae Ecclesiae patribus collecta: in memoriam septem festorum Beatissimae Virginis Mariae, per singulos dies hebdomadae distributa.* Antwerp, 1609.

Ungerer, G., ed. *A Spaniard in Elizabethan England: The Correspondence of Antonio Pérez's Exile.* 2 vols. London, 1975-1976.

Van der Essen, L. & Louant, A., eds. *Correspondance d'Ottavio Mirto Frangipani, premier nonce de Flandre (1596-1606).* Analecta Vaticano-Belgica, 2e série, section A: Nonciature de Flandre, I-II-III. 3 parts in 4 vols. Rome-Brussels-Paris, 1924-1942.

Van der Straeten, E., ed. *Den Lyste van den Musiciens van den Capelle van haer Hoocheden.* In: Van der Straeten, E. *La musique aux Pays-Bas avant le XIXe siècle. Documents inédits et annotés.* 8 vols. Brussels, 1867-1888, volume II, pp. 10-11.

Van Meerbeeck, L., ed. *Correspondance des Nonces Gesualdo, Morra, Sanseverino avec la Secrétairie d'Etat pontificale (1615-1621).* Analecta Vaticano-Belgica, 2e série, section A: Nonciature de Flandre, IV. Brussels-Rome, 1937.

Van Meerbeeck, L., ed. *Correspondance du Nonce Fabio de Lagonissa, archevêque de Conza (1627-1634).* Analecta Vaticano-Belgica, 2e série, section A: Nonciature de Flandre, XI. Brussels-Rome, 1966.

van Vervou, F. *Enige gedenckvveerdige geschiedenissen, tot nachrichtinge der nakomelingen, sommarischer wijze beschreven deur Jr. Fredrich van Vervov, dewelcke hij eensdeels gesien, om ende over geweest, anderdeels deur loffweerdige mannen gehoort ende verstaan heeft; dit alles na den ouden stijl.* Leeuwarden, 1841.

Veronelli, S., & Labrador Arroyo, F., eds. *Diario de Hans Khevenhüller, embajador imperial en la corte de Felipe II.* Sociedad Estatal para la Conmemoración de los Centenarios de Felipe II y Carlos V. Madrid, 2001.

Secondary Sources

Adams, S. 'Favourites and Factions at the Elizabethan Court,' in: Asch, R.G. & Birke, A.M., eds. *Princes, Patronage, and the Nobility: The Court at the Beginning of the Modern Age, c. 1450-1650.* Oxford U.P., 1991, pp. 265-287.

Adams, S. 'The Court as an Economic Institution. The Court of Elizabeth I of England (1558-1603),' in: Aymard, M. & Romani, M.A., eds. *La cour comme institution économique. Actes du douzième congrès international d'histoire économique, Séville-Madrid, 24-28 août 1998.* Paris, 1998, pp. 127-136.

Adamson, J. 'The Making of the Ancien-Régime Court, 1500-1700,' in: Adamson, J., ed. *The Princely Courts of Europe. Ritual, Politics and Culture under the Ancien Régime 1500-1750.* London, 1999, pp. 7-41.

Adamson, J. 'The Tudor and Stuart Courts, 1509-1714,' in: Adamson, J., ed. *The Princely Courts of Europe: Ritual, Politics and Culture under the Ancien Régime, 1500-1750.* London, 1999, pp. 95-117.

Adamson, J., ed. *The Princely Courts of Europe. Ritual, Politics and Culture under the Ancien Régime 1500-1750.* London, 1999.

Allen, P. *Philip III and the Pax Hispánica, 1598-1621. The Failure of Grand Strategy.* Yale U.P., 2000.

Allen, V. *The Bulteels. The Story of a Huguenot Family.* London, 2004.

Álvarez-Ossorio Alvariño, A. & García García, B.J., eds. *La Monarquía de las naciones. Patria, nación y naturaleza en la Monarquía de España.* Madrid, 2004.

Anderson, A.D. *On the Verge of War: International Relations and the Jülich-Kleve Succession Crises (1609–1614).* Boston, 1999.

Anselme [Père]. *Histoire généalogique et chronologique de la maison royale de France,* vol. V. Paris, 1730 [third edition].

Arroyo Martín, F. 'El marqués de Leganés. Apuntes biográficos.' *Espacio, Tiempo y Forma, Serie IV, Historia Moderna,* 15 (2002) 145-185.

Asch, R.G. & Birke, A.M., eds. *Princes, Patronage, and the Nobility: The Court at the Beginning of the Modern Age, c.1450-1650.* Oxford U.P., 1991.

Asch, R.G. ' 'The Politics of Access.' Hofstruktur und Herrschaft in England unter den frühen Stuarts 1603-1642,' in: Paravicini, W., ed. *Alltag bei Hofe* (3. Symposium der Residenzen-Kommission der Akademie der Wissenschaften zu Göttingen. Residenzenforschung 3). Sigmaringen, 1995, pp. 243-266.

Asch, R.G. 'Introduction: Court and Household from the Fifteenth to the Seventeenth Centuries,' in: Asch, R.G. & Birke, A.M., eds. *Princes, Patronage, and the Nobility: The Court at the Beginning of the Modern Age, c.1450-1650.* Oxford U.P., 1991, pp. 1-38.

Asch, R.G. 'Schlussbetrachtung. Höfische Gunst und höfische Günstlinge zwischen Mittelalter und Neuzeit. 18 Thesen,' in: Hirschbiegel, J. & Paravicini, W., eds. *Der Fall des Günstlings. Hofparteien in Europa vom 13. bis zum 17. Jahrhundert* (8. Symposium der Residenzen-Kommission der Akademie der Wissenschaften zu Göttingen. Residenzenforschung 17). Ostfildern, 2004, pp. 515-531.

Asch, R.G. 'The Court of Charles I. Some Reflections on the Social and Economic Role of the Court in Early Stuart England,' in: Aymard, M. & Romani, M.A., eds. *La cour comme institution économique. Actes du douzième congrès international d'histoire économique, Séville-Madrid, 24-28 août 1998.* Paris, 1998, pp. 139-148.

Aymard, M. & Romani, M.A., eds. *La cour comme institution économique. Actes du douzième congrès international d'histoire économique, Séville-Madrid, 24-28 août 1998.* Paris, 1998.

Babel, R. 'The Courts of the Wittelsbachs c. 1500-1750,' in: Adamson, J., ed. *The Princely Courts of Europe. Ritual, Politics and Culture under the Ancien Régime 1500-1750.* London, 1999, pp. 189-209.

Baillie, H.M. 'Etiquette and the Planning of the State Apartments in Baroque Palaces.' *Archaeologia*, 101 (1967) 169-199.

Becquart, P. *Musiciens néerlandais à la cour de Madrid. Philippe Rogier et son école (1560-1647).* Brussels, 1967.

Benigno, F. *La sombra del Rey. Validos y lucha politica en la España del siglo XVII.* Madrid, 1994.

Bérenger, J. 'Pour une enquête européenne: le problème du ministériat au XVIIe siècle.' *Annales. Economies, Sociétés, Civilisations*, 29 (1974) 166-192.

Bergé, M. 'Les bâtards de la Maison de Bourgogne et leur descendance.' *L'Intermédiaire des Généalogistes. Bulletin du Service de Centralisation des Etudes Généalogiques et Démographiques de Belgique*, 60 (1955) 316-408.

Bertelli, S. *The Courts of the Italian Renaissance.* Milan, 1985.

Birely, R. *The Jesuits and the Thirty Years' War: Kings, Courts, and Confessors.* Cambridge U.P., 2003.

Blaes, J.-B. 'La Belgique au XVIIe siècle. Le gouvernement de l'archiduc Albert,' in: Blaes, J.-B., ed. *Études historiques sur le XVIe siècle.* Brussels, 1863, pp. 133-193.

Bonenfant, P. 'Les projets d'érection des Pays-Bas en royaume du XVe au XVIIIe siècle. Aperçu sur l'évolution de ce concept politique.' *Revue de l'Université de Bruxelles*, 41 (1935-1936) 151-169.

Bottineau, Y. 'Aspects de la Cour d'Espagne au XVIIe siècle.' *Bulletin Hispanique*, 74 (1972) 138-157.

Brants, V. 'Ambroise Spinola, 1569-1630, généralissime des armes de Flandre.' *Revue Générale Belge*, 1 (1915) 172-202.

Brants, V. 'Pedro de Tolède,' in: *Biographie Nationale*, vol. XVI (1901) pp. 801-803.

Brants, V. 'Solre (Philippe de Croÿ, Comte de),' in: *Biographie Nationale*, vol. XXIII (1921-1924) pp. 126-129.

Brants, V. *La Belgique au XVIIe siècle, Albert et Isabelle. Études d'histoire politique et sociale.* Leuven, 1910.

Brants, V. *L'autonomie internationale de la Belgique sous les archiducs Albert et Isabelle (1598-1621).* Macon, 1901.

Braun, H.E. *Juan de Mariana and Early Modern Spanish Political Thought.* Aldershot, 2007.

Brockliss, L.W.B. 'Concluding Remarks: The Anatomy of the Minister-Favourite,' in: Elliott, J.H. & Brockliss, L.W.B., eds. *The World of the Favourite.* London-New Haven, 1999, pp. 279-309.

Brown, J. & Elliott, J.H. *A Palace for a King. The Buen Retiro and the Court of Philip IV.* Yale U.P., 2003.

Burke, P. *The Fabrication of Louis XIV.* New Haven-London, 1992.

Caeiro, F. *O Arquiduque Alberto de Austria. Vice-rei e inquisidor-mor de Portugal, cardeal legado do papa, governador e depois soberano dos Países Bajos.* Lisbon, 1961.

Callaey, F. [= Fredegand of Antwerp, Father O.M.F. Cap.]. *La vie religieuse et familiale en Belgique au XVIIe siècle. Étude sur le Père Charles d'Arenberg, frère-mineur Capucin (1593-1669).* Paris-Rome, 1919.

Campbell-Orr, C., ed. *Queenship in Britain, 1660-1837: Royal Patronage, Court Culture, and Dynastic Politics.* Manchester U.P., 2002.

Campbell-Orr, C., ed. *Queenship in Europe, 1660-1815: The Role of the Consort.* Cambridge U.P., 2004.

Carreras, J.J. & García García, B.J., eds. *La Capilla Real de los Austrias. Música y ritual de corte en la Europa Moderna.* Madrid, 2001.

Cartellieri, O. *La Cour des ducs de Bourgogne.* Paris, 1946.

Carter, C.H. 'Belgian 'Autonomy' under the Archdukes, 1598-1621.' *The Journal of Modern History*, 36 (1964) 245-259.

Castan, A. 'Les origines et la date du Saint-Ildefonse de Rubens.' *Mémoires de la Société d'émulation du Doubs,* 5e série, 9 (1884) 15-107.

Chaline, O. ' 'Combien de royaumes nous ignorent': la cour dans l'historiographie française.' *Annali di Storia moderna e contemporanea*, 2 (1996) 384-392.

Chaline, O. 'The Valois and Bourbon Courts c. 1515-1750,' in: Adamson, J., ed. *The Princely Courts of Europe. Ritual, Politics and Culture under the Ancien Régime 1500-1750.* London, 1999, pp. 67-93.

Chatenet, M. *La Cour de France au XVIe siècle: vie sociale et architecture.* Paris, 2002.

Clerckx, S. 'La chapelle royale de Bruxelles sous l'Ancien Régime.' *Annuaire du Conservatoire de musique de Bruxelles*, 65 (1942) 159-179.

Colas de la Noue, E. *Un Ligueur: le comte de la Fère.* Paris, 1892.

Cools, H. *Mannen met macht. Edellieden en de moderne staat in de Bourgondisch-Habsburgse Nederlanden (1475-1530).* Zutphen, 2001.

Corella Suárez, M.P. 'Orígenes históricos del marquesado de Leganés y su primer titular: Don Diego Messía de Guzmán.' *Anales del Instituto de Estudios Madrileños*, 18 (1981) 131-136.

Coremans, V. 'L'archiduc Ernest, sa cour, ses dépenses: détails sur son voyage de Prague à Bruxelles (1593-1595).' *Compte rendu des séances de la Commission Royale d'Histoire ou recueil de ses bulletins*, 13 (1847) 85-147.

Coreth, A. *Pietas Austriaca. Ursprung und Entwicklung Barocker Frömmigkeit in Österreich.* Vienna, 1959.

Costa Gomes, R. *The Making of a Court Society. Kings and Nobles in Late Medieval Portugal.* Cambridge U.P., 2003.

Crawford Volk, M. 'New Light on a Seventeenth-Century Collector: The Marquis of Leganés.' *The Art Bulletin*, 62 (1980) 256-268.

Croft, P. 'Brussels and London: The Archdukes, Robert Cecil and James I,' in: Thomas, W. & Duerloo, L., eds. *Albert & Isabella, 1598-1621: Essays.* Turnhout, 1998, pp. 79-86.

Cruz, A.J. & Suzuki, M., eds. *The Rule of Women in Early Modern Europe.* University of Illinois Press, 2009.

Cuddy, N. 'The Revival of the Entourage: The Bedchamber of James I, 1603-1625,' in: Starkey, D. et al. *The English Court from the Wars of the Roses to the Civil War.* London-New York, 1987, pp. 173-225.

Cuvelier, J. 'Don Juan de Mancicidor, secrétaire d'Etat et de Guerre de l'archiduc Albert, 1596-1618.' *Revue belge de Philologie et d'Histoire*, 4 (1925) 698-714.

Cuvelier, J. 'Les préliminaires du traité de Londres (29 août 1604).' *Revue belge de Philologie et d'Histoire*, 2 (1923) 279-304 and 485-508.

De Bock-Doehaerd, R. *Inventaire des 'Ouvrages de la Cour'. Exemplaire annoté.* Algemeen Rijksarchief, Toegangen in Beperkte Oplage 95. Brussels, 1991.

De Jonge, K. ' ' 't Hof van Brabant' als symbool van de Spaanse hofhouding in de Lage Landen.' *Bulletin van de Koninklijke Nederlandse Oudheidkundige Bond*, 98 (1999) 183-197.

De Jonge, K. 'De voornaamste residenties in Mechelen. Het Hof van Kamerijk en het Hof van Savoyen,' in: Eichberger, D., ed. *Dames met klasse. Margareta van York/Margareta van Oostenrijk.* Exhibition catalogue. Leuven, 2005, pp. 57-66.

De Jonge, K. 'Der herzogliche und kaiserliche Palast zu Brüssel und die Entwicklung des höfischen Zeremoniells im 16. und 17. Jahrhundert.' *Jahrbuch des Zentralinstituts für Kunstgeschichte*, 5-6 (1989-1990) 253-282.

De Jonge, K. 'Le palais de Charles-Quint à Bruxelles. Ses dispositions intérieures aux XVe et XVIe siècles et le cérémonial de Bourgogne,' in: Guillaume, J., ed. *Architecture et vie sociale. L'organisation intérieure des grandes demeures à la fin du Moyen Age et à la Renaissance. Actes du colloque tenu à Tours du 6 au 10 juin 1988.* Paris, 1994, pp. 107-125.

De Jonge, K. et al. 'Building Policy and Urbanisation during the Reign of the Archdukes: The Court and its Architects,' in: Thomas, W. & Duerloo, L., eds. *Albert & Isabella, 1598-1621: Essays.* Turnhout, 1998, pp. 191-215.

de la Cruz Medina, V. 'La educación de las meninas en la corte de Felipe II: algunos aspectos a través de las cartas de Ana de Dietrichstein a su madre, Margarita de Cardona,' in: Jiménez Eguizábal, A. et al., eds. *Etnohistoria de la escuela. XII Coloquio nacional de historia de la educación.* Burgos, 2003, pp. 523-534.

De Maeyer, M. *Albrecht en Isabella en de schilderkunst. Bijdrage tot de geschiedenis van de XVIIe-eeuwse schilderkunst in de Zuidelijke Nederlanden.* Verhandelingen van de Koninklijke

Vlaamse Academie voor Wetenschappen, Letteren en Schone Kunsten van België. Klasse der Schone Kunsten, IX. Brussels, 1955.

de Mogrobejo, E. et al. *Diccionario Hispanoamericano de Heráldica, Onomástica y Genealogía.* Bilbao, 1995-.

De Ridder, A. 'La Cour de Charles-Quint.' *Mémoires de la Société littéraire de l'Université Catholique de Louvain,* 14 (1889) 41-213.

De Schepper, H. & Parker, G. 'The Formation of Government Policy in the Catholic Netherlands under 'the Archdukes', 1596-1621.' *The English Historical Review,* 91 (1976) 241-254.

De Schrevel, A.-C. 'Triest (Antoine),' in: *Biographie Nationale,* vol. XXV (1930-1932) pp. 614-624.

De Sturler, J. 'Un épisode de la politique douanière des Archiducs: L'expérience de Juan de Gauna (1603-1605).' *Revue de l'Université de Bruxelles,* 42 (1936-1937) 362-386.

De Troeyer, B. 'Bio-bibliografie van de minderbroeders in de Nederlanden. Voorstudies 6: Andreas de Soto.' *Franciscana,* 37 (1982) 69-96.

de Vegiano, J.-C.-J. & de Herckenrode, J.S.F.J.L. *Nobiliaire des Pays-Bas et du Comté de Bourgogne.* 4 vols. Ghent, 1862-1868.

Dean, T. 'The Courts. A Historiographical Problem.' *The Journal of Modern History,* 67 (1995) 136-151.

Degryse, K. & Janssens, P. 'Le rôle économique de l'aristocratie belge aux XVIIe et XVIIIe siècles,' in: Núñez, C.E., ed. *Aristocracy, Patrimonial Management Strategies and Economic Development, 1450-1800.* Seville, 1998, pp. 43-53.

del Río Barredo, M.J. 'De Madrid a Turín: el ceremonial de las reinas españolas en la corte ducal de Catalina Micaela de Saboya,' in: Gómez-Centurión Jiménez, C., ed. *Monarquía y Corte en la España Moderna.* Cuadernos de Historia Moderna, 2003 (Anejo II), pp. 97-122.

Delen, M.-A. *Het hof van Willem van Oranje.* Amsterdam, 2002.

Demeester, J. 'Le domaine de Mariemont sous Albert et Isabelle (1598-1621).' *Annales du Cercle Archéologique de Mons,* 71 (1978-1981) 190.

den Boon, T. & Geeraerts, D., eds. *Van Dale Groot woordenboek van de Nederlandse taal.* Utrecht, 2005.

Descimon, R. & Ruiz Ibánez, J.J. *Les Ligueurs de l'exil. Le refuge catholique français après 1594.* Seyssel, 2005.

Dickens, A.G., ed. *The Courts of Europe. Politics, Patronage and Royalty, 1400-1800.* London, 1977.

Diels, A. 'De familie Colaert (ca. 1555-1630) en de prentkunst in Antwerpen.' *Archives et bibliothèques de Belgique,* extranummer 88. Brussels, 2010.

Discailles, E. *La légende des bons souverains: les archiducs Albert et Isabelle.* Brussels, 1910.

Domínguez Nafría, J.C. *El Real y Supremo Consejo de Guerra (siglos XVI-XVIII).* Colección Historia de la Sociedad Política. Madrid, 2001.

Duerloo, L. & Janssens, P. *Wapenboek van de Belgische adel van de 15de tot de 20ste eeuw.* 4 vols. Brussels, 1992-1994.

Duerloo, L. & Thomas, W., eds. *Albrecht & Isabella, 1598-1621: Catalogus.* Exhibition catalogue. Turnhout, 1998.

Duerloo, L. & Wingens, M. *Scherpenheuvel. Het Jeruzalem van de Lage Landen.* Leuven, 2002.

Duerloo, L. ' 'Pietas Albertina.' Dynastieke vroomheid en herbouw van het vorstelijk gezag.' *Bijdragen en Mededelingen betreffende de Geschiedenis der Nederlanden,* 112 (1997) 1-18.

Duerloo, L. 'Archducal Piety and Habsburg Power,' in: Thomas, W. & Duerloo, L., eds. *Albert & Isabella, 1598-1621: Essays.* Turnhout, 1998, pp. 267-283.

Duerloo, L. 'Boerenbruiloft met Infante: Breughels genrestukken tussen belegering en propaganda,' in: Blondé, B., De Munck, B. & Vermeylen, F. eds. *Doodgewoon. Mensen en hun dagelijks leven in de geschiedenis. Liber Amicorum Alfons K.L. Thijs.* Published in: *Bijdragen tot de Geschiedenis,* 87 (2004) 255-267.

Duerloo, L. *Dynasty and Piety. Archduke Albert (1598–1621) and Habsburg Political Culture in an Age of Religious Wars.* Farnham, 2012.

Duindam, J. 'De herontdekking van het vorstelijk hof.' *Tijdschrift voor Geschiedenis,* 108 (1995) 361-376.

Duindam, J. 'The Burgundian-Spanish Legacy in European Court Life. A Brief Reassessment and the Example of the Austrian Habsburgs,' in: Cauchies, J.-M. & Noflatscher, H., eds. *Pays bourguignons et autrichiens (XIVe-XVIe siècles): une confrontation institutionelle et culturelle.* Publication du Centre Européen d'Études Bourguignonnes (XIVe-XVIe s.) 46: Rencontres d'Innsbruck (29 septembre au 2 octobre 2005). Neuchâtel, 2006, pp. 203-220.

Duindam, J. 'Van cohabitatie naar coëxistentie? Hofhouding en staatsbestuur in vroeg-modern Europa.' *Tijdschrift voor Geschiedenis,* 115 (2002) 254-273.

Duindam, J. *Myths of Power. Norbert Elias and the Early Modern European Court.* Amsterdam U.P., 1995.

Duindam, J. *Vienna and Versailles. The Courts of Europe's Dynastic Rivals, 1550-1780.* Cambridge U.P., 2003.

Duindam, J., Artan, T. & Kunt, M., eds. *Royal Courts in Dynastic States and Empires.* Leiden, 2011.

Ebben, M. 'Portuguese Merchant Bankers and the Court of the Archdukes, 1596-1633,' in: Thomas, W. & Duerloo, L., eds. *Albert & Isabella, 1598-1621: Essays.* Turnhout, 1998, pp. 303-307.

Echevarría Bacigalupe, M.A. 'Los gastos de un gobernador general en Flandes: el archiduque Leopoldo Guillermo (1647-1652).' *Letras de Deusto,* 33 (1983) 175-186.

Edelmayer, F. 'Honor y dinero. Adam de Dietrichstein al servicio de la Casa de Austria.' *Studia Histórica. Historia Moderna,* 10-11 (1992/93) 89-116.

Edelmayer, F. *Söldner und Pensionäre. Das Netzwerk Philipps II. im Heiligen Römischen Reich.* Munich, 2002.

Eichberger, D. 'A Cultural Centre in the Southern Netherlands: The Court of Archduchess Margaret of Austria (1480-1530) in Mechelen,' in: Gosman, M., MacDonald, A. & Vanderjagt, A., eds. *Princes and Princely Culture 1450-1650.* 2 vols. Leiden, 2003, volume I, pp. 239-258.

Eichberger, D., ed. *Dames met klasse. Margareta van York/Margareta van Oostenrijk.* Exhibition catalogue. Leuven, 2005.

Elias, H.J. *Kerk en Staat in de Zuidelijke Nederlanden onder de regeering der aartshertogen Albrecht en Isabella, 1598-1621*. Antwerp, 1931.

Elias, N. *Die Höfische Gesellschaft. Untersuchungen zur Soziologie des Königtums und die höfische Aristokratie*. Neuwied, 1969. [English edition: Elias, N. *The Court Society*. Translated by E. Jephcott. Oxford, 1983.]

Elliott, J.H. & Brockliss, L.W.B., eds. *The World of the Favourite*. London-New Haven, 1999.

Elliott, J.H. 'Introduction,' in: Elliott, J.H. & Brockliss, L.W.B., eds. *The World of the Favourite*. London-New Haven, 1999, pp. 1-10.

Elliott, J.H. 'La sociedad cortesana en la Europa del siglo XVII: Madrid, Bruselas, Londres,' in: Brown, J., ed. *Velázquez, Rubens y Van Dyck. Pintores cortesanos del siglo XVII*. Madrid, 1999, pp. 15-31.

Elliott, J.H. 'Power and Propaganda in the Spain of Philip IV,' in: Wilentz, S., ed. *Rites of Power. Symbolism, Ritual and Politics since the Middle Ages*. Philadelphia, 1985, pp. 145-173.

Elliott, J.H. 'The Court of the Spanish Habsburgs: A Peculiar Institution?' in: Mack, Ph. & Jacob, M.C., eds. *Politics and Culture in Early Modern Europe: Essays in Honour of H.G. Koenigsberger*. Cambridge U.P., 1987, pp. 5-24.

Elliott, J.H. *Imperial Spain*, 1469-1716. London, 2002 [original edition: London, 1963].

Elliott, J.H. *The Count-Duke of Olivares. The Statesman in an Age of Decline*. New Haven-London, 1986.

Elton, G.R. 'Tudor Government. The Points of Contact, III: The Court.' *Transactions of the Royal Historical Society, 5th series*, 26 (1976) 211-228.

Elton, G.R. 'Tudor Government.' *The Historical Journal*, 31/2 (1988) 425-434.

Elton, G.R. *Studies in Tudor and Stuart Politics and Government, papers and reviews 1946-1972*. 2 vols. Cambridge, 1974.

Escudero López, J.A., ed. *Los validos*. Madrid, 2005.

Esteban Estríngana, A. *Guerra y finanzas en los Países Bajos católicos. De Farnesio a Spinola (1592-1630)*. Madrid, 2002.

Esteban Estríngana, A. *Madrid y Bruselas. Relaciones de gobierno en la etapa postarchiducal (1621-1634)*. Leuven, 2005.

Evans, R.J.W. 'The Court. A Protean Institution and an Elusive Subject,' in: Asch, R.G. & Birke, A.M., eds. *Princes, Patronage, and the Nobility: The Court at the Beginning of the Modern Age, c.1450-1650*. Oxford U.P., 1991, pp. 481-491.

Evans, R.J.W. *Rudolf II and his World. A Study in Intellectual History, 1576-1612*. Oxford, 1973.

Fantoni, M. 'The Courts of the Medici 1532-1737,' in: Adamson, J., ed. *The Princely Courts of Europe. Ritual, Politics and Culture under the Ancien Régime 1500-1750*. London, 1999, pp. 255-273.

Fantoni, M. 'The Future of Court Studies: The Evolution, Present Successes and Prospects of a Discipline.' *The Court Historian*, 16/1 (2011) 1-6.

Feros, A. 'Lerma y Olivares. La práctica del valimiento en la primera mitad del seiscientos,' in: Elliott, J.H. & García Sanz, A., eds. *La España del Conde-Duque de Olivares*. Valladolid, 1990, pp. 195-224.

Feros, A. 'Twin Souls: Monarchs and Favourites in Early Seventeenth-Century Spain,' in: Kagan, R.L. & Parker, G., eds. *Spain, Europe and the Atlantic World*. Cambridge U.P., 1995, pp. 27-47.

Feros, A. *Kingship and Favoritism in the Spain of Philip III, 1598-1621*. Cambridge U.P., 2000.

Fischer, J. 'Die Erbteilung Rudolfs II. mit seinen fünf Brüdern vom. 10 April 1578. Nach bisher unbekannten Archivalien.' *Ferdinandeums-Zeitschrift*, III. Folge, 41. Heft. Innsbruck, 1897, pp. 5-14.

Gachard, L.-P. 'L'incendie du palais royal de Bruxelles (3 février 1731),' in: Gachard, L.-P., ed. *Études et notices historiques concernant l'histoire des Pays-Bas*, vol. III. Brussels, 1890, pp. 194-232.

Galesloot, L., ed. *Troubles de Bruxelles de 1619. Justification apologétique pour l'advocat Rombaut van Uden*. Brussels, 1868.

García Carraffa, A. & García Carraffa, A. *Diccionario heráldico y genealógico de apellidos españoles y americanos*. 86 vols. Madrid, 1920-1963.

García García, B.J. 'La Corte de los Archiduques en Bruselas.' *Torre de los Lujanes*, 44 (2001) 59-75.

García García, B.J. *La Pax Hispanica. Política exterior del Duque de Lerma*. Leuven, 1996.

García Rey, H. 'Alonso Vázquez, soldado e historiador.' *Boletín de la Real Academia de Bellas Artes y Ciencias Históricas de Toledo*, 11 (1919) 1-25.

Garganigo, A. ' 'Coriolanus', the Union Controversy, and Access to the Royal Person.' *Studies in English Literature, 1500-1900*, 42 (2002) 335-359.

Ghéret, D. 'Le produit des licentes et autres impôts sur le commerce extérieur dans les Pays-Bas espagnols (1585-1621),' in: Arnould, M.-A., Despy, G., Ghéret, D. et al., eds. *Acta Historica Bruxellensia. Recherches sur l'histoire des finances publiques en Belgique*, 3 vols. Brussels, 1968-1974. Volume II, pp. 43-122.

Ghys, I. *De Antwerpse magistraat in een laat-humanistische en contra-reformatorische periode: 1585-1621. Een institutionele, sociaal-economische en culturele analyse*. Unpublished master's thesis, Katholieke Universiteit Leuven, 1988.

Goemans, L.V. *Het Belgische Gezantschap te Rome onder de regeering der aartshertogen Albrecht en Isabella (1600-1633), naar onuitgegeven diplomatische bronnen*. Ekeren-Donk, s.d.

Gómez Centurión, J. 'Jovellanos y las Órdenes Militares, VI.' *Boletín de la Real Academia de la Historia*, 61 (1912) 370-431.

Gómez-Centurión Jiménez, C. & Sánchez-Belén, J.A., eds. *La herencia de Borgoña: La hacienda de las Reales Casas durante el reinado de Felipe V*. Madrid, 1998.

Gómez-Centurión Jiménez, C. 'Etiqueta y ceremonial palatino durante el reinado de Felipe V: el reglamento de entradas de 1709 y el acceso a la persona del rey.' *Hispania*, LVI/3, 194 (1996) 965-1005.

Gossart, E. *La domination espagnole dans les Pays-Bas à la fin du règne de Philippe II*. Brussels, 1906.

Gossart, E. *L'auberge des princes en exil. Anecdotes de la cour de Bruxelles au XVIIe siècle*. Brussels, 1905.

Grattan Flood, W.H. 'New Light on Late Tudor Composers: XL. Peter Philips.' *The Musical Times*, 70 (1929) 312-314.

Guillaume, G. 'Croy (Charles de),' in: *Biographie Nationale*, vol. IV (1873) pp. 544-552.

Guillaume, G. 'Croy (Charles-Alexandre de),' in: *Biographie Nationale*, vol. IV (1873) pp. 555-558.

Gunn, S.J. & Janse, A., eds. *The Court as a Stage. England and the Low Countries in the Later Middle Ages*. Woodbridge, 2006.

Gunn, S.J. 'The Courtiers of Henry VII.' *The English Historical Review*, 108 (1993) 23-49.

Henne, A. & Wauters, A. *Histoire de la ville de Bruxelles*. 3 vols. Brussels, 1845.

Hennequin de Villermont, M. *Le duc et la duchesse de Bournonville et la cour de Bruxelles*. Brussels, 1904.

Hennequin de Villermont, M. *L'Infante Isabelle, gouvernante des Pays-Bas*. 2 vols. Paris-Tamines, 1912.

Henrard, P. *Henri IV et la princesse de Condé*. Brussels, 1885.

Herman, A.L. 'The Language of Fidelity in Early Modern France.' *The Journal of Modern History*, 67 (1995) 1-24.

Hildebrand [Father O.M.F. Cap.]. 'Capucins belges et comtois, prédicateurs de la cour de Bruxelles sous Albert et Isabelle (1617-1633).' *Études franciscaines*, 49 (1937) 333-341.

Hirschbiegel, J. & Paravicini, W., eds. *Das Frauenzimmer. Die Frau bei Hofe in Spätmittelalter und Früher Neuzeit* (6. Symposium der Residenzen-Kommission der Akademie der Wissenschaften zu Göttingen. Residenzenforschung 11). Stuttgart, 2000.

Hirschbiegel, J. & Paravicini, W., eds. *Der Fall des Günstlings. Hofparteien in Europa vom 13. bis zum 17. Jahrhundert* (8. Symposium der Residenzen-Kommission der Akademie der Wissenschaften zu Göttingen. Residenzenforschung 17). Ostfildern, 2004.

Hofmann, C. *Das Spanische Hofzeremoniell von 1500-1700*. Frankfurt, 1985.

Hoppe, H.R. 'John Bull in the Archduke Albert's Service.' *Music & Letters*, 35 (1954) 114-115.

Hortal Muñoz, J.E. 'La casa del Archiduque Ernesto durante su gobierno en los Países Bajos (1593-1595),' in: Álvarez-Ossorio Alvariño, A. & García García, B.J., eds. *La Monarquía de las Naciones. Patria, nación y naturaleza en la Monarquía de España*. Madrid, 2004, pp. 193-205.

Hortal Muñoz, J.E. 'La Noble Guarda de Archeros de Corps en el contexto de la Casa Real de los monarcas Austrias Hispanos,' in: Vermeir, R., Fagel, R. & Ebben, M., eds. *Agentes e Identidades en Movimiento. España y los Países Bajos, siglos XV-XVIII (Actas del VII Congreso de Historiadores Españoles, Belgas y Neerlandeses, 27-29 septiembre 2007)*. In press.

Hortal Muñoz, J.E. 'Las guardas palatino-personales de los monarcas Austrias hispanos.' *Reales Sitios*, 179 (2009) 4-21.

Hortal Muñoz, J.E. 'The Household of Archduke Albert of Austria from his Election as Governor of Flanders until his Investiture as Sovereign Prince of the Low Countries: 1570-1598.' *Revue belge de Philologie et d'Histoire*, in press.

Hortal Muñoz, J.E. *El manejo de los asuntos de Flandes. Las relaciones entre las Cortes de la Monarquía Hispánica y de los Países Bajos durante el siglo XVI*. Saarbrücken, 2011.

Houben, B. & Raeymaekers, D. 'Women and the Politics of Access at the Court of Brussels. The Infanta Isabella's Camareras Mayores (1598-1633),' in: Akkerman, N. & Houben, B., eds. *The Politics of Female Households: Ladies-in-Waiting across Early Modern Europe*.

Leiden, 2013, pp. 123-145.

Houben, B. *Wisselende gedaanten. Het hof en de hofhouding van de landvoogden Isabella Clara Eugenia (1621-1633) en de kardinaal-infant don Fernando van Oostenrijk (1634-1641) te Brussel.* Unpublished doctoral dissertation, Universiteit Gent, 2009.

Israel, J. 'Chapter 1: The Court of Albert and Isabella, 1598-1621,' in: Israel, J. *Conflicts of Empires. Spain, the Low Countries and the Struggle for World Supremacy 1585-1713.* London, 1997, pp. 1-21.

Israel, J. 'Het tijdperk van de Aartshertogen, 1598-1621,' in: Janssens, P., ed. *België in de Zeventiende Eeuw. De Spaanse Nederlanden en het prinsbisdom Luik.* 2 vols. Ghent, 2006, volume I, pp. 28-32.

Israel, J. 'The Courts of the House of Orange, c. 1580-1795,' in: Adamson, J., ed. *The Princely Courts of Europe. Ritual, Politics and Culture under the Ancien Régime 1500-1750.* London, 1999, pp. 119-139.

Jacobs, M. *Parateksten, netwerken en conventies in de Spaanse Nederlanden en Franche-Comté (1621-1678): de familie Chifflet uit Besançon.* Unpublished doctoral dissertation, Vrije Universiteit Brussel, 1998.

Janssens, P. 'Het vorstelijk hof,' in: Aerts, E., Baelde, M., Coppens, H. et al., eds. *De centrale overheidsinstellingen van de Habsburgse Nederlanden (1482-1795).* 2 vols. Brussels, 1994, volume I, pp. 163-171.

Jordan Gschwend, A. 'In the Shadow of Philip II, *El Rey Lusitano*: Archduke Albert of Austria as Viceroy of Portugal (1583-1593),' in: Thomas, W. & Duerloo, L., eds. *Albert & Isabella, 1598-1621: Essays.* Turnhout, 1998, pp. 39-46.

Jouanna, A. 'Faveur et favoris: l'exemple des mignons de Henri III,' in: Sauzet, R., ed. *Henri III et son temps.* Paris, 1992, pp. 155-165.

Jurado Sánchez, J. 'La financiación de la Casa Real española y sus repercusiones sobre la Hacienda y la economía (1561-1808),' in: Aymard, M. & Romani, M.A., eds. *La cour comme institution économique. Actes du douzième congrès international d'histoire économique, Séville-Madrid, 24-28 août 1998.* Paris, 1998, pp. 57-64.

Justus, K.L. 'Gilded Palace, Gilded Playpen: Louis XV's Use of Palatial Space to Control his Rebellious Children and Their Politics.' *The Journal of Family History*, 21 (1996) 470-495.

Kagan, R.L. 'The Count of Los Arcos as Collector and Patron of El Greco.' *Anuario del Departamento de Historia y Teoría del Arte*, 4 (1992) 151-159.

Kaiser, M. & Pečar, A., eds. *Der Zweite Mann im Staat. Oberste Amtsträger und Favoriten im Umkreis der Reichsfürsten in der Frühen Neuzeit.* Zeitschrift für Historische Forschung, Beiheft 32. Berlin, 2003.

Kantorowicz, E.H. *The King's Two Bodies: A Study in Mediaeval Political Theology.* Princeton U.P., 1957.

Keller, K. *Hofdamen. Amtsträgerinnen im Wiener Hofstaat des 17. Jahrhunderts.* Vienna, 2005.

Kerkhoff, J. *Maria van Hongarije en haar hof (1505-1558). Tot plichtsbetrachting uitverkoren.* Hilversum, 2008.

Kettering S. 'Gift-Giving and Patronage in Early Modern France.' *French History*, 2 (1988) 131-151.

Kettering, S. 'Brokerage at the Court of Louis XIV.' *The Historical Journal*, 36 (1993) 69-87.

Kettering, S. 'Friendship and Clientage in Early Modern France.' *French History*, 6 (1992) 139-158.

Kettering, S. 'The Historical Development of Political Clientelism.' *The Journal of Interdisciplinary History*, 18 (1988) 419-447.

Kettering, S. *Patronage in Sixteenth and Seventeenth Century France*. Aldershot, 2002.

Kettering, S. *Patrons, Brokers and Clients in Seventeenth-Century France*. New York, 1986.

Kettering, S. *Power and Reputation at the Court of Louis XIII. The Career of Charles d'Albert, Duc de Luynes (1578-1621)*. Manchester U.P., 2008.

Klingenstein, L. *The Great Infanta: Isabel, Sovereign of the Netherlands*. London, 1910.

Krausman Ben-Amos, I. 'Gifts and Favors: Informal Support in Early Modern England.' *The Journal of Modern History*, 72 (2000) 295-338.

Lagomarsino, D. *Court factions and the Formulation of Spanish Policy towards the Netherlands (1559-1567)*. Unpublished doctoral dissertation, Cambridge University, 1973.

Lamet, P.M. *Yo te absuelvo, Majestad. Confesores de reyes y reinas de España*. Madrid, 1991.

Lanoye, D. 'Structure and Composition of the Household of the Archdukes,' in: Thomas, W. & Duerloo, L., eds. *Albert & Isabella, 1598-1621: Essays*. Turnhout, 1998, pp. 107-119.

Le Roux, N. 'Courtisans et favoris: l'entourage du prince et les mécanismes du pouvoir dans la France des guerres de religion.' *Histoire, Économie et Société*, 17 (1998) 377-387.

Le Roux, N. *La faveur du roi. Mignons et courtisans au temps des derniers Valois (vers 1547-1564)*. Paris, 2000.

Lefèvre, J. 'Don Juan de Mancicidor, secrétaire d'État et de Guerre de l'archiduc Albert (1596-1618).' *Revue belge de Philologie et d'Histoire*, 4 (1925) 697-714.

Lefèvre, J. 'La Cour de l'Archiduc Léopold-Guillaume, 1647-1652.' *Archives, Bibliothèques et Musées de Belgique*, 5 (1928) 65-77.

Lefèvre, J. 'La souveraineté d'Albert et d'Isabelle.' *Revue Générale Belge*, 89 (1953) 967-983.

Lefèvre, J. 'L'aumonerie militaire à l'époque de l'archiduc Albert, 1598-1621.' *Revue belge de Philologie et d'Histoire*, 7 (1928) 113-129.

Lefèvre, J. 'Le ministère espagnol de l'Archiduc Albert, 1598-1621.' *Bulletin de l'Académie Royale d'Archéologie de Bruxelles*, 1 (1924) 202-224.

Lefèvre, J. 'Les ambassadeurs d'Espagne à Bruxelles sous le règne de l'archiduc Albert (1598-1621).' *Revue belge de Philologie et d'Histoire*, 2 (1923) 61-80.

Lefèvre, J. 'Les chatelains militaires espagnols des Pays-Bas à l'époque de l'archiduc Albert (1598-1621).' *Revue belge de Philologie et d'Histoire*, 9 (1930) 831-852.

Lefèvre, J. 'Les livres de raison de l'archiduc Albert (1612-1618).' *Archives et bibliothèques de Belgique*, 42 (1971) 156-163.

Lefèvre, J. 'L'intervention du duc de Lerme dans les affaires des Pays-Bas (1598-1618).' *Revue belge de Philologie et d'Histoire*, 18 (1939) 463-485.

Lefèvre, J. 'Maes (Engelbert),' in *Biographie Nationale*, vol. XXXVII (1971-1972) pp. 566-569.

Lefèvre, J. *La Secrétairie d'État et de Guerre sous le Régime espagnol (1594-1711)*. Brussels, 1934.

Lefèvre, J. *Spinola et la Belgique 1601-1627*. Brussels, 1947.

Lewis, P.S. 'Être au Conseil au XVe siècle,' in: Paviot, J. & Verger, J., eds. *Guerre, pouvoir et noblesse au Moyen Age. Mélanges en l'honneur de Philippe Contamine.* Paris, 2000, pp. 461-469.

Leyder, D. *Les archives du Grand Conseil des Pays-Bas à Malines (vers 1445-1797).* Brussels, Algemeen Rijksarchief, Guides 73, 2010.

Liesenborghs, P. 'Het edele vermaak. De jacht in de hofcultuur van de Spaanse Nederlanden onder de Aartshertogen.' *Ons Heem,* 60 (2007) 6-14.

Liesenborghs, P. *Het edele vermaak. De jacht in de Spaanse Nederlanden onder de Aartshertogen.* Unpublished master's thesis, Katholieke Universiteit Leuven, 2005.

Loades, D. *The Tudor Court.* London, 1986.

Lombaerde, P. 'Pietro Sardi, Georg Müller, Salomon de Caus und die Wasserkünste des Coudenberg-Gartens in Brüssel.' *Die Gartenkunst,* 3 (1991) 159-173.

Lonchay, H. 'Le serment de fidélité prêté par les Belges à Philippe III en 1616,' in: *Mélanges Paul Frédericq. Hommage de la Société pour le progrès des études philologiques et historiques.* Brussels, 1904, pp. 311-317.

Lonchay, H. 'Philippe II et le mariage des archiducs Albert et Isabelle.' *Académie Royale de Belgique, Bulletin de la Classe des Lettres et des Sciences Morales et Politiques et de la Classe des Beaux-Arts,* 6 (1910) 364-388.

López Álvarez, A. 'Organización y evolución de la caballeriza,' in: Martínez Millán, J. & Fernández Conti, S., eds. *La Monarquía de Felipe II: La Casa del Rey.* 2 vols. Madrid, 2005, volume I, pp. 293-339.

López Álvarez, A. *Poder, lujo y conflicto en la Corte de los Austrias. Coches, carrozas y sillas de mano, 1550-1700.* Madrid, 2007.

López-Cordón Cortezo, M.V. 'Entre damas anda el juego: las camareras mayores de Palacio en la edad moderna,' in: Gómez-Centurión Jiménez, C., ed. *Monarquía y Corte en la España Moderna.* Cuadernos de Historia Moderna, 2003 (Anejo II), pp. 123-152.

Maçzak, A. & Müller-Luckner, E., eds. *Klientelsysteme im Europa der frühen Neuzeit.* Munich, 1988.

Marini, M. 'Anna van Croÿ (1563-1635). Een spilfiguur in de Arenberggeschiedenis,' in: Neu, P., ed. *Arenberger Frauen. Fürstinnen, Herzoginnen, Ratgeberinnen, Mütter. Frauenschicksale im Hause Arenberg in sieben Jahrhunderten.* Koblenz, 2006, pp. 85-109.

Martin, C. & Parker, G. *The Spanish Armada.* London, 1988.

Martin, C. 'La Trinidad Valencera: An Armada Invasion Transport Lost off Donegal.' *International Journal of Nautical Archeology,* 8 (1979) 13-38.

Martínez Hernández, S. 'Significación y trascendencia del género epistolar en la política cortesana: la correspondencia inédita entre la infanta Isabel Clara Eugenia y el marques de Velada.' *Hispania,* 64/2, no. 217 (2004), 467-514.

Martínez Millán, J. & Fernández Conti, S., eds. *La Monarquía de Felipe II: La Casa del Rey.* 2 vols. Madrid, 2005.

Martínez Millán, J. & Pizarro Llorente, H. 'La capilla real: integración social y definición de la ortodoxia religiosa,' in: Martínez Millán, J. & Fernández Conti, S., eds. *La Monarquía de Felipe II: La Casa del Rey.* 2 vols. Madrid, 2005, volume I, pp. 517-544.

Martínez Millán, J. & Visceglia, M.-A., eds. *La Monarquía de Felipe III: La Casa del Rey.* 2 vols. Madrid, 2008.

Martínez Millán, J. 'El archiduque Alberto en la corte de Felipe II (1570-1580),' in: Thomas, W. & Duerloo, L., eds. *Albert & Isabella, 1598-1621: Essays*. Turnhout, 1998, pp. 27-37.

Martínez Millán, J. 'Grupos de poder en la corte durante el reinado de Felipe II: la facción ebolista, 1554–1573,' in: Martínez Millán, J., ed. *Instituciones y élites de poder en la Monarquía Hispana durante el siglo XVI*. Madrid, 1992, pp. 183–197.

Martínez Millán, J. 'La Emperatriz Maria y las pugnas cortesanas en tiempos de Felipe II,' in: Belenguer Cebriá, E., ed. *Felipe II y el Mediterráneo. Vol. III: La Monarquía y los reinos (I)*. Madrid, 1999, pp. 143-162.

Martínez Millán, J., ed. *La Corte de Carlos V*. 5 vols. Madrid, 2000.

Martín-Peñato Lázaro, M.J. 'Los Laso de la Vega y su vinculación con la ceca de Toledo.' *Numisma*, 250 (2006) 525-535.

Martyn, G. 'Het recht ten tijde van de aartshertogen: codificatie en enkele fundamentele wetten,' in: Thomas, W. & Duerloo, L., eds. *Albert & Isabella, 1598-1621: Essays*. Turnhout, 1998, pp. 249-254.

Martyn, G. *Het Eeuwig Edict van 12 juli 1611: zijn genese en zijn rol in de verschriftelijking van het privaatrecht*. Brussels, 2000.

Mayoral López, R. *La Casa Real de Felipe III (1598-1621). Ordenanzas y Etiquetas*. Onuitgegeven doctoraatsproefschrift Universidad Autónoma de Madrid, 2007.

Mears, N. 'Courts, Courtiers, and Culture in Tudor England.' *The Historical Journal*, 46 (2003) 703-722.

Menčík, F. 'Beiträge zur Geschichte der Kaiserlichen Hofämter.' *Archiv für Österreichische Geschichte*, 86 (1899) 449-563.

Mertens, J. & Aumann, F., eds. *Krijg en Kunst. Leopold-Willem (1614-1662). Habsburger, landvoogd en kunstverzamelaar*. Exhibition catalogue. Bilzen, 2003.

Midelfort, H.C.E. 'A Melancholy Emperor and His Mad Son,' in: Midelfort, H.C.E., ed. *Mad Princes of Renaissance Germany*. Virginia U.P., 1996, pp. 125-143.

Miller, P.N. 'Friendship and Conversation in Seventeenth-Century Venice.' *The Journal of Modern History*, 73 (2001) 1-31.

Minois, G. *Le confesseur du roi. Les directeurs de conscience sous la monarchie française*. Paris, 1988.

Morgan, D.A.L. 'The House of Policy: The Political Role of the late Plantagenet Household, 1422-1485,' in Starkey, D. et al. *The English Court from the Wars of the Roses to the Civil War*. London-New York, 1987, pp. 25-70.

Mörke, O. 'De hofhouding van het huis Oranje-Nassau in de zeventiende eeuw,' in: Frijhoff, W., Burke, P. & te Boekhorst, P., eds. *Cultuur en maatschappij in Nederland 1500-1850. Een historisch-antropologisch perspectief*. Heerlen, 1992, pp. 39-77.

Mörke, O. 'Sovereignty and the Authority. The Role of the Court in the Netherlands in the First Half of the Seventeenth Century,' in: Asch, R.G. & Birke, A.M., eds. *Princes, Patronage, and the Nobility. The Court at the Beginning of the Modern Age, c. 1450-1650*. Oxford U.P., 1991, pp. 455-477.

Nader, H. 'Habsburg Ceremony in Spain: The Reality of the Myth.' *Historical Reflections*, 15 (1988) 293-309.

Nelson, B. 'Ritual and Ceremony in the Spanish Royal Chapel, c. 1559-c. 1561.' *Early Music History*, 19 (2000) 105-200.

Newton, W.R. *L'espace du roi. La cour de France au château de Versailles 1682-1789*. Paris, 2000.

Nijsten, G. *Het hof van Gelre. Cultuur ten tijde van de hertogen uit het Gulikse en Egmondse huis (1371-1473)*. Kampen, 1992.

Noens, V. *Het standpunt van het Madrileense hof inzake de onafhankelijkheid van de aartshertogen met betrekking tot binnenlandse aangelegenheden*. Unpublished master's thesis, Universiteit Gent, 2006.

Onnekink, D. *The Anglo-Dutch Favourite: The Career of Hans Willem Bentinck, 1st Earl of Portland (1649-1709)*. Aldershot, 2007.

Oresko, R. 'The House of Savoy in Search for a Royal Crown in the Seventeenth Century,' in: Oresko, R., Gibbs, G.C. & Scott, H.M., eds. *Royal and Republican Sovereignty in Early Modern Europe: Essays in Memory of Ragnhild Hatton*. Cambridge U.P., 1997, pp. 272-350.

Oresko, R. 'The Sabaudian Court, 1563-c. 1750,' in: Adamson, J., ed. *The Princely Courts of Europe. Ritual, Politics and Culture under the Ancien Régime 1500-1750*. London, 1999, pp. 232-253.

Osborne, T. *Dynasty and Diplomacy in the Court of Savoy. Political Culture and the Thirty Years' War*. Cambridge U.P., 2002.

Papy, J. & Van Houdt, T. 'The Image of Archduke Albert in Seventeenth-Century Funeral Literature,' in: Thomas, W. & Duerloo, L., eds. *Albert & Isabella, 1598-1621: Essays*. Turnhout, 1998, pp. 319-334.

Paravicini, W. 'Die Hofordnungen Philipps des Guten von Burgund.' *Francia*, 10 (1982) 131-166; 11 (1983) 257-301; 13 (1986) 191-211; and 15 (1987) 183-231.

Paravicini, W. 'Die Residenzen der Herzöge von Burgund, 1363-1477,' in: Patze, H. & Paravicini, W., eds. *Fürstliche Residenzen im spätmittelalterlichen Europa*. Sigmaringen, 1991, pp. 207-263.

Paravicini, W. 'Europäische Hofordnungen als Gattung und Quelle,' in: Kruse, H. & Paravicini, W. *Höfe und Hofordnungen 1200-1600* (5. Symposium der Residenzen-Kommission der Akademie der Wissenschaften zu Göttingen. Residenzenforschung 10). Stuttgart, 1999, pp. 13-20.

Paravicini, W. 'Expansion et intégration. La noblesse des Pays-Bas à la cour de Philippe le Bon.' *Bijdragen en Mededelingen betreffende de Geschiedenis der Nederlanden*, 95 (1980) 298-314.

Paravicini, W. 'The Court of the Dukes of Burgundy. A Model for Europe?' in: Asch, R.G. & Birke, A.M., eds. *Princes, Patronage and the Nobility: The Court at the Beginning of the Modern Age, c. 1450-1650*. Oxford U.P., 1991, pp. 69-102.

Parker, G. *The Army of Flanders and the Spanish Road, 1567-1659*. Cambridge U.P., 2004 [Original edition: Cambridge U.P., 1972].

Parker, G., ed. *The Thirty Years' War*. London, 1984.

Pasture, A. *La restauration religieuse aux Pays-Bas catholiques sous les archiducs Albert et Isabelle (1596-1633)*. Leuven, 1925.

Persson, F. 'Splendour at a Price. The Economy of the Swedish Court in the Early Modern Period,' in: Aymard, M. & Romani, M.A., eds. *La cour comme institution économique*.

Actes du douzième congrès international d'histoire économique, Séville-Madrid, 24-28 août 1998. Paris, 1998, pp. 151-159.

Persson, F. 'The Courts of the Vasas and Palatines,' in: Adamson, J., ed. *The Princely Courts of Europe. Ritual, Politics and Culture under the Ancien Régime 1500-1750*. London, 1999, pp. 275-293.

Piot, C. 'Maes (Charles),' in: *Biographie Nationale*, vol. XIII (1894-1895) pp. 130-131.

Piot, C. 'Melun (Pierre de),' in: *Biographie Nationale*, vol. XIV (1897) p. 332.

Pirenne, H. *Geschiedenis van België*. 7 vols. Ghent, 1902-1933. [Accessed via Digitale Bibliotheek voor de Nederlandse Letteren, http://www.dbnl.nl/]

Pollentier, F. *De Admiraliteit en de oorlog ter zee onder de Aartshertogen (1596-1609)*. Brussels, 1972.

Porteman, K. 'Albrecht en Isabella in de letterkunde van hun tijd,' in: Thomas, W. & Duerloo, L., eds. *Albert & Isabella, 1598-1621: Essays*. Turnhout, 1998, pp. 309-318.

Poullet, E. 'Les gouverneurs de province dans les anciens Pays-Bas Catholiques.' *Bulletin de l'Académie Royale de Belgique*, 2e série, 35 (1873) 362-436 and 810-921.

Proesmans, K. 'Muziek aan het hof van Albrecht en Isabella 1598-1621.' *Musica Antiqua*, 6/1 (1989) 4-8; 6/2 (1989) 82-86 and 6/3 (1989) 123-127.

Proesmans, K. 'The Key Role of the Archducal Court in Spreading a New Musical Style in the Low Countries,' in: Thomas, W. & Duerloo, L., eds. *Albert & Isabella, 1598-1621: Essays*. Turnhout, 1998, pp. 129-135.

Proesmans, K. *Het muziekleven aan het hof van Albrecht en Isabella*. Unpublished master's thesis, Katholieke Universiteit Leuven, 1988.

Put, E. 'Les archiducs et la réforme catholique: champs d'actions et limites politiques,' in: Thomas, W. & Duerloo, L. *Albert & Isabella, 1598-1621: Essays*. Turnhout, 1998, pp. 255-265.

Raeymaekers, D. 'The 'Gran Privado' of Archduke Albert: Rodrigo Niño y Lasso, Count of Añover (c. 1560-1620),' in: Vermeir, R., Fagel, R. & Ebben, M., eds. *Agentes e Identidades en Movimiento. España y los Países Bajos, siglos XV-XVIII*. Madrid, 2011, pp. 129-149.

Raeymaekers, D. 'The Households of Habsburg Europe: Conference Report.' *The Court Historian*, 12/1 (2007) 91-94.

Raeymaekers, D. 'The Power of Proximity: The Cámara of Albert and Isabel at their Court in Brussels,' in: Van Wyhe, C., ed. *Isabel Clara Eugenia. Female Sovereignty in the Courts of Madrid and Brussels*. London, 2011, pp. 258-279.

Rahlenbeek, C. 'Bournonville (Alexandre de),' in: *Biographie Nationale*, vol. II (1868) pp. 860-862.

Rahlenbeek, C. 'Longueval (Charles-Bonaventure de),' in: *Biographie Nationale*, vol. XII (1892-1893) pp. 359-368.

Redworth, G. & Checa, F. 'The Courts of the Spanish Habsburgs 1500-1700,' in: Adamson, J., ed. *The Princely Courts of Europe. Ritual, Politics and Culture under the Ancien Régime 1500-1750*. London, 1999, pp. 43-65.

Ríos de Balmaseda, A. 'La Capilla de Reliquias de Cuerva y el cuadro de la Sagrada Cena de Tristan.' *Toletum: Boletín de la Real Academia de Bellas Artes y Ciencias Históricas de Toledo*, 27 (1991) 129-143.

Rodríguez-Salgado, M.J. ' 'Una perfecta princesa.' Casa y vida de la reina Isabel de Valois (1559-1568). Primera parte,' in: Gómez-Centurión Jiménez, C., ed. *Monarquía y Corte en la España Moderna*. Cuadernos de Historia Moderna, 2003 (Anejo II), pp. 39-96.

Rodríguez-Salgado, M.J. 'Honour and Profit in the Court of Philip II of Spain,' in: Aymard, M. & Romani, M.A., eds. *La cour comme institution économique. Actes du douzième congrès international d'histoire économique, Séville-Madrid, 24-28 août 1998*. Paris, 1998, pp. 67-86.

Rodríguez-Salgado, M.J. 'The Court of Philip II of Spain,' in: Asch, R.G. & Birke, A.M., eds. *Princes, Patronage, and the Nobility: The Court at the Beginning of the Modern Age, c.1450-1650*. Oxford U.P., 1991, pp. 205-244.

Rodríguez Villa, A. 'Don Francisco de Mendoza, almirante de Aragón (1547-1623),' in: Valera, J., ed. *Homenaje a Menéndez y Pelayo en el año vigésimo de su profesorado. Estudios de erudición española*. 2 vols. Madrid, 1899, volume II, pp. 486-610.

Rodríguez Villa, A. *Ambrosio Spínola, primer Marqués de los Balbases*. Madrid, 1904.

Roegis, E. *Het hof van don Juan José de Austria, landvoogd in de Habsburgse Nederlanden (1656-1658)*. Unpublished master's thesis, Universiteit Gent, 2006.

Russell, E. 'Pedro Rimonte in Brussels (c. 1600-1614).' *Anuario Musical*, 28-29 (1973-1974) 181-194.

Saintenoy, P. *Les arts et les artistes à la cour de Bruxelles*. 3 vols. Brussels, 1932-1935.

Sánchez, M.S. 'Confession and Complicity: Margarita de Austria, Richard Haller, S.J. and the Court of Philip III.' *Cuadernos de Historia Moderna*, 14 (1993) 133-150.

Sánchez, M.S. 'Empress Maria and the Making of Political Policy in the Early Years of Philip III's Reign,' in: Saint-Saëns, A., ed. *Religion, Body and Gender in Early Modern Spain*. San Francisco, 1991, pp. 139-147.

Sánchez, M.S. 'Sword and Wimple. Isabel Clara Eugenia and Power,' in: Cruz, A.J. & Suzuki, M., eds. *The Rule of Women in Early Modern Europe*. University of Illinois Press, 2009, pp. 64-79.

Sánchez, M.S. *The Empress, the Queen and the Nun: Women and Power at the Court of Philip III of Spain*. Johns Hopkins U.P., 1998.

Schutte, J.G. & Light, J.M. 'The Relative Importance of Proximity and Status for Friendship Choices in Social Hierarchies.' *Social Psychology*, 41 (1978) 260-264.

Smith, H. 'Court Studies and the Courts of Early Modern Europe.' *The Historical Journal*, 49 (2006) 1229-1238.

Smolar-Meynart, A., Vanrie, A., Soenen, M. et al. *Het paleis van Brussel. Acht eeuwen kunst en geschiedenis*. Exhibition catalogue. Brussels, 1991.

Smuts, M., ed. *The Stuart Court and Europe. Essays in Politics and Political Culture*. Cambridge U.P., 1996.

Soetaert, P. *De Bergen van Barmhartigheid in de Spaanse, de Oostenrijkse en de Franse Nederlanden (1618-1795)*. Brussels, 1986.

Spangler, J. 'Aulic Spaces Transplanted: The Design and Layout of a Franco-Burgundian Court in a Scottish Palace.' *The Court Historian*, 14 (2009) 49-62.

Starkey, D. 'A Reply: Tudor Government: The Facts?' *The Historical Journal*, 31/4 (1988) 921-931.

Starkey, D. 'Introduction: Court History in Perspective,' in: Starkey, D. et al. *The English Court from the Wars of the Roses to the Civil War*. London-New York, 1987, pp. 1-24.

Starkey, D. et al. *The English Court from the Wars of the Roses to the Civil War*. London-New York, 1987.

Starkey, D. *The Development of the Privy Chamber, 1485-1547*. Unpublished doctoral dissertation, Cambridge University, 1973.

Stengers, J. 'Le mythe des dominations étrangères dans l'historiographie belge.' *Revue belge de Philologie et d'Histoire*, 59 (1981) 382-401.

Steurs, F. *Het Keizershof en het hof van Margareta van Oostenrijk te Mechelen*. Mechelen, 1879.

Sturmberger, H. 'Die Anfange des Bruderzwistes in Habsburg.' *Mitteilungen des Oberösterreichischen Landesarchivs*, 5 (1957) 143-188.

Swett, K.W. ' 'The Account Between Us': Honor, Reciprocity and Companionship in Male Friendship in the Later Seventeenth Century.' *Albion*, 31 (1999) 1-30.

Thieffry, S. 'La Chapelle royale de Bruxelles de 1612 à 1618 d'après les Libros de la Razón de l'archiduc Albert.' *Belgisch Tijdschrift voor Muziekwetenschap*, 55 (2001) 103-126.

Thomas, W. & Duerloo, L., eds. *Albert & Isabella, 1598-1621: Essays*. Turnhout, 1998.

Thomas, W. 'Andromeda Unbound: The Reign of Albert & Isabella in the Southern Netherlands, 1598-1621,' in: Thomas, W. & Duerloo, L., eds. *Albert & Isabella, 1598-1621: Essays*. Turnhout, 1998, pp. 1-14.

Thomas, W. 'La Corte de los Archiduques Alberto de Austria y la Infanta Isabel Clara Eugenia en Bruselas (1598-1633). Una revisión historiográfica,' in: Crespo Solana, A. & Herrero Sánchez, M., eds. *España y las 17 provincias de los Países Bajos. Una revisión historiográfica (XVI-XVIII)*. Córdoba, 2002, pp. 358-386.

Thomas, W., ed. *De val van het Nieuwe Troje. Het beleg van Oostende, 1601-1604*. Exhibition catalogue. Leuven, 2004.

Thompson, I.A.A. 'The Institutional Background to the Rise of the Minister-Favourite,' in: Elliott, J.H. & Brockliss, L.W.B., eds. *The World of the Favourite*. London-New Haven, 1999, pp. 13-25.

Thurley, S. *The Royal Palaces of Tudor England. Architecture and Court Life 1460-1547*. London-New Haven, 1993.

Van Durme, M. *Les Archives générales de Simancas et l'histoire de la Belgique (IXe-XIXe siècles)*. Commission Royale d'Histoire: Collection de chroniques belges inédites et de documents inédits relatifs à l'histoire de la Belgique. 4 vols. Brussels, 1964-1990.

Van Honacker, K. 'Reorganisatie in Brussel of de strijd om de privileges. Het conflict tussen de ambachten en de aartshertogen van 1619.' *Bijdragen tot de Geschiedenis*, 73 (1990) 299-312.

Van Honacker, K. *Lokaal verzet en oproer in de 17de en 18de eeuw. Collectieve acties tegen het centraal gezag in Brussel, Antwerpen en Leuven*. Standen en Landen, 98. Kortijk-Heule, 1994.

van Sas, N.C.F., ed. *Vaderland. Een geschiedenis van de vijftiende eeuw tot 1940*. Amsterdam, 1999.

Van Wyhe, C. 'Between Chastity and Passion. The Impact of the French Exiles on the Cult of Courtly Love at the Brussels Court in the 1630s,' in: Steiger, J.A., ed. *Passion, Affekt un Leidenschaft in der Frühen Neuzeit. Wolfenbütteler Arbeitungen zur Barockforschung*, vol.

11. Wiesbaden, 2005, pp. 951-980.

Van Wyhe, C. 'Court and Convent: The Infanta Isabella and her Franciscan Confessor Andrés de Soto.' *Sixteenth Century Journal*, 35 (2004) 411-445.

Van Wyhe, C. 'Court, City and Countryside: Jan Brueghel's Peasant Weddings as Images of Social Unity under Archducal Sovereignty,' in: Thomas, W. & Duerloo, L., eds. *Albert and Isabella, 1598-1621: Essays*. Turnhout, 1998, pp. 151-160.

Vander Linden, H. 'Spinola (Gaston de),' in: *Biographie Nationale*, vol. XXIII (1921-1924) pp. 426-428.

Vanhemelryck, F. 'Hofrechtbanken (15de eeuw-1794),' in: Aerts, E., Baelde, M., Coppens, H. et al., eds. *De centrale overheidsinstellingen van de Habsburgse Nederlanden (1482-1795)*. 2 vols. Brussels, 1994, volume 1, pp. 180-187.

Varey, J.E. 'Further Notes on Processional Ceremonial of the Spanish Court in the Seventeenth Century.' *Iberomania*, 1 (1974) 71-79.

Varey, J.E. 'Professional Ceremonial of the Spanish Court in the Seventeenth Century,' in: Körner, K.-H., ed. *Studia Iberica. Festschrift für Hans Flashe*. Bern-Munich, 1973, pp. 643-652.

Vázquez Gestal, P. *El espacio del poder. La corte en la historiografía modernista española y europea*. Valladolid, 2005.

Verlinden, C. et al., eds. *Dokumenten voor de geschiedenis van prijzen en lonen in Vlaanderen en Brabant. Deel II (14de-19de eeuw)*. Bruges, 1965.

Vermeir, R. *In staat van oorlog. Filips IV en de Zuidelijke Nederlanden, 1629-1648*. Maastricht, 2001.

Verschaffel, T. 'The Embellishment of Brussels under Leopold I and Leopold II.' *The Court Historian*, 12/2 (2007) 193-214.

Vocelka, K. 'Matthias contra Rudolf. Zur politischen Propaganda in der Zeit des Bruderzwistes.' *Zeitschrift für Historische Forschung*, 10 (1983) 341–351.

Volk, M.C. 'New Light on a Seventeenth-Century Collector: The Marquis of Leganés.' *The Art Bulletin*, 62 (1980) 256-268.

Völkel, M. 'The Hohenzollern Court,' in: Adamson, J., ed. *The Princely Courts of Europe. Ritual, Politics and Culture under the Ancien Régime 1500-1750*. London, 1999, pp. 211-229.

Wangermee, R. 'La musique à la Chapelle royale des Pays-Bas,' in: Wangermee, R. & Mercier, P., eds. *La musique en Wallonie et à Bruxelles*. 2 vols. Brussels, 1980-1982, pp. 201-211.

Watanabe-O'Kelly, H. 'Der Fall des Günstlings. Hofparteien in Europa vom 13. bis zum 17. Jahrhundert (book review).' *The English Historical Review*, 121 (2006) 1529-1530.

Wauters, A. *Histoire des environs de Bruxelles*. 3 vols. Brussels, 1855-1857.

Weiser, B. *Charles II and the Politics of Access*. Woodbridge, 2003.

Wellens, R. 'Deux documents relatifs à l'agrandissement du domaine de Mariemont sous les Archiducs Albert et Isabelle.' *Annales du Cercle archéologique du Canton de Soignies*, 23 (1964) 1-14.

Whitelock, A. & MacCulloch, D. 'Princess Mary's Household and the Succession Crisis, July 1553.' *The Historical Journal*, 50 (2007) 265-287.

Williams, P. *The Great Favourite. The Duke of Lerma and the Court and Government of Philip III of Spain, 1598-1621*. Manchester U.P., 2006.

Winterling, A. *Der Hof der Kurfürsten von Köln, 1688-1794. Eine Fallstudie zur Bedeutung 'absolutistischer' Hofhaltung.* Bonn, 1986.

Wirth Marvick, E. 'Favorites in Early Modern Europe: A Recurring Psychopolitical Role.' *The Journal of Psychohistory*, 10 (1983) 463-489.

Wirth Marvick, E. 'Psychobiography and the Early Modern French Court: Notes on Method with Some Examples.' *French Historical Studies*, 19 (1996) 943-965.

Zagorin, P. 'The Court and the Country: A Note on Political Terminology in the Earlier Seventeenth Century.' *The English Historical Review*, 77 (1962) 306-311.

Zandvliet, K. 'Het hof van een dienaar met vorstelijke allure,' in: Zandvliet, K., ed. *Maurits. Prins van Oranje.* Zwolle-Amsterdam, 2000, pp. 36-63.

Zedler, J.H. *Grosses vollständiges Universal-Lexikon.* 68 vols., 1731-1754. [Accessed via http://www.zedler-lexikon.de/]

Zijlmans, J. 'Aan het Haagse hof,' in: Keblusek, M. & Zijlmans, J., eds. *Vorstelijk vertoon. Aan het hof van Frederik Hendrik en Amalia.* Zwolle-The Hague, 1997, pp. 30-45.

Papers

Carlos Morales, C.J. *The Economic Foundations of the Royal Household of the Spanish Habsburgs, 1556-1621.* Paper presented at the colloquium *A Constellation of Courts: The Households of Habsburg Europe, 1555-1665*, organized by the universities of Antwerp and Ghent (Brussels, Paleis der Academiën, November 3-4, 2006).

Duerloo, L. *Patronage and Ethos at the Habsburg Courts of Europe.* Paper presented at the colloquium *A Constellation of Courts: The Households of Habsburg Europe, 1555-1665*, organized by the universities of Antwerp and Ghent (Brussels, Paleis der Academiën, November 3-4, 2006).

Duindam, J. *Palace, City, Dominions: The Spatial Dimension of Habsburg Rule.* Paper presented at the colloquium *The Politics of Space: Courts in Europe and the Mediterranean, ca. 1500-1750* (San Marino, The Huntington Library, January 26-27, 2007).

Lebrecht, F. *Les Lalaing, une famille au service des archiducs.* Paper presented at the colloquium *Les 'Trente Glorieuses' (ca. 1600 – ca. 1630) dans les Pays-Bas méridionaux et la France septentrionale*, organized by the Université Charles-de-Gaulle – Lille 3 (Lille, Maison des Sciences de l'Homme, March 22-23, 2007).

Thomas, W. *The Court of the Archdukes and the Spanish Faction.* Paper presented at the conference *A Constellation of Courts: The Households of Habsburg Europe, 1555-1665*, organized by the universities of Antwerp and Ghent (Brussels, Paleis der Academiën, November 3-4, 2006).

Websites

Centre de Recherche du Château de Versailles: http://www.chateauversailles-recherche.fr/

Centro Studi Europa delle Corti: http://www.europadellecorti.it/

Instituto Universitario 'La Corte en Europa' (Universidad Autónoma de Madrid): http://www.iulce.es/

La Cour de France du Moyen Âge au XIXe siècle: http://cour-de-france.fr/

Patronage- und Klientelsysteme am Wiener Hof (Institut für Geschichte, Universität Wien): http://www.univie.ac.at/geschichte/wienerhof/

Residenzen-Kommission der Akademie der Wissenschaften zu Göttingen: http://resikom.adw-goettingen.gwdg.de/

Rudolstädter Arbeitskreis zur Residenzkultur: http://www.rudolstaedter-arbeitskreis.de/

The Society for Court Studies: http://www.courtstudies.org/

Index

C

Gallery

Plate 1 – Portrait of Archduke Albert. Frans Pourbus the Younger II. Oil on panel, 42 x 60 cm. (Bruges, Musea Brugge-Groeningemuseum. © Lukas – Art in Flanders VZW.)

Plate 2 – Portrait of the Infanta Isabella. Frans Pourbus the Younger II. Oil on panel, 42 x 60 cm. (Bruges, Musea Brugge-Groeningemuseum. © Lukas – Art in Flanders VZW.)

Plate 3 – View of the Coudenberg palace in Brussels circa 1649.
(© Amsterdam, Scheepvaartmuseum / National Maritime Museum, Collection Atlas van Loon.)

Plate 4 – Anne de Croÿ, princely countess of Arenberg, afterwards duchess of Aarschot (1564-1635).
(© Enghien, Arenberg Archives and Cultural Centre. Photo: Studio Berger.)

Plate 5 – Charles of Arenberg and Anne de Croÿ and their five children ca. 1601. Frans Pourbus the Younger II.
(© University of Leuven, Collection Arenberg. Photo: Hugo Maertens.)

Plate 6 – Charles, princely count of Arenberg, afterwards duke of Aarschot (1550-1616).
(© Enghien, Arenberg Archives and Cultural Centre. Photo: Studio Berger.)

Plate 7 – Antoinette-Guillemette of Arenberg, countess of Isenburg-Grenzau (1557-1626).
(© Enghien, Arenberg Archives and Cultural Centre. Photo: Studio Berger.)

Plate 8 – Wedding Banquet Presided Over by the Archdukes, ca. 1612-1613. Jan Breughel the Elder.
(© Madrid, Museo Nacional del Prado.)